NOVELS
for Students

Advisors

Jayne M. Burton is a teacher of English, a member of the Delta Kappa Gamma International Society for Key Women Educators, and currently a master's degree candidate in the Interdisciplinary Study of Curriculum and Instruction and English at Angelo State University.

Mary Beth Maggio teaches seventh grade language arts in Schaumburg, Illinois.

Tom Shilts is the youth librarian at the Okemos branch of Capital Area District Library in Okemos, Michigan. He holds an MSLS degree from Clarion University of Pennsylvania and an MA in U.S. History from the University of North Dakota.

Amy Spade Silverman has taught at independent schools in California, Texas, Michigan, and New York. She holds a bachelor of arts degree from the University of Michigan and a master of fine arts degree from the University of Houston. She is a member of the National Council of Teachers of English and Teachers and Writers. She is an exam reader for Advanced Placement Literature and Composition. She is also a poet, published in *North American Review*, *Nimrod*, and *Michigan Quarterly Review*, among others.

Mary Turner holds a BS in Secondary Education from East Texas State University and a Master of Education from Western Kentucky University. She teaches English 7 and AP English 12 literature and composition at SBEC in Southaven, Mississippi.

Brian Woerner teaches English at Troy High School in Troy, Ohio. He is also a Program Associate of the Ohio Writing Project at Miami University.

NOVELS
for Students

**Presenting Analysis, Context, and Criticism
on Commonly Studied Novels**

VOLUME 41

Sara Constantakis, Project Editor

Foreword by Anne Devereaux Jordan

GALE
CENGAGE Learning

Detroit • New York • San Francisco • New Haven, Conn • Waterville, Maine • London

Novels for Students, Volume 41

Project Editor: Sara Constantakis

Rights Acquisition and Management: Mary Snell, Robyn Young

Composition: Evi Abou-El-Seoud

Manufacturing: Rhonda Dover

Imaging: John Watkins

Product Design: Pamela A. E. Galbreath, Jennifer Wahi

Content Conversion: Katrina Coach

Product Manager: Meggin Condino

For product information and technology assistance, contact us at **Gale Customer Support, 1-800-877-4253.**
For permission to use material from this text or product,
submit all requests online at **www.cengage.com/permissions.**
Further permissions questions can be emailed to
permissionrequest@cengage.com

Gale
27500 Drake Rd.
Farmington Hills, MI, 48331-3535

ISBN-13: 978-1-4144-9484-5
ISBN-10: 1-4144-9484-X

ISSN 1094-3552

This title is also available as an e-book.
ISBN-13: 978-1-4144-9270-4
ISBN-10: 1-4144-9270-7
Contact your Gale, a part of Cengage Learning sales representative for ordering information.

Printed in Mexico
1 2 3 4 5 6 7 16 15 14 13 12

Table of Contents

The Informed Dialogue: Interacting with Literature

When we pick up a book, we usually do so with the anticipation of pleasure. We hope that by entering the time and place of the novel and sharing the thoughts and actions of the characters, we will find enjoyment. Unfortunately, this is often not the case; we are disappointed. But we should ask, has the author failed us, or have we failed the author?

We establish a dialogue with the author, the book, and with ourselves when we read. Consciously and unconsciously, we ask questions: "Why did the author write this book?" "Why did the author choose that time, place, or character?" "How did the author achieve that effect?" "Why did the character act that way?" "Would I act in the same way?" The answers we receive depend upon how much information about literature in general and about that book specifically we ourselves bring to our reading.

Young children have limited life and literary experiences. Being young, children frequently do not know how to go about exploring a book, nor sometimes, even know the questions to ask of a book. The books they read help them answer questions, the author often coming right out and *telling* young readers the things they are learning or are expected to learn. The perennial classic, *The Little Engine That Could, tells* its readers that, among other things, it is good to help others and brings happiness:

"Hurray, hurray," cried the funny little clown and all the dolls and toys. "The good little boys and girls in the city will be happy because you helped us, kind, Little Blue Engine."

In picture books, messages are often blatant and simple, the dialogue between the author and reader one-sided. Young children are concerned with the end result of a book—the enjoyment gained, the lesson learned—rather than with how that result was obtained. As we grow older and read further, however, we question more. We come to expect that the world within the book will closely mirror the concerns of our world, and that the author will *show* these through the events, descriptions, and conversations within the story, rather than *telling* of them. We are now expected to do the interpreting, carry on our share of the dialogue with the book and author, and glean not only the author's message, but comprehend how that message and the overall affect of the book were achieved. Sometimes, however, we need help to do these things. *Novels for Students* provides that help.

A novel is made up of many parts interacting to create a coherent whole. In reading a novel, the more obvious features can be easily spotted—theme, characters, plot—but we may overlook the more subtle elements that greatly influence how the novel is perceived by the reader: viewpoint, mood and tone, symbolism, or the use of humor. By focusing on both the obvious and more subtle literary elements within a novel, *Novels for Students* aids readers in both analyzing for message and in determining how and why that message is communicated. In the discussion on Harper Lee's *To Kill a Mockingbird* (Vol. 2), for example, the mockingbird as a symbol of innocence is dealt with, among other things, as is the importance of Lee's use of humor which "enlivens a serious plot, adds depth to the characterization, and creates a sense of familiarity and universality." The reader comes to understand the internal elements of each novel discussed—as well as the external influences that help shape it.

"The desire to write greatly," Harold Bloom of Yale University says, "is the desire to be elsewhere, in a time and place of one's own, in an originality that must compound with inheritance, with an anxiety of influence." A writer seeks to create a unique world within a story, but although it is unique, it is not disconnected from our own world. It speaks to us *because* of what the writer brings to the writing from our world: how he or she was raised and educated; his or her likes and dislikes; the events occurring in the real world at the time of the writing, and while the author was growing up. When we know what an author has brought to his or her work, we gain a greater insight into both the "originality" (the world of the book), and the things that "compound" it. This insight enables us to question that created world and find answers more readily. By informing ourselves, we are able to establish a more effective dialogue with both book and author.

Novels for Students, in addition to providing a plot summary and descriptive list of characters— to remind readers of what they have read—also explores the external influences that shaped each book. Each entry includes a discussion of the author's background, and the historical context in which the novel was written. It is vital to know, for instance, that when Ray Bradbury was writing *Fahrenheit 451* (Vol. 1), the threat of Nazi domination had recently ended in Europe, and the McCarthy hearings were taking place in Washington, D.C. This information goes far in answering the question, "Why did he write a story of oppressive government control and book burning?" Similarly, it is important to know that Harper Lee, author

of *To Kill a Mockingbird,* was born and raised in Monroeville, Alabama, and that her father was a lawyer. Readers can now see why she chose the south as a setting for her novel—it is the place with which she was most familiar—and start to comprehend her characters and their actions.

Novels for Students helps readers find the answers they seek when they establish a dialogue with a particular novel. It also aids in the posing of questions by providing the opinions and interpretations of various critics and reviewers, broadening that dialogue. Some reviewers of *To Kill A Mockingbird,* for example, "faulted the novel's climax as melodramatic." This statement leads readers to ask, "Is it, indeed, melodramatic?" "If not, why did some reviewers see it as such?" "If it is, why did Lee choose to make it melodramatic?" "Is melodrama ever justified?" By being spurred to ask these questions, readers not only learn more about the book and its writer, but about the nature of writing itself.

The literature included for discussion in *Novels for Students* has been chosen because it has something vital to say to us. *Of Mice and Men, Catch-22, The Joy Luck Club, My Antonia, A Separate Peace* and the other novels here speak of life and modern sensibility. In addition to their individual, specific messages of prejudice, power, love or hate, living and dying, however, they and all great literature also share a common intent. They force us to *think*—about life, literature, and about others, not just about ourselves. They pry us from the narrow confines of our minds and thrust us outward to confront the world of books and the larger, real world we all share. *Novels for Students* helps us in this confrontation by providing the means of enriching our conversation with literature and the world, by creating an *informed* dialogue, one that brings true pleasure to the personal act of reading.

Sources

Harold Bloom, *The Western Canon, The Books and School of the Ages,* Riverhead Books, 1994.

Watty Piper, *The Little Engine That Could,* Platt & Munk, 1930.

Anne Devereaux Jordan
Senior Editor, TALL (Teaching and Learning Literature)

Introduction

Purpose of the Book

The purpose of *Novels for Students* (*NfS*) is to provide readers with a guide to understanding, enjoying, and studying novels by giving them easy access to information about the work. Part of Gale's "For Students" Literature line, *NfS* is specifically designed to meet the curricular needs of high school and undergraduate college students and their teachers, as well as the interests of general readers and researchers considering specific novels. While each volume contains entries on "classic" novels frequently studied in classrooms, there are also entries containing hard-to-find information on contemporary novels, including works by multicultural, international, and women novelists. Entries profiling film versions of novels not only diversify the study of novels but support alternate learning styles, media literacy, and film studies curricula as well.

The information covered in each entry includes an introduction to the novel and the novel's author; a plot summary, to help readers unravel and understand the events in a novel; descriptions of important characters, including explanation of a given character's role in the novel as well as discussion about that character's relationship to other characters in the novel; analysis of important themes in the novel; and an explanation of important literary techniques and movements as they are demonstrated in the novel.

In addition to this material, which helps the readers analyze the novel itself, students are also provided with important information on the literary and historical background informing each work. This includes a historical context essay, a box comparing the time or place the novel was written to modern Western culture, a critical essay, and excerpts from critical essays on the novel. A unique feature of *NfS* is a specially commissioned critical essay on each novel, targeted toward the student reader.

The "literature to film" entries on novels vary slightly in form, providing background on film technique and comparison to the original, literary version of the work. These entries open with an introduction to the film, which leads directly into the plot summary. The summary highlights plot changes from the novel, key cinematic moments, and/or examples of key film techniques. As in standard entries, there are character profiles (noting omissions or additions, and identifying the actors), analysis of themes and how they are illustrated in the film, and an explanation of the cinematic style and structure of the film. A cultural context section notes any time period or setting differences from that of the original work, as well as cultural differences between the time in which the original work was written and the time in which the film adaptation was made. A film entry concludes with a critical overview and critical essays on the film.

To further help today's student in studying and enjoying each novel or film, information on media adaptations is provided (if available), as well as suggestions for works of fiction, nonfiction, or film on similar themes and topics. Classroom aids include ideas for research papers and lists of critical and reference sources that provide additional material on the novel. Film entries also highlight signature film techniques demonstrated, and suggest media literacy activities and prompts to use during or after viewing a film.

Selection Criteria

The titles for each volume of *NfS* are selected by surveying numerous sources on notable literary works and analyzing course curricula for various schools, school districts, and states. Some of the sources surveyed include: high school and undergraduate literature anthologies and textbooks; lists of award-winners, and recommended titles, including the Young Adult Library Services Association (YALSA) list of best books for young adults. Films are selected both for the literary importance of the original work and the merits of the adaptation (including official awards and widespread public recognition).

Input solicited from our expert advisory board—consisting of educators and librarians—guides us to maintain a mix of "classic" and contemporary literary works, a mix of challenging and engaging works (including genre titles that are commonly studied) appropriate for different age levels, and a mix of international, multicultural and women authors. These advisors also consult on each volume's entry list, advising on which titles are most studied, most appropriate, and meet the broadest interests across secondary (grades 7–12) curricula and undergraduate literature studies.

How Each Entry Is Organized

Each entry, or chapter, in *NfS* focuses on one novel. Each entry heading lists the full name of the novel, the author's name, and the date of the novel's publication. The following elements are contained in each entry:

Introduction: a brief overview of the novel which provides information about its first appearance, its literary standing, any controversies surrounding the work, and major conflicts or themes within the work. Film entries identify the original novel and provide understanding of the film's reception and reputation, along with that of the director.

Author Biography: in novel entries, this section includes basic facts about the author's life, and focuses on events and times in the author's life that inspired the novel in question.

Plot Summary: a factual description of the major events in the novel. Lengthy summaries are broken down with subheads. Plot summaries of films are used to uncover plot differences from the original novel, and to note the use of certain film angles or other techniques.

Characters: an alphabetical listing of major characters in the novel. Each character name is followed by a brief to an extensive description of the character's role in the novel, as well as discussion of the character's actions, relationships, and possible motivation. In film entries, omissions or changes to the cast of characters of the film adaptation are mentioned here, and the actors' names—and any awards they may have received—are also included.

Characters are listed alphabetically by last name. If a character is unnamed—for instance, the narrator in *Invisible Man*—the character is listed as "The Narrator" and alphabetized as "Narrator." If a character's first name is the only one given, the name will appear alphabetically by that name.

Variant names are also included for each character. Thus, the full name "Jean Louise Finch" would head the listing for the narrator of *To Kill a Mockingbird*, but listed in a separate cross-reference would be the nickname "Scout Finch."

Themes: a thorough overview of how the major topics, themes, and issues are addressed within the novel. Each theme discussed appears in a separate subhead. While the key themes often remain the same or similar when a novel is adapted into a film, film entries demonstrate how the themes are conveyed cinematically, along with any changes in the portrayal of the themes.

Style: this section addresses important style elements of the novel, such as setting, point of view, and narration; important literary devices used, such as imagery, foreshadowing, symbolism; and, if applicable, genres to which the work might have belonged, such as Gothicism or Romanticism. Literary terms are explained within the entry but can also be found in the Glossary. Film entries cover how the director conveyed the meaning, message, and mood of the work using film in comparison to the author's use of language, literary device, etc., in the original work.

Historical Context: in novel entries, this section outlines the social, political, and cultural climate in which the author lived and the novel was created. This section may include descriptions of related historical events, pertinent aspects of daily life in the culture, and the artistic and literary sensibilities of the time in which the work was written. If the novel is a historical work, information regarding the time in which the novel is set is also included. Each section is broken down with helpful subheads. Film entries contain a similar Cultural Context section because the film adaptation might explore an entirely different time period or culture than the original work, and may also be influenced by the traditions and views of a time period much different than that of the original author.

Critical Overview: this section provides background on the critical reputation of the novel or film, including bannings or any other public controversies surrounding the work. For older works, this section includes a history of how the novel or film was first received and how perceptions of it may have changed over the years; for more recent novels, direct quotes from early reviews may also be included.

Criticism: an essay commissioned by *NfS* which specifically deals with the novel or film and is written specifically for the student audience, as well as excerpts from previously published criticism on the work (if available).

Sources: an alphabetical list of critical material used in compiling the entry, with full bibliographical information.

Further Reading: an alphabetical list of other critical sources which may prove useful for the student. It includes full bibliographical information and a brief annotation.

Suggested Search Terms: a list of search terms and phrases to jumpstart students' further information seeking. Terms include not just titles and author names but also terms and

topics related to the historical and literary context of the works.

In addition, each novel entry contains the following highlighted sections, set apart from the main text as sidebars:

Media Adaptations: if available, a list of audiobooks and important film and television adaptations of the novel, including source information. The list also includes stage adaptations, musical adaptations, etc.

Topics for Further Study: a list of potential study questions or research topics dealing with the novel. This section includes questions related to other disciplines the student may be studying, such as American history, world history, science, math, government, business, geography, economics, psychology, etc.

Compare and Contrast: an "at-a-glance" comparison of the cultural and historical differences between the author's time and culture and late twentieth century or early twenty-first century Western culture. This box includes pertinent parallels between the major scientific, political, and cultural movements of the time or place the novel was written, the time or place the novel was set (if a historical work), and modern Western culture. Works written after the mid-1970s may not have this box.

What Do I Read Next?: a list of works that might give a reader points of entry into a classic work (e.g., YA or multicultural titles) and/or complement the featured novel or serve as a contrast to it. This includes works by the same author and others, works from various genres, YA works, and works from various cultures and eras.

The film entries provide sidebars more targeted to the study of film, including:

Film Technique: a listing and explanation of four to six key techniques used in the film, including shot styles, use of transitions, lighting, sound or music, etc.

Read, Watch, Write: media literacy prompts and/or suggestions for viewing log prompts.

What Do I See Next?: a list of films based on the same or similar works or of films similar in directing style, technique, etc.

Other Features

NfS includes "The Informed Dialogue: Interacting with Literature," a foreword by Anne Devereaux Jordan, Senior Editor for *Teaching and Learning*

Literature (*TALL*), and a founder of the Children's Literature Association. This essay provides an enlightening look at how readers interact with literature and how *Novels for Students* can help teachers show students how to enrich their own reading experiences.

A Cumulative Author/Title Index lists the authors and titles covered in each volume of the *NfS* series.

A Cumulative Nationality/Ethnicity Index breaks down the authors and titles covered in each volume of the *NfS* series by nationality and ethnicity.

A Subject/Theme Index, specific to each volume, provides easy reference for users who may be studying a particular subject or theme rather than a single work. Significant subjects, from events to broad themes, are included.

Each entry may include illustrations, including photo of the author, stills from film adaptations, maps, and/or photos of key historical events, if available.

Citing Novels for Students

When writing papers, students who quote directly from any volume of *NfS* may use the following general forms. These examples are based on MLA style; teachers may request that students adhere to a different style, so the following examples may be adapted as needed.

When citing text from *NfS* that is not attributed to a particular author (i.e., the Themes, Style, Historical Context sections, etc.), the following format should be used in the bibliography section:

> "*Night*." *Novels for Students*. Ed. Marie Rose Napierkowski. Vol. 4. Detroit: Gale, 1998. 234–35.

When quoting the specially commissioned essay from *NfS* (usually the first piece under the "Criticism" subhead), the following format should be used:

> Miller, Tyrus. Critical Essay on "*Winesburg, Ohio*." *Novels for Students*. Ed. Marie Rose Napierkowski. Vol. 4. Detroit: Gale, 1998. 335–39.

When quoting a journal or newspaper essay that is reprinted in a volume of *NfS*, the following form may be used:

> Malak, Amin. "Margaret Atwood's *The Handmaid's Tale* and the Dystopian Tradition." *Canadian Literature* 112 (Spring 1987): 9–16. Excerpted and reprinted in *Novels for Students*. Vol. 4. Ed. Marie Rose Napierkowski. Detroit: Gale, 1998. 133–36.

When quoting material reprinted from a book that appears in a volume of *NfS*, the following form may be used:

> Adams, Timothy Dow. "Richard Wright: 'Wearing the Mask.'" In *Telling Lies in Modern American Autobiography*. University of North Carolina Press, 1990. 69–83. Excerpted and reprinted in *Novels for Students*. Vol. 1. Ed. Diane Telgen. Detroit: Gale, 1997. 59–61.

We Welcome Your Suggestions

The editorial staff of *Novels for Students* welcomes your comments and ideas. Readers who wish to suggest novels to appear in future volumes, or who have other suggestions, are cordially invited to contact the editor. You may contact the editor via e-mail at: **ForStudentsEditors@cengage.com**. Or write to the editor at:

Editor, *Novels for Students*
Gale
27500 Drake Road
Farmington Hills, MI 48331-3535

Literary Chronology

1802: Alexandre Dumas is born on July 24 in Villers-Cotterêts, France.

1812: Charles Dickens is born on February 7 in Landport, Hampshire, England.

1819: Herman Melville is born on August 1 in New York, New York.

1836–1837: Charles Dickens's *The Pickwick Papers* is published serially.

1847: Bram Stoker is born on November 8 in Dublin, Ireland.

1847–1850: Alexandre Dumas's *The Man in the Iron Mask* is published in serial form in *Le Siècle* as part of *The Vicomte de Bragelonne, or Ten Years After*.

1855: Herman Melville's novella "Benito Cereno" is published in *Putnam Monthly*.

1870: Charles Dickens dies of a stroke on June 9 at Gadshill, near Rochester, Kent, England.

1870: Alexandre Dumas dies of a stroke on December 5 in Dieppe, France.

1873: Willa Cather is born on December 7 in Back Creek Valley, Virginia.

1890: Boris Pasternak is born on February 10 in Moscow, Russia.

1891: Herman Melville dies of natural causes on September 28 in New York City, New York.

1897: Bram Stoker's *Dracula* is published.

1906: R. K. Naryan is born on October 10 in Madras (modern Chennai), India.

1912: Bram Stoker dies of a series of strokes on April 20 in London.

1914: John Hersey is born on June 17 in Tientsin, China.

1915: Willa Cather's *The Song of the Lark* is published.

1922: Willa Cather is awarded the Pulitzer Prize for *One of Ours*.

1931: The film *Dracula* is released.

1940: Frank Chew Chin is born February 25 in Berkeley, California.

1944: Buchi Emecheta is born on July 21 in Lagos, Nigeria.

1944: John Hersey's *A Bell for Adano* is published.

1945: John Hersey is awarded the Pulitzer Prize for *A Bell for Adano*.

1947: Willa Cather dies of a cerebral hemorrhage on April 24 in New York City.

1947: Salman Rushdie is born on June 19 in Bombay, India.

1948: T. C. Boyle is born on December 2 in Peekskill, New York.

1957: Boris Pasternak publishes *Doctor Zhivago*.

1958: Boris Pasternak is awarded the Nobel Prize for Literature on October 23.

1960: Boris Pasternak dies of lung cancer at his dacha on May 30, in Peredelkino, near Moscow, Russia.

1962: Julie Otsuka is born in Palo Alto, California, on May 15.

1965: The film *Doctor Zhivago* is released.

1968: M. T. Anderson is born on November 4 in Cambridge, Massachusetts.

1972: R. K. Naryan's *The Ramayana* is published.

1979: Buchi Emecheta's *The Joys of Motherhood* is published.

1981: Salman Rushdie is awarded the Booker Prize for *Midnight's Children*.

1990: Salman Rushdie's *Haroun and the Sea of Stories* is published.

1991: Frank Chin's *Donald Duk* is published.

1993: John Hersey dies of cancer on March 22.

1993: Salman Rushdie is awarded the Booker of the Bookers Prize for *Midnight's Children*.

1995: T. C. Boyle's novel *The Tortilla Curtain* is published.

2001: R. K. Naryan dies of congestive heart failure on May 13 in Chennai.

2002: M. T. Anderson's *Feed* is published.

2002: Julie Otsuka's *When the Emperor Was Divine: A Novel* is published.

2006: M. T. Anderson is awarded the National Book Award for Young People's Literature for *The Astonishing Life of Octavian Nothing, Traitor to the Nation*.

2008: Salman Rushdie is awarded the Best of the Booker Award for *Midnight's Children*.

Acknowledgements

The editors wish to thank the copyright holders of the excerpted criticism included in this volume and the permissions managers of many book and magazine publishing companies for assisting us in securing reproduction rights. We are also grateful to the staffs of the Detroit Public Library, the Library of Congress, the University of Detroit Mercy Library, Wayne State University Purdy/Kresge Library Complex, and the University of Michigan Libraries for making their resources available to us. Following is a list of the copyright holders who have granted us permission to reproduce material in this volume of *NfS*. Every effort has been made to trace copyright, but if omissions have been made, please let us know.

COPYRIGHTED EXCERPTS IN *NfS*, VOLUME 41, WERE REPRODUCED FROM THE FOLLOWING PERIODICALS:

America, no. 23, March 11, 1944. Copyright © 1944 by America Press. Reproduced by permission.—*Booklist*, September 1, 2002. Copyright © 2002 by the American Library Association. Reproduced by permission.—*Cultural Critique*, spring, 2007. Copyright © 2007 by the Regents of the University of Minnesota. All rights reserved. Reproduced by permission.—*Dickens Quarterly*, March, 2008. Copyright © 2008 by the Dickens Society. Reproduced by permission.—*Edinburgh Review*, October, 1838.—*English Language Notes*, March, 2004. Copyright © 2004, Regents of the University of Colorado. Reproduced by permission.—*History Today*, January, 2006. Copyright © 2006 History Today Ltd. Reproduced by permission.—*Horn Book Magazine*, no. 5, September/October, 2002. Copyright 2002 by The Horn Book, Inc., Boston, MA, www.hbook.com. All rights reserved. Reproduced by permission.—*International Fiction Review*, January, 2002. Copyright © 2002 International Fiction Association. Reproduced by permission.—*Journal of Adolescent & Adult Literacy*, September, 2003. Copyright © 2003 International Reading Association. Reproduced by permission of the International Reading Association.—*Kliatt*, January, 2004; May, 2004. Copyright © 2004 by *KLIATT*. Reproduced by permission.—*Legacy: A Journal of American Women Writers*, June, 2000. Copyright © THE UNIVERSITY OF NEBRASKA PRESS, 2000. Reproduced by permission of the University of Nebraska Press.—*Library Journal*, September 1, 2002. Copyright © 2002. Library Journals LLC, a wholly owned subsidiary of Media Source, Inc. No redistribution permitted.—*Magazine of Fantasy and Science Fiction*, April, 1993 for "Bram Stoker's 'Dracula'" by Kathi Maio. Copyright © 1993 by Kathi Maio. Reproduced by permission of the author.—*MELUS*, winter, 1999. Copyright MELUS: The Society for the Study of Multi-Ethnic Literature of the United States, 1999. Reproduced by permission.—*Migration World Magazine*, January/February, 1996. Copyright © 1996 by The Center for Migration Studies. Reproduced by permission.—*New Statesman & Society*,

November 10, 1995. Copyright © 1995 New Statesman, Ltd. Reproduced by permission.—*Parabola*, May, 1991. Copyright © 1991 by the Society for the Study of Myth and Tradition. Reproduced by permission.—*Publishers Weekly*, August 26, 2002. Copyright © 2002 by PWxyz, LLC. Reproduced from *Publishers Weekly*, published by the PWxyz, LLC, by permission.—*Queen's Quarterly*, winter, 2007 for "Re-reading 'Doctor Zhivago'" by Richard Teleky. Copyright © 2007 by Richard Teleky. Reproduced by permission of the author.—*Research in African Literatures*, fall, 2004. Copyright © 2004 Indiana University Press. Reproduced by permission.—*Santa Fe New Mexican*, January 12, 2003. Copyright © 2003 by *The Santa Fe New Mexican*. Reproduced by permission.—*Southwest Review*, 1991. Copyright © 1991 Southern Methodist University. Reproduced by permission. —*Studies in Short Fiction*, spring, 1993; summer, 1998. Copyright 1993, 1998 by *Studies in Short Fiction*. Reproduced by permission.—*Teaching English in the Two Year College*, v. 28.1, September, 2000. Copyright © 2000 by the National Council of Teachers of English. Reproduced by permission of the publisher.—*Twentieth-Century Literature*, winter, 2001 for "Fairy Tale Politics:

Free Speech and Multiculturalism in 'Haroun and the Sea of Stories'" by Andrew S. Teverson. Copyright © 2001 by Andrew S. Teverson. Reproduced by permission of the author.—*World Literature Today*, summer, 1996. Copyright © 1996 by *World Literature Today*. Reproduced by permission of the publisher.

COPYRIGHTED EXCERPTS IN *NfS*, VOLUME 41, WERE REPRODUCED FROM THE FOLLOWING BOOKS:

Robinson, Harlow. From *Russians in Hollywood: Hollywood's Russians*. University Press of New England, 2007. Copyright © 2007 by University Press of New England, Hanover, NH. All rights reserved. Reproduced by permission of the publisher and author.—Sanders, David. From *New Voices in American Studies*. Purdue University Studies, 1966. Copyright © 1966 by Purdue Research Foundation. Reproduced by permission.—Wade, Pamela Christine. From *"As If It Mattered!": Discovering the Effect of the Fairytale in Willa Cather's "The Song of the Lark"*. Proquest, 2008. Copyright © 2008 by Proquest. Reproduced by permission.

Contributors

Bryan Aubrey: Aubrey holds a PhD in English. Entries on *A Bell for Adano* and *When the Emperor Was Divine*. Original essays on *A Bell for Adano* and *When the Emperor Was Divine*.

Catherine Dominic: Dominic is a novelist and a freelance writer and editor. Entries on *The Man in the Iron Mask* and *The Song of the Lark*. Original essays on *The Man in the Iron Mask* and *The Song of the Lark*.

Diane Andrews Henningfeld: Henningfeld is a professor of English at Adrian College who writes widely for educational publications. Entries on *Feed* and *Haroun and the Sea of Stories*. Original essays on *Feed* and *Haroun and the Sea of Stories*.

Michael Allen Holmes: Holmes is a writer with existential interests. Entry on *The Joys of Motherhood*. Original essay on *The Joys of Motherhood*.

Sheri Metzger Karmiol: Karmiol teaches literature and drama at The University of New Mexico, where she is a lecturer in the University Honors Program. Entries on *Doctor Zhivago* and *Donald Duk*. Original essays on *Doctor Zhivago* and *Donald Duk*.

David Kelly: Kelly is an instructor of literature and creative writing. Entry on *Dracula*. Original essay on *Dracula*.

Michael J. O'Neal: O'Neal holds a PhD in English. Entry on *The Pickwick Papers*. Original essay on *The Pickwick Papers*.

Christopher Russell: Russell is a freelance writer with a bachelor's degree in English literature. Entry on *Benito Cereno*. Original essay on *Benito Cereno*.

Bradley A. Skeen: Skeen is a classicist. Entry on *The Ramayana*. Original essay on *The Ramayana*.

Rebecca Valentine: Valentine is an award-winning author whose writing has been published by Dell, St. Martin's Press, and Reader's Digest, among others. Entry on *The Tortilla Curtain*. Original essay on *The Tortilla Curtain*.

A Bell for Adano

JOHN HERSEY

1944

A Bell for Adano is a war novel by American author John Hersey, published in 1944 and currently available as a version published by Vintage in 1988. It is based in the fictional town of Adano at the time of the Allied invasion of Sicily in July 1943. Hersey had covered the invasion as a journalist for *Time* magazine.

Adano is based on the real-life town of Licata, and the protagonist of the story, Major Victor Joppolo, is based on some of the experiences of Major Frank E. Toscani, the American Army officer who was Licata's military governor at the time. Hersey spent several days visiting Toscani, who told him of replacing the town's much-loved seven-hundred-year-old bell, which had been taken from the town by the Fascists to be melted down and used in the war effort.

Another character in the novel, General Martin, is based on a real-life model, in this case General George S. Patton, Jr., commander of the U.S. Seventh Army at the time. The incident in which Martin orders the shooting of a mule is based on a real incident during the war.

A Bell for Adano revolves around the efforts of Joppolo to reestablish civilian trust in the authorities. He believes in the power of democracy, and he makes great efforts to get the town back on its feet after its citizens have been beaten down by decades of Fascist rule. His sincerity and decency win the townspeople over, and the novel is a tribute to how people can learn to cooperate with one another under benevolent American tutelage.

John Hersey (© *AP Images*)

AUTHOR BIOGRAPHY

John Hersey was born in Tientsin, China, on June 17, 1914, the son of Roscoe and Grace Baird Hersey, who were missionaries. In 1924, the family moved back to the United States and settled in Briarcliff Manor, New York. Hersey attended public schools and then earned a scholarship to attend Hotchkiss School. Later he entered Yale University, graduating in 1936. He began working as a journalist for *Time* magazine in 1937, and during World War II, he covered the fighting in the South Pacific as well as Europe for *Time* and *Life* magazines. In 1942, he was cited by the secretary of the Navy for helping to evacuate the wounded from Guadalcanal. He accompanied Allied troops in the invasion of Sicily in 1943, surviving several plane crashes. In 1944, he covered the war in Moscow. After the war ended, he spent time in Japan in 1945 and 1946.

Hersey's first two books were journalistic accounts of the war in the Pacific. His first novel was *A Bell for Adano* (1944), based on what he had witnessed in Sicily. The novel was awarded the Pulitzer Prize in 1945 and was made into a film the same year. His next work was a nonfiction book, *Hiroshima* (1946), an account of the dropping of the atomic bomb on that Japanese city the previous year and the effects it had on six survivors. The book had a major impact worldwide. Hersey followed this with *The Wall*, a novel about the Warsaw Ghetto during World War II. The novel was awarded the Anisfield-Wolf Award (1950) and the Sidney Hillman Foundation Award (1951).

During the 1950s and continuing until a few years before his death, Hersey wrote prolifically, both fiction and nonfiction, producing a book every two or three years on a wide variety of topics, including war, democracy, education, and racism. Among his most notable works are the novels *The War Lover* (1959), *The Child Buyer* (1960), *White Lotus* (1965), *Under the Eye of the Storm* (1967), *The Conspiracy* (1972), *My Petition for More Space* (1974), *The Walnut Door* (1977), and *The Call* (1985). Nonfiction works include *Aspects of the Presidency* (1980).

From 1965 to 1970, Hersey was master of Pierson College at Yale University, during which he opposed U.S. involvement in Vietnam. For several decades, he taught at Yale as an adjunct professor of English. Hersey married Frances Ann Cannon in 1940, and they had three sons and a daughter. They were divorced in 1958, and Hersey married Barbara Day Addams Kaufman that year, by whom he had one daughter. Hersey died of cancer in Key West, Florida, on March 23, 1993.

PLOT SUMMARY

Chapter 1

A Bell for Adano starts in the fictional town of Adano, Italy, on the first day of the Allied invasion in July 1943. The Americans are soon in charge, and Major Victor Joppolo, the senior civil affairs officer, and Sergeant Borth, in charge of security, arrive at the former Fascist headquarters in the town square. Joppolo meets the local people. He appoints Giovanni Zito, who claims to be anti-Fascist, as his usher. Zito tells him that two weeks ago, Mussolini's forces took the seven-hundred-year-old town bell so it could be melted down and used in the war effort.

The major then appoints Ribaudo Giuseppe as his interpreter. Joppolo speaks Italian but not all the Americans do. An old man named Cacopardo, who owns sulfur refineries, enters with a fat man named Craxi. When Joppolo asks them what the town most needs, Craxi says food, but

MEDIA ADAPTATIONS

- *A Bell for Adano* is available as an unabridged Audiobook, read by David Green, published by Recorded Books in 2010.
- The novel was made into a movie, starring John Hodiak as Joppolo and Gene Tierney as Tina, in 1945. The film was directed by Henry King and produced by Twentieth Century Fox Film Corporation.
- The novel was also adapted into a play by Paul Osborn on Broadway in 1944, at the Cort Theater, with Fredric March as Joppolo.

Cacopardo says the bell, and the two men argue. Zito says the bell is more important. Father Pensovecchio arrives, having been sent for by Joppolo. He says the bell is important because the sound of it governs all the daily activities of the town. Joppolo says he will try to replace it.

Chapter 2

Joppolo meets Mercurio Salvatore, the town crier, who has been a Fascist but is now is willing to serve the Americans. Joppolo gives him an assignment to tell the people they must read the proclamations he will be posting around town. The proclamations describe the changes the Americans will be making in how the town is run. People must obey the proclamations or face punishment.

Chapter 3

Father Pensovecchio begins mass in his church in the morning. More people are there than usual, because word has spread that the American major will be attending, but the major has not arrived and the priest gets anxious. Joppolo has been talking with Zito about the bell and has forgotten he said he would attend mass. When he remembers, he runs to the church and arrives breathless. The priest tells the congregation the Americans have come as liberators. Joppolo's attention is caught by a blonde woman in the congregation.

Chapter 4

Gargano, the chief of police, enters a crowded baker's shop and goes to the front of the line. People protest, but he insists he still has the authority to do so. A woman named Carmelina continues to protest, and Gargano arrests her and takes her to Joppolo's office. Joppolo sympathizes with her but does not want to undermine Gargano's authority, since he wishes to keep him in office. On the charge of disturbing the peace and questioning authority, Joppolo sentences Carmelina to one day's imprisonment, suspended. She is relieved at the light sentence. Joppolo explains to local officials the principles of democracy.

Chapter 5

The major learns from Giuseppe that the blonde woman in church was Tina, the daughter of Tomasino, the best fisherman in town. Joppolo says he wants to meet Tomasino and get the fishermen going out again to improve the food supply.

Chapter 6

General Marvin arrives in town. When his armored car is obstructed by a slow-moving cart, he orders the cart to be pushed into the ditch and the mule to be shot. When he meets Joppolo, he orders that all carts be banned from the town. Joppolo knows this will have a bad effect and later tells the town officials he will try to get the order revoked. Three men come to Joppolo's office, saying that if they cannot bring their carts into town, people will not have enough food or water. Joppolo decides to countermand Marvin's order.

Chapter 7

At the military police headquarters, Captain Purvis complains about Joppolo's order, fearing the wrath of General Marvin should he find out. Sergeant Trapani, however, thinks the major was correct. Purvis orders Trapani to make out a report, saying they were only following Joppolo's orders when they let the carts back in town. On Corporal Schultz's suggestion, they let the report get lost in a pile of Purvis's papers, so it is never delivered, and therefore Joppolo will not get into trouble.

Chapter 8

Tomasino the fisherman refuses to go to see Joppolo, so Joppolo visits him at his boat, followed by a crowd of townspeople. The fisherman thinks Joppolo has come to arrest him, but Joppolo says he just wants him to resume fishing. Tomasino is skeptical, thinking he will have to pay corrupt authorities, because that is the way it was under the Fascists. Joppolo explains that this is not so, and that there will be no special taxes either. He takes Tomasino to see Lieutenant Livingston in order to get the Navy's permission to let the fishing boats go out. Livingston is suspicious of Tomasino but agrees to find a way to allow the boats out. Tomasino overcomes his suspicions and is delighted at the prospect of going fishing again.

Chapter 9
Joppolo hears from a colonel at nearby Vicinamare that the bell of Adano has already been used to create gun barrels.

Chapter 10
The former mayor, Nasta, comes down from the hills where he has been hiding. He is bedraggled, and the townspeople, who hate him, taunt him. Joppolo has Nasta arrested. Nasta says he wants to serve the American forces, but Joppolo is not interested. Instead, he makes Nasta report every day to Sergeant Borth. Borth has him confess his sins against the townspeople, one sin a day. The townspeople overhear this and are delighted at the humiliation of their former oppressor.

Chapter 11
Tomasino invites Joppolo to his home for dinner with his wife and two daughters, Tina and Francesca. When he arrives Joppolo is surprised to see Captain Purvis and Giuseppe already there. It proves a convivial occasion, with plenty of wine and dancing. Captain Purvis drinks too much and is frustrated in his attempts to get to know Francesca because he has to use Giuseppe as a translator, while Joppolo, who speaks Italian, has a more successful time with Tina.

Chapter 12
The next morning, Captain Purvis has a hangover and is in a bad mood. He complains to Trapani that the major made him go home the previous evening. Then he finds the report Trapani made about the carts and is angry that it has never been sent. He orders Trapani to send it to division headquarters, but Trapani deliberately addresses it to the wrong person.

Chapter 13
Cacopardo visits Joppolo saying he has important information about German troop positions. Joppolo sends him to see General Marvin in another town. Cacopardo has to get through much red tape at headquarters before he is permitted to see the general. Angered by the long delay, he insults the general. Furious, Marvin throws him out of his office, but not before he finds out from the old Italian that the man who sent him there was Major Joppolo, whom Marvin remembers in relation to the incident with the cart.

Chapter 14
Joppolo and Purvis visit the Tomasino family again, wanting to get to know the two daughters better. Tina tells Joppolo that she has a boyfriend who is missing. She does not know whether he has been captured or killed. She asks Joppolo if he could help in locating him. Joppolo takes offense, thinking this was the only reason he had first been invited to the family home. He insists on leaving, with Purvis, but later he regrets his petulance.

Chapter 15
Schultz and his friends Bill and Polack get drunk on wine. They get the idea that Joppolo is soon to be demoted because he countermanded an order from General Marvin, and they decide they want to give him a gift as a going-away present. They are billeted in the house of a wealthy man named Quattrochi, and they go around the house searching for suitable gifts among the heirlooms. Because they are drunk, they succeed only in breaking a lot of valuable items.

Chapter 16
Joppolo is visited by a British officer, Lord Runcin. Joppolo explains he is helping the town. He has improved the food supply, developed a public assistance program, and solved a refugee problem. The people are learning to trust the authorities. Joppolo explains the need for a bell, and Runcin tells him to write to General Wilson in Algiers, who is good at getting supplies. After Runcin leaves, Quattrochi complains to Joppolo over the damage in his home. Furious, Joppolo goes to see the damage, tells Quattrochi to make a claim for payment, and reprimands the men responsible.

Chapter 17
Joppolo tackles the problem of the black market in Adano, which is caused by Americans who casually overpay for services because they do not know what the correct price is. Joppolo bans U.S. soldiers from going into the town.

Chapter 18

The report about the countermanded order gets read and filed at division headquarters. Lieutenant Butters takes note of it and believes Joppolo was right in countermanding the order. He sends the report to headquarters in Algiers, hoping that, like many things, it will get lost in transit.

Chapter 19

Former mayor Nasta spreads rumors that the Germans are about to counterattack and claims the Americans are no good at fighting. He also spreads rumors about Joppolo, hoping to undermine his authority. Joppolo has Nasta arrested and put in a makeshift prisoner of war camp in the local park, which contains mostly Italians but some Germans as well. One night, the Germans help Nasta to escape, but he is soon recaptured by Sergeant Borth.

Chapter 20

The artist Lojacono paints names and small figures on the fishing boats. On Agnello's boat, he paints the major riding a porpoise. The next day, the boats go out and the catch is good. The fishermen send Tina to Joppolo to thank him. Joppolo apologizes for his previous behavior and says he may have word of her boyfriend soon. Tina is happy and forgets to pass on the gratitude of the fishermen.

Chapter 21

One afternoon, Errante Gaetano is driving his mule and cart through town. He is distracted by some children, and the mule stops in the middle of the street, blocking the approach of some American amphibious trucks. Police Chief Gargano hits the mule to get it to move, Errante fights back, and Gargano arrests him.

Chapter 22

Acting on a suggestion from Cacopardo, Joppolo uses his diplomatic skills to enlist Lieutenant Livingston for help in raising the Anzio, a motor ship with a valuable cargo of sulfur that has sunk in shallow waters only a mile or so from the beach at Adano.

Chapter 23

At the Quartermaster Depot in Algiers, General William B. Wilson is exasperated by Joppolo's request for a bell and tells a member of his staff to write him a churlish letter of refusal.

Chapter 24

Joppolo acts as judge in trials of petty offenders in the town. He is good at getting people to tell the truth. When Errante Gaetano is brought before him, Joppolo sympathizes with him and dismisses the case over Gargano's protests.

Chapter 25

Joppolo tells Tina about the impending release of some Italian prisoners of war, but he has no news of her boyfriend, Giorgio.

Chapter 26

The town officials assemble in Joppolo's office and tell him he has forgotten to do something. He has no idea what it might be. They send him to a house in the town where he encounters a rude and crotchety old photographer named Spataforo, who takes his picture while telling him he is ugly. Joppolo does not know what the townspeople plan to do with the photo.

Chapter 27

Lieutenant Livingston has succeeded in raising the Anzio onto a floating dry dock. However, a stranger spreads rumors among the laborers that the Germans are counterattacking that morning. He says they will drop poison gas on the harbor from a plane at eleven o'clock. When a courier plane passes overhead at about eleven, the stranger says he can smell gas and runs toward the town. Panic ensues as the people believe there has been a gas attack. The disturbance is quieted only after Joppolo informs everyone that the rumor is false.

Chapter 28

At headquarters in Algiers, a mail clerk comes across the report about the countermanded order and wonders what he should do with it. His superior tells him to throw it away, but the clerk puts it in the pouch to return to the front.

Chapter 29

Joppolo goes to the Navy Club for drinks. He appeals to the Navy officers for help in getting a bell for Adano. Commander Robertson thinks he can get a suitable bell from a destroyer, the U.S.S. *Corelli*.

Chapter 30

Captain Purvis wants to spend some time alone with Francesca, so he gets Giuseppe to organize a big party at Quattrocchi's house for Joppolo, inviting many of the townspeople. Purvis hopes to sneak out unnoticed.

Chapter 31

Italian prisoners of war are released and return joyfully to Adano. However, Tina's Giorgio is not among them. His friend Nicolo tells Tina that Giorgio is dead. He was a good patriotic soldier, and the night before the Americans were due to attack, he scolded some drunken Italian soldiers. They turned on him, throwing bottles, and killed him. Joppolo does his best to comfort Tina.

Chapter 32

Lojacono paints a portrait of the major from the photograph taken by Spataforo. A delegation of town officials goes to his studio and criticize his work as he tries to finish it. They plan to present the portrait at the party.

Chapter 33

General Marvin gets Lieutenant Byrd to read some items to him taken from the pouch that has arrived from Algiers. Byrd happens to read the report of the countermanded order. Furious, Marvin issues an order for Joppolo to report to Algiers for reassignment.

Chapter 34

Three fishermen, Agnello, Merendino, and Sconzo, are fishing outside the designated zone when their boat hits a mine. All three men are killed. Tomasino breaks the news to Joppolo and tells him he will not be able to attend the party the following day.

Chapter 35

A woman comes to Joppolo's office carrying a dead child. The boy has been hit by an American military truck as he and others scrambled for candy thrown to them by the U.S. soldiers. Joppolo tells Gargano to round up the children on the street and keep them in the police station for a few hours to deter them.

Chapter 36

The bell from the *Corelli* is delivered to Adano. Joppolo tells the engineer battalion to install the bell in the clock tower. Borth reads the mail and finds the order from Marvin telling him to report to Algiers for reassignment. In the afternoon, town officials present Joppolo with his portrait. In the evening, Gargano rounds up the children. Then the party at Quattrocchi's house in honor of Joppolo begins, and Joppolo arrives with Tina. They both leave for a while to visit the children at the police station, work out a better way for them to receive candy, and then return to the party.

Chapter 37

Having received news of his reassignment, Joppolo regretfully leaves Adano. When he is four miles outside of town he hears the newly installed bell chiming, and it sounds good.

CHARACTERS

Agnello

Agnello is a fisherman. He likes to exchange insults with Tomasino. He is one of the men killed when his boat strikes a mine.

Bellanca

Bellanca is an inoffensive old man, a former notary, who is appointed mayor of the town following the American invasion.

Bill

Bill is a friend of Schultz and Polack and a member of the engineer battalion. Like his two friends, he gets drunk and damages Quattrocchi's house.

Sergeant Borth

Sergeant Borth is a member of the military police, and he is put in charge of security in Adano. His parents are Hungarian, although he is a U.S. citizen. He has done many jobs before enlisting in the U.S. Army, including being a journalist in Rome, a secretary in Marseille, and a salesman of radios in San Francisco. He is not yet thirty years old. Fearless and plain-spoken, he thinks the war is a joke and likes to get people to lighten up.

Lieutenant Butters

Lieutenant Butters forwards to division headquarters the report about Joppolo overturning Marvin's order, hoping it will be lost because he believes Joppolo was right to countermand the order.

Lieutenant Byrd

Lieutenant Byrd is a member of General Marvin's staff. It is he who reads Marvin the memorandum that reveals how Joppolo countermanded Marvin's order.

Cacopardo

Eighty-two-year-old Cacopardo is one of the town's wealthiest citizens, since he owns the sulfur refinery. He offers himself to Joppolo as an advisor on many matters. When Cacopardo says he has information about the whereabouts of German troops, Joppolo sends him to General Marvin, but Cacopardo is treated poorly there and ends up insulting the general and getting thrown out of his office.

Carmelina

Carmelina is the wife of Fatta. More formidable than her lazy husband, she protests when Gargano goes to the front of the line at the bakery. She is arrested but receives only a suspended sentence.

Craxi

Craxi is a resident of Adano. He is about forty years old and is very fat. He is married with seven children and is an enthusiastic supporter of the Americans. He even wants Joppolo to send a telegram he has composed to President Roosevelt thanking him for liberating the town.

Fatta

Fatta is a resident of Adano known for being lazy. He is also illiterate and a bit of a fool. He is easily convinced by a stranger that the Germans have dropped poison gas on the town, and he plays a role in spreading panic. Fatta is married to Carmelina.

Francesca

Francesca is one of two daughters of Tomasino. She is pursued by Captain Purvis.

Errante Gaetano

Errante Gaetano is a simple man who drives a mule and cart. It is his mule that is shot on the order of General Marvin. Errante acquires another mule and is involved in another incident in which he inadvertently blocks the road when a convoy of amphibious trucks need to pass. He is arrested by Gargano, but Joppolo takes his side and dismisses the case.

Gargano

Gargano is the chief of police in Adano. He is not very popular with the townspeople, but Joppolo allows him to retain his position. He is nicknamed "The Man With Two Hands" because of his constant gesturing. Gargano arrests Carmelina for challenging his authority and later arrests Errante Gaetano, but in each case, Joppolo's sympathies are with the defendants.

Giorgio

Giorgio is Tina's boyfriend. He does not appear directly in the story. His fate is related by his friend Nicolo. A patriotic Italian soldier, Giorgio was killed by some drunken soldiers after he scolded them for their poor behavior.

Giuseppe

Giuseppe is Major Joppolo's interpreter. He looks like an Italian gangster, but he is not a bad man. He lived in Cleveland, Ohio, for a while but was repatriated after it was discovered he had entered the country illegally. He is anxious to please his new employer.

Major Victor Joppolo

Major Victor Joppolo is an officer in the U.S. Army who is in charge of Adano during the American occupation. He is an efficient administrator and improves life in the town in many respects. He also makes great efforts to replace the lost bell that is so important to the townspeople. He is a great believer in the virtues of American democracy, which he explains to the town officials. He is not presented as perfect, however; his major weakness is that he wants too much to be liked. He certainly succeeds in that goal, winning the trust and affection of the townspeople, so much so that they have his portrait painted and throw a party in his honor. Eventually he is reassigned, away from Adano, because he countermanded an order from General Marvin. He acted in that way solely because he knew it was in the town's best interests.

Major Joppolo is an Italian American who speaks fluent Italian. His parents were originally from Florence, Italy, and immigrated to the United States. Poor in Italy, they prospered in their new country, after settling in the Bronx in New York City. Joppolo left high school when he was sixteen. He lied about his age in order to get a driver's license and worked as a truck driver until he was twenty. Then he injured himself lifting something heavy and switched to working in a grocery store for a while, after which he became a clerk, working for the New York City government in the taxation department. After being laid off from that job, he borrowed some money and bought a grocery store, but economic times were bad and that business failed after a couple of years. He returned to work for New York City government and then joined the U.S. Army. Joppolo is married, to a woman of Italian parentage, but this does not stop him from feeling lonely abroad and developing an affection for Tina.

Lieutenant Livingston

Lieutenant Livingston is an officer in the U.S. Navy who is in charge of harbor facilities in Adano. He is a Yale graduate and a snob who at first looks down on Joppolo because of his more humble background. Later, however, he changes his mind when Joppolo, needing his assistance, is especially charming to him.

Locajano

Locajano is an old painter who can paint almost any subject. His work is considered beautiful, although the townspeople like to criticize it as well. It is Locajano who paints the portrait of Joppolo.

Margherita

Margherita is the wife of Craxi. She is described as formidable. When the baker throws a piece of woodcoke and accidentally hits Margherita in the stomach, she advances toward him, shaking her fists, and he wisely retreats.

General Marvin

General Marvin, commander of the 49th U.S. Army Division in Sicily, is an irascible, impatient, vindictive man. He orders the unnecessary shooting of a mule, and because he was inconvenienced by the slow-moving cart the mule was pulling, he orders that all carts be kept out of Adano, even though this will have negative consequences for the town. Marvin takes a dislike to Joppolo, and when he finds out that the major countermanded his order, he orders him to report to Algiers for reassignment.

Merendino

Merendino is a fisherman who is Agnello's assistant. He is killed along with Agnello when their boat hits a mine.

Colonel Middleton

Colonel Middleton is General Marvin's chief of staff. He sometimes tries to get Marvin to modify an unreasonable order even though he knows it is hopeless to try to reason with him.

Nasta

Nasta is the former mayor of Adano who fled to the hills when the Americans invaded. He is roundly disliked by everyone because of his abuse of his office. When he wanders back into the town, he is taunted by the townspeople. Joppolo makes him report to Sergeant Borth every day, but this does not stop Nasta from making mischief. When he spreads damaging rumors about a German counterattack and undermines the Americans in other ways, he is arrested and put in a prisoner-of-war camp in Adano. He escapes but is soon recaptured.

Nicolo

Nicolo is a returning prisoner of war who was friends with Tina's boyfriend Giorgio. He gives Tina an account of how Giorgio died.

Father Pensovecchio

Father Pensovecchio is the priest of the Church of Sant' Angelo. He has a reputation for being the best priest in town, and at mass one morning, he hails the Americans as liberators.

Polack

Polack is a friend of Schultz. He is in the engineer battalion and is billeted at Quattrocchi's house. Along with Schultz and Bill, he gets drunk and breaks many valuable items in the house.

Captain Purvis

Captain Purvis is an officer who serves under Joppolo. He is in charge of the military police in Adano. He has only recently been commissioned, and he believes strongly in military discipline. It is he who has the idea of writing a memo explaining that Joppolo countermanded the order of General Marvin, so that he does not get into trouble because of it. Purvis and Joppolo have little in common, but they learn to get along well with each other. Purvis drinks a lot and tries to seduce Francesca.

Quattrocchi

Quattrocchi is a wealthy merchant who lives in a large town house. Three soldiers are billeted there, and while drunk, they destroy many valuable items. When Quattrocchi, who has been living elsewhere, discovers the damage, he complains furiously to Joppolo. Joppolo tells him he can claim compensation, and Quattrocchi is satisfied at the way the case is handled.

Commander Robertson

Commander Robertson is a Navy officer who meets Joppolo at a small party at the Navy villa. To help Joppolo, the commander has the idea of acquiring the bell from the U.S.S. *Corelli* and donating it to Adano.

Lord Runcin

Lord Runcin is a British army officer who is part of the Allied military government in Sicily. He visits Joppolo and tells the major to write to General Wilson and request a bell.

Mercurio Salvatore

Mercurio Salvatore is the town crier. He is a former Fascist and is not expecting to keep his position under the American administration, but Joppolo allows him to stay on, and he does his job conscientiously.

Corporal Chuck Schultz

Corporal Chuck Schultz is a military policeman. He is one of the three men billeted at Quattrocchi's house who get drunk and break many valuable items in the house.

Sconzo

Sconzo is another one of the fishermen killed when Agnello's boat hits a mine.

Spataforo

Spataforo is the irritable photographer who takes Joppolo's picture and tells him he is ugly. Apparently, he says the same thing to everyone.

Tina

Tina is the attractive blonde daughter of Tomasino, and Major Joppolo becomes fond of her. However, he suspects that Tina may be using him to discover the fate of her boyfriend, Giorgio. Nonetheless, she and Joppolo form a friendship, and Tina accompanies him to the party in his honor.

Tomasino

Tomasino is the leader of the fishermen. He is a morose man who does not trust authority, but he is delighted when Joppolo allows him and the other fishermen to resume their activities.

Sergeant Frank Trapani

Sergeant Frank Trapani is a military policeman who keeps records for Captain Purvis and acts as his secretary.

General William B. Wilson

General William B. Wilson is in charge of the Quartermaster Depot in Algiers. He does not take kindly to Joppolo's request for a bell and refuses to do anything to help.

Giovanni Zito

Giovanni Zito was the usher at Fascist headquarters in Adano, but he tells Joppolo he hated the Fascists. Joppolo allows him to retain his position in what is now Joppolo's headquarters.

THEMES

Democracy

When the Americans, with a long tradition of democracy in their own country, arrive in Adano, the townspeople have been living under a Fascist dictatorship for two decades. The new military governor, Major Joppolo, is a great believer in democracy, and he sees it as his task to teach these values to the townspeople, who have long been mistrustful of authority. One of the first things Joppolo does is assemble the town officials and tell them he intends to create an open form of government. He will inform them of what he thinks rather than leaving them in the dark.

He explains the principles of democracy, as he understands them: "Democracy is that the men of the government are no longer the masters of the people. They are the servants of the people." He points out to the officials that their wages are paid by the citizens of the town, through the taxes that the citizens pay. Therefore they must learn to think of themselves as the servants of the people, not their masters. Up to that point, people in Adano had had very different ideas of authority. This is illustrated in the small incident in which Gargano, the chief of police, goes straight to the head of the line in the bakery, assuming that his position gives him the authority to do so. Joppolo pointedly tells the officials that if he has to go to the bakery, he will wait in line, like everybody else.

Throughout the novel, Joppolo does his best to live up to this democratic ideal. Everything he does is for the good of the people he serves. He even countermands an order from General Marvin because he knows the town will suffer if he does not. He makes extensive efforts to replace the town bell because he knows how much it means to

TOPICS FOR FURTHER STUDY

- Using Internet research, create a timeline for the Sicily campaign in 1943.

- Go to UMapper.com and create a map of Sicily, marking the dates and places of the landings and the main lines of the Allied assault.

- Imagine that the movie of *A Bell for Adano* is to be reissued. Go to Glogster.com and make a poster advertising it.

- Research the military career of General George S. Patton on the Internet and then write an essay in which you discuss whether Hersey's negative portrayal of him as General Marvin is fair or unfair.

- Read *The Boys from St. Petri*, by Bjarne Reuter, a novel for young-adult readers set in occupied Denmark in World War II. How does this story of resistance to German occupation by a group of high-school boys compare with *A Bell for Adano*? Which novel presents the more realistic portrayal of war? Write a short essay in which you present your opinions.

the citizens. He has other accomplishments, too, and he proudly explains some of them to Lord Runcin. The people:

> can congregate in the streets any time they want and talk about whatever they want to. They can listen to their radios. They know they can get a fair trial out of me. They can come to the City Hall and talk to me any time they want.

Justice

Along with democracy goes justice. For years, the people in Adano have lived with injustice. The Fascists abused the power they held over people. The people were cowed, used to being hauled into court for petty matters and being frightened of officials. The previous mayor, Nasta, for example, imposed an exorbitant fine on Zito the usher

simply because Zito left a map of North America open on the table, and Nasta thought Zito was mocking him. Tomasino the fisherman makes it clear to Joppolo that, in the past, the authorities have been corrupt, demanding protection money or instituting special, unjust taxes. Joppolo quietly explains to him that none of this will happen under the American occupation.

Joppolo makes every effort to ensure that justice replaces the arbitrary and corrupt use of power. He imposes a very light sentence on Carmelina for her part in the ruckus in the bakery, and she remarks that such a mild sentence is unheard of in Adano. Joppolo throws out unjust charges brought against Errante Gaetano, even though those charges were placed by the chief of police. He tells a grateful Quattrocchi that he can claim compensation for damage done to valuables in his house by soldiers billeted there. "I know I can always get justice from you," says Quattrocchi. Joppolo is not afraid, however, to be tough when the situation demands it. He fines a baker three thousand lira for various offenses that have interfered with the bread supply to the people. The heavy fine was warranted because of the negative effect of the man's actions on the community.

One irony in the novel is that Major Joppolo, the dispenser of justice, does not receive justice himself, since he is unfairly relieved of his duties and reassigned because of the petulance of General Marvin. In this sense, the Americans, because of an arrogant commander, fail to live up to their own ideals.

STYLE

Symbol of the Bell

The bell is important for Adano. It was there for seven hundred years. In the sixteenth century, the sound of the bell warned the people of an imminent invasion by the French and the Turks. Father Pensovecchio explains the significance of the bell in the daily life of the town:

> This bell was the center of the town. All life revolved around it. The farmers in the country were wakened by it in the morning, the drivers of the carts knew when to start by it, the bakers baked by it, even we in the churches depended on that bell more than our own bells.

Adano is a small, coastal Italian town and the setting for the novel. *(© Andre Goncalves | Shutterstock.com)*

Joppolo immediately sees the significance of the bell for the townspeople, and he sees it as a symbol of freedom. Wanting to replace it, he thinks first of a replica of the Liberty Bell, the bell that symbolizes American freedom.

In the end, the bell Joppolo acquires symbolizes not only freedom but also Italian-American friendship and cooperation. Vincent Corelli was an Italian American who in World War I commanded a destroyer and went to the aid of an Italian frigate that was in difficulties during a storm. The bell from the U.S.S. *Corelli* is therefore rich with historical associations. The fact that it also symbolizes freedom is clear because it is the last sound Joppolo hears as he leaves the town. He may be leaving, but he is leaving a town that is now free from oppression.

Point of View

The story is told from the point of view of an omniscient third-person narrator. This means that the narrator, who is outside the story, has the ability to get inside the minds of all the characters and explain to the reader what they are thinking or feeling, as well as what they do or say. On one occasion, the narrator becomes what is called an intrusive narrator. An intrusive narrator comments directly on his characters, evaluating their behavior and offering his or her own opinion of them and other matters. This occurs at the beginning of Chapter 6, in reference to General Marvin, who is about to appear in the story for the first time. The narrator addresses the reader directly: "I don't know how much you know about General Marvin. Probably you just know what has been in the Sunday supplements." He proceeds to make a judgment about Marvin before the character actually appears: "I can tell you perfectly calmly that General Marvin showed himself during the invasion to be a bad man, something worse than what our troops were trying to throw out." Addressing the reader directly in this way, the narrator brings attention to himself and his own role in shaping the judgments of the reader.

COMPARE
&
CONTRAST

- **1940s:** World War II is being fought over much of the globe. It involves all the great powers and many smaller nations. When the war ends in 1945, the death toll as a result of the conflict is about fifty million, higher than that of any conflict in human history.

  Today: Although a number of wars have been and are being fought in the twenty-first century, none of them have come close to being a world war. The war in Iraq, begun when a United States-led international coalition invaded Iraq in 2003, is the biggest war of the century, as of 2012.

- **1940s:** Before the Allied invasion of 1943, Sicily, like the rest of Italy, is under the rule of Fascism. Fascism is a nationalistic, authoritarian, anti-democratic ideology similar to Nazism. Italy and Germany are allies in the war and are known as the Axis powers.

  Today: Italy is a parliamentary democracy, a U.S. ally, and a member of NATO, the Western military alliance. Sicily is one of five autonomous regions within Italy, with its own president and regional assembly.

- **1940s:** In North Africa, in Sicily, and in the Normandy Campaign, General George S. Patton establishes his reputation as a military strategist and outspoken leader who fires up his troops with sometimes profanity-laced speeches and a ruthless approach to fighting the enemy.

  Today: General Patton retains his reputation as one the greatest army commanders in U.S. history. His speeches to his men are preserved and revered by many.

HISTORICAL CONTEXT

The Sicily Campaign

During World War II, British and American forces landed on the Mediterranean island of Sicily on the night of July 9–10, 1943, after a week-long aerial bombardment. The invasion was a prelude to the invasion of Italy. Sicily was defended by nine Italian divisions and four German divisions, making up a total of four hundred and five thousand men.

In *Closing the Ring*, the fifth volume of Sir Winston Churchill's *The Second World War*, Churchill, who was the British prime minister at the time, emphasized the critical importance of the Sicily campaign: "The capture of Sicily was an undertaking of the first magnitude. . . . [I]ts importance and its difficulties should not be underrated." In the initial assault on Sicily, three thousand ships and landing craft took part, carrying one hundred and sixty thousand men, fourteen thousand vehicles, six hundred tanks, and eighteen hundred guns, according to Churchill. Churchill continued, "These forces had to be collected, trained, equipped, and eventually embarked, with all the vast impedimenta of amphibious warfare, at widely dispersed bases in the Mediterranean, in Great Britain, and in the United States."

When the invasion got underway, the British Army and a Canadian division attacked the eastern part of the island; the American Seventh Army, under General S. Patton, attacked on the west. The town of Licata, on which Adano in the novel is based, was a landing point for the American forces. Licata, as well as the town Gela, was quickly captured. U.S. forces faced some resistance from the Germans, but this did not stop them from pushing west to Marsala and north to Palermo. Churchill wrote that, in mid-July, the Americans "were advancing steadily under the spirited leadership of General Patton." Palermo was captured by U.S. forces on July 22. On August 3, General Sir Harold Alexander, the British commander of

What the townspeople want most is a replacement bell for their bell tower.

(© bddigitalimages / Shutterstock.com)

the 15th Army Group, telegraphed to Churchill that "General Patton . . . is in great heart. The Seventh American Army have done a grand job of work and are fighting really well." On August 17, 1943, Alexander telegraphed Churchill: "By 10 a.m. this morning . . . the last German soldier was flung out of Sicily and the whole island is now in our hands."

The Sicily campaign had taken thirty-eight days. Churchill acknowledged the difficulty of the campaign, in which the Allied forces had to battle outbreaks of malaria as well as the enemy, but wrote that success was never in doubt once the Allied troops were ashore and were operating their air forces from captured airfields.

In late July, Italy signed an armistice agreement with the Allies after dictator Benito Mussolini was ousted. Italy then switched sides, joining with the Allies and declaring war on Germany. Allied forces landed in Italy in early September, where they faced stiff opposition from German troops. The American Fifth Army captured Naples on October 1, but strong German resistance continued elsewhere in Italy, and Allied progress was slow for the remainder of the year and into 1944. Rome was captured on June 4, 1944.

CRITICAL OVERVIEW

A Bell for Adano was a best seller and received high praise from many contemporary reviewers. The reviewer for *Time* made this assessment: "Angry and intense, it is half sharp-eyed, unsparing war reporting and half fast-moving, self-consciously hard-boiled fiction." The reviewer notes that Hersey paints his characters in black and white, with few shades in between. Joppolo is "unqualifiedly good," while Patton is "unqualifiedly bad." Concluding that the mood of the novel is "bitter," the reviewer writes, "Its humor is raucous and wild. At its worst, it descends to college humorous magazine slapstick. At its best it is a superb piece of reporting."

Later views have tempered the early enthusiasm. In *John Hersey*, David Sanders comments that the novel "seems not to have deserved the praise given it in 1944 when reviewers were apparently overwhelmed by the prospect of affirmative war fiction." Sanders notes that the novel is "didactic from the first page" but also acknowledges that Hersey writes "plainly, entertainingly, and feelingly."

Sam B. Girgus, in *Dictionary of Literary Biography*, also modified earlier views. He commented on how Joppolo was seen by early readers of the novel as a hero who brought democracy to Adano, but Girgus modifies this point of view, arguing that in the novel,

> there is a basic conflict . . . between the traditional idea of democracy and the new concept of social control and political organization typified by the American military government. In dramatizing this conflict Hersey anticipated the radical attack on the liberal social programs of the 1960s.

WHAT DO I READ NEXT?

- Hersey's *Hiroshima* is the book for which he is best known, and it is as powerful today as when it was first published in 1946. In an objective, dispassionate style, Hersey describes the aftermath of the atomic bomb dropped on Hiroshima in August 1945. He tells the stories of six people who survived the blast. Forty years after his first visit to Hiroshima, Hersey returned to that city and then wrote an additional chapter to his book in which he brought the stories of the six survivors up to date. The additional chapter is available in the 1989 Vintage Books edition.

- *The Moon Is Down* (1942), a novel by John Steinbeck, is set in an unnamed small town that has just been conquered by a small invading army. Although it is never explicitly stated, the town is in Norway, and the invaders are the German Nazis. The Germans invaded Norway in April 1940, seven months after World War II began in 1939. In 1942, Norway was still under occupation, and Steinbeck wrote the novel in order to show that a free, democratic people would eventually rid itself of the invaders who live under a nondemocratic, dictatorial system.

- *The Day of Battle: The War in Sicily and Italy, 1943–44* (2007), by Rick Atkinson, is a riveting account of the Allied invasion of Sicily and Italy. Atkinson traces how the U.S. Army developed into a formidable military force during the course of the campaign. The account is enlivened by the stories of individual soldiers who fought in the battles, and Atkinson makes a case for the central importance of the Mediterranean campaign in producing the final, successful outcome of the war.

- Stephen Ambrose's *The Good Fight: How World War II Was Won* (2001) is a history of World War II by a renowned historian that is suitable for middle-school and high-school readers. It contains many maps and photographs and describes the significant campaigns and battles of World War II, as well as related events such as the relocation of Japanese Americans to internment camps and the Manhattan project that developed the atom bomb. Events before and after the war, such as Hitler's rise to power and the Nuremberg trials, are also included. The vivid, fast-paced narrative gives young readers a clear understanding of what World War II was like for those who fought in it and those who lived through it.

- *Code Talker: A Novel about the Navajo Marines of World War Two* (2006), by Joseph Bruchac, is a novel for young readers told in the manner of a Native American storyteller. It tells of Ned Begay, a Navajo boy who joins the Marines in World War II and is trained as a "code talker" to use codes based on the Navajo language to radio or telephone communications to U.S. forces in the Pacific. Ned vividly describes his wartime action in the Pacific Theater.

- *The Cruel Sea* (1951) is a classic war novel by Nicholas Monsarrat about British sailors who are involved in the Battle of the Atlantic in World War II. Two British ships escort convoys across the Atlantic, trying to avoid being sunk by German U-boats. The novel is based on the author's own experience during the war.

CRITICISM

Bryan Aubrey

Aubrey holds a PhD in English. In the following essay, he examines how a modern reader's reaction to A Bell for Adano *might be rather different from that of a reader in the 1940s.*

In 1998, Robert Kanigel published *Vintage Reading: From Plato to Bradbury: A Personal Tour of Some of the World's Best Books.* This was a collection of short essays gathered from columns Kanigel wrote for the *Baltimore Sun* and the *Los Angeles Times.* One of the books Kanigel discusses is *A Bell for Adano.* Kanigel recommends the book and makes an interesting comment about it. Rejecting the notion that it is a propaganda novel, he regrets "the cynicism with which many readers are apt to greet Hersey's story." He pointed out the change that had taken place in social and political attitudes in the United States in the fifty years since the novel was published:

> [M]aybe half a century ago, the gap between "propaganda" and how Americans saw themselves as a nation was not so wide as it is today. Maybe Americans back then had not yet grown distrustful of noble sentiments.

He adds that, during World War II, it perhaps was "plainer than it sometimes is now that real differences existed between political and social systems, that those differences mattered, and that, compared to others, our system was a good one."

Strictly in that sense, World War II represented a simpler time and a simpler context. During World War II, the Axis powers presented a mortal threat to world civilization and human freedom, and the Allies represented the best hope for averting such a catastrophe. In 1944, when *A Bell for Adano* was published, it was not difficult for Americans to see themselves as fighting for the triumph of good over evil, freedom over tyranny. Many decades later, the context in which the United States operates in the world has changed. In the 1960s and 1970s, the Vietnam War clouded the easy categories of good and evil and left many in the United States unsure of the virtue of their country's cause.

Along with this, people in other countries, unlike the simple Sicilian peasants in Hersey's story, have been less willing to accept the benign nature of American intervention. A case in point occurred in Somalia just a few years before Kanigel published his book. The United States undertook a

> GIVEN THE CHANGED TIMES IN WHICH WE LIVE, IT IS PERHAPS NOT SURPRISING THAT READERS OF *A BELL FOR ADANO* MAY FIND THEMSELVES REACTING TO THE NOVEL IN WAYS THAT ARE RATHER DIFFERENT FROM HOW THE FIRST READERS RESPONDED, WHEN WORLD WAR II WAS STILL RAGING."

humanitarian intervention in Somalia that went badly wrong. A mission to provide food and other aid to a starving people resulted in the alienation of the very people the mission was intended to help, and one result was the deadly Battle of Mogadishu in 1993, in which eighteen American soldiers died at the hands of local militias.

In the early 2010s, more than a dozen years after Kanigel made his point, Americans are engaged in a "nation-building" effort in Afghanistan, just as in *A Bell for Adano*, Joppolo, in a smaller way, is trying to rebuild the social and political structures of a small Italian town. Yet the people in Afghanistan seem as resistant to and as suspicious of American intentions as the American public is of the wisdom of the ongoing U.S. presence in that country. In Afghanistan, if there are any friendly U.S. officers of the Major Joppolo variety, trying to win the hearts and minds of the people (as the government jargon has it), they are not likely to have as easy a time doing so as the fictional major does in the novel. (Indeed, one of the strategies of Hersey's novel is to decouple the Italian peasants from the Fascism that the United States is at war against; the locals are for the most part presented as ordinary, apolitical, easily persuadable folks who just want to get back to normal life again.)

Given the changed times in which we live, it is perhaps not surprising that readers of *A Bell for Adano* may find themselves reacting to the novel in ways that are rather different from how the first readers responded, when World War II was still raging. The modern reader may feel that, too often, the humor in the novel is at the expense of the Italian townspeople, who are presented in stereotypical manner as emotional, easily excitable, quarrelsome, almost childlike people who need a firm, common sense, adult American hand in order to get their town organized and functional again.

In Chapter 1, the very first Italian that Major Joppolo and Sergeant Borth encounter is the usher, Giovanni Zito, who fawns over them, anxious to please. When he is told he is to retain the position of usher, "The little Zito was delighted." Just after this, when he misunderstands a question, the narrator comments, "Little Zito was getting very mixed up." The tone is distinctly condescending. The adjective "little" refers to the man's short stature, but it carries another meaning, too. The next Italian to enter is Giuseppe, who is hired as an interpreter. Giuseppe speaks in a way that is meant to emphasize his Italian accent, but it succeeds more in making him sound foolish.

After that, Cacopardo and Craxi enter and soon get into a hot-tempered exchange about which is more important for the town at the moment, food or the bell. It is intended to be comic: oh, those excitable Italians, but the contrast with the practical, even-tempered American major, who just want the facts and a reasoned opinion, is quite marked. And so it goes on. Few of the Italians are spared, while the Americans, while not presented as being without flaws, are never figures of fun (unless Captain Purvis's crude, inebriated efforts to seduce Francesca count in that direction).

Even the serious, morose fisherman Tomasino, who has some authority himself as the leader of the fisherman and who is not prepared—or so it seems at first—to kowtow to authority and does not care if Joppolo arrests him, is made to serve the comic intentions of the author. When he is persuaded to accompany Joppolo to a meeting with Lieutenant Livingston, Tomasino, who speaks no English, salutes whenever he hears his name mentioned. The narrator drily comments that Tomasino "hated authority, but he knew it when he saw it." Tomasino salutes in this manner five times in all during this scene. Perhaps it is amusing, but it is once again humor gained at the expense of one of the Italian characters, in this case undermining the dignity of a man who had up to then shown some independence of spirit.

The most egregious example of the townspeople being presented as somehow rather ridiculous and silly comes in Chapter 27, when the gullible locals are fooled by a malicious stranger who convinces them that a German plane has just dropped poison gas over the harbor. The plane in question is just a courier plane that comes by every day at the same time, but no one realizes this, and panic spreads quickly among the men at the harbor. Lazy Fatta runs for the first time in nearly a dozen years; eight men jump into the sea, and two have to be rescued because they cannot swim. Several others, as they run to the town, become convinced that there has been a gas attack. Fatta is in distress only because he is not in good physical condition, but he thinks it is because of the gas. Soon there are hundreds of people running around in fear and panic. Fatta's wife Carmelina, skeptical at first, is soon convinced that her husband is a victim of the attack.

The panic only subsides when Joppolo, having consulted with Livingston, tells the townspeople that the rumor is untrue; there is no poison gas. He breathes deeply, just to show them the air is fine, but they do not believe him until he comes down from the balcony onto the street and does the same thing. He also patiently explains to them that the smell they detected was in fact coming from the sulfur refinery (which they would have known very well had they remained in their right minds). He even has to go down to the harbor and take some deep breaths there before all the workers are convinced. Throughout the incident, the townsfolk behave like frightened, hysterical children, and they are calmed only by the reassuring voice of the adult, the American, the major. Except for the fact that Major Joppolo is himself an Italian American, his parents hailing from Florence, it would not take much imagination to transpose the scene largely unchanged to a nineteenth-century British colony, India perhaps or somewhere in Africa, and thereby reveal the superior colonial attitude to subject peoples, the "natives" who are not all that intelligent and need the guiding hand of a race more efficient and resourceful than their own.

Such a reading may be unfair to the author, who plays the scene for comedy, perhaps without the conscious intent of making the Italians look ridiculous. They are simply the characters he has at his disposal at this point in the story, and he uses them to create the humor that will enliven the narrative. He is also intent on adding another episode that contributes to the main point he wants to make in the novel: that Major Joppolo is an outstanding man, the sort of man America

Major Victor Joppolo is an Italian American soldier who becomes the administrator for an Italian town after it is occupied by the United States. *(© Tom Antos | Shutterstock.com)*

and Europe both need at this point in their histories. This is not mere speculation about the author's intentions, since he makes it crystal clear in his Foreword, in which he writes directly to the reader, "I think it is important for you to know about Major Joppolo."

Hersey sees Joppolo as a good man who represents the "best of the possibilities" that the New World has to offer the Old. If America had more Joppolos, the nation would be able to play its part in successfully rebuilding war-ravaged Europe, just as Joppolo does so effectively in Adano. This is why the author is so careful to show Joppolo winning over the townspeople in many different ways. Joppolo wins their respect because of his decency and fairness, and he goes a long way to reestablishing their pride in their community and their acceptance of the benevolent intentions of the Americans.

For example, without being asked, the townspeople maintain the small American cemetery on the edge of town, building a fence around it, making headstones, and providing flowers to honor the American soldiers who died in the fighting to liberate the town. Their gratitude is focused on Joppolo in particular, since he is to them the face of the American occupation. If their tributes to him sometimes border on the sentimental—Lojacono says his portrait of the major shows "the wish, which is visible in this man's face, that each person in this town should be happy"—the author nonetheless wants them to be taken seriously for what they are. If, on occasion, to build his man up, he makes others seem foolish, it is a flaw in the novel that perhaps can be overlooked, bearing in mind the author's larger purpose and the time, very different from our own, in which he was writing.

Source: Bryan Aubrey, Critical Essay on *A Bell for Adano*, in *Novels for Students*, Gale, Cengage Learning, 2013.

David Sanders

In the following excerpt, Sanders discusses Hersey's writing technique as it developed throughout his war-related novels, before Hiroshima.

On May 8, 1945—V-E Day—John Hersey won the Pulitzer Prize for his first novel, *A Bell for Adano*. Twenty years later, with the appearance of his eleventh book, *White Lotus*, he has been told that while he once aspired to have a silver tongue, he has been given instead a golden touch; that instead of writing literature for all time, he has written books that make the Book-of-the-Month Club. Hersey should not have been discouraged by such remarks. They might have been said of any recent American novelist who had published several widely read novels on subjects of immediate social or historical interest. These remarks are passingly ironic only because they were made by someone employed, as Hersey once was, by *Time*.

In order to have been judged more favorably, Hersey could have blocked out a careful ground of personal experience from his missionary childhood in China to some point in his adult life and then written a WASP novel, without guilt, with just enough humor, with that special access to the theme of racial identity given only to insiders. Or he might have drawn the inescapable conclusion from everything that he reported during World War II. By adding Hiroshima to Guadalcanal, the Sicilian campaign, and the ruins of Warsaw, he should have come up with

> **"** *A BELL FOR ADANO* IS THE SORT OF BOOK ONE
> MIGHT EXPECT HERSEY TO WRITE AT THAT TIME."

the sum of absurdity, then canceled it because of its possible consequence of revolt, and settled for meaninglessness.

Instead, he proceeded less imaginatively to become a novelist. Except in such digressions as *The Marmot Drive* and *A Single Pebble*, he has taken some of the main historical events and social problems of his time as his subjects. Habits that he acquired as a reporter have gone into the writing of each novel, especially such habits as observation, memory, and research.

His second novel, *The Wall*, is probably the most thorough example of his method. He saw the ruins of Warsaw in 1944, then the ruins of Hiroshima in 1946. For two years he read documents of the Warsaw ghetto, had others translated for him, and listened for several hundred hours to the wire transcriptions recorded by his translators. He began a longhand draft as he listened to these recordings and then abandoned it because of the strange effect these recordings were having upon him. He finished a second draft after making a crucial change in response to that effect. This is the barest possible outline of how this journalist wrote what is probably his best novel; this sketch will be filled in after we have seen what kind of a journalist he was when he began writing it. Let us also be certain that *The Wall* is a novel, although "epic," "monument," and "indictment" were terms that came more readily to the people who praised it. Others called it "fictionalized journalism."

The Wall is the story of the Jews of the Warsaw ghetto during World War II. It begins with the German occupation in the fall of 1939 and ends as the last survivors of the resistance movement escape extermination in 1943. It is told in the form of a scholar's journal, the "Levinson archive," as detailed a record as Hersey might be expected to produce after all his preparation. Fact and history go directly into this fiction, but not at the expense of fiction. The novel is dominated by the brilliantly imagined character of Noach Levinson—though characterization is

not consistently Hersey's strength as a novelist Levinson, the archivist, becomes someone—a complex and compelling person—in the course of making his entries, and he comes to see far more in the characters of his acquaintances than their responses to ghetto conditions. Nor does Hersey's stubbornly acquired knowledge of what happened in the ghetto between 1939 and 1943 crowd out his understanding of how these events are related to the centuries of Jewish history since the Diaspora or keep him from convincing his readers of the timelessness of the theme of survival. *The Wall* is a novel about the events of the Warsaw ghetto as told by a wholly fictional narrator. And *The War Lover* is a novel about the conflicting impulses toward life and death that may be found in wartime aviators, *The Child Buyer* is a novel about the abuse of high intelligence in the American public-school system, and *White Lotus* is a novel about the psychology of an oppressed race.

Hersey has written these novels and three others, and yet seems less a novelist to many critics and reviewers than does the author of *Catch-22* or novelists such as Norman Mailer and James Jones. I have mentioned Hersey's choice of subjects as one reason for his situation, and certainly another might be his affirmative response to some of these subjects. Still another will be found in the praise he has been given. No one has ever condemned *Hiroshima*, a book still always referred to as "inspired journalism." In fact, no one seems to have found adequate words for praising it. It gave millions of American readers their first knowledge of the human suffering caused by the first atomic bomb; before it, they had known nothing about the explosion but statistics and photographs of mushroom clouds. Albert Einstein is said to have ordered a thousand copies of the famous issue of the *New Yorker* to distribute among his fellow townsmen in Princeton. Bernard Baruch ordered another thousand. Very few books have ever been urged upon people so suddenly and so imperatively, certainly not the wartime books, including Hersey's own *Into the Valley*, which the Office of War Information had called "imperative reading." *Hiroshima* has been praised more often as a deed than as a book. In whatever Hersey would go on to write, he would be marked by the "earnestness of his intentions"—not a novelist's earnest intentions, but a prophet's. It has been assumed, furthermore, that the earnestness that went into *Hiroshima* could never go into anything else Hersey might write. So, from *The Wall* to *White Lotus*, he has written novels that have failed when they have not instead succeeded as "inspired journalism."

Many novelists have begun as reporters and then gone back into reporting in the midst of their novel-writing. Hemingway, Crane, and Dos Passos have done so without damage, but Hersey's case is not quite like theirs. His background as a war correspondent did not disqualify him as a novelist, but the peculiar circumstances of his reporting differ significantly from those of these other reporter-novelists and they are peculiarly responsible for Hersey's flying in the face of literary taste and writing novels about contemporary history. These circumstances include his employers, his media, his beats, and the Second World War.

Hersey went to work for *Time* in October 1937, after spending the summer as Sinclair Lewis' secretary. He had waited patiently for an opening on *Time* because this magazine was, he felt, "the liveliest enterprise of its type." After a year and a half in the New York headquarters, where he became thoroughly grounded in *Time* style and *Time* editing (that process by which the news became arranged as "World Affairs" or "Miscellany"), he was sent to the Chungking bureau, a logical assignment for a man who, like Henry Luce, was a native of Tientsin. There he began reporting the Sino-Japanese war *Time* style with dispatches on Chungking air raids and interviews with the Generalissimo. Then he abruptly went off to Tokyo to interview Foreign Minister Matsuoka and United States Ambassador Joseph Grew. Reporting an air raid called for graphic details, quickly chosen and then processed by *Time*'s formular understatement. Interviews invariably led to the significant quote. All assignments required the reporter's instant adaptation to the day's new scene, no matter how much it might differ from the scene of the day before. Hersey, fresh from listening to Chiang Kai-shek's plans to win the war, could shift easily to write about Ambassador Grew's policy of "dynamic appeasement."

Hersey was not in the Philippines during the early months of the war, but after four and a half years of working for *Time* he was able to put together a book called *Men on Bataan*, which was published in June 1942. *Time*'s files, letters from servicemen, and interviews with colleagues who had been on Bataan gave him the material for a book, which was half about General Mac-Arthur and half about fifty of the other 50,000 men who fought there. Fletcher Pratt, in reviewing the book for an issue of the *Saturday Review of Literature*—an issue devoted to the question of wartime morale and guest-edited by Mrs. Roosevelt—said that it "should be read by every participant in the struggle" and that "it was literature that will not be read with shame after the war." In 1942, this meant that *Men on Bataan* was not like *Three Soldiers* or *A Farewell to Arms*. "You ought to know [these men] for they are like you," Hersey wrote in the second chapter. "They have reacted as you will react when your crisis comes, splendidly and worthily, with no more mistakes than necessary." Although the writer was plainly caught up in the war effort, turning out a book for morale's sake and, as nearly as possible, for truth's sake in a year of American defeat, he was also at the farthest point in his recent career from his best journalism or from the possibility of becoming a novelist.

Fortunately for his development in all respects, he was assigned to Guadalcanal in 1942 and was privileged to observe men he would write about. He accompanied a Marine detachment into the third battle of the Matanikau River and filled most of his next book, *Into the Valley*, with what he had seen. He was with a company when it was pinned down by sniper fire. He was in line as a false rumor of retreat was passed back eagerly from man to man. He helped to carry a litter bearing a man with a mortal abdominal wound. These things he reported, along with his own admission that if he had known what was to happen during those three days he would never have gone along. *Into the Valley* was honest reporting that anticipated *Hiroshima*, even though it had such asides on the "larger questions" as this: "If people in their homes could feel those feelings for an hour or even just know about them, I think we would be an inch or two closer to winning the war and trying like hell to make the peace permanent." Hersey balanced such a statement earlier in the book when he wrote that the Marines fought, above all, to "get this goddam thing over and get home."

Hersey stayed a month on Guadalcanal and never afterward spent any more time with a particular military unit than he did with the Marine company at the three-day battle of the Matanikau. He never again had as close and sustained a view of combat, although he would spend many hours interviewing such survivors of combat as Lieutenant John F. Kennedy. He lacked the intensive exposure of correspondents Richard Tregaskis or Ernie Pyle. But he was given a spectacular view of the war.

He went from the Solomons to Sicily and later to Russia. He interviewed men from all the American fighting services and most of the special fields within each service. He met a great assortment of the war's civilian victims. He reported occupation, liberation, and rehabilitation. *Time* and *Life* also gave him solemn duties that most other reporters were fortunate to avoid: his beats occasionally included morale and war aims. At the same time that he wrote about the Matanikau battle, he filed a story about the Marines on Guadalcanal, sections of which could have been run with the Nash-Kelvinator ad: "As a fighter, he is a cross between Geronimo, Buck Rogers, Sergeant York, and a clumsy, heartsick boy." For *Life*'s Christmas number in 1943, Hersey wrote a text to accompany reproductions of paintings by the magazine's overseas artists. Titled "Experience by Battle," the article is a curious mixture of statements. He mentions hatred of the Japanese enemy: "call it neurosis, call it hatred that consumes men and never leaves them, call it whatever you wish, the feeling of men who have fought the Japanese is permanent and terrible." The future author of *Hiroshima* and *The War Lover* also wrote: "The war will end sooner for aviators, and their scars will heal quicker, if they can concentrate on hitting the enemy carefully and well." A few pages later, he wrote:

> For American soldiers, who know their duty when they see it but who love life so very much, the Japanese warrior code is beginning to be a thing of pity. It says "Duty is weightier than a mountain, while death is lighter than a feather." The Marines who fought on Guadalcanal wanted only to live to fight victoriously another day and after the fight, to be happy and relaxed and American for many other days.

This observation lying so close to the real questions of life and death in wartime faintly anticipates what he would write years later about survival and tenacity, but in 1943 and 1944 he was incapable of pursuing its implications.

Because World War II was fought more globally than the first, because news coverage had become more extensive and instantaneous, and because he worked for publications which exploited these new conditions in capsulating the news more effectively than their competitors, John Hersey had opportunities and handicaps given no earlier writer. He stood somewhere between the wire service editor in Oklahoma who wrote a novel about the Russian front from the leavings of his teletype and Norman Mailer, who was taking notes as a rifleman for a novel he was determined to write after the war.

A Bell for Adano is the sort of book one might expect Hersey to write at that time. He finished it within six weeks after he had filed a story for *Life* on the operations of the American military governor of Licata, Sicily. The article, which took up only two of *Life*'s back pages, described a typical day at the desk of an unnamed American major, a New Yorker of Italian extraction. A merchant was told to compile a fair price list for food and clothing that had been impounded by the Fascists. A pretty girl was assured that her fiancé was a prisoner of war. Charges were dismissed in the case of a cart driver arrested for obstructing traffic. Hersey followed his training in observing these details, and then began his story in the spirit of his writing on war aims:

> For a long time we have taken pleasure in the difficulties met by Germany and Japan in organizing the conquered lands. Here at the major's desk you see difficulties, hundreds of them, but you see shrewd action, American idealism, and generosity bordering on sentimentality, the innate sympathy of common blood that so many Americans have to offer over here. You see incredible Italian poverty, you see the habits of Fascism, you see a little duplicity and a lot of simplicity and many things which are comic and tragic at one time. Above all you see a thing succeeding and it looks like the future.

This is a good precis of *A Bell for Adano*. When he turned to write the novel, Hersey borrowed General Patton, contrived a romantic interest for the major (provoking a lawsuit after the war), and added the story of replacing the town bell. Everything else is fictionalized journalism in the strictest sense. The point of the first paragraph of the article is expanded and set in italics as the foreword to the novel, and each case at the major's desk is developed into an episode. *A Bell for Adano* was a huge popular success. Even more than when he had written *Into the Valley*, Hersey was praised in terms that made him a literary 90-day wonder. He was told that he had written "a magnificent parable," and that, unlike the World War I cynics, he "could look beyond both horror and heroics to the truth of what he had seen." He "had everything needed to make a front-rank novelist," especially because of "his consuming interest in men and women and his genuine love for them."

Hersey a modest man, could not accept these tributes as a balanced critical estimate of his work. He understood better than the reviewers of *A Bell for Adano* what effect the war had had on his writing, and his understanding increased during his assignment in Moscow in 1944. There, while he was compelled to report the war by listening to the salvos in Red Square proclaiming the recapture of cities to the west, Hersey wrote an article for the *Time* book section on the activity of Russian writers in wartime. The section editor borrowed Gorki's phrase, "engineers of the soul," for the title. "Not a word is written which is not a weapon," Hersey observed, and he must have known of the old Party slogan. The books of Sholokhov, Simonov, and others that he had to summarize for his report he felt could not be criticized in conventional terms. "The only fair test," Hersey wrote, "is to see whether these writers have fulfilled their aims." He saw their aims exactly as they saw them— nothing but to defeat the hated enemy. The single determining fact about these Russian writers, Hersey insisted, was that they had been in and out of the war.

Although more of a spectator than the Russians had been, as he went in and out of the war, Hersey was more the war's product than they were. To suggest what else influenced Sholokhov, Simonov, and their colleagues in the war years is to ask if there could have [been] a Soviet novel like *A Bell for Adano*, with a Soviet major standing up for a Hungarian cart driver against a Soviet general. Hersey had only the war as milieu and guide. Such assignments as writing notes under the heading of "Experience by Battle" and producing a book on Bataan a month after the surrender of Corregidor strained Hersey as much as Russian writers had been strained in using words as weapons. While his wartime books must be judged honestly by standards applied to other American books printed in 1942 and 1944—Saul Bellow's *Dangling Man*, for example—they must also be judged by their aims for the same extenuation that Hersey sought for the Russians. When he had the opportunity to study how men survived their ordeals, as he did at the Matanikau and when he

interviewed Lieutenant Kennedy, Hersey helped himself become a novelist. Otherwise, on V-E Day, when he won his Pulitzer Prize, Hersey was a man who had had to write too much too soon. . . .

Source: David Sanders, "John Hersey: War Correspondent into Novelist," in *New Voices in American Studies*, Purdue University Studies, 1966, pp. 49–58.

Anne Stuart

In the following review, Stuart notes the factual basis for the story laid out by Hersey in A Bell for Adano.

This first novel, by the young newspaper correspondent and author of *Men on Bataan* and *Into the Valley*, who in the summer of 1943 was in Africa and accompanied the American Invasion Forces into Italy, is the first novel to be written about AMGOT (Allied Military Government of Occupied Territory), later called AMG. And while the novel is not a great one, the book is evidently based on facts as Hersey found them.

Major Victor Joppolo, U.S.A., an Italian American, formerly a clerk in the New York City Sanitation Department, was appointed senior civil-affairs officer for the town of Adano, Italy. The story tells the day-by-day task of Major Joppolo from the time he set foot on Italian soil, when he said "this is like coming home," to his departure caused by countermanding one of the unreasonable orders of the arrogant American General Marvin. As he left Adano, he had the pleasure of hearing the bell in the tower strike eleven. The Bell of Adano was seven hundred years old and was a part of the life of the people, for "it rang with a good tone every quarter hour." It was taken by Mussolini to make rifle barrels. Replacing this bell with one from the Navy, which bore the inscription "U.S.S. Corelli America et Italia" was the last act Major Joppolo did for the Italians; but the beautiful speech he had prepared about the new bell and its meaning for Adano was never uttered because instructions came ordering him back to Algiers for re-assignment.

Restoring the bell to the people of Adano was only one of Major Joppolo's accomplishments. He was familiar with the native language and knew something of the psychology of Italians and he taught the people of Adano the ways of democracy by helping them and teaching them to help themselves. His biggest obstacle was eradicating the poison of Fascism.

We are lucky to have our Joppolos [says the author in the foreword] for no other country has such a fund of men who speak the languages of the lands we must invade. This is lucky for America. America is on its way into Europe. Until there is stability in Europe, our armies and our after-armies will have to stay in Europe. Each American who stays may well be extremely dependent on a Joppolo, not only for language, but for wisdom and justice and the other things we think we have to offer Europeans.

It is a pity Major Joppolo was not permitted to stay and restore to the people of Adano the feeling of self-respect they needed so much to become better citizens.

Source: Anne Stuart, Review of *A Bell for Adano*, in *America*, Vol. 70, No. 23, March 11, 1944, p. 635.

SOURCES

"Books: After Victory," in *Time*, February 21, 1944, http://www.time.com/time/magazine/article/0,9171,774792-1,00.html (accessed October 18, 2011).

Churchill, Winston S., *The Second World War: Closing the Ring*, Houghton Mifflin, 1951, pp. 24, 36, 39, 40.

"George Patton," Biography.com, http://www.biography.com/people/george-patton-9434904 (accessed January 6, 2012).

Girgus, Sam B., "John Hersey," in *Dictionary of Literary Biography*, Vol. 6, *American Novelists Since World War II, Second Series*, edited by James E. Kibler, Jr., Gale Research, 1980, pp. 137–44.

Grant, A. J., and Harold Temperley, *Europe in the Nineteenth and Twentieth Centuries (1789–1950)*, 6th ed., revised and edited by Lillian M. Penson, Longmans, 1969, pp. 558–9.

Hersey, John, *A Bell for Adano*, Knopf, 1967.

"Italy," CIA: World Factbook, 2011, https://www.cia.gov/library/publications/the-world-factbook/geos/it.html (accessed October 25, 2011).

Kanigel, Robert, *Vintage Reading: From Plato to Bradbury: A Personal Tour of Some of the World's Best Books*, Bancroft Press, 1998, pp. 161–63.

Martin, Douglas, "F. E. Toscani, 89, Dies; Model for Hero of 'Bell for Adano,'" in *New York Times*, January 28, 2001, http://www.nytimes.com/2001/01/28/nyregion/fe-toscani-89-dies-model-for-hero-of-bell-for-adano.html (accessed October 24, 2011).

Sanders, David, *John Hersey*, Twayne's United States Author Series, No. 112, Twayne Publishers, 1967, pp. 32, 36.

FURTHER READING

Newark, Tim, *Mafia Allies: The True Story of America's Secret Alliance with the Mob in World War II*, Zenith Press, 2007.

Newark tells the story of how the Mafia, crushed by Mussolini, was able to make a comeback in Sicily after the Allied invasion.

Sanders, David, *John Hersey Revisited*, Twayne's United States Author Series, No. 569, Twayne Publishers, 1991.

This is a concise introduction to the entirety of Hersey's work.

———, "John Hersey: War Correspondent into Novelist," in *New Voices in American Studies*, edited by Ray B. Browne, Donald M. Winkelman, and Allen Hayman, Purdue University Press, 1966, pp. 49–58.

Sanders shows how Hersey's writing technique evolved over the course of his five novels related to World War II.

Walsh, Jeffrey, *American War Literature: 1914 to Vietnam*, St. Martin's, 1982.

This includes an assessment of *A Bell for Adano*, as well as *The Wall*, in the context of other books about war by American authors.

SUGGESTED SEARCH TERMS

John Hersey

A Bell for Adano

General George S. Patton

Licata

Sicily invasion 1943

Italian campaign AND World War II

World War II

Fascism

Mussolini

Benito Cereno

HERMAN MELVILLE
1855

Benito Cereno is arguably Herman Melville's most controversial story. Published in three installments between October and December of 1855 (and later in *The Piazza Tales* collection in 1856), Melville's fictionalized retelling of Captain Amaso Delano's encounter at sea with a Spanish ship overtaken by the slaves on board was disregarded for many years after publication—as was most of Melville's work—but today stands as one of the most complicated and thought-provoking stories ever written about race and slavery.

Benito Cereno is considered one of Melville's "short" novels. Melville had found fame with his earlier works but lost much of his reading audience because of the philosophical and intellectual style developments in his later works. By the time of the publication of *Benito Cereno* (1855), Melville was publishing exclusively through magazines, whereas the works of his earlier career were all published in novel form. Many of his stories deemed "too intellectual" by his contemporaries are today among the most studied stories in American fiction. *Benito Cereno* is an example of a work by Melville that was not appreciated in his lifetime but is now well regarded.

Many different interpretations have been inspired by *Benito Cereno*. According to some, the American Captain Delano is the hero, according to others, the mutinous slaves are the heroes, but all would agree *Benito Cereno* is as complicated as it is entertaining. Melville's fiction is not

Herman Melville (© *The Library of Congress*)

an easy read, but when read properly, his work is some of the most engaging and satisfying literature ever written. Copies of *Benito Cereno* are widely available for free online (http://books. mirror.org), and it has been printed in many collections including *Billy Budd and Other Stories* from Penguin Press and in *The Piazza Tales* from CreateSpace.

AUTHOR BIOGRAPHY

Melville was born in New York City on August 1, 1819. His family was among the most respected and distinguished in the city. His father, Allan Melville, was a lucrative wholesale merchant, and his mother, Maria Gansevoort Melville, was daughter to one of the richest men in Albany. In addition to being wealthy, Melville's family was also historically influential. Grandfathers on both sides were heavily involved in the American Revolution: General Peter Gansevoort was the "hero of the defense of Fort Stanwix during the American Revolution," and Major Thomas Melville participated in the Boston Tea Party.

Melville's parents thought he might be a slow learner, and his father planned for him a future in commerce rather than a professional field. However, in 1830, Melville's father had to file for bankruptcy, disrupting the family's lifestyle. His father was able to regain some of his wealth, but he died in 1832, leaving Melville and his brothers to support the family. Melville went to work at the age of thirteen for his brother's fur company. He then worked on his uncle's farm and three years later taught a single term at a small school in Albany at the age of seventeen. In 1838, Melville studied to work on the Erie Canal but could not find a job after his training.

On June 5, 1839, Melville embarked on the *St. Lawrence* but did not like sailing on a merchant ship. After returning to America and another brief attempt at teaching, Melville set sail again on a whaling ship and spent the next several years at sea, with a short stint living with the indigenous Taipis tribe in Marquesas Islands. After serving briefly with the U.S. Navy, Melville sailed home and shared exciting stories of his epic journey with friends and family. They encouraged him to write. These tales became his two first novels, *Typee* (1846) and *Omoo* (1847), which were his most widely accepted and critically acclaimed novels during his lifetime. They were essentially adventure stories but contained a little experimental writing.

Melville's third novel, *Mardi* (1849), is the first example of the type of writing by Melville that is admired today, although his contemporaries disliked it. Encouraged to return to his earlier style in order to save his career, Melville quickly published *Redburn* (1849) and *White Jacket* (1850). However, in 1851, after forming a friendship with Nathaniel Hawthorne, Melville wrote what many argue is the greatest American novel ever written: *Moby Dick*. This epic novel was brushed aside by contemporaries looking for a straightforward adventure tale without the allegories, romanticism, and philosophy. Devastated over the reading masses' inability to understand his complex works, Melville wrote *Pierre* (1852) before turning to magazine publications. This is the time in his life when he published *Benito Cereno* (1855).

Melville would publish two more novels (*Israel Potter* in 1855 and *The Confidence Man* in 1857) before retiring. He wrote poetry late in life and published some of it, but his poetry is not considered as profound as his fiction. He died on

September 28, 1891, in New York City, having spent nineteen years as an inspector of customs at the Port of New York. His obituaries stated that he was the author of *Typee* and *Omoo* but did not mention any of his other works. Not until the early 1900s was there renewed interest in Melville's work, and it was then that Melville's final novel *Billy Budd* (1927) was discovered in his office and published.

PLOT SUMMARY

The plot to Melville's *Benito Cereno* is an adaptation of Chapter 18 in Amaso Delano's *Narrative of Voyages and Travels, in the Northern and Southern Hemisphere* (1817). However, in turning the story to fiction, Melville made several changes to Amaso's narrative. The most apparent changes occur in the beginning of Melville's novel. *Benito Cereno* is set in 1799, whereas Delano's narrative happened in 1805. Also, the names of the ships have been changed: Delano's *Perseverance* becomes Melville's *Bachelor's Delight*, and Delano's *Tryal* becomes Melville's *San Dominick*. Much scholarly attention has been paid to the changes made by Melville with regards to symbolism and allegory within the story. Otherwise, the plot of *Benito Cereno* follows Delano's *Narrative* quite loyally.

Benito Cereno begins with Captain Amasa Delano, an American from Duxbury, Massachusetts, anchoring his ship, *Bachelor's Delight*, in the St. Maria harbor off the coast of Chile: "There he had touched for water." The next morning, Delano is told by his crew that "a strange sail" is heading toward the bay. Delano looks out to sea at the incoming ship. The narrative describes the grey overcast of his view, and the line "shadows present, foreshadowing deeper shadows to come" gives the reader a hint of the type of story that is being told.

Following the symbolism of color in this scene, Delano notices the ship "showed no colours," that is, they flew no flag. To a seaman, this is a peculiar sight, and certainly hints at a pirate ship or something of an unlawful and violent nature. However, Delano is a man with a "benevolent heart," and he trusts his fellow men unless given serious reason to doubt. Furthermore, when Delano observes the mysterious ship sailing "too near the land," he loses "whatever misgivings might have been obtruded on first seeing the

stranger." Simply, if they are pirates, they are not talented sailors.

When the strange ship finally enters the harbor, Delano decides he will take a small boat to see what and who is on board, giving aid if needed. He is a very nice American. Approaching the strange ship, Delano sees many dark figures walking along the bulwarks through the fog, and this sight drives him "to think that nothing less than a ship-load of monks was before him." Upon getting even closer, Delano notices that the strange ship is carrying slaves—the monk-like figures on the bulwarks are actually the cargo. After scrutinizing the ship, Delano notices that much of the maintenance of the ship has been neglected: "the spars, ropes, and great part of the bulwarks, looked woolly, from long unacquaintance with the scraper, tar, and the brush."

One of the most important symbols in this story is the stern piece Delano sees, "a dark satyr in a mask, holding his foot on the prostrate neck of a writhing figure, likewise masked." Delano wonders if the ship has "figure-head, or only a plain beak" on the nose of the ship; he cannot tell because a canvas has been wrapped over the front of the ship. Below the canvas someone has written "*Seguid vuestro jefe*" (follow your leader). Delano also notices the ship is named *San Dominick*, and the letters are "streakingly corroded with tricklings of copper-spike rust." This is a further example of the ship's state of neglect. At last, Delano's boat is hooked, and he is brought aboard the ship.

From this moment forward, *Benito Cereno* is told like detective fiction. The information gathered by Delano comes slowly, and the reader does not know exactly what is happening on the *San Dominick* until Captain Delano understands. Immediately, Delano is surrounded by a group of whites and blacks, but there are more blacks than whites, and that is unusual to Delano. The people on the ship speak Spanish. The captain, Benito Cereno, is a Spaniard. Everyone tells the same story to Delano. Most of the crew died from scurvy. "Off Cape Horn, they had narrowly escaped shipwreck, then, for days together, they had lain tranced without wind."

Upon further observation of the *San Dominick*, Delano observes many blacks working and very few Spaniards on board. He notices six black men sitting in a row, "each with a rusty hatchet in his hand." They are cleaning and sharpening the hatchets, but more importantly the sound and sight of these slaves with hatchets will remain as a major part of the background for the remainder of Delano's time spent on this ship. All the while, Delano's opinion of the blacks remains as people with "the raw aspect of unsophisticated Africans." In short, he does not believe they are capable of doing any harm, even with hatchets in their hands.

When Delano meets Cereno he understands him to be an awkward fellow, "at one moment casting a dreary, spiritless glance upon his excited people, at the next an unhappy glance toward his visitor." Nevertheless, Delano offers the Spanish captain some fish and supplies and sends his crew members back to his own anchored ship. Delano remains on the *San Dominick*, as was customary for captains of friendly ships when anchored in the same unfamiliar territory. Delano also observes that the wind is carrying the Spanish ship further away from the dock that holds his own but does not fear for his own safety at this time.

As the story continues, Delano observes more unusual behavior from Captain Benito Cereno, who is showing "symptoms of an absent or moody mind." Delano meets Babo, Cereno's body servant. Babo does not leave Cereno's side, but the American (readers should make special note of occasions where Melville refers to Delano as "the American," for these are passages that comment on American culture and the American institution of slavery, a profound debate at the time of the novel's publication in 1855) dismisses Babo's eerie presence, again thinking of blacks as unsophisticated.

It is at this time that Delano and the reader learn that Cereno gives his orders to the crew through Babo. This is a peculiar practice, but Delano ignores this as a symptom of a ship beset by illness. Delano notes "some prominent breaches not only of discipline but of decency," yet he ascribes this to the lack of officers remaining in the crew. "On these decks not so much as a fourth mate was to be seen," the fourth mate being the fifth and final crew member of any authority below the captain. Cereno is the only leader on the ship. However, when Delano asks Cereno to tell him the whole story, "Don Benito faltered."

With Babo keeping a close ear, Cereno tells Delano the story of how the ship was caught in a storm, causing it to lose some men. After the storm, much of the crew became ill and died.

Continuing his story, Cereno speaks "brokenly and obscurely, as one in a dream." After much of the crew was lost, there were some stirrings of mutiny, but Cereno credits Babo with the extinguishing of any talk about overthrowing Cereno. When Delano asks Cereno why the black slaves are permitted to walk to ship freely, Cereno says it is that way by order of their master.

After the story is told, Delano becomes suspicious of Cereno, questioning his legitimacy as captain, but he quickly forgets these fears and even contemplates offering three members of his own crew to assist the *San Dominick* on the remainder of their voyage. Babo interrupts, saying "this excitement is bad for master." Babo and Cereno walk away to discuss something privately, leaving Delano alone. He notes the sound of the "hatchet-polishers" and wonders why they are allowed to do something so noisy in the presence of the captain and a visiting captain. The bizarre behavior of the people aboard this ship makes Delano fairly nervous, but he dismisses any worries and even grows arrogant.

When Cereno returns, Delano tells him that such behavior would never be allowed on his own ship. Delano begins to give Cereno advice on how he could keep the slaves busy doing the chores of the ship, and Cereno quietly follows the flow of the conversation. All of this is said, of course, with Babo standing next to his master. It is at this point that the name of the slave owner is given: Alexandro Aranda. Aranda has died on this voyage, and when Cereno talks about him "his air was heart-broken, his knees shook; his servant supported him." Delano, seeing this as an opportunity to talk about his own experiences with dead sailors, asks if Aranda's remains are still on board the ship or if they have been cast out to sea.

Atufal, a large slave in chains, walks onto the deck, and his actions are explained to Delano. Atufal has offended Cereno in some serious way, and therefore the captain has ordered him to come every two hours until he apologizes for what he has done. Thus far, Atufal has refused to ask forgiveness and still refuses in front of Delano. Babo explains that Atufal "was king in his own land." Delano thinks this practice is silly, but Babo explains for Cereno that Atufal must not be set free. The padlock on his chains can only be unlocked by the key Cereno wears on his neck. Shortly after this scene, Cereno and Babo walk away from Delano (the rudeness of this behavior is noted by the American) and begin to whisper quietly.

Left alone, Delano looks away only to find another Spaniard on a different part of the ship. Delano notices this because the Spaniard gives an eerie stare, refusing to break eye contact. These events lead Delano to his first real suspicions in the story: the Spanish captain's behavior must be that of "innocent lunacy, or wicked imposture." However, Delano's suspicions of Cereno's place on the ship are broken when he notes the bone structure of Cereno's face; it is that of a high class in Delano's opinion. Cereno returns, and the captains continue their conversation. As they chat about the supplies on the Spanish vessel, Babo all the while remaining very close, Delano's suspicions return. With the sound of the hatchet polishers in the background, Delano decides Cereno and Babo have "the air of conspirators." It is Delano's second suspicion that drives him to act, he tells Cereno "your black here seems high in your trust." It is the reaction from the two that gives both Delano and the reader their first serious idea of what is happening on the ship: Babo holds "a good-natured grin," while Cereno acts as if he has received "a venomous bite."

Slowly the condition of who is in charge on the ship is revealed, the wind continues to carry the ship seaward, and Delano's suspicions regarding Cereno's behavior are incited and extinguished as his own opinions change. However, it must be noted that Delano does not fear any conspiracy involving the blacks that is not being led by Cereno.

When a boat from Delano's own ship is seen approaching the *San Dominick*, the people on the ship begin to make noise. Delano notices two blacks on the deck pushing a lone Spanish sailor "despite the earnest cries" of the other blacks on board. Delano asks Cereno if he saw this, and if he is going to punish the blacks. Cereno has a coughing fit, falling into the arms of Babo. Delano's next line is one of the most cited and considered passages in the story. He asks, "Tell me Benito . . . I should like to have your man here myself—what will you take for him?" Delano wants to buy Babo. It is Babo who answers, not Cereno, refusing any such transaction. Babo and Cereno leave Delano's presence.

Left alone, Delano begins to explore the ship while waiting for his own boat to arrive. A Spanish sailor gives Delano a silent message with his body movement but leaves quickly before Delano can decipher his meaning. Standing on the bulwarks, Delano leans over the railing to look in the distance, and the railing collapses, causing Delano to fall to the deck. Walking the deck, Delano finds an old Spanish sailor tying a knot. The man hands Delano the knot and tells him in broken English "undo it, cut it, quick."

When the boat from Delano's ship nears, the sailors on board first send fresh water up to the ship. Standing on the deck, Delano is pushed by a black on board, and both Cereno and the other blacks on board react with shrieks. Delano, refusing to accept any of his suspicions, waits for the supplies to be brought on board and sends his boat back to the ship. Cereno approaches Delano again, and the two captains begin to talk. Delano mentions the tragedy the *San Dominick* experienced near Cape Horn, and Cereno acts like he does not know what Delano is talking about. In short, Cereno's story about how the Spanish sailors have died has changed. Before Cereno can dig himself deeper into his story, Babo interrupts, reminding Cereno that it is shaving time. Two important things happen while Babo shaves Cereno: first, he uses the Spanish flag to wipe the Spaniard's face (which seems disrespectful to Delano, but it is not an American flag, so he dismisses it as a cultural difference), and second, Babo cuts Cereno with the blade. Cereno loses most of his strength after the shave.

The two captains sit down to eat dinner. Delano asks Babo to leave, but both Cereno and Babo refuse. After dinner, the wind begins to carry the ship back toward land and Delano's ship. Wanting to celebrate, Delano offers Cereno the opportunity to come aboard his own ship. However, Cereno refuses. Delano has lost his patience with the Spanish captain. A boat is sent to pick up Delano from the *San Dominick*. It is only after Delano is on board that Cereno runs and jumps over the edge of his ship, landing in Delano's boat. Babo follows holding a knife. Delano at first thinks they are trying to kill him, but after holding his foot on Babo's throat he sees the anger in his eyes and realizes the slaves have taken over the Spanish ship. The canvas on the front of the ship is removed to reveal a human skeleton. The crew of the American ship attacks the slaves on the Spanish ship, eventually capturing the survivors.

With the suspense removed from the story, the final chapter serves as an explanation of what happened on the *San Dominick* prior to Delano's boarding of the ship. This part of the story is presented as a court hearing. Cereno explains that Babo was the leader of the revolt, and Atufal was his assistant. After killing most of the Spanish sailors (including the master, Aranda, whose skeleton was hidden under the canvas on the front of the ship), the slaves decided they needed to keep some of the sailors in order to reach their destination. They demanded to be returned "to any Negro country." The chains Atufal wore were theater, the lock holding nothing, "in a moment the chains could be dropped." Cereno also explains that Babo planned on boarding and overtaking Delano's ship after nightfall had Cereno not ruined their scheme by jumping overboard.

After the courtroom, the final scene of the novel is a third person account of Delano and Cereno's final conversation. Cereno is still shaken, and when asked why he is still so fragile, he answers simply "the Negro." Babo is killed by the court, and his head is stuck on a post facing the church. Babo's head also faces towards the monastery "where, three months after being dismissed by the court," Benito Cereno dies.

CHARACTERS

Alexandro Aranda

Aranda does not appear in the story. He is the slave master and is killed in the revolt long before Delano arrives on board.

Atufal

Atufal is a large slave who first appears in the novel covered in chains. Delano is led by Babo and Cereno to believe that Atufal has misbehaved in some great way aboard the *San Dominick* and therefore must wear the chains until he is ready to apologize. The key to the padlock on Atufal's chains is worn by Cereno on a necklace around his neck. Atufal was a king in his homeland. During the hearing, Atufal's actions as one of the leaders of the slave revolt are revealed. The chains he wore were not locked and could have been dropped in an instant.

Babo

For much of the novel, Babo is the mysterious servant who will not leave the side of Benito Cereno. On several instances throughout the novel, Babo and Cereno walk away from Delano to hold discussions quietly, whispering so Delano cannot hear what they are talking about. Babo has more power than most slaves: he supports Cereno, keeping him from falling to the ground multiple times, he cuts Cereno with a blade while shaving the captain without being punished, he names his own price when Delano attempts to buy Babo from Cereno, and he refuses to leave the dining room when Delano asks Cereno if they can eat alone without Babo's presence. In the second part of the novel, Babo is revealed to be the leader of the slave revolt on the ship, with Atufal serving as his assistant. In the end, Babo is sentenced to death, having his head "fixed on a pole." Babo is the most controversial character in this novel. He can be seen as a villain, the epitome of a violent evil, but he can also be seen as a hero breaking free from the shackles of slavery and doing all he can to find freedom.

Benito Cereno

After the slave revolt aboard the *San Dominick*, Benito Cereno is one of the few living Spaniards on the ship. He is the captain of the ship, though he does not have any authority over the slaves. When Captain Amasa Delano comes aboard the *San Dominick*, Cereno must behave like everything is still under his control, although the constant presence of Babo by Cereno's side is suspicious to both Delano and the reader. At many moments throughout the narrative, Cereno and Babo walk away from Delano to hold discussions quietly. It is later revealed that these whispered conversations were Babo telling Benito Cereno what to say to the American Captain Delano.

Cereno is a very weak character in this novel, and that fact has led to some interesting interpretations regarding the true protagonist and antagonist of this novel. Cereno is barely able to stand during many scenes, and he faints when taken to court long after his mutinous ship has been docked and the slaves are returned to their chains. Benito Cereno dies at the end of the novel, and this is why Melville gave the novel Cereno's name. Although the novel never enters the point of view of the Spanish captain, this is his story all the way to his death.

Captain Amasa Delano

Captain Amasa Delano is the American captain of the *Bachelor's Delight*, a large sealer and general trading ship. The story is told in the third person from Delano's point of view. Delano visits the mysterious *San Dominick* and interacts with the people on the ship, including Captain Benito Cereno. Throughout the novel, Delano serves as the eyes and ears of the narration, and any clue the reader finds in the text regarding the bizarre behavior of the people on the Spanish ship is revealed as a result of Delano's actions aboard the suspicious vessel. Subsequently, much of the narrative's focus on racial issues is presented in light of Delano's opinions, giving the reader a glimpse of the common beliefs of white America in the early nineteenth century. He also speaks the most famous line in the novel: "You are saved; what has cast such a shadow upon you?"

It is through the interactions between Captain Delano and Captain Cereno that much of this story is told, making Delano one of the two most central characters in the novel. In fact, he is the first character introduced by the text, and he is also the only major character who survives at the end of the novel. Interestingly, Captain Amasa Delano was a real sailor, and his narrative about this incident is the source Melville used when writing his own fictionalized version of the story.

Dr. Juan Martinez de Rozas

Councilor of the Royal Audience, Juan Martinez plays a small role overhearing the trial in the final section of the novel.

THEMES

Race and Slavery

The most apparent and controversial theme in *Benito Cereno* is the topic of race and the differences in the reactions of the readers between the time of publication in the mid-nineteenth century and today. When *Benito Cereno* was published, the institution of slavery was still legal and widely practiced in the United States. Published at the end of 1855, six years before the American Civil War began and eight years before Lincoln issued the Emancipation Proclamation, freeing the slaves, the topic of American slavery had grown to be a serious and heavily argued topic in American politics.

In the years since the publication of *Benito Cereno*, various interpretations of Melville's story have been recorded. For example, Captain Amasa Delano's opinion of the blacks in the text has

provoked interpretations opposite in nature. Lines referring to blacks as less than human or animalistic, such as "Captain Delano took to Negroes, not philanthropically, but genially, just as other men to Newfoundland dogs," have been regarded by some critics and readers as inherently racist statements, while other critics and readers read such lines as Melville writing critically of the racial opinions that many of his contemporary Americans held, using Delano as a tragic example of their thoughts and actions.

A good argument in support of the latter interpretation is the fact that Delano refuses to acknowledge the mutiny of the blacks aboard the *San Dominick*, constantly assuming that it is Cereno who is the conspirator. Delano places himself in dangerous situations as a result of his racial bigotry. Believing the blacks to be incapable of posing any real danger, he allows himself to become surrounded by them and even attempts to purchase Babo from Benito Cereno. Surely these examples of Delano's foolish behavior encourage the reader to understand that *Benito Cereno* is not a pro-slavery text.

Class

The driving force of the plot in *Benito Cereno* is Captain Amasa Delano's insistence on maintaining and behaving in a manner acceptable to his social position as a captain and as an American. When first boarding the *San Dominick*, Delano provides multiple examples of the decency and mannerisms that were considered proper at the time. First, he is critical of Benito Cereno, looking down on the Spanish captain with American "charity . . . he had noted that there are peculiar natures on whom prolonged physical suffering seems to cancel every social instinct of kindness." Then the guilt of passing judgment on Cereno soon emerges in Delano's conscience: "Indulgent as he was at the first, in judging the Spaniard, he might not, after all, have exercised charity enough." These are the class distinctions that Melville is using both to give credibility to the characters in his story and to criticize in the same breath. After all, it is Delano's desire to follow this order of "charity," accompanied with his self-image of class, that places him on a strange foreign vessel that poses a true danger to his life.

Because Delano is blinded by his ideas of class-based behavior, he is unable to judge Cereno's situation aboard the *San Dominick*, recognizing

TOPICS FOR FURTHER STUDY

- After reading *Benito Cereno*, read Ralph Ellison's *Invisible Man*. Notice that the epigraph to *Invisible Man* is a quote from *Benito Cereno*: "'You are saved,' cried Captain Delano, more and more astonished and pained, 'you are saved; what has cast such a shadow upon you?'" The quote is from the final conversation between Captain Delano and Benito Cereno in Melville's novel, and Ellison chose not to include Cereno's response to Delano's question ("the Negro"). Why did Ellison cut this sentence from his epigraph? Is Ellison's entire novel—published nearly one hundred years later—his own version of the response Cereno was able to make in a two-word sentence? Write an essay comparing and contrasting the two novels, and pay special attention to the epigraph beginning Ellison's novel and the context of *Benito Cereno* that he borrowed for his own use.

- Differing interpretations have led to wide discussions over Melville's authorial intent regarding the institution of slavery in *Benito Cereno*. Some believe the story is an abolitionist text, while others read Delano's racism as Melville's. Create an online blog where you express your own opinion regarding the slavery in *Benito Cereno*. Visit the blogs your classmates create and start discussions on one blog with which you agree and another with which you disagree. Free blog space can be found at blogspot.com.

- Throughout the novel, Captain Delano is occasionally described as "the American Captain." Remembering that the story is set in 1799 and written in the 1850s, what aspects of eighteenth- and nineteenth-century American culture does Delano represent? Does his cultural affiliation get him into trouble when dealing with a ship from the Old World? Does Benito Cereno represent Spanish culture, or is he just a literary tool used to represent Europe and the Old World as a whole? Using the Internet to research, write an essay comparing the cultural representation of each captain, keeping the historical context of the time period in mind.

- Melville is considered by many to be a romantic. The romantics use nature in their art as a means of carrying a message. What effects does the weather have on the plot structure of *Benito Cereno*? Pay special attention to the wind and the sea. Make a list of all the moments when the weather influences the story. When finished with the list, write an essay discussing whether or not you feel this novel's plot could exist without nature. Is nature a character in *Benito Cereno*?

- Mark Twain's *Adventures of Huckleberry Finn* deals with the relationship between a poor white boy and a runaway slave traveling along the rivers of America. In Twain's novel, Huck Finn must face the social norms involving race and make his own decisions. In what ways does Huck Finn compare to Captain Delano? Is Huck a more open-minded example of American thinking than Delano? Write an essay comparing the way Huck and Delano respond when presented with a slave struggling for freedom.

"some prominent breaches not only of discipline but of decency," all the while unable to comprehend that the ship has been overthrown by slaves and both he and his ship are in danger. His first suspicions aboard the *San Dominick* are toward Cereno concerning his credibility as captain of the ship. However, after observing Cereno's face for a moment, he dismisses his early suspicions based on the bone structure of Cereno's face: "He was a true off-shoot of a true hidalgo Cereno." It is a practice like observing the bone structure of a person's face to determine his class that epitomizes the rigid social structures and faulty assumptions in this novel.

The story begins when two ships encounter each other on the sea. (© 1971yes | Shutterstock.com)

STYLE

Romanticism

In response to the scientific and technological advancements of the Industrial Revolution of the eighteenth century, the romantics produced literature, art, and music that defied the industrialization of the world. With a heavy focus on nature, the romantics used the aesthetic qualities of the organic world to give a more broad expression of humanity and earth. The most beautiful and obvious example of romanticism is in the beginning of the novel, as Delano looks out upon the sea towards the slowly approaching *San Dominick*:

> The morning was one peculiar to that coast. Everything was mute and calm; everything grey. The sea, though undulated into long roods of swells, seemed fixed, and was sleeked at the surface like waved lead that has cooled and set in the smelter's mould. The sky seemed a gray mantle. Flights of troubled gray fowl, kith and kin with flights of troubled gray vapours among which they were mixed, skimmed low and fitfully over the waters, as swallows over meadows before storms. Shadows present, foreshadowing deeper shadows to come.

This description shows the aesthetics of nature, true romanticism. In a dreary scenario like the one that unfolds in *Benito Cereno*, a setting so helpful in the telling of the story would seem unlikely, but this is the beauty of the romantic style. First, notice all that is gray in Delano's vision: "everything," "the sky," "fowl," and "vapors." Then there is a metaphor comparing the grayness of the scene to swallows in meadows. The only humanity in this paragraph is the smelter, who works with lead, a natural metal. The final sentence is a poem in itself: the shadows of this bleak scene predict "deeper shadows to come." Melville is explaining to the reader that this is going to be a dark story, and he is using nature to illustrate just how dark it will be.

Another example of romanticism in *Benito Cereno* is the way the weather coincides with events in the plot. When Delano boards the

San Dominick, the wind is slowly pushing the ship away from land and his own *Bachelor's Delight*. As the novel continues and both Delano and the reader begin to fear for the American captain's safety aboard this mysterious Spanish ship, the wind continues to push the *San Dominick* toward sea, escalating the suspense. When the suspense has been pushed as far as it can go, the wind begins to push the *San Dominick* back toward land, allowing Delano's men to bring a boat, Delano to board it, Cereno to jump onto it, and Babo to finally reveal to everyone that he is trying to kill the Spanish captain. Without the wind, the suspense is lost and the climax is impossible.

Journey at Sea

Moby Dick (1851) is seen by many as the greatest American sea story, and *Benito Cereno* is another glimmering example of Melville's accomplishments in the genre. Because Melville was a sailor for many years, his novels set at sea were largely autobiographical in the beginning of his career. Indeed, his novels *Typee, Omoo, Redburn*, and *White Jacket* provide some of the few known details about this period of Melville's life.

Benito Cereno, however, contains no trace of Melville's own life. It is widely known that Melville borrowed the plot of this novel from Captain Amasa Delano's autobiographical text. This is interesting because, at the time of publication in 1855, Melville had exhausted much of his own experiences through his fiction. Basically, there were no more stories to tell of his past, but Melville's heart was still set on the sea. So he did research, discovering a story he found interesting, and he rewrote the narrative. Of course, to write a story about the sea, it is hugely helpful to have some experience on the sea, as is evident in the grace with which Melville describes the settings, the ships, the crews, and the boats.

HISTORICAL CONTEXT

Published in 1855, *Benito Cereno* appeared six years before the first shot of the American Civil War and eight years before President Abraham Lincoln issued the Emancipation Proclamation. It is a novel about a slave ship being overthrown by the slaves, and slavery was a highly controversial topic at the time of the novel's publication. Melville was very interested in the American Civil War (being from New York, he sided with the North), and he was against slavery to some degree, so why does Amasa Delano speak in such negative terms regarding the blacks in *Benito Cereno*? An obvious explanation would be that Melville borrowed the plot from the real Captain Amasa Delano's narrative and was simply trying to replicate the captain's voice. However, a look at the historical setting of the story gives a better explanation as to what Melville was attempting to accomplish with his novel.

Amasa Delano's discovery of the ship overthrown by slaves occurred in 1805. Melville changed this date, setting his version in 1799. Perhaps the American narrator is supposed to be a naive representation of his nation. America was still a very young country—only twenty-three years old in the year *Benito Cereno* is set. Amasa embodies a young, headstrong, and slightly foolish culture that is still attempting to secure its place in the world. When *Benito Cereno* was published, America had established most of its power and image in the view of the rest of the world, but in 1799, America was still a struggling new nation. Perhaps *Benito Cereno* was meant to address the America of 1855, showing that, although the nation had progressed so far in many ways, the belief in racial inequality that justified slavery had not changed.

There is also much dispute over possible interpretations of *Benito Cereno*. While some see the behavior of the American captain as just described, believing Babo is the true hero of the tale, breaking free of his bondage, others interpret the story in the opposite way, seeing Babo as the epitome of evil and his ultimate death in the novel as representing a triumph of good over evil. Nevertheless, no matter which interpretation the reader believes, the naive characteristics of Delano's character cannot be denied. The way he continues to place himself in danger, while remaining completely oblivious to this danger until the end, forms a statement about the historical context of the American story. Without a real understanding of the workings of the world, Delano extinguishes all of his suspicions because of the ideals he holds about his own culture and the Spanish culture of the strange ship. Delano dismisses any danger he may be in, confusing it with a cultural clash between his American way of life and the behavior of the Spanish captain. This is the real historical lesson of *Benito Cereno*: America, like a young person, was still struggling to understand the behavior and workings of the older (adult) nations, especially at sea.

COMPARE
&
CONTRAST

- **1799:** America is a budding nation with little influence over the larger world. States disagree on small issues, but there is no urge to separate. In fact, a separation could kill the young and growing nation.

  1855: America is torn over the issues of the individual states' rights and the institution of slavery. The American Civil War (beginning in 1861) is the peak of these arguments.

  Today: While the citizens of America still disagree on many topics, perhaps none are as controversial as slavery, nor so serious that they will cause any separation between states. There is no threat of a civil war.

- **1799:** America is still a very young country, only twenty-three years old, and still has a small economy. America is trying to find a solid foundation in the world.

  1855: Although there is political strife inside the country, America is a large country that is becoming a powerhouse in the global picture. The industry of America is growing in strength on the back of the institution of slavery.

  Today: America is considered one of the most powerful countries in the world. Although it is still one of the youngest countries in the world, its progress in a few centuries has been monumental.

- **1799:** Melville will not be born for twenty years. His family is the epitome of New York City's upper class.

  1855: Melville is considered an author of journey stories, and the highly intellectual qualities of his later works are not received well by either scholars or the larger reading audience. Against the encouragement of his publishers, Melville continues to write fiction the way he feels he should write it, and as a result, he retires from writing thirty years before his death. When he dies in 1891, he is virtually unknown as an author.

  Today: Melville is considered one of the finest American authors. The intellectual writing style that was shunned by his contemporaries is now much admired and praised. His landmark novel, *Moby Dick*, is considered by many to be the best American novel of all time and is certainly the best American novel about life on the sea.

- **1799:** Theories based on intelligence and race—like those held by Captain Amasa Delano—are accepted on a large scale.

  1855: Beliefs in racial superiority are still rampant, but a growing number of abolitionists opposed to the inhumane aspects of slavery have emerged in American society.

  Today: It is understood that race alone has no effect on intellectual capacity.

CRITICAL OVERVIEW

When it was published in 1855, *Benito Cereno* went largely unnoticed. As biographer Tyrus Hillway writes, Melville "was writing at the end of his career almost exclusively to please himself." When Melville died in 1891, the only public remembrance for the author was a few brief obituary notices published in New York newspapers, and even these newspapers only mentioned his first novel and his lack of a career afterward.

It was not until 1919, the centennial anniversary of Melville's birth, that a few scholars, particularly Raymond Weaver, initiated a large revival of Melville's works. It was only after this revival that most of Melville's later works would be recognized as landmark works of American fiction and studied by both students and scholars.

Benito Cereno has become one of the most discussed and controversial works of fiction by the author. Many debates over the racial and cultural intention of Melville have been sparked

Benito Cereno was the captain of the San
Dominick. *(© Kletr / Shutterstock.com)*

and continue today. Yvor Winters points to the
importance of the depression Benito Cereno feels
at the end of the novel, which Cereno explains as
the fault of "the Negro." Because Cereno speaks
Spanish, "his reply...would have signified not
only the negro, or the black man, but by meta-
phorical extension the basic evil in human nature."
Therefore, Winters believes that Babo is the villain,
making *Benito Cereno* an action novel with tragic
moments.

In contrast, Darrel Abel writes, "it will not
do to interpret the mutinous blacks of *Benito
Cereno* as the representatives of evil. They rep-
resent an oppressed portion of humanity assert-
ing its equal right to life." Abel believes that
Babo and the slaves are the heroes of the novel,
and this would make *Benito Cereno* a tragic aboli-
tionist text. This debate over interpretive meanings
could continue forever, and it almost inevitably
depends on the individual beliefs of the reader,
but is that not the mark of extraordinary fiction?
It is a shame Melville was ignored in his lifetime.

The vast differences of interpretation between
Winters and Abel also coincide with the historical
context of those two texts (1947 and 1963, respec-
tively). More recent interpretations follow the

contemporary understanding by most that slavery
was wrong and the slaves were correct, though
murderously violent, in their overthrowing of the
San Dominick crew. However, a new aspect to
the story has surfaced in more recent interpre-
tations: the young American, the representative
of the New World, and his interactions at sea
with the dying Old World. These interpreta-
tions tend to focus on the year the novel is set,
1799, and the naive behavior of the American
Captain Amasa Delano. Frederick Busch's excel-
lent 1998 review of *Benito Cereno* describes Dela-
no's inability to see the true scenario aboard the
San Dominick as a reminder "at every turn that
dying Europe...encounters the most naive and
imperceptive rawness of the New World."
Busch's arguments are interesting because they
help explain two things. First, the reason Delano
is unable to fathom that the ship has been over-
thrown by slaves and his life is in danger, and
second, that Melville was being critical of Amer-
ican culture in 1855 (slavery still would exist for
eight years after publication), a culture that
desired to separate from the culture of the Old
World, yet they had not yet evolved past the
belief that slavery was a humane and justified
institution.

CRITICISM

Christopher Russell

*Russell is a freelance writer with a bachelor's degree
in English literature. In the following essay, he
explores the similarities between Captain Amasa
Delano's behavior in Melville's* Benito Cereno
*and that of the major characters in the genre of
detective fiction.*

In *Benito Cereno*, Captain Delano is investi-
gating the behavior of the people aboard the *San
Dominick*, gathering clues and trying to under-
stand the true situation aboard the ship. While
Delano is investigating, everyone aboard the *San
Dominick*, both slaves and sailors, are attempting
to veil the truth from him. Published in 1855, only
fifteen years after the invention of the detective
genre, Melville's plot follows the structure of a
detective novel. This mystery-like motif is so
prominent that even an interpretation of the
story focusing on a different aspect of the novel
will use terms that make *Benito Cereno* seem like
detective fiction. For instance, Frederick Busch
writes, "The clues that strike us at once are mis-
interpreted in multiples by Delano." So in this

WHAT DO I READ NEXT?

- Published in 1851, Melville's *Moby Dick* is considered by many to be the definitive novel about the sea. The battle between Captain Ahab and the white whale named Moby Dick became a cultural phenomenon in the twentieth century, and it remains one of the best and most-read novels by any American author.

- Though not considered a young-adult novel at the time of publication, Ernest Hemingway's 1952 novel *The Old Man and the Sea* has become a landmark introduction to the thorough reading of literature for young people. The journey of the old Cuban fisherman at sea is a cultural icon in American literature and makes an interesting comparison to the sea journeys of Melville's fiction.

- Edgar Allan Poe's only novel, *The Narrative of Arthur Gordon Pym of Nantucket* (1838), is an excellent example of one of Melville's contemporaries writing a novel about a journey at sea. Poe's novel is rich with romantic imagery and allegorical symbols, and the issue of American slavery is also a heavy motif, much like in *Benito Cereno.*

- Henry David Thoreau's 1849 essay *Civil Disobedience* has been heavily influential in social unrest since its publication. Published six years before *Benito Cereno*, Thoreau's essay gives a nice glimpse into the radical thoughts of the era in American history while also coinciding with the motif of unrest that Delano finds aboard the *San Dominick* in *Benito Cereno.*

- Ralph Ellison's 1947 novel *Invisible Man* uses a quote from *Benito Cereno* in the epigraph: "'You are saved,' cried Captain Delano, more and more astonished and pained; 'you are saved: what has cast such a shadow upon you?'" In his novel, Ellison digs into the issue of racism in American culture, saying that the main character goes beyond being unnoticed by white society: he is invisible. This novel is an excellent read, and one of the best African American novels of all time.

- Those looking to read a work of fiction by Melville that is not set at sea will enjoy his 1853 short story "Bartleby, The Scrivener." In this story about a clerk working on Wall Street, Melville takes an interesting look at human psychology. Bartleby is an early example of the American slacker, and the story is the original office comedy.

---

detective novel, the detective is clumsy, and the reader will have to work as Delano's smarter, yet silent sidekick.

Regardless of Delano's abilities as an investigator, the true word to focus on in Busch's comment is *clue*. A clue is something for a detective to find, and at the time of publication, the character of the detective, slowly gathering clues and eventually explaining the mystery, was one of the most beloved and therefore most read in fiction. Early in Melville's life, the overall failure of his experimental work caused him to avoid the poetic style he felt naturally inclined to use for something more broadly appealing; however, he was never truly able to break free from his complicated and intellectual style. By 1855, Melville was perhaps resigned to the failure of his novels but, ultimately, he could not conform. Melville, knowing he would not be widely read, decided to give a completely original and highbrow version of a genre that was quickly declining into the low-brow reading grade. Therefore, *Benito Cereno*, Melville's detective novel, mocks the type of fiction that was sold and read by the wide population of American readers who considered his work too philosophical, intellectual, and allegorical.

Edgar Allan Poe is credited with inventing the genre of detective fiction, first using the structure with his 1840 short story "Man of the

THEREFORE, *BENITO CERENO*, MELVILLE'S DETECTIVE NOVEL, MOCKS THE TYPE OF FICTION THAT WAS SOLD AND READ BY THE WIDE POPULATION OF AMERICAN READERS WHO CONSIDERED HIS WORK TOO PHILOSOPHICAL, INTELLECTUAL, AND ALLEGORICAL."

Crowd." The next year, Poe wrote "The Murders in the Rue Morgue," and in this story, his trademark detective character first appeared: C. August Dupin. Poe continued to use Dupin as his lead character for the next four years, inspiring all literary detectives that followed, including Sherlock Holmes. The detective genre was inspired by the growing American cities of the time. By the mid-nineteenth century, community watch programs were no longer sufficient in stopping crimes. Police forces were assigned but held little power. Vigilante detectives working for personal reasons became the true police, and Poe was writing their stories, reflecting on his culture with his new genre. However, after 1844, Poe quit writing detective stories.

Soon after Poe's invention of the genre, detective fiction became very popular and lost most of its literary credibility. By the time Melville wrote *Benito Cereno* in 1855, the detective genre was considered cheap. To write a traditional detective novel set in a city was unoriginal, but Melville had a better idea. Inspired by the narrative of Captain Amasa Delano's *A Narrative of Voyages and Travels*, Melville reinvented the detective genre, setting his investigator on the sea with *Benito Cereno*.

Blinded by his inexperience and prejudices, Delano struggles through much of the novel, unable to notice what is becoming more clear to the reader with each passing paragraph. Examples of Delano behaving like a detective appear in the beginning of the novel, as he rides on a boat to meet the bizarre ship, all the while scrutinizing the uncleanliness of the ship: "The spars, ropes, and great part of the bulwarks, looked woolly, from long unacquaintance with the scraper, tar, and the brush." Just as with a detective novel, the meaning of the first pages is more clear after the reader is finished with the entire text. After learning that the ship has sailed without sailors for many months, this early clue of the unkempt appearance of the ship makes more sense to the reader. There are examples of clues like this throughout the entire novel.

Another example appears towards the middle of the novel. Four clues have been gathered, and Delano lays them out for both the reader's and his own contemplation:

> First, the affair of the Spanish lad assailed with a knife by the slave boy; an act winked at by Don Benito. Second, the tyranny in Don Benito's treatment of Atufal, the black; as if a child should lead a bull of the Nile by the ring in his nose. Third, the trampling of the sailor by the two Negroes; a piece of insolence passed over without so much as a reprimand. Fourth, the cringing submission to their master of all the ship's underlings, mostly blacks; as if by the least inadvertence they feared to draw down his despotic displeasure.

After reading the novel, these four clues seem both important and flawed. It gives evidence that Delano is suspicious, though he is not totally sure what his suspicions amount to. It also helps to further explain that Delano is not a good detective. He makes the observations, but his deductions vary from wise to foolish. Also, the clues that have appeared before Delano's eyes at this point in the story vastly outnumber four: the unkempt nature of the ship, for instance, or the line of six slaves cleaning hatchets.

Suspense makes detective fiction entertaining. To send an experienced and suspicious captain aboard the *San Dominick* would make for an uneventful novel, or as the saying goes, it would be like reading a mystery backwards. It is because of Delano's bumbling that *Benito Cereno* is suspenseful and entertaining. When Delano is first suspicious of the behavior of those aboard the Spanish ship, his first impulse is to think that Benito Cereno is plotting against him, rather than the black slaves. This is an example of Delano's racism and "singularly undistrustful good nature" combining to inhibit his ability to see the truth aboard the ship, but it also gives a diversion from the final solution. Distraction and diversion, two cornerstones of the detective and mystery genre, help build suspense because they make the plot unpredictable.

Captain Delano does not see himself as a detective. He is the captain of a ship attempting

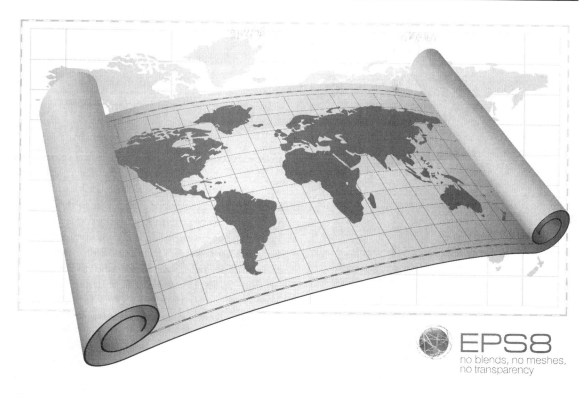

The rebellious slaves want to return the ship to Africa. (© Mushakesa / Shutterstock.com)

to meet with another captain whose ship has come within view while sailing across the ocean. The meeting of captains and the communication between ships that cross paths were common practices in 1799. When at sea for an extended period of time, interaction with a new face is welcomed by almost anyone. So Captain Delano is nothing like a detective seeking a problem to solve, he simply stumbles upon the situation. Furthermore, Delano is never able to solve the mystery, so it could be argued that to see him as a detective solving a mystery is to read too deeply. However, is it not the reluctance of readers to read deeply that resulted in the great works of Melville being ignored for so long?

It is the final chapter that gives *Benito Cereno* the full structure of a detective novel. Traditionally, the final portion of a mystery is the explanation, and this is typically given by the main character—the detective—but not always. The final section of the novel gives a thorough explanation of what happened during the slave revolt aboard the *San Dominick*. The narrative follows the string of clues Delano was able to

uncover while walking the decks of the ship and interacting with Cereno, and it fills both the reader and Delano in on the clues he was not able to uncover. The final chapter of *Benito Cereno* does give the solution to the mystery that has been built in the rest of the narrative, and although it is not given by Captain Delano, the only reason the truth is ever revealed is that Delano boarded the strange Spanish ship and was just suspicious enough, provoking exposure of the truth.

It will forever remain unclear what Melville's intentions were when he wrote novels like *Benito Cereno*. The lack of public attention during his lifetime has resulted in a lack of biographical information about an author who is now considered a canonical great. All that remains of Melville's life is his fiction, his letters, and the notes he made that are still being discovered as scholars sift through his library, desperate for more clues about the life of this brilliant and mysterious man. It is rewarding to know that Melville was aware of his skill as a writer, though it made him frustrated at the reading public's inability to see his talents. In a letter to friend and literary great Nathaniel Hawthorne, Melville wrote, "Though I wrote the Gospels in this century, I should die in the gutter." So it is not truly known whether Melville intended *Benito Cereno* to be a spin on detective fiction, but the pieces fit, and the ambiguities of this novel, the words that have inspired so many different interpretations, certainly make it mysterious.

Source: Christopher Russell, Critical Essay on *Benito Cereno*, in *Novels for Students*, Gale, Cengage Learning, 2013.

John D. Cloy

In the following review, Cloy analyzes the characterizations of the black protagonists in Benito Cereno *and* Atar-Gull, *detailing how each work handles the white characters' assumptions about race.*

Eugène Sue and Herman Melville make strong racial statements in their nautical works, *Atar-Gull* and "Benito Cereno." These pieces, published in 1831 and 1855, respectively, appeared with settings that antedate the abolition of the slave trade. For most whites, both American and European, blacks were a class apart, viewed as little more than cattle or other agricultural property. When considered as human by more liberal thinkers, their mental and emotional capacities were almost universally undervalued. Sue and Melville present in *Atar-Gull* (a novel) and "Benito Cereno" (a short story) blacks who are superior to most of their white neighbors in intelligence, cunning, patience, and fortitude. These black characters—the eponymous Atar-Gull of Sue's book and Babo in Melville's fiction—are slaves who make effectual use of whites' tendency to underestimate their abilities in order to take diabolical advantage of situations for vengeful purposes. By presenting loyal and subservient exteriors to gullible Caucasians, Atar-Gull, and Babo craftily execute murderous revenge on those who enslave them.

Although Babo and Atar-Gull use similar stratagems, their results markedly differ. Babo, who has taken over the vessel commanded by the flaccid Spanish aristocrat, Benito Cereno, fails to complete his plot to capture American captain Amasa Delano's ship and slaughter its crew. Cereno foils the scheme after Delano boards his slaver to relieve the want of the black and white sufferers who have nearly starved in a devastating calm that has paralyzed their movement for several weeks. When Delano launches his boat to return to his own ship, the *Bachelor's*

HOWEVER, BOTH SUE AND MELVILLE EMPLOY THE BLACK CHARACTERS AS JUSTIFIED REVENGE FIGURES, ALTHOUGH NOT TOTALLY POSITIVE CHARACTERS."

Delight, Cereno leaps overboard into the skiff to warn the American. Babo follows with homicidal intent, but is captured by Delano's men, who then recapture Cereno's vessel. Babo is executed at Lima for his crimes after his treachery and criminal organizational skill are brought to light. Atar-Gull, however, is totally successful. When his father, an old slave incapable of working, is wrongfully executed by Tom Wil, his English owner, the slave vows revenge. He insinuates himself into the good graces of Wil and his family by assiduous and obsequious services. With the aid of the ferocious Jamaican Maroons, he ruins Wil's crops, has his stock killed, orchestrates his daughter's death from snakebite (which results in his wife's demise from grief), and accompanies his master on a return trip to Europe after his financial ruin. The two settle in Paris, cheaper than Wil's native England, where the old man suffers a paralytic stroke that deprives him of speech. Atar-Gull then reveals his true colors to his horrified owner. Keeping neighbors at bay through a pretense of over-protection, the former slave is viewed by all as a saint, while fiendishly torturing his former master with his gloating hatred and vindictiveness. When Wil mercifully dies, the disappointed Atar-Gull is given a medal by the French citizenry, who are still unaware of his Mephistophelean machinations.

Babo and Atar-Gull belie contemporary notions of blacks' intelligence, implicitly revealing the attitudes of Melville and Sue toward slavery and the supposed inferiority of non-white people. These black characters allow themselves to be perceived as good-natured, harmless, loyal body servants to the white men they both hate and intend to destroy. By far the most resourceful and strongest figures in these works, they bide their time and reinforce their positions through seemingly assiduous care of the intended victims. Melville's American captain, Amasa Delano, reflects the then-current view of most whites regarding slaves as lesser entities. He sees the "peculiar institution" as part of the established order of things: conventional and therefore unalterable, certainly not requiring alteration. The demarcation between black and white is so great that Delano cannot even conceive of an equal association between the races. When he initially becomes uneasy at the strange happenings aboard Cereno's vessel (perhaps suggesting some evil collusion between Babo and the Spanish captain), the *San Dominick*, the American reassures himself by some "rational" reasoning:

> The whites, too, by nature, were the shrewder race. A man with some evil design, would not he be likely to speak well of that stupidity which was blind to his depravity, and malign that intelligence from which it might be hidden? Not unlikely, perhaps. But if the whites had dark secrets concerning Don Benito, could then Don Benito be any way in complicity with the blacks? But they were too stupid. Besides, who ever heard of a white so far a renegade as to apostatize from his very species almost, by leaguing in against it with negroes? ("Benito Cereno")

In a twist of racial position and power, both black characters become essentially the masters of their white overlords. Babo and his mutineers hold Cereno and the crew of the *San Dominick* hostage, their lives dependent on their good behavior while Delano and his men are aboard. Since the Spaniards have seen graphic samples of the Africans' handiwork on some of their less fortunate shipmates, they fearfully acquiesce. Atar-Gull's domination of Wil is more subtle. He succeeds by guile, and not until the old colonist is paralyzed and rendered mute by a stroke does his former bondsman declare himself. After cataloging for the horrified old invalid all the evils he has perpetrated, Atar-Gull delivers his masterstroke:

> Au-dehors je serai loué, montré, fêté, comme le modèle des serviteurs, et je te soignerai, et je soutiendrai ta vie, car elle m'est precieuse, ta vie... plus que la mienne, vois-tu; il faut que tu vives longtemps pour moi, pour ma vengeance... oh! Bien longtemps... l'éternité, si je pouvais... Et si un étranger entrait ici... ce serait pour te dire mes louanges, te vanter mon devouement a moi, qui ai tué... tué ta famille... qui t'ai rendu muet et misérable*hellip;car c'est moi... c'est moi, entends-tu, Tom Wil... c'est moi seule qui ai tout fait... moi seul.... (*Atar-Gull*)

The obtuseness of the white characters in these works borders on the unbelievable. In the American captain's case, his density probably saves him. Only after Cereno jumps into his boat as the visitors leave the *San Dominick* does Delano start to grasp the true nature of the drama around him. He still suspects the Spanish captain of perfidy at this point (grabbing him to restrain possible violence), and, until Babo leaps after his victim, attempting to poignard him, Delano is still confused. In Sue's novel, it seems unlikely that Wil and his family would not have missed Atar-Gull's overnight absences to confer with the Maroons in the mountains of Jamaica, since he was an omnipresent body-servant. Also, when one misfortune after another strikes the planter's family, the slave is never far off, in attendance at the house when Wil's daughter Jenny has her fatal encounter with the snake. Wil himself suspects nothing until Atar-Gull reveals himself in Paris as his tormentor. Neither do the neighbors in the run-down building where the two reside entertain doubts of the black's fidelity. The vastly higher intelligence and cunning of these black characters make a powerful and radical statement about Sue and Melville's beliefs in the supposed superiority of the white race.

The invidious depth of the blacks' revenge on their white owners is an accurate measure of their hatred. Both authors stress the slaves' pagan religion and foreign outlandish practices. The loosely interpreted European Christianity that allowed for the enslavement of fellow beings is contrasted with the more primal beliefs of the Africans. For the blacks, vengeance is an accepted part of their culture. The more barbarous the atrocities (including cannibalism) committed against enemies, the more successful the balancing of cosmic accounts. Thus Babo and his compatriots brutally slay the Spaniards aboard the *San Dominick*—by drowning, bludgeoning, and hacking them to death. In a particularly brutal twist, the slaves kill Don Alexandro Aranda, their former master, and install his skeleton (implying cannibalism) as figurehead on the ship, accompanied by the derisive motto "seguid vuestro jefe" (follow your leader). Atar-Gull is equally ruthless with Wil and his family, sparing no member of the Wil household. Sue and Melville subtly point out the slight distance between the ownership and degradation of slavery perpetrated by the whites to the wanton butchery of their enemies by the blacks. There seem to be no authentic Christians among the characters of either narrative, despite the claims of some of the whites themselves. After Delano has rescued Cereno from the mutineers and they are safely ashore, the Spaniard tells the American captain that he considers their passage through the adventure unscathed as a case of divine intervention:

> "Nay, my friend," rejoined the Spaniard, courteous even to the point of religion, "God charmed your life, but you saved mine. To think of some things you did—those smilings and chattings, rash pointings and gesturings. For less than these, they slew my mate, Raneds; but you had the Prince of Heaven's safe conduct through all ambuscades." ("Benito Cereno")

Benoit, whom Sue describes as a chaste and proper Catholic family man who is prone to moralizing, tries to keep his sailors in line as much as possible. When Simon, the *Catherine*'s mate, starts to blaspheme, Benoit sadly remonstrates with the offender:

> Simon . . . Simon . . . tu recommences, je n'aime pas a t'entendre blasphemer comme un païen; tu fais le philosophe, et ça te jouera un tour . . . tu verras. (*Atar-Gull*)

Though concerned with the language of his crew, Benoit nonetheless can live with the lucrative practice of slave trafficking, calling his cargo "bois d'ébene" (ebony wood), a particularly dehumanizing (and unchristian) appellation for human beings. The whites' religion seems to teem with convenient unstated precepts that allow them to act in many ways without moral restraint.

Irony figures prominently in both these fictions. Atar-Gull's receiving a prize from the Academy for his "virtuous" treatment of his master is perhaps as ironic as any event in Western literature. He emerges unscathed from his crime, like Montresor in Poe's "The Cask of Amontillado," and, like the Italian character, he gloats over his victory. Delano's dullness contains an odd variety of irony in Melville's story. That Babo and his cohorts are able to hoodwink the "superior" white captain while masquerading as slaves to their victims presents an irony of a special kind. The American's sneering attitude toward African mentality (and, to a lesser degree, that of Latins) insures his failure to perceive correctly the situation aboard the *San Dominick*. Delano is a prime example of the limitations that result from the practice of what Herbert Spencer terms "contempt prior to investigation."

The intention of the Africans in both the French and American fictions is as much concerned with control of their destinies (and their former controllers) as it is with revenge. Atar-Gull tries his mightiest to keep Tom Wil alive in order to prolong his torture (the black's sadistic control over him). Babo is willing to sacrifice his own life by leaping into Delano's boat in pursuit of Cereno; he goes to any lengths to retain his hold on the Spaniard. While Atar-Gull is devastated by Wil's death and does not long survive the Englishman, Babo dies on the scaffold for his crimes, unrepentant and silent to the last. However, his control over his victim extends beyond his death, since Cereno withdraws to a monastery, where, shattered in mind and body by his ordeal and haunted by the memory of Babo, he soon expires. Significantly, when Delano attempts to cheer the Spaniard after his rescue and the slaves' trial, the former captain's last words in the narrative (save those required at the hearing) refer to his physical and psychic captor:

> "You are saved, Don Benito," cried Captain Delano, more and more astonished and pained; "you are saved; what has cast a shadow upon you?"

> "The negro." ("Benito Cereno")

The casual reader might be initially tempted to associate the dark skin of the Africans Babo and Atar-Gull with evil, the lighter hue of Benito Cereno and Tom Wil with virtue. However, both Sue and Melville employ the black characters as justified revenge figures, although not totally positive characters. Their enslavement by whites permits the extremity of the slaves' actions, though the barbarity of their retaliation revolts modern readers. The writers sought to demonstrate a more "civilized" barbarity on the part of whites in the practice of chattel bondage. Melville's travels as a merchant seaman (and presumably Sue's as a naval physician) gave him a tolerant attitude toward people of all races. The New York writer professed sympathy with "people of all shades of color, and all degrees of intellect, rank, and social worth." Sue's republicanism has been described by detractors as opportunistic, embraced at a later period of his life after failing in an attempt at acceptance by the aristocracy. While the truth of this charge is doubtless impossible to prove after so long a period, Sue's implied sympathy with Atar-Gull and lack of empathy with Wil and his family in the novel speak volumes. Throughout the narrative the reader gets the sense that the slave is not only condoned in his vengeance by the author, but also tacitly approved.

Gothic elements are present in these sea narratives. Melville's story contains structures that exude gothic characteristics—the *San Dominick* is called a "white-washed monastery" in the narrative, and the official buildings in Lima where the rebels are tried resemble castles. The shadowy atmosphere of unreality that pervades the work supports a gothic theme; even the thick-witted Captain Delano senses that strange forces are at work. Sue's novel also features a slave vessel with many compartments, analogous to a medieval fortress. The many-storied dwelling where Atar-Gull and Wil come to live in Paris is a classic gothic house, with a concierge and numerous neighbors of various social complexions. The hint of magic involved in Atar-Gull's associations with the Maroons in the West Indies gives an added element of the macabre to this bizarre tale of ferocious revenge. Both works are shaded with religious overtones. Melville calls the slaves "black friars," and the entrance of Cereno into a monastery at the book's end is no accident. Sue's choice of a Catholic country (France) to end his story is not coincidental. The pious neighbors and associates of the odd Englishman and his black servant confer honors on the fiendish hypocrite after Wil's demise. This implied criticism of Roman blindness to reality and preoccupation with externals parallels Sue's more overt condemnation of Catholicism in *The Wandering Jew*, a scathing denunciation of the Society of Jesus. One also gets the impression that Sue does not judge too harshly the African religion that the slaves continue to embrace covertly, since the whites' faith does little to console their misery and isolation. Indeed, European Christianity viewed blacks as benighted inferiors, leaving the slaves little opportunity for an acceptable existence within the rigid hierarchical confines of the eighteenth-century great chain of being.

The surprisingly tolerant attitudes that Sue and Melville display in these works exemplify an emerging societal concern and democratization of feeling for people of color. The American Civil War was only six years away at the time of the publication of "Benito Cereno," and the French were to free their remaining slaves in the Western hemisphere in 1848, 17 years after the appearance of *Atar-Gull*. French and American ideas on freedom and personal liberty had long coincided; though the Gallic presence in the

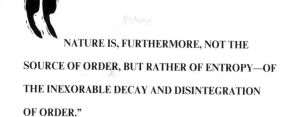

NATURE IS, FURTHERMORE, NOT THE SOURCE OF ORDER, BUT RATHER OF ENTROPY—OF THE INEXORABLE DECAY AND DISINTEGRATION OF ORDER."

American Revolution was largely one of moral support (save for notable examples like the Marquis de Lafayette), there is little doubt that the earlier French rebellion had encouraged the British colonies to revolt. These affinities of thought enabled such dissimilar authors as Melville and Sue to reach similar conclusions on the issue of racial equality—that men must be judged by their abilities alone, not their ethnic heritages.

Source: John D. Cloy, "Fatal Underestimation—Sue's *Atar-Gull* and Melville's 'Benito Cereno,'" in *Studies in Short Fiction*, Vol. 35, No. 3, Summer 1998, pp. 241–49.

Terry J. Martin

In the following review, Martin argues that this novel reveals Melville's disgust with Emersonian transcendentalism through the self-delusions of the protagonist and the personification of nature in Cereno.

Although many critics have analyzed specific natural images in Melville's *Benito Cereno*, no one has yet focused exclusively on the role of nature in the novella, nor looked fully at its problematic relation to Delano. Such an examination can both reveal much about Melville's artistry and enhance our understanding of the protagonist's special kind of self-delusion. Midway through the novella, Delano performs an act that is at once typical and revelatory of his ideology: overwhelmed by fears for his life and doubts about providence, he turns to nature for reassurance:

> As [Delano] saw the benign aspect of nature, taking her innocent repose in the evening, the screened sun in the quiet camp of the west shining out like the mild light from Abraham's tent—as charmed eye and ear took in all these, with the chained figure of the black, clenched jaw and hand relaxed.

The personal qualities that Delano attributes to nature (i.e., its "benign[ity]" and "innocen[ce]"), together with the religious associations that the sight evokes, reveal a kind of Emersonian belief in the transcendent goodness and moral providence of nature. It is, in other words, God's benignity that Delano sees suffused throughout the scene. Delano is not a thoroughgoing pantheist; he retains the idea of a personal God, noticeable especially when he later declares, "There is someone above." Nevertheless, for Delano, just as for Emerson, this transcendent spirit is shadowed forth in phenomenal nature, and Delano would no doubt agree with Emerson that "particular natural facts are symbols of particular spiritual facts." This belief in effect turns nature into a vast allegory of the divine spirit. For Delano, the mere appearance of benignity in nature warrants belief in the transcendent reality of benignity.

Delano turns to nature not only for reassurance but also for guidance and support. Nature seems for Delano to exhibit a direct interest in human affairs, in which it actively intervenes. Thus, even the most trivial occurrence, such as a pleasant tropical breeze, may convey a moral message to Delano. As Delano affirms to a despairing Cereno, "These mild Trades that now fan your cheek, do they not come with a human-like healing to you? Warm friends steadfast friends are the Trades." Delano assumes that if nature is constant in its beneficence, then Cereno's desperation must be essentially wrong and misguided. Nature seems to concur, and in Delano's estimation it openly rebukes Cereno for his moodiness:

> Meantime the sound of the parted waters came more and more gurglingly and merrily in at the windows; as reproaching him for his dark spleen; as telling him that, sulk as he might, and go mad with it, nature cared not a jot; since, whose fault was it, pray?

Delano even holds up nature as a model of human behavior. In his effort to persuade Cereno to forget the past, Delano points conclusively to the conduct of natural objects: "See, yon bright sun has forgotten it all, and the blue sea, and the blue sky; these have turned over new leaves." If nature forgets the past, then no doubt man ought to do so too.

Delano's belief that nature possesses a transcendent moral order legitimates for him the interpretation of natural signs. To be sure, Delano's behavior is no different from that of most of his contemporaries when he interprets, for example the color of skin according to this ideal order. If all things signify, then surely white, being the

opposite of black, must entail different spiritual characteristics as well. Indeed, Delano has only to look to nature to find objective corroboration for his belief that whites are "by nature . . . the shrewder race" and therefore naturally superior to blacks: the (apparent) dominance of the whites and servitude of the blacks on the *San Dominick* offers sufficient proof of Delano's premise. But Delano has also observed what he takes to be the evident inferiority even of free blacks at home. Blacks have presented themselves as "good-humor[ed]," "easy," "cheerful," and "harmonious in every glance and gesture; as though God had set the whole negro to some pleasant tune." They are, he thinks, fit "for avocations about one's person," like "natural valets and hair-dressers; taking to the comb and brush congenially as to the castanets, and flourishing them apparently with almost equal satisfaction." Furthermore, blacks are, in Delano's view, exempt "from the inflicted sourness of the morbid or cynical mind." However, he also deems them essentially "stupid," displaying the "docility arising from the unaspiring contentment of a limited mind, and that susceptibility of blind attachment sometimes inhering in indisputable inferiors." For Delano, skin color is simply the seal that providence uses to stamp inferior goods.

Of course, who knows what happens when the races are "unnaturally" mixed? Delano conjectures about the effect: "It were strange, indeed, and not very creditable to us white-skins, if a little of our blood mixed with the African's, should, far from improving the latter's quality, have the sad effect of pouring vitriolic acid into black broth; improving the hue, perhaps, but not the wholesomeness." It will be seen from this that the racially crossed offspring are at a distinct disadvantage in Delano's world, in which natural signs correlate with spiritual identity, because their identities are as uncertain as the effect of mingled magic potions. In fact, the mulatto represents a special semiotic problem for Delano precisely because the mulatto is neither black nor white and is hence unable to be interpreted with any degree of certainty. Delano is therefore even willing to consider the possibility that a mulatto with a regular European face is a devil. After all, a belief in the inherent allegorical qualities of matter requires that the mulatto be something less than white but greater than black, and devilishness at least presupposes intelligence gone astray.

For Delano, the meaning of human experience must likewise be understood in light of this allegory of divine providence, for no act can be seen apart from the divine justice that, in his eyes, actively dispenses reward and punishment in this world. Thus, his suspicion that there is a plot to kill him oddly brings about an examination of his own internal merit, as if murder could not have its root in external aggression, but rather must signify a priori some form of karmic retribution for the victim's own past transgression(s). He asks, "Who would murder Amasa Delano? His conscience is clean. There is someone above." The statement presupposes a direct empirical causality between human behavior and divine justice; with astonishing naivete Delano assumes that God would never let anything happen to the innocent (i.e., to himself), unless he had done something to deserve it. It also reveals how Delano is able to see his continued survival and good fortune as objective verification of his own innocence rather than of his cleverly disguised but nonetheless aggressive will-to-power.

Delano runs into problems, however, when the events that he witnesses often point with an almost irresistible logic to meanings that are incompatible with the existence of a benevolent providence. The whispered conversations between Babo and Benito, the nasty look of the Ashantee hatchet-polishers, the numerous signs communicated to him by the Spanish sailors, and the apparently ubiquitous presence of the imposing Atufal, along with many other equally disconcerting impressions, all suggest the existence of some sinister plot that the allegory of transcendental benignity forces him to deny. Ironically, even those spectacles that most deserve Delano's unqualified trust and sympathy, such as Benito's reduced and pathetic state, also serve to inspire the American with suspicion. In a momentary vision worthy of the completely duplicitous world of *The Confidence Man*, Delano reflects, "For even to the degree of simulating mortal disease, the craft of some tricksters had been known to attain. To think that, under the aspect of infantile weakness, the most savage energies might be couched—those velvets of the Spaniard but the silky paw to his fangs." Thus, no sign, no matter how apparently innocent, carries any absolute guarantee of its legitimacy. Later, Delano recollects similar accounts that he has heard of the mortally deceptive tactics of Malay pirates and that "now, as stories . . . recurred"—stories that have, nonetheless, a

certain power and plausibility to them that cannot easily be dismissed, and that in effect challenge his own "story."

As these examples suggest, Delano's allegorical system of understanding is not entirely self-sufficient. Although it structures and gives meaning to Delano's experience, it is also sustained by that experience—that is, it requires verification from and through his experience. It is in this way vulnerable to confutation. It is, at best, a precariously poised allegory that is in continual danger of being toppled by the logic of its tenor. And the need to read the clues around him serves to quicken the crisis of interpretation: how can he be sure that the world is not ordered according to some other allegory instead? As Delano affirms, there is in at least one sense "a difference between the idea of Don Benito's darkly pre-ordaining Captain Delano's fate, and Captain Delano's lightly arranging Don Benito's"; on that slender distinction rests the very nature of the world Delano inhabits.

Delano is not in fact able completely to dismiss the many indications of human evil throughout the story, but to admit them exacts a heavy price: as the evidence of earthly evil accumulates, so too grow his doubts about the supremacy of celestial goodness. Delano inadvertently reveals the extent of his apostasy when he repents of having too strongly doubted the good intentions of those on board the *San Dominick*, for to have given free rein to his fear, he discovers, is at once to have doubted the God that watches over him: "Once again he smiled at the phantoms which had mocked him, and felt something like a tinge of remorse, that, by harboring them even for a moment, he should, by implication, have betrayed an almost atheist doubt of the ever-watchful Providence above." Thus, Delano can only bolster his faith by denying his experience. This strategy may make both the world and himself seem better, but only at the risk of blurring the way both actually are.

Delano's very need for denial makes it evident that nature is not at all what he supposes it to be. Indeed, what Delano thinks is most "natural" or objectively self-evident is precisely what is least so. When, for example, he sees the black woman kissing the baby and speaks glowingly of "naked nature" as if it were "the thing itself"—a natural essence unshaped by either human artifice or perception—he is most fully deceived. There is nothing either "pleasant" or "sociable" about the scene, as Delano construes it. The woman is, for instance, fully a party to the plot against his life. Moreover, the scene is not even natural in the sense in which Delano takes it to be. It is only after the woman discovers him staring at her that she takes up the child and kisses it, a sequence that rhetorically suggests that the act is not at all spontaneously motivated by the "maternal transports" that Delano supposes, but is rather an entirely self-conscious artifice performed with the specific intent of placing him off his guard.

Moreover, in the world of Benito Cereno, nature is not the transcendent source of clarity that Delano imagines, but rather the source of confusion and equivocation. Significantly, our first view of nature is as a fog in which there is a continual blurring and merging of boundaries, and in which nothing can be positively identified:

> Everything was mute and calm; everything gray.... The sky seemed a gray surtout. Flights of troubled gray fowl, kith and kin with flights of troubled gray vapours among which they were mixed, skimmed low and fitfully over the waters, as swallows over meadows before storms. Shadows present, foreshadowing deeper shadows to come.

The passage serves as an analogue for the difficulty of interpretation by its evocation of grayness, of shadows, and of the inability to distinguish anything clearly. Fowl and vapors become inextricably mixed and confused. The description is indeed intended to blur the difference between them; the words "kith and kin"—with their hint of familial resemblance—and the exact syntactic repetition of the phrase "flights of troubled gray" both suggest a doubling that challenges cognitive differentiation. That Melville was employing this passage to question a certain set of epistemological assumptions is clear from its juxtaposition, for within such a background of complicated movements that become lost or fail to register, a hueless, uniform gray, and a reality that merges with, and finally becomes inseparable from, appearance, appears Captain Delano's surprise that the stranger "showed no colors."

Likewise, the morning light, which might be expected to bring clarity and illumination, merely streams "equivocally" through the vapors. Other natural signs are equally equivocal. In one of the few departures from Delano's point of view, the narrative voice states, apropos of a haggard sailor, that "whether this haggardness had ought to do with criminality, could not be determined; since, as intense heat and cold, though unlike, produce like sensations, so innocence and guilt, when, through casual association with mental pain, stamping any visible impress, use one seal—a hacked one." Thus, nature hides even what it has applied its seal to, and Don Benito warns that, truth cannot be ascertained on the basis of phenomenal evidence alone: "Even the best man [may] err, in judging the conduct of one with the recesses of whose condition he is not acquainted." In the world of Benito Cereno, one looks in vain for the natural sign that is not hopelessly equivocal.

Nature is, furthermore, not the source of order, but rather of entropy—of the inexorable decay and disintegration of order. The *San Dominick*, which has been peculiarly ravaged by natural forces that have all but transformed it to a hearse, functions as a vivid symbol of the destructive power of nature. Everything on the *San Dominick* is, indeed, in the process of becoming something other than itself and thus presents to view a strange, almost monstrous hybrid of its original form and altered state. Nothing retains its original identity, and nowhere is this more richly suggestive than in the description of the ship's name, which points both to the ultimate fate not only of the ship but of human discourse itself: "Upon the tarnished headboards, near by, appeared, in stately capitals, once gilt, the ship's name *SAN DOMINICK*, each letter streakingly corroded with tricklings of copper-spike rust." It is clearly only a matter of time until the letters dissolve completely into rust, and the sign itself is obliterated. Thus, far from being in any way the foundation of language, nature instead threatens it with utter dissolution. It is the death that constantly promises to undo the most significant assertions of human identity and language, much as it will abruptly rob of his most prized social rank the "invalid courtier tottering about London streets in the time of the plague."

Finally, although Delano assumes that his words and ideas derive their ultimate authority from nature itself, that "nature" turns out to be itself a fabrication of the language that presumes to reproduce it. In a typical scene, Melville has Delano peering into the ocean and envisioning the scene in terms of something that it is not:

> He leaned against the carved balustrade, again looking off toward his boat; but found his eye

falling upon the ribbon grass, trailing along the ship's water-line, straight as a border of green box, and parterres of seaweed, broad ovals and crescents, floating nigh and far, with what seemed long formal alleys between, crossing the terraces of swells, and sweeping round as if leading the grottoes below. And overhanging all was the balustrade by his arm, which, partly stained with pitch and partly embossed with moss, seemed the charred ruin of some summer-house in a grand garden long running to waste.

The image of a garden is especially apt here since it was a classical symbol of order. What Delano sees is, however, merely an imaginary order significantly superimposed onto a chaos of water. The scene partakes of the enchantment that Delano temporarily falls prey to, and that in turn suggests the greater "enchantment" of Delano's entire life. Delano has, it will be recalled, a "charmed eye and ear." He is, however, in this case quickly disenchanted when, forgetting that the rotting balustrade is, after all, only a rotting balustrade, he leans his weight on it and nearly topples into the sea. The scene dramatizes Delano's nearly fatal dependence on a "nature" without objective basis, and thereby reveals the radically transformative power of Delano's vision.

As we have seen, *Benito Cereno* dramatizes the vast distance between Delano's idealism and reality. Barry Philips has argued that "Emerson exhibited the same defects in his vision of the world and of providence as Delano displayed in his. In Amasa Delano, more than in any other of his major characters, Melville concentrated his contempt for the optimism of the American idealist." This is true especially of Delano's view of nature. If Melville's Delano could have read *Moby-Dick*, he would have realized that nature is complex and multifaceted, and that one might just as easily (and legitimately!) allegorize the triumph of diabolism as of benignity in nature. The most eloquent spokesman for this view is Queequeg, who states, ". . . de god was made shark must be one dam Ingin" (*Moby-Dick*). Moreover, Melville makes clear that Delano's attribution of transcendental benignity to nature works in the same way as does his refusal to accept "the imputation of malign evil in man": both, though apparent testimonials to an ennobling faith, are ultimately a means of ignoring evil—his own as well as others'. And to ignore evil is a dangerous thing to do, for whether it is in the wilderness without or the even murkier one within, the beast in the jungle eventually leaps. Delano's "innocence" is belied by his

assumption of the archetypal position of dominance modeled by the satyr in the medallioned sternpiece of the *San Dominick*—a position mirrored by Babo, whom Delano hypocritically regards as a "ferocious pirat[e]." Delano is similarly implicated in evil by his association with images of piracy, such as in the name of his boat (which was the name of the ship of buccaneer William Ambrose Cowley) and the fact that the chief mate whom he sends to retake the *San Dominick* was himself formerly "a privateer's man." Finally, although Delano, like Babo, kills no one with his own hands, he is nevertheless responsible for the deaths caused in retaking the ship, as well as for the atrocity of re-enslaving all of the blacks aboard the *San Dominick*. For especially lucid and well documented discussions of these and other dimensions of Delano's evil, see Kavanagh, Emery, and Zagarell. Melville gives the black women the status of active participants in the rebellion by noting in the deposition that "all the negroes, though not in the first place knowing to the design of the revolt, when it was accomplished, approved it." More importantly, he heightens the inflammatory role of the black women by noting that

> the negresses used their utmost influence to have the deponent made away with; that, in the various acts of murder, they sang songs and danced—not gaily, but solemnly; and before the engagement with the boats, as well as during the action, they sang melancholy songs to the negroes, and that this melancholy tone was more inflaming than a different one would have been, and was so intended; that all this is believed, because the negroes have said it.

Both passages are absent from Melville's source.

Source: Terry J. Martin, "The Idea of Nature in *Benito Cereno*," in *Studies in Short Fiction*, Vol. 30, No. 2, Spring 1993, pp. 161–68.

SOURCES

Abel, Darrel, *American Literature*, Barron's Education Series, 1963, pp. 422

Busch, Frederick, "Melville's Mail," in *A Dangerous Profession*, Broadway Books, 1998, pp. 288–90.

Hillway, Tyrus, *Herman Melville*, Twayne Publishers, 1979, pp. 17–145.

Melville, Herman, "Letter to Nathaniel Hawthorne," in *The Confidence Man*, Penguin Press, 1990, p. xi.

————, "Benito Cereno," in *Melville's Short Novels*, W.W. Norton, 2002, pp. 34–102.

Winters, Yvor, *In Defense of Reason*, Allan Swallow, 1947, p. 222.

FURTHER READING

Delano, Amasa, *A Narrative of Voyages and Travels*, Nabu Press, 2011.

> This is a reprint of the original text that inspired Melville to write *Benito Cereno*. The eighteenth chapter is the actual story of Delano boarding a Spanish ship controlled by mutinous slaves, but the entire narrative can be enjoyed as an example of what the reading audiences in Melville's time expected.

Melville, Herman, *Correspondence*, edited by Lynn Horth, Northwestern University Press, 1993.

> The largest collection of letters written by Melville, this volume gives an excellent glimpse into an author who was largely misunderstood in his lifetime. Within this collection one will find letters written to Melville's friend and literary great Nathaniel Hawthorne, among others. Arranged chronologically, this book will make an excellent companion to the reading of any work by Melville.

Weaver, Raymond, *Herman Melville, Mariner and Mystic*, Nabu Press, 2011.

> This is the definitive Melville biography by the scholar who first incited the Melville revival in the early twentieth century. Much of Weaver's work has been outdone by later scholars, but he is unquestionably the original Melville scholar. This reprint of his book on Melville is a historical and inspiring document of the invincibility of literature.

Widmer, Kingsley, *The Ways of Nihilism: Herman Melville's Short Novels*, California State Colleges Publications, 1970.

> Many scholars see Melville's short works as the three Bs: *Benito Cereno*, *Billy Budd*, and "Bartleby, the Scrivener." Widmer's book discusses the darkness and nihilism (the belief that traditional thought and values are unfounded and existence is senseless) prevalent in all three works. It is an interesting look at how Melville's fiction was able to inspire and influence such a wide variety of interpretations. Widmer's book is an excellent example of Melville's work inspiring the culture of America in the 1960s.

SUGGESTED SEARCH TERMS

Herman Melville AND *Benito Cereno*

Herman Melville AND romanticism

Herman Melville AND transcendentalism

Herman Melville AND biography

Herman Melville AND the sea

Herman Melville AND American Civil War

Benito Cereno AND slavery

Benito Cereno AND abolitionism OR pro-slavery

Benito Cereno AND detective fiction

Doctor Zhivago

1965

Doctor Zhivago is the story of a great romance that spanned several decades. The film is set in the period immediately before World War I and covers the Russian Revolution and the period immediately following; this is approximately between 1912 and 1923. However, there are a few scenes set much later, post World War II, that bring the film to a close. The film is based on the 1957 novel of the same name by Boris Pasternak and was made into a film in 1965. *Doctor Zhivago* was directed by David Lean, whose 1962 direction of *Lawrence of Arabia* had been a huge commercial success. Because the novel had been banned in the Soviet Union, much of *Doctor Zhivago* was filmed in Spain.

In turning Pasternak's 559-page novel into a film, a great many minor characters and many of the subplots were cut from the novel. Lean envisioned *Doctor Zhivago* as a film about an epic romance, which it is; however, the film can best be described as a synopsis of the novel. The focus of the film is on Yuri and Lara's relationship, rather than on the political upheaval, World War I, and the Russian Revolution, all of which are portrayed in more detail in the novel. *Doctor Zhivago*, starring Omar Sharif, Julie Christie, Geraldine Chaplin, and Rod Steiger, was nominated for ten Academy Awards and won five, for Best Art Direction, Best Cinematography, Best Adapted Screenplay, Best Costume Design, and Best Original Score.

(© AF Archive / Alamy)

The first English translation of the novel *Doctor Zhivago* was published in 1958 after it was smuggled out of Russia, where its publication had been banned. Pasternak had been well known as a poet, and the arrival of this novel was critically acclaimed by many readers; it soon became a best seller. The producer Carlo Ponti immediately wanted to film *Doctor Zhivago* as a starring vehicle for his wife, Sophia Loren, but director David Lean envisioned an unknown, Julie Christie, for the role of Lara and Peter O'Toole for the role of Yuri. When O'Toole declined, the role was given to Sharif. The film version of *Doctor Zhivago* was not shown in Russian until 1994.

PLOT SUMMARY

Doctor Zhivago is framed by the appearance of Yuri Zhivago's half-brother, General Yevgraf Zhivago, who is searching for his niece, Yuri's

illegitimate child. The story of Yuri's life is told by Yevgraf to a young woman, Tonya Komarovskaya, who he believes is Yuri's child with his mistress, Lara Guishar. The framing device that opens and closes the film is not present in the novel, which instead opens with the burial of Yuri Zhivago's mother.

As the film opens, the approximate time is the late 1940s or mid-1950s, and Yevgraf has journeyed to a dam project in search of Tonya, who works at the dam. He has an edition of Yuri's poetry, the *Lara Poéms*, and intends to speak to Tonya because he believes she is his half-brother Yuri's daughter. He tells the young woman, Tonya, that he is looking for his niece. After asking some basic questions about her childhood, Yevgraf tells Tonya the story of Yuri's life, which now unfolds for the audience, beginning with the funeral of Yuri's mother.

Yuri is a young child when his mother dies. The camera focuses on Yuri, who follows the

FILM TECHNIQUE

- Staging or *Mis en Scène*: This technique refers to all the elements that go into a camera shot that make up the composition of the shot. Most often this refers to a lengthy, uncut, and unedited sequence on film. The visual elements of the shot consist of the setting, most obviously, but also include props, actors, lighting, costumes, makeup, and movement. In *Doctor Zhivago*, the outdoor scenes of the frozen dacha, with the camera moving across the scene from one side to the next, are a good example of *mis en scène*.

- Subjective Point of View: The placement of the camera and how tightly the camera is focused on the subject or whether the view is from above or below helps to create an emotional response from the viewer. This is known as subjective camera placement. When combined with a sequence of camera shots, as in an early scene in *Doctor Zhivago*, the director is able to create a subjective point of view that elicits a planned response from the audience. For example, in the funeral scene, five-year-old Yuri walks behind his mother's coffin as the funeral procession moves toward her grave. Beginning with a long-range shot that carefully moves closer to the subject, the camera slowly moves in on the funeral so that

eventually the viewer sees exactly what the child sees—his mother's body being lowered into the ground.

- Wide Lens, Long Shots, and Close-up Shots: Lean combines wide lens, long shots, and close-up shots in several scenes of soldiers during war. The soldiers are shivering from the cold as they march past dead soldiers frozen in the snow. The ice cracks beneath their boots. For the audience, the film depicts both the suffering of war and also the frozen tundra that is Russia during the winter. The impact on the viewer, who feels as if he or she is present at the scene, is immediate. However, it is Lean's use of wide-angle camera shots that is especially effective in *Doctor Zhivago*. The film provides panoramic scenes of the Urals as the train carrying Yuri and his family plows through the snow. After Yuri is kidnapped by the Red Partisans, there is a scene in which dozens of young boys are massacred in a wheat field and their white-clothed bodies are strewn everywhere. The panoramic views of the ice palace and the vistas of white snow are also especially striking. All of these and many others in the film are the work of the wide-angle lens.

---

body of his mother to her grave. With his mother dead, all that Yuri possesses is a *balalaika*, a string instrument that is played like a guitar. His mother was an artist and had a gift for playing this musical instrument. Now that Yuri's mother has died, he has no one to care for him, since his father had previously abandoned the family and subsequently died. Alexander and Anna Gromeko, friends of Yuri's mother, offer to give Yuri a home. He will live in Moscow, with them and their daughter, Tonya.

The film now jumps ahead several years, and Yuri is studying medicine in Moscow. Yuri is an

established poet, but because he needs a job, he is studying medicine. He wants to be a general practitioner. The landscape in Moscow is icy and snow-covered. There is a brief moment when Yuri boards a trolley car on which Lara is also a passenger, but they do not meet.

The film then shifts to Pasha and Lara, whose stories are interwoven with Yuri's. Pasha is a social revolutionary, while Lara lives with her mother, Amelia, who is a dressmaker. Amelia is involved with Victor Komarovsky, who is both her financial advisor and her lover. Lara is engaged to Pasha, who distributes fliers calling for equality for workers. During a peaceful demonstration, Cossacks with sabres violently attack the demonstrators and wound Pasha in an unprovoked attack. As a result, Pasha is left with a long scar on his cheek. Yuri, who stands on a balcony, sees the entire attack and rushes into the street to help the wounded but is told to go inside his home or be arrested. While Pasha is being attacked by Cossacks, Victor takes Lara to an expensive restaurant for dinner. Her mother was supposed to attend as well, but she is unwell, so Lara and Victor are alone at dinner. She is impressed by the atmosphere and by the obvious richness of the restaurant. The film moves back and forth between Pasha's demonstration and subsequent attack, Yuri standing on the balcony watching the demonstrators, and Lara dancing with Victor. After dinner, he seduces Lara, who does not resist the advances of the much older Victor. She is only seventeen years old and is flattered by his attention (In the novel, she is sixteen).

In the next scene, the action moves to the train station, where Yuri greets Tonya, his adopted sister, who has been going to school in Paris. Alex and Anna Gromeko want Yuri and Tonya to marry. We also learn in this brief scene that Tonya's mother is unwell. The film quickly shifts to Lara and Pasha, who tells Lara that there will be no more peaceful demonstrations. Lara then goes to church to confess her sin with Victor. However, Lara continues the affair with Victor, even though she knows that her mother is in love with him. In her next scene with Victor, Lara wears a red dress, a clear symbol of her new status as a fallen woman. When Lara's mother, Amelia, discovers the affair, she drinks iodine to commit suicide. Victor finds Amelia and calls a friend, Doctor Kurt, a pathology professor, who is accompanied by Yuri. Lara stands watching as the two men treat Amelia. This is the second time in the film that Yuri and Lara's lives intersect. Yuri sees Victor with Lara and immediately knows that they are lovers. In the novel, Lara is determined to separate herself from Victor after this event; she goes to live with a friend and finishes school and even takes some college classes. This does not happen in the film.

The film continues with a meeting between Lara and Victor; Lara asks Victor for his help so that she and Pasha can marry and leave Moscow. At Lara's insistence, Pasha also meets with Victor. Pasha does not know that Victor has been involved with Lara. Pasha has become a Bolshevik, an extremist reformer, who opposes the government and especially men like Victor. Later, Victor tries to convince Lara not to marry Pasha, but when she tells him that she definitely intends to go through with the marriage, Victor rapes her. Lara arrives at a Christmas party that Victor is attending and shoots him, although he is only slightly wounded. Pasha, who has followed Lara to the party, takes her away so that she is not arrested. Yuri is also present with Tonya. Their engagement was about to be announced, but Lara's shooting of Victor interrupted the announcement. Yuri administers first aid to Victor, who asks that Yuri not reveal what has happened. This is the third time that Yuri and Lara's lives have intersected. Pasha is angry that Lara has been unfaithful with Victor but decides to marry her anyway. Eventually, they will have a daughter, Katya.

Some time has passed and World War I has begun. Yuri is now a battlefield doctor on the Eastern Front and is married to Tonya Gromeko. They have an infant son, Sasha. Pasha has also joined the army, where he is a much-admired officer. In his narration, Yevgraf explains that he has also enlisted to fight, but his purpose was really to convince the Russian Imperialist Army to defect to Vladimir Lenin's Bolshevik cause. The Bolsheviks were workers who sought equality through revolution; they later became the Communist Party of the Soviet Union. As the war progresses, the soldiers are without boots, their coats are little more than rags, and they have little food. They are ripe for revolution, according to Yevgraf's narration, and soon the film depicts this revolution in action. The February Revolution begins and soldiers begin to desert the army, but not before killing many of their superior officers. After Pasha is declared missing in action, Lara becomes a battlefield nurse and tries to find her husband. Lara travels with some deserters and again meets Yuri, who accompanies a group of soldiers headed to the front. He convinces Lara to help him care for the wounded, and they work together in a battlefield hospital until the war ends.

Soon Yuri learns that the tsar has been imprisoned and Russia is engulfed in civil war. Yuri is ordered to establish a battlefield hospital, with Lara as the nurse. There is an obvious attraction between Yuri and Lara, but she is determined to resist doing anything dishonorable. Nor does she want Yuri to do anything for which he would have to lie to his wife. When the fighting finally ends, Yuri returns to his home in Moscow, which is much changed since the beginning of the revolution. His mother-in-law is dead, and the new government has seized Yuri's home and turned it into apartments. Everyone is called comrade, and they all dress alike. Yuri has been gone a long time. The infant son that he left so long ago has grown and does not know his father.

Some time has passed and there is starvation and typhus in Moscow, but doctors are not permitted to mention that people are dying. Yuri's attitude displeases the government officials, who caution him not to talk about what he sees. Because there is no wood for the stove, Yuri steals wood. One day Yevgraf, sees Yuri and follows him to his home, where Yevgraf tells Yuri that he is his half-brother and that Yuri's poetry has been condemned as an affront to Communism. In truth, it is Yuri's attitude that is the problem. He has not adapted to the loss of the individual. Tonya knows this, but Yuri is blind to what goes on around him. Because of the policy of collective punishment, Yuri's whole family must leave Moscow as soon as possible, or they will all be arrested. Yevgraf helps Yuri with rail passes for his family, and they immediately leave for the Gromeko estate in the Urals, where they hope they will be safer.

Yuri, his wife Tonya, his father-in-law Alex, and his son Sasha all leave Moscow on a cattle train. The train has many guards, since it is also used to transport prisoners to the *gulag*. The train is packed with forced laborers headed for Siberia. In a bit of irony, the train passes through a town where Lara's husband Pasha, now calling himself Strelnikov, commands a large number of Red Party soldiers, who have just shelled the town. The train with Yuri's family continues toward the Urals. At a stop, Yuri leaves the train for a short walk and spots an armored train hidden along a railroad siding. The guards arrest Yuri and bring him to their commander, Strelnikov. Yuri recognizes Pasha, who tells him that Lara is living in Yuriatin, which is occupied by the anti-Communist White Party army. The guard who escorts Yuri back to the train tells him that most people who meet with Strelnikov are shot.

When Yuri and his family arrive at the Gromeko estate, they learn that the Red Party has seized their home. The house is boarded up.

Because they fear being shot as White Party sympathizers, Yuri and his family decide to stay in a small run-down cottage on the property. Soon they receive news that the tsar and his family have been shot, and they know that they can never return to Moscow. Yuri is unable to write poetry. In the spring, Yuri travels to Yuriatin, where he finds Lara, who works as a librarian. She is living a quiet life with her daughter, Katya. Yuri and Lara become lovers, but Yuri feels very guilty at deceiving his wife, Tonya, who is pregnant. He loves each woman, and in each home, he finds comfort. Yuri decides to end his relationship with Lara, but as he returns home from Yuriatin, he is kidnapped and forced to join the Red Partisans, who need a doctor.

After two years of combat, Yuri succeeds in deserting the army. He walks through the snow to Yuriatin, where he is told that his wife and father-in-law and children have left Gromeko. Yuri finds Lara, but he is very ill and calls for Tonya in his delirium. Lara tells Yuri that his family has returned to Moscow. She gives Yuri a letter from Tonya, in which she tells him of the birth of their daughter. Tonya also writes that the family is being deported from Russia and that Lara is a good person. Yuri and Lara resume their affair.

Victor soon appears and tells Yuri that he and Lara are being watched by the Cheka, the Communist secret police force. Yuri is a deserter from the Red Army, and his writings are considered subversive. Yuri's poetry has also put Lara at risk. The secret police are watching Lara because of her marriage to Pasha, who later became Strelnikov. The police hope that Lara will lead them to Strelnikov. Victor offers to help Yuri and Lara leave Russia, but they refuse his help and throw him out of the apartment. Instead, Yuri, Lara, and her daughter, Katya, decide to hide in Varykino, at the Gromeko estate. The house is frozen inside because the doors and windows have been left open. It is an ice house, with layers of ice and snow inside and out. This is where Yuri begins to write poetry again and where he writes the Lara poems that appear at the end of the novel.

After some time has passed, Victor shows up to tell Yuri that Lara is in danger. Victor is now the minister of justice to the White government of Baron von Sternberg. Victor explains that Strelnikov was arrested and that he committed suicide. The secret police are now looking for

Lara to arrest her as a dissident. Victor explains that Lara's husband was arrested only a few miles from the estate. This a change from the novel, since Lara's husband is not dead; in fact, he reappears at Varykino, and after telling Yuri how much he loves Lara, he commits suicide. It is not clear if Victor deliberately lies in the film about Strelnikov's death or if he was unaware of the truth. Yuri decides that Lara should leave with Victor, but Yuri remains at the estate. Lara tells Victor that Yuri would never leave Russia. She also tells Victor that she is pregnant with Yuri's child. The narration again moves to Yevgraf, who suggests that the girl before him, Tonya, is the child that Lara was carrying the day she left Yuri.

The film now jumps many years forward. Yuri once again lives in Moscow. He is very poor, but Yevgraf helps his brother find a job and buys him some clothes. On his way to work, Yuri is riding on a trolley when he sees a woman and thinks she is Lara. He jumps off the trolley and runs after the woman but soon collapses and dies of a heart attack before she sees him. In the film, the woman is Lara, but in the novel, she is just a woman who is walking along the street, parallel to the trolley. Yevgraf explains that he was astonished at how many people were at Yuri's funeral. His poetry was well loved, even though it was not widely available in Russia at that time. At Yuri's funeral, Lara tells Yevgraf that she gave birth to Yuri's daughter after she fled with Victor many years earlier. After the Baron's government collapsed, Lara was again forced to flee and lost track of her infant daughter. Lara asks for Yevgraf's help in finding Yuri's daughter. Eventually Lara disappears. Yevgraf thinks she was transported to a labor camp where she died.

Doctor Zhivago returns to the narration that Yevgraf has been relating to Tonya Komarovskaya, now identified as Yuri and Lara's orphaned daughter. While Yevgraf thinks that Tonya is Yuri's daughter, the girl is less convinced. Finally Yevgraf sees the *balalaika* that the girl is carrying and asks if she can play. Tonya's boyfriend, who has been lurking in the background, explains that she plays very well and that she is self-taught. The audience is reminded that this string instrument is what Yuri's mother also played. In this way, the film circles back to the beginning. To play this instrument is a gift. This musical talent confirms for Yevgraf that the girl before him is Yuri and Lara's daughter.

One significant difference between novel and film occurs in the concluding scenes. In the novel, Yuri returns to Moscow after Lara and Victor leave Varykino. He begins a relationship with a woman named Marina, with whom he has two daughters. This last relationship is deleted from the screenplay, so that it appears that Yuri is torn between only two women in his life—Tonya and Lara.

The film version of *Doctor Zhivago* is essentially true to the novel, but Lean chose to eliminate many of the characters and events that were secondary to the romance, the element in the novel on which he focused. The political world in which Yuri lives is significantly diminished. The novel focuses more on the war and revolution, and while no major historical characters appear, there are dozens of minor characters who move in and out of Yuri's life. There are so many of these minor characters that it is difficult to remember all of them and who they are with respect to Yuri's life. Lean left these many minor characters out of the film, which, considering the length of the novel and its complexity, was probably a good thing for the film audience.

CHARACTERS

Pavel "Pasha" Antipov

Tom Courtney plays the role of this revolutionary, who is scarred by Cossacks during a peaceful demonstration. In response, he becomes more of a political extremist. Victor describes Pasha as high-minded and an idealist. Pasha is the son of a railway worker who has been exiled to Siberia. Married to Lara, Pasha later joins the army and is presumed dead after a battle, although he is only declared missing in action. Later he reappears, having changed his name to Strelnikov. As Yuri flees to safety in the Urals, he encounters Strelnikov, who tells him that Lara is living nearby. In this way, Lara's husband helps her to find happiness with Yuri. Although Strelnikov is a revolutionary, his politics are shaped by both his belief in equality for workers and the violence of the Cossack attack on him. In the novel, he tells Yuri that he loved Lara and his daughter very much. This is less clear in the film, since he is more focused on revolution than on love.

Katya Antipova

Katya is the daughter of Lara and Pasha. This role is played by Lucy Westmore. Katya is a child and her role is minimal in the film.

Alexander Gromeko

Ralph Richardson plays Alex, a close friend of Yuri's mother. After his mother dies, Yuri is raised by Alex and his wife, Anna. Alex is important both because he is a doctor who makes it easier for Yuri to enter medical school and because he is Tonya's father, and thus, Yuri's father-in-law. His role is small, but he provides Tonya with a male presence while Yuri is off fighting. Later, after they have fled Moscow, Alex encourages Yuri to go to the library in Yuriatin, which is where he will again meet Lara. He thus unintentionally facilitates the affair between Yuri and Lara.

Anna Gromeko

Siobhan McKenna plays Alex's wife and Tonya's mother, Anna. This role is very diminished from the novel. Her job in the film is seemingly to push Tonya and Yuri together and suggest that they should marry. She dies during the war. Early in the film, she expresses the opinion that the demonstrators are to be admired for their high ideals. She has no understanding that revolution will not come without turmoil and death.

Antonina "Tonya" Gromeko

Yuri's wife is played by Geraldine Chaplin. Tonya is very beautiful but without passion. She is sweet and good but lacks the fire that defines Lara. Yuri loves Tonya, but they were raised together, and his love for her is not as passionate as his love for Lara. Tonya is primarily depicted as the dutiful wife and mother to Yuri's son. After Yuri disappears, having been kidnapped by the Red Partisans, Tonya is deported from Russia and moves to Paris. She gives birth to a daughter whom Yuri never meets. Tonya recognizes Yuri's love for Lara and acknowledges that Lara is a good person. Tonya represents the stability of home and traditions of the past.

Amelia Guishar

The role of Lara's mother is played by Adrienne Corri. She is a successful seamstress. Amelia is in love with Victor Komarovsky, a corrupt attorney, who first seduces and later rapes Amelia's daughter, Lara. When Amelia discovers Victor's affair with Lara, she tries to commit suicide, but is saved by Yuri's mentor, Doctor Kurt, who is called to her bedside. Amelia's role is more as a device. Her attempted suicide allows Yuri and Lara's lives to intersect for a second time, in what appears to be a chance encounter. Like so many other characters in *Doctor Zhivago*, Amelia simply disappears from the narration once her purpose in the story has been filled.

Larissa "Lara" Guishar

Julie Christie plays Lara, who is married to Pasha but is also in love with Yuri. Early in the film, there are a number of contrived near-meetings between Lara and Yuri. In most of them, he sees her but she is unaware of him. Her beauty attracts Yuri, but he also senses an underlying passion in her personality. As a teenager, Lara is seduced by Victor Komarovsky, with whom she has an affair. Victor also senses the passion in Lara, which in the film is revealed with a series of camera shots that focus on her face, especially the look in her eyes, as she exchanges long glances with Victor. When she finally realizes that her affair with Victor is destroying her mother, Lara tries to break it off, and he points out to her that she has always known that her mother has been hurt but has been too selfish to care how her mother feels. At this moment, Victor's assessment of Lara's personality is actually correct, but she is seventeen years old and still a schoolgirl. He is probably twice her age, although his exact age is not given in the film. Lara's emotional immaturity is especially evident on the night he seduces her. She is taken in by the expensive dinner, the dancing, and Victor's attentions. At their next meeting, she wears a red gown, which acknowledges that she knows she is a fallen woman. At the same time, her guilt takes her to a priest to confess. Thus the film reveals both Lara's pain at her choice and her desperate need for Victor's attention.

When Lara tells Victor that she will marry Pasha, Victor rapes her, after first telling her she is a tramp. Lara follows Victor to a Christmas party, where she shoots him. Pasha saves her from being arrested, and she confesses everything to him. Lara later marries Pasha, who has become a Bolshevik. In the novel, it is clear that Lara loves Pasha, but the film focuses more on her love for Yuri and pushes Pasha into the background. After Pasha is listed as missing in action, Lara becomes a battlefield nurse so that she can search for him.

Once she arrives at the battlefield, Lara once again meets Zhivago, who asks her to help him treat the wounded. The film establishes a long-simmering attraction between Lara and Yuri, but although they spend much time together, they initially resist this attraction. It is Lara who is the stronger of the two, and while they work together at the field hospital, she will not allow them to be more than friends. Lara has learned a lot from her affair with Victor, which is shown in her new emotional maturity. Much later in the film, Lara and Yuri become lovers, and she eventually gives birth to Yuri's daughter, but this happens after they are parted. The film suggests that Lara is the great love of Yuri's life and positions this love as an epic romance that endures for decades. Lara is the inspiration for many of Yuri's poems. She represents the revolution and the upheaval of Russian life. Lara loves Pasha, who is a revolutionary, but she also loves Yuri, who is the aristocrat of old Russia. Old and new worlds collide in Lara.

Victor Komarovsky

The unscrupulous Victor is played by Rod Steiger. He is an attorney who was a close friend and advisor to Yuri's father. He first seduces Lara when she is a teenager, but he is already involved with Lara's mother, Amelia, as both lover and advisor. Victor rapes Lara when she tells him she is going to marry Pasha. Later, though, he visits Lara and Yuri in Yuriatin to warn them that Lara is being watched by the secret police. He warns them once again as the police close in on them after they flee to the Gromeko estate in Varykino. He takes Lara away to protect her and, in doing so, actually saves the life of Lara and Yuri's unborn daughter. In the novel, Victor was responsible for the suicide of Zhivago's father. Victor is a survivor who can adapt to any circumstance. He is a complex character whose actions are clearly self-serving but who, in saving Lara, also demonstrates that he is not simply a villain. The complexity of this man is one of the elements of the narration that make him an especially interesting character.

Tonya Komarovskaya

Rita Tushingham plays the illegitimate daughter of Yuri and Lara. In the novel, her name is Tania. Her role is very brief, since she appears only in the framing device that opens and closes the film. She initially rejects the idea that Lara was her mother, since her mother died when Tonya was a child. She never met her father and so does not know if Yuri was her father. However, her identity as Yuri and Lara's child is confirmed when it is revealed that she plays the *balalaika*. This is the instrument that Yuri's mother also played. The suggestion is that the talent is inherited, since Tonya has never had lessons and is very talented.

Professor Boris Kurt

This role is played by Geoffrey Keen. Kurt is a pathology professor and is Yuri's mentor while he studies to be a doctor. He is also a good friend of Victor's and is called on to save Amelia's life after she attempts suicide. He understands the importance of discretion, and Victor knows that Kurt can be trusted. His role is very brief.

Yevgraf Zhivago

Alec Guiness plays Yuri's half-brother, Yevgraf, whose name is Evgraf in the novel. Yevgraf is the son of Yuri's father and his mistress. Yevgraf is someone of importance after the revolution, a general, with the authority to save those in need. Yevgraf narrates the film, appearing at the beginning as he tells Yuri's story, at several key points during the film, and then again as he concludes Yuri's story. Yevgraf appears at an opportune moment to save Yuri's life and that of his family when they must flee Moscow. Yevgraf is a risk taker and a man who makes things happen. He joins the army to create enough dissent to cause a revolution from within. In this sense, he is very different from his half-brother Yuri, who is a man of thoughts and words rather than actions. Although Yevgraf is pragmatic, he admires Yuri enough to want a copy of his half-brother's poetry. Thus we understand that there is something of the romantic in Yevgraf, which explains his efforts to locate the daughter that Yuri and Lara had together.

Yuri Zhivago

Omar Sharif plays the title character in *Doctor Zhivago*. The role of the ten-year-old Yuri is played by Tarek Sharif, the son of Omar Sharif. In the novel, Yuri's name is spelled Yurii. When he was a young child, his father abandoned his family, leaving them to live in terrible poverty. After his mother dies, her friends Alex and Anna Gromeko become parents to Yuri. Yuri is a successful and well-known poet, but he knows that writing poetry is not a job and that eventually he will need to support a family. With Alex's help, Yuri enters medical school and becomes a doctor. He then marries Tonya, with whom he has grown up as a ward in the Gromeko home, but he falls in love with Lara, with whom he has an affair. In the film there are a series of near-meetings between Yuri and Lara that seem to suggest that their destiny is to be together.

After the Russian Revolution, Yuri's poems are considered subversive and anti-Communist. The truth is that the new Communist Party does not like men like Yuri, who cannot adapt to being part of a collective mass of humanity. Yuri and his family escape to the Urals, where they can live in relative isolation. After hiding for several months, Yuri once again meets Lara and the two begin an affair. Guilt over the affair and his wife's pregnancy lead Yuri to break things off with Lara, but he is seized and forced into service by the Red Partisans. After he escapes and learns that his wife and children have fled to Paris, Yuri is again drawn back to Lara. The implication is that she is the great love of his life. Their love endures for decades and he collapses on the street in Moscow and dies after catching sight of a woman he thinks is Lara. Most of his adult life has been defined by his love for Lara, and so it is fitting that he dies trying to find her. Yuri is not a man of action and rarely makes things happen. Instead, things happen to him. He does what he is told will be best. In chasing after Lara on a Moscow street, Yuri assumes control over his life, but he falls and dies. The implication is that it is not possible for Yuri to be a man of action.

Yuri's life encompasses much of the important history of twentieth-century Russia. He is born into wealth during the tsarist rule. He is involved in World War I, the Revolution, and the subsequent civil war. He then dies in poverty. Yuri represents the aristocracy and the intelligentsia. He is a philosopher and a poet who really just wants to live and love in peace but who is drawn into war. In a sense, Yuri's life is a tragedy, since he dies alone, still seeking Lara.

THEMES

Artistic Talent

Yuri's mother plays the *balalaika*, a musical instrument that is played like a guitar. It is a very complex instrument to play, and to be able to do so is a significant artistic gift. When Yuri's

mother dies, she leaves the *balalaika* to him. It is all that remains of her property. Alex and Anna Gromeko tell Yuri that his mother was very talented and that she never took lessons to learn how to play. Tonya, Yuri and Lara's illegitimate daughter, is identified as their daughter through her ability to play the *balalaika*. She has also never had lessons, but her ability to play this instrument is so significant that her boyfriend makes a point of describing Tonya's talent as quite wonderful. The audience is supposed to recall that Yuri's mother also had this talent.

Yuri is also talented. His renown as a poet is established early in the film, when Tonya arrives in Moscow from Paris. She carries a review of Yuri's poetry that appeared in a Paris newspaper. His work is so significant that it is well known outside Russia. In Paris, his work is read and reviewed, which establishes the greatness of his talent. Throughout the film, Yuri's reputation as a poet is noted by the people he meets. However, there is little monetary value in writing poetry. While Yuri's poetry is admired, he cannot support a family as a poet. He must have a job that provides an income. After the revolution, it is his poetry and his life as a poet that endanger his family and force them to flee Moscow. Nevertheless, after Lara is compelled to flee for her safety, Yuri finds solace in writing poems about her. The *Lara Poems* are what bring him renown after his death.

The film makes clear that artistic talent fulfills the individual but offers no monetary reward. Yuri's mother dies penniless and destitute with nothing to leave to her child but the instrument that she played so well—the *balalaika*. Her granddaughter, Tonya, who also plays the *balalaika*, must work at the dam to support herself. Her talent playing the *balalaika* might be well known, but playing offers no monetary support. And lastly, Yuri's talent as a poet is personally rewarding, but there is no financial reward; there is considerable personal risk associated with writing poetry.

Nature

As a film, *Doctor Zhivago* easily evokes nature as a place of refuge, but it is also a location of great beauty and real danger. Director Lean focuses many of his camera shots on huge-scale panoramic vistas of snow and endless landscapes. Nature functions as a character in the film, appearing and reappearing in many scenes. For example,

READ, WATCH, WRITE,

- As you watch *Doctor Zhivago*, play close attention to the music and to the response that it demands of the viewer. Take careful notes on what you observe and how you feel. Answer a few questions such as: How are you supposed to feel when you hear the music? How do you feel at different times as you hear different kinds of music? Then prepare a PowerPoint presentation that includes elements of the film, as well as brief snippets of the soundtrack. First play just a brief piece of music and ask your classmates how the music makes them feel. Ask them what they think is happening when that music is playing. Then show your classmates the scene from the film without the music and ask them what emotions they feel as they watch the scene. Finally, show the scene with the music playing and query your classmates about what they feel and what they have learned from this exercise.

- *Doctor Zhivago* is a long novel, more than 550 pages. The film is just over three hours long. Director Lean chose to leave out many minor scenes and characters. With a group of three of your classmates, first divide the novel, assigning each person a series of chapters. Ask each of your classmates to make a list of the characters and scenes that were eliminated from the film. Each member of the group will create a poster presentation that shows the characters, their roles in the novel, the events in which they are involved, and what their exclusion means for the finished film. When you present the posters to your classmates, you will also discuss what you learned from this assignment and whether you think any of the eliminated

characters were important enough to have been included and why.

- Choose one scene from the film that you found especially important to understanding the entire film and write an essay explaining why the scene was important and how it would have altered the audience's understanding of the film if it had been eliminated.

- Kristina O'Donnelly's novel *The Horseman* focuses on the war between the Turks and the Kurds. Like *Doctor Zhivago*, *The Horseman* is primarily an epic romance novel, with an American teenager as the protagonist. Imagine that O'Donnelly's novel is to be turned into a film. Just as the novel *Doctor Zhivago* was cut to create a film that emphasized romance, *The Horseman* must be redacted to focus on romance. Read *The Horseman* carefully and focus on which aspects of the novel should be included in a film and what scenes and characters could best be eliminated to create a romantic epic film. Then write an essay explaining your choices and how you envision the finished film.

- Yuri has two crucial relationships in his life—his love for his wife, Tonya, and his love for his mistress, Lara. It would be helpful to compare these two relationships and what each one offers Yuri, as well as how each one fulfills his life. Create a poster that compares these two pairings, noting dates, locations, separate events, and a timeline. When you present your poster to your classmates, prepare a discussion of what you have learned about Yuri and what kind of man he was, based on these two long-term relationships.

as Yuri lies in bed on the night of his mother's funeral, the camera moves outside to his mother's grave, where a harsh wind begins to rip apart the carefully laid flowers and wreaths that adorned the grave. It is a reminder that nature can easily undo what men have done.

(© *Moviestore Collection Ltd | Alamy*)

In another scene, when Lara and Yuri part after the war ends, the camera focuses on a vase of sunflowers. As Lara's wagon moves away from the hospital, the leaves on the sunflowers begin to drop. It appears that the sunflowers are weeping as the despondent Yuri walks past the vase. When Yuri and his family are living at the Gromeko dacha near Varykino, he looks at the ice crystals on the window. He longs for Lara, which we know because the music "Lara's Theme" is playing in the background. When the ice crystals dissolve into spring flowers, viewers know that Yuri will soon find Lara, who is living in the nearby town. Both the coldness of winter and the warmth of spring are evoked in one brief scene of just over two minutes.

Lara's small apartment is filled with flowers. The home in which Yuri lives with Tonya is also surrounded with flowers. Each of the settings is idyllic and filled with sun and beauty, which makes it easy for Yuri to move from one woman to the other. In another scene, Yuri, Lara, and Katya journey to the Gromeko home, which is enclosed in ice. One night, Yuri gets up from a desk where he has been writing and walks to the ice-covered window, where he listens to the wolves howling. The wolves symbolize the risk that he and Lara face from the Red Party army, who seemingly wait in the dark for them.

STYLE

Costuming

Many of the costumes in *Doctor Zhivago* are opulent, as befits the aristocracy among whom Yuri lives. Because of the cold, there are also many furs evident. However, what is also important about the costuming is the symbolism that costumes represent. In the scene after Lara is seduced by Victor, she is wearing a red dress, which represents both her loss of virginity and her passionate nature. She is now the scarlet woman. Near the end of the film, Yuri is kidnapped by Red Partisans and all that remains of him is his cap lying alongside the road as a reminder that he was once there. The cap symbolizes Yuri's isolation. Like his cap lying alone in the snow, Yuri is now isolated from all that he loves. After the revolution, the new Communists wear plain gray clothing with no adornment. The fit is loose and poor, and men and women dress the same. The contrast with Yuri's wife Tonya and her father is notable, since they continue to dress in their own clothing and not the clothing of the Party. This sets them apart and reinforces the risk they face for their failure to adapt to the new Russia. The costuming in *Doctor Zhivago* functions as a sort of shorthand for the audience, who are able to use characters' clothing to help understand what is occurring in the film.

Framing

The opening scene of *Doctor Zhivago* serves as the first part of a framing device in the film. A framing device is a literary element designed to hold a story together. It can be used to heighten interest, to provide context, or to create resolution for a story. In *Doctor Zhivago*, the framing device opens with Yuri Zhivago's half-brother, Yevgraf, speaking to a young woman. Because Yuri and Lara do not actually meet until almost two hours into the film, it was important to make clear for the audience that the relationship between Yuri and Lara will be central to the film. The framing device helps to establish that this is a film about Yuri and Lara and their love for one another. The book of Lara poems that Yevgraf shows at the beginning establishes the importance of the relationship, even though they will not meet for two hours. In flashbacks, Yuri's story is told to the young woman. At the end of the film and the conclusion of Yuri's story, the story returns to Yevgraf and the young woman.

This is when viewers learn that the young woman is Yuri and Lara's illegitimate daughter. In this instance, the framing device heightens viewer interest, while also providing resolution at the end of the story.

Music

The music in *Doctor Zhivago* is an essential element of the film. Music helps to establish mood and atmosphere in a film. Music also enhances the performances of the actors because it helps to highlight the actor's emotions and thus evokes an emotional response from the audience. *Doctor Zhivago* is a romantic epic that requires romantic music. In particular, the romantic "Lara's Theme" is especially well known. The song dominates the film, and variations on the song appear several times during the film. One example of the effective use of music in *Doctor Zhivago* occurs after Lara and Yuri are reunited at the ice palace. Yuri begins to write a poem about Lara. As he struggles to write the first words, the musical score is tentative, but as the words begin to flow, so does the music until a full orchestra is heard as Yuri writes furiously.

Because the *balalaika* plays an important role in the film, Maurice Jarre, who scored the film, wanted to use the instrument in the orchestra. To do so, he searched in Los Angeles, where he was scoring the film, and finally found several *balalaika* players to play in the orchestra. Throughout *Doctor Zhivago*, the notes from Lara's theme are played by the *balalaika* as background to the scene. Viewers can always tell when Yuri is thinking about Lara because "Lara's Theme" can be heard on the soundtrack.

Setting

Because of the vast Russian landscapes that are seen throughout *Doctor Zhivago*, the setting is a very important part of this film. Lean spent eighteen months having craftsmen build the Moscow scenery on a ten-acre set just outside Madrid. The set for Varykino and the ice palace were also built in Spain, near Soria. This is the setting that most viewers remember best. To create the ice palace scene at the Gromeko family estate, it was necessary to cover everything in white wax, which was then sprayed with freezing cold water. Acres of white plastic were rolled out to cover the landscape so that it would look like winter. Filming took place in temperatures that were nearly 100 degrees.

The scenes in snow and ice are especially evocative in *Doctor Zhivago*. The snow tells viewers that it is cold, and thus when characters complain of the wood shortage and the lack of heat, the presence of snow reinforces the cold. The train that carries Yuri and his family away from Moscow moves through the snow-packed landscape, which is barren of other life. These scenes were filmed in Finland, where the snow and cold were legitimately felt. All the snow, for as far as the viewer can see, symbolizes the distance from Moscow. The snow also looks pure, but it hides the violence of a country torn by civil war, where the soldiers of the Red and the White parties massacre towns of people they think are politically aligned with the other side. The snow can also be romantic, as it was in a picturesque sleigh ride with Yuri and Lara bundled up in rich furs. Much of the snow was an illusion, though. Except for the train scenes, much of *Doctor Zhivago* was filmed in Spain, just outside Madrid, where the temperatures were often in the mid-80s.

CULTURAL CONTEXT

February Revolution

The 1917 February Revolution marked the beginning of a major economic, political, and social revolution in Zhivago's Russia. The setting was World War I, and the resulting anti-German hatred stemmed from the deaths of Russian soldiers and the more immediate food shortages and famine that gripped much of Russia. By 1917, Russia had been at war with Germany for three years. A million Russian soldiers had been killed and Russia had suffered several humiliating defeats at the hands of the German army. The aristocracy, which is depicted in *Doctor Zhivago* by Yuri, Tonya, and her family, did not suffer as greatly as did the families of the common workers. It was the sons of the proletariat, the wage workers, who were dying in the largest numbers, and it was their families who suffered the most because of the lack of food and other necessities.

Tsarina Alexandria was a German, and even though she had lived in Russia for decades, she was actively disliked by the people, who resented both her German birth and her life of privilege. The tsar and his wife lived well, while the people lacked food or even the wood to heat their homes and apartments during Russia's harsh winters. By mid-February 1917, demonstrators filled the street in Petrograd (formerly called Saint Petersburg). The catalyst was the International Women's Day Festival. Women left their factory jobs and filled the streets, not to celebrate but to protest the bread shortages. Soon the city came to a halt, with protestors taking over every aspect of city life. This was not the first time that the capital city was filled with demonstrators, but this time the Cossacks were tolerant and refused to disperse the demonstrators. By late February, the police had also stopped trying to maintain order. When the army deserted the monarchy, Tsar Nicholas was left with no choice but to abdicate, which he did on March 2, 1917, according to the Julian calendar. The 300-year rule of the Romanov Empire had ended at the hands of a people's revolt. Surprisingly enough, it was not Vladimir Lenin's Bolsheviks that brought down Russia's government, but the common people on the street. The treatment of the peasant class by the aristocracy, as well as poor working conditions, had made Russia ripe for revolution. The film makes clear that even after the civil war began between the White Army and the Red Bolsheviks and after Lenin and the Bolsheviks took control of Moscow, there was still no fuel for heat or food to eat. The common people continued to suffer.

(© Pictorial Press Ltd / Alamy)

The Intelligentsia

Zhivago was a member of the social and educated class defined as the intelligentsia. These were the intellectuals, the artists, academics, and politicians who formed the social and intellectual elite. The intelligentsia initially supported the idea of revolution and were opposed to the tsarist policies. The intelligentsia believed that, if the country was freed from the autocracy of their monarchy and the burdens of a corrupt government, there would follow a period of unparalleled creativity. Instead, after the temporary provisional government that replaced the abdicated tsar was toppled in the civil war of October 1917, the Bolsheviks quickly began to imprison and murder the educated professionals who formed much of the intelligentsia. The intelligentsia cared about the people, specifically about their ideological enlightenment and their cultural well-being. The goal of the new Communist government was not to create a peasant class of enlightened workers. Lenin's Bolshevik government considered the intelligentsia to be a dangerous political force that needed to be contained and eliminated. The intelligentsia

were a reminder of the old Russia, the one that existed under the tsarist regime, and as such, they had to be eliminated. Many intellectuals, including university professors and writers, were expelled or chose to emigrate to European countries. Intellectuals who protested the new government were arrested, as were those who were deemed too bourgeois. In *Doctor Zhivago*, Yuri is warned by his half-brother Yevgraf to flee Moscow because the ideas expressed in his poetry are considered contrary to the Bolshevik ideology of the new Russia.

CRITICAL OVERVIEW

Critical reviews of *Doctor Zhivago* were sometimes harsh, although not with the viewing public who made the film a big box office success. For those critics who loved Pasternak's novel, the notion that director David Lean and screenwriter Robert Bolt had cut much of the ponderous work was an unforgivable sacrilege. If the novel was perfect, why film it if it required significant cuts? That is the issue for Stanley Kauffmann, who reviewed *Doctor Zhivago* for *The New Republic*. Kauffmann suggests that, if the novel was so difficult to film in its entirety, then the only reason to have done so was to make money. After dispatching most of the leading actors as "passive and merely pleasant" (Sharif as Yuri), "passable" (Courtney as Pasha), "a joke" (Courtney as Strelnikov), and "the genes of talent have passed her by" (Chaplin as Tonya), Kauffmann turns his attention to Christie's performance as Lara. Kauffman claims that Christie's performance is very good, although he points out that her performance "does not go nearly far enough" toward capturing the essence of Lara. Although he states that director Lean was "not in top form" while directing *Doctor Zhivago*, Kauffmann is appreciative of the photography, the settings, and the sound recording, which he says are the best aspects of the film.

In his December 1965 review for the *New York Times*, Bosley Crowther writes that the film version of *Doctor Zhivago* focuses too much on the romantic entanglements of the lead characters, instead of on the political, economic, and social upheaval that was happening in Russia during this time. Crowther complains that the screenwriter has "reduced the vast upheaval of the Russian Revolution to the banality of a doomed romance." Crowther also laments the absence of the "tensions of spiritual conflict and personal tragedy" that are such an important part of the Pasternak novel. However, Crowther does admire the performances of Christie as Lara, Steiger as Victor, and Courtney as Pasha. Crowther also acknowledges that the photography, which he labels the "physical production of the film," is the film's greatest strength.

Not all critics disliked Lean's film adaptation of the Pasternak novel. A. D. Murphy's review for *Variety* was especially complimentary. After calling *Doctor Zhivago* a "meticulously designed and executed" film, Murphy notes that the film is "an excellent achievement in filmmaking" that should guarantee ticket sales. Murphy also enjoyed Sharif's performance as Yuri, which he writes is "very believable." Christie's performance as Lara is "sensitive, yet earthy and full-blooded," according to Murphy, who also compliments Steiger and Courtney for their performances. The musical score and production values are similarly noted for their strengths. Murphy is not alone in his admiration of this film. The anonymously written review in *Time* magazine refers to *Doctor Zhivago*

as a "literate, old-fashioned, soul-filling and thoroughly romantic" film. In refuting the negative reviews, this writer dismisses complaints about the cast and about the film's emphasis on the love story to the exclusion of so much of the complex history that the novel relates. In the concluding remarks, this nameless critic singles out director Lean as especially deserving of public celebration. Lean, the critic writes, "speaks for humanity in a language of unspeakably beautiful images." For this critic, there is no diminishment of the novel in this film adaptation of *Doctor Zhivago*. Although the critics might not have been able to agree on its merit, *Doctor Zhivago* did very well at theater box offices and in 2010 was still ranked as the eighth highest grossing film of all time.

CRITICISM

Sheri Metzger Karmiol

Karmiol teaches literature and drama at The University of New Mexico, where she is a lecturer in the University Honors Program. In the following essay, she discusses Yuri Zhivago's life as a poet in the film version of Doctor Zhivago.

How one man responds to a world that seems to have gone mad lies at the heart of *Doctor Zhivago*. Yuri Zhivago is an artist who seeks to remove himself from the political and military upheaval that surrounds his life. He wants only to live in freedom at a time when freedom does not exist. Yuri is a bourgeois upper-class male who has lived a life of privilege, but he does not see himself in that way. He feels that, as a poet, he is free of class distinctions, which he neither sees nor needs. Because Yuri positions himself as a poet, he is separate from those around him. As a result, he fails to react to the events that are occurring to the people in his life. He is incapable of taking action because he is not part of the world in which he lives. He is an artist who, in *Doctor Zhivago*, lives a life of passivity. Yuri is an indecisive and romantic protagonist who is more defined by his love for two women and his desire to write poetry than by his desire to survive in the world into which he has been thrust.

The isolation and passivity that define Yuri's personality begin early in *Doctor Zhivago* as he stands at his mother's grave. The mourners stand on one side of her coffin, but Yuri stands alone on the opposite side. The symbolism is clear even when he is a child. Yuri is alone. The rest of the world continues on him, but he will

WHAT DO I SEE NEXT?

- Before Director David Lean made *Doctor Zhivago*, he filmed *Lawrence of Arabia* in 1962. This film also features Omar Sharif and is often considered to be the film that made Sharif a star. This film also focuses on World War I, but moves the action to the Arabian desert. Sam Spiegel produced this film for Columbia Pictures. Since *Lawrence of Arabia* is rated PG, it is especially suitable for young-adult viewing.

- *Reds* is a 1981 film about the Russian Revolution. The film stars Warren Beatty and Diane Keaton and is also an epic romance. As in *Doctor Zhivago*, there are some wonderful scenes on trains. *Reds* was written, produced, and directed by Beatty, who won an Academy Award as Best Director for the film. *Reds* was released by Paramount and is rated PG.

- *October: Ten Days That Shook the World* is a 1928 Russian-made film about the 1917 Russian Revolution. Director Sergei Eisenstein's film was commissioned by the Soviet government to commemorate the tenth anniversary of the revolution. Today, *October* is much praised for its film techniques, including lighting, editing, and camera placement. It is largely a propaganda film to enhance the actions of the Bolsheviks, but because of the director's talents, *October* is still much admired and was released on DVD in 1998 by Egami Media. It is not rated and is suitable for young-adult viewing.

- The 1919 civil war that followed the Russian Revolution is the topic of the 1968 film *The Red and The White*. This film makes clear that there was nothing romantic about the conflict between the Bolshevik White Army and the Imperial Red Army. *The Red and The White* is a joint Russian-Hungarian film, written and directed by Miklós Jancsó and produced by Jenoe Goetz. The film was not popular in Russia, where it was considered anti-heroic, since it made clear how brutal the war had been. This film, which is not rated, was released by Kino Video.

- Leo Tolstoy's lengthy novel *War and Peace* focuses on Russia during the Napoleonic Wars of the nineteenth century. The resulting film is 427 minutes long and is considered a masterpiece. Sergei Bondarchuk wrote the screenplay and directed this 1965 Russian production, which was released by Mosfilm. *War and Peace* won an Academy Award for Best Foreign Film in 1969. It is not rated, but as a war movie, it contains violence.

- *Red Cliff* is a 2008 Chinese film about the end of the Han Dynasty in the early third century. John Woo directed and produced this nearly five-hour-long historical war epic, which was released in the United States by Lions Gate as a heavily edited shorter film. The DVD version, released by Mongolian Home Entertainment, is considered the superior film. *Red Cliff* is especially notable for its magnificently staged battle scenes, which are complex and filled with details that appeal to the viewer. The film is rated R for violence.

- The film *Empire of the Sun* tells the story of a twelve-year-old British boy who gets caught up in a civil war that erupts in China. The film was released by Warner Brothers. This PG-rated 1987 film stars Christian Bale and is directed by Steven Spielberg

---

remain separate. Through the rest of the film, Yuri will move in and out of people's lives, but in the end, he will die alone on a Moscow street. In the novel Yuri was not quite so alone. He had two close friends, Gordon and Dudorov, but the film eliminates these characters. Except for the

"

YURI IS AN INDECISIVE AND ROMANTIC
PROTAGONIST WHO IS MORE DEFINED BY HIS
LOVE FOR TWO WOMEN AND HIS DESIRE TO WRITE
POETRY THAN BY HIS DESIRE TO SURVIVE IN THE
WORLD INTO WHICH HE HAS BEEN THRUST."

two women in his life, the film focuses on Yuri as a man who exists in his own interior space, separate from those who surround him and not a part of the world that is changing so dramatically around him.

Throughout the film, Yuri simply allows things to happen to him. After his mother's funeral, he is told that he will live in Moscow with Alex and Anna Gromeko. He is a child and has no choice, but Yuri offers not a word of protest at leaving his childhood home. He becomes a doctor because his adoptive father, Alex, is a doctor. He is drafted during World War I. He operates a field hospital during the revolution because he is told to do so. After he returns to Moscow, he moves back into his old home, which is now partitioned into many small apartments, without complaint. When his half-brother Yevgraf tells Yuri he must leave Moscow, he does so. When Yuri and his family flee to Varykino, the Gromeko family dacha, he is just as happy to live in the small run-down cottage as he was to live in a beautiful mansion in Moscow. His surroundings are unimportant to him. He allows himself to passively endure all that happens to him. In the scene where Yuri deserts the Red Partisans, he leaves almost by accident. The rest of the troops move along and he is simply left alone on his horse. He actually chooses to turn his horse and ride away, but the choice was made for him when the troops moved off by themselves, leaving him alone.

The list of actions that Yuri takes at the behest of others could go on, as indeed it does, throughout the film. Yuri will do as others ask because the important things in his life occur in his mind, where he composes poetry. He has an interior life that cares little for the exterior life going on around him. Yuri cares deeply for the personal and the private, but in revolutionary

Russia, there is no place for the personal and the private to exist. In a meeting between Yuri and Strelnikov that occurs as Yuri and his family journey to Varykino, Yuri is told that "The personal life is dead in Russia." Strelnikov continues with words that have no meaning for Yuri: "The private life is dead for any man." This is the new Russia, but Yuri cannot accept this new order. He continues to write poetry and believes that his private life is of no concern to anyone else. He fails to understand that he cannot just live his life, love whoever he wishes, and exist on his own terms. There is a revolution going on and his life is no longer his own. Yuri's life is controlled by a government that cares nothing about the personal or the individual.

As change swirls around him, Yuri actually loses his ability to write poetry and struggles as he searches for words. Living in exile in Varykino with Tonya and his family should give Yuri the freedom to write, but his mind refuses to cooperate. In one scene, he sits at a table with pens and paper in front of him, but nothing flows to the paper. The problem is the yearning he feels for Lara. And yet he cannot go to her until Tonya gives him permission to go into Yuriatin. His father-in-law, Alex, even gives Yuri permission to go to the town library, where Yuri knows that Lara works. As much as Yuri longs for Lara, he cannot act on his own. He must be told that he can go into the town and that he can go to the library. There is a scene later in the film, after Yuri and Lara have taken refuge at Varykino, when he rises in the middle of the night and begins to write poetry. The film does not establish why this happens at this precise moment. In fact, there is a suggestion that it is only after he finds happiness with Lara that Yuri can again begin to write. But the novel makes clear that Yuri begins to write only after Lara tells him that he must write down all of the poems that he has been reciting to her. She gives him permission to write again. During his time with Lara at Varykino, it appears that Yuri has not given much thought to his wife and children, although there is a brief moment when he and Lara first arrive at Varykino when Yuri briefly looks with sadness at the small cottage where he lived with Tonya. Except for that brief glance at the cottage, Yuri's wife and children seem far from his consciousness. In fact, in the novel, he suffers nightmares and real grief at the loss of his family. It is only at night when he writes that Yuri seems to come alive. In the novel, Yuri explains that he knows that he and Lara

(© AF Archive / Alamy)

cannot remain long at Varykino, that the dream that they could live there together will not happen. But rather than act and create a plan by which they could escape and be together, Yuri turns to writing. He writes all night while Lara sleeps and can barely function during the day from the fatigue that results. In the novel, Pasternak writes that Yuri "was sick at heart, yet his greatest torment was his impatience for the night, his longing so to express his grief that everyone should be moved to tears." Even when faced with danger and with the loss of Lara, his first and last impulse is to write so that readers will know and understand the depth of his grief at what has been lost. The personal and the private are never far from his mind.

Several of the film reviews of *Doctor Zhivago* lamented the passivity of the title character, who seemingly drifts through the film just watching and never taking action. The poet in Yuri Zhivago is an observer who watches people and the actions surrounding him and then turns those observations into poetry. Yuri is not a man of action, a man who makes decisions, or a man who assumes control of his life. This is also true of the

novel upon which the film is based. In both novel and film, Yuri is a romantic figure, torn between two women. Initially he thinks his love for Tonya is deep but without great passion. Having grown up with Tonya, Yuri takes his love for her for granted, as if his love for his wife is simply an extension of a childhood love for an adopted sister. In contrast, Yuri's attraction to Lara, whose beauty first captivates him, is very passionate. After Yuri and his family flee Moscow for Varykino and Yuri begins his affair with Lara, Yuri is suddenly struck by how much he loves his wife. In one scene, he stands at the doorway watching his pregnant wife work in the garden, and an expression of sudden knowledge crosses his face. Yuri finally understands that he loves Tonya very passionately. Yuri's great love for Tonya is confirmed later in the film when he is delirious with illness after escaping from the Red Partisans. In his delirium, he calls out Tonya's name, not Lara's. In the film, in one of the very few decisions that he actually makes, Yuri decides to end the affair with Lara. However, in the novel, he does not choose to end the affair and is not forced to do so since he is soon captured by Red

Partisans. The irony is that the film appears to suggest that Yuri is punished for making a choice. Had he remained the passive man of inaction that he has always been, he might have continued with both women. He is truer to his passive personality in the novel, since he never chooses. When Tonya leaves Varykino, only Lara remains and it is she to whom Yuri returns after he escapes from his kidnappers. The decision of which woman he should choose is made for him.

In a review of *Doctor Zhivago* written for the *New York Times*, Bosley Crowther complains that Zhivago is never upset at what happens. He never complains or rebels; instead, he simply accepts the events that go on around him. The loss of family, of his freedom, and of his home are of little concern to Yuri. He deals with loss by writing poetry. This is his expression of loss. Perhaps, though, what Crowther condemns as passivism is Yuri's individualism, which stands alone in the face of the revolutionary Bolsheviks, who think alike, dress alike, and behave as one. Rather than think about a classless Russia, Yuri thinks about the moment in which he lives and writes. His poetry sets him apart from the classless people who surround him. In his essay on history, Ralph Waldo Emerson writes, "To the poet, to the philosopher, to the saint, all things are friendly and sacred, all events profitable, all days holy, all men divine. For the eye is fastened on the life, and slights the circumstance." Yuri is the poet of whom Emerson speaks. He cares little for the circumstances that surround him. Rather, he lives for the moments spent with the two women he loves and the opportunity to write poetry, which is not for himself but for those who will read it in the future and will know that his was a great life, filled with passion and heartache.

Source: Sheri Metzger Karmiol, Critical Essay on *Doctor Zhivago*, in *Novels for Students*, Gale, Cengage Learning, 2013.

Harlow Robinson

In the following excerpt, Robinson examines the image of Russia and Russians portrayed in the film Doctor Zhivago *and other films about Russia after the Revolution of 1917.*

Like many members of my generation, I received my first enduring images of Russia from the movies and television. In 1965, my parents took me and a school friend, both of us in those early teenage years when it is socially

> IT WAS THE PEOPLE AND THEIR STORIES
> IN *DOCTOR ZHIVAGO*, AND THE HYPNOTIC
> BEAUTY OF THE MUSICAL AND VISUAL SYNTHESIS
> ACHIEVED BY A GREAT DIRECTOR WORKING
> WITH SOME OF THE GREATEST ACTORS OF THE
> TIME, THAT REMOVED ALL BARRIERS OF
> GEOGRAPHY, HISTORY, AND IDEOLOGY."

unacceptable for boys to get excited about anything except sports, to the Elmwood Cinema in Elmwood, Connecticut, to see the just-released David Lean epic *Doctor Zhivago*. That was in the days when big, serious films had overtures and intermissions, and *Doctor Zhivago* was nothing if not serious and big, with a super-sized running time of 192 minutes and a balalaika-spiked Oscar-winning score by Maurice Jarre that contained a hit tune ("Somewhere My Love") that saturated the airwaves for months. I was enthralled.

The cinematically constructed Russia of angelic Lara and handsome Yuri and brooding Strelnikov and evil Komarovsky—full of waltzes, wars, gigantic hydroelectric dams, endless train trips, ice palaces, flowering Siberian fields, and humorless revolutionaries equipped with dramatic facial scars—seduced me utterly and forever. Lean's desperately romantic and passionate film, released at a moment when the United States and the USSR (more or less synonymous, incorrectly, in the American popular consciousness with Russia) were locked in the deadly nuclear competition of the Cold War, sent me on a quest for deeper knowledge of things Russian. I began to read the novels of Dostoyevsky and, a few years later, began studying Russian, taking the first steps on a lifelong crusade to conquer and penetrate that most challenging and rewarding of languages. *Doctor Zhivago* humanized Russia for me, transporting me far beyond the small faded New England clock city where I had spent my life to date to a vivid and exciting world that on the screen loomed so much more real and important than my own. There was Russia right on the screen just a few hundred feet away, alluring and seemingly attainable. I could almost reach out and touch it.

This Russia affected me emotionally in a way I had never been affected before, erasing whatever vague fear I had absorbed from school textbooks or daily newspaper and television news stories about the evil Commies in Moscow and their dangerous comrades in nearby Cuba who together were building missiles with which to attack us. We talked in school about building fallout shelters. Those stories seemed abstract and remote, but Dr. Zhivago's was immediate and full of very recognizable feelings. No wonder Vladimir Ilych Lenin, scheming godfather of the USSR, had once called the cinema "the most important of all the arts." For it conveys the illusion of reality like no other medium ever invented. Images seen on the screen have a way of overwhelming and superseding all others. The ability of film to shape public opinion has also been widely recognized by American politicians, including (to name only one prominent example) Senator Joseph McCarthy and members of the Un-American Activities Committee of the House of Representatives in the early 1950s, who combed through movies in search of evidence of overt and hidden pro-Communist (and therefore pro-Russian) messages.

At the time, I knew nothing about Boris Pasternak, the genius upon whose poetic and complex novel the movie *Doctor Zhivago* had been based (much too loosely for the taste of many critics, including Brendan Gill of the *New Yorker*, who called the film a "grievous disappointment"), who had died just five years earlier, engaged to the bitter end in an exhausting life-and-death struggle with Soviet totalitarian censorship. I do not believe I knew then that the novel had never been published in the USSR, or that its appearance abroad had gravely endangered Pasternak's already precarious existence, or that Pasternak had been awarded the Nobel Prize for Literature to the deep chagrin of the Soviet government. Indeed, I knew next to nothing about the Russian Revolution or Communism. Of those artists and matters I would come to know later. But such is the awesome power of the moving visual image, the vivid sense of its undeniable reality, its ability to establish immediate and direct emotional connection, that none of this mattered during my first intimate encounter with Russian at the Elmwood Cinema. It was the people and their stories in *Doctor Zhivago*, and

the hypnotic beauty of the musical and visual synthesis achieved by a great director working with some of the greatest actors of the time, that removed all barriers of geography, history, and ideology. How awful could Russia be if such people as Julie Christie and Omar Shariff lived there?

In time, I came to recognize how artificial, inaccurate, and manipulative was the image of Russia presented in *Doctor Zhivago*, and in other films about Russia that emerged from Hollywood. I came to understand that a feature film was not the same as reality, and discovered that *Zhivago* was filmed in Spain and in studios, not on the streets of Moscow and the steppes of Siberia. For the great majority of Americans, however, the image of Russia and the USSR presented in mainstream Hollywood films acquired enormous power and authority, particularly in the absence of consistently reliable alternative information on a country that because of historical and political events of the twentieth century occupied such a privileged and unusual position in the American psyche.

Hollywood films about Russia were fated to play a special role, because for most of the twentieth century, Russia/USSR was the primary "other" in the American consciousness, the ideological and military enemy, with vast and terrifying resources, by the middle of the century capable and apparently desirous of blowing us all off the planet. It is also a most curious historical coincidence that the Bolshevik Revolution of 1917 (which led to the establishment of the world's first Socialist/Communist society, one of whose avowed goals was to overthrow world capitalism, headquartered in the United States) occurred precisely at the moment when the American film industry was entering a rapid period of development, moving westward from New York toward Hollywood (farther away from Russia, even more abstract viewed from the palm-lined avenues of Los Angeles). The overthrow of the Romanov dynasty and the creation of the USSR was one of the biggest and most shocking stories of the century, so it is hardly surprising that films about Russia constituted a significant part of the output of the Hollywood studios from the very beginning of their existence.

The increasing importance of the Soviet-American relationship, especially after World War II, and its centrality in American foreign policy, ensured that films about Russia would continue to occupy a privileged position in Hollywood production, given the studios' need to make movies of a topical nature. Not surprisingly, many of these feature films about Russia engaged in a vigorous (and sometimes humorous) defense of capitalism, as we shall see. Who were the men who ran the Hollywood studios, after all, but some of the most successful capitalists that the system had ever produced?

Further complicating and enriching this phenomenon was the presence in the Hollywood film industry from its earliest days of a large number of émigrés from both pre- and post-Revolutionary Russia. Some of them anti-Soviet and some pro-Soviet in their ideological leanings, they participated (as directors, actors, composers, writers, designers, cameramen) in the making of many of the films that presented Russia and the USSR to the American audience. These Russians also worked, of course, on many other films that did not deal with Russia, joining other émigrés (from Hungary, Germany, Austria, France, England, Sweden, Czechoslovakia, Poland, and so on) in the amazing ethnic melting pot that Hollywood became. . . .

Source: Harlow Robinson, "Introduction: Meeting *Doctor Zhivago*," in *Russians in Hollywood: Hollywood's Russians*, University Press of New England, 2007, pp. 1–10.

Richard Teleky

In the following essay, Teleky compares the novel and the film, speculating on Pasternak's reactions to the changes.

At a library book sale not long ago I spotted a hardbound copy of Boris Pasternak's novel *Doctor Zhivago*. The book, which turned out to be a first edition, was in excellent condition and wore its original dust jacket. Since the novel hadn't been deaccessioned from the library's collection, it must have come from one of the boxes of books donated to the sale. I paid the two-dollar asking price, brought *Zhivago* home and started re-reading it, for the first time in over forty years, an image of the luminous Julie Christie as Pasternak's heroine in the back of my mind. I was surprised by the narrator's wry sense of humour, which I hadn't remembered, and the story kept my attention. Later I found the paperback edition read during my high school years, and its cover proclaimed it "The Novel That Made World History."

WHILE DAVID LEAN'S FILM REMOVED MANY OF THE NOVEL'S MORE ECCENTRIC IMPROBABILITIES BY CUTTING BACK ON ITS NUMEROUS MINOR CHARACTERS, HIS ADAPTATION MAINTAINED THE CURIOUS BLEND OF DOOM AND OPTIMISM THAT ANIMATES *ZHIVAGO*."

Next fall marks the fiftieth anniversary of the book's publication in English, a moment in time when a novel could draw the attention of readers around the world, with word of mouth spreading about a manuscript smuggled out of Russia. It's easy to forget the fear that shadowed the Cold War era. Just two years before *Zhivago* arrived in American bookstores, Soviet tanks drove into Budapest and ended the Hungarian uprising; two years after its arrival, Nikita Khrushchev pounded his right shoe on a podium at the United Nations and threatened to bury the West.

Begun in 1948 and originally planned for serial publication in Russia in 1956, *Zhivago* did not pass the censors. Pasternak had also given his manuscript to an agent of the Italian publisher Feltrinelli in the spring of that year, saying, "You've invited me to my own execution." The Italian translation appeared in the fall of 1957 and a Russian-language version followed, also in Milan; both were published at considerable risk to Pasternak and those closest to him An. English translation from the Russian, by Max Hayward and Manya Harari, appeared a year later, in September (from Collins in Canada and Great Britain and Pantheon in the United States) and on 23 October, the second anniversary of the start of the abortive Hungarian revolution, Pasternak was awarded the Nobel Prize for Literature.

Doctor Zhivago quickly rose to first place on the best-seller lists, bypassing a book by another Russian writer—the emigre Vladimir Nabokov's *Lolita*. Perhaps *Zhivago* better suited the Cold War atmosphere, reassuring people that, despite communism, Russians could love just like anyone else—reassurance no one was likely to find in the controversial Lolita. Naturally Nabokov despised Pasternak's novel. Stacy Schiff's biography *Vera* (Mrs Vladimir Nabokov) records the couple's dislike and distress. Nabokov considered *Zhivago* "clumsy and melodramatic, with stock situations," while *Vera* maintained that "the communists" had pushed it "into the 'Nobel prize winner' club—merely by pretending that it had been 'smuggled' out of the USSR!" (According to Brian Boyd, Nabokov's biographer, Pasternak had rejected the suggestion that Nabokov was the ideal English translator for his novel, saying, "That won't work; he's too jealous of my wretched position in this country to do it properly.")

The only other Russian writer to have received a Nobel Prize was Ivan Bunin, in 1933. This point is important, since Nobel Prizes for literature inevitably contain a political element. Russian authorities quickly saw the Nobel committee's decision as an anti-Soviet statement, and five days after accepting the prize, Pasternak declined it. As Orlando Figes wrote in *Natasha's Dance: A Cultural History of Russia*, emigres from the Russian revolution considered Bunin's work to be proof that the realist tradition of Tolstoy and Turgenev was alive in the diaspora: "As Bunin himself put it in a celebrated speech of 1924, it was 'The Mission of Emigration' to act for the 'True Russia' by protecting this inheritance from the modernist corruptions of left-wing and Soviet art." When it suits them, governments have long memories. Pasternak was even persuaded to sign a letter renouncing his creation, an act he regretted for the rest of his life.

The Nabokovs' view of *Zhivago*'s literary merits aside, they misjudged its political situation during a time of tension in the Soviet system between rigid censorship and an impulse towards liberalization. In this context, *Zhivago* became a moral as well as a literary success. Edmund Wilson, writing the *New Yorker*, called the book "One of the great events in man's literary and moral history," and similar international praise greeted its subsequent translations. But global politics alone can't account for the novel's success. It's said that everyone loves a love story, and this may help explain *Zhivago*'s popularity. Several years after reading the novel and corresponding with Pasternak, the Trappist monk and poet Thomas Merton, of *Seven Storey Mountain* fame, remained so overwhelmed by its love story that he began an affair with an attractive nurse. He probably wasn't alone in his response. Even today one

sees remnants of the novel's impact (and more likely that of David Lean's film version, released in 1965) in young women named Lara. Last year, a student of mine sighed while explaining that she was named after Pasternak's heroine—she'd yet to read the novel. It's worth noting that this "Lara" was born in the mid-1980s, decades after the novel's publication and the film's release, which must say something about Pasternak's staying power.

As a romantic couple, Zhivago and Lara are closer to Petrarch and his muse Laura than to the troubled adulterers of nineteenth-century fiction, from Madame Bovary to Anna Karenina. Readers who believed that the novel's love story matched events of Pasternak's life couldn't have been further from the truth. Pasternak's affair with Olga Ivinskaya, his model for Lara, was in fact a May-December alliance, with 22 years between them and all that such a difference entails. The couple met in 1946, when the beautiful, twice-married Olga was an editor at *Novy Mir*. Then 56, Pasternak was inspired to concentrate again on original work rather than the translations into Russian that had preoccupied him. Revered for his lyric poetry, he had been tolerated by the Soviet regime, which remained suspicious of his work. The love affair lasted until Pasternak died, in 1960, although it was interrupted in 1949 when Ivinskaya was arrested and sentenced to prison. Released in 1953, she was again sentenced to the gulag after his death, where she served four years of an eight-year sentence, punishment for her association with Pasternak, as she wrote in her memoir *A Captive of Time: My Years With Pasternak*. Whatever rumours Nabokov may have heard of that relationship, he was living safely in Ithaca, New York, and teaching at Cornell University. But safety didn't breed generosity, as Stacy Schiff showed: "Among the insults he [Nabokov] hurled at the book was the accusation that Pasternak's mistress had written the novel for him, the worst that could be said, not because Pasternak might have delegated the responsibility, but because the thing read as if written by a woman."

Movies shape our memories and even change them. As I re-read *Zhivago*, I often found myself recalling scenes from the film. The novel's powerful opening, like the movie's, is the funeral of young Yurii Zhivago's mother, although Lean adds a follow-up scene in which the child is given his mother's beloved balalaika. Nothing of this sort happens in Pasternak, but Hollywood perhaps needed an event to justify the balalaika orchestra that dominates Maurice Jarre's soundtrack, as cloying as a glass of Russian tea over-sweetened with preserves. When I reached the point in the novel where Lara and Zhivago finally admit their love, my mind, alas, switched on "Lara's Theme" from the movie. (By the mid-'60s, "Lara's Theme"—also known as "Somewhere My Love" in popular recordings by the Ray Conniff Singers and Andy Williams—played endlessly on the radio, in cocktail lounges, and at weddings, as if it were an antidote to the Beatles. In his foreword to the brochure for the thirtieth anniversary CD of his soundtrack, Jarre wrote, "I've heard a guitar player on a gondola in Venice playing 'Lara's Theme.' I've heard street musicians with primitive instruments in Central Africa playing 'Lara's Theme.'")

And what of the novel itself? Spanning half a century, *Doctor Zhivago* incorporates war, revolution, famine, collectivization, and emigration into an epic plot fuelled by implausible coincidences and reversals. Across the vast Russian landscape, quickly sketched characters bump into each other as if they lived in the same apartment building: the lawyer who drove Zhivago's father to suicide also seduced the young Lara; without comment, Zhivago's mysterious half-brother shadows him like a guardian angel, always ready with money or the things money can buy; eventually the wicked lawyer comes to the rescue of Lara and Zhivago's unborn child; and Lara's once meek husband, now turned infamous revolutionary, reappears after several reported deaths only to commit suicide after talking with Zhivago about her—to name just a few of the more spectacular contrivances. Strangely, though, these events take on a cumulative power, and implausibility ceases to matter. It's as if Pasternak followed a simple narrative aesthetic: if an incident would be unbelievable in life, then it belongs in a novel. Perhaps he felt that life often refuses the narrative niceties expected of fiction. In this sense Pasternak, who inherited the tradition of nineteenth-century realism, is closer to his (and Zhivago's) beloved Pushkin, and his sometimes surreal stories, than to Tolstoy.

Pasternak's characters are aware that something like fate propels them, and they often discuss the contorted turns in their lives. Zhivago and Lara would appear insufferable, like all lovers who mythologize themselves, if it weren't for

the terrible hardships they endure. While David Lean's film removed many of the novel's more eccentric improbabilities by cutting back on its numerous minor characters, his adaptation maintained the curious blend of doom and optimism that animates *Zhivago*. Yet there are some significant surprises for anyone re-reading the novel with the film hovering in mind. In the novel, after Lara and Zhivago separate at the wintry country home Varykino, which had once belonged to his wife's family, Zhivago ends up living in Moscow with a new "wife," Marina, and he becomes the father of two daughters; Lean's screenwriters kept the Lara-Zhivago love story in conventional focus by skipping over Marina. Instead, a decade after the lovers separate, Zhivago is riding a Moscow streetcar when he looks out the window and sees Lara walking alongside; he flees the crowded tram and has a fatal heart attack while trying to call out to his lost love.

This kind of Hollywood contrivance would never have interested Pasternak—while his Zhivago also has a heart attack after leaving a streetcar, the only person with a connection to the hero walking alongside it is an old French governess. But Pasternak had another, less sentimental, plot turn in store. Later, once Zhivago's body has been laid out in a coffin in his rented room, Lara happens to amble down the street, remember a room that had once played a role in her life, and wander up to discover her lost lover's body. At this point even Lara remarks on the piling up of improbabilities: "What an extraordinary coincidence—like predestination!" Though moments like this are shaped by Pasternak's fascination with the mystical strain in Russian Orthodoxy, they also recall literary devices favoured by Pearl Buck and Sinclair Lewis, two other Nobel Prize winners infrequently read today.

Yet literary conventions endure because they contain psychological truth. And Pasternak, who frequently spoke of truth, was writing a novel, not a memoir. He knew that people sometimes want to turn the clock back, but he refused the devices of ghosts or spirits to transcend time, though Russian literature has its share of them. Lasting fiction reflects deep psychic needs, and Pasternak surely would agree with his protagonist that "art has two constant, two unending concerns: it always meditates on death and thus always creates life." If this credo sounds like a poet's, well, Pasternak was one of Russia's leading modern poets. The 36 pages of verse that conclude his novel as "The Poems of Yurii Zhivago" are some of the book's most intense. The cycle of seasons running through them is reminiscent of the way the seasons shape the novel itself, nature a recurring motif that dwarfs human activity like an omniscient, impersonal deity. The love of the natural world that dominates *Zhivago*, the awe before all living things and their fragility, is rare in modern fiction. It may even seem old-fashioned, a quaint pastoral, unless one pays close attention to the devastation that nature also brings as *Zhivago* unfolds. There are pretty fields of golden daffodils in David Lean's film, not in Pasternak's novel.

Pasternak's critique of Soviet bureaucracy and, by implication, inhumane bureaucracy of any kind, will strike a chord with contemporary readers. Although Zhivago and Lara are obviously foils to the novel's villainous revolutionaries, it is only because Pasternak presents them as superior people—self-evidently finer, brighter, exceptional. At the same time, in his affection for Russian Orthodoxy, he may have associated the rituals of the Russian church with a less violent, pre-revolutionary world, as if the Christian socialism propounded by Tolstoy might have averted the revolution. Pasternak was born to an assimilated Jewish family, and as *Zhivago* makes clear, he had little sympathy for Judaism because it does not accept Jesus as the Messiah. At best, this strain of the novel came as a surprise. The quasi-religious, prophetic tone that runs through *Zhivago* reminds me of a remark in *Tightrope Walking*, the memoir by Pasternak's younger sister Josephine. Recalling a summer when her brother, then 23, chose the family's vacation home, she wrote, "As usual, Boris spoke in that specific voice of his, the voice of someone imparting to the world at large an esoteric experience."

The world at large no longer listens to Pasternak, and Nabokov would perhaps feel vindicated by time. *Lolita* is commonly taught in university courses and recently played a significant role in Azar Nafisi's memoir *Reading Lolita in Tehran*, while *Doctor Zhivago* has lost its claim to much public following, except through Lean's film, which regularly crops up on the Turner Classic Movie channel. In an informal telephone survey I conducted, bookstores in Boston, Cleveland, Los Angeles, and Toronto all had *Lolita* in

stock; none had *Zhivago*. (Lean's film, on DVD, is still popular, as is Stanley Kubrick's adaptation of Nabokov's novel. Both books have also received more recent film versions—*Lolita*, directed by Adrian Lyne, in 1998, and a BBC series of *Zhivago*, shown on PBS's "Masterpiece Theatre" in 2004.) Does sex sell better than war and revolution? Is Nabokov's novel the better book? The answer depends on the reader.

Re-reading is a curious act, one of memory and reassessment; it can even be a mirror to another self—in a sense, it resembles a coincidence out of Pasternak, where one comes across a once-known place decades later, like looking at old photographs. Orlando Figes quoted a pertinent remark by Igor Stravinsky, who told his friend Robert Craft that he was re-reading books he'd first read in Russia, like *Gorky's Mother*: "I read it when it was first published [in 1906] and am trying again now, probably because I want to go back into myself." The self one finds in re-reading of course depends on one's age at the first reading.

Finally, though, one puts aside a revisited book to see not just the self but the world anew. Despite the often plodding earnestness of *Doctor Zhivago*, its strength and power come from the decency of Pasternak's desire both to bear witness to the weight of history and to affirm the value of individual conscience. Thus, the novel offers readers a challenge that is still compelling: in Zhivago's place, in Lara's place, at that moment in time, in the face of all of those terrors, what might we have done? And then, what do we do today?

Source: Richard Teleky, "Re-reading *Doctor Zhivago*," in *Queen's Quarterly*, Vol. 14, No. 4, Winter 2007, pp. 584–95.

SOURCES

Crowther, Bosley, "Adaptation of Pasternak Novel at the Capital," Review of *Doctor Zhivago*, in *New York Times*, December 23, 1965.

Dancyger, Ken, "Editors Who Became Directors," in *The Technique of Film and Video Editing: History, Theory, and Practice*, 5th ed., Focal Press, 2010, pp. 71–86.

Emerson, Ralph Waldo, "History," in *Essays*, *Penn State Electronic Classics Series*, p. 10, http://www2.hn.psu.edu/faculty/jmanis/rw-emerson/essays_rwe.pdf (accessed January 1, 2012).

Fitzpatrick, Sheila, "1917: The Revolutions of February and October," in *The Russian Revolution*, 3rd ed., Oxford University Press, 2008, pp. 40–47.

Kauffmann, Stanley, "Doctoring Zhivago," Review of *Doctor Zhivago*, in *New Republic*, Vol. 154, No. 3, January 15, 1966, pp. 34–36.

Lean, David, and Robert Bolt, *Doctor Zhivago* (Two-Disc 45th Anniversary Edition), Warner Brothers, 2010.

Maxford, Howard, *David Lean*, Batsford, 2000, pp. 121–31.

Murphy, A. D., Review of *Doctor Zhivago*, in *Variety*, December 28, 1965.

Pasternak, Boris, *Doctor Zhivago*, Pantheon, 1958, p. 440.

Pasvolsky, Leo "The Intelligentsia Under the Soviets," in *Atlantic Monthly*, Vol. 126, July–December 1920, pp. 681–92.

Phillips, Gene D., "Knight Without Armor: *Doctor Zhivago*," in *Beyond the Epic: The Life & Films of David Lean*, University Press of Kentucky, 2006, pp. 321–60.

Rudova, Larissa, "*Doctor Zhivago*," in *Understanding Boris Pasternak*, University of South Carolina Press, 1997, pp. 137–77.

"To Russia With Love," Review of *Doctor Zhivago*, in *Time*, Vol. 86, No. 27, December 31, 1965.

Zubok, Vladislav Martinovich, "The Fate of Zhivago's Intelligentsia," in *Zhivago's Children: The Last Russian Intelligentsia*, Harvard University Press, 2009, pp. 1–22.

FURTHER READING

Adelman, Deborah, *The "Children of Perestroika" Come of Age: Young People of Moscow Talk about Life in the New Russia*, M. E. Sharpe, 1994.

> Pasternak would likely not recognize the Moscow depicted in this young-adult book. The author interviews Moscow teenagers in 1989 and again in 1992 to ask them about their lives in Russia and their hopes for the future and discovers that these teenagers are not very different from American teenagers. This book gives young adult-readers an opportunity to learn what it is like to live in Russia.

Barnes, Christopher, *Boris Pasternak: A Literary Biography*, Cambridge University Press, 2004.

> This is the second volume of Barnes's biography of Pasternak's life and covers the period from 1928 until Pasternak's death in 1960. Barnes discusses the controversies surrounding the publication of Pasternak's novel *Doctor Zhivago* and focuses on Pasternak's life within the cultural milieu of Russia after the Communist revolution. Barnes also explores the impact of Pasternak's being awarded the Nobel Prize for Literature in 1958.

Figes, Orlando, *Natasha's Dance: A Cultural History of Russia*, Metropolitan Books, 2002.

> This book is a survey of Russian culture that focuses on writers, artists, musicians, and intellectuals. The book begins with the founding of Russia in the twelfth century and moves forward to the twentieth century. Figes organizes the book thematically, which makes it easier for the reader to focus on specific aspects of Russian culture. This is an easy-to-understand introduction to the history and culture of Russia.

Frank, Stephen P., *Crime, Cultural Conflict, and Justice in Rural Russia, 1856-1914*, University of California Press, 1999.

> In this book, the author examines the conflict between the peasant class and local governments. Frank uses primary documents as his sources, which reveal that social class issues were an important facet of the justice system in pre-revolutionary Russia.

Ingram, Philip, *Russia and the USSR, 1905-1991*, Cambridge University Press, 1997.

> This young-adult book provides a history of Russia from the 1905 revolution though the 1917 revolution, the civil war that followed, and the many changes that occurred throughout the twentieth century. There are many photos and illustrations that help make this an easy-to-understand history.

Ivinskaya, Olga, *A Captive of Time: My Years With Pasternak*, Warner, 1978.

> Ivinskaya was Pasternak's mistress and is often cited as the inspiration for Lara in *Doctor Zhivago*. This book is a memoir of her life and her time with Pasternak.

Murphy, Dervla, *Silverland: A Winter Journey Beyond the Urals*, John Murray, 2006.

> In essence, this book is a travel guide via train through the Urals. Just as Yuri Zhivago journeys with his family through the Urals in the book and film, this writer takes a similar journey. The author records what it was like to travel through long stretches of empty snowscape by train. Since the author includes a great deal of information about the history and people who live in Siberia and her interactions with them, this book also offers readers an engaging way to learn about this part of the world.

Pasternak, Boris, *Safe Conduct: An Autobiography and Other Writings*, New Directions, 1958.

> Rather than a straightforward autobiography, this book is more reflective of Pasternak's thoughts about writing and art. Parts of this memoir are related via poetry, and some of the prose is constructed as short stories; it is not always organized chronologically. While not always an easy read, this autobiography does succeed in illustrating Pasternak's talents and his ideas about writing.

SUGGESTED SEARCH TERMS

David Lean AND *Doctor Zhivago*

Robert Bolt AND *Doctor Zhivago*

Omar Sharif AND *Doctor Zhivago*

Julie Christie AND *Doctor Zhivago*

Rod Steiger AND *Doctor Zhivago*

Russian Revolution AND Bolsheviks

Doctor Zhivago AND censorship

Doctor Zhivago AND Boris Pasternak

Lara's Theme AND Maurice Jarre

World War I AND Russia

Donald Duk

FRANK CHIN

1991

Donald Duk is a 1991 coming-of-age young-adult novel, with an almost twelve-year-old protagonist at the center of the action. The novel is set in San Francisco's Chinatown during the celebration of Chinese New Year. The author, Frank Chin, has created a contemporary novel that explores the difficulty that even second- and third-generation immigrants face when balancing two cultures: their Chinese heritage and the dominant American culture in which they live.

The protagonist hates his name, Donald Duk, which makes him the object of bullying and teasing. Throughout the novel, Chin always refers to Donald by his full name, Donald Duk, so the point of his name is never forgotten. Donald wants to fit in and be an American, but because he is Chinese, he can never fit in completely. The novel uses Donald's dreams of working on the transcontinental railroad in 1867 as a way to illustrate Donald's transition from someone who is an anti-Chinese racist to an adolescent who embraces his Chinese heritage.

Donald Duk has not received any awards, but it has proven to a useful tool for discussing ethnic and racial pride, as well as a way to explore the immigrant experience and the difficulty in fitting into American life. As a result, *Donald Duk* is often included on school reading lists. Although *Donald Duk* makes it clear that racism against Asians has been a problem in American society, Chin places an equal emphasis on

Donald's own racism with regards to his Chinese heritage and life. *Donald Duk* was originally published by Coffee House Press in Minneapolis, Minnesota. This young-adult novel is readily available in paperback additions at many booksellers.

AUTHOR BIOGRAPHY

Chin is a first-generation Chinese American author who was born in Berkeley, California, on February 25, 1940. Chin's parents were immigrants from Guandong province in China. They spent little time with their son as he was growing up in Oakland's Chinatown. Chin attended the University of California at Berkeley, left school to work, and later graduated from the University of California Santa Barbara with a bachelor's degree in English. He briefly worked as a brakeman on the Southern Pacific Railroad, which provided him with experiences that he has used in several of his plots.

Chin also worked briefly in construction in Maui, Hawaii. It was in Maui that Chin entered a playwriting contest and wrote his first play, *The Chickencoop Chinaman*, which won a five-hundred-dollar prize, providing Chin with the money that he needed to move back to the mainland. *The Chickencoop Chinaman* (1972) became the first play by a Chinese American to appear in a major New York City theater. A second play, *The Year of the Dragon*, followed in 1974.

In the 1980s, Chin turned his attention to writing short stories and novels. *The Chinaman Pacific and Frisco R.R. Co.*, a collection of eight short stories, was published in 1988 and received the American Book Award. Two novels, *Donald Duk* (1991) and *Gunga Din Highway* (1994), followed. Chin is also well known as an essayist and editor of Asian American literature. He published *Bulletproof Buddhists and Other Essays* in 1998 and co-edited two anthologies of Asian American literature, *Aiiieeeee!* (1974) and *The Big Aiiieeeee!* (1991). His most recent book is *Born in the USA: A Story of Japanese America, 1889–1947* (2002), an oral history that traces the lives of first- and second-generation Japanese Americans before the start of World War II. Chin is also well known for his controversial attacks on several contemporary Asian women writers, who Chin accuses of reinforcing Chinese American stereotypes. Chin received a second American Book Award in 2000 for lifetime achievement. Chin currently lives in California.

PLOT SUMMARY

Chapters 1–3

The opening chapter of the book introduces the narrator, Donald Duk, and his immediate family, including his parents and twin older sisters. What becomes immediately evident is how much Donald hates his name because it reminds everyone of the cartoon character, Donald Duck. When gangs of older boys pick on Donald, his father tells him that he can either fight, tell jokes, or talk like the cartoon Donald Duck. The last two choices seem like the best option for Donald, because they will make his opponents laugh and forget about beating him up.

Donald explains how embarrassing he finds his Chinese heritage. His uncle, also named Donald Duk, will be coming to visit so that he can present an opera program at the private school that Donald attends. The anticipation of this program fills Donald with horror. He never invites his best friend, Arnold, to his home because it is too Chinese, but Arnold invites himself to stay with Donald. Arnold not only expresses interest in all things Chinese but wants to participate in all of the upcoming Chinese New Year celebrations. Donald's father has been building stick and paper airplanes that he plans to burn on the last day of the celebration, illustrating the Chinese belief that the world changes and things do not last. Donald is completely uninterested in building these airplanes but decides that he will take one of the planes and burn it himself.

Donald gets up in the middle of the night and takes one of the planes up to the roof of his apartment building, where he lights the fuse, starts the plane's engine, and sends it up into the air over Chinatown. After the plane burns, Donald discovers he is not alone on the roof. He meets American Cong, a war veteran, who was exposed to Agent Orange (a chemical used in the Vietnam War by the U.S. military to kill plants, thus depriving their enemies of cover and reducing food supplies). The confrontation frightens Donald, who flees.

When Donald enters his apartment, he discovers that Uncle Donald watched his nephew take the plane and leave. When Donald begs his uncle not to tell his father about the missing

MEDIA ADAPTATIONS

- There is a video of Chin performing a reading from *Donald Duk* on YouTube. This video, http://www.youtube.com/watch?v=zuShyQzn Hjw&feature=player_embedded#!, is about 25 minutes long.

- YouTube also shows a video of Chin talking about traditional Chinese fairy tales. This video, http://www.youtube.com/watch?v=KzFAE6 onChw, is about 38 minutes long.

- Chin maintains a blog at http://chintalks. blogspot.com/, in which he writes about a large variety of subjects, including what he is working on and how he feels about current issues of Chinese and Asian stereotyping.

plane, Uncle is astonished that Donald seems to think that King would not notice the absence of one plane. Each plane represents one of the one hundred and eight outlaw heroes, and Donald's father knows the story of each outlaw. Uncle tells Donald that for the Chinese, the outlaws of the *Water Margin* legends are like Robin Hood, except that each is an individual with his own story. The plane that Donald just burned represents the outlaw Black Tornado, who killed many of his enemies. King will notice the loss of that one plane. Uncle asserts that the private school Donald attends has attempted to destroy the Chinese in him.

Donald also learns that his real surname is not Duk but Lee. Donald says that he has nightmares about railroads, and his uncle tells him that the first Lee ancestor in the United States was a young boy who came to build the railroads. When Donald sees the photograph that his uncle shows him of Chinese building the transcontinental railroad, Donald immediately realizes that he knows the place in the photo: it appears each night in his dreams. Before they return to bed, Donald's uncle tells him that he must confess the burning of the plane to his father and offer to build another. His uncle also tells

Donald that he built the Black Tornado plane that was burned.

Chapters 4–6

Donald returns to bed and dreams about his great-great-grandfather, the Lee who came to America five generations ago. Donald is transported back to the building of the Central Pacific section of the railroad. He describes the clothing that the Chinese laborers wear and the food wagons that accompany them. There is a performer who is really a traveling medicinal peddler hoping to sell his kung fu brew that will make the Chinese laborers stronger and heartier than the Irish workers who are building the Union Pacific section of the railroad.

On the first morning of the Chinese New Year, Donald's father wakes the family early so that they can go shopping for food. Arnold is going to be included in all of the Chinese New Year activities, and so he accompanies the family. Although the family restaurant is closed for the holiday, the family and all their guests will eat there. Donald decides to postpone telling his father about the plane he destroyed. Uncle Donald gives each child, including Arnold, an envelope containing fifty dollars. This gift of money is one part of celebrating the Chinese New Year. As Donald bickers with his sisters, he wonders if everyone knows about the plane and if they are waiting for him to confess.

The family first visits a fish seller, where King orders something special for the holiday dinner. All of the Chinese families are out walking in Chinatown. Everyone is dressed up and exchanges gifts of money for the children. Donald tells everyone that the Chinese need to give up being Chinese and be American. If that happened, he would not have the problems that he has. Donald's father explains that Donald may be the last Chinese boy to believe it is necessary to give up being Chinese to be American. The new immigrants know that they do not have to give up anything to be American; they can just add American to their Chinese. This is something older immigrants did not understand. They thought they must give up the old country to be accepted.

Chapters 7–9

The family stops in a Chinese restaurant for lunch. Donald thinks about his upcoming tap dance lesson, while Arnold wants to help build the airplanes. Although Arnold seems to want to learn all he can about being Chinese, Donald wants to eliminate any sign that he is Chinese. He dreams of becoming Fred Astaire and appearing in films, where people will remark that he used to be Donald Duk before he learned to dance so well. After lunch, everyone except for Donald's father returns to the family home. Donald's mother teaches Arnold how to use the pattern and cut out the balsa wood airplane parts. Donald is embarrassed at how Chinese everyone sounds and looks and how serious Arnold is about learning everything there is to know about being Chinese.

Donald escapes from the family airplane-building project to attend his dance lesson. The instructor, Larry Louie, was a famous dancer when he was younger and appeared in films. When Donald arrives, he learns that class is cancelled because of the Chinese New Year. Larry has a guest, a friend who performs for the Cantonese opera, who explains that as a result of the Cultural Revolution in China, Cantonese opera is banned and that Donald's father has always helped the opera performers. This is a surprise to Donald. As Larry and his guests and Donald walk together to the restaurant for dinner, the Frog Twins, a pair of older ladies, approach and invite the whole group up to their small apartment. One of the Frog Twins hands Donald an airplane model kit for the P-26A, the same model plane that Donald burned the previous night. After dreading all day the chore of telling his father about the plane he burned, suddenly Donald feels he has been saved by the Frog Twins.

Family and friends gather at the Duk restaurant for a celebratory dinner. Everyone bows down and offers a donation before the altar that honors the dead. Donald is upset when Larry, who is after all the Chinese Fred Astaire, also bows before the altar and acts Chinese. Donald is embarrassed, and his mother does not make him bow. Instead, she hands him a kit for a P-26A and tells him to go and confess to his father. Now Donald has two kits.

After Donald confesses that he took the plane and destroyed it, his father tells him a story about playing an important figure in Cantonese opera and how he prepared for it. The speech is a reminder of their heritage, but Donald cannot absorb the lesson. Just then his mother walks into the kitchen, and his father tells Donald that talking is not important. All that matters are

actions. Donald must work to rebuild what he has destroyed.

Chapters 10–12

The new year dinner has ended, and everyone is asleep, except for Donald, who watches television. On the television screen is a picture of American Cong, whose real name is Homer Lee. He is a Vietnam veteran and has been arrested for murder. However, Donald knows that Lee was on the roof at the time the murder took place and therefore cannot be guilty.

While he thinks about what to do, Donald falls asleep and dreams that he is his great-great-grandfather, working to build the transcontinental railroad in the spring of 1869. In Donald's dream, he watches a confrontation between Kwan, the Chinese foreman, and Crocker, the white supervisor. When the dream ends, Donald realizes that Kwan looks like Kwan Kung, the god of fighters, who is pictured on the poster for the Cantonese opera.

In the next chapter, Arnold's father has given the boys one hundred dollars to buy fireworks. The boys plan to set off fireworks as cars come down the street. The first effort produces a dud, but the second time the fireworks explode under a police car. Although the boys run, the police pick up both boys, who are met at the police station by both set of parents. The punishment is light, and soon both Donald and Arnold return to Donald's home and are immediately sent to bed.

Donald's father takes his son to visit a Chinese herbalist. King explains to the herbalist that his son hates anything Chinese, is a racist, is jumpy and disobedient, lies, and steals from his father. As the herbalist examines Donald, the moment dissolves into a conversation between Donald and Fred Astaire, and then Donald is working on the railroad. The entire visit to the herbalist and all that followed was a dream. In the morning, Donald and Arnold head to the public library where Donald asks for information about the building of the first transcontinental railroad. After dinner, Donald goes to bed early so that he can return to his dream.

Chapters 13–15

Donald's dream continues, as does the race for the Chinese laborers to complete the western section of the railroad. The men work hard to accomplish what is nearly impossible—to lay ten miles of track in one day. Watching on the sidelines are reporters, who insult the Chinese laborers in racist terms and declare that Chinese laborers cannot possibly be stronger and faster than good Christian white men, who set the previous track record of six miles. The Chinese men succeed and build over ten miles of track in one day, a new world's record. In Donald's dream, the one hundred and eight outlaw heroes of Chinese legend arrive on a cloud to applaud the achievement of their brethren. As the workers prepare to lay down the last crosstie for the railroad, every Chinese laborer signs or carves his name on the wood. In this way, the contributions of the Chinese will be remembered.

For Donald, the line between wakefulness and dreaming has grown fuzzy. When Donald is finally completely awake, he and Arnold walk to a magazine and book store in Chinatown. There Donald sees playing cards and a poster with depictions of the outlaw heroes. Donald recognizes the men he saw in his dream. In the poster, they are posed exactly as they appeared in his dream, but Donald cannot remember ever seeing this poster before.

Donald and Arnold walk to the library, where they find books about the building of the transcontinental railroad. Inside are the photos of the ceremony commemorating the completion of the railroad. The Irish workers are honored, but not one Chinese laborer is actually mentioned. The Chinese are erased from the history books. Later when they return home, Donald mentions what the history book says and that he knows that the Chinese workers were there because he was present also, in his dreams. Donald's father tells his son that the Chinese must keep their own history because white men cannot be counted on to write the history of the Chinese. King tells Donald that it is the "mandate of heaven" that the Chinese write their own history.

Donald asks his father what he means by "mandate of heaven." King quotes the ancient Chinese philosopher Confucius, who noted the transient nature of the world, which is always in a state of change. King explains that the will of the people is what constitutes heaven. When Donald sleeps, he first dreams of Fred Astaire, who has always been his ideal, but then his dream quickly shifts to the Chinese railroad workers, who are preparing to lay down the final crosstie with ten thousand Chinese names

on it. Supervisor Crocker asks Donald about the crosstie and is surprised when Donald answers in English. Donald tells the railroad men that he is an American. Once the white railmen learn about the Chinese signatures on the crosstie, they order it removed and destroyed and promise that there will be no Chinese present at the ceremony to set the golden spike in place.

Chapters 16–18

Donald and Arnold study old photographs taken at Promontory Summit on May 10, 1869. There are no Chinese faces, but there are heavily armed soldiers. The boys think that the soldiers were there to keep the Chinese out of the pictures. Suddenly Donald feels hostile to all white Americans and he picks a fight with Arnold, who calls his parents and goes home for the first time in almost two weeks. Donald is in a terrible mood, which is only slightly alleviated later in the day when he joins his father, who is distributing bags of rice. This is another of the ways that King celebrates Chinese New Year.

Donald hates to go to sleep because of the dreams he has been having. He tells his father that everything he dreams turns out to be true. The Chinese helped to build the railroad, and now he hates all white men because they deny the truth of that event. King tells Donald that he should hate only the liars and not all white men. King also tells Donald that the truth was there waiting to be discovered and that, just as he looks for the truth in the library, the truth came to his dreams. Donald now knows that he must go to the police to tell them that American Cong could not have killed anyone.

Chapter 17 opens with the completion of the ceremony at Promontory Summit, Utah. Donald wakes from his dream in a terrible mood. Arnold is gone, and Donald must go to school, but first the family stops for a waffle breakfast to celebrate everyone's birthday, which is a part of Chinese New Year. Donald can barely eat and says he will not go to school, where everyone is a racist who hates the Chinese. Of course, Donald has no real vote on whether he will attend school and soon is walking into his classroom, where his teacher, Mr. Meanwright, is delivering a patronizing lecture about the work that the Chinese did in building the railroad.

Donald cannot stand the mistakes that he hears and interrupts his teacher to correct him. Donald tells Mr. Meanwright about all of the dangers faced by the Chinese and the two hard winters that the Chinese workers survived to complete the Pacific section of the transcontinental railroad. Mr. Meanwright shows the class a picture of the Chinese workers, and Donald's image is clearly evident in the old photo. Arnold also jumps in to verify Donald's version of the events. Donald's father bursts into the classroom dressed for the opera as the great Chinese war god, Kwan Kung.

Chapter 18 opens at the Duk home. Arnold's family is visiting. They are discussing the model airplanes that hang from the ceiling. Arnold's father would like for his son to have the plane that he built rather than to have it burn, but King points out that all wooden airplanes must eventually burn, since it is an honorable end for a wooden plane. At this point, Arnold's father admits that he actually burned all the planes that he built when he was a child.

King tells Donald that Arnold is an ally. Like Donald, Arnold also dreams about Chinese workers building the railroad. The lesson is that not all white people are the enemy. After Donald and Arnold formally shake hands and make up, it is decided that Arnold will stay at the Duk home until the end of Chinese New Year. Later as the boys begin to fall asleep, Donald is met by the outlaw hero Black Tornado, who asserts that Donald is better than he himself, an outlaw hero god.

Epilogue

It is the fifteenth day of the Chinese New Year, and the celebration culminates that evening with a parade and the Cantonese opera, which includes Donald's father as the war god Kwan Kung. Donald, Arnold, and the twins will all be in the parade, running inside the dragon. After the parade and the opera, everyone heads to the old immigration station at Angel Island. The Duk family, Arnold's family, and a few friends quickly unpack all of the wooden planes and light their fuses as they send them aloft. For a brief moment, all one hundred and eight planes are in the air at the same time, and within ten minutes all of them have burned and are gone. The story ends with everyone hungry and ready to eat.

CHARACTERS

American Cong

See Homer Lee

Arnold Azalea

Arnold is Donald's classmate and best friend. He is interested in Chinese history and culture and wants to learn more. Although Arnold does not understand Donald's hatred for and embarrassment about all things Chinese, Arnold supports his best friend. Because he wants to learn more about Chinese customs, Arnold stays with the Duk family for two weeks during the celebration of Chinese New Year. Arnold also begins to dream about building the railroad. Unlike with Donald's dreams, the reader is not a witness to Arnold's dreams, and so it is not clear if, like Donald, Arnold is actively present in the dreams or if he is a only witness to the events. Arnold is loyal to Donald and aware of the bullying that Donald endures because of his name and because he is Chinese. Even after Donald fights with him, Arnold is loyal and stands up to their teacher, Mr. Meanwright, when he has the facts wrong about the Chinese immigrants who worked on the railroad.

Mr. and Mrs. Azaela

Arnold's parents contribute little to the movement of the narrative. It does not become clear until near the end of the story that Arnold's parents are very wealthy. The Azaelas like Donald, and they are willing to allow their eleven-year-old son the freedom to live at the Duk home for more than two weeks so that he can experience Chinese New Year.

Crocker

Crocker is the white supervisor in Donald's dreams of building the transcontinental railroad.

Daisy Duk

Daisy is Donald's mother. Her role is small and consists mostly of caring for her family. She helps her husband when needed and supports Donald, but she also frequently joins the twins, Venus and Penny, in teasing Donald and in engaging in sarcastic commentary. She mediates the disagreements between Donald and his father when Donald says something especially anti-Chinese. Like several other secondary characters, Donald's mother is not a well-developed character.

Donald Duk

Donald is the almost twelve-year-old protagonist who narrates the story. He hates being Chinese and wishes only to be an American. Everything that his family does that is Chinese is an embarrassment to Donald. He wants to be like Fred Astaire and dance. In part, this desire stems from selecting an icon who is as far from Chinese and Chinatown as is possible. It is not just that Donald wants to dance as well as Fred Astaire, Donald wants to be Fred Astaire.

Donald initially hates everything Chinese, from who he is to everything about his life. He especially hates his name, which makes him the object of teasing. He claims that he is neither a real duck nor a cartoon duck. At night when he sleeps, Donald begins to dream about being present at the completion of the first transcontinental railroad in late spring of 1869. In the beginning, his dreams appear more as if he is witnessing these events, but very quickly Donald is actually experiencing these events through his dreams. He becomes part of the crew of Chinese workers who are building the railroad.

Donald witnesses the racism and the humiliating way the Chinese are treated, and for the first time, he realizes that he is proud to be Chinese. He comes to understand that the Chinese have accomplished much and that their culture is rich in traditions and beliefs that are an important part of his life. By the end of the novel, Donald embraces his Chinese heritage and is willing to celebrate who he is.

Uncle Donald Duk

Uncle Donald is King's brother and Donald's uncle. Uncle Donald is a Cantonese opera entrepreneur and star. He trained King Duk as an opera star. He is present for much of novel but has a very small role. Uncle's role is primarily to support King in all that he does, but he also mediates the occasional disagreements between Donald and his father over Donald's dislike of all things Chinese. Like several other secondary characters, Donald's uncle is not a well-developed character.

King Duk

King is Donald's father. King is one of the best cooks in Chinatown and owns a successful restaurant that serves authentic Chinese food and not some American version of Chinese food, which is often served in other restaurants. King can cook anything that Donald and Arnold ask him to cook. King is also generous to those who wait outside his restaurant, hoping for food to be thrown into the garbage. He feeds the needy all year round and, during Chinese New Year, gives

fifty-pound bags of rice to many of the families in Chinatown, leaving the bags on doorsteps in the middle of the night.

King also builds model airplanes, which he will fly during the Chinese New Year. King and his family build one hundred and eight wooden model planes to honor the outlaw heroes of Chinese legend. Even though Donald claims to hate everything Chinese, King is supportive of his son and eventually helps Donald understand how important it is to honor the family's Chinese heritage. However, King does not tolerate Donald's complaints about being bullied about his name. King tells Donald that, if he walks with confidence and is proud of his name, respect will follow and the bullying will stop. King once studied Cantonese opera, and in the past, he played the most important role, that of the war god, Kwan Kong, in performances.

Penelope Duk

Penelope, also called Penny, is Venus's twin sister and Donald's older sister. The sole purpose of the twins is to deliver smart, sarcastic commentaries about everything that the other members of their family say. Both girls use references to pop culture, often indiscriminately and without real thought to the circumstances.

Venus Duk

Venus is Penelope's twin sister and Donald's other sister. Venus and her sister function as one entity; there is no attempt to create an individual personality for each girl.

Frog Twins

The Frog Twins are two poor old women who are called aunties, even though they are not relatives. Auntie is a title of respect bestowed on all older Chinese women. King gives the Frog Twins extra food and, for Chinese New Year, pays the fish seller to deliver fish to the twins, so that they can celebrate properly.

Kwan Kong

Kwan is the Chinese foreman in Donald's dreams. He works for the Union Pacific Railroad and manages the men as they lay the final ten miles of track on the way to Promontory Summit. As Donald's dreams continue, readers learn that Kwan is really the war god, the most important of the one hundred and eight outlaw heroes of Chinese legend. Kwan is fierce in protecting the rights of the Chinese railroad workers. In the Cantonese opera, Donald's father plays the role of Kwan.

Homer Lee

Also called American Cong, Homer Lee is a veteran who was exposed to Agent Orange while serving in Vietnam. Donald sees on television that Lee is arrested for murder, but the crime occurred on the night when Donald met Lee on the roof of the apartment building, so Donald becomes Lee's alibi.

Larry Louie

Larry is Donald's dance teacher. His role is minimal. Although he is teaching Donald to tap dance, Donald thinks that his teacher is a failure at his goal to be the Chinese Fred Astaire.

Mr. Meanwright

Mr. Meanwright is Donald's California history teacher. His lectures about Chinese society and history are filled with patronizing and condescending comments that are often historically inaccurate.

THEMES

Identity

Donald Duk focuses on the struggle that the adolescent title character endures as he learns to accept his Chinese identity. At the beginning of the novel, Donald hates everything Chinese, from his family's traditions to his own name. He wants to be an American, but because he is Chinese, he thinks he can never look like an American. Instead he ridicules his heritage and his home and everything Chinese that is a part of his life. Although there are other Chinese students at Donald's private school, he is the only one with a name that sets him apart. When his teachers want to celebrate Chinese New Year by teaching the students about Chinese history and traditions, Donald dislikes all the emphasis on something that he wishes would simply go away, and he especially is tired of his teacher reminding him that all Chinese people are passive and nonassertive, the victims of mysticism and Confucian philosophy.

The problem is that Donald so dislikes his heritage that he lacks sufficient knowledge to counter his teacher's erroneous information. The dreams that Donald has are Chin's way of instilling some Chinese pride and history into Donald's life. In his dreams, Donald witnesses the extraordinary hard work and danger that Chinese workers faced building the transcontinental railroad. When the workers are denied the recognition they deserve, Donald is suddenly angry at white Americans and proud of his Chinese history and traditions. It is this anger that forces Donald to accept his identity as a Chinese American. Rather than desiring to be Fred Astaire, he is proud to be Donald Duk.

Truth

Truth enters Donald's life through his dreams. After Donald begins to dream of the Chinese and the building of the transcontinental railroad, Donald hates to go to sleep because his dreams are so disturbing to him. It is the realistic quality of the dreams that makes them disturbing, and everything he dreams turns out to have been true. After he does some simple research, Donald learns that the Chinese really did help to build the railroad, but that because they were not white, they were not allowed to be present for the photograph that celebrated the completion of the railroad. As a result of this injustice, Donald now hates all white men because they deny the truth of those events.

Donald's father tells him that he should hate only the liars and not all white men. King also tells Donald that his dreams came to tell Donald the truth about the heroism of the Chinese. King says that the truth was always there waiting to be discovered. Donald's father reminds him that, just as the truth was waiting to be discovered in the library, the truth about his heritage was also waiting for Donald to discover it. The dreams are one way for the truth to be discovered. Now that he understands the importance of the truth, Donald also knows that he must go to the police to tell them that Homer Lee could not have killed anyone, because they were together on the roof when the crime happened. Donald is Lee's alibi and has an obligation to tell the truth.

Racism

Donald Duk explores racism through Donald's experiences at school. Initially Donald does not see the racism around him because he himself is a racist. He hates all things Chinese, from his home, which he believes is too Chinese, to his own appearance. Donald is embarrassed by the planned performance of the Cantonese opera at his school, which will drawn attention to his own

TOPICS FOR FURTHER STUDY

- Research the Chinese immigration center at Angel Island and prepare a PowerPoint slide presentation that focuses on when and how it functioned as a immigration center. Augment your presentation with a selection of slides of immigrants who entered at Angel Island. Discuss the more controversial aspects of this center, especially the unwarranted imprisonment of new immigrants, who were held in this facility.

- In most communities, there are a number of religious and community agencies that help immigrants on a volunteer basis. These are in addition to the official government agencies. As part of a learning and service project, research the problems that immigrant children face in your community and the resources that are available to help them. Prepare an oral presentation on what you discover. Be prepared to discuss what you and your classmates can do to help immigrant children who need extra assistance.

- The first immigration laws in the United States were directed at halting the immigration of Chinese in the nineteenth century. Research the history of Chinese immigration, and write an essay in which you discuss the reasons for these laws and how they impacted later immigration legislation.

- Read Sherman Alexie's semi-autobiographical young-adult novel, *The Absolutely True Diary of a Part-Time Indian*. Write a paper in which you compare the life of Alexie's protagonist, Arnold, with that of Chin's Donald. Consider how the boys feels about their ethnic identities and how they respond to their homes and friends and to the

challenges that they face in fitting into mainstream American life.

- Search in the library for some of the photographs that were taken during the building of the transcontinental railroad. Be sure to include photos of the "Big Four" of the Central Pacific Railroad: Leland Stanford, Collis P. Huntington, Mark Hopkins, and Charles Crocker. Use these photos and any maps, illustrations, or other visual data that you find to create a PowerPoint presentation that you will present to your classmates. During your presentation, you will trace the building of the Pacific section of the transcontinental railroad, from the first decision to build the railroad to the completion at Promontory Summit in May 1869.

- One way to get to know a character in depth is to write an obituary for that person. Write an obituary for Donald that tells readers about his journey through life, his triumphs and failures, and what kind of person you think he turned out to be in the years after this novel ended. Present your obituary as an oral report, and explain the choices that you made in constructing events after the book ends.

- PBS produced a film about building the transcontinental railroad for its series *American Experience*. The film, *The Iron Road*, provides an overview of the history of building the railroad. Watch the film and then write an essay in which you compare the film and the novel *Donald Duk*. Be sure to include some analysis of the similarities and differences that you noted between the film and Donald's dreams.

Chinese identity. Donald wants to be a complete and total American and believes that, if he can dance as well as Fred Astaire, he will become Fred Astaire and cease to be Chinese. Donald's

teacher, Mr. Meanwright, focuses his history lessons on the Chinese as passive and noncompetitive, and initially this description just makes Donald even more embarrassed to be Chinese

The novel is set in San Francisco's Chinatown.
(© aquatic creature | Shutterstock.com)

and more determined to erase the Chinese within him. Donald's dreams teach him not to hate his origins and to be proud of his history. After he embraces his own Chinese culture and history, Donald is finally able to see his teacher, Mr. Meanwright, as the racist that he is.

Donald's dreams also show him that the Chinese in the United States have been victimized by racists. The white reporters and supervisors refer to the Chinese railroad workers as "coolies," as "a heathen race," and as "inferior." Donald's dreams have shown him that the Chinese are none of these things. They risked their lives planting charges to blow up rocks in the Sierra Mountains and working in unstable tunnels, and they labored for two winters in snow and freezing weather and in the oppressive heat of the desert. After Donald understands the racism of the past, he more easily recognizes the racism of the present, including his own racism and that of his teacher. He learns that the Chinese were not passive and that they were

an important part of American history. By the end of the novel, Donald's own racism has been replaced with pride in his Chinese heritage.

STYLE

Analepsis

In telling his dreams, Donald experiences analepsis (scene from the past inserted into the narrative). Chin uses analepsis to tell stories of the past through dreams. Analepsis is not simply a flashback; instead, it is as if a memory from the past becomes the reality of the present. For instance, when Donald dreams of being present at the building of the transcontinental railroad, he is not simply an observer of these events. He becomes a participant and lives the events. In a sense, he becomes his own great-great-grandfather who was present, as if his grandfather's memories have become his own. In telling these stories, the past becomes the reality of the present and changes how Donald feels about being Chinese.

Bildungsroman *Novel*

A *Bildungsroman* novel is one that traces the growth and development of a young person from youth to adulthood. The growth of the protagonist is not only physical growth; rather this genre is focused on the emotional and psychological maturity of the protagonist. Often, *Bildungsroman* novels are autobiographical or biographical, but in *Donald Duk*, there is no biographical element. Instead the protagonist, Donald, learns about his ancestor's life through dreams, and it is Donald's dreams that change him and force him to mature. Donald's father tells him that, when he is twelve years old, he has lived though the entire Chinese zodiac calendar cycle and is thus an adult.

Children's Literature

Literature for children is written primarily for a child or adolescent audience. Usually such literature focuses on a young protagonist with whom a child or adolescent reader can identify. Children's literature also contains themes that appeal to children and that address issues in which they are interested. In addition, the vocabulary and sentence structure should be accessible to younger readers.

Donald Duk addresses several of the concerns of adolescent readers, including bullying, lack of self-esteem, and feeling like an outsider. *Donald Duk*'s narrator is an almost twelve-year-old boy who has a close friend his age. Donald's experiences appeal to youthful readers who are looking for a protagonist they recognize and with whom they might identify. Donald suffers the trauma of not fitting in with his classmates, and thus his experiences have an appeal to readers who might find comfort in knowing they are not alone in having this problem.

Chin is careful to include several exciting episodes, primarily through Donald's dreams. The prank of setting off firecrackers under a car also provides a brief episode in which the boys rebel against authority but are caught and arrested, which might also be of interest to adolescent readers.

Dream Allegory or Dream Vision

Dreams are a form of narrative used during the Middle Ages and are still employed by some authors today. The dreamer falls asleep and dreams about an event that is a real story. Dreams can function in a novel to show the past or to foresee the future. In *Donald Duk*, Chin uses dreams to show the past. Donald's dreams are a stylistic device to show Donald that the Chinese have a rich history in the United States, as well as a rich culture of their own that is separate from American life. Initially the dreams show the Chinese railroad workers, who are both assertive and hardworking. They are not the passive, nonconfrontational people that he has heard described by Donald's teacher, Mr. Meanwright. In Donald's dreams, the Chinese workers risk their lives, make demands to their supervisor, and exhibit both a bravery and a strength that Donald never knew existed. He also learns about the one hundred and eight outlaw heroes of Chinese legend and thus learns that his own heritage is richer and more complex than he had realized.

Surrealism

Surrealism is a narrative style where the narration appears to be without conscious control. The imagination and dreams are juxtaposed with what seems like reality but without any concrete narrative. There are several places in *Donald Duk* where Donald's narration seemingly dissolves between reality and dreams. For instance, in the sequence where King tells Donald he is going to take his son to an herbalist, there is some confusion about whether that really happens. This event seems to occur, but then Donald runs outside and meets Fred Astaire, and then just as quickly, the scene shifts to the dream of Chinese laborers working on the railroad. Readers know that King was threatening to take Donald to the herbalist, and so the sequence where that occurs seems like a reasonable event, but just as quickly, the shifts between scenes seem out of sync. All of this can be quite confusing, and as a narrative style, surrealism can be confusing. There might be no logic and the experiences can seem completely random, as they do in the sequence just described.

HISTORICAL CONTEXT

Chinese New Year

Chinese New year officially marks the end of the winter season and beginning of spring. The festival begins on the first day of the first month of the Chinese calendar and ends on the fifteenth day of the month. *Donald Duk* covers events that occur during this two-week period. This festival is one of the oldest and longest festivals in Chinese tradition.

The holiday is associated with a desire for good luck for the coming year, which involves a thorough cleaning of the home to wash away any bad luck that may still be lingering from the previous year. It is customary to spend money on gifts, food, new clothing, and decor for the home. The evening before the holiday begins is celebrated with a large family dinner of fancy foods. Fireworks are common throughout the fifteen days of celebration. Children are given red envelopes with money, which they receive from family members as well as close friends. Food gifts are given to friends or relatives who live nearby or who are visiting. Birthdays are also celebrated collectively during the New Year, as is the Chinese custom. Donald turns twelve during the celebration, even though the exact date of his birth is not at that time.

The color red is the predominate color, which is based on an old myth that a fierce beast that threatened a Chinese village was frightened away by the color red. In Cantonese opera, which also figures in *Donald Duk*, the important persons, such as the god Kwan, wear a red-painted face. In San Francisco, the celebration of Chinese New Year began in the 1860s when the Chinese immigrants wanted to share their culture with other residents. They created a parade, which was not a

COMPARE
&
CONTRAST

- **1990s:** In 1990, there are an estimated 583,500 Chinese-born immigrants in the United States. This makes them the seventh largest foreign-born immigrant group in the United States.

  Today: In 2008, there are an estimated 1.6 million foreign-born Chinese immigrants living in the United States. About half of these immigrants live in New York and California. The influx of foreign-born Chinese helps to raise this immigrant group to fourth place in the U.S. population.

- **1990s:** The Chinese Student Protection Act is enacted to grant permanent resident status to Chinese nationals who were in the United States after June 4, 1989, and before April 11, 1990. This legislation is in part a response to the Tiananmen Square incident of 1989.

  Today: Because so many Chinese students leave the United States after they complete their education, in 2011, the U.S. Immigration Office begins to work on a process that will ease the application process for Chinese students to extend or renew their visas and remain in the United States.

- **1990s:** Polling in the United States shows that Americans are concerned that Japanese economic power poses a threat to U.S. economic strength. A significant number of Americans think that Japan engages in unfair trade practices in their dealings with the United States.

  Today: Polling in the United States shows that Americans are now concerned that China's economic power poses a threat to U.S. economic strength. A significant number of Americans think that China engages in unfair trade practices in their dealings with the United States.

- **1990s:** A study of recent court cases shows widespread discrimination against Asian Americans as well as increasing harassment and violence. In one example, in 1989, five Indochinese children are murdered at an elementary school in Stockton, California.

  Today: Many Asian Americans who are of mixed race are describing themselves as white on their college applications because of discrimination against Asian applicants. A study by a Princeton University professor shows that Asian American students need a SAT score of 1550 to be admitted to a top U.S. college, while Caucasian students need only a score of 1410.

---

tradition in China. The parade in San Francisco is now widely considered to be the largest celebration outside Asia. The golden dragon that concluded the 2012 parade was more than two hundred feet long and required more than one hundred people to carry it.

Chinese Immigration and Chinatowns

The Chinese were the first immigrants to America to come from Asia. The early Chinese immigrants, who began arriving in 1848, were not considered true immigrants because they were Asian, and only Caucasians were considered immigrants. Most of this first wave of Chinese immigrants were male and were laborers. Stories of gold in California had crossed to China, which in turn led to plans to come to America to make a fortune and then return home. In this respect, the Chinese were different from other immigrant groups, and indeed, many Chinese did return to China but not all.

When gold mines proved too dangerous, many Chinese took jobs as domestics. This resulted in a public image of the Chinese as servants or as a docile people. One in five Chinese worked on the railroads as cheap labor and felt honored to be able to help build the railroad. However, the Chinese had a reputation as strike-breakers, who had come to America to take jobs. They faced significant discrimination and were denied citizenship. It took less than thirty-five years to cut off Chinese immigration through passage of the Chinese Exclusion Act in 1882, but before this legislation, the Naturalization Act of 1870 limited citizenship to white persons and persons of African descent. The Chinese would not become eligible for citizenship until 1943.

Chinatown in San Francisco was the first of its kind, and because of its proximity to the docks and to an important immigrant arrival point, it was also the most important Chinatown to be established. The Chinese emphasis on family also limited their movement out of Chinatowns. Unlike other immigrant groups, the Chinese found it more difficult to move away from the Chinatowns, primarily because they were not white. However, by the end of the twentieth century, many Chinatowns were experiencing a change in demographics as younger professional Chinese moved to the suburbs and away from the more urban Chinatowns. Instead, Chinatowns have become tourist attractions and home to newer and less affluent immigrants.

Building the Transcontinental Railroad

In Donald's dreams, he witnesses the completion of the transcontinental railroad and the setting of the golden spike at Promontory Summit in May 1869. When the initial decision to build the railroad was made, it was very clear that the Central Pacific Railroad Company did not have enough workers. They knew they would need five thousand workers but only had six hundred in 1864. Chinese immigrants had already helped to build the California Central Railroad, and so it was quickly decided to hire Chinese workers to augment the laborers already on the Central Pacific payroll.

The first Chinese laborers were hired in 1865 and paid twenty-eight dollars a month. Chinese workers had to provide their own tents and meals. White workers were paid thirty dollars a month, plus an extra allowance for housing and food. The terrain over the Sierras was difficult and rose seven thousand feet. In some areas, Chinese laborers were lowered in baskets, some two thousand feet above the canyon floor, to chip holes in the granite cliffs and set charges in the cliff walls. They then trusted in others to raise the baskets before the explosions. Many Chinese workers died during the building of the railroad, which was not completed until May 1869.

Donald and his father, King Duk, argue about cultural values. (© visi.stock / Shutterstock.com)

As many as twelve thousand Chinese were on the payroll during the construction years. When the final track was completed, two-thirds of the four thousand workers present were Chinese, and in what was widely considered an impossible feat, they laid the last ten miles of track in only twelve hours. Although only-one tenth of the laborers were Irish, it was the Irish who were featured in newspaper photos of the ceremony at Promontory Summit on May 10, 1869. Several of the speakers that day mentioned the Chinese laborers and how invaluable they had been in completing the railroad, but many of the official newspaper accounts of that day failed to mention the Chinese laborers.

CRITICAL OVERVIEW

The reviews of *Donald Duk* were generally favorable, with some reviewers praising Chin's ability to create meaningful social commentary in a young-adult novel, whereas others praised the novel's inclusion of the historically based sections that focused on the building of the transcontinental railroad. Typical is the review by Robert Murray Davis for the journal *World Literature Today*. Davis is especially complimentary of the segments of *Donald Duk* that focus on the railroads, which Davis says is Chin at his best. However, Davis also compliments Chin for presenting "a warmer picture of Chinatown life." Although Davis notes the novel's obvious strength as an example of "Asian-American narrative," *Donald Duk* is a novel, according to Davis, that "deserves to be read on its own merits as a lively and masterful piece of storytelling."

Also favorable was Janet Ingraham's review for *Library Journal*, which focuses on Chin's narrative voice, especially Chin's use of "flip," "clipped," and "slapstick dialog," which this reviewer suggests, transforms "tart" social commentary into "a cartoon." Ingraham highly recommends *Donald Duk* as "contemporary, regional, and YA fiction." Like Davis, Ingraham writes that the book's inclusion of the historical building of the railroad is important, since the "alluring dreams" that Donald has result in his discovery of "a new, emphatic racial pride" in his heritage.

Not all reviewers were solely focused on *Donald Duk's* obvious strengths. In his review for the *New York Times*, Tom De Haven finds both strengths and shortcomings. De Haven compliments the energetic inventiveness in *Donald Duk*, which results in a conclusion that is satisfying if somewhat "too neat and pat." He also notes that Donald's dreams are a major strength of the novel, since this is where *Donald Duk* comes "vigorously, even heroically alive." What De Haven does not like are sections of the novel that feel too forced or arbitrary, such as the story line of American Cong, which is, according to De Haven, "so awkwardly inserted" that it "does damage to the whole" novel. De Haven also points out the inadequate characterizations of Donald's sisters, his uncle, and his dancing instructor, who become little more than "caricatures." In the end, De Haven's criticisms are balanced by the elements of the novel that he especially enjoys, which are the dreams, which allow Donald and Arnold "to set the record straight" on history.

CRITICISM

Sheri Metzger Karmiol

Karmiol teaches literature and drama at The University of New Mexico, where she is a lecturer in the University Honors Program. In the following essay, she discusses how dreams in Donald Duk *are used to counter the stereotypical depiction of Chinese immigrants as a passive and nonconfrontational people.*

When Donald Duk, the adolescent protagonist of Chin's novel *Donald Duk* asserts his dislike for all things Chinese, he is echoing much of the history that has greeted the Chinese in America, since they first arrived in 1848. The Chinese were often lumped into the same category as criminals and prostitutes. They were labeled "the yellow peril," and their culture was little understood and even less appreciated by their white neighbors. Rather than trying to fit into American culture, they maintained their own traditions and beliefs.

These are the very traditions and beliefs that Donald finds so offensive. Donald has decided that to be American is to be white. Thus his goal of being Fred Astaire, which is not simply dancing as well as Astaire but inhabiting his body, is one way for him to eliminate what he dislikes the most about himself, that he looks Chinese, lives Chinese, and is the subject of ridicule for being Chinese. Chin uses dreaming as a stylistic element in *Donald Duk*, as a way to combat Donald's racism. Dreaming allows Donald to become his grandfather, to be a Lee, to be a new immigrant to America, to have pride in his heritage, and even to work alongside the mythical outlaw heroes of the ancient past.

In reading *Donald Duk*, it quickly becomes clear that Donald does not accept his Chinese heritage. He hates his name and his looks and explains that he is not a duck or a cartoon character. To have a name that calls to mind an American comedic icon is to make him feel even more Chinese, because it singles him out for unwanted attention. Attention for being Chinese is not what Donald wants. Donald hates everything Chinese and especially hates his name, which he feels proves the problem that he has with being Chinese, since "Only the Chinese are stupid enough to give a kid a stupid name like Donald Duk." His name and ethnicity bring him added attention from his teachers, who expect him to be an expert on everything Chinese.

WHAT DO I READ NEXT?

- Chin is also the author of *The Chinaman Pacific & Frisco R.R. Co.* (1988), a collection of short stories that explore what it means to be Chinese American. Many of the themes present in *Donald Duk* are also explored in these stories. The primary issue is the struggle for Chinese to fit into mainstream American life while still maintaining their own heritage and culture.

- *The Catcher in the Rye* (1951) by J. D. Salinger is the story of a teenage outsider whose experiences capture teenage cynicism and rebellion and the feeling of not belonging. Although not focused on the immigrant experience, this coming-of-age novel is well known as a traditional story of how difficult it is for many adolescent boys to fit into the world in which they live.

- Khaled Hosseini's novel *The Kite Runner* (2003) takes place in Afghanistan. It is the story of a friendship between two boys and how that friendship is tested. The novel also studies the relationships between fathers and sons.

- *Growing Up Ethnic in America: Contemporary Fiction About Learning to Be American* (1999),

edited by Maria and Jennifer Gillan, is a collection of short stories about what it means to be ethnically and or racially different in the United States. This collection of stories also deals with the experiences of immigrants, who struggle to fit in.

- *Kids Like Me: Voices of the Immigrant Experience* (2006), edited by Judith Blohm and Terri Lapinsky, is a collection of twenty-six personal narratives written by young adults, who relate their experience of trying to fit into American life. The authors are from India, Peru, Ethiopia, and China in addition to many other countries.

- *Coolie* (2001) by Yin and Chris K. Soentpiet is a children's book. The novel, set in 1869, is the fictionalized story of two young boys who come to American to help build the transcontinental railroad.

- Maxine Hong Kingston's *China Men* (1989) is a collection of stories that weave legend, myth, and history into a narrative of the lives of three generations of Chinese men in the United States.

These same teachers fail to recognize that Donald not only does not know about Chinese traditions but does not want to know about them and that he especially does not want to celebrate Chinese traditions.

Donald needs to learn to feel pride in his heritage, and it is his dreams that teach Donald what it means to be Chinese in America. It is his dreams that help Donald to counter the poorly conceived history lessons that he is learning at school. In "Dreaming as Cultural Work in *Donald Duk* and *Dreaming in Cuban*," Suzanne Leonard explains that, "since dreaming allows characters to relate both emotionally and corporeally to their cultural heritages, dreaming

can be conceived of as a mode of historiography that reshapes what counts as history and knowledge." Donald needs dreams to teach him Chinese history and to counter the racism and stereotypes that surround him. Leonard reminds readers that Donald is "surrounded by attitudes that privilege whiteness and exposed to culturally hegemonic assumptions that the Chinese are by definition a 'weak' or 'timid' people." The Chinese have a history that counters these assumptions, but Donald has tuned out that history. As a result, Donald needs "an infusion of cultural pride," because he is not interested in the Chinese mythologies and legends of his father, uncle, and ancestors.

> DREAMING ALLOWS DONALD TO BECOME
HIS GRANDFATHER, TO BE A LEE, TO BE A NEW
IMMIGRANT TO AMERICA, TO HAVE PRIDE IN HIS
HERITAGE, AND EVEN TO WORK ALONGSIDE THE
MYTHICAL OUTLAW HEROES OF THE ANCIENT PAST."

Early in the novel, Donald's uncle tells him that their surname was originally Lee, not Duk. Donald shares a name with Lee Kuey, the most famous and also the most fierce of the one hundred and eight outlaw heroes who appear in the *Water Margin* legends. However, this information is not sufficient to instill any pride in Donald. Nor is hearing that the first Lee ancestor to emigrate to America in the mid-nineteenth century helped to build the transcontinental railroad. Later, when Donald begins to dream about this first Lee immigrant ancestor, he becomes more than a witness to the building of the railroad; he actually becomes his great-great-grandfather, inhabiting his body.

As Leonard suggests, when Donald becomes his grandfather Lee, he becomes personally invested in the history of Chinese immigration. He not only witnesses the building of the railroad; he also participates as his grandfather participated. This is what Leonard labels "subjective layering," a sort of "double consciousness," in which dreams allow the dreamer to be more than just one entity. In becoming his grandfather in his dreams, Donald becomes two people within one, since he continues to be himself with all of his late-twentieth-century knowledge. Thus he also infuses his grandfather ancestor with twentieth-century knowledge, and his immigrant grandfather speaks perfect English, as does Donald.

It is not enough that Donald inhabits his ancestor; his ancestor also inhabits him, in the sense that he instills Donald with pride in his ancestor's accomplishments and pride in his Chinese heritage. Leonard notes that Donald's dreams make him understand "his Chinese heritage not as an individual burden, but rather as a collective inheritance." In a sense, Donald's racial memory of his Chinese heritage becomes stronger than his contemporary racist ideology.

This double consciousness is not unlike what John J. Su posits in "Ghosts of Essentialism: Racial Memory as Epistemological Claim" when he claims that "Chin invokes racial memory as the necessary antidote to negative social ascriptions." It is not just that Donald looks like his ancestor; he has become his ancestor, both in the past and in the present. Donald has never been interested in countering the racist teaching that he has received at his private school. When taught that the Chinese are passive and timid, Donald makes no effort to counter these allegations and seemingly accepts them. But after his dreams transport him to the past, the racial memory of who he really is impels Donald to search in the library for the documentation necessary to assert his own first-hand knowledge, which has been gained by his own journeys to his ancestor's past.

Donald has always possessed the means to explore his Chinese heritage. He lives in Chinatown. He eats in his father's Chinese restaurant and lives in a home where Chinese culture and traditions are accepted and promoted. Donald even attends a private school where there are other Chinese students present; he is not isolated from his heritage. The problem for Donald is that nothing of what he knows and understands about being Chinese is of interest to him. He is so focused on his name as a hindrance to acceptance and his Chinese race as an obstacle that he is incapable of seeing that his Chinese heritage provides many reasons to be proud. The dreams about his grandfather change all that for Donald.

Su explains, "Only after he perceives himself as personally experiencing the lives of Chinese immigrants working on the railroad is he able to reevaluate his internalized racism." Through his dreams, Donald finally sees what has always surrounded him. The planes representing the one hundred and eight outlaw heroes that hang from the ceilings of his family apartment suddenly have meaning. The posters that advertise the visiting Cantonese opera contain recognizable images of the great war god Kwan, whom Donald recognizes from his dreams. Even the neighborhood bookstore sells cards and posters with suddenly familiar images.

The dreams of those early Chinese immigrants who labored so long and hard to build a railroad are necessary because Donald has been indoctrinated at his school to believe that Chinese people lack motivation and strength. The history teacher, who thinks that he knows so much about Chinese history in California, is a bigot who fails to see the physical and emotional strength of those early Chinese immigrant experiences. Su writes,

> As long as Donald passively accepts the conception of Asian Americans presented to him, he is incapable of perceiving Chinese culture as possessing viable and fundamentally different values from those he learns in class and through the media.

Donald's dreams of the past become knowledge that has an application in his own world and where to apply that knowledge becomes easy for Donald to determine. Once his racial memories have been awakened, he must present the truth to his contemporaries at school. Donald's memories are authentic because there is undeniable truth that he was there, inhabiting his grandfather's body. As Su points out,

> The legitimacy of Donald's racial memory of the experience is ratified at the end of the novel when he and Arnold present to their class a history book that contains a photo of the Chinese workers, and Donald's face is clearly depicted among them.

Donald does not simply look like his grandfather Lee; he was his grandfather Lee, and the photograph captured that moment.

Although his father has tried to pass along an appreciation for his Chinese heritage, Donald is stubborn and heavily invested in his dreams of escaping his Chinese world for the white, homogenous world of Fred Astaire, who is completely the opposite of everything that Chinatown and Donald's life represent. Chin's use of dreams in *Donald Duk* presents the only way for Donald to legitimately appreciate his own Chinese heritage as an authentic experience. Listening to his father's or his uncle's stories is not sufficient. Certainly what he learns in school proves particularly incapable of preparing Donald to accept who he is.

In "The Remasculinization of Chinese America: Race, Violence, and the Novel," Viet Thanh Nguyen writes that Donald's exposure to real history is necessary for him to discover the truth. Nguyen claims, "In contrast to the history of passive and weak Chinese workers he is taught in school, Donald discovers a group of literate, articulate, and strong Chinese immigrants." Because these Chinese laborers must compete with the Irish laborers, they must be as strong, as aggressive, and as determined to succeed as the Irish. The Chinese crew must prove to everyone that they are as good as the Irish crew. Obviously Donald's teacher is wrong when he claims that Chinese immigrants were passive, timid, and helpless.

When Donald discovers that the truth is something far different and that the Chinese were brave and strong and that they refused to be mistreated, he cannot allow the truth to be remain hidden. When he complains to his father that lies are being told about the Chinese and they have been denied their place in history, Donald is told, "History is war, not sport! . . . You gotta keep the history yourself or lose it forever, boy." Nguyen claims that this "is the lesson Donald learns when he sees the railroad tie with the Chinese names and their claim to the railroad being torn out and destroyed." Instead of being honored for their achievement in building the railroad, their names were erased from history. This is a denial of the truth that is painful for Donald to know and to accept.

Chinese New Year last only fifteen days, but the year that Donald turns twelve years old makes this particular Chinese New Year especially important. Because Donald has lived through the entire twelve-year Chinese zodiac calendar, he is no longer considered a child in the Chinese tradition. As a young man, he needs to know the truth. The succession of dreams that Donald experiences during those fifteen days of celebration turn him from a resentful, racist Chinese boy into a historically aware Chinese adolescent with a rich cultural heritage and the strength to finally accept who he is. Gone are the dreams of Fred Astaire, of being white, of being an American without being Chinese. Donald's dreams have helped him forge a link with the past and made him truly Chinese.

Source: Sheri Metzger Karmiol, Critical Essay on *Donald Duk*, in *Novels for Students*, Gale, Cengage Learning, 2013.

Wenying Xu

In the following excerpt, Xu investigates how food and appetite assist Frank Chin in his quest to restore masculinity to his Asian American characters.

COOKING AS A MARTIAL ART

. . . The tale of Donald Duk takes place before the Chinese New Year as the title character is about to become twelve, completing his first zodiac cycle which signifies his transition from boyhood to manhood. The novel's central

Donald learns of the role of Chinese immigrants in building the transcontinental railroad, commemorated by the Promontory Summit National Monument in Utah. (© Jerry Susoeff | Shutterstock.com)

conflict is Donald's self-loathing instilled by the orientalist education he receives in a private school—"a place where the Chinese are comfortable hating Chinese." The education he receives is a process of what Frantz Fanon calls "cultural estrangement." Fanon points out,

> Colonialism is not satisfied merely with holding a people in its grip and emptying the native's brain of all form and content. By a kind of perverted logic, it turns to the past of the oppressed people, and distorts, disfigures, and destroys it.... [in] the efforts made to carry out the cultural estrangement...nothing has been left to chance. (210)

In Donald's case, his private education schools his shift of social norms and cultural allegiance to erase ethnic identification in favor of assimilation, and this cultural estrangement has rendered the ethnic practices ridiculous and shameful. He learns to regard everything Chinese as "funny": "the *funny* things Chinese believe in. The *funny* things Chinese do. The *funny* things Chinese eat" (emphasis added). In this ambivalent,

slippery word funny, he reveals what Fanon names "the colonized personality" (250).

Speaking of the affects of the culturally estranged, Fanon remarks, "the emotional sensitivity of the native is kept on the surface of his skin like an open sore" (56). Donald's debilitating embarrassment with his ancestral culture and his ethnicity, symptomatic in the word funny, exhibits his "open sore" that inflicts emotional and physical discomfort. "When Mr. Meanwright talks about Chinatown, Donald Duk's muscles all tighten up, and he wants Mr. Meanwright to shut up." The boy's ideological indoctrination has heightened his "emotional sensitivity" toward and repugnance of his home culture of Chinatown. However, his repeated use of "funny" and the lack of concrete descriptions also reveal that the process of cultural estrangement remains fortunately incomplete in him. Significantly, this leaves the possibility for the character's development and initiation into Asian American manhood.

> ONE MAY ARGUE THAT THE MASCULINIZATION OF COOKING SUCCEEDS IN BREAKING DOWN THE BINARY BETWEEN THE PUBLIC AND THE PRIVATE BY BLURRING THE DISTINCTION BETWEEN HOME AND RESTAURANT."

Donald's self-loathing is often expressed in the enmeshed lexicon of ethnicity and gender. He tends to believe that being Chinese is no different from being sissy and ridiculous. To him "Chinese are artsy, cutesy..." language that has proved durable in American culture and underpins an image fraught with the culturally enforced inferiority of Asian American men. In this adolescent character, Chin creates an allegory of the "open sore" that [afflects] many Asian American men in that Donald's self-loathing recapitulates Asian American male subjectivity as masochistic in the face of "the predicament of being yellow and male, of being formed as masculine subjects, in a culture in which most of the dominant images of manhood are white" (Kim, 293).

The novel's plot, centering on Donald's rite of passage to institute his ethnic and gender identity, hinges chiefly on three of the four father figures in his life, two real and two mythical: his father King Duk, Uncle Donald Duk, Kwan Kung, and Lee Kuey. The real men incarnate the mythical men by playing them in the Cantonese opera. In the character of Donald's father, a successful restaurateur in San Francisco's Chinatown, Chin fuses the discourse of masculinity with that of food. Eileen Fung observes this fusion and remarks, food in *Donald Duk* "has become the fetishized object of a masculine desire" (259). One of the recurring settings is King's kitchen, in which the "steam and smoke bloom and mushroom-cloud about Donald Duk's father as he tosses piles of raw shrimp paste and bowls of cold sliced fish and fruit, and waves his tools into and out of the roiling atmospheres." Larry Louie, Donald's dance teacher, appropriately describes the scene as "Godzilla versus the nuclear missiles." Alluding to the original Japanese Gojira, a cautionary

tale about nuclear escalation, Larry's image invokes a samurai-informed masculinity rising up to avenge its annihilation by America's wanton power and technology. Even though in the 1998 Hollywood remake of *Godzilla* the giant lizard is created by the French nuclear testing, it is Manhattan, the birthplace of the atomic bomb, not Paris, that gets trashed. With this allusion, Chin transforms the kitchen into a symbolic site of violence and destruction. In this kitchen the wok becomes "the hot steel," the spatula a sword, and the chef a "swordsman." The military aura surrounding this chef is further enhanced by the history of his training, for King has learned to cook "in the kitchens of the most powerful men in the world," and he often tells "the story of how he passed the war in the kitchens of presidents, prime ministers, premiers, lords and generalissimos." Chin painstakingly eradicates all feminine vestiges from King's kitchen, not only with analogies to war and martial arts but also by making King's cooking performative. King almost always cooks with an interactive audience, and it is "as if everyone in the kitchen is a player in a well-tuned orchestra and Dad is the conductor, moving in and out of the steam of his woks." Like a martial artist, King takes on challenges. Donald and his friend Arnold often sit in the kitchen and "challenge the extent of Dad's knowledge of food and cooking. Whatever the boys read about and ask for, Dad cooks without a book. Whatever it is, he cooks it."

Others often address King as "sifu," which means simultaneously a maestro chef and a kung fu maestro. The interchangeability between these two identities becomes apparent in the scene of ancestral worship, a ritual always performed via food and drink. The "family shrine" is set up on the altar table in the dining room. In front of it "stands an incense burner with smoldering sticks of incense punk. A steamed chicken on a platter and three little rice bowls filled with perfect mounds of rice... There is a bottle of Johnny Walker Red." Family and friends take turns to pay respect to the ancestors' shrine. Their stylized manner is unmistakably associated with martial arts: "He lights a stick of incense and holds it in his right hand and covers his right hand with his left, like a swordsman in a kung fu movie meeting a swordsman on the road of life." Chin transforms what has been demeaned as a demonstration of Chinese heathenness and passivity into a scene of militancy.

Metaphors of war and martial arts thus dominate the descriptions of King and his kitchen, a semiotic site where the enjoyment of masculine assertion colludes with that of cooking and eating. Chin gleefully indulges his predilection for food in this novel, set significantly around the Chinese New Year, a time of cooking, eating, and performing rituals. This is also a time when King must incarnate another of Donald's father figures, Kwan Kung, "the god of fighters, blighters and writers," by playing or, more accurately, by becoming him in the Cantonese opera. King fits this role not simply because he is a good actor but because he embodies the god's manly virtues: fierceness, loyalty, and self-discipline. It is significant that Chin makes Kwan Kung or Guan Yu, the most worthy warrior in *The Three Kingdoms*, the god of both literature and war, and thus embodies the wenwu dyad central to the historical construction of Chinese masculinities. Wen means cultural attainment, and wu martial valor. While these two qualities have been given different weight in Chinese history, their balance has never ceased to be the ideal. As Kam Louie explicates, "Ideal masculinity can be either wen or wu but is at its height when both are present to a high degree."

Chin's transformation of the god of war into the god of literature and war serves to idealize King as a cosmopolitan model of the balanced wen-wu, with his American birth, Hong Kong martial arts training, military service (presumably in Taiwan), opera performance, and culinary artistry. All of these contribute to King's Asian Americanness as the new model of Chinatown masculinity "to replace," as Ho points out, "Hop Sing of Bonanza." In *The Three Kingdoms*, however, Kwan Kung is not known for cultural attainment; his reputation as the best warrior rests on courage, loyalty, and overall discipline when it comes to women. He regards desiring/desirable women as obstacles to true brotherhood and "would rather decapitate a beautiful woman than be tempted by her" (Louie, 46). Therefore, for King to take the Kwan Kung role, he must exercise the ultimate self-control. He explains to Donald,

> nobody wants to play Kwan Kung. Too risky. What if they accidentally forget and eat a hotdog? Or one bite of a cha sin bow goes down their throat before they remember? Kwan Kung does not accept the mess up of responsibility allowed by Western psychology. Real men, real actors, real soldiers of the art don't

lose control. Just like Doong the Tattooed Wrestler in *The Water Margin*, when the most beautiful woman in the empire...coos and croons all her seductive know-how on Doong, he never gives in and never forgets his mission. Never.

Here Chin's distinction between real and fake men pivots on a man's relationship to appetite, both sexual and alimentary. The punishment for undisciplined appetite, curiously, falls on women: "There are stories about the actor who played Kwan Kung recently and did not take the part seriously, and maybe slept with his girlfriend that night before...and when he takes the stage his girlfriend's hair turns white and she has a miscarriage." Misogyny is indisputably a component in this model of contained masculinity.

Buttressing Chin's delineation of "real" Chinese manhood in *Donald Duk* is intertextuality with another Chinese classic, *The Water Margin*. This warrior tale, which portrays 108 exiled and self-exiled renegades whose code of ethics is nothing but fraternal loyalty, is essential for advancing Chin's narrative and for achieving the novel's resolution. *The Water Margin* is the source of Donald's third father figure, Lee Kuey or the Black Tornado, who represents another competing form of masculinity, the singularly wu model. Deserving the nickname, Lee is a killing machine, and Chin's adoring description runs amok: "All the Black Tornado's muscles balloon and pull at their roots pounding rage. It's the battle-axe freak who likes to run naked into one end of a battle and come out the other covered in layers of drying blood, with a bloody axe in each hand." In this presentation of a warrior is an extravagant masculinity that Chin glorifies and covets. He revises the classical character of Lee Kuey to enhance masculinity with the other extreme: undisciplined appetite. Lee boasts to Donald, "I am the only one to eat the flesh of his dead mother, because I was hungry and knew she loved me"—an episode Chin invents, despite the original character's reputation as a good son. The plot that Chin suppresses goes like this: One day Lee Kuey carries his mother over a mountain, and when his mother becomes thirsty, he leaves her sitting on a big rock while going off to find water. When he returns, his mother is gone. On a closer look, he finds blood and shreds of clothes scattered in the rock's vicinity. Following the blood trail, he comes to the opening of a cave where two tiger cubs are eating a human leg. He kills the cubs and their parents.

On the surface, Chin's deliberate reworking of this classical character serves to incarnate the male catechism: a man must do what he must do. In other words, a real man cannot be bothered by female scruples. More disturbing is its deep, subliminal root in the patriarchal religions that supplanted original matriarchal religions by killing and devouring the Mother Goddess (who bore names such as Isis, Demeter, Gaia, Shakti, Dakinis, Astarte, Ishtar, Nu Wa, Rhea, Nerthus, Brigid, and Danu). For instance, Zeus swallowed Metis, goddess of wisdom, when she was pregnant with Athena. Abundant in Greek mythology, Judeo-Christianity, Islam, Hinduism, and so on are tales of slaying dragons and demonizing serpents. Prehistoric dragons and snakes known as the energy source of life—"of healing and oracular power, fertility and maternal blessing" (Sjbb and Mor, 251)—are often associated with female deities such as the Amazonian Medusa, the Chinese Nu Wa, and the Hebrew Lilith.

With these motifs of matricide and devouring in the cultural landscape in which and against which Chin operates as a writer, his offering of a mother eater as a father figure cannot be read simply as an expression of male bravado. Male cannibalism, commencing when Zeus swallowed the pregnant Metis and striking again recently in Thomas Harris's character Hannibal Lecter, has been repeatedly enacted in literary and cultural productions (including Chin's own "Eat and Run Midnight People," which I discuss in the next section). Carol Adams defamiliarizes us with the daily representations that collapse sexuality and consumption by unveiling the linguistic, imagistic, symbolic, and literal relationship of animal slaughter and meat consumption with violence against women: "Images of butchering suffuse patriarchal culture. A steakhouse in New Jersey was called 'Adam's Rib.'... The Hustler, prior to its incarnation as a pornographic magazine, was a Cleveland restaurant whose menu presented a woman's buttocks on the cover and proclaimed, 'We serve the best meat in town!'" (60). Although in Chin, Lee Kuey's cannibalistic appropriation of his dead mother is empty of the connotation of sexual violence, the archetypal impulse to strangle and usurp the feminine power of creation is implicit. To devour Mother is to denounce one's connection with the feminine and to usurp the maternal power by attempting to give birth to oneself. (Zeus, after swallowing pregnant Metis, birthed from his head Athena, who became his obedient

mouthpiece. After killing Semele, the mother of his son Dionysus, Zeus sewed the fetus in his thigh for it to reach full term.) Chin furnishes Donald with four father figures embodying competing and yet overlapping masculinities. Their task is delivering him from his eroded and threatened psyche and giving birth to a confident and proud Chinese American man. These father figures find no rivalry in the mother Daisy Duk, who effaces herself quite jocularly. Daisy, after all, is not meant to be a mother. With its unisexual origin in Walt Disney, the Disney Duck family knows no mother figure.

That Lee Kuey is a father figure to Donald is indisputable, given claims to both Donald's ancestral history and biology. Chin insists that Lee remains a hero in Chinese history despite his senseless killing of the innocent and has Lee proclaim, "I am the only one to murder a little boy and still be counted a hero. Because I did it out of stupid loyalty..., everything sort of worked out." As it is, Chin also makes Lee Kuey Donald's ancestor, for Uncle Donald Duk tells the child, "your Chinese name is not Duk, but Lee, Lee, just like Lee Kuey." This blood connection entitles Lee's claim to Donald's education and well-being. Thus he commands, "Don't back away from me, boy. I thought you and me were alike, kid." Then "he pulls a red envelope out of his bag. 'Goong hay fot choy!'" wishing Donald Happy New Year like a regular uncle.

The novel's first resolution takes place at this moment, having established the kinship between our young protagonist and Lee Kuey, having succeeded in schooling Donald in the proper behavior and attitude that comport to masculine conduct, and having forged an ethnic identity secured in the Chinese heroic tradition. Hence, near the end of the novel, Chin revisits the scene of male competition (Donald's encounter with the Chinatown "gang kids") that initially demonstrates Donald's "sissy" self. Donald watches "a tall thin Chinatown kid in a camouflage field jacket." As this kid approaches, Donald says, "Don't mess with me, with his shoulders, his chest, his neck, his face, his eyes, and walks on. No one messes with him."

Both Donald's masculinization and ethnicization are partially made possible through an embedded discourse of food/appetite and masculinity, and this discourse becomes actualized in part by ridiculing women as well as by excluding their participation in food production and ethnic existential choices. In other words, the portrayal of women as culturally impoverished consumers is one of the necessary conditions for Chin's restoration of Chinese American male dignity. His language describing the food practices in King's kitchen evokes cooking's affinity to martial arts and war. This affinity further dissociates the two kinds of cooking—restaurant and home cooking. The traditional divide between these two modes of the same activity solidifies the system of value in gendered labor. While restaurant cooking has been regarded as male and professional, categorized as production and generating exchange value, cooking at home has been seen as female and domestic, thus belonging to the categories of reproduction and use value. These distinctions are laden with hierarchy and inequity in our commodity culture. Chin's masculinization of King's kitchen not only relies on the gendered divide between professional and domestic cooking but also attempts to banish the association of cooking with women by excluding Donald's mother and twin sisters from productive labor. These women occupy almost exclusively the position of passive consumers.

As passive consumers, these women necessarily lack individuality. All three are given character traits so identical that it is hard to tell them apart—they are cheerful, uncomplicated, theatrical, cartoon funny, callow, and whitewashed. As Fung points out, Daisy Duk's "subjectivity—if there is any sense of that at all—stems from her theatrical impersonations of performers in American cinema ... which further reinforces her distance from Chinese traditions and cultures." With the erasure of her ethnicity, Daisy Duk must relinquish her parental responsibility toward her son and must leave his education to her very ethnic husband, to Kwan Kung, to Uncle Donald Duk, and to the mother-eater Lee Kuey.

Indeed none of the women agonize over their ethnic or cultural identity as their men do. Their presence in the novel primarily comes through their naive banter with each other and cute interjections into men's conversation. "The twins often talk as if everything they hear everybody say and see everybody do is dialog in a memoir they're writing or action in a play they're directing. This makes Mom feel like she's on stage and drives Donald Duk crazy."

"Is that Chinese psychology, dear?" Daisy Duk asks. "Daisy Duk inquires," says Penelope Duk. "And Little Donnie Duk says, Oh, Mom! and sighs." "I do not!" Donald Duk yelps at the twins. "Well, then, say it," Penelope Duk says. "It's a good line . . . ."

"I thought it was narrative," Venus says. "Listen up to some Chinese psychology, girls and boys," Daisy Duk says.

"No, that's not psychology, that's Bugs Bunny," Dad says.

"You don't mean Bugs Bunny, dear. You always make that mistake." "Br'er Rabbit!" Dad says.

Although this dialog also presents King Duk in a somewhat cartoonish manner, his characterization gets plenty of time and space to develop into a unique individual. Yet the Duk women remain flat and stunted throughout the novel. Fung rightfully charges Chin with denying these women "any sense of human authenticity."

As their characterization mostly precludes agency, these women serve to set off the men as agents, producers, and providers. King's kitchen regularly feeds crowds of diners, and when it's closed for New Year it offers free dinner to more than "150" relatives and friends at one time. Such a highly productive site banishes the association of cooking with domesticity. In doing so Chin places women outside the kitchen. Except for one occasion, in which Daisy is found "shelling shrimp, busting crab, blanching chickens for Dad to finish and sauce in the woks," the women in the novel are all denied participation in the now masculine economy of cooking and feeding. King as the primary producer/provider not only cooks for armies of people but also offers free food to the community. The Frog Twin sisters "wait outside Dad's restaurant when the garbage is put out. Now and then, when Dad knows they are out in the alley, he gives them a fresh catfish to take home." On New Year's Day, King drops fifty-pound sacks of rice at his neighbors' doorsteps. Chin bestows the glory of generosity on King at the same time he assigns the disgrace of being nonconsumers or charity cases to women. Fung writes,

Here, the ethnic men are both laborers and consumers, displacing the ethnic women from both public and domestic work as well as denying them their consumption. As the men construct a kind of social reality based on the context of market economy and nationalist discourse, the women, like food, embody exchange and fetishistic values. In other words, the process of producing and consuming food constructs complex power dynamics based on gender and class differences that ultimately lead to a language of legitimacy and exclusion: namely, deciding who gets to obtain, cook, and/or eat food signals an economy of power, exchange, and desire. (256)

Chin's presentation of cooking as masculine/productive labor in this novel engenders a class divide and thus an economy of asymmetrical power relationships between men and women, between the working and the nonworking, between producers and consumers, and between consumers and charity cases. One may argue that the masculinization of cooking succeeds in breaking down the binary between the public and the private by blurring the distinction between home and restaurant. It is precisely by this breakdown, however, that Chin exiles the Duk women from the traditionally gendered space without offering them an alternative location for meaningful labor and subject formation. . . .

Source: Wenying Xu, "Masculinity, Food, and Appetite in Frank Chin's *Donald Duk* and 'The Eat and Run Midnight People,'" in *Cultural Critique*, No. 66, Spring 2007, pp. 78–104.

Susan B. Richardson

In the following excerpt, Richardson argues that Donald Duk *contains "explicit and unambiguous" cultural lessons, "especially for white readers."*

Frank Chin's *Donald Duk* is a spirited novel of education whose comic protagonist makes a welcome addition to the roster of American literary boy heroes. The novel entertains readers with its coming-of-age account of twelve-year-old Donald carping and spluttering his way to new understanding—about himself, about his community, about his place in American society. Yet beyond any entertainment value, the author clearly intends his novel to have a serious didactic purpose. Stories, according to Chin, are essential to an education that would "create informed, morally conscious citizens"; he claims that Chinese legends and stories are a "valuable tool" for reminding Chinese-Americans of their heritage and a "necessity" for bringing understanding to white Americans about the history and culture of others. The novel exemplifies his claim; *Donald Duk*'s comic strip bildungsroman becomes a novel of education for readers as well—especially for white readers. The lessons that drive the novel are explicit and unambiguous. *Donald Duk*

IT IS IRONIC THAT A DELIBERATELY BICULTURAL WORK LIKE *DONALD DUK* SHOULD ACTUALLY SUPPRESS THE READER'S EXPERIENCE OF A CULTURAL ENCOUNTER."

presents the heroic dimensions of Chinese-American history even as it exposes the invidious popular stereotypes, the prejudices, and the injustices that characterize that history. The unrelenting indictment of the status of Chinese-Americans and their treatment in American society, in the past and now, becomes an argument for social correction—a call for change dictated by respect for all and fair play as promised by American democracy.

The cultural issues explored by *Donald Duk* are not new to Frank Chin's work—Chin's role as a spokesman for Chinese America is well established. The legal and social forces that have victimized Chinese-Americans (e.g. racist U.S. exclusion laws, the nineteenth century exploitation of Chinese laborers, the distortion of classic Chinese philosophy and literature, the erasure of Chinese-American history, the emasculating stereotypes of Chinese in the American media) inform Chin's work from his earliest essays and plays to his 1994 novel, *Gunga Din Highway*.

Curiously, however, in spite of *Donald Duk*'s clear didactic purpose, Chin's narrative choices undermine the effectiveness of his argument to persuade and transform his readers. Various formal features, such as his cartoon format and the use of characters as surrogate-learners, serve to distance readers from the text and from the characters. Chin's insistence upon presenting unfamiliar ethnic material as familiar and "normal" blunts an outsider reader's encounter with Chinese-American experience and reduces the possibility of reproducing for the reader a multicultural experience. Also, Chin's repeated use of analogy between Chinese-American and mainstream cultures in order to foster white acceptance of Chinese America establishes a false homogeneity between the two cultures. These narrative strategies that simplify and homogenize also distort experience and mitigate against genuine understanding of the "other." Beyond these problems with form, moreover, the argument itself is compromised by its particularity. Even as the novel calls for the erasure of race-based prejudice and injustice, it leaves intact discrimination based on other categories such as gender or class. Voices emerge from the text that complicate the novel's seemingly simple message and that call into question the integrity of its underlying principles. The discussion of the lessons of *Donald Duk* which follows will focus first on the effectiveness of certain of Chin's narrative techniques in delivering the novel's lessons and then will consider the implications of the contending subtextual voices for the novel's didactic impact.

The style and spirit of *Donald Duk* are uncharacteristic of much of Chin's earlier work. The adversarial anger and bitterness of, for example, *The Chickencoop Chinaman* or "Come All Ye Asian American Writers of the Real and the Fake" here give way to wry humor, comic scenes of burlesque, and dialogue peppered with broad punning and the slangy, insult-laden bantering of young siblings. Although elsewhere Chin's outrage and combativeness propel him virtually to declare war on his (non-Chinese) audience—he has testified that "writing theater is like making war" (qtd. in McDonald xix), that stories are cultural weaponry, and that storytelling is a tactic to defend oneself "against all forms of oppression and exploitation" ("Uncle Frank's Fakebook of Fairy Tales")—in this novel, Chin becomes uncharacteristically solicitous of outsiders in his audience. That is, in *Donald Duk* he exchanges the role of adversary for that of teacher. Instead of a jeremiad, the novel becomes a primer with a series of lessons about Chinese-American culture.

These lessons are presumably directed at Donald although I believe that Chin's real target is his audience. Donald personifies the self-hating Chinese-American who embraces white majority attitudes as his own, including the debasement of Chinese-Americans, and the novel provides a melange of teacher figures to rectify this misguidedness. Donald's primary teacher is his father, the wise and powerful King Duk who takes pride in his name and heritage, but numerous other figures (significantly all male) provide him instruction, from Uncle Donald, the wise elder, to Crawdad Man, the teller of old Chinese stories, and Victor Lee, a Vietnam veteran.

The steady flow of explanation and advice from these many and various teachers is activated by Donald's constant refrain of "What does it mean?", a didactic structuring that places the reader in the position of onlooker. While the lessons apply to readers as well as to Donald, the audience is not addressed directly or aggressively (in the way, for example, that the audience is challenged by *The Chickencoop Chinaman*); here the arsenal of "cultural weaponry" is sheathed in the interest of the reader's comfort. Even in the case of their complete ignorance about Chinese-American culture, uninformed white outsiders are spared embarrassment since basic instruction is appropriate for a twelve-year-old like Donald. This structure, then, is one of a number of Chin's techniques to ease readers into the unfamiliar terrain of Chinese culture. The comfort gained by readers has a cost, however: a reduced potential for emotional commitment or cross-cultural understanding.

The novel's cartoon form also works to ease the reading (and sugar-coat the lessons) of *Donald Duk*. The title itself heralds the novel's identification with Disney—an identification which suggests that Donald Duk is as American and as non-threatening as Donald Duck and deserves as much attention and valorization as his namesake. The cartoon-like young protagonist expresses appropriately uncomplicated thoughts in appropriately simple syntax. Furthermore, the flattening of experience characteristic of comic books makes reading the narrative quick and effortless. The novel's progression of events is linear for, inspite of the double-layered setting of Donald's dream-world and San Francisco's Chinatown, a single protagonist and the same lessons operate in both realms. In addition, with the exception of Donald, the novel's characters are one-dimensional, static and—in some cases—parodic. Even Donald's character lacks complexity; the novel charts the change in his understanding and attitudes, yet—in part because of the lack of space in so short a work—the effect of the change upon his character is limited. Finally, as in a cartoon, *Donald Duk* exhibits a Disney-like clarity about values and morals. The novel explores issues in a humorous, non-threatening, and engaging way in which there is no ambiguity about right and wrong. Issues and behavior are clearly marked as bad or good. These features create an economy of form that allows Chin to foreground his didactic agenda; again, however, the form discourages the reader's commitment to the story or characters.

Along with Donald, Chin creates some auxiliary learner/characters who function as another important "easing" strategy. The primary example is Donald's best (white) friend, Arnold Azalea, who serves as a kind of alter ego for white readers. When Arnold is invited to spend Chinese New Year's in Chinatown with the Duk family, the family members incessantly give Arnold explanations about Chinese customs— often at length and sometimes more than once— to ensure the comfort of their uninformed guest. Arnold asks questions on behalf of the audience, and the answers he receives function in such a way as to inform the audience as well and to preclude their confusion about cultural or linguistic matters. For example, as soon as Arnold hears a Chinese term such as lay see, someone is quick to translate "lucky money in New Year's red envelopes"; when the red envelopes are distributed, Arnold receives detailed instruction as to their purpose and the protocol for behavior. Explanations to Arnold are sometimes so detailed, in fact, that the author has Donald react with embarrassment for the condescension Arnold might feel—perhaps to deflect any suspicion of condescension by the author toward his readers.

Chin introduces a second white male initiate whose presence signals the broad application of the novel's lessons. Arnold's father is characterized, even caricatured, as a rich and successful California businessman. We learn only a few facts about the Azalea family—Arnold attends an exclusive private school, his parents take expensive vacations to Hawaii, the Azaleas support Arnold's friendship with Donald—but these are sufficient to Mr. Azalea's narrative function as an adult character who takes instruction from King Duk and Uncle Donald about the meaning of things. Readers thereby understand that the novel's lessons are not only for children, but pertain even to rich, successful, white men. Although he makes a limited appearance in the narrative, Arnold's father serves the important function of validating the narrative's message for adults in the audience.

Chin never leaves his readers puzzled about the meaning of the many Chinese phrases that flavor the narrative. In general, terms are translated directly as they occur, and definitions are repeated at several places. The term may be explicitly explained to a character: "The mandate of heaven. Tien ming. 'What's that?' Donald asks.... 'The Chinese say, Kingdoms rise and

fall. Nations come and go,' Dad says." Or the synonym may appear in apposition, as in "bok gwai, the white monsters." On the rare occasion when Chin omits explanation, the context makes the meaning abundantly clear. For example, Goong hay fot choy (Happy New Year) is not defined when it first occurs during the New Year celebration, but it is unmistakably a greeting. (In case readers should miss its meaning, King Duk defines it later for Arnold.) Only with a few terms that are used continuously, like lay see [lucky money] or sifu [respected teacher], does Chin leave the reader to negotiate meaning without a (repeated) definition. Unless the reader is excessively absentminded, then, there are no instances when a Chinese term is ambiguous.

Another rhetorical technique designed to make the strange familiar in the world of *Donald Duk* is Chin's extensive use of comparison and the juxtaposition of elements from classical Chinese and American pop cultures. Beginning with the obvious identification of the hero and his family with Walt Disney characters, Chinese figures, stories, and places are regularly presented in conjunction with a mainstream American counterpart. Throughout the novel, Chinese-somethings are cited: the Chinese Fred Astaire, the Chinese Betty Crocker, the Chinese Frank Sinatra, and so on. Uncle Donald explains the Water Margin of classic Chinese legend in terms of Robin Hood: "The Water Margin was a place like [Sherwood Forest]," and "One of those 108 Chinese Robin Hoods is a hood name of Lee Kuey." Uncle Donald suggests that the band of 108 Chinese outlaws is all very much like Robin Hood, Little John and the rest of Robin Hood's Merry Men. When the Crawdad Man tells "a famous fairy tale" called *The Candlewick Fairy*, his listeners wonder if it is a "real" story. Crawdad Man authenticates it by comparing it to a Euro-American tale: "It's the real Chinese story, like 'Goldilocks and the Three Bears.' Everybody knows it" (164). The reader's ignorance is thus excused with the implication that erasing such ignorance requires very little effort.

Through their constant reference to old-time movies and Hollywood stars, including Donald's self-identification with Fred Astaire, the novel's characters ally themselves with "typical" mainstream Americans and thereby claim the same popular culture (a legitimate claim, of course, since it is also theirs). By presenting themselves as "not strange," the characters are able to dilute the strangeness of their ethnic customs and allusions. Almost invariably throughout the novel, the references to classical Chinese characters (Kwan Kung, Soong Gong, Lee Kuey, Ngawk Fay), to Chinese culture (Confucian thought, the Mandate of Heaven), to ethnic customs (New Year's firecrackers, dragons, tai chi, Cantonese opera), or to events in Chinese American history (laying railroad track in the High Sierras, detention at Angel Island) occur in tandem with names dropping from the popculture world of American television and Hollywood: Ginger Rogers, Shirley Temple, Frank Sinatra, and so on.

Again, this technique carries some risk. Chin uses a similar approach in his 1992 collection of Asian fairy tales, a project designed to introduce Asian American children to their Asian heritage and to make Asian tales palatable through a kind of homogenization: "Here," Chin writes, "you'll find we try to use the fairy tales and myths of the west, the stories you're familiar with, to take the mystery and fear of fatal exotic Orientalia out of the stories [of] the immigrants" ("Fakebook"). Shirley Geok-lin Lim reminds us that "juxtaposing ancient Chinese images and contemporary American cultural graffitti, when the Chinese allusions are unreconstructed, can only lead to uncomprehending rejection..." ("Reconstructing"). Lim's way to achieve comprehension is to place responsibility for reconstruction upon the "untrained reader." But when Chin chooses instead to aid readers' comprehension by simplifying material and removing "the mystery and fear," much of the original flavor and meaning of the Chinese folk material—in the fairy tale translations or in Donald Duk—must be lost.

By these various means, then, Chin introduces his readers to Chinese-American culture and informs them about relevant issues. As readers proceed through the narrative alongside the curious Arnold Azalea and the reluctant Donald Duk, Chin provides abundant signals for them to find their way to the proper conclusions. White readers are invited to recognize their own stereotyping attitudes in Donald and to try to disassociate themselves from them; culturally ambivalent Chinese-American readers are provided models like King Duk for taking pride in their culture. For both groups, the initial views expressed by Donald have been discredited; readers who share those views are encouraged to go through a process of re-examination and re-evaluation.

However, the author's painstaking guidance of his audience ironically subverts its goal. At the root of Chin's solicitousness, I believe, is an authorial distrust of the audience and of their capability to work out the proper conclusions on their own. Yet learning that leads to discovery and commitment requires a reader's active participation. Shirley Geok-lin Lim, in "Reconstructing Asian-American Poetry," touches on this issue when she places responsibility on the reader for doing the homework necessary to achieve comprehension of a text's unfamiliar ethnic material, and Reed Way Dasenbock makes a forcible argument (in "Intelligibility and Meaningfulness in Multicultural Literature in English") that only when a reader struggles to make sense of what is unfamiliar in a text does multicultural understanding occur. Reader response critics also, like Wolfgang Iser in "Indeterminacy and the Reader's Response," claim that the transformative power of a text depends upon the reader's active engagement with the text. Iser maintains that textual indeterminacy (or gaps in meaning) allows the reader to take a creative role in assembling meaning from the work's narrative conventions. When readers take this role, they encounter a new reality, they question the thought systems of their actual world, and they begin to change within themselves.

Surely this is precisely the outcome Chin intends for his audience. Yet readers' active engagement with *Donald Duk*, and therefore their creation of meaning, is curtailed, even preempted, by the author's preference for a predictable and pre-packaged reality and by his drive to fill in textual gaps with the correct answers for all the questions raised by the novel.

It is ironic that a deliberately bicultural work like *Donald Duk* should actually suppress the reader's experience of a cultural encounter. Despite the novel's "hyphenated" Americans, ethnic community, and foreign phrases, the novel's potential for a cross-cultural experience is subverted by the narrative techniques described above that cater to the uninformed reader. Chin himself has frequently inveighed against other Chinese-American writers for playing the role of the "tourist guide" and for making the "exotic" safe and palatable for white visitors to "Chinatown"—that is, for falsifying Chinese-American experience. Yet, by working hard to "normalize" Chinese-American life and to make it seem familiar to outsiders, *Donald Duk* seems to fall into that very role of "tourist guide." Sau-ling Cynthia Wong claims that Chin's didactic strategy in the novel "sanitizes" experience. Wong writes: "It is as if, after struggling for years with raw and impossible contradictions, Chin has decided to settle for a defanged version of Chinese-American history and the simple warm glow of ethnic pride" (Reading). But defanging experience in order to make it accessible, like removing fear and mystery, runs the risk of making it false.

Furthermore, it is dangerously misleading to suggest that encountering the "other" is effortless and not really so strange or "other." A work that confirms a reader's desire to believe that "under the skin, after all, everyone is just the same" produces an apologia for the status quo rather than a transformative or multicultural experience. To call Larry Louie "the Chinese Fred Astaire" implies he is basically the same as Fred Astaire; it downplays the "Chinese" aspect of Louie's identity and blurs his distinctiveness as, for example, a fine flamenco dancer (in contrast to Fred Astaire who was "too light on his feet"). Instead of grappling with the strange, the outsider white reader is allowed to conclude that while "they" may be a little off-center perhaps (i.e., "quaint", "exotic", "inferior"), they are, after all, "really just like us." An unfortunate corollary to this notion is that the responsibility for change is "theirs"; it is incumbent upon "them" to move toward the center, to assimilate, while "we" stay naturally, comfortably centered.

Chin shows little confidence that the readers of *Donald Duk* are willing or able to grapple with unfamiliar material. He seems, rather, to attribute to readers a "show me" stance that places the entire burden for the communicative transaction on the writer. A writer's acceptance of that burden, however, checks the learning experience of the reader. Moreover, Chin's method of "showing" is to "tell" obvious truths. In the world of Donald Duk there is one set of answers, one set of values, one interpretation of history. Mr. Meanwright's answers are unquestionably wrong, while Donald's research uncovers the "right" ones. But Donald's acquisition of truth is so easy, the lessons so superficial, that neither characters nor readers truly earn wisdom. This stance by the author results in a novel that can entertain and even edify readers, but—in spite of what I believe the author aims to do—that lacks the power to transform them.

Personal transformation involves an emotional commitment, yet the features of the novel that I have termed "easing" techniques reduce the possibilities of such a commitment from readers. The author's didactic stance makes such commitment difficult. The novel's use of cartoon, a form incompatible with a complex development of character, acts as a buffer between readers and the kind of emotional engagement with characters' lives often associated with a bildungsroman. The presence of Donald, Arnold, and Arnold's father as "readers' guides" also fosters detachment in readers in that the characters routinely behave like members of the audience—listening to stories and taking instruction about life. Consequently, readers who behave accordingly will focus their attention upon the lessons about the Chinese in America at the expense of the story about Donald and Arnold . . . .

Source: Susan B. Richardson, "The Lessons of *Donald Duk*," in *MELUS*, Vol. 24, No. 4, Winter 1999, p. 57.

SOURCES

Agiesta, Jennifer, "U.S. Views on China Reminiscent of 1990s take on Japan," in *Washington Post*, February 25, 2010.

Chin, Frank, *Donald Duk*, Coffee House Press, 1991.

"Chinese New Year Parade," in *Chinatown San Francisco Newsletter*, http://www.sanfranciscochinatown.com/events/chinesenewyearparade.html (accessed January 16, 2012).

Daniels, Roger, "Chinese," in *Coming to America: A History of Immigration and Ethnicity in American Life*, 2nd ed., Perennial, 2002, pp. 239–50.

Davis, Robert Murray, Review of *Donald Duk*, in *World Literature Today*, Vol. 65, No. 4, Autumn 1991, p. 715.

De Haven, Tom, "He's Been Dreaming on the Railroad," Review of *Donald Duk*, in *New York Times*, March 31, 1991, BR 9.

Doolittle, John T., "Chinese-American Contribution to the Transcontinental Railroad," Speech before the U.S. House of Representatives, April 29, 1999, http://cprr.org/Museum/Chinese.html (accessed January 16, 2012).

Dugger, Celia W., "U.S. Study Says Asian-Americans Face Widespread Discrimination," in *New York Times*, February 29, 1992.

Harmon, William and Hugh Holman, *A Handbook to Literature*, 11th ed., Pearson Prentice Hall, 2009, pp. 24-25, 65, 180, 536.

Ingraham, Janet, Review of *Donald Duk*, in *Library Journal*, Vol. 116, No. 3, February 15, 1991, p. 220.

"*The Iron Road*: About the Program," PBS website, http://www.pbs.org/wgbh/amex/iron/ (accessed January 16, 2012).

Kraus, George, "Chinese Laborers and the Construction of the Central Pacific," in *Utah Historical Quarterly*, Vol. 37, No. 1, Winter 1969, pp. 41–57.

Leonard, Suzanne, "Dreaming as Cultural Work in *Donald Duk* and *Dreaming in Cuban*," in *Melus*, Vol. 29, No. 2, Summer 2004, pp. 181–203.

Nguyen, Viet Thanh, "The Remasculinization of Chinese America: Race, Violence, and the Novel," in *American Literary History*, Vol. 12, No. 1/2, Spring-Summer 2000, pp. 130–57.

"Some Asians' College Strategy: Don't Check 'Asian'," in *USA Today*, December 4, 2011, http://www.usatoday.com/news/education/story/2011-12-03/asian-students-college-applications/51620236/1 (accessed January 16, 2012).

Su, John J., "Ghosts of Essentialism: Racial Memory as Epistemological Claim," in *American Literature*, Vol. 81, No. 2, June 2009, pp. 361–86.

Terrazas, Aaron, and Jeanne Batolova, "Chinese Immigrants in the United States," May 2010, http://www.migrationinformation.org/USfocus/display.cfm?id=781 (accessed January 16, 2012).

Welch, Patricia Bjaaland, *Chinese New Year*, Oxford University Press, 1997, pp. 5–40.

Xian, Yi, "U.S. Immigration Policy Speeds Up Overseas Chinese Students' Return," in *Nanfang Daily*, May 20, 2011, http://watchingamerica.com/News/104334/u-s-immigration-policy-speeds-up-overseas-chinese-students-return/ (accessed January 16, 2012).

FURTHER READING

Ambrose, Stephen E., *Nothing Like It in the World: The Men Who Built the Transcontinental Railroad 1863–1869*, Simon & Schuster, 2001.

> Ambrose's book is a history of the engineering feat that was building of the transcontinental railroad. Ambrose relates the entire story, from the investors, to the surveyors, to the laborers, including Chinese immigrants, Irish immigrants, and former Confederate soldiers. This easy-to-grasp history is perfect for young-adult readers.

Lai, Him Mark, Genny Lim, and Judy Yung, *Island: Poetry and History of Chinese Immigrants on Angel Island 1910–1940*, reprint edition, University of Washington Press, 1991; originally printed by the History of Chinese Detained on Island, 1980.

> This book provides a history of the one hundred and seventy-five thousand Chinese immigrants who were imprisoned in wooden barracks on Angel Island, some for three days and some up to three years, before they were refused entry and

deported. The book includes interviews with former prisoners, photographs, and the poetry that detainees wrote on the walls of the barracks.

Lowe, Lisa, *Immigrant Acts: On Asian American Cultural Politics*, Duke University Press, 1996.

> In this text, Lowe argues that a complete understanding of Asian immigration to the United States is important to illuminating the history of racism and discrimination that Asian immigrants have faced in America.

Nai'An, Shi, *Outlaws of the Marsh*, translated by Sidney Shapiro, Foreign Language Press, 1999.

> This book contains the stories of the one hundred and eight outlaw heroes that figure so prominently in *Donald Duk*. The book includes multiple versions of each story so that a more comprehensive legend is presented for each of the outlaw tales. This book provides an examination of fourteenth-century Chinese literature that manages to capture many different genres of literature, including romance, mystery, and heroic tales.

Theroux, Paul, *Riding the Iron Rooster: By Train Through China*, Mariner, 1988.

> This book is an account of the author's journey across China by rail. He spends a year on his journey and emerges having learned about China by watching the people he meets along his journey.

Yeh, Chio-ling, *Making An American Festival: Chinese New Year in San Francisco's Chinatown*, University of California Press, 2008.

> This book is a history of the annual Chinese New Year celebration in San Francisco, which is considered to be the largest one in the United States. The author provides an interesting sociological study of Chinese American culture and racial identity, starting with the origins of the celebration in 1953.

SUGGESTED SEARCH TERMS

Frank Chin AND *Donald Duk*

Frank Chin AND Chinese American literature

Donald Duk AND young adult novel

Donald Duk AND transcontinental railroad

Donald Duk AND 108 outlaw heroes Chinese legend

Donald Duk AND Chinese New Year

Donald Duk AND Chinese immigration

19th century Chinese immigration AND Chinese Exclusion Laws

Chinese immigration AND discrimination

Dracula

1931   Vampire stories have been told for centuries in almost every country across the globe. In the late nineteenth century, Bram Stoker wrote a vampire novel that combined the mythology of creatures who feast on human blood with tales of the historic character Vlad III, also known as Vlad the Impaler and Vlad Dracula ("son of the dragon"), a bloodthirsty Romanian warlord of the fifteenth century who subjected both his enemies and his subjects to unspeakable atrocities. Stoker's popular novel *Dracula* was adapted to the Broadway stage in the 1920s, and the stage version was adapted by Universal Studios in 1931, yielding director Tod Browning's visionary film *Dracula*, a film that has lasting impact today.

Bram Stoker's version of the vampire presents Count Dracula as a gruesome monster with pointed ears and teeth who has lived for centuries in his decaying castle, able to change his form to pass as human. Browning's film, however, focuses on the sensual attraction between the vampire and its victim. Though Hollywood censorship limited the ways in which the film could show the seduction that is inherent in the story, as the creature bites sensitive flesh of human necks and blood passes between them, actor Bela Lugosi's charisma as the title character showed the vampire's appeal to his victims. From this beginning, stories about Dracula, in film and television, in fiction and graphic novels, have viewed the character as being part monster and part charmer.

(© Moviestore Collection Ltd / Alamy)

The power that Lugosi brought to the role of Dracula has been so unwavering that it continues to assert itself, in diluted form, to this day. Familiar characters such as cereal icon Count Chocula and Count von Count from *Sesame Street* are derived from Lugosi's portrayal, showing vampires wearing capes, tuxedos, and medals, talking with variations of the actor's Hungarian accent.

PLOT SUMMARY

The opening credits of Dracula show over a stylized graphic of a bat, while the soundtrack plays a selection from Pyotr Ilyich Tchaikovsky's ballet *Swan Lake*.

The story begins with a horse-drawn coach carrying passengers through the Transylvanian mountains. A British passenger, Renfield, tells the driver to drive more carefully, but a fellow passenger who clearly knows the area insists that the coach must go quicker, to reach the inn before sundown. He warns that it is "a night of evil" and points out that they may become prey of a *nosferatu*, a word Stoker popularized in his novel as a local expression, meaning "not dead." The

carriage reaches an inn that is guarded by a gate and a large, looming cross on a hill, one of several icons of Christianity believed to protect against vampires. Renfield says that he is not stopping at this inn but is going along to Borgo Pass, where he is to be met at midnight by the carriage of Count Dracula. The locals warn him that the people of the mountains believe there to be vampires at the Dracula's castle; nonetheless, Renfield insists on going. Before he leaves, an old woman gives him a crucifix to wear around his neck.

As Renfield's coach speeds away, the scene changes to the vault beneath Dracula's castle, and the view closes in on a coffin. It is sunset. The coffin opens slightly, and a gnarled hand creeps out. Other coffins open, and Dracula's three wives emerge and approach him as he ascends the stairs to leave.

The driver drops Renfield at the crossroads in the dark and hurries away. The coach that meets him is driven by Dracula, who is silent, disguised with a scarf around his face. When this coach races too fast, Renfield leans out to speak to the driver, only to find that the driver's box is now empty. A bat flies in front of the horses, guiding them.

At the castle, the creaking front door opens by itself. Three bats, possibly representing Dracula's wives, fly near the windows, while various creatures, from rats to armadillos (which are never explained, though they are not native to Europe), crawl around the castle's ruins. Dracula comes out of an upstairs room and slowly descends the stairs to meet Renfield. As Renfield follows the count up the stairs, he notices that Dracula has passed through a spider web that spans the staircase but has not broken its strands.

A meal has already been set for Renfield in his bedroom. Dracula does not eat with him but addresses business: he has summoned Renfield from England to arrange the purchase of Carfax Abbey, near London. (In the novel, this abbey is only one of ten British properties that Dracula purchases.) As he reads the legal documents, Dracula absentmindedly notes that he is taking only three boxes with him and that he has chartered a ship that will leave for England the following evening. Renfield cuts himself on a paper clip; Dracula approaches, transfixed by the sight of blood, but he is forced to cover his eyes when the crucifix dangling from Renfield's neck drops in front of him.

Left alone, Renfield becomes dizzy from the wine Dracula has given him. He sees Dracula's three wives approach him through a fog. Standing

FILM TECHNIQUE

- At several points in the film, Lugosi's piercing stare is given even more depth and mystery by shining pinpoint lights directly on or beneath each of the actor's eyes. Without the special effects that are available today, these lights enabled the filmmakers to imply the vampire's hypnotic stare. In the novel, Bram Stoker often indicates Dracula's hypnotic power by mentioning the vampire's red, glowing eyes.

- The director, Browning, uses establishing shots to quickly indicate a scene's setting. This is most notable when the outside of Castle Dracula is shown before sundown: none of the action takes place outside the castle (except when Renfield walks to the door in the dark), but the sight of this massive, crumbling structure tells readers much about the decayed grandeur of the count's life inside. Other scenes also follow shots of the exterior of the buildings in which they take place, though none are so impressive or important to the story as the mood established by the Castle Dracula. When the geographic setting changes, this script uses a title card, like those used in silent movies, to announce "London." The establishing shot is still used commonly in films and television, but title cards are rare.

- In the early days of film, it was not unusual for studios to use repurposed footage that had been shot for a different film, even when the films did not match each other well. To establish that Dracula crossed the ocean on a turbulent sea, the film shows a ship that was originally filmed for a 1925 silent film called *The Storm Breaker*. As film historian David J. Skal points out, the two film styles are clearly different. Silent films were shot at a slower speed than sound film, and the footage had to be sped up when it was incorporated into *Dracula*.

- *Dracula* was an early film of the sound era, which began with the release of *The Jazz Singer* in 1927. Like other films of its time, *Dracula* is presented without the background music that film audiences expect today. Early sound recording techniques made it difficult to keep music and dialogue separate, jumbling the two together. Also, the tastes of filmmakers at the time were honed on the theatrical tradition of focusing on dialogue, and music would be viewed as a distraction. In 1998, composer Phillip Glass wrote a score for the 1931 movie. It was performed live by the Kronos Quartet, which toured with the film, and has been added as an alternate audio track to DVDs of the film released by Universal Studios since then.

- Karl Freund, who is credited with the photography of this film, is recognized as one of the most versatile cinematographers in the history of the movies. He was best known as an early proponent of the moving camera. In groundbreaking films such as *Metropolis* and *All Quiet on the Western Front*, Freund used the camera's motion to accentuate parts of the action and to draw attention to specific details. A good example in *Dracula* is in the first scene in Dracula's vault, when the count has not yet appeared on-screen: the camera zooms forward to the coffin as it slowly opens and a hand emerges, intensifying the scene's inherent horror. Often the camera stays still in *Dracula*, which was common for early films adapted from stage plays, but there are frequent instances of Freund's tracking shots, when the camera moves smoothly on a wheeled platform.

at the open door, a large bat swoops down on him, and Renfield faints. The women approach, but as in the novel, Dracula intervenes, silently sending them away before they can feast on him. Dracula slowly bends down over the fallen Renfield, clearly to attack him.

On a sailing ship in a raging storm, Renfield, now with a crazed look in his eyes, opens a wooden crate and whispers to his master that the sun has set. Dracula rises from the box and goes on deck to watch the sailors battle the storm.

Later the ship has sailed into London with no sign of life on deck: the dead captain has tied himself to the ship's wheel. In the hold, Renfield puts a padlock on the crate that holds Dracula's body during the daytime. When the police find Renfield below deck, he is stark raving mad. A newspaper shows that he has been admitted to Doctor Seward's Sanitarium, where he eats bugs.

In London, Dracula approaches a girl on a foggy night while she is selling flowers on a street corner. She is mesmerized as he puts his arms around her. As he walks away, a crowd of police and onlookers gathers around her dead body.

Dracula attends a performance of the symphony. He takes control of the usher's will and makes her lead him to Dr. Seward's box. At his command, she enters the box and summons Dr. Seward for a phone call, which gives Dracula the opportunity to pretend that he has overheard the doctor's name. He steps forward and introduces himself as the new resident of Carfax Abbey, which is next door to the Seward Sanitarium. (A sanitarium, also spelled sanatorium, is a general term for a convalescent home or therapy center. In this case, it is a psychiatric hospital.) Seward introduces Dracula to his daughter Mina; her fiancé, John Harker; and Mina's friend, Lucy Weston. A discussion of the abbey's decrepit state reminds Lucy of an old toast that focuses on gloom and death. The mention of death prompts Dracula to observe, "To die . . . to be really dead. That must be glorious." He tells his shocked listeners that there are worse things than death, and as the theater lights fade to indicate the end of intermission, he turns his attention to Lucy.

Later, in her bedroom, Lucy tells Mina that she finds the count fascinating. Mina leaves and Lucy goes to bed, while, outside on the street, Dracula watches her window. He enters her room as a bat and, having changed form off camera, bends down and bites her neck.

The next scene is Lucy's autopsy. A mention is made of "her last transfusion," compressing a series of measures taken to save Lucy's life in Stoker's novel, but Seward and the attending physicians cannot understand how she died of loss of blood. The bite marks on Lucy's throat are compared to similar marks on the throats of other victims.

The peaceful grounds of the Seward Sanitarium are disturbed by the screams of Renfield, who is terrified as his caretaker, Martin, takes away a spider he has captured to eat.

In Amsterdam, Professor Van Helsing is performing an experiment on blood taken from Renfield. He announces to several men seated around him that they are dealing with a vampire, the un-dead. Later, in Seward's office in London, Van Helsing explains that, although Renfield only eats small bugs when he is at the sanitarium, he escapes for hours at a time and may be eating other, larger things then.

Martin brings Renfield in, and the patient is more sane and lucid than he has been since arriving at Seward's, but his disposition quickly changes. He says that he is concerned about Mina, that his cries at night might give her bad dreams, hinting that he knows that Dracula will make her his next victim. Renfield's discussion is interrupted by the long howl of a wolf, as the film cuts to Dracula, at sunset, arising from his coffin in the abbey next door. In Seward's office, Martin steps forward to say that Renfield thinks the wolves howling in the night are talking to him, which Van Helsing understands to be a sign of vampirism; he tests his theory by taking out a bundle of wolfsbane, a plant that vampires cannot abide. On seeing it, Renfield curls up and shields himself.

Dracula enters Mina's room as a bat and then assumes his human form. Two days later, Mina relates to Harker a dream she had, with wolves howling and her bedroom filling up with mist, in which a face with red eyes approached her. Van Helsing overhears her story and talks gently to Mina, taking her scarf away from her throat to reveal the two holes that are the mark of a vampire. Just as Harker wonders what could have caused the holes in Mina's neck, the maid announces that Count Dracula has arrived.

When they are introduced, Dracula says that he is familiar with Van Helsing's scientific reputation, but he dismisses Mina's dream as the product of grim folk stories from Transylvania he has told her. Harker, disturbed to hear that Mina has been seeing Dracula, takes a cigarette, and Van Helsing looks at the mirrored lid of the cigarette case, noticing that the reflection shows Mina and Seward but not Dracula. After Mina leaves, Van Helsing confronts Dracula with the mirror, enraging him. He quickly regains his composure and apologizes, but the others comment on his animalistic rage after he leaves.

Harker goes to look where Dracula has gone and reports that he sees only a large dog or wolf. Van Helsing explains that this is one of the forms vampires often take.

As Van Helsing explains about vampires, Mina steps out into the night and into Dracula's arms, summoned by the vampire's will. Renfield enters the room and begins to tell them about the danger facing Mina, but the bat appears at the window, frightening him into silence. They all turn at the scream of the maid, who runs to Harker with the news that Mina lies on the lawn, apparently dead. The men race to Mina's side and find her just barely alive.

A policeman on a bicycle passes a cemetery and hears a child crying. Lucy, who had been buried earlier, walks past. The next day, Martin, the sanitarium caretaker, reads a newspaper story aloud about a mysterious and beautiful woman in white who has been luring small children to secluded spots at night and biting their throats.

At the sanitarium, Van Helsing questions Mina, who says she has seen Lucy after she was buried. Van Helsing promises that he can save Lucy's soul, and Mina asks him to promise to save her own soul, too, after her death. She tries to explain to Harker that she is turning into a vampire, but he is enraged and will not listen. Night approaches; Van Helsing prepares Mina's room with wolfsbane in preparation for Dracula's return, and he instructs the nurse to keep the windows closed and make sure the wolfsbane stays around Mina's neck. Harker insists that he is going to take her away from the professor's frightening stories, but Van Helsing warns that doing so will kill Mina.

Renfield enters and talks about the things that Dracula has promised him, including thousands of rats, which are the sort of small vermin that Renfield would eat. From his mysterious talk and Martin's observation that the bars of Renfield's room have been twisted, Van Helsing concludes that Dracula is in the house: as stated in the novel but not in the film, a vampire cannot enter a house unless he has been invited in by someone within.

As the others leave to protect Mina, Dracula stops Van Helsing and confronts him, trying to control his mind. He nearly succeeds, but the professor is strong enough to resist. He drives Dracula away by producing a cross from his pocket.

Harker goes to Mina's room and finds that her nurse has suffered a dizzy spell and lost consciousness and that Mina is more lively and animated than she has been in days. As Harker stares up at the stars, Mina fixates hungrily on his neck, drawing back at the last minute. Minutes after they talked about the clear, starry night, they sit on the terrace surrounded by fog. Dracula, in bat form, appears, and Mina agrees to follow his silent instructions. She stares at Harker with the look of one possessed; she is moving in to bite his throat when Van Helsing appears and stops her with his cross. Mina tearfully admits that Dracula has made her drink his blood, but her confession is interrupted by a gunshot, as Martin tries to scare off the big gray bat.

At 4:45 in the morning, Grace, the nurse, is under Dracula's spell, and she removes the wolfsbane that had made it impossible for him to enter Mina's room. Van Helsing and Harker follow Renfield to the abbey at the same time that Dracula brings Mina there. Through a barred window, Harker calls to Mina, who is under the vampire's control. Infuriated with Renfield for having led his enemies there, Dracula strangles his servant and throws his lifeless body down the abbey's huge staircase.

By the time Van Helsing and Harker reach the vault beneath the abbey, Dracula has returned to his coffin, which is actually a box of soil from his homeland. There is a box next to his, which Van Helsing and Harker assume is Mina's. While they are preparing to kill the two vampires with a stake through their hearts, however, they find that the second box is empty. Van Helsing drives a wooden stake through Dracula's heart. (This is not shown in the film, and the sound of Dracula groaning as the stake is hammered in was censored from the film for almost sixty years. It was restored in a remaster in the 1990s.) Mina, standing in the shadows, clutches her own heart and screams as Dracula is killed. Once the vampire is dead, however, she is restored to her normal self. Harker and Mina leave, but Van Helsing lingers behind, possibly to decapitate Dracula's corpse, as Stoker's novel insists must be done if he is to be prevented from ever rising again.

CHARACTERS

Count Dracula

The character of Count Dracula was originally conceived as a freakish being, more monstrous than human in his looks, with long pointed ears and fingernails and the repellent breath that is traditionally associated with legendary blood-drinking vampires. The stage version that preceded this film began the process of changing his image into that of a suave foreign gentleman, and Bela Lugosi's unforgettable film performance completed that process. Hungarian-born Lugosi, who had come to America just seven years before being cast as Dracula on stage, used his weak control of English as an asset, defining the count as someone who had studied British culture from afar, in seclusion.

In Stoker's novel, Dracula is introduced as a strange character, but he seems friendly. Dracula establishes the threat that he poses to the British Realtor who comes to meet with him only over the course of weeks. The film makes no pretense of the danger he presents right away, introducing the word "vampire" before Renfield even reaches Castle Dracula. The script gives the count sinister dialogue full of double meanings. For example, he says that he never drinks, and pauses before adding the word "wine." Audiences already know that Dracula does drink blood.

Though Dracula behaves as a member of the aristocracy—an image supported by the unexplained medallion he wears around his neck—he clearly has trouble controlling his temper at times. When confronted with a mirror, he strikes out with such force that the people discuss his animalistic rage after he leaves the room. He is soon seen running across the lawn in the form of a wolf, though the characters who do not know about vampires do not realize that this is Dracula, transformed.

Although the film version humanizes Dracula and makes him something of a romantic figure, there is still no sympathy expended for him. He surrounds himself with dark, frightening images and preys upon weak women, changing them into monsters that, in turn, prey upon children.

Dracula's Brides

Dracula's three brides are just as enigmatic in the film version of this story as they are in the novel. In both versions, they show up as if in a dream, wandering silently around in the mist. Stoker's novel is much more explicit about their attempt to seduce and attack Harker than Browning's film is in their scene with Renfield, but in both versions, Dracula intercedes, chasing them away

from the Englishman to claim the victim for himself.

John Harker

Jonathan Harker (John Harker, in the film) is the main character of the first part of Stoker's novel. He is the real estate agent who travels from England to Transylvania to work with Dracula and is then held prisoner in the castle, witness to unusual and terrifying sights. He escapes the castle and travels across the countryside to a hospital, where an attending nurse writes to his fiancée, Mina, who comes to him. The couple marries and rises in social class when Harker inherits the business that sent him to Transylvania, but they are drawn back into Dracula's circle when Mina's friend Lucy falls under the vampire's spell.

In the film, Renfield, not Harker, is the real estate agent who is held prisoner in Dracula's castle. The film introduces Harker into the story in his relationship to the Seward family. No background information is given about him, making Harker a generic romantic lead.

Harker's most significant function in the plot of the film is to insist on taking Mina away from the Seward Sanitarium. His intentions are founded in a realistic world view, giving Van Helsing the opportunity to explain the rules of vampirism that put Mina's life in danger if she were to leave. Harker is present in the final scene at Carfax Abbey, but he does not serve any important function in saving Mina or killing the vampire.

Martin

Martin, a caretaker at the Seward Sanitarium, is a character created to give the film comic relief. He is always paired with the patient Renfield, frequently commenting with a thick Cockney accent on Renfield's incredible behavior. Actor Charles K. Gerrard plays Martin with a broad range of gestures and voice, lightening the mood when the story becomes too dark.

Renfield

In Stoker's novel, R. M. Renfield is a 59-year-old inmate at the Seward Sanitarium. He is introduced into the story almost casually: Dr. Seward notes in his diary one day that he has thrown himself into his work after a romantic rejection from Lucy and chosen Renfield, among his patients, to examine more closely.

The film script gives Renfield the role that is played by Jonathan Harker in the novel: he is a real estate agent sent to Transylvania to make a sale to the mysterious count, and ends up becoming a prisoner in Dracula's castle. Unlike Harker in the novel, Renfield becomes the vampire's servant, traveling back to England with him. His apparent madness, as the only living person aboard the ship that brings Dracula to London, is what leads to his interment in the asylum. The fact that he is locked up in an asylum that is next door to a property that Dracula arranged to buy weeks earlier is treated as a coincidence.

In both works, Renfield is a complex character. Sometimes, he is mindlessly obsessed with consuming bugs and small animals, which Dwight Frye plays in the film with memorable extremism, while at other times, he is very stable. Stoker's novel explains that Renfield's manic and stable personalities coincide with midnight, when Dracula's powers are strongest, and noon, when they are weak.

As the story progresses, Renfield finds himself conflicted: he is under Dracula's control, but he also feels guilty about his part in Mina's destruction. After letting Dracula into the sanitarium, he is on the verge of revealing Dracula's plans for Mina to Van Helsing and the others, but he is stopped when Dracula appears at the window as a bat. Renfield, recognizing him, quickly points out that he has not actually told them anything useful. His crawl across the floor toward the maid, who has fainted, implies that he has evolved into a full-blown vampire himself, seeking human blood, by the end of the film, though the scene cuts before he actually touches her.

Doctor Seward

In one of the most conspicuous changes between novel and film, Dr. John Seward is altered from being one of the three men who courted Lucy to being the father of Lucy's friend, Mina. His character is accordingly aged.

In both versions, Seward is the operator of a sanitarium on the outskirts of London, next to Carfax Abbey, which Dracula purchases. His scientific background does little to help him understand what killed his daughter's friend Lucy or what is happening to Renfield, the patient who is obsessed with eating living creatures. When he brings his old professor, Van Helsing, in to consult on the Renfield case, Seward's role in the film becomes practically irrelevant.

Mina Seward

In the novel, this character is named Mina Murray and, later, after she marries, Mina Harker. The film, however, attaches her to Dr. John Seward as his daughter, simplifying Mina's connection to the Seward Sanitarium, where much of the film's action takes place.

As in the novel, Mina becomes a victim of the vampire, Count Dracula, and she is aware of the changes she is undergoing as she slips toward turning into a vampire herself. The novel points out in detail that Mina is instrumental in helping to fight Dracula, but she cannot entirely be trusted, since she might be an agent for him. The Mina of the film is more of a passive victim.

The film shows Dracula's first step in making her his servant, approaching Mina, as she sleeps, to bite her and put her under her spell. It does not show them having a social relationship, so that later, when Dracula tells Van Helsing that he has been talking to Mina and telling her legends from his homeland, audiences are as surprised as the characters on the screen are to hear that the two have been meeting, apparently in secret.

Dracula's power over Mina is so strong that he can summon her from a distance. As she weakens, he visits her in her bedroom. After being visited by him, she is refreshed and in good spirits, almost manic. Still she is losing strength overall and slipping toward death. A discussion between Dracula and Van Helsing clarifies what is happening to her: she is destined to be a vampire once she has Dracula's blood in her. The film only mentions that Dracula's blood is in Mina without explaining how. The novel, on the other hand, shows how this comes about with a graphic, gory scene in which Dracula, on Mina's bed, slits open his own vein with his sharp, clawlike fingernail. Her husband Harker sits by, powerless, as she consumes the blood.

In the end, Van Helsing and Harker wrongly assume that Mina has undergone the transformation to be a full vampire and that she is in the coffin next to Dracula's. After the count is killed and she is released from his spell, she is able to explain to them that Dracula was stopped by the coming of daylight before he could finish killing her.

Van Helsing

Professor Abraham Van Helsing (his first name is given in the novel but is not mentioned in the film) is played by character actor Edward Van Sloan, who played the role in the Broadway production of the story. Van Sloan became a familiar face to fans of Universal horror movies, playing key roles in *Frankenstein* later in 1931 and in *The Mummy* the following year.

Van Helsing is called in to look into the strange case of Renfield. The novel explains that Doctor Seward was once Van Helsing's student and summoned his former mentor from Amsterdam to consult on the Renfield case, though that fact would make little sense in the film, since the age difference between Van Helsing and Seward in the film is not great enough. Still, the first scene in which Van Helsing appears, consulting with other unnamed scientists, shows a mountain in the background behind him, indicating that he is experimenting on Renfield's blood in the Netherlands, not London.

Van Helsing is presented as a mixture of scientist and mystic. He examines Renfield's blood with a chemical experiment that helps him determine the presence of a vampire, but he also is familiar with folklore about vampires. He carries wolfsbane, knowing that it can repel the vampire, a function that is filled in the novel by garlic flowers. He knows that the vampire does not cast a reflection in mirrors (according to tradition, this is because it does not have a soul) and that icons of Catholicism, particularly the cross, render the vampire powerless. As Dracula states, Van Helsing is wise for a man who has only lived one lifetime.

Because of his knowledge and his belief in things that others would dismiss as superstition, Van Helsing becomes Dracula's only serious threat. At one point in the film, the vampire attempts to take control of his will, but Van Helsing manages to break free of Dracula's spell after a prolonged struggle.

Lucy Weston

In Stoker's novel, Lucy's last name is "Westenra," but it is shortened for the film. She is Mina's best friend and elicits marriage proposals from two men—an American adventurer from Texas and Dr. John Seward—before accepting the proposal of Arthur Holmwood, an aristocrat. She initially falls under Dracula's spell at a distance, before the count even arrives in England.

In the film, however, she first meets Dracula when he introduces himself to the Seward party at a concert, and she becomes fascinated with his mysterious air. He quickly begins feeding off of her blood. In the film, Lucy dies quickly, while

Stoker's novel has an extended sequence during which her three beaus, under Van Helsing's command, give her blood transfusions in an attempt to revive her.

Both versions refer to Lucy returning after her death, leaving her family crypt to haunt the London streets as the beautiful Lady in White, who kidnaps children and drains their blood. While the novel is graphic in its details of how Van Helsing and the others drive a stake through her heart, cut off her head, and stuff her mouth with garlic, thereby freeing her soul to go to heaven, such details could not be shown on screen in 1931. According to film historian David J. Skal, the shooting script of *Dracula* included a scene in the crypt with Van Helsing, off camera, killing the undead Lucy with a stake, but the final film leaves her fate to the audience's imagination.

THEMES

Mortality

At one point, when his true nature as a vampire has been revealed, Count Dracula observes, "For one who has not lived even a single lifetime, you are a wise man, Van Helsing." The fact that the vampire is "undead" but can remained animated for hundreds of years beyond a normal human life span is one of the most important features of vampires of legend. Like many stories of the supernatural, including stories about zombies, vampire legends attribute the creature's ability to stay alive to eating or drinking certain substances, such as human blood.

Still, the narrative structure of this story is based on the fact that Dracula can die. His life is surrounded by imagery of death everywhere, from the casket he first rises out of to the cemetery Lucy inhabits after her funeral. Dracula is shown to be, above all, human. His ultimate death, after centuries of life, is not the dramatic event it could be. In Stoker's novel, the vampire must not only have a stake driven through its heart but also have its head decapitated. Social standards of the time would never have allowed Dracula's or Lucy's physical destruction to be shown on screen, so the significance of their "eternal" lives being cut short is muted in this film portrayal.

Seduction

The stage adaptations of Dracula that preceded Browning's film began the transformation of

READ,
WATCH,
WRITE,

- Read one of the books in Melissa de la Cruz's Blue Bloods series of young-adult novels about young, wealthy New York vampires, such as *Bloody Valentine*, *Masquerade*, or *Misguided Angel*. Write a short story about this film's characters—Dracula, Van Helsing, Lucy, and John Harker—adapting de la Cruz's style to their situation.

- At one point while the action is in London, Dracula, the Transylvanian, tells Van Helsing, who is from Amsterdam, "It would be well for you to return to your own country." In what ways do these two characters represent the immigration debate in your own country? Find two contemporary opinion pieces about immigration: one about immigrants like Van Helsing and one about immigrants like Dracula, and quote from them as you write your own opinion piece about why Dracula should have been expelled from Britain.

- Write an essay that compares the attributes that this film gives to the vampire with the vampire legends of another country. For example, a good list of Asian vampire legends can be found at http://homepages.udayton. edu/~jfarrelly1/Vampires/asian.htm

- Bela Lugosi's portrayal of Dracula is different from the way the character is presented in Bram Stoker's novel. Beliefs about vampirism have evolved since then. Watch several episodes of a vampire television series, such as *The Vampire Chronicles* or *Buffy the Vampire Slayer*. Record the elements of the modern series that you think should be credited to the makers of the 1931 film, whether they are aspects of the characters or filming

techniques, and present your findings, with video clips, to your class.

- For an extended part of the novel, Mina Harker helps in the search for Dracula, as he flees back to his homeland, even as she feels herself falling increasingly under his influence. The 1931 film makes her a more traditional damsel in distress who needs to be saved by the men around her. Write and perform a short scene that adapts Mina's important contribution to the fight against Dracula to the film's story, which has Dracula remaining in London.

- The change in Renfield's behavior after he has been put under Dracula's spell is different from the way most people react to vampires. Review his early scenes in the film and then write a short story that shows readers how Renfield behaved before going to Transylvania. Make sure your depiction of him shows the personality traits that would make him go insane from the vampire's bite.

- The fact that the character of Dracula has been adapted to film and graphic novels so often indicates that there is something very visual about the vampire. At the same time, there are elements about the vampire legend, such as eternal life and the need to victimize people, that are powerful in themselves. If you had to choose, would you say that the visual elements or the character elements are the most important for the vampire's continuing popularity? Cite examples from this film and from any other appropriate media to support your point in an essay.

Stoker's character Dracula from a frightening, bat-like, foul-breathed creature to a charming gentleman. On stage, the role was played by a succession of handsome leading men, including Lugosi himself.

In the novel, Dracula's power to control others' minds is more general and not as explicitly a function of his personal charm. For instance, Stoker shows both Renfield and Lucy under Dracula's mental control before he even arrives in

England to meet them in person. In Browning's film, however, Renfield is turned into a vampire after being overcome by Dracula's brides, and Lucy is enchanted with Dracula when she meets him at the symphony. Both Lucy and, later, Mina, fall under the vampire's control when he comes to them in their bedrooms. While this hints at a sexual relationship, it avoids the exchange of blood that the novel explains is significant in the process of overpowering their will.

Good and Evil

There is no question that, charming as he may be, Dracula is the film's representative of evil. In both the film and the novel he tries, awkwardly, to convince the guest at his castle and the people at the Seward Sanitarium that he is a worldly aristocrat who is curious about English customs. Both versions of the story quickly supply reasons for their audiences to doubt his sincerity. Eventually, when confronted with evidence of his evil plans, Dracula drops his pretenses and becomes direct in his evil, as when he directly threatens Van Helsing, who knows that Dracula is a supernatural being.

In Stoker's novel, Dracula is opposed by a group of men who seek to protect Mina from him, each of whom brings a different element to the fight: the aristocrat, the hunter, the psychiatrist, and the occultist. The film simplifies the equation by countering Dracula's evil presence with Van Helsing's gentle goodness. The battle of wills they wage for the soul of Mina and for the entire world, which could be infected if vampires were left to propagate, is made clear in one specific scene in the sanitarium's library. Dracula tries to control Van Helsing's mind, using all of his evil power, and Van Helsing remains pure with the strength of his soul, giving him the ability to bring Mina back before she becomes an evil creature herself.

Supernatural

The supernatural elements of Dracula are explained to the characters in the story, and therefore to the audience, by Professor Van Helsing, a scientist who understands elements of vampirism. As in the novel, Van Helsing is clearly an educated man who can view the situation rationally, as an outsider to Mina Harker's social world. He does not abide by superstitions, but he does know enough to admit the existence of things that science is unable to measure. When he sees

(© Pictorial Press Ltd / Alamy)

that Dracula does not cast a shadow, for instance, he knows it to be a characteristic of the vampire, and he knows enough to carry with him a sprig of wolfsbane, a folk tradition said to weaken the vampire's power.

Many of the supernatural elements attributed to vampires in the novel are carried over to the film. Emphasis is given to aspects of the legend that create a striking effect on screen while staying within the film's limited budget. For instance, Dracula turns into a wolf in the novel at least as often as he turns into a bat, but the bat appears several times in the film, while his wolf presence is only talked about. His ability to control minds is visualized for audiences with close-ups on Bela Lugosi's hypnotic eyes.

The film's visual style does much to imply Dracula's supernatural abilities. The spiders and rats that infest Castle Dracula and Carfax Abbey indicate the count's age and his association with death, while the armadillos that appear in his castle prepare viewers' minds for bizarre sights to come. In particular, the film uses fog of varying density to indicate Dracula's ability to appear and disappear at will.

STYLE

German Expressionism

The fog and shadows, the huge crumbling settings, and the askew camera angles that give *Dracula* its sinister feel are all film techniques that were developed in German silent film industry during the 1920s. Today, German expressionism is recognized as one of the most distinct and influential movements in film history. This style arose in the German film industry after World War I, after Germany had suffered tremendous losses of life and economic devastation. The bleak outlook faced by the country's citizens was reflected in its films, which took on a style that came to be called expressionist: the look aimed more for subjectivity, reflecting inner emotions and turmoil, than for reality.

German expressionist films often presented stories of crime or horror: the first film made from Bram Stoker's novel, F. W. Murnau's *Nosferatu*, is one of the most solid examples of this style, as is Fritz Lang's *Dr. Mabuse, the Gambler*, which is about a criminal mastermind who can control the minds of people from a distance, through telepathy. These films generally use lighting effects and exaggerated visual elements to convey the emotional turmoil of a world that makes no sense. Though the London scenes of *Dracula* are fairly common, the exaggeration of the Transylvania settings is clearly derived from the German expressionist visual style.

Gothic Tone

The field of architecture was the first to use the word *gothic* to identify a style popularized in the Middle Ages that focused on curves instead of the straight lines of classical design. Like Castle Dracula and Carfax Abbey in this film, gothic architecture uses high, pointed arches, spires, and vaulted entryways to draw the eye up from the commonness of life on the ground.

Gothic literature is generally traced to Horace Walpole's 1765 novel *The Castle of Otranto*, which was a strong influence on the romantic movement of the early nineteenth century, who in turn influenced the Victorian writers who came after them, including Stoker. Gothic literature is generally associated with, among other things, the supernatural, which spawns from an exotic locale (such as Transylvania in this film) and often includes an ancient curse; with evil villains and noble heroes (the last is hazy in *Dracula*,

since John Harker is the handsome male lead but Van Helsing is the one who actually battles the villain); and with extremely gruesome behaviors, such as Renfield's predilection for eating insects. *Dracula* is one of the first films to translate the gothic style to a mainstream movie, bringing these literary elements into a new age.

CULTURAL CONTEXT

Bram Stoker's 1897 novel *Dracula* was certainly not the first work to dig through the ancient folk tales about vampirism for fictional purposes. In *The Dracula Book*, Donald F. Glut lists four influential vampire novels from the nineteenth century that probably influenced Stoker, going back to *The Vampyre*, published in 1919 by a secretary to Lord Byron, who started writing the original version of the tale in response to the same challenge that induced Mary Wollstonecraft Shelley to write her novel *Frankenstein*. Stoker researched his subject thoroughly throughout the 1890s, and his novel shows familiarity with legends as well as literary sources. At some point in the writing of his vampire story, he combined it with historical records of the life of Vlad "the Impaler," a Hungarian warlord who lived in Transylvania from 1430 to 1474 and earned an enduring reputation for unspeakable barbarism against his own people. Vlad, whose surname was Dracula (derived from the Latin for "dragon"), was said to have drank the blood of his enemies and to have adorned his castle with the bodies of thousands of his victims impaled on stakes. By imagining his novel's main character to be the undying Vlad Dracula, Stoker gave his vampire tale an air of historical accuracy that made it more frightening.

Stoker's novel is a product of its time. For one thing, it shows a worldview that is curious, yet naive, about the world outside of England. Transylvania, a region of Romania, is presented in the novel as a mysterious, distant, backward land, ruled by superstition, a place where supernatural powers might actually exist. Information travels from Transylvania to England by letters, which take weeks from posting to delivery. The Transylvanian terrain is not developed enough to support rail travel in Stoker's version, so people travel by coaches across the land and sailing vessels between continents. Late in the book, characters race to Dracula's castle via steamships

(© AF Archive / Alamy)

on Romanian rivers but are stopped when the ship is disabled.

The novel shows the sensibilities of Victorian England. Today, Victorianism is associated with prudishness about sexuality, reflecting the moral code of Queen Victoria, who ruled Great Britain from 1837 to 1901. When *Dracula* moves to England and the Count begins preying on first Lucy and then Mina, the novel hints at sexuality without ever openly addressing it, as in the scene in which Dracula drinks Mina's blood from her neck and opens a vein in his own chest to force her to drink his own blood. Even more strongly indicative of Victorian attitudes is the novel's strict adherence to traditional gender roles. As Elizabeth Lee puts it on *The Victorian Web*, the Victorians thought that basic biology caused male and female differentiation. They believed that "women's position in society came from biological evolution—she had to stay at home in order to conserve her energy, while the man

could and needed to go out and hunt or forage." After Lucy's death, her three suitors—Dr. Seward, Quincy Morris, and Arthur Holmwood—join Mina's husband, Harker, to protect Mina from Dracula, showing the chivalrous attitude of medieval knights to a damsel in distress. As Mina feels herself drawn into Dracula's power, which can easily be read as a growing awareness of her own sexual appetite, she frequently reflects on her need for her husband's protection, even though readers see him as more powerless and clueless than herself.

Universal Studios won the rights to the film adaptation in the late 1920s, following a successful stage version that ran in London and then on Broadway. The Transylvanian scenes, with their crumbling structures, Germanic architecture, and old-world peasants, evoke a bygone era, a mood that the London scenes do little to dispel: as David J. Skal points out in a commentary track to the DVD, the sound of car engines that herald the first London scene are the film's first indication that it is meant to take place in the modern age. There are few other modern conveniences present in the film. Electric lights and telephones are seen, but they are less important to the plot than horse-drawn carriages and kerosene lanterns.

Hollywood had successfully presented horror stories before, most notably with the 1925 silent version of Gaston Leroux's novel *The Phantom of the Opera* and a 1923 film of Victor Hugo's *The Hunchback of Notre Dame*. Stoker's story had even been filmed before, giving the basic structure to Murnau's 1922 masterpiece *Nosferatu: A Symphony of Horror*. Still, the studio was concerned that the horror elements would be too unpleasant for film audiences of the 1930s. They humanized the vampire more than Stoker or Murnau had done, presenting him as a well-mannered sophisticate who also happened to be a monster. As it turned out, the audiences of the Great Depression that had begun two years before *Dracula*'s release were turning to films for escapism, and horror movies took off. Later that year, *Frankenstein*, starring Boris Karloff and directed by James Whale, solidified the notion that monsters worked on-screen, and the following year Karl Freund, the cinematographer of *Dracula*, directed Karloff in *The Mummy*, establishing the horror monster film as a standard Hollywood genre in a way that would not have been conceivable before *Dracula*.

CRITICAL OVERVIEW

When Universal Studios bought the rights to film *Dracula* in 1930, they knew that they were dealing with a familiar, trustworthy property. The source material, Bram Stoker's novel, had been a success upon its publication 33 years earlier, and the London and Broadway shows based on the novel had both enjoyed long theatrical runs. However, the film's release on February 13, 1931—the Friday the 13th release was a publicity gimmick—saw critical responses that were uneven. For instance, Irene Thirer, writing in the *New York Daily News* (quoted by Donald F. Glut in *The Dracula Book*), points out that the film was "superbly photographed" and that Bela Lugosi, in the title role, was "simply grand." She concludes that the film's producer, Carl Laemmle, Jr., "chose director, cast, and story wisely." On the other hand, Norbert Lusk, writing for the *Los Angeles Times* (as quoted by David J. Skal in *Hollywood Gothic*) was dismissive: "Plainly a freak picture, it must be accepted as a curiosity devoid of the important element of sympathy that causes the widest appeal." Some critics were taken by the film's opening sequence, the scenes in Transylvania, and its exciting conclusion, while finding that it sagged with too much talk in the middle.

Audiences, however, found it to be the sort of escapism they were waiting for. The first week's box office earnings were nothing spectacular, and studio executives gave up hope for a financial smash, but the film proved able to pull in sizable audiences week after week. By the end of its first American release, it had earned twice what it had cost, and it was responsible for Universal turning a profit for the first time in years.

In spite of its initial success and the hold that *Dracula* has had over the popular imagination over the years, the public lost interest in it when *Frankenstein* was released at the end of 1931. Since then, *Dracula* has lived on as a part of the Universal Studios pantheon of monster films that includes *Frankenstein*, *The Mummy* (1932), and *The Wolfman* (1941), but over the years, people have remembered the character more fondly than the film. The *Time Out Film Guide* summarizes the contemporary attitude toward the film, pointing out that "the pace falters, and with the London scenes growing in verbosity and staginess, the hammy limitations of Lugosi's performance are cruelly exposed." In spite of these liabilities, *Time Out* recommends *Dracula*, with overall praise for cinematographer Karl Freund's "astonishingly fluid and brilliantly shot" camerawork and the film's "innumerable imaginative touches."

CRITICISM

David Kelly

Kelly is a novelist and an instructor of literature and creative writing. In the following essay, he compares the three most important film versions of Stoker's novel: F. W. Murnau's Nosferatu, *Tod Browning's* Dracula, *and Francis Ford Coppola's* Bram Stoker's Dracula.

The name Dracula is famous worldwide. In film alone, there have been, by some estimates, more than a hundred depictions of the character,

WHAT DO I SEE NEXT?

- The official sequel to this film was *Dracula's Daughter*, released in 1935. It is loosely based on a short story by Bram Stoker, "Dracula's Guest," but it contains none of the first film's original cast or crew except for Edward Van Sloan, returning as Van Helsing, and a brief glimpse of Lugosi's Count Dracula, dead in his coffin. Still, it follows the original in mood and setting. It is currently available on DVD from Universal and is relevant for all ages.

- Stephenie Meyer's series of *Twilight* novels shows the direct influence of Bela Lugosi, who transformed the image of the vampire from a bat-like creature to a suave gentleman. Meyer's character, Edward Cullen, is a handsome and misunderstood vampire. The first book was released as a film, *Twilight*, in 2008. It is rated PG-13 for some violence and a scene of sensuality.

- Novelist Ann Rice built a powerful international reputation for her books about vampires and the occult, especially her Vampire Chronicles series featuring the vampire Lestat. Tom Cruise plays Lestat in the 1994 film *Interview with the Vampire*. Directed by Neil Jordan, the film also stars Brad Pitt, Antonio Banderas, and Kirsten Dunst. It was given an R rating, primarily for violent imagery.

- The current trend of imagining vampire mythology in a high school setting was preceded by the acclaimed 1987 film *The Lost Boys*. It features Jason Patric and Cory Haim as teens who have moved to a new town and find themselves trapped between a gang of vampires, led by Kiefer Sutherland, and the vampire hunters who battle them. Its reputation as a classic of the genre has grown since its original release. This film is rated R because of its graphic horror elements.

- Over the decades, the reputation of *Dracula* has faded in favor of the other iconic monster film released by Universal in 1931, *Frankenstein*. Like *Dracula*, *Frankenstein* was based on a classic novel. Director Whale created a film that focuses more on action, mixing the eerie mood of *Dracula* with some of the philosophical implications of Mary Shelley's 1819 novel. Karloff's portrayal of the monster is as definitive as Lugosi's Dracula was. *Frankenstein* does not have an official rating but is appropriate for all ages.

- The 2000 film *Shadow of the Vampire* is based on the premise of a real vampire playing the role of one in one of the earliest film versions of the Dracula story, Murnau's 1922 German silent movie *Nosferatu*. Willem Dafoe turns in a stunning performance as the actor Max Schreck, whose eerie portrayal came, according to this film, from real life. John Malkovich plays the director obsessed with recording an authentic experience. This film contains horror content and some sexuality, as well as references to drug use, and may not be appropriate for younger students.

- Despite a long career in Hollywood and the dozens of movies that featured the title character of this film, Bela Lugosi himself played Count Dracula only one more time, in the 1949 comedy/drama *Abbot and Costello Meet Frankenstein*, which has the comedians battling Dracula, Frankenstein, and the Wolf Man among the same looming castle and swamp sets that established the mood for the great Universal films. This classic film is appropriate for all ages and is available on DVD.

---

showing him as anything from a lovable goofball to a heartless parasite. Most of these film appearances do not need serious attention. The vast majority are mere exploitations of the name, substituting the word "Dracula" for "vampire," or even just "monster."

THE FACT THAT *DRACULA* WAS BASED ON A
RECENT STAGE VERSION IS PAINFULLY EVIDENT,
AS IS THE FACT THAT THE STUDIO, HAVING NO
TRACK RECORD WITH SUPERNATURAL TALKIES,
WAS TIGHT WITH ITS BUDGET."

When discussing movie versions directly drawn from Bram Stoker's 1897 novel, there are three that stand out as representatives of the fine art of novel-to-film adaptation. The first screen version, F. W. Murnau's silent film *Nosferatu*, released in Germany in 1922, followed the novel's basic story line and mood, even though the producers changed the title and characters' names because they could not secure the rights to Stoker's novel (the changes did not help much: they lost a lawsuit brought by Stoker's widow, and the courts ordered all prints of the film gathered up and destroyed, though at least one survived this purge). The second version is the one that everyone thinks of when they talk about Dracula, the film released by Universal Pictures in 1932, featuring Bela Lugosi's definitive performance. The third, directed by Francis Ford Coppola, has the weight of modern filmmaking effects behind it. Its title, *Bram Stoker's Dracula*, makes it seem as if it would be more true to the novel than others, but that title is just another fluke of the copyright laws, since another studio owned the rights to the simple title *Dracula*.

Finding any of these films better than the others is, of course, a matter of taste. Some people absolutely refuse to watch a film in black and white, and they would eliminate the first two without consideration. Some will not consider a silent film. Some will not consider an R-rated film. Accepting that everyone has different subjective methods of measuring, though, it is still possible to decide on certain criteria in judging a film adaptation of a novel. The film's relation to the source material is a consideration, though that can be slippery: no one wants to see a film that merely acts out scenes from the book, but on the other hand an adaptation that strays too far from the original does not really earn its name. Even more relevant are the standards that should be applied to any film, whether it is an adaptation or not, such as its use of available technology and its focus on a relevant and moving story.

Regarding the question of technology, for instance, Coppola's film might at first seem unapproachable. In fact, the entire film seems to have no real reason for its existence than to show off the state of special effects artistry, circa 1992. Throughout the program, viewers can sit gape-jawed, watching very convincing imagery as Dracula morphs into several different people and several different species before their very eyes, while Wojciech Kilar's orchestral soundtrack hammers home the story's old-world seriousness. They can watch Dracula fly through the air while standing immobile. They can see his shadow move independently of his body's motions. They can watch conjoined women scamper from a bed in the middle of a bloody orgy, with top and bottom torsos flailing about like segments of a giant insect.

Nosferatu, though made in the early days of film, is actually a very close second to *Bram Stoker's Dracula* in technological sophistication. What Murnau did not have available to him in effects he made up for with imagination and consistency. From the vampire's make-up to the shadows to the streets of London, everything is seen as elongated, stretched, and twisted, the way it might be in a nightmare. Sound is irrelevant, and different soundtracks have been added to the film over the years, but the visuals show a solid understanding that Stoker's story, which itself is not entirely coherent, is best understood as a fevered dream. Coppola's version seems to follow this interpretation, but Murnau's accomplishment is greater since he had no earlier interpretation to follow, as Coppola did.

Film technique is clearly the weakest in Browning's *Dracula*. There are inspired visuals, mainly having to do with Dracula's castle and the mountains that were seamlessly created with two-dimensional paintings, inside and out, to imply the gothic majesty that the Count has ruled with fading influence for centuries. For every well-crafted background or set design, though, Browning presents a rubber bat—hanging in a doorway or bouncing along to lead a horse team—or a drawn-out discussion between two or three people, standing around in a room looking at each other, filmed at a distance, mid- to full-body, even though nothing is moving. Coppola's film offers several variations on the human/animal

(© Moviestore Collection Ltd / Alamy)

hybrid: Browning's, for the most part, has people standing in a doorway after Dracula has left, saying, "Look at that wolf running across the lawn." The fact that *Dracula* was based on a recent stage version is painfully evident, as is the fact that the studio, having no track record with supernatural talkies, was tight with its budget.

Where the Tod Browning film *Dracula* overtakes Coppola's *Bram Stoker's Dracula* is in solid storytelling. The Coppola version has a series of amazing special effects, but that is really all that it has. To make sense of the inexplicable way Stoker's novel moved the action to Transylvania, then to the English coast, then to London, then back to the Transylvanian countryside, Coppola's screenwriter, James V. Hart, framed the whole thing in a love story. Fifteenth-century count Vlad the Impaler is not just a bloodthirsty sadist here, nor a supernatural monster, but he is a man who has consciously become a vampire so that he can be on earth when his dead wife comes back to life. Count Dracula's focus on Mina Harking, then, is not his victimization of her,

as she comes to recognize that he is indeed her soul mate of centuries past. Aside from the liberties this takes with the character as Stoker imagined him and from what history tells about the ancient count, it also fails as a narrative device: there is no time for the film to establish a deep and passionate love between Vlad and Mrs. Vlad, but the story drives forward nonetheless, even though the character's motive and the introduction of his supernatural power are poorly explained.

In contrast, the Dracula that Lugosi created has enthralled, frightened, and amused generations for a reason. To put this version on film, Browning cut out much of Stoker's novel, removing and combining characters at will, and any remaining plot holes are filled with Lugosi's mesmerizing screen presence. Unlike Gary Oldman's always-weird Dracula in Coppola's film, Lugosi manages to be convincingly appealing and threatening in everything he does. This Dracula, at the beginning of the film, starts with the idea of moving from his ruined castle to London; he moves to London; he meets a small, closed circle of just four people (Harker, Seward, Mina, and Lucy); and he dies in London. The plot's simplification allows more room for the film's eerie attitude, while the Coppola version, trying to add much more of Stoker's plot and then adding more mood on top of that, only allows viewers room for wonder.

The limitations of storytelling in *Nosferatu* are the limitations of the silent film itself. Actors seem over-expressive, which is a result of director Murnau's style mixed with the requirements of the medium. Happiness becomes giddiness, fear becomes cowering, and menace is best shown with snarling here. In between the scenes of over-sized acting are the title cards, letting viewers know where they are and what emotions the actors are about to act out. Combining printed words with acting necessarily takes movie viewers out of the moment every now and then, reminding them that this is just a movie. Like Coppola's film, Murnau's does a fine job of offering readers visual interpretations of things they have read in the novel, but it does not have the ability to render its story as one coherent entity.

When judging a film, it would seem that the criteria should include more than just what the filmmakers are able to record, no matter how competently or even how powerfully they mix their images together. The most relevant measure should be the story they tell. Strangely, for all its affectations and limitations, Browning's version of Stoker's novel does address what is central to the book, the story of an evil man living among modern people, curious about their ways and how to exploit them. *Bram Stoker's Dracula* has its admirers, but even the most glowing reviews do little more than praise it as eye candy. *Nosferatu* changed the way film, especially horror films, could capture fear on celluloid, but it is an advanced study, a filmmaker's film. After eighty years, there is a reason people look at the Dracula presented by Tod Browning as the "real" one, which all others are simply imitating: by the time the credits roll, viewers *know* this character.

Source: David Kelly, Critical Essay on *Dracula*, in *Novels for Students*, Gale, Cengage Learning, 2013.

Kathi Maio

In the following review, Maio traces the evolving image of the vampire in film.

If asked to name a cultural indicator that this country is going to hell in a hand basket, different people would name different things: Madonna, the S & L scams, oat bran, carjacking,

> " OLD BELA LUGOSI COULD DO MORE WITH AN EYEBROW THAN GARY OLDMAN CAN DO (THROUGH NO FAULT OF HIS OWN) WITH $100,000 OF HIGH-TECH FRIPPERY."

the vote against gay rights in Colorado, the Totally Hair Barbie, the Woody Allen-Mia Farrow scandal, Ice-T, the proliferation of Espresso stands, the beating of Rodney King (and/or the Simi Valley verdict, and/or the riots in South Central L.A), the price of a pair of basketball sneakers, the fact that George Bush was elected president, the fact that George Bush wasn't re-elected president, the issuing of an Elvis postage stamp, or the shrinking size of the American candy bar.

I might add the growing popularity and evolving image of the vampire in film to that list. Once upon a time, a vampire was a monster who filled the viewer's heart with dread. Now he is a heroic figure, and a sex-symbol to boot. And I am none too pleased with his transformation. Sometimes, I am even mildly alarmed by it.

I don't like vampires. As cultural icons, they are truly disgusting. Not only would I not like to meet up with one in a dark castle, I do not even wish to see another movie about them. Vampires aren't just violent killers, they are total socio-paths. Their greatest pleasure—their only pleasure—comes from the pain of others. They enslave and murder, and can still get a good day's sleep.

And decadent? These guys and gals practically define the term. Decay is their natural element. Undead, yet not living, they are rotters who sleep in dirt-filled coffins, but who party by night in really swell (miraculously clean) outfits.

Vampires are robber-barons. Their wealth and power came at great price . . . to other people.

Is there something heroic in that? Not to me. I find the vampire hunter to be the hero of these stories. Which is why, of the current spate of blood-sucker movies, *Buffy the Vampire Slayer* is my favorite. Despite the fact that a few of the stars phoned in their performances and director Fran Rubel Kazui exhibited [a] woefully leaden hand with farce, *Buffy* was a film I genuinely enjoyed. This light-weight tale of a Valley Girl (played with winning energy and charm by Kristy Swanson) coming of age as a warrior, was about empowerment instead of surrender.

Which probably accounts, even more than the above-mentioned faults, for why it bombed at the box-office. It has reached the point where vampire tales are the ultimate romance novels.... Female leads are no longer innocent victims, violated in their sleep (as in Browning's 1931 *Dracula*). Nor are they noble wives who seek to save others by sacrificing themselves (see either *Nosferatu*). These days, they are... gals panting to have their jugular ripped, along with their bodice.

They want it. Are dying for it, in fact. They wear red see-through nighties to bed in the hopes of a visit from a demon. They offer their neck (and every other part of their anatomy) willingly. They want nothing more than to give up everything to their seducer. Their life's blood, their life, nothing is too much to sacrifice for the chance to be totally possessed by an abusive hunk.

Although this might sound like a male fantasy, they say that women are the most avid consumers of these sado-masochistic fabricators. And although I never thought I'd live to see the day when a woman would write a book (however ironic) entitled *How to Get a Date with a Vampire*, I can see how the marketing of vampires as dream-dates is made possible, given the modern woman's confusion about her life in a "post-feminist" world. So many responsibilities and choices. So much frustration and stress. The idea of giving (it) up, of being completely controlled by a "lover," can be made powerfully attractive.

Of course, I'm not trying to lay this tainted bloodlust culture directly at the feet of the women's movement. (On the contrary.) Even before the first issue of *Ms.*, in the sixties and early seventies, some vampires were already being portrayed as melancholy anti-heroes women should want to take care of. I remember how any of my baby boomer girlfriends had big crushes on Barnabas (Jonathan Frid) on *Dark Shadows*. For many of my generation, *Dark Shadows* was a campy, trashy delight. Still, I can't help but rue the day soap opera was grafted to the horror story. It only got worse from there.

In 1979, by which time feminism had made an impact on popular culture, a sterling example of what Susan Faludi has termed "backlash" was produced in the disguise of the most muddled

re-telling of Bram Stoker's story. (As an example of the plot mishigas, consider that Mina and Lucy switch identities and the vampyric Mina turns out to be Van Helsing's daughter!) But support characters in John Badham's *Dracula* could be but a trifling matter when the title star was that hunka-hunk of biting love, Frank Langella.

In this elegantly somber (and ultimately dull) film, *Dracula* is a handsome and suave fellow who possesses a mesmerizing attractiveness for the ladies. Even a strong-willed (read: feminist) Lucy, played by Kate Nelligan, can't wait to be seduced (read: drained) by the mysterious, murderous stranger who moves in next door. Although Lucy is eventually saved, it is Laurence Olivier's Van Helsing who is killed. Dracula is fried by the sunlight, but the film implies that he might still have gotten away. (No doubt to allow for the possibility of sequels.)

Thankfully, there were no sequels to this particular *Dracula*. But now we have another. *Bram Stoker's Dracula*, directed by Francis Ford Coppola, and written by James V. Hart (*Hook*). Hart is making a living at reworking other people's material. And, as far as I can tell, he's none too good at it.

The director, the writer, and everyone else associated with the movie loved to say how Hart's play was "extremely faithful to the original Bram Stoker book." I know that it's been decades since I read the novel, but somehow "faithful" is not a word I'd use for this adaptation.

The horror and dread of Stoker's late Victorian gothic have been replaced with rivers of blood, numerous acts of sexual violence, ... and a Romeo and Juliet love story. All handsomely mounted, of course. Mr. Coppola knows how to make a visually stunning movie, given a few bucks. And on this project, he was entrusted with $40 million.

The costumes by Eiko Ishioka are bizarre but beautiful, the makeup by Michele Burke and a band of magicians is some of the best I've ever seen. There are some breathtaking (and sometimes nauseating) special effects. And some lovely shots, like the one of a steam locomotive rolling across the frame over pages of Jonathan's travel diary, that do capture, briefly, the book and its time period.

Still, the folks that made this movie did not trust the power of Stoker's story. And their exploitive take on the original novel cannot be completely disguised by Coppola's operatic flourishes. Especially when so many members of the cast aren't even capable of credible accents and mannerisms.

I love Winona Ryder, but she was not quite up to the role of Mina. She was unable to portray Victorian repression, and she was little better at capturing sexual obsession. But she may, at least, comfort herself with the fact that she was ten times better than co-star Keanu Reeves. One assumes that Coppola and Columbia wanted a young American star to add a little box-office draw to their "classic" story. Reeves might have fit the bill, but he certainly didn't fit the movie.

His la-dee-dah impersonation of a nineteenth-century British professional was ludicrous. He didn't seem up-tight, he seemed petrified and embarrassed. Some of the fault must go to Hart for underwriting the role of Jonathan Harker. But Keanu didn't do his reputation as an actor, nor the reputation of the movie, any good by accepting the part.

Not every American was miscast, however. Songwriter/singer Tom Waits gives a marvelous over-the-top performance as the madman, Renfield. (Anyone who ever heard Waits perform his cover of Cole Porter's "It's All Right with Me" for the *Red, Hot & Blue* album knows that the part of Renfield was practically written for him.) But it is the British stars that make Bram Stoker's *Dracula* marginally worth viewing.

As always, Anthony Hopkins gives a brilliant turn to Dr. Van Helsing. Fighting vampires can unhinge a fellow a little. And Hopkins's Van Helsing is more eccentric and less professorial than Edward Van Sloan's kindly scientist, back in 1931. Since most Americans (who didn't see, but should have, *Howard's End*) last saw Hopkins in *Silence of the Lambs*, some may see similarities between Van Helsing and Dr. Hannibal Lecter. In reality, the two performances are shaded much differently, although both offer proof of the actor's great skill.

A generation younger, Gary Oldman gives a bravura performance as Dracula. Asked to play what amounts to five different characters (bat demon, wolf-man, and three ages of Vlad the Impaler/Dracula), Oldman captured each role with equal intensity. His ancient Count was especially fine. He's the only actor I've ever seen who could make me completely forget the layers of rubber and paint and fake hair and see the natural character hidden there.

Any actor would give his eye teeth to play a vampire with that much range. But that doesn't mean the audience will enjoy seeing that many representations of one character in a single movie. The many faces of this Dracula are indicative of Hart's showy screenplay and Coppola's style-defeats-substance approach to bringing *Dracula* to the screen.

One Dracula is enough, when he is genuinely scary. Old Bela Lugosi could do more with an eyebrow than Gary Oldman can do (through no fault of his own) with $100,000 of high-tech frippery. Split into so many pieces, Dracula's personality falls apart. And, personally, I was in no mood to try to put them all together again.

Especially since Hart and Coppola were obviously trying to sell me a bill of goods about how Dracula was actually a good guy with a broken heart, a fallen searching for his one true soulmate. That being the case, why would this lovelorn gentleman brutally rape.... the best friend of his beloved? Perhaps there could be a reason for this action. The film-makers do not, however, provide us with one.

The heady mix of sex and violence needs no explanation or justification in Hollywood these days. And the vampire story provides the perfect mythic narrative framework to which the gents of tinseltown may readily attach repeated lush images of eroticized bloodletting.

Columbia's pricy production of *Dracula* is full of its own self-importance. Francis Coppola's involvement guarantees that fact. Yet it is no less exploitive than a low-budget schlocker like *The Blood of Dracula's Castle* (1967). It is only more pretentious, with spiffier special effects.

Give me a vampire film like Germany's *Jonathan* (1973)—one that portrays bloodsuckers for the fascists they are. Preserve us from high-toned trash like *Bram Stoker's Dracula*. It's the kind of movie that can leave you wondering what this world is coming to.

Source: Kathi Maio, "Bram Stoker's *Dracula*," in *Magazine of Fantasy and Science Fiction*, Vol. 84, No. 4, April 1993, p. 75.

Joyce Carol Oates

In the following excerpt, Oates describes the differences between the film and the novel versions of Dracula.

. . . Anyone opting to see a movie after forty years risks discovering that the movie will prove disappointing, if not embarrassing. I'd worried that *Dracula* as a film of 1931 would be too dated to justify discussing it in the speculative terms of an essay.

Not at all. The film is riveting throughout, intelligently and shrewdly constructed; it certainly deserves its classic status, and Bela Lugosi his fame. (As a yet more sinister, because wholly unsympathetic, brother-rival to Boris Karloff's immortal Frankenstein monster.) In terms of contemporary cinema, of course Tod Browning's film is excessively melodramatic and stagey—the presentation of visual horror, in contrast to the more subtle psychological horror that prose fiction can render, is notoriously difficult. Yet, in a darkened movie theater, with an audience, if such an audience might exist, unfamiliar with the vampire legend, how much more effective than on the screen of one's household television where all images are domesticated, thus diluted. My initial response to the film is surprise that it moves so swiftly—too swiftly? Did early audiences catch the vampire exposition flung out at them, by frightened Transylvanian peasants on the eve of Walpurgis Night? In a mode very different from the mock-Gothic, systematically digressive Stoker novel, narrated from the viewpoint of numerous diarists and letter writers, the film reveals its secrets within the first five minutes, so that there is never any suspenseful doubt about the nature of Count Dracula: we soon see him and his three wives, dressed as for a formal evening, rising from their coffins amid a nervous scuttling of rats and spiders. (These creatures are shown fleeing the vampires!) What an eerie, yet elegant sight, and how disquieting it would have been, years ago, to a child unfamiliar with the conventions of vampire lore: for, if there is anything "forbidden" about adults in the night, in their beds, in privacy and secrecy, the vision of Dracula and his wives rising from their coffins would confirm it.

A technique Tod Browning uses throughout the film, no doubt for economy's sake, is nonetheless very dramatic: we see the initial movements of an action (Dracula rising from his coffin, for instance), then the camera cuts elsewhere, then back, and now Dracula is standing composed as if he'd been there all along. His later metamorphoses from bat to man—a bat hovering in the opened French windows of a young woman's bedroom—are even more striking.

The subliminal message is: Blink just once, and the vampire is already there.

The film *Dracula* differs substantially from the novel *Dracula*, having been adapted from a play, by Bram Stoker, now apparently forgotten; it is rather sharply truncated in terms of plot development, not rushed exactly but with an air, in the concluding minutes especially, of incompletion. In place of Jonathan Harker visiting Castle Dracula for business reasons we have the less fortunate Renfield, who is quickly overcome by his sinister host, and, by way of a bloodsucking scene we are not allowed to see—the screen fades discreetly as Dracula stoops over his fallen prey—is transformed into a slave of Dracula's for the remainder of his life. Back in London, after the storm-tossed channel crossing, Renfield becomes the "zoophagous" patient of the asylum director Dr. Seward; the man is mad, exhibiting the grimaces, grins, and twitches that are the cinematic cliches of madness, yet he is mystically enlightened and even, at times, eloquent: his impassioned talk of life, life devouring life, life drawing sustenance from life, is a distillation of Darwinian theory, disturbingly contrary to Christianity's promise of spiritual redemption/ bodily resurrection. In the film, Renfield eats flies and spiders to provide him with "blood"; in the novel, he catches flies and feeds them to spiders, feeds his spiders to sparrows, and, one day, astonishes his keepers by eating the sparrows raw, and alive. Renfield's finest scene in the film is a speech of radiant madness, made to Dr. Seward and Van Helsing, a report of Dracula's Luciferian promise to him: "'Rats! Thousands of rats! All these will I give you, if you will obey me!'"

Once Dracula has relocated to London and becomes acquainted with, and attracted to, the beautiful young women Lucy Westerna and Mina Seward, Dr. Seward's daughter, the story is an erotic fantasy in which the Stranger—the Non-Englishman—seduces one too-trusting woman, and then the other, beneath the noses of their male keepers. (The men are Dr. Seward, Mina's fiance Harker, and the scientist Van Helsing, an early prototype of the "wise scientist"—as distinguished from the "mad scientist"—without whom horror and science-fiction films could not exist.) The erotic triangle is a recognizable one: the "good" (i.e., gentlemanly, proper, Christian) man and the "evil" (i.e., sensuous, duplicitous, ethnically exotic, unChristian) man compete for Woman (i.e., virginal, Christian, and of the right social class). Woman per se is naturally passive, childlike, maybe a bit stupid; the contest is solely among men of varying degrees of enlightenment and courage. Van Helsing emerges the victor, saving Mina for his friend Jonathan Harker; in another mode of the fantasy, Van Helsing would marry beautiful Mina himself.

In the novel, Lucy Westenra's seduction/ victimization/gradual death is the focus of much narrative concern; in the movie, the young woman is dispatched quickly, after a single visualized nocturnal appearance of Dracula in her room. Lucy's subsequent career as a vampire (who preys upon small children) is sketchily treated, and the extraordinary scene in the novel in which Van Helsing and his friends drive a stake into her heart, in a lurid, prurient mock-rape, is omitted entirely. (So violent, brutal, erotically charged, and, indeed, horrific a scene could scarcely have been filmed in 1931, though it would be a delight for our special-effects movie technicians to prepare today.) So abstract is this Dracula in its depictions of vampire-assault and ritual vampire-killing, so greatly does it depend upon dialogue summary, it might be possible for an uninformed or a very young viewer to miss the point altogether. What are those people in evening dress doing to one another?

It is the subtle, suggestive, disturbing appeal of the vampire that makes of the Dracula legend a very different fantasy from, for instance, that of the werewolf or the golem (Frankenstein's monster being a species of golem), whose grotesque physical appearance is sheerly repugnant and could never be construed as "seductive." The most insidious evil is that which makes of us, not victims, or not victims merely, but accomplices; enthusiastic converts to our own doom. The way of the vampire is the way of an absolute addiction—for the taste of blood one might substitute virtually any other substance, legal or otherwise. One of the special strengths of the vampire, Van Helsing warns in the film, is that people will not believe in him—"rational" people— but it is primarily women who resist believing in his evil; like Lucy Westenra (whose name is transparently obvious—she suggests "Westernization," rebellious female doubt of patriarchal tradition), who becomes a vampire, and Mina Seward, who, but for the zeal of her male protectors, would have succumbed to the same fate. The beautiful blond actress Helen Chandler plays the role of Mina in the film as convincingly as one might do in so circumscribed a context; her one animated scene, when she is infused with a bit of Dracula's rich, centuries-old, Transylvanian blood,

shows her surprising and exciting her staid English fiance with an unexpected erotic intensity otherwise absent from the film. The struggle is not really between the forces of good and evil, or even between Christianity and paganism, but between "propriety" and "the forbidden."

Dracula is, on the surface at least, a resolutely chaste film. If lovely female bodies are violated by Dracula, the actions are never visually depicted; no skin is punctuated; the "two small holes" said to be discovered on the throats of victims are never shown. In the novel, Dracula's wives speak lasciviously of their bloodsucking as "kisses"—the most voluptuous scene in the entire novel occurs in Castle Dracula, as a beautiful young female vampire stoops over to "kiss" the semi-conscious Harker ("I closed my eyes in languorous ecstasy and waited—waited with beating heart")—but in the film Dracula's power seems primarily that of the master hypnotist, eyes gleaming, fingers outstretched like talons, capable of bending others to his will. His stylized movement as he bends toward a victim's throat only symbolically suggests a kiss, and only a psychoanalytic theorist, committed to seeing sexual imagery in all things, could argue that the vampire's "kiss" is a metonymical displacement for rape, or any physical, genital act. Is the vampire's "kiss" simply a "kiss"?—not on the lips, which might signal both complicity and adulthood, but on the throat, as a child is kissed, blessed, with no expectation of a response? Certainly the vampire legend, like many such classic-horror legends, has about it the air of the nursery. At their cores, these are cautionary tales for the infant in us all.

I note in passing how truly oblique this 1931 *Dracula* is: in a film in which blood is so crucial, no blood at all is ever shown on screen, except when Renfield, in Castle Dracula, accidentally cuts his finger as Dracula stares hungrily.

The true horror of Dracula, as I've suggested, lies in the man's will. He has an uncanny ability, which Bela Lugosi makes credible, to mesmerize his victims, thus to make them want him— this, one of the vampire's secrets, that the virtuous victim, who is us, can so readily be transformed into the evil accomplice-disciple. (As moviegoers are "seduced" by screen actors and actresses— otherwise, why movies at all?) Not mere destruction of the sort other, ugly, "monstrous" villains threaten, but the awakening of desire in the victim; an unholy, loathsome, yet clearly enormously exciting complicity in being damned. Civilization is a structure of artfully coded taboos, and taboos entice us to violate them, if for no other reason than to rebel against our parents, teachers, spiritual leaders who have indoctrinated us, or tried to, into the accumulated wisdom of the tribe. There is a yet more pernicious, because so romantic, sense that Dracula's interest in a woman is a consequence of her beauty. The most beautiful woman is the most desired woman, the most desired woman is not killed, but made a bride: this is her, and (our?) reward.

It's a matter of social class, too. The hapless little flower-girl, a street vendor, is a victim of Dracula's, but, unlike Lucy and Mina, she is merely killed. No mystery why.

The wish that desire of a brutal, primitive, Darwinian sort be rooted in physical attractiveness, thus in our individuality—this is surely one of mankind's most tragic, because infantile and enduring, fantasies, the secret fuel of sado-masochistic relations, in life as in art. To be raped—to be murdered—to be devoured—because we are irresistible: what solace! That we might simply be devoured, as Renfield devours his flies, for the "life" in us, and at once forgotten, is too terrible a truth to be articulated.

Art, by its selectivity, is always a matter of fabrication: thus its great value, its solace. Lie to us, we beg of our cruder fantasies, collective no less than private.

"There are far worse things awaiting man than death."

Dracula's enigmatic remark, made in Dr. Seward's drawing room, passes virtually unheard in that context, though it is perhaps the most disturbing idea in the Dracula-legend. In other versions of *Dracula* (Werner Herzog's 1978 remake *Nosferatu the Vampyre*) the isolated and tragic nature of the vampire is explored; the vampire is less villain than suffering victim of a curse; an oblique kinship is suggested between Dracula and the rest of humanity—for aren't we all blood-drinkers?—carnivores—don't we all, in a myriad of ways, prey upon one another? This, the vampire's most startling secret, allows us to feel a tug of sympathy for Dracula, seeing that he is not really immortal or supranatural, but trapped in flesh, condemned to forever feed upon the warm blood of living creatures. Tod Browning's film is of course a conventional one structurally, and does not explore this theme. As the film moves to its prescribed ending scenes are accelerated, condensed; there is a chase scene of a sort, Dracula with Mina in his arms, Van Helsing and Harker in pursuit; as Dracula lies helpless in his coffin, Van Helsing, unassisted, quickly dispatches him with a stake through his heart, and the story is over. Fear has been aroused, fear has been protracted, fear is now banished: THE END is truly the end.

Strange, and revealing of the habits of mind to which we are all heir, that images that may endure in the memory for decades can be discovered, upon a re-examination, to have been strung out like beads on an invisible yet always palpable "plot"—the tyranny, not just of genre, but perhaps of film generally. Its great, raw, even numinous power resides in images; its weakness is virtually always narrative, plot. There is a new theory of dreaming that argues that dream-images are primary, culled from the day's experiences or from memory and imagination; the dream itself, as a story, is a pragmatic invention to string together these images in some sort of coherent causal sequence. If this is true, it argues for an even closer relationship between film and dreaming than film theorists have speculated upon.

I should probably confess that, contrary to the spirit of this collection of essays on film, I can't really claim that any film made an impression on me commensurate with that of the books I'd read as a child and a young adolescent; it's likely that, had I somehow never seen a movie at all, in my entire life, my life would not be very different from what it has been and is. Had I never read a book, however—that's unimaginable.

Yet movies, comprised of images, among these images the enormously inflated faces of men and women of striking physical appearance, have the power of lingering in the memory long after all intellectual interest in them has been exhausted. Nostalgia is a form of sentimentality; sentimentality is over-evaluation; the "over-evaluation of the loved object" is Freud's deadpan definition of romantic love. To be haunted by images out of one's own remote past is perhaps a form of self-love, which is after all infinitely better than self-loathing. We seem, once we pass the approximate age of thirty, to be involved in a ceaseless and bemused search for the self we used to be, as if this might be a way of knowing who and what we are now. For me this contemplation of a 1931 *Dracula* first seen sometime in the early 1950s, when I was twelve or thirteen years old, seen again now when I'm fifty-two, has become a kind of conduit into the past, which deflects me from analyzing it in purely intellectual terms; I'm tugged by memory, as by gravity, to the old Rialto Theatre there at the corner of Pine and Walnut Streets, Lockport, New York, as if these early memories are fated always to be stubbornly rooted in time, place. Especially place.

As it happened, my father Frederic Oates worked through high school in the display departments of both the Rialto and the Palace Theatres, helping prepare the marquee and lettering signs (in water-color, on a black-lacquered and easily washable surface—the era of mass-printed cardboard posters hadn't yet arrived), and he tells me a fact that seems astonishing: both theaters, in a city of about only twenty-five thousand inhabitants, changed their bills three times a week. And these bills were double-features, plus a newsreel and a cartoon or comic short. So we're speaking of quantity, sheer quantity, in those pre-television, pre-Depression years. He tells me too, as explanation rather than apology, that he'd soon grown to be bored by movies since he had to see each new bill three times a week, in order to prepare publicity; and, since the display department was in the theater, in fact in the Rialto building, he had to listen to film dialogue again, again, again, to the point at which the entire phenomenon must have seemed—and here I am speaking for him, supplying my own metaphor—horribly like the maya of Oriental religion, the ceaseless flood of diversionary dream-shadows and delusions that constitutes life at the surface of being, not spiritual life, at the core. So, as an adult, he stopped seeing movies entirely, rarely watches television, and spends as much of his time as he can reading. Only once did he overcome his revulsion for the medium and see a movie, in my memory—*On the Waterfront*, in 1954, at my urging, and because the movie had drawn so much praise. (Did he like *On the Waterfront?*—well, it was "all right.")

Perhaps it's simply the case that, where romance isn't operant, our susceptibility to dreams is lessened. We see through them. We can't detect our own images in them. Our human propensity for "over-evaluation" shifts elsewhere.

Source: Joyce Carol Oates, Review of *Dracula*, in *Southwest Review*, Vol. 76, No. 4, 1991, pp. 498–510.

SOURCES

Dracula: The Legacy Collection, 1931, DVD, Universal Studios, 2004.

"The Gothic Experience," in *Literary Gothic*, 2002, http://www.litgothic.com/LitGothic/general.html (accessed December 29, 2011).

Glut, Donald F., *The Dracula Book*, Scarecrow Press, 1975, pp. 38, 119–20.

Hudson, David, "German Expressionism," in *Green Cine*, 2005, http://www.greencine.com/static/primers/expressionism1.jsp (accessed December 29, 2011).

Lee, Elizabeth, "Victorian Theories of Sex and Sexuality," in *Victorian Web*, 1996, http://www.victorianweb.org/gender/sextheory.html (accessed January 11, 2012).

Review of *Dracula*, in *Time Out Film Guide*, 2011, http://www.timeout.com/film/reviews/65736/dracula.html (accessed December 29, 2011).

Skal, David J., "Commentary," in *Dracula: The Legacy Collection*, Universal Studios, 2004.

———, *Hollywood Gothic: The Tangled Web of "Dracula" from Novel to Stage to Screen*, W.W. Norton, 1990, p. 144.

FURTHER READING

Byers, Thomas B., "Good Men and Monsters: The Defense of Dracula," in *Dracula: The Vampire and the Critics*, edited by Margaret L. Carter, UMI Research Press, 1988, pp. 148–57.

> Though this article analyzes the character as presented in the novel and not the film, many of the psychological and sociological points Byers raises are just as relevant to both versions of the story.

Beresford, Matthew, *From Demons to Dracula: The Creation of the Modern Vampire Myth*, Reaktion Books, 2008.

> Unlike McNally and Florescu in their definitive work about the historic image of the vampire, Beresford focuses on the image of the vampire that the twentieth century has come to cultivate, mostly because of the novel and film versions of *Dracula*.

Clements, Susannah, *The Vampire Defanged: How the Embodiment of Evil Became a Romantic Hero*, Brazos Press, 2011.

> Viewers who see the differences between the horrible creature Dracula is in Stoker's novel and the charming continental gentleman he is in Browning's film will already sense the transformation that Clements tracks across the twentieth century, from *Nosferatu* to *Twilight* and beyond.

Lennig, Arthur, *The Immortal Count: The Life and Films of Bela Lugosi*, The University Press of Kentucky, 2010.

> Lugosi's career started with *Dracula*, and he never reached such international popularity again. There are many studies of his life by fans of horror, but Lennig's book takes a serious look at his career and the effect that his one perfect role has had on our culture.

McNally, Raymond T., and Radu Florescu, *In Search of Dracula: The History of Dracula and Vampires*, Houghton Mifflin, 1994.

> This book, by authors who have previously written books about the historic Vlad Dracula and Stoker's vampire creation, gives readers a comprehensive background to the vampire tradition and Dracula in general.

Skal, David J., *Dark Carnival: The Secret World of Tod Browning*, Anchor Books, 1995.

> The director of *Dracula* was famous for his silent classics *The Unholy Three* (1925) and *The Unknown* (1927) when he attached himself to this project, but his reputation today rests with this film, which he was reputedly reluctant to take, and with his one more sound film, the classic horror film *Freaks*, from the following year.

———, *The Monster Show: A Cultural History of Horror*, Faber & Faber, 2001.

> Skal brings his encyclopedic knowledge of horror movies to a comprehensive study of how the genre has affected, and has been affected by, the evolving media culture of the last century.

SUGGESTED SEARCH TERMS

Dracula AND Bram Stoker

Dracula AND Tod Browning

Dracula AND Lugosi

Lugosi AND Tod Browning

Lugosi AND vampire

Dracula AND Victorian age

Universal Studios AND classic horror

Vlad the Impaler

Dracula AND Van Helsing

Feed

M. T. ANDERSON

2002

In M. T. Anderson's best-selling young-adult novel *Feed* (2002), young people in the future have microchips implanted in their brains shortly after birth connecting them wirelessly to an Internet-like feed supplied by the megacorporation Feed-Tech. In this future world, everyone is encouraged to buy consumer goods. Inspired by what he sees as a loss of intelligence in youth culture, Anderson created a cautionary tale about what happens when people submit to consumerism and information overload. Titus and Violet, a young couple from radically different backgrounds, discover that love is not enough to overcome the feed. While the opening scenes can be humorous, the book becomes increasingly grim and dark by the end. Readers should be aware that the book includes off-color language and some references to drug use inappropriate for younger readers.

AUTHOR BIOGRAPHY

Anderson was born as Matthew Tobin Anderson on November 4, 1968, in Cambridge, Massachusetts, to Will Anderson, an engineer, and his wife, Juliana Anderson, an Episcopal priest. When he was young, the family lived in Italy for a period, and he became fascinated with ruins. He attended St. Mark's School, in Southborough, Massachusetts, before entering Harvard University in 1987. He proceeded to study at Cambridge University

Titus is the unintelligent, isolated, non-curious first-person narrator and protagonist in Feed.
(© Tamara Kulikova / Shutterstock.com)

in England, where he was awarded a BA in 1991. Between 1993 and 1996, Anderson worked as an editorial assistant at Candlewick Press, in Cambridge, Massachusetts.

At the age of thirty, Anderson published his first young-adult novel, *Thirsty* (1997), the story of a high-school student who suddenly thinks he is becoming a vampire. This debut earned him significant attention. After earning a master of fine arts degree from Syracuse University, in New York, in 1998, he followed *Thirsty* with another young-adult novel, *Burger Wuss*, in 1999. Next, Anderson wrote the text for a picture book for children, *Handel, Who Knew What He Liked*, published in 2001. This book was named a Boston Globe–Horn Book Honor Book for Nonfiction in 2002. Meanwhile, from 2000 to 2006, Anderson taught courses in writing for younger readers in the MFA program at Vermont College in Montpelier.

With the 2002 publication of *Feed*, Anderson became a very well-recognized writer of literature for young people. The book was named a finalist for the 2002 National Book Award. In 2003, *Feed* won a Los Angeles Times Book Award and was also named a Boston Globe–Horn Book Honor Book for Fiction. After penning several more children's books, Anderson returned to young-adult fiction with *The Astonishing Life of Octavian Nothing, Traitor to the Nation*. The first volume of this title, *The Pox Party*, was published in 2006, as followed by volume two, *The Kingdom on the Waves*, in 2008. The first volume of the series won for Anderson the National Book Award for Young People's Literature in 2006.

Since then, Anderson has been prolific in his work, publishing five books between 2009 and 2011, notably pursuing his "Pals in Peril" series, including the 2011 title *Zombie Mommy*. Anderson lives in New England and enjoys traveling.

PLOT SUMMARY

Part 1: Moon

Titus is the protagonist of *Feed*. He is presented as an ordinary teenager in some future time. He has a father, mother, and a brother he calls "Smell Factor." The family is clearly wealthy and spends money without thought. Nevertheless, at the beginning of the book, Titus seems to be searching for something, though he does not know what.

Titus has friends named Link, Marty, Quendy, Calista, and Loga. They speak a slangy version of English that seems lacking in vocabulary. As the story opens, the friends are on the moon for a spring break trip. It becomes clear, as the story continues, that each of the teenagers is fitted with a microchip in their brain that wirelessly connects to something like the Internet, called the "feednet." The information that inputs directly to their brains is called "the feed." Through the feed, run by FeedTech corporation, the teenagers are able to chat with each other, listen to music, purchase consumer goods, watch video— all of the things available today through the Internet. However, in the future of *Feed*, the young people can access this information and engage in these activities just by thinking about them, since the feed is implanted in their brains. In addition, since the feed always knows where they are and what they are doing, it posts banner ads concerning restaurants, hotels, clubs, and goods that reference the teens' location and activity.

Titus seems bored by the trip. He is not enjoying the Ricochet Lounge, where patrons can bounce around in the moon's low gravity and slam into each other. One reason for this is because he is generally unhappy that Loga and he are no longer a "diad," or couple.

Suddenly, Titus sees a beautiful girl watching them. She is wearing wool, not plastic, and there is something different about her. Titus is intrigued. Meanwhile, the girls begin to talk about their "lesions." Although it is never fully explained, it seems that everyone in the culture is beginning to experience open sores on their faces and bodies. It also becomes apparent that the lesions are being touted by the feed as beautiful and signs of status.

The beautiful girl is near the group, and Quendy approaches her to discuss lesions. The girl, obviously very intelligent, uses a much more extensive vocabulary than the others. Titus falls for the new girl and wants to be with her.

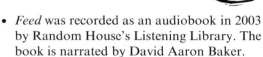

MEDIA ADAPTATIONS

- *Feed* was recorded as an audiobook in 2003 by Random House's Listening Library. The book is narrated by David Aaron Baker.

The beautiful girl's name is Violet, and the group asks her to come with them. She reveals that she is on the moon all alone, observing. The group decides to find other clubs to visit. During the cab ride to the new club, they see a group of protesters waving banners with slogans. It is the first inkling that all is not fun and games in this future time. Titus says that his father calls these kinds of people "Eurotrash." The glimpse of the protest is also a brief foreshadowing of the next event.

The group arrives at the club and begins dancing. Suddenly, a man appears screaming, "We enter a time of calamity!" He touches the youths' necks with a metal device, and then all of them begin screaming the same phrase. The police arrive and tell Titus that they are going to have to turn him off. All goes black.

Part 2: Eden

The second section opens with the sentence, "The first thing I felt was no credit." Evidently each person's bank account is accessed through the feed. Tellingly, in this consumer-oriented culture, Titus's first thought is for the amount of money available to him, or his credit, as it is called here. Then he realizes that he is in a room, in a bed, and that the feed is not transmitting. This is horrifying. He is used to the feed telling him where he is, supplying him with all the information he needs, and making communication with other people possible. Titus is unable to find himself or his friends. All he finds is a message saying there is no transmission signal.

Titus discovers he is in a hospital, and he finds Violet. He also discovers that their feeds have been hacked by a terrorist and that everyone (except Loga, who was not touched by the terrorist) is in the hospital. The police are there to try to solve the crime. Eventually Titus learns that the hacker was part of a group called the Coalition of Pity.

During the time in the hospital, Titus and Violet grow emotionally close. She reveals that her family is not wealthy and her upbringing has been very different from that of Titus and his friends. Her father has homeschooled her. Lamenting the circumstances, Violet declares that she came to the moon to "try to have fun like a normal person, a normal person with a real life—just for one night you want to live, and suddenly you're screwed."

Titus's father arrives the next day. At this point, the reader discovers that Dad speaks in the same slanging, empty language as the teenagers. He calls Titus "Dude," and uses the word "like" repeatedly. All of the other parents are arriving as well, except for Violet's. Her parents have jobs, she says, and cannot come.

Later, Violet reveals that her father is a professor of dead languages, such as BASIC and FORTRAN. These are two computer languages dating from the 1950s and 1960s. Titus is surprised to discover that Violet can read and write. Titus says, "I can read. A little. I kind of protested it in School™. On the grounds that the silent 'E' is stupid."

Titus enjoys his time with Violet, but what he calls the "salad days" are soon over, as the feed is returned in a rush. All the young people are thrilled, including Violet and Titus. Everyone dances and laughs.

Part 3: Utopia

In "Utopia," everything seems to be back to normal. Titus is still enthralled by Violet, and he brings her to a party at Quendy's house. While there, Titus feels some discomfort. He seems uneasy that everything has gone back to the way it was before the attack, and he reveals this to Violet.

Later that night, Titus has what he thinks is a dream. However, the intrusion into his sleep by someone or something that calls itself the police signals to the reader the invasiveness of the feed. Changes to the feed and to a person's brain can be made remotely, without the person's knowledge or permission, in much the same way that computers connected to the Internet will sometimes upgrade software automatically.

In the following scenes, Titus and Violet continue to spend time together. Violet reveals that she is trying to see what happens to the feed if she shops for a strange assortment of items. At first, it just seems like a practical joke, an attempt to outwit FeedTech and prevent the corporation from really knowing who she is.

Titus's parents seem a bit worried about him, and it is revealed that parents can check their children's feeds. They decide he needs a bit of cheering up, and so Titus's father buys him an "upcar," a transportation device that flies through the air, piloted by the owner. This means that Titus can give his friends rides and also go to visit Violet, who lives several hundred miles away.

Violet comes with him to shop for the upcar. Titus tells Violet that his parents are buying him the car for being brave and because he will have to go to court to testify against the hacker. Violet looks at him strangely and tells him that there will be no court case because the hacker is dead. They all saw him get beaten to death by the police with clubs. Titus has no memory of this. The reader can surmise that the late-night fixes to Titus's feed can also alter, delete, or download "memories."

Over the weeks, Violet and Titus visit the country and spend countless hours chatting and becoming ever closer. Violet has dinner with Titus's family, and Titus visits her home. Violet lives in a lower-class neighborhood with old houses and none of the amenities of Titus's neighborhood. He finds Violet's father to be very strange and says he "looked like a crank." Violet's father wears his feed in a backpack and must use special glasses to access it. It is not implanted in his brain. Violet's father uses archaic (for the time of the story) vocabulary. He is a highly educated, very intelligent man. Later, when Titus inquires as to her mother's whereabouts, Violet reveals that she has left the country and lives in South America or some other warm clime. When Titus asks if her parents are divorced, she tells him they were never married. This diverges from the social norms of the time and establishes that Violet's family is radically different from Titus's. They are, in many ways, a subversive element in a culture controlled by FeedTech.

One night, Titus is again awakened by terrible images of pollution, violence, and devastation. Violet awakens him and is very frightened. She believes someone is tapping into her feed.

When she tries to report it to FeedTech, she only receives automated help.

Shortly thereafter, at a party, Titus's friends are mean to Violet, and she demands they leave. Titus and Violet have a terrible argument; then Violet reveals that her feed is malfunctioning. She is losing control of parts of her body.

As part 3 concludes, Violet is also losing control of her mind. She freaks out at a party with Titus and his friends, and then she has a terrible seizure. Things become highly confused until finally Titus realizes he is in an ambulance with Violet speeding to a hospital.

Part 4: Slumberland

Part 4 is divided into smaller chapters, each titled by a percentage. Soon, the reader discovers that this is the percentage of Violet's brain that is working.

While Violet is in the hospital, the doctors explain that because her feed was not installed until she was seven years old and because it was a less expensive model, the hacking she experienced has done permanent damage. Her feed will continue to deteriorate until it becomes entirely corrupt and malfunctioning. It cannot be removed from her brain, however. This means that she will die.

Violet's father attempts to access help from FeedTech. They tell him that, because of Violet's erratic shopping habits, they are unable to establish a profile for her and therefore cannot fix her feed.

Violet is understandably frightened. She reaches out to Titus for support and tries to share with him what she is feeling. She tells him she loves him, and she sends him long messages.

Titus does not react well. He deletes her messages without reading. Finally the two of them decide to go away together to a college town in the country. They rent a cottage but again have an argument. Titus does not want to be bothered with Violet's problems. When he returns her to her home, her father is waiting and takes her hand. But she removes her hand from his and stands alone between her father and Titus.

The rest of the summer, Titus is unhappy. He spends a lot of money and tries to be with his friends, but he is restless and deeply disturbed; still, he does not get in touch with Violet. Finally, one night at dinner, he receives a message from Violet's father, who says that Violet wanted him to contact Titus when she was near death. Titus goes to Violet's home, where she is comatose in bed. Her father blames Titus for Violet's condition. He sends Titus terrible memories of what the last months have been like for Violet as she has grown progressively weaker. Titus denies that he has done anything wrong, although the reader knows that Titus is guilty of everything Violet's father accuses him of. Violet's father is inconsolable over the imminent loss of his daughter.

Titus is very upset. When he gets home, he goes into a frenzy of purchasing pairs of pants and tracking them until he expends all of his credit. Two days later, he goes back to visit Violet, who is dying. He sits on her bed and talks to her aloud. He attempts to ignore all the messages coming in through his feed. He tells her stories, although the stories are only one sentence long. Finally, he tells her the story of their relationship as if it were the trailer for a movie, complete with a happy ending:

> "It's about the feed.... It's about this meg normal guy who doesn't think about anything until one wacky day, when he meets a dissident with a heart of gold.... Set against the backdrop of America in its final days, it's the high-spirited story of their love together, it's laugh-out-loud funny, really heartwarming, and a visual feast.... Together, the two crazy kids grow, have madcap escapades and learn an important lesson about love. They learn to resist the feed."

A message from the feed comprises the last two pages. It is an advert for the Blue-Jean Warehouse's final sale. The sentence "Everything must go!" is repeated five times, in increasingly small print.

CHARACTERS

Link Arwaker

Link is one of Titus's friends. He is a large, not very attractive boy; however, he is popular with his friends. The reason he is named Link is that his parents had him cloned from the blood on Mary Todd Lincoln's shawl from the assassination of Abraham Lincoln. His parents have spent a fortune to have him so conceived.

Calista

Calista is one of Titus's female friends who accompanies him on a trip to the moon at the opening of the book. She, along with the others, has her feed hacked by a terrorist while on the moon.

Dad

Dad is Titus's father. His language usage is nearly identical to his son's. He is a wealthy man who is employed by a large corporation. At the end of the novel, when he is sharing via the feed his memories of a whale-watching trip he took with colleagues, there is some hint that he may be having an affair with a coworker.

Loga

Loga is Titus's ex-girlfriend. She accompanies the group on the trip to the moon. Her feed, however, is not attacked by the terrorist. When she visits her friends in the hospital after the attack, she seems more interested in chatting about the news with her friends on Earth than she does in commiserating with her friends who have been the victims of the attack.

Marty

Marty is one of Titus's friends and a member of the group that goes to the moon.

Mom

Mom is Dad's wife and Titus's mother. She does not appear to have a job but rather stays at home, goes out with friends, and spends money. Her vocabulary is also very limited, and her thoughts seem very shallow. Her main responsibility seems to be taking care of Titus's younger brother.

Quendy

Quendy is one of Titus's female friends. Although it is a little difficult to distinguish one girl from the other, due to their limited vocabularies and shallow conversation, Quendy seems to be the ringleader of the group. The group often gathers at her home, and she appears to be something of a trendsetter. Not only does she wear culottes, something none of them have seen before, but she also has her body inflicted with artificial lesions. Lesions have begun appearing on the bodies and faces of everyone in the culture; through the feed, lesions have begun to be associated with high-status individuals such as movie stars and models. Thus, when Quendy chooses to have herself mutilated and cut up with the artificial lesions, it indicates how far she is willing to go to associate herself with the newest trend. Quendy is the one who is the cruelest to Violet, making fun of her vocabulary and calling her stupid. She obviously sees Violet as an outsider and resents her admission to their group of friends.

Smell Factor

"Smell Factor" is the name Titus gives to his younger brother; he is never referred to by any other name throughout the book. When Titus calls him Smell Factor at one point, his mother retorts that that is not his name, but she does not supply the name. Smell Factor engages in head banging, food throwing, and singing along with the feed nonstop. While it is likely that his behavior is typical for youngsters in this society, in present-day society, his behavior would be seen as reason for alarm.

Titus

Titus is the protagonist and first-person narrator of the novel. He is a teenager who comes from an affluent family. Although he does not refer to his family's affluence, he has all the possessions of a wealthy teenager, including his own personal flying device and a hefty bank account. He is also able to take expensive trips with his friends. Despite all of his belongings, he nevertheless is often bored and unhappy, particularly in the first part of the book before he meets Violet.

As the novel opens, he is on the moon with his friends for spring break. He spots Violet at a club and quickly becomes enamored with her. He is able to speak to Violet, although his limited vocabulary also limits the depth of their relationship. Violet introduces him to all kinds of new ideas and thoughts. At one point, the couple goes shopping for unlikely items in an attempt to resist the feed. Titus finds such rebellion exciting, although it is unlikely that he understands very much about Violet's motivation.

When Violet falls ill and reaches out to him for support, Titus reveals a very unattractive side of his personality. He deletes her messages without reading them and cuts her off. He has grown uncomfortable with the way his friends treat Violet, but he is also unwilling to stand up for her with them.

After he has a final fight with Violet, he does not go to see her again until her father sends him a message that she is dying. He goes to their home and is unable to bear her father's anger at him. Tellingly, in order to soothe himself after the event, he begins to madly purchase many pairs of pants, all the same style in different colors. He returns to Violet's home two days later and tries to ease her death by telling her stories.

Whether or not Titus learns anything over the course of the novel is up for debate. He is alternately naive, insensitive, tender, and cruel. Although the happy ending he supplies for Violet when he tells her their final story ends with resisting the feed, it is unlikely that he will have the courage or strength to ever do so.

Violet

Violet is a girl the group meets while they are on the moon. Violet is very pretty, although she dresses in wool rather than plastic. She is not from the same social class as the rest of the group and is utterly astounded when she hears Titus say that he has been to Mars and it was dumb. The trip to the moon is her first trip off planet.

Violet lives with her father, who is a university professor. They are not wealthy people, and Violet did not receive her feed until she was seven years old. Her father had to save and save to get the money together for the feed for her. He also sacrificed greatly to send her on the trip to the moon.

When the terrorist attacks Violet and the other teenagers while on the moon, she has the worst reaction, since her feed is a less expensive model and because she received it later in life. Eventually, her feed begins to fail, and she loses cognitive and motor abilities. Although this is the explanation given to Violet and her father, there is also the hint that she is being put out of commission by the feed because she refuses to use the computerized personal shopping assistant supplied by the feed. Further, she shops for unconventional and unwanted items and does not even purchase them. She does this for fun to prevent FeedTech from profiling her. Ironically, she eventually discovers that, because FeedTech cannot build a profile for her, they cannot (or will not) help her when her feed fails.

Meanwhile Violet and Titus form a relationship. She comes to love Titus and shares her thoughts and ideas with him. As her feed begins to malfunction more often, she finds herself in serious difficulty and tries to reach out to Titus for emotional support. She sends him long messages that he deletes. By the time Titus finally decides to visit her, she is in a coma. It is impossible to tell if she hears any of the words that Titus speaks to her as she is dying.

Violet's Father

Violet's father is a university professor of dead languages. These languages include BASIC and FORTRAN, computer languages dating from the 1950s and 1960s. The father has a hunched back from wearing a very old model of feed scanner in a backpack. He must also wear special glasses in order to read the feed. Although he loves his daughter, his homeschooling and dissident ideas have prevented her from having a life like Titus's. She does not receive her feed until she is seven years old, long after other children. However, the fact that she receives the feed at all speaks to her father's deep love for her.

When Violet is sick, her father does everything in his power to find help. He fails. In his anger, he blames Titus for her condition. He is extraordinarily cruel to Titus, when he finally comes to visit Violet; however, Titus's behavior leading up to the confrontation was reprehensible, so perhaps the father's outburst can be justified.

THEMES

Consumerism

One of the main themes of *Feed* is consumerism. As James Blasingame states in his review of *Feed* in the *Journal of Adolescent & Adult Literacy*, "Science fiction writers often extrapolate present-day trends to show disastrous results in the future." Anderson, Blasingame argues, draws on present-day consumerism to create a future in which young people are constantly blasted with advertising and encouragement to buy goods.

The definition of consumerism has two parts. First, consumerism is the theory that a society's increasing consumption of goods is economically desirable. The economic downturn in the United States beginning in late 2007 demonstrated the role of consumerism in the economic health of the nation. Many of the steps taken to avert further economic catastrophe were designed to encourage the purchase of consumer goods among the population. Only through increased consumption of goods could the country pull itself out of its economic problems, because increased consumption translates into a better employment rate with more money circulating through the system. This is, at least, the theory.

Consumerism also describes a preoccupation with, and an inclination toward, the buying of consumer goods. In order to encourage people to buy consumer goods, corporations use advertising to instill desire for their goods. Advertisers use a variety of techniques to persuade people to buy, and thus contribute to and increase consumerism.

TOPICS FOR FURTHER STUDY

- Read George Orwell's novel *1984*, paying particular attention to the descriptions of Newspeak. What are the principles of Newspeak? Why does the government mandate the use of Newspeak? How does Newspeak compare to the language spoken by Titus, his family, and his friends? Write a brief story in your own language. Now rewrite the story in Newspeak. Finally, write it again in the language used by Titus. What do you notice about what happens to your story? Report on your findings to the class.

- Gather together at least four or five copies of magazines that target teen audiences. With a small group of your peers, analyze the magazines by noting the products that are advertised, the subjects of the articles, and the vocabulary used by the writers. What are the magazines trying to sell? How do these magazines both reflect and create their audiences? Write an essay that answers these questions, using examples from your research.

- Read selections from the young-adult anthology *The Best Japanese Science Fiction Stories*, edited by John L. Apostolou and Martin Harry Greenberg and published in 1997. How do the thirteen Japanese authors represented characterize the future? What do they seem to be the most afraid of? How do their visions compare and contrast with Anderson's *Feed*? Using paints, pastels, charcoal, colored pencils, or other art supplies, create a series of images that represent a few of these visions. Set up an exhibit of your work and write a catalog explaining each image.

- William Gibson's *Neuromancer* (1984) is an adventure story of an ace cybercowboy who can link directly into the Internet in order to hack the defenses of corporations and organizations. Anderson's *Feed* tells the story of a future world where the Internet connections are hardwired into people's brains just after birth and where corporations and media control the culture. Read *Neuromancer* and take notes on Gibson's vision of the future. Do you think that Anderson was influenced in any way by *Neuromancer*? How does the future presented by Anderson resemble or diverge from the future imagined by Gibson? Prepare a presentation for your classmates, using PowerPoint or other presentational software, that compares and contrasts these visions of the future. Select appropriate images and music to accompany your presentation.

In *Feed*, the characters have all been fitted out with an implanted microchip that receives a wireless Internet feed transmitted directly to their brains. Moreover, the feed works both ways: information from the individual's brain is transmitted directly to the corporation that supplies the feed. Thus advertising can be custom-tailored to the teen. That is, if a teen thinks that he or she would like a new pair of jeans, immediately banner ads for various kinds of jeans and places where they can be bought flood the teen's brain.

The world that Anderson creates strikes contemporary readers as horrifying, largely because of the ruthlessness of the consumerist message. He has tracked the growth of consumerism across time, and by projecting that same rate of growth into the future, he presents a picture of a culture completely consumed by consumption. His message seems clear: unless the rapid and rampant growth of consumerism is slowed, our world will be largely unlivable.

Social Class

The world of *Feed* is a society built on status and class. Anderson has used what he has observed in present-day Western culture, a culture enmeshed

Titus meets Violet during spring break on the moon. *(© martin | | fluidworkshop | Shutterstock.com)*

in the demands of consumerism. One necessity for consumerism is distinctions of class and social status. Such distinctions build desire for consumer goods, as corporations attempt to link certain products with higher social status so that they can sell more and charge more. Thus, goods are stamped with brand names, and the brand names are subsequently associated with wealthy and high-status individuals. This path can be illustrated using the example of women's purses. Women traditionally carry bags to hold their wallets, identification, makeup, and other essentials that they need through the day. In recent years, such bags have been designed and branded by companies bearing the names of their designers, such as Kate Spade and Calvin Klein. Although designer bags are very similar in efficacy and style to non-designer bags, companies can charge significantly more money for the designer bags simply because they are associated with higher social status. Similarly, certain tourist locations have higher social status than others. People who travel to places such as Fiji, for example, are generally considered to have higher social status than people who travel to Branson, Missouri.

Anderson extrapolates the way class functions in contemporary Western culture to imagine the near future. The main characters in *Feed*, excepting Violet, are from wealthy families of high social standing. They spend their spring break on the moon. They own small personal flying devices for transportation. They do not have to hesitate to buy any of the hundreds of clothing items that flood their feeds, regardless of cost. Worst of all, they do not seem to be in any way aware of their privilege.

Violet, on the other hand, comes from a less wealthy, lower social class. She does not have the consumer goods to signify herself as a member of the higher class. Most important for the story, her feed is inferior to those of Titus's group of friends. Moreover, her feed was installed late, when she was seven, leading to her problems after the hacker damages her feed. Because of her inferior social standing, Violet is considered an outsider by Titus's group of friends. They discriminate against her and seem to dislike her. Titus himself is discomfited by Violet's father's social standing. The refusal of the feed corporation to help Violet recover, when her feed fails, sends the message that her social standing and her refusal to buy the goods that flood the feed make her an expendable member of the society.

STYLE

First-Person Narration

Narration is the device a writer uses to tell his or her story. Sometimes in a story, writers will choose to narrate the events through an authorial voice that provides all of the details. In other stories, such as *Feed*, the author chooses to have one character serve as the narrator. The first-person narrator of *Feed* is Titus. According to Clare Bradford in an essay appearing in *Jeunesse: Young People, Texts, Cultures*, Titus can be "identified through a style of language that combines Californian youth English with invented idioms." Titus's language can be initially difficult to follow because of the invented vocabulary. This technique, however, draws readers in and forces them to engage with the text to understand its meaning.

The narrative moves forward with the introduction of Violet, when Titus and his friends go to the moon for spring break. Because Violet is of a different social class, she has different norms of behavior. The contrast between Violet and Titus then becomes an opportunity for the reader to make judgments about the world being presented. In addition, because of Anderson's construction of the narrative in the first person, readers are not included in the protagonists' group. That is, they occupy a position on the outside. As a result, readers are invited to think critically about Titus as a character. While Titus makes many assumptions about the society in which he lives, the reader, as an outsider, does not. Rather, the reader in many cases will find Titus's decisions and reactions to be either unattractive or unethical. Indeed, the entire group of friends generally behave badly, something that cannot escape the reader's notice. This becomes particularly apparent when Titus's friends interact with Violet, when they are openly mean to her.

As the narration continues, it becomes clear that Titus is not a reliable narrator, though he does appear to intend to tell the truth. Yet many of his assumptions just seem wrong. Bradford writes that this is a "key narrative strategy" on Anderson's part. Because readers may not identify

with him or have much sympathy for him, they are able to objectively consider and judge Titus, his friends, and their values.

In addition to Titus's first-person narration, *Feed* also relies on advertisements, news flashes, and other interruptions to the action that come through the feed. These interruptions are not mediated by Titus, and so they present the reader with more evidence by which to form judgments about the culture presented in the novel.

Dystopia

To understand the term *dystopia*, it is perhaps best to consider first the earlier, opposite term, *utopia*. In the sixteenth century, the English writer and philosopher Thomas More coined the term to title a book describing a fictional, ideal community located on an island in the Atlantic. Although More's *Utopia* marks the first recorded use of the term, the concept of the ideal society extends back to Plato's *Republic*, written circa 380 BCE. Utopias, while generally fictional, describe societies that the writers imagine as being better than the society in which they live. Often, utopias are didactic; that is, they are designed to teach a lesson or advocate a particular position.

The term *dystopia*, on the other hand, is a fairly new coinage. The word refers to an imaginary place or condition in which the essence and actualities of life are as bad as can be imagined. The *Oxford English Dictionary* credits philosopher John Stuart Mill with using the word "dystopian" in 1868, while the first published used of the word "dystopia" occurred in 1952.

Dystopian fiction is a twentieth- and twenty-first-century phenomenon, extending back to Aldous Huxley's *Brave New World*, written in 1931 and published in 1932. George Orwell followed with *1984*, published in 1949. Orwell's concern with language and the limiting of human thought has many connections to *Feed*. More recently, Canadian writer Margaret Atwood has written a series of dystopias, beginning with her 1985 novel *The Handmaid's Tale* and continuing with *Oryx and Crake* (2003) and *The Year of the Flood* (2009). Cormac McCarthy's 2006 novel *The Road* is also classified as a dystopia.

The world of *Feed* is generally considered to be a dystopia by reviewers, critics, and readers. Unlike the main characters in the previously mentioned works, however, Titus probably would not consider himself to be living in a terrible society. For much of the book, Titus simply has fun with his friends. Certainly, he has some worries about Violet, but for the most part, he lives a highly energetic life, filled with all the extras afforded someone of high social standing. He has plenty of money, plenty of friends, and the ability to travel as he wants. Because the feed essentially keeps him ignorant of history, politics, and current events, he does not seem to notice the pollution nor have a problem with the lesions that have been breaking out on the skin of his friends. Neither is he sickened or alarmed by the filet-mignon farms where cattle meat is cloned for human consumption.

For readers, however, the world of *Feed* is a nightmare. Titus's ignorance does not blind the reader to the serious and sometimes deadly problems of the society. Violet's eventual death serves to point out how dangerous a consumerist culture can be for the nonaffluent members of the society. In addition, readers have no choice but to notice how stunted the vocabulary of the teenagers and how shallow their thinking are. One of the most horrifying parts of the novel is the language and thinking of Titus's parents. Their lives are just as stunted and just as shallow as their children's. Consequently, the reader must conclude that the entire society is under the control of a megacorporation that, through the feed, can pacify and placate the population.

Feed joins other popular dystopian young-adult novels of the present century such as *The Hunger Games* (2008), *Catching Fire* (2009), and *Mockingjay* (2010), by Suzanne Collins, and *Uglies* (2005), by Scott Westerfeld. That dystopian fiction is so popular among young people suggests that real-world youth, unlike the teenagers portrayed in *Feed*, are ready and able to examine their own culture critically.

HISTORICAL CONTEXT

The Internet

The Internet, as evolved into a more invasive entity called feednet, plays an essential role in *Feed*. The feed that is connected wirelessly to the brains of all of the characters is an extrapolation of present-day Internet technology. The Internet had its origins in the early 1960s. According to the Internet Society's "Brief History of the Internet," "The first recorded description of the social interactions that could be enabled through networking was a series of memos written by J. C. R. Licklider of MIT in August 1962."

The first usage of what would become the Internet was by scientists at places like the Massachusetts Institute of Technology and Stanford University. At this time, the networks were closed, except to those scholars who could access them. By the mid-1980s, Internet connections were spreading among scholars of all disciplines. Indeed, according to the Internet Society, it became a requirement of National Science Foundation funding to American universities that Internet connections paid for by the foundation be available to all qualified users on campus, regardless of discipline. However, searching the World Wide Web at this time was difficult for those not skilled in technology. At the same time, a growing number of people began to use electronic mail, or e-mail.

The development of web browsers such as Netscape in the early 1990s greatly increased the use of the Internet. In addition to text, users could now access images and sound. At the same time, the Internet began to be increasingly commercialized. Businesses such as America Online provided an easy interface with the web for a monthly charge.

In 1995, Yahoo!, developed at Stanford, offered not only a portal for computer users but also a search engine. The development of search engines changed the face of the Internet dramatically. In 1998, Google was developed, also at Stanford. In the years since, Google has become the premier presence on the Internet. Although Google is a free service, data mining and advertising make it a very profitable venture. With the advent of search engines such as Google, businesses clamored to get online and establish a web presence.

Between 2000 and 2011, Internet usage in North America grew 151 percent, according to the Internet Society. An astounding 78.3 percent of the North American population had access to the Internet by 2011. In that year, it was entirely possible for an individual living in the United States to purchase all Christmas and birthday presents, plan trips, book flights, balance a check book, listen to music, watch videos, and perform many other activities without ever getting up from the couch.

Data Mining

Data mining, according to the *Encyclopædia Britannica*, is "the process of discovering interesting and useful patterns and relationships in large volumes of data." Currently, many businesses

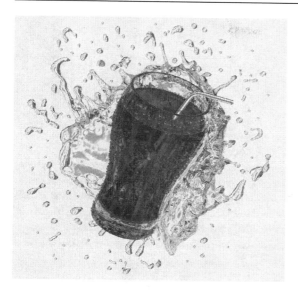

One of Titus's schemes involves a promotion by the Coca-Cola company. (© Guido Vrola | Shutterstock.com)

employ firms to mine data in order to target customers and increase sales. The advent of the Internet has made data mining a very profitable business.

One of the ways that data is mined is through affiliation cards. These include cards given out at grocery stores, drugstores, and other venues offering users special discounts on certain items. When the user swipes the card to receive the discount, the computerized cash register records the user's name and contact information as well as every item in the order. In some stores, this results in instant coupons for additional goods based on what the consumer usually buys.

Data mining is also present every time someone uses free e-mail accounts. For example, on Google, if a user writes to many of his or her friends about a trip he or she intends to take to Hawaii, banner ads along the side of the e-mail screen will tout restaurants and hotels in Hawaii. Because of the speed of the Internet and the possibility of crunching huge amounts of data, it is possible for individuals to be targeted directly. Indeed, consumer information is a valuable commodity for corporations and businesses that try ever harder to tailor their products to their customers.

The lucrative nature of data mining was just entering the public consciousness at the time that Anderson began writing *Feed.* In the years since its publication, data mining has grown dramatically and to such an extent that ads featured in social media such as Facebook seem spookily accurate in predicting what products will be most attractive to the individual user.

CRITICAL OVERVIEW

When Anderson's *Feed* was published in 2002, it generated considerable critical interest in the field of young-adult literature. Many teachers and librarians found in the book an important message for young readers. Young readers found an enjoyable, funny, and ultimately tragic look into the future. In a positive review appearing in the *New York Times Book Review,* Elizabeth Devereaux notes the mixture of comedy and tragedy, calling *Feed* "subversive, vigorously conceived, painfully situated at the juncture where funny crosses into tragic."

Similarly, James Blasingame comments on how the somewhat carefree tone of the early passages gives way to tragedy, in a review appearing in the *Journal of Adolescent & Adult Literacy.* He concludes that, "although the novel opens as the semblance of a lighthearted romp through the teenage experience of the future, it soon changes into a dark prediction of times to come."

Other critics have focused less on the humor in the book in noting that, thematically, *Feed* is concerned with the effects of consumerism on the culture and youth. For example, in reviewing another Anderson title in the *New York Times Book Review,* Jenny Davidson refers to *Feed* as "a surprisingly affecting commodity-culture satire." Likewise Paula Rohrlick, in a review appearing in *Kliatt,* comments that *Feed* portrays "consumerism carried to its logical extreme." A review appearing in *Publishers Weekly* concludes that *Feed* "offers a thought-provoking and scathing indictment that may prod readers to examine the more sinister possibilities of corporate- and media-dominated culture." These critics found much to applaud in the novel, although some found *Feed* to be deeply disturbing.

Other reviewers have highlighted Anderson's detailed creative portrayal of a near-future Earth. One such critic, Lauren Adams, applauds Anderson's conception of the future world, in a review appearing in *Horn Book* magazine: "The world of the novel is wholly and convincingly realized. . . . Inventive details help evoke a world that is chillingly plausible." Adams concludes, "The reflections the novel shows us may be ugly and distorted, but they are undeniably ourselves."

Not all reviews were so wholeheartedly positive. Frances Bradburn, for example, writing in *Booklist*, calls the novel "didactic"and argues that it "plays on every negative teen stereotype." Although she admits that *Feed* works as a "cautionary tale," she finds it a "less successful" example of young-adult literature.

Feed's popularity with critics and educators alike is evidenced by its inclusion by Ian Chipman in a 2009 listing of core modern works of dystopian fiction for youth appearing in *Booklist*. Chipman states that Anderson's premise "seems to be more scarily relevant almost by the minute." In addition, *Feed* was a finalist for the National Book Award in 2002.

In more recent years, scholars have examined the text more closely. For example, in 2010 in her article appearing in *Jeunesse*, Bradford first notes that *Feed* "thematizes corporate power and consumerism." She then makes two persuasive arguments. First, she asserts that *Feed* "positions its readers simultaneously to advert to and to critique the processes whereby young people are inducted into consumerism." In other words, by engaging readers as "active participants in meaning-making," the novel forces the reader to pay attention to and consider critically how corporations and governments initiate young citizens into a society of consumers. Her second argument, on the other hand, undercuts the novel itself. She notes that Anderson paints a scathing portrait of a consumerist society and positions himself as a critic of that society, while at the same time, he used media and devices of the consumerist society to market his book. She writes, "The novel itself is a product marketed to young people and to the adults (parents, teachers, librarians) who mediate texts to them."

WHAT DO I READ NEXT?

- Anderson won the National Book Award for his 2006 novel *The Astonishing Life of Octavian Nothing, Traitor to the Nation*, Vol. 1, *The Pox Party*, set in pre-Revolution Boston. The protagonist is a young black man living with a houseful of radical philosophers.

- Canadian author Margaret Atwood's *Oryx and Crake* (2003) and *The Year of the Flood* (2009) are dystopias that tell the story of a future Earth destroyed by genetic engineering, global warming, pollution, class warfare, and human greed.

- *Consumed: How Markets Corrupt Children, Infantilize Adults, and Swallow Citizens Whole* (2008) by Benjamin R. Barber is a book that, though sometimes difficult, is one of the best analyses of the effects of global markets and consumerism on individuals.

- *Brave New World* (1933) by Aldous Huxley is one of modern literature's first superficial utopias, where the citizens appear to be happy, that is better described as a dystopia. Huxley's book examines the impact of technology on all aspects of life in the near future.

- The *Clone Codes* by Patricia C. Mckissack, Fredrick Mckissack, and John Mckissak, is a young-adult science fiction series with volumes published in 2010 and 2012. The series tells the story of a future earth where cyborgs and clones are treated like slaves.

- *Beyond the Curve* is a collection of stories from Japan's premier science fiction writer, Abe Kobe. The book, translated by Julia Winters Carpenter, was first published in English in 1993.

CRITICISM

Diane Andrews Henningfeld

Henningfeld is a professor of English at Adrian College who writes widely for educational publications. In the following essay, she examines the various ways Anderson uses language in the novel Feed.

Ernie Tucker, reporting on an interview with *Feed* author Anderson for *Reading Time*,

asserts, "Anderson loves to play with language." It is true that the reader who picks up the novel *Feed* for the first time is likely to be confused and disconcerted by the language. The story is told from the point of view of Titus, a teenager living at some unspecified time in the future. His language is filled with unfamiliar slang, and he seems to be deficient in vocabulary. It soon becomes clear, however, that Anderson is using this strange language for several important and serious reasons. First, language is an important device in creating characters. Second, the language of the characters in *Feed* serves specific thematic purposes. Third, the language of *Feed* requires a particular critical strategy from readers.

Through the process of characterization, an author brings to life the people of his or her story. Characterization is achieved in a variety of ways: First among them is what a character says and thinks. Another way characterization is achieved is through what other characters in the story say and think about the character. As such, language becomes the medium through which characterization takes place. A writer's ear for the language used by his characters must be keen. When asked by James Blasingame, in an interview, how he created "the slang that Titus and the others speak," Anderson replied that he "read a lot of magazines like *Maxim*, *Stuff*, and *Teen*. I watched a lot of cable." Thus, the inspiration for the slang in *Feed* came directly from twenty-first-century published and televised teen-speak.

In the same interview, Anderson also commented on how slang is often used by Americans, noting that "there are certain linguistic positions that we as Americans tend to fill with a slang term." He offers several examples:

> Like the "buddy" position, used as a filler to reaffirm the connection between interlocutors—there's one in every age in America as we move through time: sir/sirrah, b'hoy . . . , friend, pal, buddy, man, guy, dude. Same thing for a string of positive intensifiers: capital, bully, swell, groovy, cool, awesome, . . . phat, tight. I started to think about these idiomatic place-holders, and I just inserted fabricated ones—"unit" and so on.

In *Feed*, readers are able to learn a great deal about the main characters, Titus and Violet, through what the two characters say and what the other characters say about them. Titus presents himself early on as a young man of very limited vocabulary. Readers soon learn, however, that he speaks in the same way as his peer group, suggesting that the language they speak is widespread among teenagers. Titus uses in-group slang as his primary means of communication. At the same time, since readers are privileged to Titus's thoughts, readers are also able to access what he thinks. In this case, readers discover that Titus seems to be longing for

THE STORY OF TITUS AND VIOLET IS NOT HEARTWARMING BUT TRAGIC AND PATHETIC; IT IS NOT A HIGH-SPIRITED STORY OF LOVE BUT RATHER A LOW-SPIRITED TALE OF REJECTION AND BETRAYAL; AND MOST OF ALL, THE STORY OF TITUS AND VIOLET SHOWS THAT RESISTING THE FEED IS FUTILE."

more meaning in his existence; his boredom and ennui suggest that he is searching for something he does not have the language to describe. Violet, on the other hand, uses slang, but in a way suggestive of a second language user. Her first language, or her mother tongue, is much richer in vocabulary. Consequently, she has the ability to think deeply about current social issues, solve problems, and imagine a different kind of life. Her language reveals her sharp intelligence and ready wit.

Language also plays an important thematic role in the story. As Elizabeth Devereaux notes, in a review of *Feed* appearing in the *New York Times Book Review*, "Anderson uses the mechanics of the narrative and the vocabulary to advance both the premise and the story line. . . . Consumerism has laid waste to language and thought." Devereaux's point is that the constant input from the feed, flooding people with advertisements and so-called "news" stories that are little more than governmental propaganda stunts the ability of people to learn and grow. They are unable to think critically or deeply because they simply do not have the vocabulary to do so. The problem is not only with the young people either; Titus's father and mother speak the same vacuous language their son does. This suggests that among people of their social class, such language is not only acceptable but the norm. They are incapable of analysis or careful thought and live their lives simply reacting to the feed. As James Blasingame writes, in a review appearing in the *Journal of Adolescent & Adult Literacy*, "With such information and stimulation flying into their minds at the speed of light, . . . the characters have no time for critical thinking."

Anderson is not the first writer to draw these connections between language, thought, and culture. Paula Rohrlick, writing in *Kliatt*, argues that Anderson's "provocative SF take on the excesses of our consumer society has echoes of [Anthony Burgess's 1962 novel] *A Clockwork Orange*, as Anderson . . . creates his own vocabulary." Perhaps an even stronger comparison can be made with George Orwell's 1949 novel *1984*. In Orwell's dystopia, the common people are fed a constant stream of bad literature, advertising, and propaganda composed in Newspeak. This language has as its goal the elimination of as many words as possible, particularly words having to do with liberty and freedom. By eliminating words, the totalitarian government of *1984* also limits the ability of the population to think or revolt. The overarching power structure in *Feed*, while not necessarily governmental, is corporate and megalithic. There is no part of the culture that is not controlled and mediated by corporate greed, bent on inculcating all citizens with the desire for new products on which to spend their money.

Anderson also uses language to establish his thematic concern with class and social structure. Titus, his friends, and his family are all clearly of the upper middle class. They have more money than they know what to do with and plenty of leisure time. When they want something, they merely think about it and it is ordered. The feed not only entices them to buy but also makes the process exceedingly easy, thus pandering to the desire for instant gratification. No one in this social class has to wait for anything.

Violet, on the other hand, comes from a much poorer background. Her father is a university professor of dead languages. He uses long words and complicated sentences to get at complex ideas. He has homeschooled Violet, and she also has a much larger vocabulary than Titus and his group of friends, who attend schools owned and operated by FeedTech. Tellingly, she is also the only one among them who can actually read. Her language sets her apart. When she attends a party with Titus and his friends, Quendy, Calista, and Loga complain that she uses long words. They say they think it is stupid. It is difficult to discern if their real complaint is with her language, however; it is likely that they subconsciously view her language as a class marker. Moreover, her language also marks her as an outsider to their peer group. Violet, in short, is an interloper, and the girls turn against her.

Further, Violet's use of long words also suggests that she is a subversive element, someone who is a dissident concerning the feed. She and her family violate social norms, and the culture represented by Titus's friends and family rejects her.

That these are serious thematic concerns for Anderson seems clear from his acceptance speech for the 2002 Boston Globe–Horn Book Award for *Feed*. In that speech, Anderson asserted,

> We live in a world where our nation's operational vocabulary is on a plummeting decline, where Dunkin' Donuts has replaced the cruller with a "glazed stick" and Horace's own famous injunction, "Carpe diem—seize the day" has been trademarked by a cereal company.

He continued this line of thought in his interview with Blasingame:

> In my low moments, I worry that we're producing a nation and a generation that is inarticulate and clumsy in their thought; self-absorbed; incapable of subtlety; constructed by products; unable to learn from the past, because the past is forgotten; blind to global variation; violently greedy and yet unaware of how much we ask for already.

The language of *Feed* signals to readers that they must employ a different strategy for reading the text. Readers are dropped directly into an unknown future world. They do not know the slang, nor do they know anything about the social structure or context of the world they find themselves reading about. As a result, they must become active, engaged readers. They must follow the clues sprinkled through the text and read between the lines. Anderson leaves gaps in his texts, gaps that readers must fill in order to piece together the meaning of the story. By the end of the novel, the careful and engaged reader will have participated with Anderson in a collaborative act of meaning making. The narrative requires the reader to be actively involved in the storytelling.

What Anderson requires of his readers is exactly what Titus and his friends are no longer capable of doing; the feed has destroyed their ability to piece together stories coherently. They have lost the ability to narrate their lives, as is evident from the final pages of the book. As Titus sits on Violet's bed as she is dying, he tries to say something to her that will be meaningful, but all he is able to do is salvage bits and pieces:

> I told her stories. They were only a sentence long, each one of them. That's all I knew how to find. So I told her broken stories. The little pieces of broken stories I could find. I told her what I could.

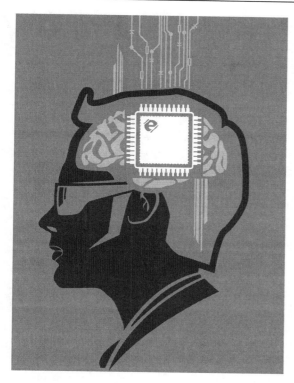

Nearly thee-quarters of the citizens have a computer chip, called a feed, implanted in their brains. (© Anton Novik | Shutterstock.com)

Sadly, even his story of their relationship cannot be told in his own language; rather he must co-opt the language of the feed to piece together the way he understands their relationship. The result is a story that sounds like a movie trailer rather than a real-life relationship:

> It's about this meg normal guy who doesn't think about anything until one wacky day, when he meets a dissident with a heart of gold. . . . Set against the backdrop of America in its final days, it's the high-spirited story of their love together, it's laugh-out-loud funny, really heartwarming, and a visual feast . . . .Together, the two crazy kids grow, have madcap escapades, and learn an important lesson about love. They learn to resist the feed.

This scene is highly emotional and suggests superficially that Titus has matured over the course of the book. He wants to provide for Violet (and for the reader) a happy ending. However, at closer inspection, Anderson's ideal engaged reader will understand that this passage demonstrates the *opposite* of what it says. Titus is unable to communicate a story without resorting to the language of the feed. He uses the clichéd and conventional language the feed would use to advertise a movie. Moreover, it is patently dishonest. The story of Titus and Violet is not heartwarming but tragic and pathetic; it is not a high-spirited story of love but rather a low-spirited tale of rejection and betrayal; and most of all, the story of Titus and Violet shows that resisting the feed is futile.

Source: Diane Andrews Henningfeld, Critical Essay on *Feed*, in *Novels for Students*, Gale, Cengage Learning, 2013.

Paula Rohrlick

In the following review, Rohrlick deems Feed *a "provocative SF take on the excesses of our consumer society."*

To quote from the review of the hardcover in *Kliatt*, November 2002: It's spring break, and Titus and his teenage friends are partying on the moon when he spots a beautiful girl. He and Violet are just getting to know each other when a hacker causes their feeds to malfunction—the chips in their brains that barrage them with ads and direct their thoughts and dreams. Titus recovers, but Violet's feed is damaged; she hasn't always had a feed, and she openly questions the poisoning of the planet, why everyone is developing lesions, and the way in which the feed insidiously feeds off them. This is a new way of looking at the world for Titus, who has never before questioned his technologically enhanced way of life, hanging out with his shallow, trendy friends. Violet and Titus enter into a relationship, each trying to understand the other, even as Violet starts to decline and die as her feed stops working. This provocative SF take on the excesses of our consumer society has echoes of *A Clockwork Orange*, as Anderson (author of the YA novels *Thirsty* and *Burger Wuss*) creates his own vocabulary ("It was brag," for example, meaning "great"; there are some old-fashioned expletives here as well). The invented words are not hard to understand, though, and the flashes of humor as well as the cleverly imagined grim future world should quickly draw readers into this look at teenage love and loss, and at consumerism carried to its logical extreme.

Source: Paula Rohrlick, Review of *Feed*, in *Kliatt*, Vol. 38, No. 3, May 2004, p. 26.

James Blasingame

In the following review, Blasingame argues that Anderson presents a "cautionary tale" about the dangers of the information age.

Science fiction writers often extrapolate present-day trends to show disastrous results in the future. In this cautionary tale, society's appetite for communication technology, rampant consumerism and marketing, and adolescents' thirst for rapid-fire sensory stimulation and pre-digested information result in a future world in which solicited and unsolicited information is delivered directly to the human brain in a wireless Internet feed. Every young person has the implanted microchip, as do most adults, and the result is a constant bombardment of information from advertisers and marketing concerns. The protagonist, Titus, and his teenage friends experience this as something like MTV, telemarketing, and Internet access all happening simultaneously. A ubiquitous corporate entity maintains a consumer profile of every individual and never stops making purchase suggestions for this or that product and the happiness each product will bring, such as this ad for a musical recording: "If you liked 'I'll Sex You In;' you'll love these other slouch-rock epics by hot new storm 'n chunder band Beefquake, full of riffs that . . . ." All information is not unsolicited, however, and Titus and his friends can "chat" in pairs or as a group, as well as get the news or research any topic just by thinking about it.

With such information and stimulation flying into their minds at the speed of light, however, the characters have no time for critical thinking, and have unwittingly become little more than cattle feeding on whatever the faceless creators of what comes over "the feed" send their way. Hair, clothing, and body art (which in the future will be in the form of oozing lesions—an evolution from today's tattoos, perhaps?) change so fast that fashions actually change during the course of an evening out.

When Titus meets Violet, he has no idea that she does not fit the profile of a normal teenager; in fact, in that future world, she doesn't have a (consumer) profile at all in the sense that most others do. She has purposely vexed the anonymous corporate entity by creating such an unpredictable buying history that the constant individualized consumer manipulation that comes over everyone else's feed cannot be successfully created for her. This rebellious stance eventually causes her downfall when she needs medical attention, and the corporate entity that seems to control everything tells her that until she becomes a better consumer (with a solid profile), she is on her own. She is told to make more purchases until a reliable consumer

profile can be created for her at which point the issue of medical attention will be revisited.

Violet and her father seem to be the only people who question what the world has become. In this future, people have clones to provide spare body parts when they need them, forests have been razed to make room for air factories, and beef does not come from a cattle ranch but rather from "a filet mignon farm . . . tissue spreading out for miles . . . these huge hedges of red" being fed by irrigation tubes that bring artificial blood to the steak. Perhaps Violet and her father are different because their experience with the feed is different. Violet didn't get hers as an infant but rather when she was 7 years old, and her father does not have an implant at all but a portable unit with virtual reality glasses that he can remove. This ultimately leads to a family disaster in the form of their abandonment by the (anonymous) powers that be.

The author's premise is right on target. The Information Age and its rapidly expanding technology seem to be enhancing the role consumerism plays in our lives and especially in the lives of young people. Anderson has also attempted to extrapolate slang, computer games, and teen fashion trends into the future, and only time will tell how accurate he has been. At some point the reader will begin to feel a sense of hopelessness; this story is a tragedy just as much as it is science fiction. Violet's individualism does not improve her life nor does her sacrifice appear to have any impact on the dehumanizing of mankind when information technology, consumerism, and corporate greed become indistinguishable. Although the novel opens as the semblance of a lighthearted romp through the teenage experience of the future, it soon changes into a dark prediction of times to come.

Source: James Blasingame, Review of *Feed*, in *Journal of Adolescent & Adult Literacy*, Vol. 47, No. 1, September 2003, pp. 88–90.

Lauren Adams

In the following review, Adams illustrates what she sees as "Anderson's feel for American teens" in Feed.

M. T. Anderson has created the perfect device for an ingenious satire of corporate America and our present-day value system. Titus and his friends are connected to one another, to merchandise, entertainment, even School[TM], through the "feed," an implant in the brain that provides instantaneous communication and information. As the group arrives on the moon for spring break, they are barraged with banner ads on the feed—images of hotels, restaurants, casinos; the "braggest" styles and places to be. The scene is like a nightmarish cross between *Valley Girl* and *The Matrix*: bored suburban teenagers with painfully limited vocabularies seeking new stimuli, oblivious to the vast technological infrastructure that controls their decaying world. While partying on the moon, Titus meets Violet, a girl noticeably different from his friends; that same night they are all "attacked" by a dissident who hacks into their feeds. Anderson wisely refrains from explaining the workings of the feed for the first thirty pages; instead he immerses the reader in Titus's head—a frenzy of sight-, smell-, and sound-bytes—so that when Titus wakes in the hospital with his feed temporarily shut off following the attack, the reader, too, can feel the immense quiet that Titus has never known. "Normal" life on Earth resumes quickly, however, once the feed is reconnected. Anderson's feel for American teens translates easily to this new dystopic arena ("Omigod! Like big thanks to everyone for not telling me that my lesion is like meg completely spreading"). Between chapters, snips from the feed broadcast advertisements but also reveal the state of the world: destruction in Central and South America, hatred for America and threats from the "Global Alliance," whole suburbs vanishing mysteriously. Anderson's hand is light throughout; his evocation of the death of language is as hilarious as it is frightening. "Could we like get a thingie?" the doctor asks while treating Titus. Reading and writing are as outmoded as speech; Titus is perplexed by Violet's use of pen and paper. After all, the feed "knows everything you want and hope for, sometimes before you even know what those things are." Violet's efforts to enlist Titus in resisting the feed compete with tremendous peer pressure from his friends, who turn the oozing skin lesions they're developing into a fashion rather than consider what might be causing them. In a dramatic outburst (strongly recalling Charlton Heston in *Soylent Green*) Violet screams, "Look at us! You don't have the feed! You are feed! . . . You're being eaten!" Yet here there is no climactic uprising, no heroic transformation. Titus is a believable teenager, both intrigued and threatened by Violet's intelligence and new ideas. And when Violet reaches out to Titus while dying from a technical malfunction of the feed, he fails her

utterly, heartbreakingly, by closing himself off. Right there, Anderson hands us the worst of ourselves—erecting blinders to the pain and suffering of others in order to protect our own way of life. The world of the novel is wholly and convincingly realized: on an Earth that no longer supports life, suburbs are stacked vertically upon one another, each home with its own bubble of sun, sky, and air; Titus and Violet stroll through fields of genetically grown filet mignon, "huge hedges of red," while other lifeforms mutate to survive—"slugs so big a toddler could ride them side-saddle." These inventive details help evoke a world that is chillingly plausible. Like those in a funhouse mirror, the reflections the novel shows us may be ugly and distorted, but they are undeniably ourselves.

Source: Lauren Adams, Review of *Feed*, in *Horn Book*, Vol. 78, No. 5, September-October 2002, pp. 564–65.

SOURCES

Adams, Lauren, Review of *Feed*, in *Horn Book*, Vol. 78, No. 5, September–October 2002, p. 564.

Anderson, M. T., *Feed*, Candlewick Press, 2002.

————, M. T. Anderson website, 2012, http://mt-anderson.com (accessed January 1, 2012).

————, "On the Decay of the Language and the Rise of the Insect Overlords," 2002 Boston Globe–Horn Book Award acceptance speech, M. T. Anderson website, http://mt-anderson.com/blog/he-talks-talks-2/on-the-decay-of-language-and-the-rise-of-the-insect-overlords/ (accessed January 2, 2012).

Blasingame, James, "An Interview with M.T. (Tobin) Anderson," in *Journal of Adolescent & Adult Literacy*, Vol. 47, No. 1, September 2003, pp. 98–99.

————, Review of *Feed*, in *Journal of Adolescent & Adult Literacy*, Vol. 47, No. 1, September 2003, pp. 88–90.

Bradburn, Frances, Review of *Feed*, in *Booklist*, Vol. 99, No. 4, October 15, 2002, p. 400.

Bradford, Clare, "'Everything Must Go!': Consumerism and Reader Positioning in M. T. Anderson's *Feed*," in *Jeunesse: Young People, Texts, Cultures*, Vol. 2, No. 2, Winter 2010, pp. 128–37.

Chipman, Ian, "Core Collection: Dystopian Fiction for Youth," in *Booklist*, Vol. 105, No. 18, May 15, 2009, p. 50.

Clifton, Christopher, "Data Mining," in *Encyclopædia Britannica Online*, 2012, http://www.britannica.com/EBchecked/topic/1056150/data-mining (accessed January 12, 2012).

Davidson, Jenny, Review of *The Astonishing Life of Octavian Nothing, Traitor to the Nation*, Vol. 1, *The Pox Party*, in *New York Times Book Review*, November 12, 2006, p. 42.

Devereaux, Elizabeth, Review of *Feed*, in *New York Times Book Review*, November 17, 2002, p. 47.

Leiner, Barry M., et al., "Brief History of the Internet," Internet Society website, 2012, http://www.internetsociety.org/internet/internet-51/history-internet/brief-history-internet (accessed January 4, 2012).

Mattson, Jennifer, "Top 10 Fantasy Books for Youth: 2005," in *Booklist*, Vol. 101, No. 16, April 15, 2005, p. 1467.

"Q&A: M.T. Anderson Says Series Fiction Fits in Children's Literature," in *Kirkus Reviews*, Vol. 74, No. 23, December 1, 2006, pp. S20–22.

Review of *Feed*, in *Publishers Weekly*, Vol. 249, No. 29, July 22, 2002, p. 181.

Rohrlick, Paula, Review of *Feed*, in *Kliatt*, Vol. 36, No. 6, November 2002, p. 5.

Tucker, Ernie, "Interview with M. T. Anderson," in *Reading Time*, Vol. 53, No. 3, August 2009, pp. 12–13.

FURTHER READING

Anderson, M. T., *Thirsty*, Candlewick Press, 1998.
    Anderson's first novel is the story of Chris, a high-school freshman in Massachusetts who realizes he is becoming a vampire. The book is both scary and funny.

James, Edward, and Farah Mendlesohn, eds., *The Cambridge Companion to Science Fiction*, Cambridge University Press, 2003.
    James and Mendlesohn present twenty essays tracing the history of science fiction, summarizing critical approaches to science fiction and discussing various genres and subgenres of science fiction.

McLuhan, Marshall and Quentin Fiore, *The Medium Is the Massage: An Inventory of Effects*, Gingko Press, 2005.
    First published in 1968, McLuhan's book is still considered one of the most influential volumes on media, technology, and their impact on society.

Roberts, Adam, *Science Fiction*, "New Critical Idiom" series, Routledge, 2000.
    This book is an excellent introduction to the field of science fiction, offering both the history of science fiction as well as chapters on gender, race, and technology. Each chapter closes with a case study of a particular seminal science-fiction work.

Ryan, Johnny, *A History of the Internet and the Digital Future*, Reaktion Books, 2010.
    Ryan argues that politics, economics, and culture are undergoing drastic changes due to the development of the Internet. Ryan traces the history of the Internet from 1950 to 2010.

SUGGESTED SEARCH TERMS

M. T. Anderson

M. T. Anderson AND *Feed*

Feed AND Titus AND Violet

young adult AND science fiction

dystopia

M. T. Anderson AND National Book Award

consumerism

class AND social standing

history of the Internet

data mining AND *Feed*

privatization of schools AND *Feed*

Haroun and the Sea of Stories

SALMAN RUSHDIE

1990

Salman Rushdie's *Haroun and the Sea of Stories* (1990) is a children's story that also has great appeal for adults. Not only is the novel a first-rate quest adventure but also provides a meditation on the importance of free speech and the value of storytelling. Often funny, sometimes sad, *Haroun and the Sea of Stories* concerns young Haroun Khalifa and his father, Sharif Khalifa, who is a master storyteller. When Sharif loses the ability to tell stories, partially because of his wife's betrayal and partially because of Haroun's insensitive remarks, Haroun sets out to help his father regain his craft. His journey takes him to the far side of the hidden moon Kahani and back.

Although the novel is light-hearted and filled with jokes, Rushdie wrote the book while in hiding. In 1988, Rushdie published *The Satanic Verses*, a novel that included a parody of the Prophet Muhammad, something considered blasphemous by conservative Muslims. In response to the publication, the Ayatollah Khomeini of Iran issued a *fatwa*, or death sentence, against Rushdie. The threat was real: others connected with the publication of the book were attacked and murdered. Consequently, Rushdie found himself living in a series of safe houses in England, separated from his son and unable to appear in public. *Haroun and the Sea of Stories* was Rushdie's first post-*fatwa* work, and many readers identify the villain of the story with the Ayatollah.

Salman Rushdie (© *UK History | Alamy*)

Haroun and the Sea of Stories is an excellent introduction to the body of Rushdie's work. Whether read as political allegory, a fantastical quest adventure, or a coming-of-age story, the novel is both engaging and thought provoking.

AUTHOR BIOGRAPHY

Rushdie was born on June 19, 1947, in Bombay, India, to Anis Ahmed and Negin Rushdie. Although the family was from Kashmir, they moved to Bombay shortly before the writer's birth. When the subcontinent gained its independence from Britain in 1947, Muslims moved to the newly formed Muslim nation of Pakistan, while Hindus moved to an independent India. Despite this, Rushdie's Muslim family chose to stay in Bombay. Rushdie's education was in both English and Urdu.

Rushdie attended the Cathedral Boy's High School before continuing his education in England at the Rugby School, a prestigious private boys' school, and later at King's College, Cambridge. Upon graduation, he remained in England, where he worked as an actor for several years before turning to writing copy for an advertising agency to support himself. During this period, he wrote the novel *Grimus* and married Clarissa Luard in 1976. The couple had a son, Zafar, in 1980. Although *Grimus* was not a success, it set the stage for Rushdie to work on *Midnight's Children*, published in 1981 and dedicated to Zafar.

The novel was a huge success, garnering both critical praise and a wide readership. It won several important awards, including the Booker Prize and the James Tait Black Memorial Prize. It eventually went on to win the Best of the Booker awards in 2008. In addition, the book became a best seller, selling more than 250,000 copies within the first three years of publication. *Midnight's Children* was also quickly translated into more than twelve languages. Rushdie followed the publication with his novel *Shame* in 1983 and a nonfiction book, *The Jaguar Smile: A Nicaraguan Journey*, in 1987.

Rushdie's home life was less successful. In 1985, he separated from Luard and began an affair with the Australian author Robyn Davidson. By the time his divorce from Luard was finalized in 1987, he had broken off with Davidson and begun living with the American writer Marianne Wiggins, whom he married shortly thereafter.

On September 26, 1988, Rushdie's novel *The Satanic Verses* was published. This event set in motion a whole series of consequences that irrevocably altered Rushdie's life. The book was offensive to religious Muslims, and in 1988, India banned the book. From there, other Muslim countries followed suit, either requiring heavy censorship of the book or banning it all together. The most devastating blow, however, occurred on February 14, 1989. The Iranian Ayatollah Khomeini (famous in the United States for his role in the deposition of the Shah of Iran and the U.S. Embassy hostage crisis of 1979–1981), issued an edict called a *fatwa* against Rushdie and *The Satanic Verses*. He pronounced that Rushdie and all those involved in any way in the publication, printing, and selling of the book were sentenced to death.

Rushdie and his wife went into hiding immediately, protected by the British Special Branch. They constantly moved locations, and it is likely that the stress placed on the couple by the danger and instability in their lives caused the breakup of the marriage by 1993. The *fatwa* continued for years, remaining in effect even after the death of Khomeini in 1989. The danger continued as well: in 1991, Rushdie's Japanese, Italian, Norwegian, and Turkish translators were all attacked, resulting in the death of Hitoshi Igarashi and the severe wounding of the others. According to Norbert

Schürer, writing in *Salman Rushdie's "Midnight's Children,"* about sixty people died in all as a result of what came to be known as the Rushdie Affair.

It was under these circumstances, in hiding and separated from his son, Zafar, that Rushdie began writing *Haroun and the Sea of Stories*, a children's book he published in 1990. It is easy to read into the novel the themes of censorship and violence elicited by the *fatwa*.

Since 1990, Rushdie has published eleven more books and experienced two additional marriages and divorces. He emerged from hiding, cautiously at first, in 1993, and by 1995, was making public appearances again. In 1998, the Iranian government officially lifted the *fatwa*.

Rushdie has won most of the world's most prestigious literary awards. In 1993, he won the Booker of the Bookers for the best novel of all the Booker Award–winning novels published to date. In 2008, he repeated the honor by winning the Best of the Booker award. Both were for *Midnight's Children*. In 2007, Rushdie was knighted by Queen Elizabeth II for services to literature.

Rushdie's books are of great interest to scholars and students as well as to the general public. He continues to be one of the most important writers living in the twenty-first century.

PLOT SUMMARY

Chapter 1: The Shah of Blah

The story opens in the country of Alifbay. A boy named Haroun Khalifa lives in a sad city in that country. The city is "so ruinously sad that it had forgotten its name." Although the city is sad, Haroun lives happily with his father, Rashid, who laughs easily and his mother, Soraya, who sings beautifully. Rashid is a storyteller known by two names: to those who enjoy his stories, he is called Rashid the Ocean of Notions; to those who wish him ill, however, he is known as the Shah of Blah. Like many teenagers, Haroun is sometimes embarrassed by his father and his stories.

The Khalifa family's upstairs neighbors are Mr. Sengupta and his wife, Oneeta, a childless couple. Mr. Sengupta is very thin and whiny while Oneeta is large and generous. Mr. Sengupta is a minor city bureaucrat who loudly criticizes Rashid and his stories. "What's the use of stories that aren't even true?" he asks.

MEDIA ADAPTATIONS

- Tim Supple and David Tushingham adapted *Haroun and the Sea of Stories* for the stage. The play was performed at the Royal National Theatre in London in 1998.

- An abridged audiobook version of the novel was read by Salman Rushdie and released by Penguin Audio in 1997.

- An opera based on *Haroun and the Sea of Stories* by Charles Wuorinen and libretto by James Fenton premiered at the New York City Opera in Fall 2004.

Rashid never pretends that his stories are anything other than fiction. Politicians often employ Rashid to speak on their behalf because everyone loves Rashid's stories, despite the fact that Rashid always admits that everything he says is made up.

One day, Haroun comes home from school to find that his mother has run off with Mr. Sengupta. Rashid is completely heartbroken, as is Haroun, who now can no longer concentrate on anything for more than eleven minutes. Haroun is also bitter toward his father, believing that his mother has left because of him. Haroun throws Mr. Sengupta's words at his father: "What's the use of stories that aren't even true?" Haroun immediately regrets his unkind words, but the damage is done. Soon Rashid is unable to think of any more stories, and the politicians grow angry. They order Rashid to go to the Valley of K and redeem himself by telling stories or there will be real trouble for the Shah of Blah. Haroun feels terribly guilty over his father's situation and resolves to fix the problem himself.

Chapter 2: The Mail Coach

Because Rashid has fallen from favor, he and Haroun must travel to the Valley of K by mail bus. It is very crowded at the bus station, and it is difficult to find tickets. However, Haroun meets Mr. Butt, the mail coach driver, and hits it off with him. Mr. Butt puts them on the bus and asks if there is anything that Haroun wants. Haroun asks for a sunset view, thinking it will cheer his father. Butt then drives the bus at frightening speeds in order to reach the Valley of K in time for sunset. Everyone is terrified, and Haroun blames himself for his request. However, the sunset is truly magnificent and worth the terror. Rashid says that he thought that they were going to be killed. He uses the words "khattam-shud." When Haroun asks what that means, his father says,

> Khattam-Shud . . . is the Arch-Enemy of all Stories, even of Language itself. He is the Prince of Silence and the Foe of Speech. And because everything ends, because dreams end, stories end, life ends, at the finish of everything we use his name.

As they enter the Valley of K, Haroun notices that someone has painted the words "Kosh-Mar" over the sign reading "Valley of K." Rashid shows himself to be an expert in ancient languages by recalling that, in the ancient tongue of Franj, the valley was once called Kosh-Mar or Kache-Mer. He also admits that, in the old tongue, that was the word for nightmare.

They are met by a shifty politician called Mr. Snooty Buttoo who takes them across Dull Lake. Haroun does not like Mr. Buttoo and is uncomfortable that there are so many soldiers needed to protect Mr. Buttoo. On Dull Lake, a terrible-smelling mist engulfs them.

Chapter 3: The Dull Lake

The mist is so thick and smells so bad that no one can stand it. Haroun calls it a Mist of Misery. When the weather suddenly changes, he realizes that the lake is in Moody Land, a place where people's moods affect the weather. It is one of Rashid's most beloved stories. However, Rashid denies that they are in Moody Land, saying that it was only a story. Haroun tells his father that he must think happy thoughts, and when he does, the weather clears. Haroun no realizes that "the real world was full of magic, so magical worlds could easily be real."

They finally arrive at a luxurious houseboat that will be their accommodation for the night. In the library is a copy of *The Oceans of the Streams of Story*, a collection of tales. (This collection is, in fact, a real eleventh-century collection of Indian legends, folk tales, and fairy tales.)

Although the houseboat is comfortable, neither Haroun nor his father can sleep. Rashid is very depressed and anxious. They decide to switch bedrooms. Just as Haroun is finally dropping off to sleep, he is awakened by a Water Genie named Iff who has come to disconnect Rashid from his supply of story water from the great Story Sea. Haroun snatches Iff's Disconnector tool (an instrument something like a wrench) and refuses to return it until Iff takes him to Gup City on the hidden Moon Kahani to get the decision to disconnect Rashid reversed. Haroun now knows that his father's explanations about the Sea of Stories are true.

Chapter 4: An Iff and a Butt

The Genie tells Haroun to choose a bird and name it. The Genie has in his pocket tiny birds, and Haroun chooses a Hoopoe. Iff throws the tiny creature out the window, where it expands to a very large bird that looks a little like Butt the mail coach driver. Haroun thus calls the bird Butt the Hoopoe. Iff and Haroun jump on its back, and the bird flies away. Haroun discovers that Butt the Hoopoe is mechanical and that it can communicate with him telepathically.

They approach the Moon of Kahani and have a beautiful view of the Ocean of the Streams of Story, where they land. Iff tells Haroun to collect wish in a bottle, then drink it. It might save them the trouble of going to Gup City if Haroun can wish his father's troubles away. However, Haroun is not able to concentrate long enough to do so. He saves the wish water.

As they approach Gup City, Iff tells Haroun that the Ocean is being polluted and that many of the stories no longer make sense. He attributes the poisoning to Khattam-Shud, also known as the Cultmaster of Bezeban, from the dark side of Kahani.

Chapter 5: About Guppees and Chupwalas

In this chapter, Butt the Hoopoe explains the geography and details of Kahani. The rotation of Kahani has been brought under control by the Eggheads so that it is always light in Gup City and always dark in Chup City. As they continue on their journey across the ocean, they meet Mali, the Floating Gardener, and Bagha and Goopy, plentimaw fish. The plentimaw fish eat the stories in the ocean and then their digestive tracts make new stories out of the elements of the old. However, the pollution in the ocean is causing stories to be lost and damaged.

When they arrive in Gup City, the beauty of the palace and gardens entrances them. However, they soon discover that the Guppees are preparing for war with the Chupwalas.

King Chattergy and Prince Bolo, along with General Kitab and the Walrus, prepare to address the crowds gathered at the palace. Bolo reveals that his fiancée, the Princess Batcheat, has been kidnapped by the servants of the Cultmaster of Bezeban. They have sent messages to Khattam-Shud demanding her return and the cessation of the poisoning of the Ocean of the Streams of Story, but neither demand has been met. They declare war.

Suddenly there is a commotion, and a man with a sack over his head and his hands tied behind his back is led onto the balcony. He is identified as a captured spy. When the sack is removed, Haroun is startled to see his father, Rashid.

Chapter 6: The Spy's Story

Haroun pushes his way through the crowd and shouts at his father. The Guppees fall silent and Haroun tells them his father is not a spy at all. Haroun and Iff are taken by a page named Blabbermouth. All the pages wear tunics with the texts of famous stories on them. When Haroun arrives in the Throne Room, he finds his father telling his story to Prince Bolo, General Kitab, and the Walrus. Rashid says that he transported himself to Gup in dream but made an error in calculation, ending up in the Twilight Strip between Gup and Chup. He reports that there are bad things happening there. A Cult of Muteness has developed, wherein followers of the Idol of Bezeban devote themselves to a lifetime of silence, sewing their lips together so that they cannot ever speak. In addition, Rashid saw Batcheat kidnapped while he was in the Twilight Strip. Rashid offers to lead the Gup army to the place where he saw the Chupwala army assembled. Haroun shouts that he will go with him.

Blabbermouth is appointed to take him back to his room. When the page's hat is dislodged, however, Haroun discovers that Blabbermouth is a girl, not a boy. Blabbermouth is beside herself and makes Haroun promise not to reveal her gender. Blabbermouth next entertains Haroun with a juggling act.

Chapter 7: Into the Twilight Strip

The next morning, Blabbermouth awakens Haroun to join the army of pages assembling in the Pleasure Garden. Haroun finds his father with Iff, and the Guppee forces prepare to depart. The members of the army all chatter away about the causes of the war and how it should be fought. Haroun takes issue with this, but Butt the Hoopoe argues that, once you give a people freedom of speech, you must expect them to use it.

As Haroun and the rest of the forces enter the Twilight Strip between Gup and Chup, his spirits fall. Butt tells him not to worry, that the Twilight Strip has this effect on everyone seeing it for the first time. The armies come ashore in Chup. Haroun, Blabbermouth, General Kitab, and Rashid begin to scout the area. They come across a warrior who is fighting his shadow in a silent, graceful dance. When the warrior becomes aware of them, he stops and gestures to them quickly. They do not understand him. The warrior then attempts to speak.

Chapter 8: Shadow Warriors

Bolo wants to fight the warrior, but Rashid quickly realizes that the gestures are a kind of language. Rashid is then able to communicate with the warrior, whose name is Mudra (a word that means sacred hand gestures in yoga). Mudra has left the army of the Cultmaster and is willing to assemble an army of other warriors and their shadows who will fight on the side of Gup against Khattam-Shud. The Warrior insists, however, that they must decide what to do first: save the Ocean from poison or save the Princess Batcheat. They decide to save Batcheat, but Haroun volunteers to go to the Old Zone to investigate the poisoning of the water. He volunteers because of his love for the stories his father tells. He says that he has only recently begun believing in the reality of the Ocean but now feels it is his duty to try to save it.

Thus, Haroun, Iff, Goopy, Bagha, and Mali with Butt the Hoopoe set off to the Southern Polar Ocean, where the Wellspring or Source of Stories is located. Before their journey is over, however, Goopy and Bagha cannot swim in the grossly polluted waters of the Southern Ocean. The rest of the companions continue. As they try to make their way through a weed-jungle, they are trapped by a Web of Night, a Chupwala weapon. The companions are taken prisoner.

Chapter 9: The Dark Ship

Iff breaks down in grief when he sees how poisoned the Ocean is here.

We are the Guardians of the Ocean and we didn't guard it.... The oldest stories ever made and look at them now. We let them rot, we abandoned them, long before this poisoning. We lost touch with our beginnings, with our roots, our Wellspring, our Source.

The group is surrounded by Chupwalas and led to a huge black boat, the flagship of Khattam-Shud. They are ordered on board. Iff manages to hand Haroun a small Bite-a-Light, a device that will give him two minutes of light if he bites down on it. Everything is in shadows and dark.

Finally, Haroun and Iff are confronted by Khattam-Shud himself, a "skinny, scrawny, measly, weasely, snivelling clerical type." Haroun identifies him as Mr. Sengupta and begins to shout at him. The Cultmaster then changes shape and frightens all. Next he tells them he might as well show them what they came to see, since they will never be able to report back to the Guppees.

Chapter 10: Haroun's Wish
Khattam-Shud shows them vast machinery that manufactures poison. Since every story must be ruined in a different way, they have need of a great many poisons. He tells them about the Plug. He intends to plug the Wellspring of Stories itself, meaning that stories will cease.

At this minute, Mali's long tendrils begin to enter the ship. He quickly jumps on the ship's power generator, bringing the whole operation to a halt. Haroun bites on the Bite-a-Lite and blinds all the Chupwala soldiers who are used only to darkness. He dons a protective wet suit and dives into the ocean, catching a glimpse of the workers constructing the Plug. He remembers the wish water vial in his pocket and suddenly knows what to do. He returns to the surface and wishes that the Moon Kahani would spin normally so that both Gup and Chup would share equal hours of light and dark. Within eleven minutes, the light begins to pour down on Chup. The Chupwalas and the ship begin to melt. Haroun rescues Iff and Mali, and they all escape on Butt the Hoopoe. The poison has been destroyed and the Ocean will be able to heal.

Chapter 11: Princess Batcheat
Meanwhile, after Blabbermouth saves Bolo from a bomb, the armies of Gup who have been so chatty and honest fight together in a coordinated fashion and defeat the armies of Chup. Their silence has been their downfall because they were unable to communicate strategy. At the end of the battle, there is an earthquake caused by the spinning moon. A large statue of Bezeban crushes the real Khattam-Shud (the Khattam-Shud on the boat being the Shadow of the Cultmaster). As the Guppees enter Chup City, they hear Batcheat singing. They recover Batcheat, and peace is declared.

Haroun, however, is summoned to the office of the Walrus. His wish has destroyed all of the Eggheads' machinery, and he is being called to answer for himself.

Chapter 12: Was It the Walrus?
Haroun is terrified. He tries to persuade Iff and Mali to go with him, but they refuse. When he finally walks into the Walrus's office, he finds the Walrus, King Chattergy, Prince Bolo, Princess Batcheat, Blabbermouth, General Kitab, Iff, Mali, and Rashid, along with several others all assembled. He asks if he is in trouble, and the room erupts with laughter. They are pulling a joke on him. The real reason for the summons is so that he can be honored for his bravery and his saving of the Ocean of Stories. The Walrus tells him he can have anything he wants.

Haroun wants a happy ending but knows they cannot give it to him. The Walrus disagrees. He says that by a Process Too Complicated To Explain, they can make up a happy ending for him.

Butt the Hoopoe flies them back to Dull Lake, and when Haroun enters the houseboat, he immediately falls asleep. When he awakens, he finds his father sipping tea and talking about a strange dream. Mr. Buttoo arrives to take Rashid to his speaking engagement, and Haroun, wondering if the whole night was a dream, returns to his room. He finds a letter from Blabbermouth and signed by all his friends from Kahani telling him to return again. Enclosed is a tiny bird, Butt the Hoopoe, who will transport him wherever he wishes.

Rashid finds his voice again and announces that he will tell the story *Haroun and the Sea of Stories*. He begins with the first sentence of Rushdie's *Haroun and the Sea of Stories*. The story turns the people of the Valley of K against the corrupt Mr. Buttoo, and Haroun and Rashid return safely to their home. Everyone there is happy.

Haroun suddenly realizes that his wish has come true. The name of his city has been remembered. It is called Kahani. When Rashid and Haroun arrive at their apartment, Oneeta Sengupta tells them that they must hurry to celebrate.

Soraya has returned home. When he awakens the next morning, he remembers that it is his birthday. He hears his mother singing in the living room.

CHARACTERS

Bagha

Bagha is a plentimaw fish, a type of fish with several mouths that consumes stories in the Ocean of the Stream of Stories. The stories are reassembled in the guts of the plentimaw fish and become new stories. Bagha is always with its partner, Goopy. The pair is named after two heroes from a movie by Satyajit Ray, according to Rushdie's glossary located at the end of the novel.

Princess Batcheat

Princess Batcheat is the daughter of King Chattergy and is engaged to Prince Bolo. Her terrible singing voice is an ongoing joke throughout the book, as are her unattractive nose and mouth. Her kidnapping sets in motion the war between Gup and Chup. According to Rushdie's glossary at the end of the novel, her name means "chit-chat."

Blabbermouth

Blabbermouth is a page in service to Prince Bolo, disguised as a boy. She is a talkative, intelligent, and courageous young woman. At first, she appears ill tempered with Haroun, but ultimately they become friends. She develops an infatuation and admiration for the warrior Mudra. Haroun has a crush on Blabbermouth and is happy when she kisses him.

Prince Bolo

Bolo is a prince in Gup who is engaged to the king's daughter Batcheat. He is a silly man, overdressed in the garb of royalty. He is not very smart and rarely judges his situation accurately. For example, at one point, he grants would-be assassins immunity against the advice of Blabbermouth and others. Only Blabbermouth's quick action saves him. He overrates his own courage and swordsmanship. On the other hand, although he is laughable, he loves Batcheat with all his heart despite her many shortcomings. Nor is he an evil character. Rather, he is a parody of a fairy-tale hero. According to Rushdie, his name means "Speak!"

Mr. Butt

Mr. Butt is the mail coach driver. He and Haroun become friends early in the book, and he promises him that Haroun and his father will see a beautiful sunset over the Valley of K. To do so, however, he drives excessively fast and recklessly. He is Butt the Hoopoe's counterpart in the "real" world.

Butt the Hoopoe

Butt the Hoopoe is a large mechanical bird who can communicate with Haroun telepathically. He provides transportation from Earth to Kahani for Haroun and Iff. He resembles the mail coach driver in both appearance and speech patterns.

Snooty Buttoo

Snooty Buttoo is a corrupt politician who hires Rashid to speak on his behalf, in order to win reelection. He is arrogant and cruel and does not deserve reelection. While in the Valley of K, Rashid and Haroun stay on a houseboat that Snooty Buttoo provides. When Rashid returns from Kahani, the story he tells turns the people against Buttoo, and Buttoo leaves the Valley of K, never to be heard from again.

King Chattergy

King Chattergy is Batcheat's father and the figurehead ruler of Gup.

The Eggheads

The Eggheads are a group of scientists and engineers who have devised all of the Processes Too Complicated to Explain (P2C2E). They are responsible for altering Kahani's orbit so that Gup is always in daylight and Chup is always in darkness. They can also create happy endings for stories, and they have developed a method for distributing story water across the face of the Earth.

Goopy

Goopy is a plentimaw fish, a type of fish with several mouths who consume stories in the Ocean of the Stream of Stories. The stories are reassembled in the guts of the plentimaw fish and become new stories. Goopy is always with its partner, Bagha. The pair is named after two heroes from a movie by Satyajit Ray, according to Rushdie's glossary located at the end of the novel.

Iff

Iff is a Water Genie dispatched to disconnect Rashid from the supply of water coming from the Stream of Stories. When Haroun takes his Disconnector from him, he is obliged to take Haroun to the Moon Kahani and Gup City to plead Rashid's case with the Walrus. Iff's pattern of speech includes many clichés and synonyms. Although at first annoyed with Haroun for the theft of his Disconnector, Iff proves to be a boon companion.

Haroun Khalifa

Haroun is the protagonist of *Haroun and the Sea of Stories*. While his age is not given, events in the story imply that he is probably twelve or thirteen. That is, he is young enough to still be in school and live at home, but also old enough to be embarrassed by his father and interested in girls. Haroun's parents believe that he is an exceptional child, although he refuses to believe it. Nonetheless, the events of the story prove that his parents' assessment is not wrong. He is compassionate and responsible, feeling deeply for the trouble his words cause his father. He takes it upon himself to try to solve his father's problem, since he feels responsible for having caused it. Haroun is also resourceful. He quickly snatches the Water Genie's Disconnector tool, in order to preserve his father's access to stories as well as to give him an edge in negotiating with Iff to take him to Gup City. Finally, Haroun is a very brave boy. Although it is dangerous, he volunteers to go to the Old Zone to spy on Khattam-Shud, and while there, he escapes from capture, figures out a way to win the war, and saves his friends. Haroun grows over the course of the story and realizes that all that really matters to him is that his father and mother are happy with each other again.

Rashid Khalifa

Rashid is Haroun's father, variously known as the Ocean of Notions and the Shah of Blah for his talent in creating stories on the spot. He earns his living as a storyteller, often working for politicians who want him to help them win reelection. After a period of being completely absorbed in his career, he loses his wife to another man and is heartbroken. His heartbreak results in his being unable to tell stories. Rashid is a kind father who loves his son and his wife. In addition, he is a brave man himself. On Kahani, he defends himself against charges of spying and subsequently leads the Guppee armies to the location of the Chupwala tents. He regains his ability to tell stories after his visit to Kahani. More importantly, the stories he tells after he returns from Kahani

no longer support corrupt politicians but put them in their places. Thus, the novel allows not only Haroun to mature and grow, it also allows Rashid to become a better father, husband, and storyteller.

Soraya Khalifa

Soraya is Haroun's mother and Rashid's wife. Although initially happy in the story, she grows weary of Rashid's stories over the years. She stops singing and then runs away with Mr. Sengupta. At the end of the story, she realizes her error and returns to the family and resumes singing in the living room.

Khattum-Shud

Khattum-Shud is the evil villain of the novel. He is also referred to as the Cultmaster of Bezaban. (Bezaban, according to Rushdie, means "Without-a-Tongue.") Khattum-Shud hates stories and words and wants silence. He is the enemy of free speech and the ruler of Chup. He has started a religion in which practitioners must sew their lips together to prevent them from speaking. His "real-world" counterpart is Mr. Sengupta. According to Rushdie's glossary, his name means "completely finished" or "over and done with."

General Kitab

General Kitab is the leader of the Guppee army. He is a good man and a strong leader who supports the rights of his troops to question his authority and debate strategy. He is frequently embarrassed by Prince Bolo's over-the-top and inappropriate responses to battle situations and diplomatic negotiations.

Mali

Mali is a floating gardener, a species made up of vines and water plants. His major task is to make sure stories do not become too complicated or knotted up. He does this by cutting away weeds and straightening out root systems. He is a boon companion to Haroun and is responsible for saving the day when Haroun is held captive by Khattam-Shud.

Mudra

Mudra is a warrior who defected from Khattam-Shud's army. He has learned how to disconnect his shadow from himself and has trained the entire army to do so. He and his shadow practice martial arts with each other. Mudra has difficulty speaking with his voice but is eloquent in an ancient language of gestures. He and his fellow warriors and shadows join the Gup forces in their war against the Chupwalas. According to Rushdie's glossary, Mudra "speaks Abhinaya, the Language of Gesture" used in classical Indian dance. Rushdie continues, "a 'mudra' is any one of the gestures that make up the language."

Mr. Sengupta

Mr. Sengupta is the Khalifas' upstairs neighbor. He is a skinny, whiny, minor civil servant who hates stories and has an eye for Soraya. He persuades her to run away with him, setting the rest of the events of the story in motion. He is the "real-world" counterpart of Khattam-Shud.

Oneeta Sengupta

Oneeta Sengupta is Mr. Sengupta's wife. She is a large, compassionate woman who loves Haroun as a son. Her husband's desertion causes her both embarrassment and pain.

The Walrus

The Walrus is the head of the Eggheads, so called because of his mustache.

THEMES

Storytelling

Janet Mason Ellerby, writing in *Lion and the Unicorn*, identifies storytelling as an important theme in *Haroun and the Sea of Stories*. She writes, "Rushdie addresses the serious theme of storytelling and its critical link to cultural emancipation within his own rollicking story of a boy's fabulous adventures."

Early in the novel, Mr. Sengupta says, "What are all these stories? Life is not a storybook or joke shop. All this fun will come to no good. What's the use of stories that aren't even true?" After Soraya leaves the family and Rashid is heartbroken, Haroun shouts the same question at his father, blaming him for his mother's unhappiness. The remaining pages of the novel attempt to answer that very question.

Haroun discovers on his journey first to the Valley of K, later to Kahani, and finally back to his hometown again, that stories carry great power. Without stories, all is silence. Stories connect the past to the present and the present to the future. They carry in them the bits and pieces of

TOPICS FOR FURTHER STUDY

- With a group of your classmates, choose several scenes from *Haroun and the Sea of Stories* that seem particularly vivid to you. Using paints, pastels, and other media, create illustrations for the book. Mount the exhibit and invite others in your school to view your creation.

- Read Isabelle Allende's young-adult novel *City of the Beasts* (2002). The story features two young people who travel to the magical world of the Amazon. Analyze the novel as a coming-of-age story and write an essay in which you compare and contrast what Haroun has learned with what the main characters of *City of the Beasts* have learned.

- Using the Internet and your school library, research the region known as Kashmir. Why has this region been so troubled since 1947? Using software such as Glogster, create a poster that embeds important issues, illustrations, news reports, and other relevant materials so that others in your class can learn about this area of the world.

- With a group of your classmates, write a play adaptation of *Haroun and the Sea of Stories*. Record your presentation of your play and post to YouTube for others to view.

- Read *The Annotated Alice: The Definitive Edition* by Lewis Carroll, with introduction and notes by Martin Gardner. This is a fully annotated edition, revealing all of Carroll's political, historical, philosophical, and literary allusions. Now, return to *Haroun and the Sea of Stories*. Prepare similar annotations for several chapters of *Haroun*. If you are able, work with others so that you can create a fully annotated version of the novel.

- With a small group, research the Ayatollah Khomeini, the *fatwa*, and the Rushdie Affair. Write a news script and present a newscast reporting on the incident.

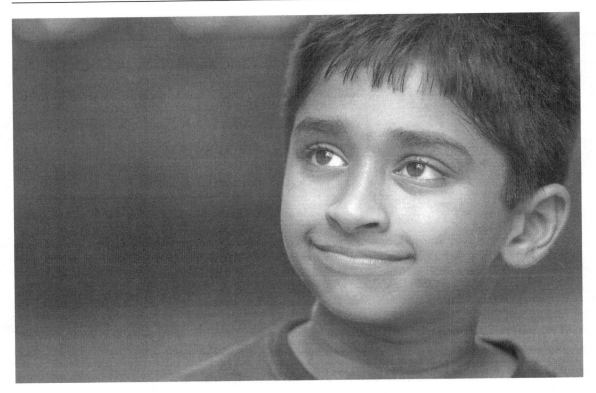

The main character, Haroun, is an energetic, curious boy with a short attention span.

(© Arvind Balaraman | Shutterstock.com)

all human experience. Through the creative act of storytelling, humans recreate themselves.

Likewise, as Haroun makes his journey, he discovers that the stories his father has told him since he was a child are true, although they seem fantastic to him. He learns that there really is a Sea of Stories and that the archenemy Khattam-Shud, the enemy of all language, exists. Rushdie's point seems to be that fiction has a purpose and that stories carry truths even when, paradoxically, they are not true.

Throughout the novel, Rushdie also reiterates his philosophy of storytelling. No story is new; all stories are made up of bits and pieces of other stories. "Any story worth its salt," exclaims Butt the Hoopee, as Haroun and his companions travel to Gup City, "can handle a little shaking up!" Iff the Water Genie expands on this comment. He tells Haroun, "Nothing comes from nothing, Thieflet; no story comes from nowhere; new stories are born from old—it is the new combinations that make them new." Thus, for Rushdie, every act of storytelling is simultaneously one

of destruction and then reconstruction. Storytelling is recycling; the new story is created out of old elements.

Finally, storytelling serves yet another purpose in the novel. David Appelbaum, writing in a review appearing in *Parabola* tells the reader that "story telling is the antidote for sadness in Salman Rushdie's delightful new novel." Stories allow humans to escape the drudgery of their daily lives, experience adventures they could not in real life, and feel emotions absent in their humdrum existences. Stories not only educate their listeners, they also make them happy.

Language

Throughout *Haroun and the Sea of Stories*, Rushdie plays with language, using puns, onomatopoeia, allusion, and other figures of speech. The use of these techniques in the novel runs deeper than mere stylistics, however. The subject of language serves as a serious thematic concern for Rushdie. In an interview with Davia Nelson, Rushdie suggests that his experience with the *fatwa* during the writing of *Haroun* deeply affected how he felt about language. He states, "I guess [I] had become involved myself in a sort of war between language and silence—I suddenly understood the meaning of the story that I hadn't previously understood."

The purpose of the *fatwa* issued against Rushdie was to shut him up, permanently. By killing Rushdie, the Ayatollah would put an end not only to the storyteller but also to the stories. Indeed, during the early days of the *fatwa*, Rushdie was in deep hiding and did not appear to his audiences. Gradually, this changed. Rushdie chose to write *Haroun and the Sea of Stories* in retaliation.

It is not surprising that the arch villain of the novel is Khattam-Shud, the Prince of Silence and the Foe of Speech. Many scholars agree that this villain is a stand-in for Khomeini. Just as Khattam-Shud wants to stop all stories, Khomeini wanted to censor and silence any who disagreed with him and his belief system.

Thus, for Rushdie, hiding from death, the importance of being able to speak and tell stories became ever clearer. When the voice is silenced, everything ends. As he writes in *Haroun*, "Because dreams end, stories end, life ends, at the finish of everything we use his name. 'It's finished,' we tell one another, 'it's over. Khattam-Shud: The End.'" For Rushdie, the end of the language is the end of everything.

STYLE

Magical Realism

One of the most important styles found in late twentieth- and early twenty-first-century literature and art is magical realism (sometimes referred to as "magic realism.") While the work might seem realistic on the surface, fantasy, myth, magic, the supernatural, and dreams invade and at times coopt the work. Magical realism had its earliest articulations in the works of South American writers; perhaps the best-known magical realist in the world is Colombian writer Gabriel García Márquez, who was in turn influenced by Argentine writer Jorge Luis Borges. Other important writers of magical realism include Italian writer Italo Calvino, English writer John Fowles, and German writer Günter Grass.

In *Haroun and the Sea of the Stories*, Rushdie clearly draws on magical realism to create his story. As the novel opens, Haroun lives in a realistic household consisting of his father, his mother, and his upstairs neighbors. Although the city where Haroun lives sounds like many industrial cities, the element of magical realism enters in quickly: "In the north of the sad city stood mighty factories in which (so I'm told) sadness was actually manufactured, packaged, and sent all over the world."

The truly magical part of *Haroun*, however, happens after Haroun and his father travel to the Valley of K and are taken to a houseboat where they are to spend the night. In the middle of the night, Haroun is awakened by a supernatural being, Iff the Water Genie. While Iff is obviously magical, he is also realistic, behaving like the plumber he is, come to turn off the water. The combination of the realistic elements with the purely fantastical serves to make the scene more humorous and also more meaningful.

Further, when Haroun travels to the moon Kahani and experiences his amazing adventures, readers might wonder if all of the action is part of a fantastic dream, similar to the one experienced by Dorothy in *The Wizard of Oz*. However, like Dorothy, Haroun finds evidence after his return that the journey was real, regardless of how magical it seemed. Haroun's return to his home signals the return to the so-called real; however, his mother's return and the return of the family unit are by far the most magical events Haroun could ever have hoped for. Perhaps Haroun's most important lesson is the one he learns on his journey: "He knew what he knew: that the real world was full of magic, so magical worlds could easily be real."

The Journey of the Hero

In creating *Haroun and the Sea of Stories*, Rushdie drew on one of the oldest story devices known, the journey of the hero. Since humans have begun telling and recording stories, the heroic journey has been the core of the repertoire. Stories such as *The Epic of Gilgamesh*, *The Iliad*, *The Odyssey*, and *Beowulf* all feature a young hero who leaves home, travels far, learns much, shares his adventures with boon companions, and returns home, a wiser and more experienced person. Joseph Campbell, in his groundbreaking 1949 book *The Hero with a Thousand Faces*, detailed the stages and characteristics of the heroic journey. Susanna Schrobsdorff, writing in *Time*, comments, "Campbell drew from ancient allegories in dozens of cultures and codified [them] into one rollicking human epic, a universal saga that he referred to as the monomyth."

One of the best-known heroic journey stories in contemporary culture is that of George Lucas's *Star Wars*. Likewise, the *Harry Potter* novels follow Campbell's descriptions of the hero and his or her journey.

Haroun demonstrates many of the stages described by Campbell. The heroic quest always starts with a challenge or call to the journey, usually because of some important need or desire. In the case of Haroun, he begins his journey because he feels that he must help his father. Heroes often also receive supernatural help. Haroun is helped by Iff the Water Genie and a host of other supernaturally talented allies. Heroes often find themselves in a dark, difficult place where it is uncertain whether they will survive. For Haroun, this comes when he is on board ship with Khattam-Shud. Sometimes Rushdie's use of the heroic journey is deliberately satirical. For example, heroes generally run into some sort of goddess who helps them on their way. Haroun runs into Blabbermouth, a chatty girl disguised as a boy, serving as a Guppee page. Many heroic stories include reconciliation with a father figure. In the novel, Haroun first denigrates his father and then later comes to admire and respect him. Indeed, the impetus for his journey is to atone for his transgression against his father, a transgression that takes away his father's gift of storytelling.

Finally, the heroic journey story ends with the hero returning home. Through his or her journey, he or she has grown in significant and important ways. Haroun demonstrates his growth through the maturity of his wish, that his family be reunited. As a result of his journey, his town is no longer sad. Everyone benefits from his contribution, and he has proved himself to be, though a young boy, heroic in every sense.

HISTORICAL CONTEXT

Kashmir

In both his fiction and nonfiction, Rushdie often refers to Kashmir, a highly contested area located on the northern border of India and the northeast border of Pakistan. In *Haroun and the Sea of Stories*, several locations can be identified with Kashmir, including The Valley of K, also known as Kache-Mer and Kosh-Mar. The glossary written by Rushdie and included in the text of *Haroun*

and the Sea of Stories also notes that the fictional Dull Lake is named for Dal Lake in Kashmir. Rushdie's association with Kashmir runs deep; his family lived in Kashmir until just before Rushdie's birth in 1947, and Rushdie continues to comment on the situation in the beleaguered region. An article in the September 24, 2001, issue of the British newspaper the *Telegraph* provides a brief history of the region's conflicts, shedding light on Rushdie's ongoing fascination with Kashmir.

In 1947, India gained independence from Britain. Part of the agreement included the creation of the state of Pakistan. The partition of the Indian subcontinent was largely along religious lines, with Pakistan becoming a Muslim state and India becoming a Hindu one, based on the religious affiliation of the majority of the population in each area. The partition was not neat, however; according to the *Telegraph*, there were some 650 princely states, including Kashmir, within the new countries. The states were forced to join one or the other of the new countries, depending on their location. Located on the border of both India and Pakistan, Kashmir had a choice of whether to join with India or Pakistan. The choice was not peaceful. In 1947 and 1948, Indian and Pakistani armed forces fought a war over the region.

In 1948, the United Nations intervened and asked both warring parties to remove their troops in anticipation of a vote by the inhabitants of Kashmir as to their preference. Pakistan refused to stop fighting. In 1949, the countries observed a cease-fire. At this point, about 65 percent of the territory was held by India, with the remaining 35 percent held by Pakistan; the Kashmir Valley was claimed by both countries, according to an August 11, 2011, article appearing in the *New York Times*.

Since 1949, India and Pakistan have engaged in all-out war over Kashmir several times. One of the most serious outbreaks of fighting began with an insurgency of Kashmiris in 1989, eventually resulting in the deaths of more than 60,000 people. The *New York Times* further reports that the insurgency was "partly fueled by training, weapons, and cash from Pakistan," which wanted to use the Kashmiri independence movement to wrest control of the region from India. During this period, thousands of people, mostly young Kashmiri men, went missing. (In August 2011,

COMPARE
&
CONTRAST

- **1990s:** In Kashmir, an independence movement, aided by funding from Pakistan, continues an insurgency resulting in the deaths of many people.

  Today: Although in a period of relative peace, the situation in Kashmir is still volatile. A mass grave with thousands of bodies from the 1990s is uncovered in 2011.

- **1990s:** Rushdie is in hiding after the Ayatollah Khomeini issues an edict called a *fatwa*, encouraging all Muslims to murder Rushdie in response to the publication of his book *The Satanic Verses*.

  Today: The *fatwa* is lifted, and Rushdie has come out of hiding. He is still, however, considered to be in some danger from radical Islamists who do not recognize the lifting of the *fatwa*.

- **1990s:** Rushdie is under the protection of the British government's Special Branch security teams in response to the *fatwa*.

  Today: Rushdie is awarded a knighthood by Queen Elizabeth II for his contributions to literature. The event touches off protests and riots among Muslims.

- **1990s:** Rushdie wins the Booker of the Bookers award for *Midnight's Children* in 1993. The award signifies that this book is considered the best among all of the books awarded the Booker Prize since the award's inception.

  Today: By public vote, *Midnight's Children* wins the Best of the Booker award, commemorating the prize's fortieth anniversary.

---

mass graves containing the bodies of more than two thousand people were found in Kashmir.)

It was against this backdrop of intrigue, violence, and contested territory that Rushdie wrote *Haroun and the Sea of Stories*. The conflict between India and Pakistan over the Kashmir Valley clearly parallels the conflict between the fictional Guppees and the Chupwallas in the novel.

The Ayatollah Khomeini and the Fatwa

Ruhollah Khomeini was an Iranian religious scholar, born in 1900, who achieved the title of "ayatollah" in the 1920s, according to the *BBC History* website. An *ayatollah* is a high-ranking Shiite Muslim scholar. In the 1960s, Khomeini became politically active in opposing the rule of the Shah of Iran, whose regime was pro-Western. Khomeini pushed for a return to conservative Islam and for Iran to be governed by Islamic law. In 1962, the Shah had Khomeini arrested, immediately making him a hero to those who opposed the Shah. Released into exile

in 1964, Khomeini continued to agitate from abroad for the Shah's overthrow.

In 1979, Khomeini and his party were successful in bringing down the Shah. Khomeini returned to Iran and was elected the country's religious and political leader. He maintained his anti-American, anti-Western stance, and under his influence, radical students stormed the U.S. Embassy in Tehran on November 4, 1979, taking a number of Americans hostage. The Americans were held for over a year.

In September 1988, Rushdie's *The Satanic Verses* was published in Britain. Reviewers were immediately concerned about the potential Muslim backlash against the novel because Muslims found the content of the book highly offensive. By early October, India had banned the book and Rushdie began receiving death threats. The furor continued over the following months, leading to riots and book burnings across the world, even in England. Finally, on February 14, 1989, Khomeini, speaking as the ruler of Iran and the religious head of all Shiite Muslims, issued a

Haroun and his father catch a ride on the mail bus to go to the Valley of K before sunset as the novel begins. *(© Jeremy Richards / Shutterstock.com)*

fatwa against Rushdie. Khomeini called on Muslims around the world to execute all who were involved in the writing, publication, and distribution of *The Satanic Verses*. An Iranian religious foundation offered a $1-million USD reward for anyone who murdered Rushdie.

Khomeini died in June 1989 without revoking the *fatwa*. As a result, Rushdie remained in hiding under close protection for many years, including the years during which he wrote *Haroun and the Sea of Stories*. Most critics agree that the arch villain Khattam-Shud is a caricature of Khomeini.

CRITICAL OVERVIEW

When *Haroun and the Sea of Stories* was published in 1990, reviewers responded very favorably. Rushdie wrote the book under extraordinary circumstances. The Ayatollah Khomeini of Iran had issued a sentence of death (known as a *fatwa*) on Rushdie in response to the 1988 publication of *The*

Satanic Verses. Rushdie immediately went into hiding under stiff protective custody. He moved house constantly and was separated from his family, particularly his son, most of the time. The knowledge of these circumstances seems to have affected many reviewers. Indeed, most early reviews focus on the parallels between the *fatwa* and Rushdie's story. Edward Blishen, for example, writing in *New Statesman and Society*, asserts, "It's a tale that springs clearly enough out of the predicament of a writer who, by elaborate chance, has taken upon his shoulders the whole implicit peril of the storyteller's trade." Likewise, Sybil Steinberg, writing in *Publishers Weekly*, references the "unprecedented controversy generated by *The Satanic Verses*," noting that, in *Haroun and the Sea of Stories*, "Rushdie offers as eloquent a defense of art as any Renaissance treatise."

At the same time, many critics agree with Denis Donoghue, who, in an early review appearing in the *New Republic*, suggests, "There is something for everybody in *Haroun and the Sea of Stories*." Both adults and children could enjoy the story, the critics seem to agree. For example, Rosalia Baena, writing in *Journal of Commonwealth Literature*, reads *Haroun and the Sea of Stories* as a work aimed at a "double audience: on the one hand a young reader can enjoy the story of Haroun and his father Rashid." Baena continues, "On the other hand, an adult reader and a literary critic perceive at least two other layers of meaning, at a political and a metafictional level."

In a slightly later study, James Harrison, writing in his *Salman Rushdie* (1992), comments on the similarity between Rushdie's situation and the plot of *Haroun*, noting, however, that the book plays with language as well as providing political commentary. Moreover, according to Harrison, Rushdie's work does not fall into the trap of being overly preachy and didactic:

> Never, as one reads the book, does such potential didacticism displace, or overshadow, or even diminish the pleasure one derives from the playful inventiveness of the fantasy and the sheer vigor and "jump" of the story.

Indeed, many scholars comment on the allegorical nature of *Haroun*. Eva König, for example, writing in *International Fiction Review*, asserts, "The interpretation of the novel as an allegory about democratic and artistic freedom is favored in the Anglocentric world." König, however, finds another reading more satisfying. Though she believes that the allegorical reading "in the shadow of the *fatwa*" reflects the construction of the story, she also argues that Rushdie "simultaneously sets up and deconstructs such a simple allegorical interpretation." For König, the novel's importance is as a commentary on colonialism:

> It can be argued that this novel is also about an ex-colony waking up to a new understanding of the postcolonial condition.... Seen in this light, *Haroun and the Sea of Stories*, a 'minor' novel according to some critics, takes its rightful place among Rushdie's others works dealing with the postcolonial condition.

Likewise, Patricia Merivale, writing in *ARIEL*, notes that *Haroun* is "strikingly postcolonial: it subverts, or at least gives a little twist to, an eclectic amalgam of colonial 'classical' Children's Literature."

Other scholars provide various additional commentaries. Suchismita Sen, for one, focuses on the act of communication in *Haroun and the Sea of Stories*: "In Haroun's story, Rushdie provides a child's-eye view of the intricate and often intangible nature of interpersonal communication."

Daniel Roberts, writing in *ARIEL*, suggests that *Haroun and the Sea of Stories* "makes sophisticated use of a number of literary allusions from various Romantic-period texts." Roberts also argues that the use of these allusions creates a stronger political statement, particularly with regard to Kashmir.

In an innovative and interesting article, Aron R. Aji, writing in *Contemporary Literature*, looks at the "legacy of Islam" in the narrative details of *Haroun*. He raises two important questions concerning the text: first, he wonders if there is a "kinship" between stories and religion, since both stories and religion speak so fully to what it means to be human. Second, he asks whether this kinship can "serve as grounds for reconciliation between the Islamic faith and the pluralistic cultural traditions of its community." Aji answers both questions with a resounding "yes."

Finally, David Applebaum, writing in *Parabola*, finds that *Haroun and the Sea of Stories* shares many features with *The Arabian Nights*. He also reads the story of young Haroun as a classic story of a heroic journey.

CRITICISM

Diane Andrews Henningfeld

Henningfeld is a professor of English at Adrian College who writes widely for educational publications. In the following essay, she examines the role of allusion in Haroun and the Sea of Stories.

In *Haroun and the Sea of Stories*, Rushdie creates an imaginary world with some very recognizable similarities to this one. It is a world that children delight in and a world that adults can read with wry smiles, recognizing Rushdie's word play and sly allusions to other writers and other tales. Indeed, one of the most enjoyable features of *Haroun and the Sea of Stories* is Rushdie's use of allusions. The allusions, however, are more than just a stylistic device, and they do more than merely identify what works have influenced Rushdie. A clue to the real role of allusions in the novel comes from Iff the Water Genie: "Nothing comes from nothing, little Thieflet; no story comes from nowhere; new stories are born from old—it is the new combinations that make them new."

Before examining the metafictional nature of the novel, it might be wise to review the definition

WHAT DO I READ NEXT?

- Lewis Carroll's children's classics, *Alice's Adventures in Wonderland* and *Through the Looking Glass*, first published in 1865 and 1871, bear similarities to *Haroun and the Sea of Stories* in their use of puns, satire, fantastic occurrences, and sly comments on contemporary politics. A particularly interesting one-volume edition of the two books is *The Annotated Alice* (2000), with introduction and notes by Martin Gardner.

- Rushdie draws heavily on the famous collection of stories *One Thousand and One Arabian Nights* for source material for *Haroun and the Sea of Stories*. Geraldine McCaughrean provides a one-volume selection of the stories designed for readers ten and up in *One Thousand and One Arabian Nights* (Oxford Story Collections), published in 2000.

- In 2002, Chilean writer Isabelle Allende published the young-adult novel *City of the Beasts*. The novel tells the tale of fifteen-year-old Alexander Cold and twelve-year-old Nadia Santos, who journey to the magical world of the Amazon with a party of people, including Alexander's grandmother, a doctor, a guide, a soldier, and native peoples looking for the mythical creature known as The Beast.

- *Luka and the Fire of Life* by Salman Rushdie, published in 2010, is a sequel to *Haroun and the Sea of Stories*. The novel features Luka, Haroun's younger brother, who must embark on a dangerous journey to the Magic World in order to save his father's life.

- *Islam in the World*, 3rd edition (2006), by Malese Ruthven provides a lucid overview of the major issues surround Islam in the world today. In this edition, the author covers the Rushdie Affair, considering both the events and the consequences of the publication of *The Satanic Verses*.

- British writer Jasper Fforde has created a fantastic alternate reality in his series of "Thursday Next" novels. In these books, literary detective Thursday Next takes on cases that protect characters and stories of famous books by entering the Book World, the place where all stories originate. *The Well of Lost Plots* (2003) offers the best description of the Book World.

---

of allusion, and to identify a number of key allusions in *Haroun and the Sea of Stories*. A literary allusion is a reference, without explicit identification, to a fictional character, another writer, a person, a place, an historic event or another literary text or passage. According to M. H. Abrams, writing in *A Glossary of Literary Terms*,

> Allusions of course imply a fund of knowledge that is shared by an author and an audience. Most literary allusions are intended to be recognized by the generally educated readers of the author's time, but some are aimed at a special coterie.

A number of critics, including Sybil Steinberg in *Publisher's Weekly*, Janet Mason Ellerby in *Lion and the Unicorn*, Daniel Roberts and Patricia Merivale in separate articles appearing in *ARIEL*, and David Applebaum in *Parabola*, among others, note that Rushdie uses many allusions in *Haroun and the Sea of Stories*. Most commonly cited are references to *Arabian Nights*, *Alice's Adventures in Wonderland*, *The Wizard of Oz*, Aesop's *Fables*, and *Pinocchio*, although there are additional works, writers, and events alluded to throughout the novel.

Literary allusions can sometimes function as inside jokes between the writer and the reader. The reader who is unaware of the person, place, or thing to which the writer refers can still enjoy the story, but this reader nevertheless misses out

> " THE ULTIMATE MESSAGE OF *HAROUN* IS THAT
> SOMETHING OF INESTIMABLE VALUE WILL BE LOST
> AND THE WORLD WILL GROW DIM, LIKE THE DARK
> SIDE OF KAHANI, SHOULD HUMANS EVER FORGET
> THE IMPORTANCE OF OUR STORIES AND LEGENDS."

on the special significance of the reference. For example, the army of pages in *Haroun* alludes to the army of playing cards in *Alice's Adventures in Wonderland*, a book written in 1865 by Charles Dodgson, under the pseudonym of Lewis Carroll. Carroll's book and its sequel *Through the Looking Glass*, in turn, are chock-full of additional allusions.

Rushdie offers many additional humorous allusions aimed at an educated, literate audience. At the beginning of chapter eight, for example, the Shadow Warrior tries to speak. All he manages to croak out, however, are the words "Gogogol" and "Kafkafka." Readers in the know will recognize the allusions to Nikolai Vasilievich Gogol, a Ukrainian-born Russian novelist and playwright, and Franz Kafka, the Bohemian writer of short stories and novels. Both writers were known for their surreal, grotesque, and strange subject matter. The later references to the Valley of K also echo Kafka: in his novel *The Trial*, Kafka's protagonist is referred to only as K.

A few paragraphs later, the Shadow Warrior says, "Spock Obi New Year." Again, readers familiar with *Star Trek* and *Star Wars* will recognize the brief reference to Mr. Spock, the Vulcan science officer of the *Enterprise*, and Obi Wan Kanobi, the old Jedi knight who becomes Luke Skywalker's mentor. While this is a brief allusion, it nevertheless serves to reinforce the thematic understanding of *Haroun* as a quest story. In addition, the description of the Shadow Warrior practicing martial arts with his shadow brings to mind scenes from *Peter Pan* by J. M. Barrie. Peter becomes separated from his shadow in that book.

Thus, these instances demonstrate that, in addition to providing a secret wink to the knowledgeable reader, allusions can serve a thematic

purpose. An allusion can be used to insert into a new work all of the thematic and stylistic concerns of the alluded-to text or writer. For example, in 1962, Ray Bradbury titled one of his best-known novels *Something Wicked This Way Comes*. The title is an allusion to William Shakespeare's play *Macbeth*. In this play, there are witches, the second of whom speaks the line, "By the pricking of my thumbs, something wicked this way comes" just before Macbeth enters the scene. Bradbury's use of the phrase as his title signals that the novel will probably contain some sort of supernatural element, just as the witches provide in *Macbeth*. Moreover, readers familiar with the play know that it is the story of a man who loses his honor and his life in thrall to blind ambition created by the prediction of the three weird sisters. Thus, before the reader even begins to read Bradbury's novel, he or she is already prepared for the thematic concerns Bradbury will address.

In *Haroun and the Sea of Stories*, Rushdie provides many such instances. As the armies of Gup enter the Twilight Strip, for example, Rushdie writes, "On those twilit shores, no bird sang. No wind blew. No voice spoke. . . . Thorn-bushes clustered around white-barked, leafless trees, trees like sallow ghosts." The description in general and the phrase "no bird sang" in particular call to mind the poem "La Belle Dame sans Merci," written by John Keats in 1819. Keats uses the phrase "and no birds sing" throughout the poem as a refrain. Within the poem, a young knight errant tells of being lulled into a dream where he sees ghostly figures in a desolate landscape. (This, of course, is an allusion on the part of Keats to the legends of the Waste Land encountered by King Arthur's young knights Percival, Galahad, and Bors, who travel through an enchanted waste land in search of the Holy Grail.) Thus, with the allusion, Rushdie inserts into *Haroun and the Sea of Stories* the theme of the brave knight on a quest, encountering danger and enchantment.

Perhaps the most important allusion in *Haroun and the Sea of Stories* is to the *Kathasaritsagara*, roughly translated as *Oceans of the Streams of Story*. This is an eleventh-century collection of Indian legends, folk tales, and fairy tales. In addition, there are many important allusions to *One Thousand and One Nights*, an ancient collection of Middle Eastern and South Asian folk and fairy tales. By so clearly referencing these collections, Rushdie signals that he is entering the streams of

The Moon, Kahani, is half light and half darkness throughout the novel, and contains a spring thought to be the source of all the stories.

(© Triff | Shutterstock.com)

story himself. Like Rashid, he gulps in the water from the streams of story and uses elements of many old stories to create a totally new work.

By so doing, *Haroun and the Sea of Stories* becomes a lesson in not only the value of fiction but also how fiction is created. It is a commentary on the nature of fiction itself, a form of literature known as "metafiction." While this is not a feature that most children reading the novel will likely observe, it is one of the most interesting features for adult readers and scholars who observe in the novel Rushdie's formula for writing fiction. Indeed, Rushdie's formula overturns all notions that fiction can be created new out of whole cloth. Rather, he demonstrates, not only in what his characters say but also in what he does himself in the writing, that there is nothing new under the sun. This is not to say that his writing is not original. It is the new combination of old elements that infuses the novel with life and depth. Readers who are familiar with the great traditions of literature will recognize and enjoy these elements in the story. The recognition deepens the experience of reading and joins humans across cultures.

At the same time, *Haroun and the Sea of Stories* can be read as a metafictional cautionary tale. The villain of the piece, Khattum-Shud,

does not have the destruction of the world as his goal but rather the destruction of all of the basic elements of story construction. He is poisoning the deep wells of tradition, the place from which all stories spring. For contemporary readers, this goal poses a question: what happens when readers cease to share any common cultural touchstones? What happens when readers fail to recognize the bits and pieces of the old traditions? The ultimate message of *Haroun* is that something of inestimable value will be lost and the world will grow dim, like the dark side of Kahani, should humans ever forget the importance of our stories and legends.

Source: Diane Andrews Henningfeld, Critical Essay on *Haroun and the Sea of Stories*, in *Novels for Students*, Gale, Cengage Learning, 2013.

Andrew S. Teverson

In the following excerpt, Teverson describes the novel as a literary fantasy that uses elements of traditional fairy tales along with the author's imagination.

A SEA OF STORIES

...*Haroun and the Sea of Stories* can be described as a short literary fantasy that combines traditional elements of fairy tale with the author's own creative and surreal imaginings. It operates as a children's quest narrative that features a young boy traveling to distant lands in search of a happy ending and as a potent political allegory that confronts pertinent contemporary issues, ranging from the restrictions on freedom of speech imposed by fundamentalist regimes to the pollution of the environment by irresponsible multinational corporations. As such it can be located in the subgenre, suggested by Jean-Pierre Durix, of "the children's story which only adults can really understand" (343), a tradition that incorporates Jonathan Swift's *Gulliver's Travels* (1726) and Lewis Carroll's *Alice in Wonderland* (1865).

The influence of both these predecessors is evident in the style and the structure of *Haroun and the Sea of Stories*. All three narratives use fantastical and nonsensical scenarios to conceal (or reveal) a satirical intention, and all three are organized around the adventures of a central hero who begins the tale in a comfortable domestic environment, travels out of that environment to visit a fantasy world full of peculiarities and marvels—though strangely parallel to his or her own world—and then returns home to find that

> ON SEVERAL LEVELS, THEREFORE, RUSHDIE
> HAS CREATED IN *HAROUN* A COMPLEX ALLEGORY
> THAT EMPHASIZES THE IMPORTANCE OF EXCHANGE
> BETWEEN DIFFERENT CULTURAL GROUPINGS."

his or her understanding of the home world has been clarified.

Despite the similarities between *Haroun* and texts such as *Gulliver's Travels* and *Alice in Wonderland*, however, Carroll's and Swift's tales, unlike Rushdie's, both derive from a predominantly English storytelling tradition. *Alice in Wonderland* was heavily influenced by previous Victorian "juvenile" literature such as Catherine Sinclair's *Holiday House* and Frederick Marryat's *Masterman Ready*, and also reveals a debt to the fantastical, nonsensical situations portrayed in popular British fairy tales and nursery rhymes. Swift's novel, similarly, is influenced by popular British oral or chapbook fairy tales such as *The History of Tom Thumbe* and *The History of Jack and the Giants*. Rushdie's fantasy, by contrast, demonstrates a resistance to the tradition's exclusive reliance on European narrative forms and European modes of perception by taking this tradition, saturated in British folklore and fairy tale, and merging it with an equivalent tradition in Indian storytelling that derives from Indic, Persian, or Arabic oral and literary sources. In addition to a host of character types and scenarios reminiscent of Western fairy tales, for instance, Rushdie gives us plot motifs and expressions from *The Arabian Nights*, Bhatta Somadeva's eleventh-century *Ocean of Streams of Story (Katha Sarit Sagara)*, and, as we have seen, Attar's *The Conference of the Birds*.

There are, of course, elements in *Alice in Wonderland* and *Gulliver's Travels* that also derive from texts such as these. *The Arabian Nights* first became popular in Britain in the early eighteenth century, and, since Swift, as Peter Caracciolo notes, was among its first English readers, it is probable that oddities recalling "the wonderful East" in *Gulliver's Travels*, such as the floating island populated by transcendentalist astronomers, owe something to *The Nights*. The figure

of the caterpillar in *Alice in Wonderland*, similarly, with his hookah and his "languid, sleepy" voice, draws upon stereotypes of the drug-addled oriental that narrative collections like *The Nights* have been associated with since their introduction into Europe by Antoin Galland. These orientalist elements, however, do not represent attempts to incorporate the non-European narrative into the substance and body of the story; neither do they represent attempts to convey the spirit of Arabic or Sanskrit storytelling to a new readership. On the contrary, they isolate fantastic or absurd features of the non-European narrative tradition to emphasize their strangeness, and to play upon European ideas of the foreign and exotic. Rushdie, by contrast (although this is a contentious point), aims to transform the genre by placing both narrative traditions on an equal footing, by showing how the two are interdependent and intertwined.

Rushdie's attempt to demonstrate the compatibility of tales from different cultures is most apparent in the episode in which Haroun takes a drink from the story sea. Haroun is miserable, having failed to wish hard enough for the return of his father's storytelling abilities, so Iff, the Water Genie, extracts a story from the water to cheer him up. Haroun drinks the story water and finds himself transported to a virtual landscape in which the story is being played out before him. First he has to dispatch several monsters, which he does with considerable ease; then he finds himself at a white stone tower:

> At the top of the tower was (what else but) a single window, out of which there gazed (who else but) a captive princess. What Haroun was experiencing, though he didn't know it, was Princess Rescue Story Number S/1001/ZHT/420/41(r)xi; and because the princess in this particular story had recently had a haircut and therefore had no long tresses to let down (unlike the heroine of Princess Rescue Story G/1001/RIM/777/M(w)i, better known as "Rapunzel"), Haroun as the hero was required to climb up the outside of the tower by clinging to the cracks between the stones with his bare hands and feet.

Rushdie is clearly being playful here. This passage creates a comic effect by drawing attention to the formulaic conventions of fairy tale and then confounding those conventions by introducing the extravagant device of a princess with a haircut. Despite this frivolous approach, however, Rushdie's parodic fairy tale notation suggests a serious point. The first notation, S/1001/ZHT/420/41(r)xi, calls to mind *The Arabian Nights*. The number 1001 evokes the thousand

and one nights, and the letters ZHT (possibly) signify Scheherazade. The second notation, G/1001/RIM/777/M(w)i, also suggests the presence of *The Arabian Nights* (1001) but then alludes to the Brothers Grimm, the capital letters spelling GRIMM unambiguously, the lowercase *w* standing for Wilhelm. Both are variants, as Rushdie notes, of the "princess rescue story" that has become popularized as "Rapunzel."

This playful notation alerts the reader to the fact that the tale "Rapunzel" is not exclusive to the Grimms' collection, and that different variants of the tale, such as the mysterious S/1001, are also floating around in the veins of the story sea. The variant of "Rapunzel" that is now most popular is undoubtedly that which was collected by Grimm in 1812, but—as Rushdie reminds the reader cryptically—this is not the only version, nor indeed is it the first. Grimm took the tale from a story by Friedrich Schultz, who had in turn borrowed it from a French tale, "Persinette," by Mlle. Charlotte-Rose de la Force (published anonymously in *Contes des Contes* in 1692) (Zipes 729). It is unclear where de la Force took it from, although there is an Italian variant in Basile's *Pentamerone*, and it is probable that Basile's version, through various complex paths, is related to early Indian versions of the tale. Just as Rushdie implies in his parody, therefore, there are Indian and Middle Eastern precedents for a tale that is now predominantly thought of as European. The implication of this is that the tales of different cultures are not separated from one another by rigid cultural divides and "walls of force" but may share a number of significant features.

Perhaps this is giving too much weight to what is, arguably, little more than a passing joke on Rushdie's part. S/1001/ZHT/420/41(r)xi and G/1001/RIM/777/M(w)i are, perhaps, only jests at the expense of folklore indexers such as Antti Aarne and Stith Thompson that were not meant to be subjected to rigorous analysis. However, there are other ways that *Haroun* suggests to the reader that narratives evolve through a process of cultural exchange and fruitful intermingling, and are not (as the Brothers Grimm and later the Nazis were eager to suggest) indications of the purity of the national voice. This idea is presented to the reader pictorially in the image of the story sea that Haroun examines only a page before he drinks the princess rescue stories. The story waters, as Haroun observes, are "made up of a thousand thousand thousand and one different currents, each one a different colour, weaving in and out of one another like a liquid tapestry of breathtaking complexity." As Iff explains:

> Different parts of the Ocean contained different sorts of stories, and as all the stories that had ever been told and many that were still in the process of being invented could be found here, the Ocean of the Streams of Story was in fact the biggest library in the universe. And because the stories were held there in fluid form they retained the ability to change, to become new versions of themselves, to join up with other stories and so become yet other stories; so that unlike a library of books, the Ocean of Streams of Story was much more than a storeroom of yarns. It was not dead but alive.

It is this livingness, for Rushdie, that characterizes storytelling. Stories may seem to be "fixed" or "stable" if they are fixed artificially—by a canon of "official" narratives, or by direct censorship. The most cursory investigation of a story's genealogy, however, will reveal that the borders and boundaries we have erected around the stories of different peoples and nations are permeable, and that a serious assessment of a narrative's ancestry must include a recognition of the process and performance of cultural interaction. It is in this respect that the story sea as an image of Rushdie's hybrid sources comes to reflect one of the dominant arguments presented in the plot of *Haroun*—that the establishment of strict and impermeable boundaries between different cultures gives a false impression of the "purity" of each culture and prevents cultural groups from discovering that their respective *social* narratives provide as much of a basis for dialogue and communication as they do for segregation and separation. As a testament to this, the troubles that Haroun encounters on the moon of Kahani are largely the result of the separation of the moon into two halves. There is a light side populated by the talkative Guppees (derived from *gup*, gossip in Hindustani) on which the sun always shines, and a dark side populated by the silent Chupwalas (quiet fellows in Hindustani) that is in perpetual darkness. The division between the two sides is maintained by a wall of force erected by the Guppees to keep the Chupwalas out, and it is this wall that is responsible for the tensions between the two communities. Its name, "Chattergy's Wall," after the king of the Guppees, recalls the Roman emperor Hadrian's barrier against the Picts and the Scots, but it also invokes the Berlin wall separating communist East Germany and democratic West Germany which had come down the year before Rushdie published *Haroun*. Its symbolic function is the same as that of the wall constructed by the king in Edward Bond's play *Lear* (1972): it is meant to ensure the safety of the populace, but it ends up being a cage, a trap, which causes hatred, suffering, and brutality.

The Guppees, in Rushdie's tale, seem to have justice on their side, since they are defending their moon Kahani against the tyranny of Khattam Shud. As the tale progresses, however, it becomes increasingly apparent that the Guppees are as much responsible for Khattam Shud's reign as the Chupwalas, because it is their machinery that has created the division between the two cultures. They developed techniques with which to bring the moon's rotation under control, separating day from night and Chupwala from Guppee, and it is this separation that has allowed Khattam Shud's fanatical opposition to the Guppees to flourish. The success of Haroun's quest, therefore, depends on his being able to undo this binary opposition, which he does in the end by causing the moon to turn "so that it is no longer half in light, half in darkness." Light shines down on Chup for the first time, causing all Khattam Shud's shadow battalions to melt away to nothing.

Once the binary is undone, the people of Gup and Chup devise a peace settlement that permits "a dialogue" between the two groups. "Night and Day, Speech and Silence," according to this peace, "would no longer be separated into Zones by Twilight strips and Walls of Force." This radical transformation in the way that the two cultures interact is prelude to a total reassessment of their understanding of one another. Each realizes that the other is not as bad, or as different, as they first thought—and both realize that the distinctive differences between the two cultures can provide opportunities for productive exchange rather than destructive enmity. This is something that the perceptive young Haroun has realized several chapters previously while watching Mudra, the shadow warrior from the "enemy" city of Chup, do his martial dance. At first he thinks:

> How many opposites are at war in this battle between Gup and Chup! Gup is bright and Chup is dark. Gup is warm and Chup is freezing cold. Gup is all chattering and noise, whereas Chup is silent as a shadow. Guppees love the Ocean, Chupwalas try to poison it. Guppees love Stories, and Speech; Chupwalas, it seems, hate these things just as strongly....

And yet, he recognizes,

> it's not as simple as that . . . because the dance of the Shadow Warrior showed him that silence had its own grace and beauty (just as speech could be graceless and ugly); and that Action could be as noble as Words; and that creatures of darkness could be as lovely as the children of light. "If Guppees and Chupwalas didn't hate each other so," he thought, "they might actually find each other pretty interesting. Opposites attract, as they say."

In a tale that is largely about oppositions—between fantasy and reality, between child and adult, between good and bad—Rushdie is being careful to suggest that there can be "dialogue" and "crossover" between categories.

On several levels, therefore, Rushdie has created in *Haroun* a complex allegory that emphasizes the importance of exchange between different cultural groupings. At the level of theme, he has shown how Guppees and Chupwalas are able to create a better society when rigorous separation is not enforced; at the level of symbolism, he has given us the potent image of the story sea that is only healthy when stories from diverse places are permitted to intermingle freely; finally, and perhaps most innovatively, he has created a story sea in his own text by drawing eclectically from diverse narrative traditions (Arabic, Persian, Indian, and European) and allowing those traditions to cross-pollinate one another. The allegory of *Haroun*, in this sense, is one that works, like traditional fabular allegories, by creating situations in the plot that "speak otherwise" about social, cultural, and political events; but it is also possible to argue that Rushdie has extended the reach of the traditional fable by making intertextuality serve an additional allegorical function. Not only is the story of *Haroun* about the dangers of ethnocentrism and its terrible impact on a fantastical other world, but the eclecticism of *Haroun* as a piece of writing also operates as material evidence of the benefits (in terms of lively and dynamic storytelling) that can be accrued from a willingness to traverse freely across the boundaries of diverse cultural traditions. The real tragedy of Khattam Shud, in this respect, must be that he is not only confounded by the opponents he comes up against *within* the tale—Haroun and the representatives of the story sea—he is also confounded by the very materiality of the story within which he finds himself. He is thus, we might say, completely finished before he is even begun....

Source: Andrew S. Teverson, "Fairy Tale Politics: Free Speech and Multiculturalism in *Haroun and the Sea of Stories*," in *Twentieth-Century Literature*, Vol. 47, No. 4, Winter 2001, pp. 444–66.

David Appelbaum

In the following review, Appelbaum posits that Haroun and the Sea of Stories *echoes several questions of purpose that may have confronted Rushdie during his battle over* The Satanic Verses.

Story telling is the antidote for sadness in Salman Rushdie's delightful new novel. With an adventure of youthful heroics straight out of *The Arabian Nights*, Rushdie opens his tale in the saddest of cities, "a city so ruinously sad that it had forgotten its name." In this place, telling and spinning tales have—as they did for Scheherazade—life-giving powers. For both her and Rushdie, a story celebrates life's unfolding and its triumph over the sentence of death ordained by the Sultan Schahbriar.

Haroun shares other aspects with *The Arabian Nights*. Talking birds, water genies, a kidnapped princess, and a maniacally evil adversary—all favorites of Scheherazade's storytelling—reappear in Rushdie's saga. Even the names of the boy-hero and his father, Haroun and Rashid, play on Haroun al-Raschid, Caliph of Baghdad, in the *Nights*.

The story begins with Rashid Khalifa. Rashid is the Shah of Blah, or alternately the Ocean of Notions, the consummate storyteller. He enjoys fame, good fortune, and domestic tranquillity in spite of an environment of global melancholy. As a conduit of the life-force, Rashid alone appears immune to ungrateful, drab, and routinized existence. The key to his precarious happiness lies in Soraya, his wife, whose singing sustains Rashid's own poetry even in the wasteland.

One day, the songs suddenly stop. Shortly thereafter, Soraya runs off with Mr. Sengupta, the upstairs neighbor, a clerk and a disparager of Rashid's storytelling. Despairing over the loss of his mother, Haroun defiantly confronts Rashid with the literalist's question: "What's the use of stories that aren't even true?" With that final blow, the spigot from which gushed Rashid's splendid creations is shut off—*khattam shud*, completely finished, as Rushdie says. Rashid, the Shah of Blah, no longer has a story to tell.

The stage is set for young Haroun to redeem himself and save his father. The hero's journey begins with a barnstorming tour of a distant city.

Rashid has been hired to aid a questionable candidate's campaign. Just before the dangerous insinuations that his father is *khattam shud* can be verified, Haroun discovers the way to the other world.

For Rushdie as for Lewis Carroll, the other realm is the reverse of the ordinary one. Instead of the visual reversal (which takes place when Alice goes through the mirror into the Looking Glass World), Rushdie features metaphoric reversal. Metaphor becomes reality and reality, when Haroun enters the land of Kahani, is the substantiation of everything that metaphor describes. By contrast, "the literal meaning" is not simply an unintelligent response but the pathological and shadowy denial of what is.

Rushdie has us enjoy Haroun's repeated amazement at the facts of reversal. Haroun discovers that Rashid's tales do indeed spring forth from the story waters. In Kahani, there is an ocean of stories which by a P2C2E (A Process Too Complicated To Explain) is connected to Rashid's sink—or was, while harmony reigned. Haroun is able to travel about by (metaphorically) giving his thoughts wings. He quickly uncovers an ominous fact: his father's dry spigot is the local effect of a global phenomenon of pollution. The sea of stories is being poisoned!

Rushdie's treatment of the final part of Haroun's journey—redemption and return—is accomplished with affection and humor. The adversary is Khattam Shud incarnate. He appears strangely like Mr. Sengupta, clerkish, literal-minded, unable to bear the element of play, trying to rid the world of yarn-spinning. Khattam Shud repeats Haroun's own taunting question to him: "What's the use of a story that isn't even true?" A cavernous, floating poison factory works night and day. How can a single boy make a difference? Haroun's victorious act inserts his own story-line into the scheme of things (by a P2C2E), thereby insuring that the sea of stories will be ever-renewed by the incorruptible source. With that reassertion of willful imagination, Khattam Shud dissolves forever.

Haroun is more than a piece to be included in a collection of traditional tales. It borrows its transparently allegorical style from another genre, the moral fable. The purpose of a moral fable is to alert us to forces corrosive to self-inquiry, good will, and hope. The fables of Aesop dwell on traditional obstacles to a search for meaning: the likes of greed, arrogance, spite, and sloth. Rushdie, however, discloses a thoroughly modern toxin—at least never felt until modern times. *Haroun* gently and with good humor concerns itself with safeguarding storytelling from powers presently abroad in ourselves and in the world (since the two are connected by a P2C2E) that would leave us, like Rashid, story-less. "What's the use of a story that isn't even true?" is a question that must have confronted Rushdie in the face of the fanatical outrage prompted by *The Satanic Verses*. What about the option of knuckling under and falling mute, *khattam shud*?

To betray the power of spinning a yarn *is* to sever the connection with the other world. The literal mind, with its parsing of things into black and white, its refusal of ambiguity and uncertainty, its demand for control and definition, thereby triumphs. The course of present-day history threatens such an ending. The story, through the enjoyable and disturbing, fascinating and unsettling play of imagination, reminds us of how to live differently. Its elements guide us indirectly back to the forgotten avenues and lost pathways of our inner life, and reawaken the need—felt so strongly in childhood—to be. *Haroun* recalls such a function and through its fabulous creations nourishes the impulse to tell useless tales. Small wonder that fascist and fanatic alike—always alert to deviations from *the* literal truth—cry for the suppression of the story. The real power of subversion lies in our freedom to respond to a suggested but unstated meaning.

Source: David Appelbaum, Review of *Haroun and the Sea of Stories*, in *Parabola*, Vol. 16, No. 2, May 1991, pp. 126–32.

SOURCES

Abrams, M. H., "Allusions," in *A Glossary of Literary Terms*, 6th ed., Harcourt Brace Jovanovich, 1993, pp. 8–9.

Aji, Aron R., "'All Names Mean Something': Salman Rushdie's *Haroun* and the Legacy of Islam," in *Contemporary Literature*, Vol. 36, No. 1, Spring 1995, pp. 103–29.

Applebaum, David, Review of *Haroun and the Sea of Stories*, in *Parabola*, Vol. 16, No. 2, May 1991, pp. 126–32.

"Ayatollah Khomeini (1900–1989)," in *BBC History*, 2012, http://www.bbc.co.uk/history/historic_figures/khomeini_ayatollah.shtml (accessed January 1, 2012).

Baena, Rosalía, "Telling a Bath-Time Story: *Haroun and the Sea of Stories* as a Modern Literary Fairy Tale," in *Journal of Commonwealth Literature*, Vol. 36, No. 2, 2001, pp. 65–76.

Ball, John Clement, "Salman Rushdie: Overview," in *Contemporary Popular Writers*, edited by Dave Mote, St. James Press, 1996, pp. 344–45.

Banville, John, "An Interview with Salman Rushdie," in *New York Review of Books*, Vol. 40, No. 5, March 4, 1993, pp. 34–36.

Blishen, Edward, Review of *Haroun and the Sea of Stories*, in *New Statesman and Society*, Vol. 3, No. 120, September 28, 1990, p. 32.

Brennan, Timothy, "Salman Rushdie," in *British Writers: Supplement 4*, edited by George Stade and Carol Howard, Scribners, 1997.

"A Brief History of the Kashmir Conflict," in *Telegraph*, September 24, 2001, http://www.telegraph.co.uk/news/1399992/A-brief-history-of-the-Kashmir-conflict.html (accessed January 2, 2012).

Donoghue, Denis, Review of *Haroun and the Sea of Stories*, in *New Republic*, Vol. 203, No. 24, December 10, 1990, pp. 37–38.

Durix, Jean-Pierre, "'The Gardener of Stories': Salman Rushdie's *Haroun and the Sea of Stories*," in *Journal of Commonwealth Literature*, Vol. 28, No. 1, 1993, pp. 114–22.

Ellerby, Janet Mason, "Fiction under Siege: Rushdie's Quest for Narrative Emancipation in *Haroun and the Sea of Stories*," in *Lion and the Unicorn*, Vol. 22, No. 2, April 1998, pp. 211–20.

Harrison, James, "Chapter 1: Biography," in *Salman Rushdie*, Twayne's English Authors Series 488, Twayne Publishers, 1992.

"Kashmir," in *New York Times*, August 10, 2011, http://topics.nytimes.com/top/news/international/countriesand territories/kashmir/index.html (accessed January 1, 2012).

Keats, John, "La Belle Dame Sans Merci," The Poetry Foundation website, 2011, http://www.poetryfoundation.org/poem/173740 (accessed January 7, 2012).

König, Eva, "Between Cultural Imperialism and the Fatwa: Colonial Echoes and Postcolonial Dialogue in Salman Rushdie's *Haroun and the Sea of Stories*," in *International Fiction Review*, Vol. 33, 2006, pp. 52–63.

Merivale, Patricia, "The Telling of Lies and 'the Sea of Stories': 'Haroun,' 'Pinocchio,' and the Postcolonial Artist Parable," in *ARIEL*, Vol. 28, No. 1, January 1997, pp. 193–208.

Nelson, Davia, "Salman Rushdie and the Sea of Stories: An Interview," in *American Theatre*, Vol. 20, No. 3, March 2003, pp. 26–40.

Roberts, Daniel, "Rushdie and the Romantics: Intertextual Politics in *Haroun and the Sea of Stories*," in *ARIEL*, Vol. 38, No. 4, October 2007, pp. 123–47.

Rushdie, Salman, *Haroun and the Sea of Stories*, Penguin, 1990.

Schrobsdorff, Susanna, "Ideas: *The Hero with a Thousand Faces*," in *Time*, August 30, 2011, http://entertainment.time.com/2011/08/30/all-time-100-best-nonfiction-books/slide/the-hero-with-a-thousand-faces-by-joseph-campbell/#the-hero-with-a-thousand-faces-by-joseph-campbell (accessed January 9, 2012).

Schürer, Norbert, *Salman Rushdie's "Midnight's Children": A Reader's Guide*, Continuum, 2004, p. 10.

Sen, Suchismita, "Memory, Language and Society in Salman Rushdie's *Haroun and the Sea of Stories*," in *Contemporary Literature*, Vol. 36, No. 4, Winter 1995, pp. 654–75.

Shakespeare, William, *The Tragedy of Macbeth*, in *The Complete Works of William Shakespeare*, Massachusetts Institute of Technology, 1993, http://shakespeare.mit.edu/macbeth/macbeth.4.1.html (accessed January 3, 2012).

Steinberg, Sybil, Review of *Haroun and the Sea of Stories*, in *Publisher's Weekly*, Vol. 237, No. 41, October 12, 1990, p. 47.

FURTHER READING

Grant, Damian, *Salman Rushdie* (Writers and their Work), Northcote House Publishers, 1999.

> This brief book summarizes Rushdie's life from 1947 to 1999 and provides background information on his writings.

Gurnah, Abdulrazak, ed., *The Cambridge Companion to Salman Rushdie*, Cambridge University Press, 2007.

> This book has two major sections: the first offers thematic readings of Rushdie's novels while the second discusses Rushdie as a postcolonial writer. The book also includes a detailed chronology of Rushdie's life and a useful bibliography.

Pipes, Daniel, *The Rushdie Affair: The Novel, the Ayatollah, and the West*, 2nd ed., postscript by Koenraad Elst, Transaction Publishers, 2003.

> Pipes examines the events leading to the *fatwa* issued by the Ayatollah Khomeini upon the publication of *The Satanic Verses*. He discusses specifically why the novel was considered blasphemous and the repercussions of the *fatwa* on Rushdie's life

Rushdie, Salman, *Midnight's Children*, Knopf, 1981.

> *Midnight's Children* was Rushdie's first critical success. In 1993, it won the Booker of the Bookers award as the best Booker award winner to date. In 2008, the novel was again named the best book ever to be awarded a Booker Prize.

———, *The Wizard of Oz* (BFI Film Classics), British Film Institute, 1992.

> In this short book, Salman Rushdie provides first an essay on the famous American film followed by a short story called "The Ruby Slippers." Rushdie has claimed in many interviews that *The Wizard of Oz* was highly influential in his life, and particularly in the composition of *Haroun and the Sea of Stories*.

Teverson, Andrew, *Salman Rushdie* (Contemporary World Writers), Manchester University Press, 2008.

> Teverson provides historical, cultural, and literary contexts for Rushdie's works as well as detailed critical readings of each. He also offers a biographical section to connect Rushdie's life to his novels.

SUGGESTED SEARCH TERMS

Salman Rushdie

Haroun and the Sea of Stories

India

Kashmir

Pakistan

Haroun and the Sea of Stories AND Magical Realism

Salman Rushdie AND the Best of the Bookers

Salman Rushdie AND storytelling

Satanic Verses

Salman Rushdie AND *fatwa*

Salman Rushdie AND Ayatollah Khomeini

The Joys of Motherhood

BUCHI EMECHETA

1979

The Nigerian author Buchi Emecheta's novel *The Joys of Motherhood*, first published in 1979, is recognized as a work of the highest rank in the canon of African literature. Emecheta began publishing novels in 1972 while living in London, and critics agree that she had mastered her narrative powers by the time she broached this work, which many consider her best. After her first two autobiographical novels, she began tackling major Nigerian societal themes in her next two, as reflected in their titles: *The Bride Price* (1976) and *The Slave Girl* (1977). Though she would have much more to say about women's lives and their roles in society, her fifth novel constitutes something of a culmination of her initial womanist trajectory, focusing on a theme that speaks to the very heart and soul of a culture, motherhood. *The Joys of Motherhood* relates the hardscrabble life of Nnu Ego, whose experiences as a young woman leave her desperate to claim and secure her status as a mother. Nnu Ego's destiny is shaped by the circumstances of mythical dimensions in which she was conceived; by the Ibo patriarchal tradition, from which she has little power to escape; and by the ways in which her children respond to their mother's devotion and their family's poverty. The novel does include several scenes of a sexual nature, including one that is elaborated in some detail; these scenes are not gratuitous but integral to Emecheta's broader depiction of the experiences of women within a polygamous tradition. A revised edition of *The Joys of Motherhood* was published as part of the African Writers Series in 2008.

Buchi Emecheta (© *Art Directors & TRIP / Alamy*)

AUTHOR BIOGRAPHY

Emecheta was born on July 21, 1944, in Lagos, Nigeria. Her parents had come to Lagos from the village of Ibuza seeking work. Emecheta and her younger brother Adolphus were thus raised partly in the city and partly in the village, where they would go, during the rainy seasons, to help with family farming and learn the traditional ways. In her essay "Feminism with a Small 'f!," Emecheta reports, "If I lived in Lagos I could start to have loose morals and speak Yoruba all the time. So my parents wanted me to learn the rigorous Ibo life." Her first exposure to Ibo storytelling was in the home, where her aunt, referred to as her "big mother," would relate mesmerizing tales of ancestors' heroic deeds, tales that often explained Ibo mores and customs. As a child, Emecheta imagined that storytellers like her aunt were inspired by spirits, and she determined to become one herself. Although, at first, only her brother was enrolled in school, she paid a pointed visit to a nearby Methodist school one day, and her parents then enrolled her as well. She

persevered in improving her storytelling in what was her fourth language, English, even after an English teacher who revered William Wordsworth responded to Emecheta's claim that she too would write, like Wordsworth, by telling the young Ibo girl to go pray for forgiveness for her pride.

When Emecheta was nine, her father died, and her mother was inherited by his brother. Emecheta was separated from her immediate family and raised by her mother's cousin in Lagos. Using food money to pay for an application, Emecheta secured admission to the prestigious Methodist Girls' High School, and she hoped to proceed to a university. When that did not prove an option, she married a young man named Sylvester Onwordi, and they started a family. After Emecheta worked at the American embassy for a time, she and her children joined her husband, who was studying accounting in London in 1962; the couple would eventually have five children. Still intent on writing, Emecheta completed a manuscript of a novel, titled *The Bride Price*— but it was burned by her husband, who thought it would shame the family. As soon as she saved enough money, she left her husband and began writing again, meanwhile raising her five children independently.

After amassing piles of rejection slips, Emecheta was finally able to start serially publishing autobiographical recollections in the *New Statesman* in 1972. That year, she was able to publish these as her first novel, *In the Ditch*. A second autobiographical novel, *Second-Class Citizen*, appeared in 1974. Emecheta then revived her burned manuscript as her third novel, *The Bride Price* (1976). She would write and publish prolifically through the 1970s, with *The Joys of Motherhood* appearing in 1979, and the 1980s, with her works including plays as well as young-adult novels. She lectured as a visiting professor at various universities in England, the United States, and Nigeria through the 1970s and early 1980s. Living in London, she has run the Ogwugwu Afor Publishing Company, which has a branch in Ibuza, along with her son. She was awarded the Order of the British Empire in 2005.

PLOT SUMMARY

1. The Mother

The opening chapter of *The Joys of Motherhood* introduces Nnu Ego, who, in 1934 in Lagos, Nigeria, backs out of her house in a stupor. She proceeds to bolt across town toward a bridge, where she intends to end her life by jumping into the water below.

2. The Mother's Mother

The next chapter occurs a generation earlier in the town of Ibuza, which includes the village of Ogboli, where Nwokocha Agbadi, an Ibo chief, resides. A dominant wrestler and powerful speaker, Agbadi is greatly respected and has obtained seven wives, but his heart has been captured by a mistress, Ona. Ona's father, Obi Umunna, who has no sons, will not allow Ona to marry: if she bears a son, it is to be under Obi Umunna's name.

When Agbadi is gored during an elephant hunt and near death, Ona stays by his side for days to nurse him back to health. In the midst of his recovery, he rouses himself one night to roughly induce her to welcome his advances, which she eventually does, and as their intercourse concludes, she cries out and wakes the whole compound. That very night, Agbadi's first wife, Agunwa, becomes ill—many blame Ona's insolence—and some twenty days later, when Agbadi himself has just recovered, Agunwa dies. According to custom, Agunwa's personal slave is to be killed and buried alongside her, but when the woman's protests provoke Agbadi's son to strike her brutally, Agbadi intervenes. The slave woman thanks him and promises to return to his household as a legitimate daughter—but she is nonetheless fatally struck from behind and duly buried. Just then, Ona is beset by sickness, and Agbadi soon realizes she is pregnant. In time, a daughter, Nnu Ego, is born. In accord with her father's demands, Ona still refuses to marry or live with Agbadi.

A year later, Obi Umunna dies, yet Ona still respects his wish that she refuse marriage. But one day, Nnu Ego becomes stricken with a strange headache, and a *dibia*, or medicine man, explains that a lump on her head is evidence that she is indeed Agunwa's slave woman returned. The slave woman is thus her *chi*, or personal god, and the *dibia* advises that the girl be brought to Agbadi's compound so that she can worship her *chi* there. Ona at last agrees to join Agbadi, and at his home, Nnu Ego gets better. Ona gets pregnant again, but she is beset by unshakable illness and gives birth prematurely; Ona's dying wish is that Nnu Ego be allowed to marry and thus live the life of a fulfilled woman. A day after Ona's death, her weak son dies as well.

3. The Mother's Early Life

At sixteen, Nnu Ego (whose age-mates are already having children) is so hounded by suitors that Agbadi at last agrees to marry her off, to Amatokwu, in a neighboring village. But she fails to get pregnant, and every *dibia* they visit blames Nnu Ego's *chi*, the slave woman, who had been dedicated to a river goddess. Amatokwu takes a second wife, who does soon bear a child and, a year later, is pregnant again. Helping care for the first baby, Nnu Ego begins offering her breast to stop the boy's crying, and the stimulation eventually produces milk—but one time, Amatokwu catches her and beats her. Agbadi then takes Nnu Ego back to his home, and she recovers her health. Instead of sending her back to Amatokwu, Agbadi sends back the bride price and arranges for Nnu Ego to marry a man living in Lagos, Nnaife Owulum. She discreetly leaves the village, with Nnaife's elder brother to guide her.

4. First Shocks of Motherhood

Arriving in the Yaba neighborhood in Lagos, Nnu Ego discovers, to her disappointment, that Nnaife is a chubby, undignified man who washes white people's clothes for a living. The other people from Ibuza living in Lagos congratulate Nnaife for acquiring such a beautiful wife. Nnaife insists on exercising his marital rights on her first night there, even with his older brother sleeping in the same room. Slowly, Nnu Ego adapts to life in Yaba, with Nnaife working most of the time. Soon after dreaming of being taunted with an unreachable baby boy by her *chi*, Nnu Ego becomes pregnant. She meanwhile borrows from a women's fund and begins selling cigarettes on the street. She delivers a baby boy, Ngozi, with Cordelia's help, and soon, carrying him on her back, she resumes her petty trading. But within a month, she finds the boy lying dead.

5. A Failed Woman

The narrative picks up after the events of the first chapter. Crossing the bridge in Lagos on his way home from a night shift, Nwakusor, an Ibo, happens to recognize a woman who is struggling against passersby who are trying to stop her from jumping. When the woman, Nnu Ego, reveals that her baby has died, people excuse her seeming madness, and Nwakusor leads her home.

6. A Man Is Never Ugly

Back in Yaba, Cordelia finds Ngozi's body and goes to the Meers' kitchen to tell her husband,

Ubani. To break the news to Nnaife, Ubani leads him to the sight of the body, and everyone wonders where Nnu Ego is.

7. *The Duty of a Father*

Three months later, the mourning Nnu Ego's old friend Ato, Nwakusor's wife, drops by and laughingly stirs Nnu Ego back to proper spirits. A few months later, for a second time, Nnu Ego dreams about finding a child by a stream, but this time she is allowed to take the dirty, chubby boy. Realizing she is pregnant, she imagines that she is carrying a son who will live and be successful. Reluctant to threaten this baby's health, she declines to resume her trading. She indeed bears a son, in the mold of Nnaife, who names the boy Oshiaju.

8. *The Rich and the Poor*

In July 1939, Mrs. Meers informs Nnaife that, because England will be fighting Germany (with the onset of World War II), the Meers will be leaving permanently. Resolved to wait for new masters to arrive, Nnaife reluctantly watches Oshiaju while Nnu Ego goes back to petty trading. When Ubani gets work with the railways, his family moves out, leaving Nnaife's family alone in the unkempt compound. When Nnaife begins occupying himself with an old guitar left behind by the Meers, Nnu Ego finally insults him until he goes out looking for work. In a European neighborhood on the island part of Lagos, Nnaife encounters white people playing golf and begins picking up their balls unbidden. When they confront him, he flashes his recommendation letter from Dr. Meers and pathetically begs for work; pitying him, they agree to employ him on their journey to Fernando Po (an island in the Bight of Biafra) and let him have some pocket change. He leaves the next day. Before long, British soldiers arrive to claim the compound, ordering Nnu Ego to move her family elsewhere. Nnu Ego finds a room on Little Road under a Yoruba landlord, and Cordelia and Ubani help her move their belongings. There, being so poorly attired, Oshia is shunned during a communal feast.

9. *A Mother's Investment*

Oshia wakes one morning to find a neighbor, Iyawo, attending him; Nnu Ego has given birth to another boy, Adimabua. Nnu Ego can only make so much as a petty merchant, and Oshia becomes malnourished and grows seriously ill. He is near death, but Iyawo's hearty cooking revives him. Other neighbors extend charity, and Nnu Ego is able to resume trading. One of the neighbors, Mama Abby, takes Oshia for a day trip to the island, and when Nnu Ego returns that evening, she finds that Nnaife has returned.

10. *A Man Needs Many Wives*

Flush with wages from the journey, Nnaife splurges on alcohol, and Nnu Ego buys several outfits. Oshia begins attending the Yaba Methodist school, while Nnaife declines to look for more work. One evening, Nnaife returns with Nwakusor and others, and they relate that Nnaife's elder brother has died—meaning that Nnaife has inherited his several wives. Ubani offers to help Nnaife get work at the railways as a grass cutter, and Nnaife accepts. Among the elder Owulum's wives, the eldest, Adankwo, will remain in Ibuza for the time being, but the newest, Adaku, will come to Lagos. One day, Nnu Ego finds Adaku and her four-year-old daughter, Dumbi, waiting there, and Adaku submissively assists Nnu Ego. Nnaife beams over his new wife, and Nnu Ego tries to adjust to the new polygamous family dynamic, which proves especially difficult at night.

11. *Sharing a Husband*

In 1941, Nnu Ego has twins, named Taiwo and Kehinde, and Adaku gives birth to a boy; but the boy dies within weeks, leaving Adaku depressed. Nnu Ego and Adaku begin to support each other. Oshia, though, comes to fear Adaku, a fear that a *dibia* confirms as legitimate. Adaku suggests that Nnaife's nighttime guitar playing might attract evil spirits. After the guitar seems to play itself one night, Nnaife duly smashes it, and they consult a *dibia*, who instructs them to conduct a sacrifice. Only Oshia knows that the noise came from mice he had hidden in the guitar. Objecting to their meager food allowance, Nnu Ego and Adaku resolve to go on strike and refuse to cook for Nnaife. But when Oshia tears up what little money they have to "make more money," Nnaife just laughs. The next day, Nnu Ego cooks him a nice dinner after all, but Nnaife never shows up.

12. *Men at War*

That day, soldiers and Korofos (military police) are milling about the rail yard, and when work finishes, the Korofos round up the workers and shuttle them off for unexplained inspections. The men are forcibly enlisted in the army but are at least accorded decent pay. Permitted to dictate a letter, Nnaife directs Nnu Ego to use the first twenty pounds to cover school fees, allow Adaku to start trading, and cover expenses indefinitely. Nnu Ego will travel to Ibuza to spend time at home with her ailing father.

13. A Good Daughter

Arriving near Ibuza after a few days' journey, Nnu Ego's family gets help walking the last five miles from members of the Owulum and Agbadi households. After seeing his favored daughter one last time and taking pride in her womanhood, Agbadi remarks that he will rejoin his daughter's family and even bring Ona with him, and he dies. Nnu Ego soon gives birth to another boy, who is recognized as Agbadi returned and is named Nnamdio. Meanwhile, Adaku gives birth to a girl.

14. Women Alone

Seven months later, Adankwo urges the contented Nnu Ego to return to Lagos before Adaku has a chance to usurp her position as head of Nnaife's household. Indeed, back in Lagos, Adaku has gained status as a merchant in the market while neighbors have claimed the business space outside their home; thus, Nnu Ego is reduced to the backbreaking work of selling firewood. When a well-off relation of Adaku's drops by on a rainy day to visit, Nnu Ego first treats her with derision, then puts on friendly airs when Adaku returns. When Adaku hears of Nnu Ego's insulting behavior, she summons their male peers from Ibuza to judge the matter. But Nwakusor scolds Adaku, telling her that her friend was insensitive for displaying such (relative) wealth and reminding her that only Nnu Ego has yet provided Nnaife with sons to immortalize his name. Nnu Ego is merely asked to pay a small fine. Humiliated by this treatment, Adaku resolves to quit Nnaife's household and ensure decent education for her daughters by becoming a prostitute.

15. The Soldier Father

While Adaku flourishes in her new circumstances, Nnu Ego is just getting by, and even when the war ends, Nnaife remains absent. The boys are reduced to taking cheap private lessons, while the girls must help their mother run the household. One day, a postman drops by with a summons to collect a package, and with Mama Abby's help, Nnu Ego discovers that Nnaife is still recovering from water-snake bites, while there are sixty pounds being held on her behalf.

Nnu Ego is enabled to now sell clothing instead of firewood. A year later, Nnaife finally returns. Nnu Ego gets pregnant again, but Nnaife nonetheless travels to Ibuza to give Adankwo some company. When he returns, he brings a new sixteen-year-old wife, Okpo, whose bride price was thirty pounds. Nnaife commits to spending much of the rest of his funds to put Oshia through a good secondary school (referred to as college). Nnu Ego gives birth to another set of twin girls, Obiageli and Malachi.

16. A Mother of Clever Children

Three months later, Nnu Ego's family moves to a mud house in Onike, with no running water or electricity but more room. Oshia is sent off to boarding school, and the jealous Adimabua is told he can only get an education when Oshia starts earning money. But during a trip home, Oshia says he next wants to attend university abroad. Nnu Ego is pregnant again, but this time the baby, whom she perhaps had not wanted, is stillborn. Okpo, pregnant for a second time herself, becomes good friends with the now-teenage Adim.

17. A Daughter's Honour

Oshia does exceptionally well in school and gets a job at the Technical Institute—but a few months later, he wins a scholarship to attend college in the United States. Nnaife is growing impatient for income from Oshia so that he might retire himself, so the news that his son will leave Nigeria outrages him. Nnaife effectively disowns Oshia, who soon flies to America. A marriage is arranged for the fifteen-year-old Taiwo, but Kehinde tells her father she has fallen in love with the Yoruba butcher's son, Ladipo. Nnaife and Nnu Ego quarrel, and, that night, Kehinde goes missing. When the women cannot find her, Nnaife is awakened, and he grabs a cutlass to go threaten the butcher's family. The Yorubas restrain him, but Nnaife wounds one young man and threatens murder and the police come and take him away.

18. The Canonised Mother

Nnu Ego participates as a witness in the trial, and Nnaife is thoroughly disgraced by the revelations and sentenced to five years. But the lawyer drops by to tell Nnu Ego that Nnaife may be released after three months, in which case he must proceed quietly to Ibuza. Upon marrying, Taiwo and her husband persuade Nnu Ego to leave Obiageli with them. Proud of her elder daughters, Nnu Ego returns to Ibuza, along with Nnamdio and Malachi, in style—riding in the front seat. But she never hears from Oshia in America, nor from Adim, who ends up in Canada, and can only boast unknowingly about them around Ibuza as her senses begin failing her. On the way back home one night, she lies down by the side of the road and dies. Her children return to give her a glorious funeral, but in death, when prayed to for the gift of fertility, she never grants people's wishes.

CHARACTERS

Mama Abby

Referred to not by her own name but as the mother of her son, Abby, Mama Abby has been well provided for by Abby's European father. Being literate, she helps Nnu Ego read her mail and with other neighborly concerns.

Adaku

Originally the third wife of the elder Owulum, Adaku becomes Nnaife's second wife living in Lagos. Seen as ambitious, Adaku is shunned by Nnu Ego at first, and they naturally compete with each other not only for Nnaife's attention but also for his money, to feed, clothe, and school their respective children. When Nnaife's friends make clear that Adaku will always be inferior to the woman who has already borne Nnaife two sons (Nnu Ego), Adaku refuses to be stifled any longer and claims to choose one of the few paths open to a woman who rejects the husband chosen for her, prostitution. Yet she also becomes an accomplished merchant, and in ensuring her daughters' education and well-being, she proves content.

Adankwo

Though inherited by Nnaife after the elder Owulum's death, the senior wife Adankwo remains in Ibuza with her children. When Nnu Ego returns to Ibuza for a long spell, Adankwo, as her elder co-wife, is the one to kindly urge her to finally return to Lagos or risk losing her children's inheritance to the ambitious Adaku.

Adimabua

With Oshia as his role model, Nnu Ego's second surviving son, known as Adim, strives to succeed in what little schooling his family can afford.

Like his older brother, Adim confirms the quality of his upbringing by gaining admission to university abroad, in Canada.

Nwokocha Agbadi

The father of Nnu Ego is the epitome of traditional African masculinity, a chief who is of great physical stature, successful in the raiding of other villages, admired for his speaking abilities, and surrounded by a trophy-case collection of wives. His affection for the only daughter of Ona, his greatest love, compels him to reclaim Nnu Ego when she is mistreated by her first husband. But his honorable resentment of that mistreatment is what motivates him to send his daughter not back to Amatokwu but to an unknown man in Lagos—Nnaife—a choice that proves ill advised.

Agunwa

Agbadi's senior wife, Agunwa, is struck by a fatal illness precisely when Nnu Ego is conceived by Agbadi and his mistress Ona—who is blamed for appreciating the conception too vocally—casting a moral pall over the origin of Nnu Ego's life.

Amatokwu

Nnu Ego's first husband is acutely mindful of his family's expectation that his new wife bring a new child to the family. Thus, when months pass without Nnu Ego getting pregnant, he accepts the new wife his family finds for him, and as she promptly gives birth, Amatokwu favors her. After he abuses Nnu Ego for letting the baby nurse at her breast, Nnu Ego is glad to leave. But once she is stuck with Nnaife, Nnu Ego thinks back to Amatokwu with fondness as well as admiration for his rural integrity.

Ato

An old friend of Nnu Ego's from Ibuza, Ato drops by a few months after Ngozi's death and helps Nnu Ego overcome the trauma. Ato is Nwakusor's wife.

Cordelia

The wife of Ubani, the Meers' cook, Cordelia establishes a friendship with Nnu Ego that lasts even when they no longer live side by side.

Dumbi

Dumbi is the daughter Adaku brings with her from Ibuza to Lagos.

Nnu Ego

With Nnu Ego introduced in the first chapter title as "The Mother," the reader is well aware from the onset that this book will revolve around her (though the point at which her life will end is left uncertain). She is initially depicted as sweet, obedient, and polite, and her desire for children—precisely what her first husband and father also desire of her—is made clear. Internalizing the community's functional perspective on the usefulness of women, she considers herself a failure when she cannot provide Amatokwu with a child. In that she is then effectively banished from the peaceable countryside and condemned to live a harrowed urban life with a husband she has little respect for and no attraction toward, Nnu Ego unsurprisingly proceeds to invest her entire life in her children. Her hardships are many, from suffering malnourishment to performing arduous labor to make ends meet to enduring the humiliation of her husband's sleeping with another woman in her presence. With the cards she is dealt, Nnu Ego does everything in her power for her children's sake, but her sons, at least, do little to recognize her devotion until after her death, when she is given a glorious burial.

Folorunsho

A child of Nnu Ego's Yoruba landlords on Little Road, Folorunsho at first befriends but later inspires envy in Oshia, who is kicked out of a communal gathering by Folorunsho's mother for being so poorly attired.

Obi Idayi

One of the chiefs of Ogboli, Idayi is Agbadi's closest friend. When Agbadi and Ona quarrel, Idayi helps them resolve things.

Iyawo Itsekiri

A neighbor of Nnu Ego's at Little Road, Iyawo helps revive Oshia with hearty food when he is deathly ill.

Kehinde

The second of Nnu Ego's first set of twin girls, Kehinde eventually falls in love with Ladipo, the Yoruba son of the butcher. Her objection to any arranged marriage and subsequent running away from home inspire Nnaife to attack the butcher's family with a cutlass, landing him in jail. But Kehinde ends up happy with her new family.

Ladipo

Kehinde falls in love with the Yoruba butcher Aremu's son, Ladipo, and insists on marrying him, which infuriates her father.

Malachi

One of Nnu Ego's second set of twins, Malachi, along with Nnamdio, returns to Ibuza when Nnu Ego moves back there.

Dr. Meers

Although his title attests to his intelligence in white people's terms, Dr. Meers snickers like a schoolboy upon addressing Nnaife as "baboon," and the author aptly characterizes him as "lower than the basest of animals" for disrespecting Nnaife's feelings and dignity.

Mrs. Meers

The wife of Dr. Meers talks to Nnaife as simply and briefly as possible, even when telling him that the Meers are leaving the country.

Ngozi

Nnu Ego's first baby, a boy, dies of unexplained causes after only a few weeks.

Nnamdio

Nnu Ego's third boy is recognized as the return of Agbadi, who died only weeks before his birth and told his daughter he would rejoin her family.

Nwakusor

A dockworker, Nwakusor crosses the Carter Bridge, heading home after a night shift, just when Nnu Ego is attempting to jump over the side, and he helps summon her back to reality and escorts her home. After Nnu Ego and Adaku quarrel, he chastises Adaku in the name of patriarchy, deeming her inferior for having borne no sons yet.

Nweze

Nnaife's lawyer, Nweze, helps prepare Nnu Ego for testimony and afterward helps arrange for Nnaife to be released early.

Obiageli

One of Nnu Ego's second set of twins, Obiageli stays in Lagos with Taiwo's family when her mother returns to Ibuza.

Okpo

When Nnaife returns from military service to find that Adaku has left, he promptly journeys to Ibuza, both to enjoy the company of Adankwo and to purchase a new wife, the sixteen-year-old Okpo. Unlike Adaku, Okpo is truly both respectful and submissive to Nnu Ego.

Ona

A headstrong woman whose contrary nature is part of what Agbadi appreciates, Ona—a nickname meaning "priceless jewel"—is not appreciated by Agbadi's legitimate wives. In this patriarchal culture, Ona is resigned to her father Obi Umunna's insistence that she never marry, even beyond his death. But her dying wish is that her own daughter, Nnu Ego, be allowed to find fulfillment as both wife and mother, a wish that Agbadi honors.

Oshiaju

Known as Oshia, Nnu Ego's first surviving son ends up defining his life as an attempt to escape the dire circumstances he is raised in. He resents his mother, Nnu Ego, for their poverty and her inability to keep him in school, even though she does all she can for his sake. Oshia surely absorbs some of Nnaife's condescending attitude toward his mother. Yet his heroic soldier father loses his stature as well when, itching to retire, Nnaife berates Oshia for daring to prioritize his own education over the economic needs of his family. Once Oshia makes it to an American university, only his mother's funeral can inspire him to return to his origins.

Owulum

The elder brother of Nnaife, referred to simply as Owulum, escorts Nnu Ego to Lagos. When he dies, Nnaife inherits his wives Adankwo and Adaku (while Owulum's second wife returns to her own people).

Nnaife Owulum

Emecheta partly deceives the reader at first in presenting a small portion of the narrative from Nnaife's perspective, making him seem quite like an ordinary respectable man. But Dr. Meers's characterization of Nnaife as a "baboon" proves more than just a demeaning epithet, hinting at both his animal-like slovenliness and his expanded physique. Nnaife seems to want little more from life than to do as little as possible. When he loses his job with the Meers, he is content to coast along idly until Nnu Ego practically kicks him out to look for work. When he returns from his first journey by sea, he likewise lazes and drinks heavily until circumstances—the death of his older brother—force his hand. He allows his wives meager allotments of cash to care for the family, yet he claims glory for himself when his military pay lets him buy a new wife and put his son through a junior college. But after he snaps and attacks the butcher's family for supposedly kidnapping his daughter, the truth comes out with a vengeance during his trial, as the questioning of Nnu Ego, in particular, allows the entire courtroom to realize just what kind of a father Nnaife has been.

Slave Woman

The moral pall cast over Nnu Ego's conception by Agunwa's illness and death is embodied by the slave woman who is condemned to die alongside Agunwa. Promising to return to Agbadi's family, the slave woman becomes Nnu Ego's *chi*, or personal god, and coming from a people devoted to the powerful river goddess, she is blamed for Nnu Ego's initial inability to get pregnant.

Taiwo

The first of Nnu Ego's first set of twins, Taiwo has the good fortune to be married to a college-educated man, Magnus, who gains employment with the nation's treasury.

Ubani

At first the Meers's cook, Ubani wisely finds employment with the railways when the Meers skip town. He later helps Nnaife get his grass-cutting job.

Obi Umunna

Ona's father is another chief, but one whose wives give him few children, and only Ona survives through adolescence. Aggrieved by his lack of sons, Umunna thus forbids Ona to marry, so that any son she might bear would belong not to a husband but to Umunna himself.

THEMES

Female Identity

Thematically, *The Joys of Motherhood* is a tour de force on female identity and motherhood in colonial Africa, set in a specifically Nigerian context that is readily universalized to reflect much of the rest of the continent—at least, any

TOPICS FOR FURTHER STUDY

- While she has companions at different periods in her life, Nnu Ego meets a tragic end owing in part to the absence of any close friends who might have helped her stay emotionally grounded when her motherhood-centered world started to unravel. Investigate the dialogue in *The Joys of Motherhood* to explore how Nnu Ego's interactions with others reflect and/or determine her emotional state. Begin with her first husband, Amatokwu, and proceed through commentary on each of her friends and companions through the remainder of the story, including Nnaife, Cordelia, Ato, Mama Abby, and Adaku (and others if you choose), discussing how Nnu Ego's interactions with each person affect her psychological state, what the benefits and drawbacks of each relationship are, and the impact each person's absence has on Nnu Ego.

- Read Emecheta's young-adult novel *The Moonlight Bride* (1980), which is set amid the preparations for a wedding in an Ibo village. Write an essay in which you compare and contrast the ways that traditional culture is depicted by Emecheta in this novel and in *The Joys of Motherhood.* Address how the setting frames Emecheta's cultural commentary, and offer your opinion on which book is more approving of traditional ways and why.

- Write a historical research paper examining how World War II affected native Africans throughout the continent, in any and all nations that were involved owing to the actions of their colonizers. If possible, include statistics identifying the number of Africans who lost their lives in World War II.

- Peruse Dr. Edward M. Hallowell's book *The Childhood Roots of Adult Happiness: Five Steps to Help Kids Create and Sustain Lifelong Joy* (2003), familiarizing yourself with the most salient aspects of the five parenting concepts the author highlights as essential. Generally speaking, Hallowell does not have in mind the sort of situation in which Nnu Ego is obliged to raise her children. Write an essay in which you assess Nnu Ego's parenting in view of Hallowell's theoretical framework, discussing the extent to which she is able to follow his precepts, how much her circumstances limit her ability to do this, and the effects of these limitations on the development of her children.

- Use the Internet to compile statistics on the quality of life in twenty-first-century Nigeria. One useful resource is Planned Parenthood's "Nigeria Country Program" page. Also compile similar statistics regarding the quality of life in the United States, and create a digital presentation, such as using spreadsheet graphs and PowerPoint or other software, to illustrate the differences between the American and Nigerian figures. If appropriate, include downloaded photographs of American and Nigerian scenes that represent or correspond to the figures you include.

region where polygamy has been practiced. The identities of women as well as men must be understood within the constructs imposed on them by their culture, and the Ibos' traditional family structure, wherein a man may welcome as many wives as he chooses into his home, plays a fundamental role in shaping the identities of maturing women like Nnu Ego. This shaping can begin as early as a girl's birth. With Nnu Ego, although her father, Agbadi, means to honor how "priceless" she is, his giving her a name meaning "twenty bags of cowries" in fact precisely puts a price on her. In justifying this name by asserting that his daughter "is a beauty and she is mine," Agbadi reveals two significant facets of the traditional male perspective on women: beauty is considered their most essential quality, and ultimately they are seen as possessions, ones that are bought and sold and that belong to whoever owns them. Nnaife confirms this perspective in rhetorically asking a rebellious Nnu Ego, "Did I not pay your bride price? Am I not your owner?"

Nnu Ego, then, must construct her identity in the face of such misogynistic treatment passed off as tradition. A number of comments suggest the degree to which Nnu Ego internalizes the female identity that is expected of her. Especially in the absence of her birth mother, her father's influence over her is made clear by her submissiveness toward him and her consideration for his expectations in moments of uncertainty. As a young wife of sixteen years, she surely believes, as he affirms, that "when a woman is virtuous, it is easy for her to conceive." When months pass without her becoming pregnant (despite her confirmed premarital virtue), she tells Amatokwu, "I am sure the fault is on my side. . . . How can I face my father and tell him that I have failed?" After her relationship with Amatokwu flounders, when she is recovering her health, the narrator acknowledges that men "wanted women who could claim to be helpless without them." When the married Nnu Ego is instructed to down a glass of alcohol as a precursor to bad news, "like a good woman, she must do what she was told."

It is no wonder, then, that Nnu Ego never manages to resolve the contradictions between the expectations placed on her by her father, Nnaife, and Ibo culture and her own natural impetus toward self-fulfillment. In fact, she gradually abandons any hope of finding true self-fulfillment in realizing how her circumstances dictate her every action: with Nnaife so frequently absent, Nnu Ego must use all her energy to both provide for her family financially and care for her children physically (a plight known to single mothers the world over). Upon giving birth to her second set of twin girls and witnessing her husband's disappointment at the lack of a son, Nnu Ego experiences a sort of identity crisis. She prays, "God, when will you create a woman who will be fulfilled in herself, a full human being, not anybody's appendage?" In lieu of self-fulfillment, Nnu Ego attains here a height of self-knowledge, recognizing, "That's why when I lost my first son I wanted to die, because I failed to live up to the standard expected of me by the males in my life." She also attains a height of cultural knowledge, recognizing that for African women of the future to be released from the patterns that restrict female

identity to the confines of tradition, women of the present must bring about the necessary cultural redirection: "Until we change all this, it is still a man's world, which women will always help to build." As her own life draws to an end, Nnu Ego can take solace only in confirming her identity not merely as a woman but as a mother.

Motherhood

That the ideal of motherhood is central to the concept of female identity constructed for Ibo women by their culture is made clear throughout *The Joys of Motherhood*. Beyond the book's title, nearly every chapter title refers to women, men, or their roles within the family. Thus, the construct of the family is foregrounded in the reader's mind, and even before she is introduced, Nnu Ego is designated an archetype by the first chapter's title, "The Mother." Ibo culture's emphasis on motherhood is evinced in comments from nearly every male Ibo character, all of whom frame the bearing of children, especially sons, as paramount to a woman's identity. But Emecheta does not deny that this is also a natural female instinct, as suggested by the narrator's comment on Nnu Ego in her first marriage that "all she wanted was a child to cuddle and to love." As combined with cultural expectations, Nnu Ego's yearning for motherhood is so strong that, when she at last gives birth to Ngozi, his being a son "gave her a sense of fulfillment for the first time in her life." And yet Emecheta's title is rendered ironic by the circumstances of Nnu Ego's motherhood, in which the palpable joys prove few and far between. Ultimately, in her moment of prayer, she recognizes, "Yes, I have many children, but what do I have to feed them on? On my life. . . . I have to give them my all." She further asks, "'When will I be free?' But even in her confusion she knew the answer: 'Never, not even in death. I am a prisoner of my own flesh and blood.'"

In view of Nnu Ego's experiences as a young woman, it is not surprising that she ends up such a prisoner to motherhood. The threefold traumatic circumstances that she endures in forging her first and second marriages can be seen as marking a psychological defining phase in her life. Blessed with what seems an ideal union with Amatokwu, she first experiences the trauma of being labeled barren and dismissed in favor of a second wife in a matter of months. In turn, she is sent away from her homeland and the support of her family members to unite with a man, Nnaife, who repulses her. And thirdly, after her first son

The novel reflects on the changing role of Nigerian women in the twentieth century. *(© Oleg Znamenskly / Shutterstock.com)*

is born, suddenly embodying the justification for her very existence, this justification is torn away from her by the child's death weeks later. That Nnu Ego is driven to a suicide attempt—which might have been successful had Ngozi's death occurred earlier in the morning—signals the supreme importance motherhood has assumed in her life. Indeed, until the end, Nnu Ego can only cling to her status as mother to psychologically survive. Through all her trials, only her motherhood seems to lift her spirits at all, such as when she witnesses the newly married Taiwo's contentment. The narrator then remarks of Nnu Ego, "Her cup of happiness was full. Yes, this was something. She was happy to see her children happy." Still, without any other friends to look after her when she moves back to Ibuza, "so busy had she been building up her joys as a mother," Nnu Ego dies a most lonesome death by the side of the road.

Tradition

The Ibos' patriarchal, polygamous tradition is highlighted in Emecheta's novel, especially with respect to how that tradition shapes gendered roles and expectations. The author also offers a great deal of insight into how the imposition of British mores in urbanized Lagos serves to suppress, neutralize, or counteract various aspects of traditional rural Ibo life. This happens in part because the polygamous family structure does not translate well from the rural compound, where the open air and the adults' individual huts allow for relative peace of mind, to urban rental units that often consist of a single room. Other culture-shifting factors include the Christianity of whites like the Meers, who demand that their employees share their religion, and the capitalistic, wage-earning existence that supplants the communal village economy, in which virtually all people farm to feed their families and/or produce or provide something of benefit to the community.

Male Identity

The Western culture that infiltrates life in Lagos seems to have its most pernicious effects on the African men who find themselves there, some of whom are, at length, literally consumed by it, as with Nnaife, who is abducted from his place of employment to serve overseas in a white country's war. Although Nnu Ego's father, Agbadi, is partly framed as being so traditionally masculine as to be antiquated or obsolete, before he sends his daughter to Lagos, he makes remarks about city life that prove especially insightful: "They say any fool can be rich in such places. I don't trust men who can't make it here in Ibuza." He feels that "only lazy men who could not face farm work went to the coast to work" in city jobs. Sure enough, Nnu Ego recognizes just such a man in Nnaife, leading her to characterize the city as "this place where men's flesh hung loose on their bones, where men had bellies like pregnant women, where men covered their bodies all day long." Nnu Ego cannot help but think that there is something wrong with a place where a sedentary lifestyle denies men the opportunity to achieve admirable fitness through the performance of labor that the human body has evolved over countless generations to perform regularly. This tragedy of masculinity is intensified by the fact that the average urban African man is so wrapped up in surviving that he cannot realize how much he is compromising his identity. As Nnu Ego laments, "How could a situation rob a man of his manhood without him knowing it?" Nnu Ego's friend Cordelia echoes this sentiment, remarking of African men in Lagos, "Their manhood has been taken away from them. The shame of it is that they don't know it. All they see is the money, shining white man's money." Cordelia advances this line of thought when she adds that urbanized African men "stopped being men long ago. Now they are machines." In having these village women voice such thoughts when gauging the appeal of their men, and considering that sexual attraction is the driving force behind reproduction and the continuation of a species, Emecheta makes the point that humankind's adaptation to the urban environment represents perhaps the evolution of the "civilization" but moreover the devolution of the human being.

STYLE

Biographical Narrative

The Joys of Motherhood is essentially the story of Nnu Ego's life, with close attention devoted throughout to her roles, responsibilities, expectations, and sentiments as daughter, wife, and mother. The third-person narration tracks Nnu Ego's activities foremost but also often reveals the thoughts and even subconscious inclinations of other characters; the narrator's insightfulness sheds light on much that the Western reader in particular would not necessarily realize might be passing through the mind of a Nigerian in the given circumstances. Emecheta, who has resided mainly in England since moving there in 1962, is widely recognized as writing with Western, as well as African, audiences in mind. Overall, the story is presented in chronological fashion, beginning with the events surrounding her conception, passing over her childhood to show her on the cusp of marriage, and then proceeding through adulthood to her life's end. Only the first chapter comes out of sequence, opening the novel with what is perhaps the most emotionally intense scene, the aftermath of Nnu Ego's discovery of her first baby's death. The presentation of this particular scene in the first chapter shapes the reader's understanding of the novel in several ways. To begin, the scene's primacy suggests that this episode, spurred by whatever has driven Nnu Ego to this fraught, panicked state, is a significant moment in her life, even a turning point. The reader comes to realize the psychological truth of this as her life unfolds. Furthermore, while the title is *The Joys of Motherhood*, the first chapter makes clear that the book will be far from a paean to maternity, instead suggesting that the book will stress the heights of anguish and other emotions inspired in women by the state of motherhood, juxtaposed with whatever joys may also be there. Thirdly, in presenting such a turbulent scene so well integrated with and dependent on the urban environment of Lagos before shifting back in time to the rural village, the first chapter positions another major theme of the book at the forefront of the reader's mind, namely, the sociological contrast between the traditional rural and modernizing urban Nigerian environments.

Irony

In a certain respect, the irony inherent in Emecheta's title becomes evident as early as the first chapter, which fails even to hint at the joys that will accompany motherhood for this panicked archetypal mother. And yet Emecheta does not overplay the title's significance—she does not pile on tragedy in a way that turns that title into an ironic punch line. She does foreshadow tragedy to come, such as with the *dibia*'s remarking of the very young Nnu Ego, who is ailing from a head-ache linked to her *chi*, "She will always have trouble with that head. If she has a fortunate life, the head will not play up. But if she is unhappy, it will trouble her both physically and emotionally." Still, Emecheta does not then turn heavy-handed with symbolism by invoking constant headaches as a way of tracking Nnu Ego's descent toward an early death. The narrative subtlety is such that the reader is given room to sustain the (perhaps subconscious) hope that the title will not prove ironic after all—that Nnu Ego's many trials will result in the reward of an idyllic period of life, one in which she can indeed bask in her motherly joys. But the emotional confusion she experiences when her eldest boys drift beyond the family's reach, and when a last daughter is stillborn, eventually leave her senses adrift. The narrative's ironic edge is drawn out through the final pages, with the taxi driver who presumes that with a son in America she "must be full of joy" and "very rich," and even with the treatment Nnu Ego receives after her sorrowful death, marked by a glorious funeral that she cannot enjoy and by her spirit's refusal to answer prayers for children—as if her spirit cannot bear to grant these requests in light of the way her own motherhood used up her entire life. With the tension of the ironic title sustained until the book's closing paragraphs, the reader is made to feel all the more acutely through Nnu Ego's death the injustice that Ibo and British society should conspire to allot such a trying life to such a selfless woman.

African Feminism

By the time Emecheta came to write *The Joys of Motherhood*, her fifth novel, she was certainly aware of her burgeoning status as a contributor to the African literary canon. The era of modern African literature may be said to have opened with the publication of the landmark 1959 novel *Things Fall Apart* by Chinua Achebe, a Nigerian writing about the convergence of Ibo society and British colonization. The first English-language novel by an African woman was *Efuru* (1966) by Flora Nwapa, also Nigerian. In *Efuru*, the title character is a woman who matures to a greater understanding of the world but never establishes an identity as a mother. Emecheta derived her title from that book's final passage, in which the closing question, referring to the lake goddess, leads the reader to consider the full extent of women's conceptions of the nature of motherhood:

Efuru slept soundly that night. She dreamt of the woman of the lake, her beauty, her long hair and her riches. She had lived for ages at the bottom of the lake. She was as old as the lake itself. She was happy, she was wealthy. She was beautiful. She gave women beauty and wealth but she had no child. She had never experienced the joy of motherhood. Why then did the women worship her?

Thus, Emecheta deliberately positions her own novel as a literal response to Nwapa's novel, suggesting that women like Nnu Ego would perhaps worship a childless goddess as a means of spiritual escape from the never-ending obligations of motherhood.

Emecheta is often considered in the light of feminism, in both Western and African molds. In *Emerging Perspectives on Buchi Emecheta*, Shivaji Sengupta offers an anecdote about an interaction with a Nigerian cabdriver in New York City that reveals much about Emecheta's role as a female African author. Asked about Chinua Achebe, the man "broke into the glorious laughter of a proud Nigerian" and praised Achebe as "a national hero." Asked about Emecheta, the cabdriver grew visibly angered and shouted, "Emecheta is no writer! The woman is a troublemaker!" He proceeded to declare that all Emecheta wants to do is "turn all the women against men." In general, Emecheta is indeed recognized as portraying strong women and less admirable men, and *The Joys of Motherhood*, for instance, offers much critical commentary on men's roles in preserving the patriarchal oppression of women. Yet the novel's protagonist, Nnu Ego, is not recognized as a feminist model, in that she never manages to assert her own identity or achieve true self-fulfillment. Instead, the secondary character Adaku offers such a model, in abandoning the patriarchal insistence that she define herself by bearing sons, escaping her inherited polygamous marriage with Nnaife, and earning her own way in life to ensure that her daughters receive a modern education. And as if with a feminist flourish, Adaku is portrayed as spiritually buoyed by her independence. Yet the reader understands that Adaku is only able to achieve this plateau at great personal cost, as she voices her intent to support her family through prostitution. Curiously, after this declaration, the novel offers no confirmation that Adaku actually follows through with her threat, and she seems to do well enough in the marketplace to not necessarily need to.

In her essay "Feminism with a Small 'f!,'" Emecheta speaks directly to the fact that she approaches women's issues not in an idealistic, Western-style, feminist way but in a way marked by realism:

> If I am now a feminist then I am an African feminist with a small f. In my books I write about families because I still believe in families. I write about women who try very hard to hold their family together until it becomes absolutely impossible.

In her novels, she points out, she has not approached matters from an explicitly feminist angle but has nonetheless demonstrated her support of women and women's issues in portraying female characters who, for example, respond to polygamy by evolving beyond desire; who counter indifferent husbands by forging powerful bonds with other women, including co-wives; and who ensure their culture's future by collectively raising children in as loving an environment as possible.

HISTORICAL CONTEXT

Colonial Nigeria

While the chapter tracing Agbadi's relationship with Ona and the birth of Nnu Ego is understood to take place beginning around 1909, *The Joys of Motherhood* otherwise takes place from the later 1920s through the early 1950s in Nigeria, in west-central Africa. Within the novel, the historical context is stressed only in so far as it affects the lives of the Ibo (also spelled Igbo) characters. The pre-independence era is established in the first chapter, but no attention is given to political actions leading toward independence. And while World War II is a major historical marker that greatly affects Nnaife in particular, Emecheta largely follows the local perspective on the time period, which revolves not around the war itself but its effects on the local economy: supplies became harder to procure, and with so many white employers vacating the country, paid work became harder to find. Still, Emecheta has much to say about how the urban environment of Lagos, as shaped by the colonizing British, affected the lives of Nigerians who lived there as well as the lives of their rural families, so the nation's history of colonization is relevant to the novel.

The coast of what is now Nigeria was first reached in 1472 by Portuguese explorers, who made trade connections, and from the sixteenth through the eighteenth centuries European slave traders purchased or abducted millions of the region's people to be transported to the Americas with the status of property. The British Empire abolished slave trading on British ships and in British colonies (which Nigeria was not at that time) in 1805. Through the early nineteenth century, British explorers led the way into the interior of the Nigerian area, especially following the course of the Niger River. In 1849, the British installed their first imperial representative in the region on the island of Fernando Po (now called Bioko), in the Bight of Biafra, the bay just southeast of the Nigerian coast. With the intent of putting a stop to the slave trade still being conducted by American ships and others, the British invaded the island of Lagos, which was key to the trade, in 1851. The king at Lagos soon agreed to abolish commerce in slaves. By 1862, the British were charting out urban infrastructure and had made Lagos and the environs a colony, which was assigned a governor in 1886. The colonized region proceeded to expand and evolve through various polities under the British until it became the Colony and Protectorate of Nigeria in 1914. When World War I broke out, the lack of trade with German agents stifled the economy, while the local Nigeria Regiment was mobilized to attack the neighboring German colony of the Cameroons. After the war, the Nigerian economy rebounded.

The most significant event in Nigeria between the world wars was an uprising among women known as the Aba Riots or Aba Women's War of 1929. Disgruntled with the oppressive colonial administration and an expected tax targeting women, many staged aggressive (but nonviolent) sit-in protests, a traditional form of political maneuvering on the part of women. The British responded with police and military force, and many women were killed; ultimately, the colonial administration was reorganized to better reflect indigenous customs. When World War II flared in 1939, the Nigeria Regiment was again mobilized, as bolstered by what the Anglophilic Sir Alan Burns calls, in his *History of Nigeria*, "voluntary recruitment"—that is, as Emecheta clarifies in her novel, often forcibly conscripted recruitment, as with Nnaife. Detachments were sent to Somaliland and Ethiopia to fight the Italians and to Burma to fight the Japanese. As with

COMPARE
&
CONTRAST

- **1940s:** Under the British governor Arthur Richards, in 1947 a new constitution is promulgated in Nigeria, establishing a preliminary legislative structure featuring a central Legislative Council and three regional Houses of Assembly.

  1970s: After military ruler Murtala Ramat Mohammed is assassinated in 1976, Olusegun Obasanjo takes control of the country and oversees the passage of a new constitution that establishes an American-style elective presidency.

  Today: In the wake of Obasanjo's controversial victory returning him to the presidency for a second term in 2003, President Goodluck Jonathan, elected in early 2011, seeks to amend the constitution to limit the president to a single, longer term in office.

- **1940s:** Being governed as a British colony, the Nigerian military is mobilized to participate in World War II, with regiments fighting in northeast Africa against the Italians and in Burma against the Japanese.

  1970s: After civil war closed out the 1960s, with the Federal Republic of Nigeria defeating the three states that seceded to become the Republic of Biafra in 1970, Nigeria experiences a period of peace that allows for major development of infrastructure and a boom in the exploitation of oil resources.

  Today: With the terrorist Islamist group Boko Haram seeking to impose sharia (Islamic law) on the entire nation, Christians (mostly in the south) and Muslims (mostly in the north) are increasingly clashing in Nigeria, especially in the central city of Jos, with hundreds of people killed in 2010 and 2011.

- **1940s:** Perhaps the world's most famous person of Ibo descent is the American actor and singer Paul Robeson, performing such roles as the lead in Shakespeare's *Othello* on Broadway.

  1970s: In the wake of his 1959 publication of *Things Fall Apart*, Chinua Achebe is likely the world's most famous Ibo, with Emecheta advancing on the literary horizon.

  Today: While Emecheta now rivals Achebe for the honor of most famous Ibo in the realm of literature, in the field of entertainment, the American actor Forest Whitaker, who won an Academy Award for playing Ugandan dictator Idi Amin in *The Last King of Scotland* (2006), is also of Ibo descent.

---

the previous war and as related in Emecheta's novel, World War II brought hardship to the Nigerian economy and to the families of Nigerian soldiers. In the decade after the war, several constitutions were promulgated as local and federal political structures were refined to allow the country to progress toward self-rule. Independence was achieved in 1960 under Prime Minister Abubakar Tafawa Balewa. Since then, Nigeria has experienced several distinct historical phases, including civil war in the late 1960s, an oil boom in the late 1970s, scattered military coups into the 1980s, and heightened tension between Christians and Muslims as well as militant attacks on the oil industry in the twenty-first century.

CRITICAL OVERVIEW

Most literature scholars and critics speak of Emecheta in glowing superlative terms. In the *Dictionary of Literary Biography*, Kirsten Holst Petersen affirms that "Emecheta is to date the most important female African writer. The extent of her output and the centrality of her subject matter—the role of women in present-day Africa—have put her in this position." *The Joys of Motherhood* is considered her "most accomplished book," one that Petersen praises as "a testimony to its author's growing radicalization and willingness to consider unorthodox means of change." The fact that Emecheta's

The protagonist of the novel, Nnu Ego, sees her role as a mother and wife changing as colonialism ensues. *(© Hector Conese | Shutterstock.com)*

novels' commentaries on patriarchy have "enraged some male African critics to a vitriolic attack on her books" is considered by Petersen evidence that "her books are, indeed, of vital importance."

In his essay "Buchi Emecheta: The Shaping of a Self," Chikwenye Okonjo Ogunyemi affirms that Emecheta is "the most prolific and controversial of all black African female novelists." Considering the trajectory of her first five novels, Ogunyemi notes that, with *The Joys of Motherhood*, Emecheta "has come into her own. It is a much more substantial work than its predecessors. . . . There is a marked technical development in the writing with its wry humor and underlying irony." Ogunyemi concludes that "*The Joys of Motherhood* foreshadows what can legitimately be expected of a mature, Nigerian feminist literature," as "the dynamic Emecheta might help to launch a feminist revolt having at last found her place in the Nigerian artistic world."

A wide variety of scholarly essays have been devoted to *The Joys of Motherhood*, both alone and in comparison with other works, illuminating the array of thematic strains within Emecheta's narrative. For example, Lisa Friedli-Clapie, in "Undercurrents of Mammy Wata Symbolism in Buchi Emecheta's *The Joys of Motherhood*," explores how the death of the slave girl who becomes Nnu Ego's *chi* is pivotal to the plot, as the river goddess in a sense both inhabits Nnu Ego—in arriving in Lagos she is seen as "a 'Mammy Water,' as very beautiful women were called"—and also directs at Nnu Ego wrath intended for her father, who oversaw the murder of the slave woman, a river goddess worshipper. In "Procreation, Not Recreation: Decoding Mama in Buchi Emecheta's *The Joys of Motherhood*," Marie Umeh analyzes how the book, considered the author's "*magnum opus*," illustrates the ways that men in patriarchal Ibo society construct motherhood as something that should adequately fulfill whatever desires women have, subordinating women's sexuality (but not men's) to a strictly functional role.

In "Technique and Language in Buchi Emecheta's *The Bride Price*, *The Slave Girl*, and *The*

Joys of Motherhood," Ernest N. Emenyonu focuses on the last of these novels, in which the author "achieves her best writing." The critic states that "the irony is well conceived and exploited," the language "is well controlled," similes and metaphors are precise and appropriate, and the author offers exacting moral commentary without turning didactic. In general, her "style is also much more secure and confident.... Her mastery of the art of suspense is complete." Emenyonu concludes that, in light of the "strong artistry" of her novels, Emecheta is "one of the best storytellers in modern Africa."

CRITICISM

Michael Allen Holmes

Holmes is a writer with existential interests. In the following essay, he considers the significance of Nnu Ego's children in The Joys of Motherhood.

While Buchi Emecheta's novel *The Joys of Motherhood* has been considered in academic reviews from an array of angles, relatively little attention has been paid to Nnu Ego's children. This may be because their roles and significance are well enough developed in the course of the novel as to be deemed self-explanatory. The individual reader may even feel that, in the unceasing growth of Nnu Ego's family, Emecheta verges on overextending the narrative. The first son, Oshia, is fully realized as a character, and Adim, appearing halfway through, also becomes an individual with distinct traits, though he makes fewer appearances. Progressing to the third and fourth (living) children, the twins Taiwo and Kehinde are depicted only rarely through their earliest childhood: speaking in a few scattered scenes, they are present in the narrative mostly through the work they perform with their mother. Yet the girls are more fully realized as characters when they reach their teenage years and attain husbands for themselves. The fifth through seventh children, however—Nnamdio, Obiageli, and Malachi—are given very little characterization, making their function in the narrative seem vague or unconsidered. And regarding their function, the scholar Chikwenye Okonjo Ogunyemi, in "Buchi Emecheta: The Shaping of a Self," finds that the children's symbolic value, as reflected in their names, is too ambivalent to enhance the novel's meaning or moral direction. Ogunyemi contends that Emecheta

"confuses the reader about her own stance in her naming of some of the characters." For instance, where the names of Obiageli and Malachi seem to send contrasting messages—one traditional dependence, the other feminist optimism—the critic concludes, "It is as if Emecheta herself is not sure of what she wants or is nostalgic about the past with its own order." But a closer look at both the names and the patterning of all of Nnu Ego's children suggests that their roles have been intricately conceived by the author, and they hold more, not less, meaning than one might at first guess.

In her autobiographical and nonfiction writing, Emecheta makes clear the societal and spiritual importance she attaches to raising children. A mother of five children herself, whom she raised in London with virtually no help from their philandering father (who denied having fathered them in trying to avoid paying child support), Emecheta lived an existence that only other single parents can fully understand, being the sole support, financially, physically, and emotionally, on whom her children depended. During the hardest times—escaping the abuse of their father, looking for livable apartments in a city where no one would rent to black people—this pressure might have broken Emecheta, but as she relates in her autobiography, *Head Above Water*, her children proved her most essential inspiration. Upon her arrival in London by ship on a cloudy day in 1962, the sheer damp chill and grayness of it all was almost enough to sap her will to survive, but she realized, "I was not going to allow myself to perish because if I did, who was going to look after the babies I'd brought this far?" When she first learned of her husband's unfaithfulness a couple of years later, she thought she "would die of sorrow." And yet, she writes, "I knew that I could not afford to die of sorrow. My kids would suffer.... I must, please God, be around until my kids needed me no more." Again, when she and the children were first getting on their feet in the absence of their father, she realized, "I had to pull myself out of the ditch for their sake.... I could not afford to wallow in the mire of our powerlessness for long."

Despite her devotion to her family, Emecheta eventually found herself at odds with her eldest daughter, Chiedu, who, as a teenager felt that she needed to attend a more expensive school in order to succeed, which would have required money that the family simply did not

WHAT DO I READ NEXT?

- Having taught at her home nation's University of Calabar in 1980–1981, Emecheta proceeded to write *Double Yoke*, a novel that addresses prejudice against women in higher education in Nigeria by relating the experiences of a female college student.

- Emecheta made a stylistic departure from her early family-centered novels with *Destination Biafra* (1982), which addresses the confluence of events that led to the secession of the Republic of Biafra from Nigeria in the late 1960s.

- To examine the Nigerian roots of Emecheta's literary works, the reader can turn to both Chinua Achebe's *Things Fall Apart* (1958), which focuses on the colonizing experience more from the perspective of the Ibos of the villages, and Flora Nwapa's *Efuru*, which follows a young Ibo woman who is fated to travel down turbulent paths in life.

- The Zimbabwean author and filmmaker Tsitsi Dangarembga's 1988 novel *Nervous Conditions* won the Commonwealth Writers Prize for Africa in 1989. It relates the coming of age of Tambu, who leaves her rural home to study at a missionary school run by her British-educated uncle in colonial Rhodesia in the 1960s.

- Emecheta has been considered alongside the Indian author Nayantara Sahgal, whose novel *The Day in Shadow* (1972) depicts a Hindu mother who is oppressed by her capitalist and patriarchal husband.

- A classic American novel depicting the domestic oppression of women is Alice Walker's *The Color Purple* (1982), set among African Americans in rural Georgia in the 1930s and presented in the form of letters by the protagonist, Celie, to God. The story includes some violent episodes and may be more appropriate for older teenagers.

- The Nigerian author Remi Adedeji assembled a collection of stories based on Nigerian folktales titled *Moonlight Stories* (1999), appropriate for young adults, relating why the tortoise's shell is cracked and other such legends.

- Another well-regarded female African author is Mariama Bâ, of Senegal, whose novel *Une si longue lettre* (1980), translated as *So Long a Letter*, consists of a letter from a widowed woman who must share her mourning with her deceased husband's younger second wife.

---

have. Emecheta's communicating this to Chiedu led the girl to throw a milk bottle through a window in their home, letting in the cold winter air, and then leave for a spell to stay with her father. Emecheta found herself thinking, "This was going to be my lot. I was going to give all I had to my children, only for them to spit on my face and tell me that I was a bad mother." It was during the ensuing six weeks that Emecheta channeled her overflowing emotions and took stock of her own life by writing *The Joys of Motherhood*, the conclusion of which she describes (in her autobiography) as an envisioning of the worst

that could ever happen to her. She originally dedicated the novel to Chiedu, with whom she reconciled, but her daughter objected, so the dedication is instead to all mothers. Chiedu, surely seeing herself in the portrait of the ungrateful Oshia, asked her mother not to publish the novel, but Emecheta politely refused. Chiedu assured her mother that she would never allow her to suffer a lonesome fate like Nnu Ego's. Tragically, Chiedu would not have time to give the world much more than the inspiration for her mother's powerful novel; she died in her early twenties, while living away from her mother,

CONSIDERED COLLECTIVELY, NNU EGO'S CHILDREN DO NOT SIMPLY OVERFLOW FROM THE FAMILY AT RANDOM BUT REPRESENT A COMPREHENSIVE ARRAY OF TRAJECTORIES OF MATURITY PRODUCED BY THE INTERSECTION OF TRADITIONAL IBO VILLAGE CULTURE AND WESTERNIZED URBAN CIVILIZATION."

owing to complications from anorexia. Emecheta's dedication in *Head Above Water* reads, "For Chiedu's Memory," and in a prose poem there, Emecheta acknowledges, "A part of a mother dies with her child."

Given Emecheta's experiences with her own children, one cannot underestimate the significance she must attribute to all the children she has created, in her life as well as in her fiction. In real life, a caring parent invests so much in his or her children that each child is in certain respects, quite literally, a reincarnation of one or both parents. The parents' time and energy spent working translate into the money that translates into the food that sustains the children—or among farmers, which, at the village level is nearly everyone, the parents may themselves produce through their own physical labor most of the food that the children eat. In either scenario, the parents' energy is transformed into the children's energy. And every word spoken by the parent is absorbed by the child, each shared thought and moral lesson is refigured in the child's brain (sometimes inversely), becoming a portion of the child's subconscious mental and emotional framework.

Emecheta holds the highest respect for the work of raising children, the realm of women in traditional Ibo culture. In her 1988 essay "Feminism with a Small 'f'!" (first delivered as a conference speech), she affirms, "It is our work to bring the next generation into the world, nurture them until they are grown old enough to fly from the nest and then start their own life." When a feminist photojournalist objected to Emecheta posing in her work space because it happened to be her kitchen, as she relates,

> I tried to tell her in vain that in my kitchen I felt I was doing more for the peace of the world than the nuclear scientist. In our kitchens we raise all Reagans, all Nkrumahs, all Jesuses. In our kitchens we cook for them, we send them away from home to be grown men and women, and in our kitchens they learn to love and to hate.

Emecheta concludes that "those who wish to control and influence the future by giving birth and nurturing the young should not be looked down upon.... If I had my way, it would be the highest paid job in the world."

Turning from Emecheta's thoughts on raising children to the children in *The Joys of Motherhood*, one would imagine that Emecheta has written them to embody (as do her own second-generation immigrant children) the confluence of their parents' efforts and their environment. In this regard, an analogy posited by Emecheta in her essay helps illuminate the manner in which a novel (and the characters therein) can take on a life of its own:

> A book is akin to a child on his mother's back. The mother knows she is carrying a baby on her back but the child can use its hands to lift anything that passes by, without the mother knowing.

In other words, however much control one thinks one has over one's children, or writing, once the most formative phases have passed, the child, like the book, will independently draw toward and figure its own destiny. Accordingly, through and beyond an author's conscious intents in his or her writing, the resulting work—especially if the author, like Emecheta, has a great store of cultural knowledge and experience—may hold even greater meaning to be extracted by the reader. In this novel, such meaning may be encoded in the archetypal protagonist's children. While Nnu Ego dies a sad death as an underappreciated mother, her children are still the fruits of her labors, and their accomplishments reflect on her. The narrator relates that Nnu Ego "had been brought up to believe that children made a woman." And as she herself states in speaking with Adim late in the book, "The fact is that parents get only reflected glory from their children nowadays."

Oshiaju's name is well justified in the context of his following the departed Ngozi (who is figuratively cast into "the bush" at death), with Nnaife proud that "the bush has refused this." The novel's realization of Oshia's character is aided by the detour into his consciousness on the morning that his little brother Adim is born.

The reader is given insight into how a sort of eldest sibling complex, whereby the child comes to feel the burden of always being the responsible one, can be intensified by a family's poverty, where the responsibilities of the eldest may expand to include child care, cooking, and other housework. Oshia, however, ultimately feels the reverse of this complex, since his mother prioritizes his schooling and allows him to shirk chores that his sisters perform. Oshia, then, represents the confluence of traditional Ibo masculinity and the sort of modern Western independence cultivated in urban, long-colonized Lagos. Thus, given the opportunity and the encouragement to better himself as fully as possible, it is unsurprising that he elects to do so in a developed Western nation, America. As such, his name is doubly significant, as the bush refuses him both in his survival at birth and in his self-imposed exile as a young adult—or rather, perhaps, Oshia refuses the bush.

Nnu Ego's next child is also a boy, Adimabua, meaning "now I am two." The name is given by Nnaife to reflect the doubling of his progeny; he now has two young boys who will grow up to replace their father as the men of the Owulum line. But in light of Adim's destiny, his name, too, has a doubled significance: just as if he were Oshia's twin, he neatly follows in his brother's footsteps (though without the same advantages in schooling), earning the right to attend a university in Canada and achieve the highest possible degree of self-fulfillment.

While Oshia and Adim are figuratively twinned, Nnu Ego's next children are actual twins, given the traditional names of Taiwo, "she who tasted the world first," and Kehinde, "the second to arrive." These names, too, prove suitable given the children's fates. Taiwo becomes the first of Nnu Ego's children to be matched to a husband (although Kehinde does marry and become pregnant first); and in effectively adopting one of her young sisters when the rest of the family returns to Ibuza, Taiwo becomes the first to get a taste of motherhood. Her name thus suggests Emecheta's implication elsewhere that the world revolves around motherhood, that motherhood is the central institution in any culture. While Taiwo's husband is Ibo, his status as a treasury employee in Lagos lends the sense that Taiwo is also moving beyond Ibo culture to get a taste of the Westernized capitalist world. Kehinde's fate diverges from her sister's somewhat, in that she branches out to marry a man from another ethnic group, a Yoruba. Together, then, these twins represent traditional Ibo womanhood as modified by the mixed urban environment of Lagos.

The next child is Nnamdio, meaning "this is my father," as the boy is recognized as a reincarnation of Agbadi, who, in dying, assured his daughter that he would return to her family. Unlike his siblings, Nnamdio is born back in Ibuza, and accordingly, he comes to signify a return to traditional Ibo roots. His one standout characteristic is his disinclination toward sedentary Western schooling: at age six he "would not even sit still for five minutes at a private lesson," and when his mother takes him back to Ibuza several years later, he "still refused to go to school." Thus, instead of being assimilated into Western, urbanized civilization like his elder brothers, Nnamdio instinctively rebels against those confines, and the reader easily imagines that Nnamdio will flourish in the physically fulfilling life of the village to become, like his grandfather Agbadi, an accomplished, respected farmer and chief in the traditional mold.

The last of Nnu Ego's surviving children are Obiageli, "she who has come to enjoy wealth," and Malachi, "you do not know what tomorrow will bring." Indeed, Obiageli is the one to be raised in what will surely be financially comfortable circumstances by Taiwo and her husband, Magnus—another significant name, meaning "great" in Latin. The scholar Ogunyemi reads Obiageli's name as thus reflecting a return to women's traditional dependence on a patriarchal provider, in this case her brother-in-law, the one to earn the wealth. But Emecheta's comments in "Feminism with a Small 'f'!" suggest that Obiageli's name might be read another way. Although Nnu Ego, acceding to the patriarchal culture represented by her father, does not send any of her daughters to school, Emecheta assures the reader of her essay that she believes education for women to be of the utmost importance. She remarks, "I want very much to further the education of women in Africa, because I know that education really helps the women. . . . It helps them to rear a generation. It is true that if one educates a woman, one educates a community, whereas if one educates a man, one educates a man." The reader of *The Joys of Motherhood* may imagine that Obiageli, in the household of her sister and brother-in-law, who is recognized by Adim as "an enlightened man," will be just such a young woman to benefit from an education and (likely not going so far as to become a career-oriented Western-style feminist) pass what she learns on to her children. Her education, then, will be the "wealth" that she comes to enjoy. Magnus confirms that in Lagos, Obiageli "will be able to start school and will help her sister in running the house." Thus, Obiageli, as a character, is portrayed as uniting the educated Western and traditional Ibo domestic spheres of womanhood. Malachi, finally, is Emecheta's wild card, with her name suggesting only uncertainty about her fate. Given a taste of life in Lagos from an unschooled girl's perspective, Malachi will be raised back in Ibuza, ultimately by relatives instead of her mother. But where the return to the village roots bodes well for Nnamdio, allowing his maturation into traditional, virile African manhood, for Malachi this return could potentially mean submersion back in the restricted bounds of patriarchal, polygamous society. Perhaps, rather than signal such a pessimistic fate for this girl through her name, Emecheta wished to leave her future more open to possibility and optimism on the part of the reader.

Considered collectively, Nnu Ego's children do not simply overflow from the family at random but represent a comprehensive array of trajectories of maturity produced by the intersection of traditional Ibo village culture and Westernized urban civilization. Their patterning, too, seems significant. The first two boys are born years apart, but Adim essentially follows the same path as Oshia. Emecheta thus identifies the masculine means of cultural transmission to be ultimately based on imitation—the young man sees what proves successful for another and follows his lead. Both pairs of twins, on the other hand, see divergent fates. Taiwo and Kehinde follow similar trajectories, but one is paired with an Ibo with modern employment in the treasury, while the other rebelliously pairs herself with a Yoruba from a family grounded in the traditional employment of a butchery. And where Obiageli will be raised in modern urban circumstances, Malachi will be raised in traditional village circumstances. Thus, both pairs of twins start united but end up separated, in ways that push gently beyond the family's traditional boundaries—as opposed to the total rupture in the family's boundaries accomplished by Oshia and Adim. And it is the emotional pain caused by the boys' silence overseas that prefigures Nnu Ego's early death.

Several of Nnu Ego's children move to the west, leaving her to feel abandoned in her old age.
(© iofoto | Shutterstock.com)

In sum, in the diversified configuration of the fates of the children of the archetypal mother Nnu Ego, Emecheta seems to chart out the means by which the traditional African family will branch out into the modern world. And above all it is the triad of Taiwo, Magnus, and Obiageli, adapting to modernity at a moderate pace while remaining aligned with the family and its traditions, with supportive parents to guide girls and boys alike through education, that bodes well for this and all African families' futures.

Source: Michael Allen Holmes, Critical Essay on *The Joys of Motherhood*, in *Novels for Students*, Gale, Cengage Learning, 2013.

Stéphane Robolin

In the following excerpt, Robolin investigates the role of gender in postcolonial textual analysis by examining how supernatural characters and incidents construct the protagonist's colonial identity in The Joys of Motherhood.

Buchi Emecheta's 1979 novel, *The Joys of Motherhood*, opens with a haunting scene. The protagonist, Nnu Ego, flees her home in great distress and despondency, frantically placing as much distance between herself and the latest of the misdeeds attributed to her spiteful "spirit": the sudden death of her newly-born son. Running "like someone pursued"—here, by the absent presence of her vengeful *chi*, the guiding spirit from the realm of the living-dead who has rendered her life unbearable—Nnu Ego seeks to terminate the excruciating pain that accompanies her long succession of failed attempts at motherhood. Her arduous efforts to achieve motherhood, the very standard of success for women according to the customs of Nnu Ego's community, have yielded nothing but grievous loss, culminating in the death of her first (neonatal) son. Faced with this failure, presumably orchestrated by her harassing *chi*, she prepares to throw herself off the extended Carter Bridge in the port city of Lagos.

The *chi* in this scenario actively contributes to Nnu Ego's misery by ceaselessly haunting her, but neither the spirit nor the dreadful iniquities it carries out are isolated phenomena in this novel. Spectral figures in this text, more often than not, register a grave injury resulting from structured social inequalities. Most curiously, they also materialize around issues of interpretation that run through the novel—Nnu Ego and her community read her situation as resulting from her spirit's malevolence (as explored below)—thus drawing our attention to the connections between questions of interpretation, constructions of justice, and Emecheta's career-long preoccupation with gender. This essay draws on the metaphor of haunting and the way Emecheta's novel deploys spectral irruptions to consider the multiply configured intersections of gender, interpretation, and justice, loosely referred to here as gendered hauntings. This notion of gendered hauntings, I will point out, applies as much to the content within the text—thus facilitating an exploration of this nexus within the plot and details of the narrative—as it does to the theoretical dynamics surrounding the text, thereby enabling us to seize upon the metaphorical ghosts that exist beyond the text and haunt certain acts of interpretation.

I understand Emecheta's explicitly feminist novel to be engaged in a (fictionalized) theoretical enterprise in its own right, one which posits a specific nexus of political, cultural, economic, sexual, and religious forces that constitute a colonial society and elucidates how such forces bear upon the individuals within it. Placing Emecheta's text in conversation with cultural theory proper permits an interrogation into the premises and conclusions of both theoretical enterprises. I demonstrate that certain postcolonial

> THE *DIBIA*'S INTERPRETATION LINKING THE SLAVE WOMAN AND NNU EGO—AND, BY CATEGORICAL EXTENSION, WOMANHOOD AND SLAVEHOOD—IS A CRITICAL ELEMENT THAT RESONATES THROUGHOUT *THE JOYS OF MOTHERHOOD*."

articulations of liminality—particularly those advanced by Homi Bhabha—prove remarkably productive in helping to elucidate Emecheta's famed novel. However, I argue, *The Joys of Motherhood* has as much to offer contemporary conceptions of liminality, for its representational work poses implicit challenges to the latter. Through the theoretical tension it generates, this particular juxtaposition of novel and theory returns us to basic questions of resistance and subjectivity. Moreover, the particularly gendered contours of haunting in Emecheta's novel help focus our attention on the ways that sexual politics of interpretation are practiced in cultural and postcolonial studies.

An overview of Nnu Ego's life reveals a narrative saturated with pathos. In her struggle to achieve the ideal of motherhood, she encounters many obstacles. Along the way, she is apparently plagued by her *chi*, who offers her the worst of both worlds: when desirous of children and economically capable of providing for them, she is rendered barren; but "now that [she] cannot afford them," Nnu Ego gives birth to nine children. Emecheta's text, then, chronicles Nnu Ego's difficulties and functions as a powerful testimony regarding the undue burden placed on her and the women she represents. The opening haunting scene—which takes place at the narrative's chronological midpoint—affords Emecheta the opportunity to level a powerful critique against the workings, and trappings, of gender as encoded and structured in a multilayered social hierarchy. For we learn the source of Nnu Ego's misery is the "sins" of her father, Nwokocha Agbadi—namely, his hand in the slave trade and, in particular, his "unfair" "acquisition" of one woman who had been "promised to a river goddess." The Slave Woman is placed in Agbadi's compound as primary servant to Agunwa, Agbadi's first wife. Upon Agunwa's untimely death, however, the Slave Woman is forced to accompany her mistress into the spirit world, as local custom dictates. This form of "slave suttee" marks respect for the woman who is to be buried, but the Slave Woman, fearful and unwilling to abdicate her own life, struggles and refuses to submit voluntarily. For the latter's intransigent resistance to the custom, Agunwa's outraged eldest son indignantly beats the Slave Woman to death, but before passing out, she vows to return to this family in a new form. And so she apparently does, in the form of *chi* to Nnu Ego upon her birth and, in the process, turns Nnu Ego's life into an enormous trial.

African religious scholar John Mbiti has established the centrality of the "living-dead" in a number of African societies. The spectral presence of the recently (physically) deceased "are the 'spirits' with which African peoples are most concerned: it is through the living-dead that the spirit world becomes personal to men" (82). As mediators of the human and spirit world, the living-dead, then, become the arbiters of justice, restitution, and punishment. In this way, the presence and retributive deeds of the murdered Slave Woman as *chi* signal the calculated disciplinary action against wrongs or transgressions—among them being Agbadi's kidnapping of a river goddess's subject, his profitable participation in slavery, and the murder of an innocent woman who was without fault. Traditionally, according to Mbiti, "when punishment comes, it comes in the present life. For this reason, misfortunes may be interpreted as indicating that the sufferer has broken some moral or ritual conduct against God, the spirits, the elders or other members of his society" (205). The twist in this otherwise simple schema, of course, comes in Emecheta's decision to situate Nnu Ego as the bearer of this punitive burden, a twist that highlights the differential sexual politics that are, to a great extent, Emecheta's focus. Indeed, the history of Nnu Ego's recent past communicates a complex dynamics of gender and power that sets into motion a chain of reactions: the neglect of Agbadi's head-wife for the company of his mistress leads to the former's premature death, which in turn creates the circumstances for the Slave Woman's own death. Shortly after, the Slave Woman returns in the form of the *chi* of Nnu Ego, Agbadi's daughter, who subsequently pays for her father's own

indiscretions and faults. This decidedly gendered form of haunting attests to the unjust displacement of responsibilities onto women, whereby the misfortunes of a woman are foisted upon the subsequent generation.

Nnu Ego's unfortunate gendered haunting is established through the act of interpretation: The tie between Nnu Ego and the Slave Woman is underscored, in part, in the *dibia*'s (medicine man's) analysis of the infant Nnu Ego's seemingly abnormal lump on her head. Given the cause of the Slave Woman's death (a blow to the head by Agunwu's first son), the young protagonist's physical characteristic leads the *dibia* to an unsettling conclusion:

> "The child *is* the slave woman who died with your senior wife Agunwa. She promised to come back as a daughter. Now here she is. That is why this child has the fair skin of the water people, and the painful lump on her head is from the beating your men gave her before she fell into the grave." (emphasis added)

The Slave Woman figures not simply as the guiding spirit of Nnu Ego; she *is* Nnu Ego. The protagonist, in other words, becomes an avatar of this captive servant, so that one embodies the other. The rest of the novel teases out the implications of this ostensibly metaphorical association, through which Emecheta eventually conjoins the condition of slavehood and the condition of womanhood. Indeed, not only does the protagonist eventually accept "worn outfits for [her] newly-born baby"—a custom reserved only for slaves—but also, it eventually occurs "to Nnu Ego that she [is] a *prisoner*" and that "men cleverly [use] a woman's sense of responsibility to *enslave* her" (emphasis added). To her own vexed and astonished realization, Nnu Ego acts and feels like a slave.

The *dibia*'s interpretation linking the Slave Woman and Nnu Ego—and, by categorical extension, womanhood and slavehood—is a critical element that resonates throughout *The Joys of Motherhood*. But distinguishing between interpretation as a conclusion (a fait accompli) and interpretation as an act of reading helps to elucidate an altogether different aspect of Emecheta's message. For, while the text gives evidence of this *dibia*'s accuracy, it also troubles any presumption that the *dibia* is a universally reliable truth-sayer/soothsayer. Indeed, the later claims by another *dibia* about the "mysterious ghosts" summoned by the amateurish guitar-playing of Nnu Ego's second husband, Nnaife, are exposed as misled at best, fraudulent at worst ("Maybe some medicine men could see into the future, but that man from Abeokuta [. . .] was not so truthful"); mice that Oshia, the eldest son, had temporarily placed in the guitar in fact were responsible for the "mysterious" noise. Later in the text, he refrains from "telling h[is duped mother] that most of those *dibias* only told her what she wanted to hear." Under optimal circumstances, however, the *dibia* is responsible for interpreting the actions that exist within the liminal space that lies between "the living" and "the dead." If the living-dead act as mediators between the living and God (and God's realm of the spirit world), the medicine man functions as the interpreter of the elusive but significant relations between the living and the living-dead. John Mbiti points out that medicine men are not only trained to decipher the root of "sickness, disease, and misfortune," but also help to implement preventative measures against misfortunes, remove curses, and control the spirits and living-dead (165–66). Medicine men's social function, then, lies in their capacity to properly "read" the signs of the world(s) around them. In this way, Emecheta also places under her critical lens the interpretive work of the mediator between the living people and the ghostly matter, the seething absent presence, that surrounds them (Gordon 195). . . .

Source: Stéphane Robolin, "Gendered Hauntings: *The Joys of Motherhood*," in *Research in African Literatures*, Vol. 35, No. 3, Fall 2004, pp. 76–92.

Teresa Derrickson

In the following excerpt, Derrickson illustrates how female characters in The Joys of Motherhood *are doubly exploited by both Ibo and European institutions.*

Much of the written scholarship on Buchi Emecheta's *The Joys of Motherhood* (1979) focuses on the novel's critique of traditional Ibo society. Specifically, such articles read Emecheta's text as a denunciation of the reproductive practices of the Ibo people, practices that do harm to women by promoting (and indeed institutionalizing) the idea that a proper wife should seek only to beget and care for her offspring. As critical texts that recognize Emecheta's attempt to expose the gender politics operating within indigenous Africa, these readings are important. They collectively validate *The Joys of Motherhood* as a work of socio-historical import, as a novel that fills noticeable gaps in the historical record of African women's

> THE TITLE OF EMECHETA'S NOVEL IS PATENTLY IRONIC, FOR IT WOULD SEEM THAT THERE ARE FEW JOYS ASSOCIATED WITH MOTHERHOOD AFTER ALL."

experiences. Nevertheless, the scholarly consensus that valorizes this work obscures other thematic threads that are equally important in the recovery of African women's history. As S. Jay Kleinberg discusses in his introduction to *Retrieving Women's History*, the effort to rectify women's erasure in history entails not only an analysis of their work and their role in the family, but also an analysis of "both formal and informal political movements and . . . their impact upon women, women's participation in them and the ways in which they shape male-female interactions and men's and women's roles in society."

Kleinberg's call for an analysis of the way in which women's experiences are impacted by local politics encourages us to return to Emecheta's text to analyze a question that most critics of this book raise but do not fully explore: to what extent does colonialism impinge upon the lives of Ibo women? One compelling answer to this question is introduced by Rolf Solberg, who suggests that the lives of the Ibo women in *The Joys of Motherhood* are determined by the tensions of a "culture collision" between the institutions of traditional Ibo society and the institutions of western Europe. The focus of this paper will be to develop this suggestion and to argue its validity. In particular, I will demonstrate that the hardships endured by the women of Emecheta's novel do not emanate from an oppressive cultural practice regarding women's role in Ibo villages, but from a historical moment of political and economic transition, a historical moment in which the values and priorities of British culture clash destructively with the values and priorities of indigenous Africa.

The Joys of Motherhood bears out the fact that this transitional period was particularly disadvantageous for African women. As the plight of the novel's key character reveals, colonialism was a costly reality for those who were forced to walk a fine line between that which was demanded of them by their village communities and that which was demanded of them by the rules of a European political regime. This paper will demonstrate that the Ibo women of Emecheta's novel find themselves in this very predicament: specifically, they are subjected to new forms of exploitation as they are asked to assume traditional duties and responsibilities under a newly imported economic system that—unlike their native system—fails to validate or reward them for such work. In essence, this paper traces the destructive influence of Western capitalism and its associated ideologies on the relative power and autonomy of Ibo women. Colonialism, I hope to show, was a far greater threat to their collective well-being than the strictures of village patriarchy.

Set in the British colony of Nigeria in the 1930s and 1940s, *The Joys of Motherhood* details the life story of an Ibo woman named Nnu Ego who escapes the ignominy of a childless first marriage by fleeing to the distant city of Lagos to start anew with a second husband. Nnu Ego's simple dream of becoming a mother—a dream rooted in the cultural values of Ibo society, where motherhood is the primary source of a woman's self-esteem and public status—is happily realized several times over in this new setting. The pleasures associated with motherhood that the protagonist so eagerly anticipates, however, are ultimately negated by the difficult economic conditions of her new urban environment. In short, there are so few job opportunities for her husband to pursue (and so little ambition on his part to pursue them) that Nnu Ego spends her entire life alternately birthing children and working day in and day out as a cigarette peddler to stave off the hunger and poverty that invariably haunt her household. The novel focuses on this grueling battle, a battle that ends in a loss for Nnu Ego, as she witnesses her beloved sons grow up and leave Nigeria for good and her daughters marry and move away. Nnu Ego's hopes of living out her final years in the company of her grandchildren disappear before she turns forty, and she dies at the side of a country road, alone and unnoticed.

The title of Emecheta's novel is patently ironic, for it would seem that there are few joys associated with motherhood after all. And yet while that reality is certainly one message the novel imparts, there is far more to the text than a critique of motherhood. The fact that Emecheta's novel moves beyond this critique to explore the costs of colonialism for women in urban Nigeria is summarized in a crucial passage midway through the novel in which Nnu Ego pauses to assess the injustices of her life in Lagos: "It was not fair, she felt, the way men cleverly used a woman's sense of responsibility to actually enslave her.... [H]ere in Lagos, where she was faced with the harsh reality of making ends meet on a pittance, was it right for her husband to refer to her responsibility? It seemed that all she had inherited from her agrarian background was the responsibility and none of the booty." This excerpt is key in locating the source of Nnu Ego's anguish not in her position as a mother per se, but in her position as a woman who is asked to assume the same obligations of her "agrarian background" within a new cultural setting that confers "none of the booty" normally associated with such labor. Nnu Ego is able to interpret the inequity of this exchange as something that "enslaves" and "imprisons" her. She is also able to identify, at least on some level, the political economy of colonial Lagos as the Western construct of "the new" that proves to be unaccommodating of her traditional role as wife and mother: she notes, for example, that it is the "harsh reality of making ends meet on a pittance" that secures her thralldom.

Before discussing in further detail the political dynamics underwriting this thralldom, it might be useful to review the role women played in Ibo society before the widespread influence of British rule. As Kamene Okonjo points out, the popular belief that African women were impotent and/or trivial in the male-dominated communities of Ibo culture is a gross misconception. While men's labor was widely considered to be more prestigious than women's labor, and while the practice of polygamy and patrilocal domicile (married women dwelling in their husbands' villages rather than in their own) secured men's power over women in general, Ibo women still wielded considerable influence both within their marriages and within the larger community. Women, for example, were a major force in the society's agrarian economy: they planted their own crops, sold their crop surplus (as well as that of their husbands), and exerted exclusive control over the operation and management of the village market, the site where all local commerce took place. In addition, women were active participants in the dual-sex political system of Ibo society, a system in which Ibo men and Ibo women governed themselves separately, both sexes selecting their own set of leaders and cabinet members to legislate issues relevant to the members of their respective constituencies.

Women's formidable presence in the economic and political realms of the village gave them significant say in how the village was run and ensured that their needs would not be ignored. Surprisingly, the practice of polygamy worked in subtle ways to contribute to this outcome. While polygamy was not a perfect marital arrangement, it was well-suited to the agrarian lifestyle of the Ibo people and contained several built-in mechanisms that allowed women to better cope with the burdens of that type of lifestyle. As Janet Pool observes, polygamy allowed co-wives, for example, to "form a power-bloc within the family," a power-bloc that was notoriously effective in coercing an otherwise stubborn husband to behave in ways congenial to his wives. Polygamy also eased the workload of Ibo women by making it a common practice for women of the same union to share domestic chores, such as cooking and babysitting. This benefit was particularly advantageous in the context of Ibo society, for Ibo women were encouraged to have numerous children—far more children than they were probably able to manage on their own. Finally, in addition to the cultural prestige conferred upon those associated with such a union, polygamy protected the economic interests of women by ensuring that a given family had enough members, that is, sufficient manual labor to produce and harvest a bountiful crop.

It would be incorrect to assert, even in light of the foregoing facts, that the status of women in precolonial Ibo society matched the status of men, for this was simply not the case. However, as Leith Mullings argues, although women of African agrarian societies did not enjoy the same roles and privileges as men, they were equal to men in all the ways that counted: they had equal access to resources and to means of production. As Mullings goes on to explain, the shift of indigenous Africa from subsistence-based societies to money-based societies (a shift precipitated by British colonialism) upset this power balance by introducing a new type of production called cash-cropping. Planting crops for cash (as opposed to planting crops for food or exchange) was a form of labor that was quickly taken up and dominated by African men. Cash-cropping proved so superior to other forms of productive labor within the context of the new capitalist economy that it immediately undercut the value of women's work (which was not aimed at producing cash) and rendered such work practically superfluous.

These facts are crucial to understand the hardships experienced by the female protagonist of Buchi Emecheta's novel. As the novel makes evident, Nnu Ego is a victim of this newly imported capitalist society, a society in which African women are required to continue performing traditional duties and responsibilities in an economic setting where that labor is no longer of any market value. In other words, Nigeria's transition from a tribal culture and a tribal moral value system to a Western capitalist system with all its benefits and pitfalls has occurred at the expense of women like Nnu Ego, who have exchanged one form of patriarchy with another, while being stripped of former privileges and denied the right to new ones.

Ketu Katrak's analysis of the effects of the colonial capitalist system on women's sociopolitical situation in Nigeria confirms that the local economy was indeed a major force in contributing to the subjugation of women like Nnu Ego. Katrak explains, for example, that while African men were allowed to enter the formal economy of colonial Nigeria by acquiring jobs that paid standard wages, African women were excluded from this sphere and were edged instead into the informal and highly unstable economy of streetside peddling: "Women were forcibly kept outside of the wage market dominated by men in this Nigeria of the 1930s and 1940s."

The gender bias inscribed in the new, dominant capitalist system proves to be devastating for Nnu Ego, who is pressured to maintain her role as a traditional wife and mother regardless of the fact that this new system works against the success of that role. Nnu Ego's barred access from reliable modes of production confines her to levels of poverty that make it nearly impossible for her to feed, clothe, and educate her eight children. This would not have been the situation in her tribal village of Ibuza, where Nnu Ego's crop yield would have sustained her large family, and where Nnu Ego and the other women of the community would have controlled key sectors of the local economy through the production and exchange of household goods and services.

Women's influence over the economic affairs of their community gave them significant political leverage and allowed them to participate in village-wide decisions that affected their well-being as women. . . .

Source: Teresa Derrickson, "Class, Culture, and the Colonial Context: The Status of Women in Buchi Emecheta's *The Joys of Motherhood*," in *International Fiction Review*, Vol. 29, No. 12, January 2002, pp. 40–51.

SOURCES

Allan, Tuzyline Jita, "*The Joys of Motherhood*: A Study of a Problematic Womanist Aesthetic," in *Womanist and Feminist Aesthetics: A Comparative Review*, Ohio University Press, 1995, pp. 95–117.

"Buchi Emecheta," in *British Council Literature*, http://literature.britishcouncil.org/buchi-emecheta (accessed January 20, 2012).

Burns, Alan, *History of Nigeria*, 7th ed., Allen & Unwin, 1969, p. 247.

Busby, Margaret, Foreword to *Emerging Perspectives on Buchi Emecheta*, edited by Marie Umeh, Africa World Press, 1996, pp. xiii–xix.

Daymond, M. J., "Buchi Emecheta, Laughter and Silence: Changes in the Concepts of 'Woman,' 'Wife,' and 'Mother,'" in *Emerging Perspectives on Buchi Emecheta*, edited by Marie Umeh, Africa World Press, 1996, pp. 277–88.

Emecheta, Buchi, "Feminism with a Small 'f!,'" in *Criticism and Ideology: Second African Writers' Conference*, edited by Kirsten Holst Petersen, 1988, pp. 173–85.

———, *Head Above Water*, Heinemann, 1994, pp. v, 27, 30, 39, 224.

———, *The Joys of Motherhood*, George Braziller, 1979.

Emenyonu, Ernest N., "Technique and Language in Buchi Emecheta's *The Bride Price, The Slave Girl*, and *The Joys of Motherhood*," in *Emerging Perspectives on Buchi Emecheta*, edited by Marie Umeh, Africa World Press, 1996, pp. 251–66.

Ezeigbo, Theodora Akachi, "Tradition and the African Female Writer: The Example of Buchi Emecheta," in *Emerging Perspectives on Buchi Emecheta*, edited by Marie Umeh, Africa World Press, 1996, pp. 5–26.

Friedli-Clapie, Lisa, "Undercurrents of Mammy Wata Symbolism in Buchi Emecheta's *The Joys of Motherhood*," in *West Virginia University Philological Papers*, Vol. 51, Fall 2005, pp. 83–90.

"The History of Nigeria," in *Total Nigeria*, http://www.ng.total.com/01_about_nigeria/0103_history.htm (accessed January 22, 2012).

Loflin, Christine, "Mother Africa: African Women and the Land in West African Literature," in *African Horizons: The Landscapes of African Fiction*, Greenwood Press, 1998, pp. 35–54.

"Nigeria Profile," in *BBC News Africa*, http://www.bbc.co.uk/news/world-africa-13949550 (accessed January 22, 2012).

Nwapa, Flora, *Efuru*, Heinemann, 1966.

Ogunyemi, Chikwenye Okonjo, "Buchi Emecheta: The Shaping of a Self," in *Komparatistische Hefte*, Vol. 8, 1983, pp. 65–78.

Petersen, Kirsten Holst, "Buchi Emecheta," in *Dictionary of Literary Biography*, Vol. 117, *Twentieth-Century Caribbean and Black African Writers, First Series*, edited by Bernth Lindfors and Reinhard Sander, Gale Research, 1992, pp. 159–66.

Robolin, Stéphane, "Gendered Hauntings: *The Joys of Motherhood*, Interpretive Acts, and Postcolonial Theory," in *Research in African Literatures*, Vol. 35, No. 3, Fall 2004, pp. 76–92.

Stratton, Florence, "The Shallow Grave: Archetypes of Female Experience in African Fiction," in *Emerging Perspectives on Buchi Emecheta*, edited by Marie Umeh, Africa World Press, 1996, pp. 95–124.

Umeh, Marie, Introduction to *Emerging Perspectives on Buchi Emecheta*, edited by Marie Umeh, Africa World Press, 1996, pp. xxiii–xlii.

———, "Procreation, Not Recreation: Decoding Mama in Buchi Emecheta's *The Joys of Motherhood*," in *Emerging Perspectives on Buchi Emecheta*, edited by Marie Umeh, Africa World Press, 1996, pp. 189–206.

FURTHER READING

Basden, G. T., *Among the Ibos of Nigeria*, Barnes & Noble, 1966.

> First published in 1921, this is a thorough ethnological study, addressing the roles of men and women and many cultural practices, conducted through the author's extensive habitation with the Ibo at a time when rural areas were virtually untouched by colonization. While from a modern perspective Basden's phrasings may be considered politically incorrect, he offers legitimate insight into the psychology of tribal minds.

Crittenden, Ann, *The Price of Motherhood: Why the Most Important Job in the World Is Still the Least Valued*, Macmillan, 2001.

> In this volume, Crittenden analyzes the costs of motherhood from a Western capitalist viewpoint, framing mothers' efforts in terms of lost wages and their unrewarded exploitation by the rest of society.

Jell-Bahlsen, Sabine, *The Water Goddess in Igbo Cosmology: Ogbuide of Oguta Lake*, Africa World Press, 2008.

> This volume provides a comprehensive discussion of all aspects of the Igbo (or Ibo) water goddess known as Ogbuide or Uhammiri, including mythical tales, theology, and religious practices of the Igbo people.

Oyewùmí, Oyèrónké, *The Invention of Women: Making an African Sense of Western Gender Discourses*, University of Minnesota Press, 1997.

> This scholarly study by a Yoruba author explores the history of gender identity in Yoruba culture as a means of reconsidering the legitimacy of using approaches shaped by Western views of gender to judge African circumstances.

SUGGESTED SEARCH TERMS

Buchi Emecheta AND *The Joys of Motherhood*

Buchi Emecheta AND interview

Buchi Emecheta AND review

The Joys of Motherhood AND criticism

Nigerian literature

African literature

Ibo OR Igbo AND culture

Ibo OR Igbo AND history

Buchi Emecheta AND London

Buchi Emecheta AND feminism

Buchi Emecheta AND Flora Nwapa

The Man in the Iron Mask

ALEXANDRE DUMAS

1847–1850

Alexandre Dumas's *The Man in the Iron Mask* is the final story in the series that features the Musketeers Aramis, Athos, Pathos, and d'Artagnan. In *The Three Musketeers*, published in 1844, d'Artagnan joins the famous three, and together they diffuse a plot hatched by Cardinal Richelieu. In the next installment, *Twenty Years After*, published in 1845, the four heroes are caught up in the civil wars in France known as the Fronde and fail in an attempt to rescue King Charles I of England from death. The final work in Dumas's series, *The Vicomte de Bragelonne, or Ten Years After*, was published in installments from 1847 through 1850 and includes three books often published individually: *Bragelonne, or the Son of Athos*; *Louise de la Vallière*; and *The Man in the Iron Mask*.

In the final book, *The Man in the Iron Mask*, Dumas focuses on the struggle for power among the individuals surrounding King Louis XIV. Aramis, now a bishop, seeks to rise ever higher in the ranks of the Order of the Jesuits, a secret religious organization, and in the Roman Catholic Church, hoping one day to become pope. The king's financial ministers, Fouquet and Colbert, meanwhile, attempt to outmaneuver one another and ingratiate themselves further with the king. In addition to exploring these political power struggles, Dumas also examines the romances of key figures in the novel and studies the way love and passion often lead to turmoil and destruction. The key plot in the novel, however, centers on

Alexandre Dumas

the existence of a twin brother to the king. The child, Philippe, was whisked away at birth, sequestered, and imprisoned, until Aramis rescues him with the hope of installing him in Louis XIV's place on the throne of France. The plot fails, with disastrous consequences, one of which is Philippe's return to prison. Now as ordered by his brother the king, he must wear a mask of iron to conceal his identity.

Originally published as *L'homme au masque de fer* in serial form from 1847 through 1850 in the journal *Le Siècle* as the last part of *The Vicomte de Bragelonne, or Ten Years After*, *The Man in the Iron Mask* is available in a 1998 Oxford University Press edition, introduced and annotated by David Coward.

AUTHOR BIOGRAPHY

Dumas was born on July 24, 1802, in the town of Villers-Cotterêts, near Paris. In 1806, Dumas's father, who served as a general in Napoleon's army, died, leaving the family in poverty. After briefly attending school between 1811 and 1813, Dumas began working as an attorney's clerk in

1816. He collaborated on several theatrical works in 1820 and 1821 with Adolphe de Leuven. In 1823, Dumas moved to Paris and secured a position as the secretary to the Duc d'Orléans, who would later become king. A year later, a son was born to Dumas by his mistress Marie-Catherine Laure Labay. The son, Alexandre Dumas (fils), would later become a famous author as well. The year 1829 marked Dumas's first success as an author, when his play, *Henri III et sa cour* debuted. A revolution in 1830, in which Dumas participated, ousted King Charles X. The former Duc d'Orléans then became King Louis-Philippe.

For the next several years, Dumas continued to write and to travel, recovering from cholera in Italy in 1832. He married Ida Ferrier in 1840 and published an eight-volume essay collection, *Celebrated Crimes*, in 1841. Two years later, the first installments of *The Three Musketeers* were published in serialized form to popular acclaim. Dumas separated from Ferrier in 1844. The same year, he published another of his most famous works, *The Count of Monte Cristo*. In 1845, the sequel to *The Three Musketeers*, titled *Twenty Years After*, was published. From 1847 through 1850, the final volume in the Musketeer trilogy was published in installments under the name *The Vicomte de Bragelonne*; this volume contained the work *The Man in the Iron Mask*, which would later be published as a stand-alone volume.

Despite the success of these works, Dumas's income dropped considerably during the Revolution of 1848. By 1850, Dumas's theater fell into bankruptcy. The author fled to Brussels the following year to escape his creditors; he remained there for two years. Upon returning to Paris in 1853, Dumas founded the daily paper *Le Mousquetaire*, which lasted until 1857. He then began a weekly paper, which survived for three years. In 1860, Dumas traveled to Italy in order to aid in the struggle for independence there. He lived in Naples following this war and worked as a keeper of the museums. Back in Paris, his debts continued to mount. Dumas died of a stroke on December 5, 1870, in Dieppe, France, in his son's home.

PLOT SUMMARY

Chapters 1–5

Aramis and the Duchesse (Madame de Chevreuse) discuss their past involvements and plots. Aramis is one of the famous "four," as he, Athos, Porthos, and d'Artagnan are known. He is now a

MEDIA ADAPTATIONS

- A MP3 downloadable version of the *The Man in the Iron Mask*, read by Simon Vance, was published by Audio Audible in 2010.

- An unabridged audio CD of *The Man in the Iron Mask*, also available as an MP3 download, read by Geoffrey Sherman, was published by Brilliance Audio in 2006.

- *The Man in the Iron Mask* was adapted for film in 1998. Directed by Randall Wallace, who also wrote the screenplay based on Dumas's novel, the film starred Leonardo DiCaprio as King Louis XIV and his imprisoned twin, Philippe, and featured Jeremy Irons as Aramis, John Malkovich as Athos, Gérard Depardieu as Porthos, and Gabriel Byrne as d'Artagnan. The DVD was released in 1998.

- A second film adaption of Dumas's *The Man in the Iron Mask* produced in 1998 was written and directed by William Richert and starred Nick Richert as Louis and Philippe.

- In 1985, an animated television movie adaption of *The Man in the Iron Mask* was released. It was written by Keith Dewhurst and featured the voice of Colin Friels as Philippe and Louis XIV.

- *The Man in the Iron Mask* was produced as a television movie in 1977 and was written by William Bast and directed by Mike Newell. The movie stared Richard Chamberlain as Louis and Philippe.

- In 1968, *The Man in the Iron Mask* was adapted as a television series, starring Nicolas Chagrin as Louis XIV. The nine-episode series was directed by Hugh David and written by Anthony Stevens.

- A 1939 film adaptation of *The Man in the Iron Mask* was directed by James Whale and written by George Bruce.

- A 1928 film adaption of *The Man in the Iron Mask* was directed by George J. Banfield and Leslie Eveleigh and was written by Banfield, George A. Cooper, and Anthony Ellis. The film was released in the United Kingdom.

bishop. Chevreuse suspects that Aramis is also the new General of the Order, that is, the Jesuits. The Duchesse, who needs money, tells Aramis of incriminating letters she possesses written by the late Cardinal Mazarin regarding some misappropriation of funds. She threatens to show these letters to Monsieur Fouquet, whom the letters incriminate. Aramis does not participate in this blackmail.

The Duchesse visits Colbert, the Intendant of Finances, and accuses him of having ambitions to become the Surintendant, a position currently held by Fouquet. He denies it. She tells Colbert that she has letters implicating M. Fouquet in a scandal involving Cardinal Mazarin, which could send Fouquet into exile or prison if discovered. Chevreuse bargains with Colbert for money and an audience with the Queen Mother in exchange for the letters. Confident that he will soon procure Fouquet's post after purchasing the letters, Colbert offers to sell a high-ranking position to Monsieur Vanel.

The Queen Mother (Anne of Austria), the Queen (Maria-Teresa, wife of King Louis XIV), and their ladies-in-waiting are conversing when a visitor is announced. It is Madame de Chevreuse, disguised as a nun and promising to cure the Queen Mother's cancer. Once alone with Anne, Chevreuse reveals her knowledge that King Louis XIV has a twin brother who was hidden away at birth on the advice of Cardinal de Richelieu. Chevreuse then reveals her identity, and the Queen Mother embraces her as an old friend.

The Queen Mother believes that the twin died as a child. The Duchesse discusses a rumor that he survived but dismisses this notion out of deference to Anne. Chevreuse asks Anne to visit and then hints that she needs money to repair her estate prior to Anne's visit. The Queen Mother insists that M. Fouquet will pay the sum.

Chapters 6–10

Jean de La Fountaine owes a debt to Fouquet and gives money from book sales to help Fouquet. La Fountaine reveals to Fouquet that Vanel wishes to purchase Fouquet's Procureur-General post, and Fouquet agrees. Vanel is waiting outside, and the deal is soon settled.

Fouquet presents his lover, Madame Belliere, with the jewels she once sold in order to help him. Aramis (also known as Monsieur d'Herblay and the Bishop of Vannes) arrives and warns Fouquet that Chevreuse has letters indicting him in the misappropriation of state funds. Fouquet cannot find the receipt that would prove his innocence. Aramis tells him not to worry, because such a case would be tried in Parliament by the Procureur-General, a post Fouquet himself holds. Fouquet reveals that he has just sold the post to Vanel in order to repay Madame Belliere.

Vanel refuses to be bribed into owing Fouquet a favor as part of the purchase of the post. The papers are signed, and Vanel leaves at once. Aramis advises Fouquet to go through with a large party he planned on giving for the king, and Aramis promises to pay for the enormous expense of such an affair. He also says he will help Fouquet escape rather than face prosecution.

Chapters 11–15

The narration switches to Raoul, Vicomte de Bragelonne, the son of Athos and Chevreuse. Raoul has recently returned from England, going against the king's orders. His former lover, Louise de la Vallière, has recently become the king's mistress. Despondent that Louise is deceiving him, Raoul visits d'Artagnan and asks for information about the affair. d'Artagnan (Captain of the Musketeers) refuses to help. Louise's friend Mademoiselle Montalais arrives seeking Raoul.

Mademoiselle Montalais takes Raoul to the quarters of Henrietta of England, the wife of King Louis's brother, who is referred to only as Monsieur. Henrietta asserts that Louise is in love with King Louis and he with her. Raoul still doubts that Louise has been unfaithful to him. To provide proof, Henrietta takes Raoul to

the chamber where Louis and Louise have been secretly meeting.

Raoul seeks the help of Porthos (Monsieur le Baron du Vallon de Bracieux de Pierrefonds), his father's friend and a former Musketeer. Porthos agrees to help Raoul set up a duel with Monsieur le Comte de Saint-Aignan, who has supported the affair.

Chapters 16–20

Porthos visits Saint-Aignan and relays Raoul's message. The duel is delayed, however, for the king has requested Saint-Aignan's presence. King Louis XIV is conversing with Fouquet and Colbert. Fouquet invites the king to the party, as Aramis has instructed him to do, and asks for the king's forgiveness, admitting that he sold the position of Procureur-General to Vanel.

Saint-Aignan tells Louis that Raoul has challenged him to a duel because he abetted the affair between Louis and Louise. Louis vows to protect Saint-Aignan and to avenge the challenge to his own honor. He tells Saint-Aignan to find Louise and assure her of Louis's continued affection and protection. Athos arrives and accuses the king of exiling Raoul to England to free Louise for himself. Athos asserts that Louis has now become their enemy and departs. Louis summons d'Artagnan, who is captain of the Musketeers.

Athos speaks with Raoul after meeting with the king. Raoul gives up any further thoughts of revenge and resigns himself to the loss of Louise. When d'Artagnan arrives, Raoul confesses he thought the man appeared not as a friend but as the Captain of the Musketeers, come to arrest him or his father. d'Artagnan denies this but advises Raoul to leave Paris.

Chapters 21–25

Still lamenting his loss, Raoul returns home and finds Louise there. She begs Raoul for forgiveness and confesses that, while she loved him once, she loves Louis now, more deeply than she ever loved Raoul. He describes the depth of his feelings for her and asks her to leave.

Back in Athos's quarters, d'Artagnan reveals that he has indeed been ordered to arrest Athos. He offers him the opportunity to escape, which Athos rejects. Athos believes that his imprisonment may teach the king to regret his abuse of power.

d'Artagnan escorts Athos to the Bastille, the prison in Paris. They are surprised to see Aramis descending from a carriage. d'Artagnan asks Athos to go along with a plan he is devising, and the two make their way to the quarters of the prison governor, Baisemeaux, where Aramis is to dine. d'Artagnan convinces the habitually forgetful Baisemeaux that he has actually invited him to dinner. Baisemeaux welcomes them to stay. Athos agrees, but d'Artagnan rushes off, saying he will return for dessert. He departs for the palace.

d'Artagnan confronts the king about his imprisonment of Athos. He describes the king's actions as dishonorable and even tells the king that he planned to help Athos escape. He tells the king to imprison him in the Bastille as well. He tenders his sword to Louis, who throws it on the ground. Claiming to be dishonored, d'Artagnan picks up the sword and prepares to kill himself with it. Louis stops him, returns the sword to d'Artagnan's sheath, and signs an order to free Athos.

Chapters 26–30

d'Artagnan returns to the dinner at the Bastille and reveals that Athos had been a prisoner but has now been released. Meanwhile, Raoul and Athos's servant, Grimaud, realize that d'Artagnan must have come to arrest Athos. They retrieve Porthos and ride to the Bastille. They see d'Artagnan's carriage and prepare to overtake it. Inside, d'Artagnan and Athos deduce what is happening and, with some amusement, wait to see how Porthos and Raoul will handle themselves in their rescue attempt. They capture the carriage, and the truth is revealed. Raoul and Athos prepare to leave immediately for their estate outside of Paris, while d'Artagnan and Porthos return to the city.

Back at the Bastille, Aramis and Baisemeaux continue their discussion. Aramis alludes to a secret order, the Jesuits, of which he suspects Baisemeaux is a member. Aramis asserts that one of the prisoners is ill and has asked for a confessor. Baisemeaux, clearly frightened of Aramis and his power, allows Aramis access to the prisoner.

Aramis is led to the prisoner's cell and enters alone. As they converse, Aramis reveals that the young man is in fact Philippe, the twin of King Louis XIV. Aramis vows to free Philippe, yet only after Aramis shows him both a small mirror and a portrait of Louis does he truly believe he is Louis's twin.

Chapters 31–35

d'Artagnan takes Porthos to Monsieur Percerin, Paris's most sought-after tailor, to be measured for new clothes for Fouquet's party for the king. Aramis arrives and convinces Percerin to provide sketches of the new suits he is making for the king and samples of the fabric. Porthos relates how he was once measured by Molière, the French playwright and actor, who worked for Percerin and who is Fouquet's friend.

Aramis asks Fouquet for a note releasing a prisoner named Seldon from the Bastille, which Fouquet readily gives. Aramis arranges the release form for Seldon to be delivered to the Bastille while he dines with Baisemeaux. Aramis urges the intoxicated Baisemeaux to follow the order at once and, when his back is turned, replaces the order with another.

Chapters 36–40

Baisemeaux is startled to see that the name on the release order is not "Seldon" but "Marchiali," the name given to the prisoner Aramis recently visited. Baisemeaux suspects that the signatures on the form have been forged and wants to confirm the order. Aramis then reveals that he is in fact the General of the Order. Baisemeaux recognizes this authority and allows the prisoner to be released. Aramis and Philippe escape.

Aramis offers Philippe money and a quiet estate where he could live in anonymity. Alternatively, he offers to put Philippe on the throne in his brother's place, and Philippe agrees. They review their plan, and Philippe is quizzed about members of his family and the court. He will simply replace Louis, who will be sent away. Aramis promises to serve Philippe faithfully and, in return, expects to be aided in his continued rise to power within the Church.

Fouquet and Aramis, at Vaux, discuss the arrival of Louis and the impending party. The king and his entourage make their way toward Vaux.

Chapters 41–45

Fouquet entertains the king and his guests with a banquet. After the king retires for the evening, d'Artagnan accuses Aramis of plotting something. Aramis allays his concerns to some degree, assuring d'Artagnan that he means the king no harm. After d'Artagnan departs, Philippe emerges from his hiding place. Aramis opens a secret panel through which the king in his chambers on the floor below may be observed.

They observe Colbert revealing to Louis the assertion that Fouquet has misappropriated state funds for personal gain. Louis grows increasingly angry. Louis and Louise discuss the matter with Colbert. Louise advises against taking action against Fouquet in his own house. Colbert, who violently disagrees with her, drops a letter as she leaves the scene and tells Louis that she must have dropped it. In reality, the letter was written by Fouquet some time ago, when he sought Louise's affections himself. The letter, never delivered to Louise, fell into Colbert's hands. The king, jealous and incensed, calls d'Artagnan to his chambers. The king orders d'Artagnan to arrest Fouquet, but d'Artagnan convinces Louis to wait until morning and reconsider.

Porthos and Aramis, both disguised, use a series of trapdoors and secret passageways to abduct Louis and take him to the Bastille. Aramis tells Baisemeaux that the recently released prisoner is mad and has attempted to impersonate the king. King Louis is thus imprisoned in Philippe's place.

Chapters 46–50

In the Bastille, Louis panics and behaves like a mad man. d'Artagnan, sent to guard Fouquet till morning, finds himself sympathetic to Fouquet's plight but guards him nonetheless.

The narration turns to Philippe, now acting as king. Although he suffers from guilt over what he has done, he reminds himself of the treachery he has endured since birth. Aramis returns in the morning, and the men discuss how events will unfold. When d'Artagnan arrives to meet with the king as previously arranged, Aramis answers the door. After a brief discussion, Aramis hands d'Artagnan the king's order for Fouquet's release. He then accompanies d'Artagnan from the room.

In Fouquet's quarters, d'Artagnan issues the release and departs. Aramis gradually reveals all to Fouquet, who responds with horror, seeing in Aramis's actions a hideous crime. Fouquet gives Aramis four hours to escape. Stunned, Aramis flees with Porthos.

Fouquet proceeds to the Bastille and threatens Baisemeaux until he allows access to the prisoner known to him only as Marchiali, who is, in fact, Louis. Louis calls out that he is the king and that Fouquet is a traitor. Having taken the keys from Baisemeaux, Fouquet enters Louis's cell.

Chapters 51–55

Fouquet explains Aramis's treachery to Louis. Louis vows vengeance, and Fouquet reveals that he has helped Aramis and Porthos escape. Fouquet and Louis leave the prison, unimpeded by a confused Baisemeaux.

Back at Vaux, Philippe converses with his family members, who suspect nothing. Fouquet and Louis arrive through a secret staircase, and all are shocked. Both Louis and Philippe address Anne of Austria, their mother, who is near fainting. Louis commands d'Artagnan to determine which of the two brothers is paler, suggesting that the more pale of the two is the imposter. d'Artagnan identifies Philippe as his prisoner. King Louis orders Philippe to be taken away and to forevermore wear an iron mask to hide his identity.

Aramis and Porthos make their way to Athos's estate. Athos has been joined by his son Raoul, and they have grown closer in the wake of Raoul's heartbreak. Aramis relates the whole affair to Athos, who gives Aramis and Porthos two fresh horses to further their escape to the stronghold of Belle Isle.

Athos is visited by the Duke, Monsieur de Beaufort, who is about to leave on a military mission to Africa for the king. Raoul is invited to go along; he assents, which saddens Athos.

Chapters 56–60

Raoul bids farewell to his friend Monsieur de Guiche, who is having an affair with Henrietta, the king's sister-in-law. Athos and Raoul unsuccessfully seek d'Artagnan in Paris, at the shop of a mutual friend, Planchet. Planchet tells them that d'Artagnan has recently been to see him and that he has been journeying through France. Raoul is given command of a fleet by Monsieur de Beaufort and accepts his father's help in making the necessary preparations for departure.

Raoul and Athos scour the countryside looking for men to press into naval service for the expedition to Africa and seeking d'Artagnan as well. They find d'Artagnan with a contingent of soldiers guarding a prisoner wearing an iron mask, Philippe. To protect his friends, d'Artagnan tells the governor of the island prison that Raoul and Athos are Spanish nobleman and understand no French. d'Artagnan, Athos, and Raoul discuss the secret that surrounds the prisoner; d'Artagnan has not, to this point, believed it, but Athos and Raoul maintain that the prisoner is, in fact, Louis's brother.

Chapters 61–65

d'Artagnan receives a summons from the king and departs for Paris. Beaufort's flotilla is ready now to leave for Africa, and Athos and Raoul exchange an emotional farewell. d'Artagnan seeks Louise in Paris and describes Raoul's devastation in the wake of her deception. The king sends d'Artagnan with his Musketeers to a meeting of the States of Brittany at the castle at Nantes.

Fouquet, surrounded by close friends, receives d'Artagnan with an order for money for his expenditures for the impending journey to Nantes. Not long after, a courier arrives with a message from the king, seeking the gold necessary for him to make his own departure. Fouquet, already impoverished, sees in these events his own ruin and is encouraged by his friends to flee the country.

d'Artagnan spies the Duchesse conversing in a carriage with Colbert's mistress but rides on. Colbert enters the carriage, and he and Chevreuse discuss the impending fall of Fouquet and the need to imprison Aramis. Chevreuse has just met with the Queen Mother, presumably confirming that Fouquet and Aramis must be eliminated, because of their knowledge of the secret of Louis's twin.

Fouquet intends to arrive early in Nantes and to attempt to garner support there. If unsuccessful, he plans to flee to Belle Isle. On the way, he is followed by Colbert.

Chapters 66–70

In Nantes, Fouquet and d'Artagnan meet prior to the king's arrival. d'Artagnan attempts to give Fouquet time to escape before the king's arrival, but the king arrives earlier than expected and summons Fouquet. Their conversation convinces Fouquet that the king will imprison him. As soon as Fouquet is dismissed, the king orders d'Artagnan to arrest him.

d'Artagnan soon discovers that Fouquet has escaped on a horse left for him by his loyal friend Monsieur Gourville. A long chase ensues that leaves both horses dead. Eventually, d'Artagnan escorts Fouquet to the barred carriage and off to prison.

The king expresses to d'Artagnan his intentions toward Colbert. d'Artagnan tells Louis that Fouquet has been arrested but admits that he has attempted to place the means of escape within Fouquet's grasp. Louis orders d'Artagnan to send Fouquet to prison with a guard of Musketeers and to take control of Belle Isle.

At Belle Isle, an island fortress, Aramis and Porthos discuss the recent disappearance of the island's boats. Aramis rightly suspects that their escape is being thwarted. Porthos, who still understands little of what he and Aramis have done, remains confused. When royal ships are spotted, a messenger comes with word from d'Artagnan. Aramis begins to relate the truth to Porthos.

Chapters 71–75

d'Artagnan arrives on the island to speak with Aramis and Porthos. They discuss options for escape. d'Artagnan claims to have an idea, despite the bleak outlook.

Colbert has anticipated the ways in which d'Artagnan might deceive the king and free his friends and has issued a series of orders that correspond with every attempt d'Artagnan takes to liberate Aramis and Porthos. When d'Artaganan states that he will resign, he is escorted under guard back to the shores of France, while Belle Isle is attacked by the king's forces.

Porthos fears he is coming to the end of his life, suffering from a weakness in his legs that portended the deaths of his father and grandfather. He and Aramis take a prisoner, Monsieur Biscarrat, who becomes friendly when he realizes that Porthos and Aramis are in fact former Musketeers with whom his own father served. He warns them that the island is about to be attacked and that all who resist will be shot or hung. Aramis pleads with the people of the island not to fight and then asks Biscarrat to return to his commander and tell him that he will not be opposed. Aramis and Porthos then agree to escape by means of a boat hidden in a secret cavern.

Three of Aramis's men wait in the cavern for Aramis and Porthos. Aramis begins to craft a plan as the men realize they are being hunted by hounds. After the animals have infiltrated the grotto, the men kill the dogs and prepare to kill the king's men who will surely follow.

Chapters 76–80

Aramis and Porthos kill some of the soldiers attacking them. Biscarrat informs them what they are up against and enters unarmed, hoping to be killed for the dishonor of having betrayed the Musketeers.

Aramis and Porthos plan to escape by taking their small boat to the beach. Porthos, using an iron bar and hiding behind a pillar, kills man after man as the king's soldiers approach. The confused soldiers begin to fire their weapons, which makes rocks and dust from the cavern walls fall upon them.

Aramis rigs a barrel of explosives, which he instructs Porthos to cast into the cavern. Porthos does so, but as he flees, his legs weaken and he is crushed by the collapsing cavern. Aramis and the other men free Porthos from the debris, but he dies from his injuries.

Aramis and his men escape but are followed by another ship. They surrender to the ship's commander, Louis Constant de Pressigny. Aramis greets him with a mysterious sign and shows his ring. From this point, the commander treats him with reverence, apparently recognizing Aramis's authority as General of the Order of the Jesuits.

d'Artagnan returns to Nantes and attempts to see the king, who continues to rebuff him. d'Artagnan tenders his resignation and prepares to leave but is apprehended by Monsieur de Gesvre, the head of the guard at Nantes, who tells him the king wishes to see him.

Chapters 81–85

The king accuses d'Artagnan of disloyalty, and d'Artagnan expresses dismay at the king's lack of faith in him. Louis offers d'Artagnan either exile or continued service, but on the king's terms alone. d'Artagnan commits himself to the king's service.

d'Artagnan learns of Porthos's death and Aramis's flight. Louis gives d'Artagnan a leave of absence to set Porthos's affairs in order. d'Artagnan is present at the reading of Porthos's will, which provides for Aramis, Athos, d'Artagnan, Raoul, and his friend and servant Mousqueton, who dies of grief.

Athos slips into illness and depression in his son's absence. He dreams of Raoul telling him of Porthos's death and then receives a letter confirming the death. Athos collapses and has a vision of Raoul ascending to heaven.

Chapters 86–88

Grimaud returns and tells Athos of Raoul's valiant death. Athos dies, moments before d'Artagnan arrives. Following the funerals given for Raoul and

Athos, d'Artagnan finds Louise weeping in the chapel for the deaths she believed she caused.

Epilogue

Four years have passed. The Queen Mother has died during a hunting expedition, and Fouquet is exiled. The king has a new romantic interest, much to the annoyance of the queen and the despair of Louise. Colbert informs d'Artagnan of the arrival of the Duc d'Almeda, the ambassador from Spain, who is in fact Aramis. Henrietta and Louis discuss how she might persuade her brother, the English King Charles, to aid France in a dispute with the Dutch. Colbert and Aramis discuss French and Spanish relations, along with the campaign against the Dutch. d'Artagnan, for his role in the military endeavors, is offered a promotion by Colbert.

The Death of d'Artagnan

The narrator relates the details of d'Artagnan's death in battle against the Dutch.

CHARACTERS

Anne of Austria, the Queen Mother

Anne was the queen of Louis XIV's father, King Louis XIII. Historically, she served as regent during Louis childhood and was heavily aided by Cardinal Mazarin. In Dumas's tale, the night she gave birth to Louis, she also bore another son, Louis's twin. With some reservations, she allowed the second child to be taken away and raised in isolation and later imprisoned. She is physically ill, as well as sick at heart over her actions.

Aramis, Monsieur d'Herblay, Bishop of Vannes, and later, Duc d'Almeda

Aramis, one of the original three Musketeers that Dumas wrote about in earlier volumes, is now a bishop. Although it is a secret he keeps well, Aramis is also the General of the Order, a secret order of Jesuits. Aramis engineers a variety of intrigues throughout the novel and is behind the plot to remove Louis XIV from the throne and install there instead his imprisoned twin, who has equal rights to the throne as Louis XIII's son. Motivated by his interests as a Jesuit and by his quest for power, Aramis seeks promotion to the level of cardinal and hopes to eventually be elected pope. Although his plot fails, Aramis is able to escape both death and exile by fleeing to Spain. He eventually acquires the role of Spain's ambassador to France, with the title of Duc d'Almeda.

Athos, Comte de la Fère

Athos is one of the original three Musketeers of Dumas's earlier writings and Raoul's father. Unlike his former Musketeer companions Aramis and Porthos, Athos is uninvolved in the plot to trade the imprisoned Philippe for his brother, Louis XIV. Athos confronts King Louis on behalf of his son, accusing the king of dishonoring those who have loyally served him by duping Raoul and taking up with Raoul's former fiancée, Louise. The king responds by arresting Athos, but through d'Artagnan's efforts, Athos is released, and he retreats to his estate outside of Paris. He later dies of grief after his son is killed.

Baisemeaux

Baisemeaux is the governor of the Bastille, who historically served with the king's Musketeers, and who, in Dumas's earlier writing, served with Aramis, Athos, Pathos, and d'Artagnan. Baisemeaux's cooperation and loyalty to Aramis are instrumental in the initial success of Aramis's plan, that is, the swapping of Louis and Philippe. Yet Baisemeaux later succumbs to Fouquet's threats and allows Fouquet to remove Louis from prison. At no point does Baisemeaux seem to understand the royal identities of his prisoners or to glean that there are indeed two men who have alternately occupied cell number twelve.

Monsieur de Beaufort

Beaufort is a duke who, prior to his departure on a military venture to Africa, asks Raoul if he would like to come with him on the campaign.

Madame Belliere

Madame Belliere is Fouquet's mistress. Fouquet sells a key government post in order to pay Madame Belliere back for money she once loaned him.

Monsieur Biscarrat

Biscarrat is one of the king's men. He is taken prisoner by Aramis and Pathos on Belle Isle and tells them of the king's plan to attack the island. Aramis and Porthos allow him to return to his battalion. Biscarrat later discovers Aramis and Pathos in their escape attempt and tries to dissuade the members of his party from searching the grotto where Aramis and Porthos are hidden.

Biscarrat fails and allows himself to be killed by Porthos.

Madam de Chevreuse, the Duchesse

Chevreuse's former affair with Athos resulted in the birth of Raoul, who has been raised by his father. Chevreuse seeks power and wealth and, having been involved in political intrigues for many years, has come into possession of correspondence between Fouquet and the late Cardinal Mazarin. The letters suggest that Fouquet used state funds to loan to Mazarin without paying the money back to the government. When Aramis exhibits no interest in the letters, Chevreuse turns instead to Colbert, who has his ambitions set on Fouquet's own position. Colbert purchases the letters from Chevreuse. She then, with Colbert's help, succeeds in visiting with the Queen Mother, who is a former friend, and reveals her knowledge of the secret surrounding Louis's birth. Anne welcomes Chevreuse back into her confidence and lends Chevreuse money to repair her estate. Chevreuse later impresses upon Anne the importance of imprisoning Fouquet, to whom Aramis has revealed the secret of Louis's twin.

Monsieur Colbert

Colbert is the Intendant of Finances who seeks to ruin Fouquet and thereby attain his position of Surintendant. His manipulations throughout the novel aid in Fouquet's ruin, and he becomes an invaluable adviser to Louis XIV.

d'Artagnan, Captain of the Musketeers

d'Artagnan, in Dumas's earlier work, *The Three Musketeers*, joins forces with Aramis, Athos, and Porthos in adventures filled with deception and intrigue. By the time *The Man in the Iron Mask* begins, d'Artagnan has been made Captain of the Musketeers, while his friends have since left the famous guard. Loyal to King Louis XIV, d'Artagnan suspects a plot in which Aramis is involved, but he is very much loyal to his old friends, as well as to the king. d'Artagnan confronts Louis on Athos's behalf, thereby freeing the latter from the Bastille, and attempts to aid Aramis and Porthos in their escape from Belle Isle after their plot to usurp the king is foiled by Fouquet. d'Artagnan additionally understands Fouquet's loyalty to Louis and, in sympathy, attempts to aid in Fouquet's escape as well, after he has arrested Fouquet. Near the end of the story, d'Artagnan is sent by Louis to Philippe, who is held in an island prison and wears an iron mask as ordered by Louis. d'Artagnan, however, later seems to doubt that Philippe can truly have been Louis's twin, when Athos and Raoul argue to the contrary. At the end of the work, Dumas relates the details of d'Artagnan's death in battle.

Monsieur Fouquet

Fouquet is a key player in *The Man in the Iron Mask*. For much of the book, he is a friend and ally to Aramis. As the Surintendant of Finances, he keeps diligent records, although he cannot find a key receipt, the one that could have cleared him of the crimes suggested by the letters Chevreuse sells to Colbert. Fouquet faces financial and political ruin. Aramis involves the unwitting Fouquet in his plot to replace Louis with Philippe, and when Aramis reveals the truth to Fouquet, Fouquet is enraged, despite the fact that, under Philippe, Fouquet would have remained free. Fouquet allows Aramis and Porthos a chance to escape to his fortress at Belle Isle and then proceeds to retrieve the distraught king from the Bastille. Nevertheless, Fouquet is eventually arrested by Louis, imprisoned, and later exiled.

Monsieur de Gesvre

Gesvre is the leader of the military guard at Nantes. He is tasked with bringing d'Artagnan to the king after d'Artagnan has tendered his resignation.

Monsieur Gourville

Gourville is a friend of Fouquet. He tries to help Fouquet escape from Nantes after the king has issued an order for his arrest.

Grimaud

Grimaud is Athos's valet and devoted friend. He accompanies Athos's son, Raoul, on his expedition to Africa and returns to Athos to relate the details of Raoul's death.

Monsieur de Guiche

Guiche is Raoul's friend. He is having an affair with the king's sister-in-law, Henrietta.

Henrietta

Often referred to simply as "Madame," Henrietta is the wife of the king's brother (Monsieur), and the sister of King Charles II of England.

Jean de La Fontaine

La Fontaine is a friend of Fouquet's and a member of the group of poets and playwrights known as the Epicureans.

Louise de La Vallière

Louise was once affianced to Raoul but fell in love with King Louis, thereby breaking Raoul's heart and setting into motion a chain of events that threatens Raoul and his father, Athos.

Louis XIV, King of France

Louis XIV is a young king who struggles under the weight of his responsibilities and the confusing web of intrigues that surrounds him. Dumas depicts Louis as perpetually suspicious and as seeking to consolidate his power by squelching the rights of those who oppose him. Louis is repeatedly astounded by the ways in which his father's Musketeers, notably d'Artagnan, Athos, Aramis, and Porthos, openly defy him through word and action. Because of Fouquet's devotion, Louis does not lose the throne to his twin Philippe. Rather, the king grows increasingly powerful and eventually imprisons and then exiles Fouquet. He bends d'Artagnan to his will, and his pursuit of Aramis and Porthos results in Porthos's death.

Marchiali

Marchiali is the name given to Philippe when he is brought to the Bastille as a young teenager. Later, after Aramis has freed Philippe and brought Louis to the Bastille, Louis takes the place of the prisoner known as Marchiali.

Maria-Teresa, Queen of France

King Louis's bride, Maria-Teresa has little direct interaction with Louis in the novel. Although publicly Louis treats his queen with respect, his romantic interests lie elsewhere.

Cardinal Mazarin

Mazarin has died before *The Man in the Iron Mask* begins. Historically, Mazarin was named by Richelieu as his successor, and he aided Anne of Austria in ruling France during Louis XIV's childhood. Mazarin further arranged Louis XIV's marriage to his Spanish queen, Maria-Teresa. In Dumas's novel, Mazarin, along with Fouquet, is implicated in the letters Chevreuse sells to Colbert.

Molière

Molière, the actor and playwright, makes an appearance in Dumas's novel as one of the poets Fouquet counts among his close friends.

Monsieur, Duc d'Orléans

The king's younger brother is referred to by the name "Monsieur" throughout the novel. He is the husband of Henrietta.

Mademoiselle Montalais

Mademoiselle Montalais is a friend of Louise de La Vallière. She plays a role in revealing to Raoul the truth of the king's relationship to Louise.

Mousqueton

Mousqueton is Porthos's servant. He dies of grief after Porthos's death.

Monsieur Percerin

Percerin is the king's tailor. He reluctantly provides Aramis with cloth samples and drawings of the suit of clothes he is making for the king for the party at Vaux.

Philippe

Philippe is the twin brother of King Louis XIV. Upon his birth, his father and his father's adviser, Richelieu, agree that, as the second twin, Philippe must be sent away to avoid civil war later. He is raised in seclusion by the midwife who delivered him and one of his father's lords, both of whom are later murdered. When he is fifteen years old, Philippe is taken to the Bastille, where he languishes for another eight years. Aramis, privy to the secret of Philippe's birth, reveals to him his true identity and offers to help him escape prison and rise to power. Philippe deliberates and agrees. He is discovered, however, after Fouquet releases Louis from prison. Louis is able to convince d'Artagnan that Philippe is the imposter and orders d'Artagnan to take Philippe to a faraway island prison, where his identity will forever be concealed by an iron mask. Once d'Artagnan has been recalled from the prison by Louis, and d'Artagnan, Athos, and Raoul depart the island, Philippe is forgotten; the narrative never returns to him.

Planchet

Planchet is a businessman and a friend to Athos and Raoul. He tells the pair of them, who are seeking d'Artagnan, that d'Artagnan has recently been to see him.

Porthos, Monsieur le Baron du Vallon de Bracieux de Pierrefonds

Porthos is one of the original three Musketeers Dumas wrote of in his earlier work. Characterized as a large, strong man, more brave than cunning, Porthos is extremely loyal to his friends. Without knowing the full extent of his actions, Porthos aids Aramis in kidnapping and imprisoning Louis and establishing Philippe in his place. Porthos flees with Aramis after Fouquet becomes aware of the scheme and is later killed in the attempt to escape from Belle Isle.

Louis Constant de Pressigny

Pressigny is the commander of the ship that overtakes Aramis's escaping vessel as he leaves Belle Isle. Aramis knows Pressigny to be in the secret Jesuit order and reveals himself to Pressigny as the general of that order, thereby commandeering Pressigny's ship and traveling to Spain.

Raoul, Vicomte de Bragelonne

Raoul is the son of Chevreuse and Athos. Loved as dearly by his father's friends as by his own father, Raoul is hopelessly in love with Louise de La Vallière. He is exiled to England by King Louis XIV, as the king seeks to woo Louise himself. Raoul and Louise, once betrothed, are thus separated, and Louise falls in love with the king. Raoul returns secretly and learns the truth. He spends the remainder of the novel tormented by the way Louise deceived him. He accepts a commission with Beaufort to fight in Africa in order to escape France. He is killed in the line of duty, which breaks Athos's heart.

Cardinal de Richelieu

Richelieu does not appear in *The Man in the Iron Mask* but is referred to as the predecessor to Cardinal Mazarin, who was Richelieu's protégée. Richelieu was a powerful adviser to King Louis XIII.

Le Comte de Saint-Aignan

Saint-Aignan is a friend and confidante to King Louis and aids in arranging secret meetings between Louis and his lover, Louise.

Seldon

Seldon is, like Philippe, a prisoner of the Bastille. Aramis uses a signed order for Seldon's release as a way of convincing Baisemeaux that the king has signed an order for the release of the prisoner known as Marchiali. Aramis takes care to ensure that Seldon is in fact finally granted his freedom.

Monsieur Vanel

Monsieur Vanel is a minister in Louis's administration who purchases a cabinet post from Fouquet.

THEMES

Friendship

As the last installment of a lengthy series, *The Man in the Iron Mask* opens with the history of the friendships among its protagonists already in place. When the book is read on its own, readers must draw on references in the text to the earlier experiences of Aramis, Athos, Porthos, and d'Artagnan to fully understand the weight of this history. However, the actions of the men in defending and aiding one another throughout the novel underscore the deep sense of brotherly love and affection they still share. Significantly, Dumas depicts the bonds of friendship among the men as able to withstand suspicions and deceptions and as deeper than most other loyalties.

The naive Porthos does as his friends ask him to do, without question, and this loyalty extends as well to Athos's son, Raoul. When the heartsick Raoul asks for help, d'Artagnan sends word to Athos, and Porthos aids Raoul by setting up the duel with the king's accomplice, Saint-Aignan. Although the king does not allow this duel to happen, Porthos's unquestioning devotion is displayed, as is d'Artagnan's concern for Raoul.

Repulsed by the king's deceptions where Raoul is concerned, Athos exchanges bitter words with the king, despite the threat of imprisonment. In order to save his friend from the Bastille, d'Artagnan—who first offers Athos a chance to escape (a chance Athos rejects)—shares his low opinion of the king's actions with the king. Appealing to King Louis in this way, d'Artagnan is successful in freeing Athos. As Aramis begins to set his plan to rescue Philippe into motion, d'Artagnan grows suspicious of Aramis's actions. He confronts Aramis, who reassures d'Artagnan that he will soon be told everything, and indeed, Aramis has earlier indicated that d'Artagnan will eventually be told the truth. Aramis does not have the chance, however, to reveal all to d'Artagnan, as Fouquet threatens to expose him, once he discovers that Aramis has swapped Louis for

Philippe. After Aramis and Porthos escape, d'Artagnan is eventually tasked with capturing them. Despite d'Artagnan's fealty to Louis, he attempts to devise a plan to allow Aramis and Porthos to escape the fortress at Belle Isle.

Although the escape effort is unsuccessful, d'Artagnan was ready to face Louis's wrath in order to aid his friends. In fact, he is forced to answer for his actions when he returns to Louis. So loyal to his friends is d'Artagnan that he argues with the king, saying, "It was a cruelty on your Majesty's part to send me to take my friends and lead them to your gibbets." d'Artagnan goes on, telling the king, "Mine is a rebel sword when I am required to do ill." The friendships among the men are worth risking imprisonment and death for, and in spite of all other motivations, the four friends continue to value and protect these relationships.

Love

Dumas's treatment of love in *The Man in the Iron Mask* is one in which romantic love is depicted as foolish and destructive and familial love is characterized by either deception or devotion but always associated with pain. Raoul's love for Louise is a torment to him. She deceives him by allowing him to still believe in her fidelity, even after she has become the king's lover. His sorrow is such that his father is moved to confront the king, and Raoul is so devoured by his pain that he flees France to lose himself, and eventually his life, in a war in Africa. Athos is so grief-stricken after his son's departure that he instantly begins to wither with despair. When word comes of Raoul's death, Athos can no longer retain his grasp on his own life, and he too dies. Louise later blames herself for both of their deaths.

Dumas offers the reader another portrait of the grieving parent in the figure of Anne of Austria, who is depicted as uneasy with her decision to have one of her twin boys sent away and imprisoned while the other rules as king. She is tormented by disease, which Dumas suggests has taken hold as a result of her grief over her loss. Nevertheless, when confronted with the reality of Philippe's tormented existence, Anne does nothing. Philippe addresses her by saying, "If I were not your son I should curse you, my mother, for having rendered me so unhappy." Anne makes no reply but allows her son to be taken away by d'Artagnan, even after King Louis's orders—to have Philippe's face covered for the rest of his existence by an iron mask—are read. Dumas

TOPICS FOR FURTHER STUDY

- Dumas's Aramis reveals himself to be the General of the Order, a secret Jesuit organization that wields considerable power throughout Europe. Research the history of this organization. To what date can scholars trace the beginnings of the Order of the Jesuits, also known as the Society of Jesus? How did the organization become so powerful during King Louis XIV's reign? How did it evolve over time? In what way did the Order of the Jesuits come into conflict with the Roman Catholic Church? Create either a report or a timeline in which you examine this organization and highlight the major events in its history.

- Nineteenth-century Mexico was as affected by imperialism (on the part of Spain), rebellion, and political conflict, as Europe was during that same century. Mexican journalist Jose Joaquin Fernandez de Lizardi explored these turbulent events in his novel *The Mangy Parrot: The Life and Times of Periquillo Sarniento, Written by Himself for His Children* (1816). Like Dumas, Lizardi was as much commenting on his nation's political struggles as writing to entertain his readers, and like Dumas's work, Lizardi's became a classic in his country. Read Lizardi's novel and write a report on the work in which you summarize the plot and the major characters. Also discuss the political themes

of the work. Present your work to the class as an oral report or as a web page or Power-Point presentation.

- Like Dumas, nineteenth-century author Mark Twain explored the genre of historical fiction. Twain's young-adult historical novel *The Prince and the Pauper* (1881) is set in sixteenth-century England. Like *The Man in the Iron Mask*, it features twins, royalty, and a case of mistaken identity. With a small group, read Twain's novel and compare it to *The Man in the Iron Mask*. Consider the ways in which the authors employ the characters who resemble members of a royal family. In what ways do the authors use the double of a prince or king to comment on the notions of power and justice? Create an online blog to use as a forum for your book discussion.

- Dumas portrays a political power struggle between two members of King Louis XIV's government, Fouquet and Colbert. Research the historical figures of Fouquet and Colbert, their relationships to King Louis XIV, and their roles within his administration. Discuss the way history is similar to or different from Dumas's fiction in a detailed report. Be sure to cite all print and online sources.

---

characterizes all love, save the loving bonds of friendship shared by the four friends, as harbingers of grief, despair, and suffering.

STYLE

Historical Fiction

Like much of Dumas's work, *The Man in the Iron Mask* may be categorized as historical fiction, a genre that became widely utilized during

the nineteenth century. Dumas employed a variety of historical sources to invent plots and characters that were rooted in historical events of the mid-seventeenth century, during the early years of King Louis XIV's reign. As Barbara T. Cooper states in her introductory essay to the Barnes & Noble Classics edition of *The Man in the Iron Mask*, "There is much in this story that is historically true." Cooper goes on to highlight the specific plot points that accurately represent French history, such as the king's visit to Vaux.

The story of the man in the iron mask is a part of the legend of the Three Musketeers. (© Feliks Kogan / Shutterstock.com)

Yet as Francine du Plessix Gray observes in a critical introduction to the Penguin Classics edition, Dumas's novel cannot be regarded as "true to history." Gray states that Dumas had "no pretension whatsoever at being either a scholar or a researcher" and identifies areas in which Dumas rearranged historical events to suit the narrative needs of his novel. Dumas drew on historical personages, such as King Louis XIV and ministers Fouquet and Colbert, and was inspired by allegedly historical materials regarding Musketeers d'Artagnan, Athos, Aramis, and Porthos in his fictionalization of their characters, personalities, motivations, and relationships. In doing so, as Brian Hamnett observes in *The Historical Novel in Nineteenth-Century Europe: Representations of Reality in History and Fiction*, Dumas, along with other authors like Sir Walter Scott, shaped the development of the genre of nineteenth-century historical fiction.

Romanticism in Fiction

Dumas's treatment of French history in *The Man in the Iron Mask* is influenced by the romanticism prevalent in fiction of this time. Nineteenth-century romanticism focused on the concerns of the individual and his or her personal motivations, was rooted in a sense of idealism, and often drew inspiration from nature. Hamnett asserts, "The historical novel, with its emphasis on wild scenery and rebels, was ripe for further development by the Romantics." As Dumas explores the personal histories and psychological motivations for the actions of his Musketeers and other characters, he draws on the romantic ideals of the time and incorporates the tragedy often characteristic of romantic fiction.

d'Artagnan is driven by multiple claims on his sense of loyalty and honor and is often tormented by this conflict. Aramis's ambitions are rooted in both political convictions and the quest for personal power, yet he witnesses the death of one of his closest friends, Porthos, as a result of his scheming. Athos is moved to grief and death by the loss of his son, Raoul, while Raoul himself is tortured by his love for Louise. Porthos's blind devotion to his friend Aramis leads to his own demise. Further, all four of the protagonists—Athos, Aramis, Porthos, and d'Artagnan—rebel in some way against the king, and it is this rebellious nature that often characterizes the heart of the romantic hero.

The Man in the Iron Mask contains an additional romantic element, as Cooper explores. She states,

> Twins, doubles, and doppelgangers were a frequent Romantic motif. Indeed, whether used to examine individual, familial or collective breakdowns or schisms, or to explore social, sexual, or national politics—or some combination of these—the trope of duality and division, of identity in crisis, resonated in a particularly meaningful way with French writers in the first half of the nineteenth century.

Dumas uses the motif of twins with the characters of Louis and Philippe as means of exploring not only the divided sense of identities the characters possess but also the nature of kingship and the right to rule.

HISTORICAL CONTEXT

The Reign of Louis XIV of France

Louis was born in 1638 and became king at the age of four when his father, Louis XIII, died. Louis XIV's mother, Anne of Austria, serving as regent, ruled France during Louis's childhood. Anne was aided in her role as regent by Cardinal Mazarin, who had been Louis XIII's chief minister. During Louis XIV's youth, a series of rebellions sent the royal family and Mazarin into exile. After they returned to Paris and King Louis XIV was restored to the throne, he married Maria-Teresa in 1660. Maria-Teresa was the daughter of King Philip IV of Spain. A year later, upon Mazarin's death, Louis, now twenty-three years old, embarked upon his rule without the aid of a chief minister. Louis regarded himself as a divinely ordained monarch, and he employed the sun as his image and emblem, becoming known as the Sun King.

With the help of his finance minister, Jean-Baptiste Colbert, Louis tightened his government's control over France and employed regional officers, or attendants, to help manage the financial administration of the various regions in France. After the death of King Philip of Spain, Louis embarked on an increasingly aggressive approach to foreign affairs and sought to gain control of the Spanish Netherlands, putting France at war with the Dutch. Louis was a devout Catholic, and in 1685, he revoked an edict that had given French Protestants the freedom of worship they had previously enjoyed; many fled to Holland and England. During the last thirty years of his reign, Louis involved France in a series of lengthy wars, including the War of the League of Augsburg (1688–1697), which brought France into conflict with an alliance led by Anglo-Dutch, Spanish, and Holy Roman Empire forces. This war was followed by the War of the Spanish Succession (1701–1714). Louis died in 1715 and was succeeded by his great-grandson, who became Louis XV.

The Musketeers

The Musketeers of the Guard were a group of soldiers organized in 1622 as a personal guard to the royal family of King Louis XIII. The soldiers were soon divided into two regiments, those designated as the protectors of the State and the monarch, and those designated as the protectors of the Church and the cardinal. The soldiers were armed with muskets (hence the name "musketeers"), as well as with swords. Unlike admission to other military regiments, admission to the Musketeers of the Guard was open to the lower classes of French nobility. The Musketeers of the Guard existed as a regiment for approximately two hundred years and were romanticized and popularized by Dumas's *The Three Musketeers*. A detailed personal history, claimed to be compiled from the papers, real-life Musketeer Captain d'Artagnan, was published in 1700 by Gatien Courtilz de Sandras under the title *The Memoirs of Monsieur d'Artagnan, Captain-Lieutenant of the 1st Company of the King's Musketeers*. Dumas states in the preface to *The Three Musketeers* that he utilized Sandras's work as source material for his novel. Many scholars doubt the authenticity of Sandras's work but recognize that Sandras was d'Artagnan's contemporary and likely had access to some accurate source material from which he drew for his work.

COMPARE & CONTRAST

- **1660s:** France is ruled by King Louis XIV. In these early years of his reign, the king is regarded as an effective ruler who has consolidated his power and reduced his reliance on ministers and advisers.

  1850s: After the Revolution of 1848, the monarchy falls, and the Second Republic of France is established. The nephew of Napoleon Bonaparte, Charles Louis Napoleon Bonaparte, is voted into office. He is ousted but returns to power, and in 1852 he reinstates the Empire and reigns under the title of Napoleon III.

  Today: The French Republic is governed by a presidential-parliamentary system. It is headed by Prime Minister Francois Fillon and President Francois Hollande, who in May 2012 ousted former president Nicolas Sarkozy.

- **1660s:** Paris is exalted in popular fiction of this time. The French capital is depicted as a metropolis in which foreigners and people from far off provinces may pursue their dreams. Other works describe everyday life in the city, while still other novels are inspired by King Louis XIV's court. Popular novelists include Jean Donneau de Visé, Antoine Furetière, and Jean de Préchac.

  1850s: Popular fiction includes both historical fiction and romantic literature and poetry. France's tumultuous past, the monarchy of Kings Louis XIII and XIV, and the historical Musketeers of the Guard are fodder for the novels of the day. Popular authors writing in this mode include Victor Hugo and Alexandre Dumas.

  Today: Twenty-first-century fiction draws on many sources and traditions. Experimental and historical fiction are both popular modes. At the same time, there is a return to traditional narrative techniques. Popular authors include Annie Ernaux, Patrick Modiano, and Marie Redonnet.

- **1660s:** During the reign of Louis XIV, a masked prisoner whose name is unknown is imprisoned in one of the French government's distant prisons, Pignerol, Exiles in the Alps, or island of Sainte-Marguerite, although this prisoner's existence will not be known to the world at large until after his death.

  1850s: Bastille records indicate that, in 1698, the governor of the Bastille escorted a masked prisoner to the Bastille from another prison and that the unknown prisoner died in 1703, still masked. The notion of this man in the iron mask rises to mythic status. Speculation about the identity of the prisoner remains high in the 1850s, and popular writers speculate who he might have been and what his crimes were.

  Today: The unsolved mystery of the man in the iron mask continues to captivate conspiracy theorists and writers alike as evidenced by the fact that the myth still inspires new fictional explorations, including a 2008 Marvel comic book, several audio recordings, and nonfiction explorations of such mysteries, including the 2002 book *Who Was the Man in the Iron Mask? and Other Historical Mysteries*, by Hugh Ross Williamson.

The Masked Prisoner

Dumas was one of many people who speculated on the identity of the masked prisoner, who, during the reign of Louis XIV, was escorted to the Bastille in 1698. As David Coward explains in the introduction to the Oxford World's Classics edition of *The Man in the Iron Mask*, Monsieur M. de Saint-Mars, the former governor of the prisons of Pignerol, Exiles in the Alps, and island of Sainte-Marguerite, arrived in Paris in

The Fleur de Lis was the symbol of French royalty. *(© Tairy Greene | Shutterstock.com)*

1698 to take over the command of the Bastille. Coward states, "He brought with him, 'in his litter' a long-term prisoner 'whom he kept masked at all times and whose name is not spoken.'" Coward quotes the "unofficial register kept by the Deputy Governor of Bastille, Étienne du Junca." Coward goes on to cite the record of the prisoner's death in 1703. The unknown prisoner was still masked.

When de Junca's records and the correspondence between Saint-Mars and the king's ministers were later discovered, speculation began as to the identity of the high-security, unknown prisoner. Coward notes that it was French intellectual and writer Voltaire who asserted, based on sources he would not reveal, that the prisoner was Louis XIV's older brother. As the story grew to mythic proportions, the reported velvet mask was alternately identified as a mask of fur, glass, and iron. In 1790, when memoirs of the Duke de Richelieu were published by questionable sources, it was revealed that an unnamed courtier suggested that Louis XIV had a twin brother who was sequestered from birth. By the early to mid-nineteenth century, the myth of the man in the iron mask and the theory that King Louis XIV had a twin had gripped the imaginations of French romantic writers, including Dumas.

CRITICAL OVERVIEW

By the time Dumas had published the first two volumes of the works concerning the Musketeers, he had established himself as a popular author whose works were eagerly anticipated. In an essay for *Dictionary of Literary Biography*, Barbara T. Cooper states, "Dumas's success during this period produced resentment among some of his contemporaries." Dumas's conclusion to the story of the Musketeers as it stands in *The Man in the Iron Mask* was examined by nineteenth-century critics from a variety of angles.

Arthur Fitzwilliam Davidson, in *Alexandre Dumas (père): His Life and Works*, summarizes Dumas's treatment of his Musketeers but asserts that the Dumas's focus was on Porthos. Davidson maintains, "The book is the book of Porthos." Davidson regards Dumas's treatment of Porthos's death as "true epic pages." Similarly, Louise Stockton in an article for *The Critic* contends that

> Dumas did not like Aramis from the beginning...and he did not admire Athos half as much as he pretended. He loved Porthos, and of d'Artagnan he was so proud he almost crowed for joy when he wrote his name.

Although these nineteenth-century critics were focused on Dumas's characterizations, later critics center their studies on Dumas's inspirations for the novel's plot. Don D'Ammassa, in the *Encyclopedia of Adventure Fiction* describes the historical story of the prisoner who wore a mask of either velvet or iron during Louis XIV's reign. Touching on the various speculations this prisoner inspired, D'Ammassa insists that Dumas's identification of the man in the iron masks as Louis's twin was "a clever innovation." D'Ammassa additionally explores the novel's themes and comments on the way the notion of the conflict between duty and honor is exemplified in d'Artagnan's character. Like D'Ammassa, Cooper, in a critical introduction to *The Man in the Iron Mask*, describes the novel as "a complex tapestry of fact and fiction and of the personal and the political" and finds the work to be "a moving and psychologically nuanced conclusion to the *Musketeer* trilogy."

CRITICISM

Catherine Dominic

Dominic is a novelist and a freelance writer and editor. In the following essay, she examines the complexities of Aramis's character in The Man in

WHAT DO I READ NEXT?

- *Three Musketeers* is the novel in which Dumas first introduces the characters of Aramis, Porthos, Athos, and d'Artagnan. The work was published in 1844.

- *Twenty Years After*, published in 1845, is Dumas's second installment in the *Musketeer* trilogy.

- *The Vicomte of Bragelonne: Ten Years After*, is the final installment in Dumas's chronicles of the four Musketeers. It was published in serial form between 1847 and 1850. In addition to *The Man in the Iron Mask*, the volume contains two other books that situate the events of *The Man in the Iron Mask* within the context of the Musketeers' history.

- *Count of Monte Cristo* is another of Dumas's best-loved works. An adventure novel set in France, Italy, and several Mediterranean islands, the work takes place in the early decades of the nineteenth century and was published in 1844.

- Victor Hugo, a contemporary of Dumas and a fellow author of historical fiction, published *The Hunchback of Notre Dame* in 1831. The historical romance is set in fifteenth-century Paris.

- David L. Smith's young-adult nonfiction resource, *Louis XIV*, published in 1992, uses both primary and secondary sources to explore the reign of King Louis XIV and to examine his pursuit of absolute power.

- *The Twentieth Wife*, the 2003 novel by Indu Sundaresan, is set in India in the seventeenth century and explores the fate of Mehrunissa, who rises above the traditional roles of women during that time and becomes the Empress Nur Jahan. Set roughly during the same time period as *The Man in the Iron Mask*, Sundaresan's novel, like Dumas's, examines the nature of power and the political machinations that occur in a royal palace.

- Emmanuel Le Roy Ladurie's *Saint-Simon and the Court of Louis XIV*, translated by Arthur Goldhammer and published in 2001, is an exploration of Louis XIV's court and is based on the memoirs of one of his courtiers, the Duke of Saint-Simon.

- Wendy G. Lawton's 2002 young-adult novel, *The Tinker's Daughter: A Story Based on the Life of Mary Bunyan*, explores the religious conflicts rending England during the reign of Charles II, who was King Louis XIV's contemporary. (Readers of *The Man in the Iron Mask* will recall that Henrietta, Charles II's sister, was married to King Louis XIV's brother.)

---

the Iron Mask *and explores his tragic flaw and its consequences.*

Critics have noted that, of the four Musketeers—Athos, Aramis, Porthos, and d'Artagnan—Dumas seems to have liked Aramis the least. Louise Stockton states this clearly in *The Critic*, noting, "Dumas did not like Aramis from the beginning." This judgment is perhaps rooted in the author's treatment of the characters throughout the course of the trilogy consisting of *The Three Musketeers*, *Twenty Years After*, and *The Vicomte de Bragelonne, or Ten Years After*. Barbara T. Cooper likewise observes the way

Dumas characterizes Aramis more negatively than he does the other friends, stating in an introduction to the Barnes & Noble Classics edition of *The Man in the Iron Mask* (the final book in *The Vicomte de Bragelonne*) that Aramis is "the most enigmatic and sinister of the former Musketeers." Cooper additionally suggests that, by allowing Aramis to be the only former Musketeer left alive at the end of the novel, Dumas was signaling "the end of an age and a system of values." In *The Man in the Iron Mask*, the character of Aramis is arguably the most deeply nuanced of the four friends; he is

"
WHILE THE OTHER MUSKETEERS ARE, IN
MANY WAYS, TREATED AS EXEMPLIFYING
PARTICULAR TRAITS—HONOR IN THE CASE OF
D'ARTAGNAN; LOYALTY IN THE CASE OF PORTHOS;
AND LOVE IN THE CASE OF ATHOS—ARAMIS IS
DRAWN IN A MORE COMPLEX MANNER."

also incredibly flawed. While the other Musketeers are, in many ways, treated as exemplifying particular traits—honor in the case of d'Artagnan; loyalty in the case of Porthos; and love in the case of Athos—Aramis is drawn in a more complex manner.

Although many of his actions may be regarded by as manipulative and ambitious, Aramis nonetheless is driven as much by his own quest for personal power as by his sense that he can influence political outcomes that are better for France than those outcomes in which he has not played a role. Egotistical and infused with a sense of his own moral superiority, Aramis seems to believe that he pursues a course of action that will be better for France than the path the country is currently on under Louis XIV's rule. Yet his egotism foils his plot, and his ambition leaves Philippe in a worse position than the one in which Aramis originally found him.

Upon Aramis's meeting with Philippe in prison, after initial plans to free Philippe are made, Philippe expresses his gratitude to Aramis. Aramis replies,

> It is not you who will have to thank me, but rather the nation whom you will render happy, the posterity whose name you will make glorious. Yes; I shall indeed have bestowed upon you more than life, as I shall have given you immortality.

In this statement, Aramis's twin aims are revealed: a better France, a happy France, as well as Aramis's own personal glory, which he will have achieved by bestowing upon France a king who will make of the country all it deserves to be.

Later, after securing Philippe's release, Aramis further reveals to Philippe his motivations and his belief that, in committing certain acts, such as the removal of Louis XIV from power, he is justified. He asserts that Louis "will be a bad king." Because of the deprivations he suffered as a child during France's civil wars, Louis "will devour the means and substance of his people; for he has himself undergone wrongs in his own interest and money." Aramis believes himself right in condemning the king for these faults, and maintains, "If I condemn him, my conscience absolves me."

After asserting the need for Philippe to take Louis's place, based on political concerns, and the notion that this course of action would be best for France, Aramis resumes his justification, this time based on a religious and moral foundation. "All that Heaven does, Heaven does well," Aramis states. He views himself as the "instrument" of "Providence" (that is, God's divine will) and therefore sees it as his duty to act, because Heaven chose him to be a "depositary of the secret" of Philippe's birth. Aramis's religious argument goes on, as he describes the Christian people he has at his command and explains that he does their bidding in saving Philippe "from the abyss for a great purpose... to raise you above the powers of the earth—above himself [Aramis]." Philippe acknowledges that Aramis is speaking of the order of the Jesuits when he refers to the people he commands, and he further understands Aramis's power as the General of the Order.

After Philippe expresses his fear that Aramis, because of his position within the order, will have the power to crush him just as easily as he has raised him, Aramis assures Philippe that this will not happen. Candidly, Aramis states that with Philippe's power will come his own, as he is confident that Philippe will judge him worthy and that together they "will do such great deeds, that ages hereafter shall long speak of them." Aramis is fully convinced that placing Philippe on the throne is the right thing for France because Louis will be a bad king; that by allowing him to know the secret of Philippe's birth, Heaven has acknowledged that Aramis has a duty to act; that he possesses not only a moral imperative, but the power to act; and that by allowing Aramis to rise in power with him, Philippe will be empowered to further greatness with Aramis at his side.

Philippe makes his decision to follow Aramis's plan. Once they are hidden in the room above the king's at Vaux for Fouquet's party, the two discuss their ambitions once again. Aramis states plainly that he aims to become Philippe's prime minister and, in such a way, be able to carry out his own interests, as well as aid Philippe with pursuing his goals for France. Aramis intends to rise to the level of cardinal and, with Philippe's assistance, become pope: "I shall have given you the throne of France, you will confer on me the throne of St. Peter." The strength of this alliance, in Aramis's view, is inestimable. He tells Philippe, "I will simply say to you: The whole universe is our own; for me the minds of men, for you their bodies." Aramis has thus fully outlined the grand nature of his ambitions and presented them to Philippe as mutually beneficial, assuring Philippe that he, Aramis, will never put his own success above Philippe's. He maintains, "I shall never ascend the ladder of fortune, fame, or position, until I shall have first seen you placed upon the round of the ladder immediately above me."

Although the increasingly trusting Philippe embraces Aramis as he would a father, Aramis's plans are thwarted, and through his own arrogance. He and Porthos succeed in removing Louis from his room and incarcerating him in the Bastille. Philippe slips into Louis's bed and the next morning signs the papers securing Fouquet's release (Louis had placed him under arrest the previous evening). Aramis accompanies d'Artagnan to Fouquet's quarters to deliver the release. After d'Artagnan departs, a relieved but surprised Fouquet asks Aramis to explain how his release has come to pass.

Aramis's next actions are those that condemn him. He has certainly proven himself clever enough to have presented an explanation—a lie—to Fouquet that would ease the minister's mind and could remind him of the very fact of his freedom and the debt he owes Aramis. Yet Aramis seems to delight in the gradual revealing of his plan to a shocked Fouquet. He unravels the secret of the twin births to Fouquet and further tells him how he, during the night, swapped one son of Louis XIII for the other. He even smiles as he gradually makes his secrets known to Fouquet. Aramis seems to truly relish this story that highlights his cunning intelligence and power.

The boasting nature of Aramis's revelations to Fouquet is suggestive of Aramis's supreme confidence that Fouquet's response will be admiration, even delight. Yet when Fouquet fully understands what has transpired and labels it

The famed prison, Sainte Marguerite, off the coast of France (© Sean Nel | Shutterstock.com)

nothing less than a crime, Aramis is "stupefied." Even as he flees, Aramis seems stunned by the turn of events. He and Porthos make their escape from Vaux. In explaining his actions to Porthos, Aramis makes an admission that reveals to some extent a sense of self-awareness, stating, "My crime was being an egotist." Porthos later dies as the two attempt to flee from Belle Isle. Aramis, because of his position as the General of the Order, manages to sail to Spain, where he eventually, through his connections with the Jesuits and the king of Spain, becomes Spain's ambassador to France. In this capacity, he will later, with King Louis XIV and d'Artagnan, make plans for France's war with the Dutch.

Aramis falls, but not far. His flaws have tragic and fatal consequences, but not for him. Although his ambitions to elevate Philippe for France's benefit and his quest for the papacy fail, Aramis enjoys life, liberty, and power at the novel's conclusion. This is far more than can be said for Porthos or Philippe, the man in the iron mask. As a result of Aramis's revelations to Fouquet, Aramis and Porthos become fugitives, and Porthos dies an agonizing death in their escape attempt. Further, as far as Dumas is concerned, Aramis never gives poor Philippe another thought. Imprisoned on an island in complete seclusion with only his jailor and fated to wear the mask of iron until his death, Philippe is forgotten. As a youth whose true identity was unknown to him, Philippe's existence in the Bastille was bleak, but he wore no mask and did not have to endure the thoughts of what might have been had Aramis not bragged of his exploits to Fouquet.

Aramis seems to have little understanding of what he has done to Philippe, as the would-be king is never spoken of again after d'Artagnan has been recalled to King Louis's side. Yet Aramis's parting words to d'Artagnan at the close of the novel's epilogue suggest at least that the weight of the past is settling upon Aramis. He tells his friend, "And you will, perhaps, never see me again, dear d'Artagnan . . . if you knew how I have loved you! I am old, I am extinguished, I am dead."

Source: Catherine Dominic, Critical Essay on *The Man in the Iron Mask*, in *Novels for Students*, Gale, Cengage Learning, 2013.

Roger MacDonald

In the following excerpt, MacDonald investigates the origins of the protagonist in The Man in the Iron Mask.

. . . Unaware of Athos' true fate, Dumas kept the Three Musketeers and d'Artagnan in robust health until almost the end of the third book in his trilogy, *The Man in the Iron Mask*. For the central figure of that tale (which fictionalizes an essentially true story of a mysterious prisoner of Louis XIV) he followed the most popular current theory of the prisoner's identity, that of an identical twin of the King. In Dumas' version, d'Artagnan, who remains loyal to Louis, escorts the royal twin to the remote Mediterranean island of Sainte-Marguerite and locks him into the mask.

It is unlikely that this theory of the prisoner's identity could be correct. The arrival of an unexpected second child, allegedly nine hours after the first, could surely not have remained undetected in the goldfish bowl of the French court, and infant mortality was so high that the birth of a second son to Anne of Austria would have been more welcomed than feared. Later, Hollywood scriptwriters gave the story a sinister

> "D'ARTAGNAN WAS SUPPOSED TO BE DEAD BUT NONE OF THE PURPORTED EYEWITNESS ACCOUNTS OF HIS DEMISE WITHSTAND CLOSE SCRUTINY."

twist by imprisoning Louis himself in the same mask the King had supposedly devised for his innocent brother.

In the novel, the switch of one twin for the other takes place during the spectacular party at Vaux-le-Vicomte in August 1661, held by Nicholas Fouquet, the French finance minister, to celebrate the completion of his extravagant new château. The real event, attended by Louis XIV, proved the catalyst for Fouquet's arrest—by d'Artagnan—on the King's orders almost three weeks later. D'Artagnan had been employed by Mazarin to carry by word of mouth his most private messages. Consequently, d'Artagnan knew better than most the extent to which Mazarin, aided and abetted by finance minister Colbert (1619–83), had also used the state's money as though it were his own, persuasively demonstrated by Daniel Dessert in *Colbert el le serpent venimeux* (2000). The Gascon believed Fouquet was no guiltier than either of them and wanted nothing to do with the hypocrisy of his arrest. D'Artagnan therefore feigned or, at the least, exaggerated illness but Louis had no one else he could trust—even the duc de Gesvres, captain of his palace guard, was in Fouquet's pocket—and simply waited until he had recovered. Nonetheless the arrest was perilously close to being a fiasco, for d'Artagnan missed Fouquet's departure from the royal council and had to pursue him down the street. Acting as Fouquet's jailer for the next three years, d'Artagnan became increasingly partisan in his prisoner's interest. Obliged by Colbert to remain within earshot of his charge, d'Artagnan refused point-blank to report on Fouquet's conversations with his lawyers. In 1664, when Fouquet escaped the death penalty, Louis sent him to the remote Alpine prison of Pignerol and as a sign of royal displeasure at his insubordination, d'Artagnan was instructed to lead his escort of a hundred Musketeers across the mountains in savage winter conditions. Olivier Lefevre d'Ormesson, the only trial judge who had believed Fouquet to be innocent of all the charges, wrote in his journal that d'Artagnan was 'angry at being ordered to travel to Pignerol and would have got out of it if he could.'

Despite now being out of royal favour, d'Artagnan had a stroke of good fortune. For him the post of Captain of the Musketeers, who had been revived under Cardinal Mazarin's nephew, Philippe- Julien Mancini, in 1657, remained completely out of reach. Early in 1667, however, Mancini stoked up a row between his sister, Hortense Mancini and her husband, thereby hoping to gain control of Hortense's spectacular inheritance, left by her uncle the cardinal. Louis impulsively decided to make an example of Philippe and early in 1667 forced him to relinquish his company of Musketeers in favour of d'Artagnan—even though in doing so he was giving d'Artagnan a promotion the King did not feel he deserved. Colbert was outraged by Louis' perverse decision as D'Ormesson commented:

> M. de Colbert does not like d'Artagnan . . . the King's decision in this respect is surprising, he knows d'Artagnan is a friend of Fouquet and Colbert's enemy.

Far from becoming subservient to the King, however, in 1671 d'Artagnan repeated his defiance by refusing to arrest a fellow Gascon, the comte de Lauzun, who had dared to court, even possibly to marry in secret, Louis' ageing but wealthy cousin, the Grande Mademoiselle, whose lands the King coveted for his illegitimate offspring. Lauzun was contemptuously dismissive of their mother, Louis' most durable mistress, Athénaïs de Montespan. When the outraged monarch responded by sending Lauzun to Pignerol, once again d'Artagnan was ordered to escort the prisoner there in the depths of winter. What the manipulative Lauzun told d'Artagnan on the journey left the Captain of the Musketeers disillusioned with his king. The two Gascons may have reached the conclusion that Louis was not entitled to sit on the French throne. In his biography, *Louis XIV* (2000), Anthony Levi offers persuasive evidence that Mazarin, not the homosexual Louis XIII, was the Sun King's real father: perhaps Lauzun was in a position to know the truth.

On his return, d'Artagnan was disrespectful to Louis, and the King decided to remove him from court once more by making him governor of Lille. D'Artagnan lacked the education and guile to make a success of the job, and within a few weeks he had fallen out with the King's favourite, the siege engineer, Vauban. Although recalled in disgrace, at court d'Artagnan automatically returned to the position he held for life as Captain of the Musketeers whose men provided protection for the royal entourage outside the palace walls. They can scarcely have failed to notice when in March 1673 Athénaïs de Montespan, her position as *maitresse en titre* threatened by younger concubines, took part naked in a Black Mass designed to retain the royal favour, at a secluded château south of Paris. It was the most extraordinary incident in what would become known as the Affair of the Poisons, when many of the high and mighty of France were accused of dabbling in black magic and administering lethal substances. Long before the poisons scandal broke, d'Artagnan almost certainly knew what was going on. His reluctance to precipitate a political crisis did not include preserving Athénaïs' reputation and Louis had to take action. In his history of seventeenth-century France, W. H. Lewis concludes that 'Ridicule was perhaps the only thing in the world that Louis feared.'

D'Artagnan, a loose cannon, had to go. In June 1673 an opportunity presented itself when the King personally oversaw the successful siege of the formidable Dutch fortress, Maastricht. The Musketeers, led by d'Artagnan, were ordered prematurely into a night attack and suffered heavy casualties: perhaps Louis was hoping to arrange d'Artagnan's glorious death on the battlefield as a way out of their difficulties. D'Artagnan had a charmed life, and survived unscathed. However, on the following morning, to foil a Dutch counterattack he was drawn into a near-suicidal charge across open ground by the small English contingent on the French side, led by the Duke of Monmouth and John Churchill, the future Duke of Marlborough. While saving Monmouth during 'the bravest and briskest action they had seen in their lives,' d'Artagnan was hit in the neck by a stray bullet and reported dead.

Within a few months, a rumour swept Paris of a secret prisoner in the Bastille. He was said to be the playwright Molière, who had challenged the establishment, attacking the hypocrisy and pretentiousness of both the Roman Catholic Church and the court through his comedies. When Molière supposedly died on February 17th, 1673, he did not receive a proper funeral: no burial service took place and the entry in the church register remained unsigned; his body was taken directly to the cemetery of Saint-Joseph late at night. In 1792 his presumed grave would be exhumed and found to be empty and two historians, Anatole Loquin and Marcel Diamant-Berger, writing in 1883 and 1971 respectively were convinced that it was he who became the Man in the Iron Mask. In view of the notoriously poor state of his health, however, it is extremely unlikely that Molière could have survived in prison for more than thirty years. Rather, the Catholic Church may have arranged for him to be buried in unconsecrated ground, as a petty retribution after death for his ridiculing of them in life. The year when the rumour about a mysterious captive began, 1673, and not Molière himself, was the clue.

The state prisoners at Pignerol, Fouquet and Lauzun, were now being guarded by Bénigne de Saint-Mars, d'Artagnan's former quartermaster sergeant, who was forbidden to leave his post for even a single day. In July 1673, however, he sent from Maastricht a coded letter to Louvois about the state of health of a wounded third party, one so important that Saint-Mars himself and some of his men had been sent from Pignerol to the Maastricht battlefield to watch over him.

D'Artagnan was supposed to be dead but none of the purported eyewitness accounts of his demise withstand close scrutiny. One was by a fellow Musketeer who had been injured and missed this part the action; the second by a notorious liar; and the third by a drunken Irish peer. The story of d'Artagnan's Musketeers risking life and limb under withering fire in order to recover the body of their fallen commander was not reported at the time. There would have been no need for such heroics, because frequent truces were declared so that dead and injured combatants could be removed from the battlefield under a white flag. When in 1674 *le Mercure Galant* said that the Musketeers had failed to retrieve d'Artagnan's corpse, the gossip sheet was promptly shut down by the authorities and its editor imprisoned.

In 1873 an army officer, Théodore Iung, published his research into *The Man in the Iron Mask*, which established that Saint-Mars had been his jailer at four successive prisons. The names of only two of Saint-Mars' prisoners eluded Iung. The first, surely the Mask himself, had arrived at Pignerol from Paris in March 1674 amid extraordinary precautions, 'manacled at

night' and 'kept from view' in such a way that he could neither 'shout out or write...who he was.'. The second, a prisoner in the Bastille at the beginning of 1699, proved to be Gatien de Courtilz de Sandras, the author of the *Mémoires de Monsieur d'Artagnan.*

Courtilz went to such lengths to conceal his identity that the authorities were unsure of his real name. After his military career, he became a writer of pamphlets, political tracts and biographies, more than one hundred works in all, printed outside France to escape censorship. He called Louis XIV '*Le Grand Alcandre*,' a reference to Corneille's comedy '*L'Illusion Comique*,' in which the old sorcerer, Alcandre, lives in a cave with his deaf and dumb servants. The Sun King would not have liked the analogy. Courtilz was sent to the Bastille in 1693. He was still a prisoner, although he was given the freedom to go more or less where he liked within its walls, thanks to his influential wife, Louise Pannetier, when Saint-Mars arrived with the Iron Mask in September 1698.

Twenty-five years had elapsed since d'Artagnan's last military campaign, the siege of Maastricht, and outside the senior ranks of the armed forces he was long since forgotten. There is no evidence that Courtilz had ever met d'Artagnan during his military service and Courtilz was never a Musketeer. Courtilz showed no signs of husbanding information on potential subjects for future use, let alone a quarter of a century after the event. Arthur de Boislisle, editor of Saint-Simon's diaries; Jules Lair, author of the definitive biography on Fouquet; and Charles Samaran, who undertook a great deal of original research on the Musketeers, all rejected the cynical view that Courtilz' autobiography of d'Artagnan was pure fiction. Samaran concluded that, 'not only on general events, but on the deeds and actions of individuals, there are amazingly accurate details.' Jurgain determined that Courtilz's collective reference to Aramis, Athos and Porthos, the first mention of them anywhere, was also founded on fact. Courtilz wrote d'Artagnan's biography while in jail, and his wife smuggled out the manuscript. The only rational explanation is that Courtilz had a prime source of information among the prisoners in the Bastille; but none of his nineteen fellow inmates listed in the prison register had the remotest connection with d'Artagnan. That left the sole prisoner not accounted for, the Man in the Iron Mask, confirming, given the wealth of detail he supplied, that he could only be d'Artagnan himself.

In 1687, during his transfer from another Alpine prison, Exiles, to the island of Sainte-Marguerite, off Cannes, a priest at Grasse saw the prisoner in his mask, made not of iron, but steel. His eyewitness account appeared in a newsletter circulated by clerics, which also reported an unguarded remark made by Saint-Mars about the identity of his charge that 'All the people one believes to be dead are not.' This meant that the man in the Mask had to be sufficiently well-known to attract comment, for his supposed death to have been widely reported and for him to be held in the utmost secrecy. D'Artagnan, almost alone of all the credible candidates, meets this criteria.

Just before embarking on his spectacular series of historical novels, Dumas produced *Celebrated Crimes*, a series of eight volumes on dark deeds from history. Volume Six included *The Man in the Iron Mask*. Like much of Dumas's prodigious output, it owed a great deal to the work of others, in this instance his closest collaborator, Auguste Maquet, a former history teacher. As was often the case, Dumas undermined Maquet's meticulous research by some impulsive contributions of his own. Dumas confessed that in writing an earlier play about the Iron Mask, he had been forced to 'choose one view of a dramatic situation to the exclusion of all others . . . and . . . by the inexorable laws of logic to push aside everything that interferes with its development.' He had selected, and would stick with, the notion of an identical twin in the mask, because 'it was incontestably the most dramatic.' How ironic, then, that the qualities of loyalty and honour that d'Artagnan possessed, brilliantly captured by Dumas in fiction, proved the Musketeer's eventual undoing in fact: and that Dumas, in failing to give credit to Courtilz, ensured that an even better story would slip through his fingers, the astonishing secret that d'Artagnan himself was the Man in the Iron Mask.

Source: Roger MacDonald, "Behind the Iron Mask," in *History Today*, Vol. 55, No. 11, November 2005, pp. 30–36.

Lionel Lackey

In the following excerpt, Lackey examines Dumas's characterization of the man in the iron mask.

In the later books of the Musketeer series, *Twenty Years After*, and the three parts of *Le*

> WHATEVER HIDDEN AGENDA A POLITICAL CRITIC MIGHT SUSPECT DUMAS OF HAVING—SUCH AS A DESIRE TO STAY IN FAVOR WITH BOURGEOIS READERS, CRITICS, AND PUBLISHERS—DUMAS DOES NOT PRETEND THAT SOCIAL JUSTICE IS PRESENT OR CAN BE BYPASSED IN ADMIRATION OF THE HEROICS OF FOUR FEUDAL SOLDIERS."

vicomte de Bragelonne, Dumas gives a darkening, chaotic view of a materialistic environment which infects, disunites, and finally destroys the four heroes who in *The Three Musketeers* had seemed inseparable and invincible. While I shall not take a purely historicist approach, I shall refer to some historicist tenets which I think Dumas illustrates.

Historicism assumes a connection between materialistic or economic concerns and all human activity. Historicist or political critics often imply that a writer has a hidden (perhaps unconscious) agenda which may counteract his seemingly high-minded thesis and which inadvertently appears through signs and semiotics. According to Fredric Jameson, "there is nothing that is not social or historical," and the duty of the critic is "the unmasking of cultural artifacts as socially symbolic acts." In the same vein, Terry Eagleton faults George Eliot, who "strives for organic closure" by smoothing over unresolved social or cultural conflicts. Dickens is better, Eagleton feels, because of "the clarity with which . . . conflicts inscribe themselves in the fissures and hiatuses of the texts." My thesis is that Dumas is unusually straightforward (like Eagleton's view of Dickens) in showing problems caused by economic needs and honest about the difficulty of finding fair, satisfying solutions.

On the other hand, F.W.J. Hemmings says of *The Three Musketeers*,

> we are given a particularly rose-tinted, partial, not so much distorted as disinfected view of the past. . . Dumas' picture of the seventeenth century omits everything that would have made it a most uncomfortable age for any of his nineteenth-century readers . . . . Even war is reduced

to a gay picnic.... none of the usual dull con-
cerns of adult humanity have any hold. Money
and possessions are not merely of no account,
they are things one does not need to trouble his
head about, for in the last resort God will
provide. . . .

This is mostly true of the first and most
popular Musketeer novel. But it is to Dumas'
credit that in the others of the series—written in
the same decade as the first gloriously successful
book—he did not repeat his formula of easy
triumph for his four romantic heroes, who age
in both years and worldly preoccupation.

A. Craig Bell calls Dumas "republican by
reason, royalist by instinct," adding that "his pol-
itics were an uneasy compromise between the
two." David Coward says that "his political
enthusiasms were brief and shallow," those of
"a champagne socialist"; his antidote to bourgeois
materialism was not so much a proletarian revolu-
tion as a return to "the values of nobility and chivalry
which had freed men's spirits in a way no amount of
money and business and industry will ever match."
Dumas is not didactic, so to find out what he favors
one must look to his characterizations—often so
mixed as to approach that whirling confusion that
critical theorists call "carnival."

. . . The darkest descent of a Musketeer
occurs in *The Man in the Iron Mask*, when Aramis
the bishop uses his connections with the Jesuits
and Fouquet to attempt the substitution of Louis'
unknown, hitherto-hidden twin Philippe on the
throne, with the hope of getting himself made
Cardinal and eventually Pope. Seeds of this
grand conspiracy had been sown as early as
"The Second Floor of La Bertaudiere" (Louise),
when Aramis had shown some pity for one young
prisoner named Seldon (in the Bastille for writing
satirical verses) but had taken a greater interest in
another called Marchiali. In "The State Secret"
(Louise), Aramis had persuaded a dying Jesuit
general (whom he may have poisoned) to name
him his successor on the strength of Aramis'
knowing of a possible pretender to the throne.
He makes loans to Baisemeaux, Governor of the
Bastille, and effects the release of "Marchiali" (the
twin Philippe). The latter is an inoffensive young
man who has made himself fairly content with
his unexplained imprisonment (ordered by his
parents and Richelieu to avoid a quarrel over
succession). With the help of the gullible Por-
thos, who still thinks that his services will earn
him a dukedom, Aramis switches the twins. But
Fouquet, who Aramis thought would rejoice

since Louis was about to impeach him, will
not go along, orders Aramis and Porthos to
flee, and releases Louis from the Bastille. Por-
thos dies in an explosion in a cave where he and
Aramis are eluding their pursuers. Aramis buys
off the arresting naval officer with his Jesuit
influence and escapes to Spain but sheds the
first tears of his cynical, opportunistic life over
the death of his friend. Philippe is punished with
a fate more dreadful than his former incarcer-
ation: he becomes Man in the Iron Mask for life,
Dumas never bringing himself to divulge whether
it was Louis, Fouquet, or Colbert who devised
this Cruel and Unusual Punishment. Louis' grat-
itude to Fouquet is short lived, and d'Artagnan,
who admires Fouquet, is forced to arrest him;
Fouquet behaves gallantly in defeat. As a good
side effect of his frustrated grander designs, Ara-
mis has brought about the release of the unfortu-
nate satirist, Seldon. But the final chapters are full
of sad leave-takings among the old friends.

With Fouquet no longer posing a threat to the
French economy, Colbert can re-emerge as the
wise, forward-looking economist he had seemed
at first. In "The Squirrel Falls—the Adder Flies,"
he begins to convince the skeptical d'Artagnan
that he is after all not evil, that his moves against
Fouquet have been born of historical necessity:

> I have many ideas M. d'Artagnan; you will see
> them expand in the sun of public peace; and if
> I have not the certainty and good fortune to
> conquer the friendship of honest men, I can at
> least be certain, monsieur, that I shall obtain
> their esteem. For their admiration, monsieur,
> I would give my life.

Colbert obtains a pardon for Aramis, who
in the Epilogue visits France and d'Artagnan as
a Spanish diplomat, the Duc d'Almeda. Colbert
needs d'Artagnan for a military side of his proj-
ects, a war with Holland; in return he promises
and obtains for d'Artagnan the long-desired
promotion to Marshal of France. D'Artagan
receives a congratulatory letter and a marshal's
baton from him just before being hit by a fatal
bullet at the siege of a Dutch fortification. Perhaps
his material prosperity has made him lower his
guard. His penultimate thought is of his pro-
motion, but then

> he . . . fell back, murmuring these strange
> words, which appeared to the soldiers cabalis-
> tic words—words which had formerly repre-
> sented so many things upon earth, and which
> none but the dying man longer comprehended:
> "Athos—Porthos, farewell till we meet again!

Aramis, adieu forever!" Of the four valiant men whose history we have related, there now no longer remained but one single body; God had resumed the souls.

Well do I remember my dismay and distress one Saturday morning long ago when, an eleven-year-old boy, I checked the last Musketeer book out of the library and looked ahead to the end. The kind, gentle woman who tried to console me that day was partly right in saying not to take this book too seriously, because it was "not their story." In a way it is not, because the four late-middle-aged, self-serving men who die (or, in the case of Aramis, survives, never to be reunited with the others) are not the four young idealists who had scorned money and defied politics thirty years earlier. But part of the sadness lies in the inevitability of their change.

Whatever hidden agenda a political critic might suspect Dumas of having—such as a desire to stay in favor with bourgeois readers, critics, and publishers—Dumas does not pretend that social justice is present or can be bypassed in admiration of the heroics of four feudal soldiers. Colbert may modernize his country's economy, but there will still be street people run over or buffeted about; unjust incarcerations like those of Seldon and Philippe; exploitation of the naive by the sophisticated as with Porthos and Aramis; self-deception as to motive as shown by d'Artagnan and Athos; and the scapegoating of the weak and vulnerable as is done to Louise. David Coward is of course right in noting Dumas' love of "nobility and chivalry," but it is not a love blind to their limitations or corruptibility. The disintegration of the four popular heroes has an almost naturalistic, existentialist aura which shows that idealism cannot always prevail against society or against self-interest and the striving for security that seems to advance with age. Yet the later *Musketeer* novels are not entirely a surrender to cynicism. Besides flashes of humor, there are times when not only Athos, Porthos, Aramis, and d'Artagnan but also Fouquet and Colbert act altruistically and magnanimously; they even shed tears over lost ideals and friendships and induce some readers to do the same. These moments of light and warmth enable the four heroes not so much to grow old gracefully as to stay young gracefully, and they preserve some remnants of romance in the concluding chronicles of Dumas' historically correct *Musketeers*.

Source: Lionel Lackey, "The Death of D'Artagnan: Dumas' Realistic Musketeers," in *English Language Notes*, Vol. 41, No. 3, March 2004, pp. 41–50.

SOURCES

Cooper, Barbara T., "Alexandre Dumas," in *Dictionary of Literary Biography*, Vol. 119, *Nineteenth-Century French Fiction Writers: Romanticism and Realism, 1800–1860*, edited by Catherine Savage Brosman, Gale Research, 1992, pp. 98–119.

———, Introduction to *The Man in the Iron Mask*, by Alexandre Dumas, Barnes & Noble Classics, 2005, pp. xiii–xxviii.

Coward, David, Introduction to *The Man in the Iron Mask*, by Alexandre Dumas, Oxford University Press, 1998, pp. ix–xxiii.

D'Ammassa, Don, "*The Man in the Iron Mask*," in *Encyclopedia of Adventure Fiction*, Facts on File, 2009, pp. 135–37.

Davidson, Arthur Fitzwilliam, "The Great Novels," in *Alexandre Dumas (père): His Life and Works*, J. P. Lippincott, 1902, pp. 216–56.

Dumas, Alexandre, *The Man in the Iron Mask*, Oxford University Press, 1998.

———, Preface to *The Three Musketeers*, George Routledge and Sons, 1878, pp. iii–iv.

"France," in CIA: *World Factbook*, https://www.cia.gov/library/publications/the-world-factbook/geos/fr.html (accessed January 12, 2012).

"From Messrs. H. S. Nicholas, Ltd.," in *The Publishers' Circle and Booksellers' Record of British and Foreign Literature*, Vol. 71, December 1899, p. 295.

"From the Three Glorious Days to the Third Republic," Musée d'Orsay website, http://www.musee-orsay.fr/en/collections/courbet-dossier/historical-context.html (accessed January 12, 2012).

Gray, Francine du Plessix Gray, Introduction to *The Man in the Iron Mask*, by Alexandre Dumas, translated by Joachim Neugroschel, Penguin, 2003, pp. vii–xxv.

Hamnett, Brian, Introduction and "Romanticism and the Historical Novel," in *The Historical Novel in Nineteenth-Century Europe: Representations of Reality in History and Fiction*, Oxford University Press, 2011, pp. 1–16,100–24.

"Louis XIV (1638–1715)," in *Historic Figures*, BBC website, http://www.bbc.co.uk/history/historic_figures/louis_xiv.shtml (accessed January 12, 2012).

Stockton, Louise, "The Treatment of the Plot," in *The Critic*, No. 753, July 25, 1896, pp. 51–52.

Welch, Ellen R., "Cosmopolitan Seductions: City Guides and Parisian Novels," in *A Taste for the Foreign: Worldly Knowledge and Literary Pleasure in Early Modern French Fiction*, University of Delaware Press, 2011, pp. 51–82.

Yair, Gad, "Introduction: Bordieu's Politics of the Revolution," in *Pierre Bourdieu: The Last Musketeer of the French Revolution*, Lexington Books, 2009.

FURTHER READING

Bell, A. Craig, *Alexandre Dumas: A Biography and Study*, Cassel, 1950.
>   Bell's biography of Dumas offers a detailed discussion of the author's life and career.

Dunlap, Ian, *Louis XIV*, St. Martin's Press, 2000.
>   Dunlap's acclaimed and extensive biography of King Louis XIV details the monarch's reign and provides the social, historical, and political context in which the king's life may be understood.

Hahn, H. Hazel, *Scenes of Parisian Modernity: Culture and Consumption in the Nineteenth Century*, Palgrave Macmillan, 2009.
>   Hahn outlines the cultural and economic developments occurring in Paris during the nineteenth century, discussing such topics as the consumption of literature and art and the factors that contributed to the modern urbanization of the city. Hazel references Dumas as an iconic figure of the literary establishment during this time.

Wright, Jonathan, *God's Soldiers: Adventure, Politics, Intrigue, and Power: A History of the Jesuits*, Image, 2005.
>   Wright traces centuries of the Jesuit order's history and examines the political machinations with which the order has allegedly been involved.

SUGGESTED SEARCH TERMS

Alexandre Dumas AND *The Man in the Iron Mask*

Alexandre Dumas AND *The Three Musketeers*

Alexandre Dumas AND *The Memoirs of d'Artagnan*

Alexandre Dumas AND Louis XIV

Alexandre Dumas AND historical fiction

Alexandre Dumas AND romanticism

Alexandre Dumas AND Order of the Jesuits

Alexandre Dumas AND French history

Alexandre Dumas AND The Vicomte de Bragelonne

Alexandre Dumas AND man in the iron mask myth

The Pickwick Papers

CHARLES DICKENS

1836–1837

Popularly referred to as *The Pickwick Papers*, Charles Dickens's first novel is actually titled *The Posthumous Papers of the Pickwick Club*. The novel's protagonist is Samuel Pickwick: wealthy, unworldly, unmarried, portly, bespectacled, slightly aging, and benevolent but naive. Pickwick founds and leads the Pickwick Club and joins a group of the club's members to travel throughout England in search of antiquities and other curiosities. The conceit of the novel, established in the first chapter, is that it is a record of the club's adventures and that its "posthumous papers" have been edited by the author. The novel was originally conceived as commentary for sporting illustrations drawn by the popular caricaturist Robert Seymour, but it quickly took on a life of its own, particularly after Seymour's untimely death. The illustrations for most of the rest of the novel were drawn by H. K. "Phiz" Browne, who would work with Dickens for more than two decades.

The novel, in common with many novels of the Victorian era, was first published serially—in this case, in monthly parts from April 1836 to November 1837. Often, serially published novels appeared a few chapters at a time in magazines, but *The Pickwick Papers* was published (in London) in small booklets that could be purchased for a shilling each. Later, novels that first appeared this way were published as bound books.

The Pickwick Papers launched Dickens's career as one of the Victorian age's preeminent novelists. Particularly after the first appearance of

Charles Dickens

Pickwick's servant, Sam Weller, interest in the novel swelled, and by the end of its run a phenomenal forty thousand copies of each part were printed. In time, Dickens became a household name and almost a revered public figure. Although many critics regard Dickens's later novels—*Great Expectations, Bleak House, Little Dorrit, Our Mutual Friend*—as richer and more complex, *Pickwick* continues to hold an honored place in Dickens's canon among the author's fans for its warm comedy, beloved characters, and gentle wisdom. The novel spawned a host of imitators and illustrators, and still today, people can purchase knickknacks and gift items—coffee cups, Christmas ornaments, T-shirts, wall clocks, pillows, note cards, posters, ceramics, canes—with themes and illustrations from *The Pickwick Papers*. The Pickwick Papers is available in numerous editions, including one published by Oxford University Press in 2008.

AUTHOR BIOGRAPHY

Dickens was born in Landport, near Portsmouth, Hampshire, England, on February 7, 1812, the second of eight children of John Dickens and Elizabeth Barrow; the house in which he was born is now the Charles Dickens Birthplace Museum. When Dickens was twelve years old, his father, a clerk in the Navy Pay Office, encountered financial troubles and was imprisoned for debt in Marshalsea Prison (an experience Dickens drew on in having Pickwick imprisoned in the Fleet debtor's prison). Charles was sent to work for several months in a shoe-blacking warehouse, interrupting his education and giving him a lifelong sympathy for the plight of child laborers. He began his career as a solicitor's clerk and then a court reporter. In 1832, he was a reporter for an evening newspaper, and he later became a reporter for the *Morning Chronicle*.

Dickens's first short story, "A Dinner at Poplar Walk," was published in 1833. In 1836, drawing on his experience as a journalist, he published *Sketches by Boz*, a series of descriptions of London life. That year, he also became the editor of a new magazine, *Bentley's Miscellany*, and married Catherine Hogarth, the daughter of the editor of the *Evening Chronicle*. They had ten children but would separate in 1858, a separation that was likely triggered, at least in part, by his relationship with the actress Ellen Ternan.

Dickens's first novel was *The Pickwick Papers* (1836–1837), which, like most of his fiction, was published serially. The success of this novel encouraged Dickens to continue writing, and in the following years, he wrote *Oliver Twist* (1837–1839), *Nicholas Nickleby* (1838–1839), *The Old Curiosity Shop* (1840–1841), and *Barnaby Rudge* (1841). His work was popular in both England and North America and in 1842, he took his first trip to Canada and the United States. The travelogue *American Notes* (1842) and some episodes of his novel *Martin Chuzzlewit* (1843–1844) were based on his impressions, many of them unfavorable, from his American tour.

During the 1840s and 1850s, Dickens continued to write with an almost feverish intensity, publishing *A Christmas Carol* (1843), *Dombey and Son* (1846–1848), *David Copperfield* (1849–1850), *Bleak House* (1852–1853), *Hard Times* (1854), *Little Dorrit* (1855–1857), and *A Tale of Two Cities* (1859). He was also the editor of *Household Words*, a magazine he founded in 1850. When that magazine ceased publication in 1859, he became editor of a new magazine, *All the Year Round*. He continued to enjoy great popularity and, in the 1850s and 1860s, traveled throughout England, Scotland, and Ireland giving highly successful public readings from his novels. He also gave readings in Paris in 1863, and in 1867–1868, he went on a five-month reading tour in the United States.

In the final decade of his life, even as his health declined, Dickens wrote *Great Expectations* (1860–1861) and *Our Mutual Friend* (1864–1865). In 1870, he was working on *The Mystery of Edwin Drood*, which had begun publication but remained unfinished, when he suffered a stroke. He died at his country home, Gads Hill Place (near Rochester, Kent), on June 9, 1870, at age fifty-eight.

PLOT SUMMARY

The chapter groupings correspond to those in the twenty parts of the original publication of *The Pickwick Papers*. The text used for this summary is *The Pickwick Papers* in the Oxford Illustrated Dickens, first published by Oxford University Press in 1948.

Chapters 1–2

On May 12, 1827, the Pickwick Club of London votes to form a traveling society that will include Samuel Pickwick, Tracy Tupman, Augustus Snodgrass, and Nathaniel Winkle. On his first journey, Pickwick rides in a horse-drawn cab to meet his friends, taking notes on the driver's fabrications about his horse. The cabbie believes Pickwick is an informer, and after reaching the destination, he arouses a crowd against the Pickwickians. The men are rescued by a young stranger, who joins them on their journey to Rochester and entertains them with stories. At Rochester, the Pickwickians invite the stranger to dinner. A dance is in progress, and Tupman lends the stranger Winkle's dress coat. The stranger wins a middle-aged widow away from Dr. Slammer, a local army man, who vows to exact revenge. The next day, a lieutenant searches for the man wearing Winkle's coat. He finds Winkle and challenges him to a duel on Slammer's behalf. That evening, with Snodgrass as his second, Winkle goes to meet Slammer, who calls off the duel because he sees that Winkle is the wrong man.

Chapters 3–5

Back at the inn, Winkle and Snodgrass find Pickwick and Tupman with the stranger and a friend of his—a strolling actor called "Dismal Jemmy," who tells a story about an alcoholic

MEDIA ADAPTATIONS

- The British composer and conductor Albert Coates wrote an operatic version of *The Pickwick Papers*, titled simply *Pickwick*. The opera holds the distinction of being the first to be shown on television, when the BBC broadcast it on November 13, 1936. That year, it was also staged at Covent Garden by the British Music Drama Opera Company, directed by Vladimir Rosing.

- *Mr. Pickwick* is the title of a play written by Stanley Young and published by Random House in 1952. The play was produced that year by the Playwright's Company under the direction of John Burrell and starring George Howe.

- A 1952 movie version of *The Pickwick Papers*, directed by Noel Langley, starred James Hayter in the title role. The movie, produced by Noel Langley and George Minter and with music by Antony Hopkins, was released on DVD by VCI Entertainment in 2009. Running time is 109 minutes.

- In 1985, England's BBC produced a twelve-part, 350-minute television adaptation of *The Pickwick Papers*, starring Nigel Stock, Clive Swift, Alan Parnaby, and Jeremy Nicholas. The series was produced by Barry Letts and directed by Brian Lighthill. It was released on DVD by BBC Worldwide in 2006.

- AudioGo released an abridged audiobook version of *The Pickwick Papers*, narrated by Clive Francis, Peter Jeffrey, Norman Rodway, and Trevor Peacock, in 2008. Running time is two hours and forty-three minutes.

- In 2010, Saland Publishing released an audio CD of an abridged version of *The Pickwick Papers* read by Charles Coburn. The reading is available as an MP3 download and runs for fifty-three minutes.

- An unabridged version of *The Pickwick Papers*, narrated by Simon Prebble, was put out by Blackstone Audio in 2010. It is available as two MP3 CDs, with a running time of thirty hours and forty-seven minutes.

pantomime who beats his wife and son, cannot support himself, and dies insane. Dr. Slammer and two companions arrive and recognize Tupman and the stranger. A dispute erupts, and Pickwick has to be restrained.

The Pickwickians go to nearby Chatham to watch army maneuvers, but they are caught up in the confusion of a mock battle. They meet Mr. Wardle, a country squire, and his family. Wardle invites them to take part in a picnic. Snodgrass is attracted to Wardle's daughter, Emily, while Tupman is attracted to Wardle's spinster sister, Rachael. Wardle invites the Pickwickians to his farm at Dingley Dell.

Chapters 6–8

The Pickwickians meet Wardle's mother and several neighbors, and the group plays cards and other games. After the card games are finished, a minister tells the story of "The Convict's Return," about a man who serves fourteen years for theft. When he is released, he returns home, where he and his father get into a violent fight, during which the father dies. The man repents until his death.

A group gathers to go crow hunting, but Winkle is fearful of his lack of skill. He accidentally shoots Tupman, who is cared for by Rachael. The other Pickwickians accompany Wardle to Muggleton to see a cricket match, where they again meet the stranger, who introduces himself as Alfred Jingle.

Tupman takes Rachael to a bower, where he declares his love for her. Joe the Fat Boy sees him kissing her. Wardle and the rest return home from the cricket match in the company of Jingle, who favorably impresses Rachael. The next day, Joe tells old Mrs. Wardle about Tupman's romance. Jingle overhears and, assuming that Rachael has money, tries to convince her that Tupman is a greedy conniver and tries to persuade Tupman to pursue Emily instead.

Chapters 9–11

Jingle elopes with Rachael, and Pickwick and Wardle unsuccessfully pursue the couple. Jingle encounters Sam Weller at the White Hart Inn in London and asks him the way to Doctors' Commons for a marriage license. Jingle purchases the license, but Wardle arrives at the inn with Pickwick and his lawyer, Mr. Perker. They learn Jingle's whereabouts from Sam and confront him in a room with Rachael. Perker suggests

that Wardle compromise with Jingle, so Wardle buys Jingle off. Pickwick and Wardle then return to Manor Farm at Dingley Dell with Rachael.

Pickwick learns that Tupman has left Manor Farm, intending to commit suicide in romantic despair. The Pickwickians hurry after Tupman, whom they find dining and looking well, and matters are resolved. At Cobham, Pickwick finds a stone with a strange inscription, which he mistakenly assumes to be ancient. Unable to sleep, Pickwick reads a manuscript, "A Madman's Manuscript," that the clergyman at Wardle's farm gave him. The story, written by an insane author, recounts his plot to murder his wife and children, but he was captured and consigned to an asylum before he could carry out the plot.

Chapters 12–14

In London, Pickwick's widowed landlady, Mrs. Bardell, mistakenly assumes that he has proposed marriage to her. She throws herself into his arms just as the other Pickwickians enter the room, putting Pickwick in an awkward situation. Pickwick then hires Sam Weller as his manservant.

At Eatanswill, a contentious election is occurring between the Blues and the Buffs. The next day, voting takes place, with the successful candidate winning because of bribes.

In the commercial room at the Peacock Inn at Eatanswill, Snodgrass and Tupman listen to a one-eyed bagman tell a story about a poor commercial traveler who is caught in a storm but finds shelter in an inn owned by a buxom widow. The traveler, under advice from a high-backed chair in his room, manages to cut out an adulterous suitor who is courting the widow, and marries her.

Chapters 15–17

Still at Eatanswill, the Pickwickians attend a costume breakfast held by Mrs. Leo Hunter, a wretched poet. Among the guests is Alfred Jingle, who leaves hastily when he encounters Pickwick, who pursues him to Bury St. Edmunds with Sam. At Bury St. Edmunds. Sam meets Jingle's servant, Job Trotter, who tells Sam of Jingle's plan to elope with a rich girl from a nearby boarding school. Job then suggests a plan to save the girl. Pickwick waits in the boarding school garden to surprise Jingle in the act, but he is caught in a storm and escapes by entering the school. There, the hysterical students, having no idea who he is or of Jingle's plan, lock him in a closet. Wardle and Sam arrive to straighten out the matter.

Chapters 18–20

Pickwick, laid up with rheumatism, writes a humorous story, "The Parish Clerk—a Tale of True Love," which he then reads to Wardle. The story involves a schoolmaster who wants to marry but whose father objects to the marriage. Winkle becomes embroiled in a dispute with the editor of an Eatanswill newspaper because of a false accusation that he is having an affair with the editor's wife. Wardle invites the Pickwickians to spend Christmas at Manor Farm to celebrate Trundle's wedding to Isabella Wardle. Pickwick receives a letter informing him that Mrs. Bardell is suing him for breach of promise. He resolves to return to London to get legal assistance. The next day, the ailing Pickwick falls asleep in a wheelbarrow during a hunting expedition and is arrested by an irascible neighbor. Once again, Sam and Wardle rescue him.

In London, Pickwick goes to the offices of Dodson and Fogg, Mrs. Bardell's lawyers. He indignantly refuses to settle the matter by paying damages. Later, Sam encounters his father, who tells Pickwick that he has seen Jingle and Job Trotter.

Chapters 21–23

A law clerk tells stories of dead bodies and ghosts in the chambers of the Inns of Court. He also narrates "The Old Man's Tale About the Queer Client," the story of a client imprisoned in the Marshalsea and his efforts to seek vengeance against his father-in-law.

Tony Weller tells Sam about the evangelist with whom his wife has taken up. Pickwick arrives at Ipswich and, that night, loses his way trying to find his room. He mistakenly enters a woman's bedroom, undresses, and leaves after the woman panics. The next morning, Sam encounters Job Trotter, who unsuccessfully tries to evade him. He tells Sam that his master is planning to marry a cook for her savings. Sam tells Pickwick about a plan he has in mind, although he does not provide his employer with any details.

Chapters 24–26

Pickwick has breakfast with a man who turns out to be the fiancé of the woman whose room he entered the previous night. A dispute erupts, and the woman files a complaint with the local magistrate, who arrests Pickwick and Tupman. Pickwick disentangles himself by telling the officer that Jingle is after his daughter, a fact revealed to him by Sam. Sam, meanwhile, dines with the servants and strikes up a romance with the pretty housemaid, Mary. Pickwick and Sam thwart Jingle's plan to marry the cook. Pickwick and Sam return to London.

Pickwick moves out of Mrs. Bardell's house and into a hotel. Sam learns that Mrs. Bardell intends to take Mr. Pickwick to court and that Dodson and Fogg have a good chance of winning.

Chapters 27–28

Sam visits his father at Dorking, where he finds his stepmother with a gluttonous evangelist, Reverend Stiggins. The Pickwickians travel to Dingley Dell for Christmas. Several young women, friends of the Wardle girls, arrive to attend the marriage of Isabella and Trundle. Winkle begins a romance with one, Arabella Allen, and Snodgrass is glad to see Emily again. Wardle narrates "The Story of the Goblins Who Stole a Sexton."

Chapters 29–31

One morning, Pickwick finds two medical students in the Wardle kitchen. Bob Sawyer and Ben Allen, Arabella's brother, are ill-mannered, high-spirited young men. Winkle grows jealous of Bob Sawyer's attentions to Arabella. During a skating party, Pickwick is saved after falling through the ice. The next morning, the party breaks up. Sawyer invites Pickwick to a bachelor party at his rooms in London, and Winkle and Snodgrass take leave of their sweethearts. In London, Pickwick learns that the lawsuit is on and that the Pickwickians will all be called as witnesses.

Bob Sawyer is harangued by his landlady because he cannot pay the rent. The Pickwickians arrive at his party, which includes a number of medical students, turns out to be a disaster, and breaks up when the landlady throws all the men out.

Chapters 32–33

Sam Weller writes a valentine to Mary, but his father believes Sam should avoid women. Sam signs the valentine, "Your love-sick Pickwick." Tony invites Sam to a temperance meeting, where the Reverend Stiggins becomes drunk and quarrelsome. A fight breaks out, and Tony lands some blows on Stiggins.

Pickwick's trial on the charge of breach of promise begins. Serjeant Buzfuz represents Mrs. Bardell, while Pickwick is represented by Sergeant Snubbin. Buzfuz manages to elicit damaging evidence from Winkle, Snodgrass, and Tupman. The jury finds Pickwick guilty and set damages at £750. Pickwick says that he would rather go to debtors' prison than pay.

Chapters 34–36
Pickwick learns that it will be two months before he can be imprisoned, so he takes his companions to Bath, where he attends a ball and takes part in a card game. One evening, Mr. Pickwick reads "The True Legend of Prince Bladud," the legendary founder of Bath whose tears, shed because his sweetheart has married another man, are the source of Bath's mineral waters. Sam becomes the life of the party at a soiree held by a number of footmen. Pickwick learns that Winkle has run off to Bristol and dispatches Sam to pursue him and bring him back.

Chapters 37–39
Winkle becomes embroiled in a misadventure with Arabella. He has to flee when he, Pickwick, and Sam are mistaken for robbers. At Bristol, Winkle winds up at the medical shop of Bob Sawyer and Ben Allen, who wants his sister, Arabella, to marry Bob. Sam arrives and puts Winkle under lock and key. After Pickwick catches up with them in Bristol, Winkle declares his love for Arabella, who reciprocates.

Chapters 40–42
In London, Pickwick is taken into custody and imprisoned in the Fleet debtor's prison after having repeatedly refused to pay damages to Mrs. Bardell. He is given a room, where he is disturbed by his boisterous roommates. He eventually obtains the use of a private room. When he goes to the section of the prison that houses people who cannot afford to pay for better accommodations to find someone willing to run errands for him, he discovers Jingle and Trotter. Pickwick feels sorry for them and gives them money. He tries to dismiss Sam from service to him, but Sam refuses to abandon Pickwick. In order to remain near Pickwick, Sam arranges to have himself arrested for debt (by his father) and imprisoned at the Fleet. He refuses to tell Pickwick the identity of his creditor.

Chapters 43–45
Later, the other Pickwickians arrive, and it is clear that Winkle has something on his mind. In the months that follow, Pickwick witnesses the squalor and misery of prison life and resolves to keep to his room. On a legal technicality, Mrs. Bardell is imprisoned at the Fleet for debt; she never paid her attorneys, Dodson and Fogg.

Chapters 46–48
Pickwick learns that what had earlier been on Winkle's mind was the fact that he had eloped with Arabella. Mrs. Bardell agrees to release Pickwick from his debt to her if he will pay her lawyers' fees, the source of her debt. Pickwick agrees, and the next morning, he and Sam leave the prison.

Ben Allen continues to want his sister to marry Bob Sawyer. He is disturbed to learn that she has secretly married Winkle, but he becomes resigned to the marriage.

Chapters 49–51
Pickwick, Sawyer, and Winkle travel to Birmingham to obtain the blessing of Winkle's father for the marriage. At a small town, the party encounters the editors of the two Eatanswill newspapers, which ends in a brawl.

Chapters 52–57
Sam learns that his stepmother has died and left £200 to him and the remainder of her money to Tony. Pickwick arranges to have Jingle and Trotter released from prison. Wardle announces that he is resigned to a marriage between Snodgrass and Emily. Tony and Sam take care of the legalities involving their inheritances. Tony wants to give his money to Pickwick, and Pickwick considers taking it to set up Sam in a business. Sam refuses, wanting to remain in Pickwick's service. Old Mr. Winkle finally consents to the marriage of his son and Arabella.

Pickwick announces to his friends that he is settling down in a home at Dulwich. The Pickwick Club has disbanded. The wedding of Snodgrass and Emily Wardle will take place in his new home. Winkle obtains a position in London from his father, who is reconciled to his son's marriage and pleased with his new daughter-in-law. Snodgrass becomes a country gentleman, and Tupman remains a bachelor. Bob Sawyer and Ben Allen head off to India as surgeons. Jingle and Job Trotter reform and find success in the West Indies. Tony Weller retires, and after two years, Sam weds Mary. Both remain in service to Pickwick.

CHARACTERS

The Pickwick Papers contains a large cast of characters, both major and minor. This list includes only those who play an ongoing role in the narrative.

Arabella Allen

Arabella Allen, Ben Allen's pert and pretty sister, becomes Winkle's sweetheart and wife.

Ben Allen

Ben Allen, a young medical student, is Arabella Allen's loutish brother.

Mrs. Martha Bardell

Mrs. Martha Bardell is Pickwick's widowed landlady. She mistakenly assumes that he has proposed marriage to her, and much of the continuing action of the novel involves her lawsuit against Pickwick for breach of promise. She is later imprisoned for debt for failing to pay her lawyers, but Pickwick benevolently arranges for her release.

Serjeant Buzfuz

Serjeant Buzfuz is Mrs. Bardell's prosecuting barrister. He, along with Mrs. Bardell's solicitors, Dodson and Fogg, is part of the author's indictment of the legal profession.

Dodson and Fogg

Dodson and Fogg are Mrs. Bardell's unscrupulous solicitors.

Alfred Jingle

Alfred Jingle is a rascal and adventurer with a gift for imposture who devises schemes to make a mercenary marriage, which Pickwick tries to thwart. At one point, he tries to elope with Rachael Wardle, but Mr. Wardle buys him off. Near the end of the novel, he is sentenced to Fleet Prison, where Pickwick takes pity on him, gives him money, and rehabilitates him. Jingle is a foil to Pickwick: As Jingle is street smart and conniving, Pickwick is innocent and naive. Jingle is immediately recognizable in the book for his staccato way of speaking.

Joe the Fat Boy

Joe the Fat Boy is Mr. Wardle's gluttonous, sleepy servant.

Mary

Mary is Sam Weller's sweetheart and eventual wife.

Mr. Perker

Perker is Pickwick's attorney.

Samuel Pickwick

Samuel Pickwick is the founder of the Pickwick Club and the protagonist of the novel. He is portly, bald, elderly, innocent, generous, and benevolent, though naive as well. Unaware of deception, he lives in a spiritual Eden, leading to misadventures. He undergoes a moral education, yet he remains benevolent and a man of goodwill, even to the extent of giving money to the imprisoned Alfred Jingle and rehabilitating him. The principal ongoing action in which he is involved is the lawsuit filed against him by his landlady, Mrs. Bardell, for breach of promise to marry her. Near the end of the novel, he is imprisoned in the Fleet debtor's prison because he refuses to pay damages to Mrs. Bardell. He is released from prison when Mrs. Bardell promises to forgive his debt to her if he will pay the lawyers' fees she is unable to pay, which led to her own imprisonment for debt.

Bob Sawyer

Bob Sawyer is a medical student and prankster who wants to marry Arabella Allen. Eventually, with the help of Pickwick, he and his friend, Ben Allen, find success in India as surgeons.

Dr. Slammer

Dr. Slammer is an army man who challenges Winkle to a duel at Rochester based on mistaken identity.

Augustus Snodgrass

Augustus Snodgrass, a young man, takes on the role of the Pickwick Club's poet, although he never writes poetry. He eventually marries Emily Wardle and becomes a country gentleman.

Serjeant Snubbin

Serjeant Snubbin is Pickwick's absent-minded, ineffective courtroom attorney.

Reverend Stiggins

The Reverend Stiggins is Mrs. Weller's avaricious, alcoholic, evangelist minister. He is clearly an object of satire and part of the author's indictment of evangelical religion that emphasizes doctrine over charity and simple human kindness.

Job Trotter

Job Trotter is a wily actor Alfred Jingle employs as a servant.

Mr. Trundle

Mr. Trundle is Isabella Wardle's fiancé and then husband.

Tracy Tupman

Tracy Tupman is portly and middle-aged, and he adopts the role of the Pickwick Club's romantic adventurer, although he is never quite successful. Ironically, he remains a bachelor to the end of the novel. He carries on a flirtation with Rachael Wardle.

Emily Wardle

Emily Wardle is Mr. Wardle's pretty daughter and Snodgrass's sweetheart. Eventually they marry.

Isabella Wardle

Isabella Wardle is Mr. Wardle's pretty daughter who marries Mr. Trundle during the Christmas festivities.

Mr. Wardle

Mr. Wardle is a benevolent country squire at Dingley Dell who entertains the Pickwickians at Manor Farm.

Rachael Wardle

Rachael Wardle is Mr. Wardle's spinster sister who tries to elope with Jingle. The pair are caught, however, and Mr. Wardle buys off Jingle.

Sam Weller

Sam Weller is a clever, shrewd Cockney boot cleaner who becomes Pickwick's servant and, eventually, his closest friend. He is in many respects a foil to Pickwick. After Weller's introduction, sales of the novel, which was serially published, increased, and Weller remains one of the author's most popular characters. The term "Wellerism" is often used to refer to his words of wisdom. Weller is so loyal to Pickwick that he arranges to have himself arrested and imprisoned so that he can be with his master in Fleet Prison. At the end of the novel, he marries Mary, a servant girl, and the two remain in service to Mr. Pickwick.

Tony Weller

Tony Weller, a coachman with marital troubles, is Sam Weller's kindly but irresponsible father. In some ways, he resembles Mr. Pickwick, who is a father figure to Sam Weller. But just as Pickwick is optimistic and straightforward, Tony Weller is sardonic and cynical.

Nathaniel Winkle

Nathaniel Winkle is supposedly the sporting member of the Pickwick Club, but his sporting efforts are consistently inept. Winkle has a flair for misadventures. He eventually marries Arabella Allen. Initially, his father is opposed to the marriage, but eventually Winkle obtains his father's consent.

THEMES

Nostalgia

The Pickwick Papers was written at a time when England was undergoing significant changes. The Industrial Revolution was under way, people were flocking to the cities, and old ways of life in the countryside were passing. The age of the steam engine was beginning, and many Britons looked back to a former time when people held to older customs and traditions; traveled in coaches and stayed at comfortable, hospitable roadside inns; and, in particular, knew and accepted their place in a stable social order, one that linked the past with the future. The novel, then, depicts a way of life that was passing, the "good old days" that were times of stability in contrast to the disruptions and uncertainties of modern life. A good example of the nostalgia that pervades the novel can be found in chapter 28:

> We write these words now, many miles distant from the spot at which, year after year, we met on that day, a merry and joyous circle. Many of the hearts that throbbed so gaily then, have ceased to beat; many of the looks that shone so brightly then, have ceased to glow.

In thinking about Christmas, the narrative voice goes on:

> The most minute and trivial circumstance connected with those happy meetings, crowd upon our mind at each recurrence of the season. . . . Happy, happy Christmas, that can win us back to the delusions of our childish days.

Passages such as these are undoubtedly sentimental, but this sentimentalism was one of the appeals Dickens held for his readers.

TOPICS FOR FURTHER STUDY

- Conduct research into parliamentary elections in England, both today and in the nineteenth century. When were elections held? Why? Who typically might have run for a seat in Parliament? What kind of backing might a candidate have had? Was it commonplace to bribe voters with drink and other favors? Present your findings in a written report.

- Using a tool such as UMapper.com, trace the route of the Pickwickians on their journey. Share your map with your classmates.

- One of Mr. Pickwick's tribulations is his trial for breach of promise (to marry). Investigate courtship and marriage customs in Victorian England. Was it realistic for Dickens to depict a lawsuit for Pickwick's "breach of promise"? What sorts of courtship and engagement rituals were common, and did those rituals differ depending on social class? Present the results of your findings in an oral report to your class.

- *The Pickwick Papers* was a nostalgic work for its nineteenth-century readers because it is set in a time before railroad travel became commonplace, so the characters travel in more leisurely style by horse-drawn carriages and stagecoaches. Locate images of the earliest trains in England, as well as of the kinds of unmotorized conveyances in which people traveled. Also include images of typical coaching inns at which people stopped. Share your images with your classmates using a tool such as Picasa.com, Blogspot.com, or Flickr.

- A modern classic with a journey motif, one that has been enjoyed by young adults, is Richard Adams's *Watership Down*. The novel tells the tale of a group of rabbits that, facing the destruction of their warren in Sandleford, England, travel to Watership Down, the name of a hill in Hampshire, England. Along the way, they encounter dangers, but Hazel, the group's quiet leader, wins the loyalty and respect of the group, while Fiver, a "runt," displays the wisdom of a Sam Weller. Read the novel, then prepare a chart specifying similarities and differences between it and *The Pickwick Papers* along a dimension that you choose: leadership, danger, duplicity, the quest, or any other element.

- Another travel narrative that has become a modern classic is *Blue Highways: A Journey into America* by William Least Heat-Moon. The narrative describes the author's three-month soul-searching tour throughout the United States, sticking to smaller back roads (drawn in blue in old atlases). After reading *Blue Highways*, prepare an essay in which you compare how Heat-Moon and Dickens present visions of their culture and society.

Evangelicalism

Dickens had little use for evangelical religion, particularly when he believed that evangelical preachers were duping their congregants for their own worldly ends and when their focus was on the hellfires of damnation rather than peace, justice, and genuine charity. Throughout his novels, he presents satirical portraits of these kinds of preachers. In *The Pickwick Papers*, he places his critique of evangelicalism in the mouth of Tony Weller, Sam's father, whose wife is in the clutches of such a preacher, Mr. Stiggins, whose red nose—a characteristic of which the reader is repeatedly reminded—indicates that he drinks heavily. Talking about the preacher to Sam, Tony says:

> The worst o' these here shepherds is, my boy, that they reg'larly turns the heads of all the young ladies, about here. Lord bless their little hearts, they thinks it's all right, and don't know no better; but they're the wictims o' gammon, Samivel, they're the wictims o' gammon.

1970s English postage stamp honoring Pickwick Papers *(© rook76 | Shutterstock.com)*

He goes on to say:

> ...and wot aggrawates me, Samivel, is to see 'em a wastin' all their time and labour in making clothes for copper-coloured people as don't want 'em, and taking no notice of flesh-coloured Christians as do. If I'd my vay, Samivel, I'd just stick some o' these here lazy shepherds behind a heavy wheelbarrow, and run 'em up and down a fourteen inch-wide plank all day.

This passage also expresses Dickens's impatience with evangelical do-goodism that overlooked poverty at home in England and instead focused on the ills of faraway countries.

Legal System

Dickens had little respect for the legal profession, perhaps in part because of the imprisonment of his father for debt. Throughout his novels, he depicts most lawyers as venal, deceptive, and fraudulent. In *The Pickwick Papers*, the law firm of Dodson and Fogg, who represent Mrs. Bardell in her lawsuit against Pickwick for breach of promise, is no exception. The reader knows that Pickwick is innocent of having deceived or misled Mrs. Bardell, yet her lawyers refuse to compromise. Dickens perhaps expresses his own view of the duplicity of the legal profession when he has Pickwick give Dodson and Fogg a piece of his mind, saying to them, "I said, sir, that of all the disgraceful and rascally proceedings that ever were attempted, this is the most so. I repeat it, sir." The injustice of the legal system is then emphasized by Pickwick's imprisonment in the Fleet debtor's prison and his observations of the other inmates.

STYLE

Picaresque Novel

The Pickwick Papers is not a tightly plotted novel. Rather, it is episodic as the Pickwickians travel about to various locations in the country. The plotline involving Mrs. Bardell and her action for breach of promise ties together portions of the novel, and the appearance and reappearance of Mr. Jingle lend continuity. Otherwise, the novel adopts some of the conventions of the picaresque novel, which originated in Spain with a sixteenth-century work by an unknown author titled *The Life of Lazarillo de Tormes and of His Fortunes and Adversities* (1554). At the heart of the picaresque novel is the *picaro* (feminine form: *picara*), a usually lowborn or roguish character who narrates his story as he moves about from place to place in an effort to survive in differing social circumstances. By the eighteenth century, the picaresque novel had begun to decline in popularity as novelists were placing more emphasis on elaborate plots and character development, but some of the characteristics of this type of fiction survived, and Dickens's earliest reading would have included novels by Henry Fielding, Tobias Smollett, and Daniel Defoe that employed the conventions of the picaresque form. In *The Pickwick Papers*, Samuel Pickwick is not the narrator, he is not lowborn, and he is anything but a rogue. Nevertheless, he and his band of Pickwickians travel about, encountering adventures and people from various classes and social milieus, usually with great comic effect. These encounters allow the author to comment satirically on rogues and imposters in a way that does not require him to construct a tight plot.

Satire

Portions of *The Pickwick Papers* are highly satirical (although many portions, such as the events surrounding the Christmas celebration at Dingley Dell, are not). Satire in literature is the use of humor, exaggeration, or ridicule to highlight people's foibles, follies, abuses, shortcomings, or stupidity. In chapter 13, Dickens presents a highly satirical depiction of a parliamentary election at the borough of Eatanswill, a name that echoes the words "eating," or "eatin'," and "swill," or pig food consisting of scraps. In describing the election contest, Dickens maintains a flow of facetious and deliberately overblown language; for example:

> It appears, then that the Eatanswill people, like the people of many other small towns, considered themselves of the utmost and most mighty importance, and that every man in Eatanswill, conscious of the weight that attached to his example, felt himself bound to unite, heart and soul, with one of the two great parties that divided the town.

The narration goes on to describe the Blues and the Buffs, the two parties that are bent on obstructing and vilifying each other in any way they can, often through the incendiary language used in the town's two newspapers, one representing the Blues and the other the Buffs. The election is corrupted because of bribery. Mr. Perker, the agent for one of the candidates, describes electioneering practices to Mr. Pickwick: "We have opened all the public-houses in the place, and left our adversary nothing but the beer-shops—masterly stroke of policy that, my dear sir, eh?" Later, Mr. Pickwick's servant, Sam Weller, tells his employer that one of the parties has bribed the barmaid at one of the public houses to "hocus the brandy and water of fourteen unpolled electors as was a stoppin' in the house." When Mr. Pickwick asks for clarification, Weller explains that "hocusing" means adding laudanum—an opiate drug—to the brandy, putting the voters to sleep so that they could not cast their votes. This kind of satire is indicative of the author's dissatisfaction with some of the social and political institutions of early Victorian England.

Narrator as Editor

The narrator of a work of fiction can be either one of the characters or a third person—a narrative voice—who may or may not allow himself access to the thoughts of the characters. In *The Pickwick Papers*, Dickens adopts narrative conventions that were popular at the time but became less popular in later fiction. One of these conventions is the pretense that the narrative voice has investigated and is reporting on the activities of the characters. This pretense is established in the novel's very first paragraph, where the narrative voice calls himself "the editor of these papers" and goes on to say that he is laying them before his readers "as a proof of the careful attention, indefatigable assiduity, and nice discrimination, with which his search among the multifarious documents confided to him has been conducted." The hyperbolic language, too, establishes a tone of comic facetiousness that pervades the novel.

Interpolated Tales

Another narrative convention used in *The Pickwick Papers* is that of the interpolated story. As the Pickwickians travel about, they encounter curious characters and documents. From time to time, the narration is turned over to one of these characters, or the document is reproduced. These interpolated stories include "The Stroller's Tale" (chapter 3), "The Convict's Return" (chapter 6), "A Madman's Manuscript" (chapter 11), "The Bagman's Story" (chapter 14), "The Parish Clerk—A Tale of True Love" (chapter 17), "The Old Man's Tale about the Queer Client" (chapter 21), "The Story of the Goblins Who Stole a Sexton" (chapter 29), "The True Legend of Prince Bladud" (chapter 36), and "The Story of the Bagman's Uncle" (chapter 49). The interpolated tales are generally dark, gloomy, ghostly, or violent, placing them in sharp contrast to the sunniness and good humor of the main narrative. The suggestion is that beneath the humor and lightness of the world inhabited by the naive and unworldly Pickwick lies a darker realm of madness, murder, and mayhem.

HISTORICAL CONTEXT

The Pickwick Papers was published at the very beginning of the Victorian era; chapters 40–42 would have been released about ten days after Queen Victoria assumed the throne on June 20, 1837. Victoria remained on the throne for nearly sixty-four years, the longest reign in British

COMPARE & CONTRAST

- **1830s:** Although the first railroads were built in England in the early 1800s, most people continue to travel by horse-drawn carriages and stagecoaches.

  Today: Great Britain's National Rail network is considering plans for high-speed trains that could make the journey from London to Birmingham—about 120 miles—in less than fifty minutes.

- **1830s:** Under English common law, a man may be successfully sued and required to pay damages for failing to fulfill a promise to marry.

  Today: Under the Matrimonial Proceedings and Property Act of 1970, English laws pertaining to breach of promise have been abolished and replaced by laws that apply strictly to property disputes between the parties.

- **1830s:** At the start of the decade, the number of eligible voters in England is small, about 4,500 men in a population of 2.6 million. Some large cities have no members of Parliament, while "rotten boroughs" (depopulated or unpopulated districts) do.

  Today: All men and women age eighteen and older are eligible to vote in British general elections in England, each of 533 constituencies is represented by a member in Parliament.

history. The age to which she gave her name was one of peace, industrial and population growth, the expansion of the British Empire, and relative prosperity, although beneath the veneer of prosperity was crushing poverty in the nation's cities and mining towns and the extensive exploitation of child labor, as reflected by Dickens's experience working in a shoe-blacking factory at age twelve.

Some historians mark the beginning of the Victorian era five years earlier, in 1832, when the first electoral reform bill was passed in England, a reform that in time would change English society. The issue of electoral reform is relevant to *The Pickwick Papers* because, in chapter 13, Dickens gives a highly satirical account of a corrupt election in the pocket borough of Eatanswill and of the contending Blue and Buff (Whig and Tory) political parties. During the 1830s, the issue of parliamentary reform was very much on the front burner in England. In the late eighteenth and early nineteenth centuries, very few people in England had the right to vote. In 1831, on the eve of reform, less than 1 percent of the nation's population was eligible to vote for parliamentary representatives. Further, representation throughout England was highly unequal. Such large cities as Manchester, Birmingham, and Leeds had no members in Parliament, but members were sent to Parliament from a scandalously large number of "rotten" and "pocket" boroughs. Rotten boroughs were districts with very small populations, usually because the population had declined; a pocket borough was one that was in the "pocket" of a single rich or powerful landowner who could dictate to voters the outcome of a parliamentary election.

In the late eighteenth century, pressures for reform grew, primarily from manufacturers and country landowners who believed that their interests were not represented under the current system. After the French Revolution, which began in 1789, radical reformers in England were calling for universal suffrage—the right of every man to vote. (Note that women were not included in their demands.) Such organizations as the Sheffield Corresponding Society and the London Corresponding Society amped up pressure on the government to extend the franchise. In 1819, the authorities fired on a crowd attending a political meeting at St. Peter's Field in Manchester, killing eleven. This event, referred to as the

Members of the Pickwick Club travel and make reports back on their adventures. *(© Kisialiou Yury /*
Shutterstock.com)

Peterloo Massacre, led to a series of repressive laws against agitators, but it contributed to a climate of anxiety on the part of the government that revolution could erupt in England.

In this environment, the British prime minister, Lord Charles Grey, backed a reform bill that passed in 1832. Called the Great Reform Act, the law extended voting rights to all men who occupied property with a value of at least £10. While £10 does not sound like very much, in 1830, £10 was roughly equivalent to more than £11,000 (about $17,500) today as a per capita share of the nation's income and more than £30,000 (about $47,900) as a share of the nation's gross domestic product. Accordingly, the Great Reform Act was quite moderate, extending the franchise to about one in seven men—but for moderates, it was a step in the right direction. The Great Reform Act would be followed by later bills extending the franchise. A second reform act was passed late in Dickens's life, in 1867; at that time, about two of five men were eligible to vote. A third reform act, passed in 1884, extended the franchise to all male house owners and added about six million men to the voting roles. It was not until 1928 that universal adult suffrage—for men and women—became a reality in England. These reform bills, however, contributed to a cultural ethos in Britain based on a belief in the nation's stability and continuity—in contrast to the violent revolution that had rocked a country such as France.

CRITICAL OVERVIEW

Contemporary critics and reviewers were not initially enthusiastic about *The Pickwick Papers.* Kathryn Chittick, in *Dickens and the 1830s,* notes that reviewers tended to regard the novel as little more than a sketchbook and gave it scant attention. Chittick quotes some of these notices, many of them just a line or two. *The Times* wrote that *Pickwick* was "distinguished by much humour rich and genuine, though somewhat coarse and uncultivated." *The Sun* characterized the book merely as "tales and sketches of characters," as "amusing periodical sketches," and as "sketches of low life."

Nevertheless, it is difficult to overstate the popularity of *The Pickwick Papers* with readers when it was first published—and after. Paul Davis, in *Critical Companion to Charles Dickens*, notes that just a thousand copies of the first part were printed, but that number swelled to nearly forty thousand by the end of the novel's run. Davis quotes Philip Collins, the editor of *Dickens: The Critical Heritage*, who termed *The Pickwick Papers* a "cult novel." In Louisa May Alcott's *Little Women* (1868–1869), the four March daughters, admirers of Dickens, called themselves the Pickwick Club, a suggestion of the novel's continuing popularity.

The popularity of the novel persisted into the twentieth century with such distinguished critics as G. K. Chesterton and W. H. Auden. Chesterton, in a 1906 essay on the novel, "*The Pickwick Papers*," writes that

> *Pickwick*, indeed, is not a good novel; but it is not a bad novel, for it is not a novel at all. In one sense, indeed, it is something nobler than a novel, for no novel with a plot and a proper termination could emit that sense of everlasting youth—a sense as of the gods gone wandering in England.

Later in the essay, Chesterton writes, "*Pickwick* is supremely original in that it is the adventures of an old man. It is a fairy tale. . . . The result is both noble and new and true."

In a seminal essay first published in 1962, "Dingley Dell & the Fleet," Auden speculated on why the novel held little appeal for him as a child and much more as an adult:

> The conclusion I have come to is that the real theme of *Pickwick Papers* . . . is the Fall of Man. It is the story of a man who is innocent, that is to say, who has not eaten of the Tree of the Knowledge of Good and Evil and is, therefore, living in Eden.

Auden goes on:

> He then eats of the Tree, that is to say, he becomes conscious of the reality of Evil but, instead of falling from innocence into sin . . . he changes from an innocent child into an innocent adult who no longer lives in an imaginary Eden of his own but in the real and fallen world.

Modern critics have also tried to account for the fascination that *Pickwick* continues to hold. In "Language into Structure: Pickwick Revisited," for example, Steven Marcus discusses the spontaneity with which the novel was written and concludes, "What we have, in short, is something rather new

and spectacular." He calls the novel a "breakthrough" and states that, in creating the novel, Dickens was "regularly spontaneous and self-generatingly creative on demand" as he faced the pressure of writing a new part each month. Angus Wilson focused on characterization in Dickens in an article titled "The Heroes and Heroines of Dickens." Wilson comments that "Dickens never produced so satisfactory a hero as Mr. Pickwick" and that "no article on Dickens' heroes should fail to salute the perfection of Mr. Pickwick."

CRITICISM

Michael J. O'Neal

O'Neal holds a PhD in English. In the following essay, he examines parental roles in The Pickwick Papers.

The fiction of Charles Dickens is a gold mine for readers interested in the intersections between an author's biography and his literary output. In Dickens's case, it is apparent that aspects of his personality and background had a profound influence on his psychology and that psychology in many respects shaped his fiction.

The Dickens psychological narrative goes something like this: young Charles was a sensitive boy who was deeply affected by the events of his early life. His father's imprisonment for debt made him, in essence, an absentee father at a crucial time in his son's life. The Dickens family was under financial stress, forcing Charles to leave school and go to work in a shoe-blacking factory, where he was surrounded by coarse, vulgar boys with whom he had nothing in common—a demeaning experience for him. His mother, Elizabeth, seemed indifferent to her son's humiliation and even wanted him to return to work in the blacking factory after his father was released from prison. Meanwhile, he came to resent his sister, Fanny, who was allowed to continue to attend the Royal Academy of Music. Dickens's resentment of his mother persisted into his adulthood. She made frequent demands on him for money and shamed the author with her tendency to dress in an inappropriately girlish manner.

All of this motivated Dickens's desire to escape from his family and become a gentleman. It also, so the narrative goes, contributed to his view of women, principally a psychological need to see women as "angels in the house"—that is, as

WHAT DO I READ NEXT?

- One of Dickens's most popular novels is *A Tale of Two Cities* (1859), a drama of romance and sacrifice set against the menacing backdrop of the French Revolution and its Reign of Terror. The novel is available in numerous editions, including one published by Penguin Classics in 2003.

- Many critics see parallels between *The Pickwick Papers* and *Don Quixote* (1605/1615) by the Spanish author Miguel de Cervantes. In particular, the relationship between Cervantes's title character and his sidekick, Sancho Panza, is similar to that between Pickwick and his manservant, Sam Weller. The novel is available in numerous editions (and translations), including one published by Penguin Classics in 2003.

- Ann Selby's *The Victorian Christmas* (Remember When, 2008) discusses many of the Christmas practices of the Victorian period and how Dickens (along with Prince Albert, Queen Victoria's husband) essentially created British Christmas traditions that survive today through such works as *The Pickwick Papers, A Christmas Carol,* and various other sketches and stories.

- Young adults will enjoy a pair of Spanish picaresque novels published by Penguin in 2003. The novels are contained in the volume *Lazarillo de Tormes and The Swindler: Two Spanish Picaresque Novels.*

- Christopher Paul Curtis's young-adult novel *Bud, Not Buddy* (Laurel Leaf, 2004) is a contemporary picaresque / travel story that narrates the adventures of Bud ("not Buddy") Caldwell as he travels through Depression-era Michigan in search of his father and, like the Pickwickians, gets into scrapes along the way.

- Jerome K. Jerome's novel *Three Men in a Boat* (Penguin Classics, 2004) has remained immensely popular with readers of all ages since it was first published in 1889. The novel narrates the misadventures of three men, accompanied by a dog named Montmorency, on a hilarious boat trip from London to Oxford.

- Perhaps one of the most loved American travel books is Mark Twain's memoir *Life on the Mississippi* (1883). Twain used his travel experiences as a steamboat pilot on the Mississippi River to, like Dickens, comment on greed, duplicity, and the changes taking place in his world. The book is available in a 2009 Library of America edition.

---

feminine, docile, delicate, and good homemakers and mothers. His marriage to Catherine Hogarth was doomed because she failed in his estimation to live up to his Victorian ideal of womanhood: he regarded her as a negligent mother and, particularly after giving birth to ten children, as somewhat dowdy and fat, though it is likely no woman could have met Dickens's impossible standards. It was little wonder that the marriage collapsed after he met a young actress named Ellen Ternan in 1857. Dickens took part in amateur theatricals, including productions of a play titled *The Frozen Deep* in which Ellen symbolically died in his arms onstage every night.

Out of this stew of psychological impulses came at least two prominent features in Dickens's work. One is the depiction of women. Critics generally agree that for all his genius, Dickens was not particularly successful in depicting women, although by the time he reached his last completed novel, *Our Mutual Friend*, he had managed to depict two convincing female characters, Bella Wilfer and Lizzie Hexam, who are more or less normal. In most of his fiction, women fall into one of two types: either they are the docile, delicate, domestic creatures of his imagination (Esther Summerson in *Bleak House*, Lucie Manette in *A Tale of Two Cities*, Agnes Wickfield in *David Copperfield*,

> IN DICKENS'S CASE, IT IS APPARENT THAT ASPECTS OF HIS PERSONALITY AND BACKGROUND HAD A PROFOUND INFLUENCE ON HIS PSYCHOLOGY AND THAT PSYCHOLOGY IN MANY RESPECTS SHAPED HIS FICTION."

Amy Dorrit in *Little Dorrit*) or they are fairy tale witches and shrews (Miss Havisham in *Great Expectations*, Mrs. Skewton in *Dombey and Son*, Madame Defarge in *A Tale of Two Cities*). Sometimes he consigns his mothers and mother figures to horrible deaths, like Miss Havisham in *Great Expectations*. His most sympathetic women are mother figures who are not biological mothers, such as Betsy Trotwood in *David Copperfield* and Mrs. Boffin in *Our Mutual Friend*.

The other feature is a succession of surrogate father types, represented by Mr. Brownlow in *Oliver Twist* and John Jarndyce in *Bleak House*. In *Little Dorrit*, Amy Dorrit marries Arthur Clennam, who is much older and treats her in many ways as a protective and benevolent father would treat a child. These and other men are usually (but not always) aging, unmarried, benevolent, and wealthy, though rarely is the source of this wealth specified—and never is any attention given to the rough-and-tumble world of commerce by which wealth might be earned and accumulated. These men are always just "there," *sui generis*, in a way that Dickens's father was not, at least in the young boy's imagination.

Readers can begin to see these psychological impulses being played out in *The Pickwick Papers*. At the center of the novel is Samuel Pickwick, the first in a long line of elderly bachelor or widowed men who assume the role of a father figure to the surrounding characters. It is noteworthy that all of the other Pickwickians are considerably younger than Pickwick. Throughout the novel, he treats them as would a kindly father, one who often has to get them out of scrapes. At times he becomes angry with them when they fail to live up to his expectations of gentlemanly behavior. He functions as a father figure to Sam Weller. Sam has a father, Tony, who, in many respects, is an inverse mirror image of Pickwick; like

Pickwick, he is aging and overweight, but the two men, in many regards, share similar values. In the end, Pickwick is a generous father who rehabilitates Jingle and Trotter, presides over the marriages of the younger characters, and ultimately acquires a large number of godchildren while continuing to function as a kind of father to Sam and his wife, Mary. According to the narrative of Dickens's life, Pickwick—and to some extent, Mr. Wardle—is the father the author never really felt he had.

Mothers and wives, though, often receive very different treatment in Dickens's fiction, and *The Pickwick Papers* is no exception. The novel, by definition, focuses on a group of unmarried men, so women do not play as important a role in this novel as they do in some of the author's later novels, yet readers can see Dickens's incipient attitudes. First, the novel contains essentially no mothers. Among the women characters are two types. The younger women—the Wardle sisters, Mary, and Arabella Allen—are all pert, pretty, and vivacious, but they are stereotypes, without any depth, and their primary role is the one they have in relation to the male characters who pursue them.

Among the older women the picture is not a very pretty one. The most sympathetic is old Mrs. Wardle, who, while beloved, is deaf and ineffectual. Rachael Wardle is made to be faintly ridiculous in running off with Alfred Jingle. Anticipating the author's later witches and shrews is Mrs. Weller, Tony's second wife and Sam's stepmother. Although, at the end of the novel, she does the right thing in bequeathing her money to her husband and stepson, in the meantime she falls under the influence of the duplicitous and gluttonous Reverend Stiggins, and her ongoing annoyance with Tony presents a picture of an unpleasant marriage. Mrs. Bardell is, at best, deluded and, at worst, conniving in her lawsuit against Pickwick for breach of promise. And numerous other minor characters, among them the wives of the newspaper editors in Eatanswill and Bob Sawyer's landlady, are not the type of women who would conform to Dickens's ideal of womanhood. Instead, they are often bitter and contentious.

What is the modern reader to make of these stereotypes, whether benign or malevolent? Do they diminish the reader's sense of Dickens's skill as a novelist? Ultimately, each reader has to decide the answers to these questions for him- or herself. All novelists depict a world that is the outgrowth of their experiences melded with imagination. That Dickens was damaged by the events of his early life can hardly be held against him. Dickens's defenders, while not able to defend the author's treatment of parental figures with a straight face, will point to other riches in his novels: his lively wit, his close observation, his keen dissection of social class, his passion for justice, his optimism, his flow of language that can alternately beguile, amuse, arouse, and move to tears. Perhaps without the stresses of his early life, Dickens would never have been impelled to translate his unique imaginative vision into the shelf of novels that generations of readers have loved.

Source: Michael J. O'Neal, Critical Essay on *The Pickwick Papers*, in *Novels for Students*, Gale, Cengage Learning, 2013.

Leslie Simon

In the following excerpt, Simon examines the themes of human interaction with the material world versus subjective consciousness in The Pickwick Papers.

We begin not where Dickens invites us to begin—that is, on page one of *The Pickwick Papers*, where a ray of light illumines fiction's gloom—but in the adventure stories of the eighteenth century that paved the way for Dickens's first novel. We begin with Lovelace declaring himself an emperor and Clarissa "his conquest"; we begin along Tom Jones's pilgrimage toward "home" and a sense of domestic stability. And we begin with travelers who defy the boundaries of fair Britannia: with Robinson Crusoe, whose original sin was in leaving home in the first place, and his appropriation of an island in a masterstroke of homemaking and empire-building; and Gulliver, whose travelogues relate a number of imaginative journeys into imperial recesses—ranging from make-believe Laputa to make-believe Japan.

Though what are considered the true fictions of empire are over a century in the making at this point—G. A. Henty's youthful exploratory parties have yet to tame the wilds of brutish South Africa, Rider Haggard's Holly and Leo are years from uncovering the erotic mysteries of Ayesha and the Amahaggar, and even Wilkie Collins's moonstone is yet safe and sound in the bosom of a Hindu moon shrine—the romances and travel writing of the eighteenth century prepare the way for Dickens's own tale of travel, exploration and movement toward some better

> " PICKWICK, WE FIND, IS SOMEHOW ALWAYS BLINDED JUST AT THE MOMENT OF OBSERVATION. WHETHER BY DUST OR BY HUMAN BODIES OR BY HIS OWN UNRULY HAT, THIS GREAT OBSERVER OF THINGS AND PEOPLE MANAGES TIME AND TIME AGAIN *NOT* TO SEE."

understanding of what it means to be "at home." Amidst their excursions, pursuits, human and archival discoveries, and persistent use of imperial rhetoric and imaging, these novels introduce what will be the nineteenth-century fetishization of home and its other. As G. K. Chesterton has said of Pickwick, "He has set out walking to the end of the world, but he knows he will find an inn there" (67). In other words, traveling away from home ultimately leads back to it, whether necessitating or being in and of itself a return.

In the final chapter of Dickens's inaugural novel, *The Pickwick Papers*, the ironically (though endearingly) distinguished Samuel Pickwick abandons the "pursuit of novelty" that has inspired his recent peregrinations across the provincial landscapes of England and into the spiraling, fog-smothered cityscape of London, for the comforts of middle-class domesticity (871–72; ch. 57). Until his naïve queries and unwitting intrusions lead him to his final site of exploration, Fleet Prison, this bumbling bourgeois retiree commits himself to "enlarging his sphere of observation" by means of travel and discovery, proving tirelessly invested in his wanderings to "the advancement of knowledge, and the diffusion of learning" (2; ch. 2).

Indeed, the papers that we read are—in the style of the ostensibly biographical travel writing of the eighteenth century—records of Pickwick's movement across England and his collection of "discoveries worthy of being noted down" (8; ch. 2). What I would like to argue is that Mr. Pickwick's tale of exploration works very similarly to contemporary narratives of imperial adventure: though the geographical movement of the narrative subject takes the novel out and away from home, nominally exploring tracts of otherness and uncovering signs of difference, the story continuously and persistently moves *inward*, exploring the narrative subject himself and revealing much more about the explorer than the explored.

Just as fictions of empire travel into unknown territories to collect information supplemental to imperial understandings of human existence—largely, of course, only to reify pre-existing conditions of imperial normativity—Pickwick and his friends leave hearth and home for the purposes of exploratory travel, committed to their duty as pioneers of empirical wisdom and truth. The novel, however, quickly makes clear with such examples as the stone "of unquestionable antiquity" that the conclusions drawn from Pickwick's material discoveries are more often erroneous than not, and that meaning has been ascribed to these findings by subjective impressions rather than by objective analysis (158; ch. 11).

In fact, the novel operates structurally as an archive, revealing the discovery of scientific objects and literary manuscripts alike, blurring the line between things that record objective and those that record subjective histories, as Mr. Pickwick collects them all indiscriminately. The "facts" of the story—these fragments of the physical world that are presumed to provide a sense of fixed reality for Pickwick and his fellow travelers—are exposed as inconclusive signifiers more telling of modes of investigation than of those things being investigated. Imagination, memory and emotional experience as recorded in manuscript and reported to Pickwick through the intimate voices of subjective narration, on the other hand, gain significance as the novel continues, and indeed ultimately overtake material objects as determiners of human reality.

I suggest that, by demonstrating the tension between human engagement in an objective world of facts and materialities, and individualized journeys into subjective consciousness, *The Pickwick Papers* describes how explorations of reality must always begin with the personal, as the personal is inevitable, inescapable. In fact, I would go further to argue that experiential knowledge and reflection provide a more dependable reality than does anything labeled "empirical," simply by accounting for the mutable, unfixed quality of human life. As Edward Said has taught us that orientalism says much more about the orientalist than the so-called oriental, so we might also conclude that the discovery and fetishization of material things is more symptomatic of the cultural drive to discover and fetishize than of the things themselves.

So that the real object of observation in this novel is Mr. Pickwick, the subject and observer himself, as we travel with him into his own heart of darkness—or playfulness and lightness, as this case may be—and toward an awakening into selfhood and interior reflection.

Many scholars label this first of Dickens's novels as anything and everything but a novel. Perhaps they take their cue from Dickens whose 1867 preface to *The Pickwick Papers* notoriously expresses his desire that the novel's chapters had been "strung together on a stronger thread of general interest" (833; Appendix B). Despite his disavowal and critics' laudatory skepticism of the novel's narrative cohesion, I suggest that its very structure of miscellany and collection marks this a narrative of imperial discovery. The novel begins by promising to enlighten the world, "convert[ing] into a dazzling brilliancy that obscurity" that is the pages of British fiction, by shining its spotlight on Samuel Pickwick, just as Pickwick promises to shed light on truth and knowledge (1; ch. 1). The novel, it seems, has made a discovery and is going to reveal it to us—and that discovery is the story of a middle-aged, middle-class, middle-weight (or am I being to generous?), *over*-weight, middling sort of romantic adventurer, who, in his escapades across England, ultimately discovers—himself.

Over the course of his career, Dickens provides us with a number of collectors. From Mr. Venus who by trade collects carcasses and bones, to Krook who specializes in rags, bottles and documents of ranging importance; from Gradgrind who incites his students to cram their minds with facts, facts and more facts, to Chancery and the Circumlocution Office which both do their duty in collecting heaps and heaps of dust—these characters and institutions share a common forefather in narrative collection: Mr. Pickwick. Indeed, the principal Pickwickians in the novel are themselves a motley crew of individuals: the rusty romantic Tupman, the—shall we say—inexpert sportsman Winkle, the curiously-dubbed "poetic" Snodgrass. And, of course, Samuel Pickwick himself, the keeper of notebooks, which are, in turn, keepers of the "facts" unearthed by this always attentive, most times sightless, "observer of men and things" (20; ch. 2).

The novel's opening scene reveals a party of gentlemen congregated to lionize in unison their General Chairman—Mr. Pickwick—for his sensational breakthroughs in the world of science: namely, tracing "to their source the mighty ponds of Hampstead" and introducing his celebrated Theory of Tittlebats (5; ch. 1). The sensationalism of the discoveries, indeed, is well marked by the singular naysayer of the group, Mr. Blotton, who indicates his general skepticism of Pickwick by labeling the amateur explorer a "humbug"—and a humbug in the purest Pickwickian sense (6–7; ch. 1). Blotton's role throughout the novel is to offer doubtful commentary on Pickwick's scientific discoveries, and to serve (naturally) as a blot on the Chairman's impeccable reputation, on more than one occasion upsetting his fanfare by exposing weaknesses in Mr. Pickwick's theoretical conclusions.

However, in the moment, the novel allows this one layer of irony to be overshadowed by another, as Pickwick's observations on the current state of domestic travel provide a humorous comparison to the quite authentic dangers involved in sailing the high seas, as described by imperial adventure stories. He warns his three companions that travelling "was in a troubled state," that "the minds of coachmen were unsettled," that "horses were bolting" and overturning stagecoaches in all directions—that their journey, in short, would in all probability be a dangerous one (6; ch. 1). Spoken like a true hero, like a captain, perhaps, in Her Majesty's royal fleet.

Not that the three gentlemen are in any way to be discouraged, especially in the company of such leadership. Nay, they board their coach without more ado, at which time Pickwick cracks his notebook and immediately begins taking notes on the age and longevity of his coachman's horse, facts that are almost instantaneously converted into a Pickwickian theory on "the tenacity of life in horses" (9; ch. 2). And this theory is not to be left long alone on the blank pages of Pickwick's notebooks. He and his group collect information everywhere. They fill their pages with poems, descriptions of ruins and old castles, and even the details of city streets. As they pass through Stroud, Chatham, Brompton and Rochester, Pickwick compiles—in quintessentially Dickensian form—a list, the effect of which is to document the principal productions of these towns. Common to these localities are "soldiers, sailors, Jews, chalk, shrimps, officers, and dock-yard men" and such commodities as "hard-bake, apples, flat-fish, and oysters," all available in surrounding marine stores. Mr. Pickwick even finds a way to rationalize the dirt that characterizes these towns, concluding that those who view the consumption of

tobacco and smell pervading the streets "as an indication of traffic, and commercial prosperity," will find the atmosphere "truly gratifying" (20; ch. 2).

This preliminary note-jotting and fact-finding is a prelude to what proves the highlight of Pickwick's artifactual discoveries, made on his return from Dingley Dell while stopping over briefly in Cobham. Establishing Pickwick as "the envy of every antiquarian in this or any other country," the text boasts, his "immortal discovery" (156; ch. 11) of a stone fragment engraved illegibly with what Pickwick infers to be writing of ancient date leads to "ingenious and erudite speculations on the meaning of the inscription," including twenty-seven of Pickwick's own readings of the text across ninety-six pages of his original theory (167; ch. 11). When he first makes the discovery, happening upon the strange fragment while passing the door of a poor man's cottage, Mr. Pickwick behaves as any explorer of imperial treasure does: he commodifies the object, paying for it in cash; he further appropriates it by removing it from its natural environment and cleaning it with soap and water, thereby baptizing the object into its new life of spectacular display; and he fetishizes it by ascribing transcendental meaning to its muted material reality.

Once again, the ubiquitous Blotton surfaces, bent on tarnishing "the lustre of the immortal name of Pickwick" (168; ch. 11). Much to the dismay of Pickwick's admirers—who presume him to have uncovered a relic of man's past, and more specifically to have produced a trace of British social ancestry and linguistic history—Blotton makes the journey to Cobham himself. And there he learns, while meeting with the stone's merchandiser, that the inscription in fact bears the man's own name crudely spelt and crudely written—and bears, if anything else, testimony to his own near illiteracy and Pickwick's questionable perspicacity. Our clumsy explorer has read what he has wanted to read, and has unwittingly written this dull rock a romantic history to be consumed by antiquarians nationwide. "Bill Stumps, his mark" truly does stump poor Mr. Pickwick, and the mark most remembered is not the one left by Bill, but by Pickwick in his awkward voyage toward scientific truth. Readers are assured, however, that this insult to Pickwick's understanding is quickly *blotted out* by his supporters, who prefer—we can assume—to be entertained by adventure stories than to be disabused of them by "ignorant meddlers" like Blotton (169; ch. 11). This chapter of the novel ends by drawing the appropriate conclusion that "the stone remains an illegible monument of Pickwick's greatness," as it indeed is rather a signifier of his own pursuit of observation and discovery than of any quality the rock naturally possesses (169; ch. 11).

Very soon after, the Pickwickians travel to Eatanswill where the principal character's finding himself enmeshed in political warfare adequately (and *satirically*) demonstrates his powers of observation. Amidst the parade-like confusion of Buff and Blue marketeering, Pickwick—an innocent observer of the procession—has his

> hat knocked over his eyes, nose, and mouth, by one poke of a Buff flag staff, very early in the proceedings. He describes himself as being surrounded on every side, when he could catch a glimpse of the scene, by angry and ferocious countenances, by a vast cloud of dust, and by a dense crowd of combatants. He represents himself as being forced from the carriage by some unseen power, and being personally engaged in a pugilistic encounter; but with whom, or how, or why, he is wholly unable to state. (191; ch. 13)

Pickwick, we find, is somehow always blinded just at the moment of observation. Whether by dust or by human bodies or by his own unruly hat, this great observer of things and people manages time and time again *not* to see.

At the beginning of this same chapter, the editors of these papers even denote themselves inheritors of an archival conundrum, unable to make Pickwick's records cohere with their own as they search for the fictitious Eatanswill on certified British maps: "Knowing the deep reliance to be placed on every note and statement of Mr. Pickwick's," they claim, "and not presuming to set up our recollection against the recorded declarations of that great man, we have consulted every authority, bearing on the subject, to which we could possibly refer" (177; ch. 13). And still, we find, record is set against record, and recorded truth is demonstrated as something not always so easily determined. The material reality of Pickwick's observations does not account for the material reality of Eatanswill's absence on the British map, and the editors finally—throwing up their hands—conclude that the town in Pickwick's notebooks is "a fictitious designation" substituted for another (178; ch. 13).

And we finally—throwing our hands in the air as well—conclude that Dickens is quite overtly offering his readers an example of how material reality is often too blindly consumed (Eat-and-

swill, you know). Students of empire for decades past have maintained that literature of imperial discovery operates similarly to imperial discovery itself, which often fictionalizes the meaning of the discovered according to imperial projects of self-aggrandizement. The discovered, in the hands of the discoverer, becomes no longer just a "thing," as Elaine Freedgood would claim, but a commodity—something, even if it be only an idea, available to consumers for literal or ideological purchase. This, the novel informs us, is how material is so often manipulated into reality and ascribed a history not intrinsic to its originary construction. Things willfully misread become cornerstones in history, and that great tome of supposed realities sets into motion a system of enforced normativities—creating, perhaps, what the novel refers to humorously as "legal fiction" (623; ch. 40). The archives that are "The Pickwick Papers" shed light on the history of Pickwick and his critical discoveries, and Mr. Pickwick, moreover, bears a light of his own—a lantern, in fact, whose beam awakens further erroneous theorizing in scientific gentlemen similarly inclined to gaze "abstractedly on the thick darkness" of the world, in search of invention (612; ch. 39). In much the same way, the General Chairman of the Pickwickians in his official capacity as truth-teller carries on the tradition (the torch, we might say) of legalizing fiction so satirically reckoned with in the novel....

Source: Leslie Simon, "Archives of the Interior: Exhibitions of Domesticity in *The Pickwick Papers*," in *Dickens Quarterly*, Vol. 25, No. 1, March 2008, pp. 23–36.

T. H. Lister

In the following essay, Lister offers a critique of all aspects of Dickens's The Pickwick Papers *at the time of its publication.*

Mr. Charles Dickens, the author of *Sketches by Boz, The Pickwick Papers, The Life and Adventures of Nicholas Nickleby,* and *Oliver Twist,* is the most popular writer of his day. Since the publication of the poems and novels of Sir Walter Scott, there has been no work the circulation of which has approached that of the *Pickwick Papers....* They seem, at first sight, to be among the most evanescent of the literary *ephemerae* of their day— mere humorous specimens of the lightest kind of light reading, expressly calculated to be much sought and soon forgotten—...'good nonsense,'—and nothing more. This is the view which many persons will take of Mr Dickens's writings—but this is not our deliberate view of them. We think him a very original writer—well entitled to his popularity—and not likely to lose it—and the truest and most spirited delineator of English life, amongst the middle and lower classes, since the days of Smollett and Fielding. He has remarkable powers of observation, and great skill in communicating what he has observed—a keen sense of the ludicrous—exuberant humour—and that mastery in the pathetic which, though it seems opposed to the gift of humour, is often found in conjunction with it. And to these qualities, an unaffected style, fluent, easy, spirited, and terse—a good deal of dramatic power—and great truthfulness and ability in description. We know no other English writer to whom he bears a marked resemblance. He sometimes imitates other writers, such as Fielding in his introductions, and Washington Irving in his detached tales, and thus exhibits his skill as a parodist. But his own manner is very distinct—and comparison with any other would not serve to illustrate and describe it. We would compare him rather with the painter Hogarth. What Hogarth was in painting, such very nearly is Mr Dickens in prose fiction. The same turn of mind—the same species of power displays itself strongly in each. Like Hogarth he takes a keen and practical view of life—is an able satirist—very successful in depicting the ludicrous side of human nature, and rendering its follies more apparent by humorous exaggeration—peculiarly skilful in his management of details, throwing in circumstances which serve not only to complete the picture before us, but to suggest indirectly antecedent events which cannot be brought before our eyes. Hogarth's cobweb over the poor-box, and the plan for paying off the national debt, hanging from the pocket of a prisoner in the Fleet, are strokes of satire very similar to some in the writings of Mr Dickens. It is fair, in making this comparison, to add, that it does not hold good throughout; and that Mr. Dickens is exempt from two of Hogarth's least agreeable qualities—his cynicism and his coarseness. There is no misanthropy in his satire, and no coarseness in his descriptions—a merit enhanced by the nature of his subjects. His works are chiefly pictures of humble life—frequently of the humblest. The reader is led through scenes of poverty and crime, and all the characters are made to discourse in the appropriate language of their respective classes—and yet we recollect no passage which ought to cause pain to the most sensitive delicacy, if read aloud in female society.

> THE *PICKWICK PAPERS* ARE, AS THE AUTHOR ADMITS IN HIS PREFACE, DEFECTIVE IN PLAN, AND WANT THROUGHOUT THAT POWERFUL AID WHICH FICTION DERIVES FROM AN INTERESTING AND WELL CONSTRUCTED PLOT."

We have said that his satire was not misanthropic. This is eminently true. One of the qualities we the most admire in him is his comprehensive spirit of humanity. The tendency of his writings is to make us practically benevolent—to excite our sympathy in behalf of the aggrieved and suffering in all classes; and especially in those who are most removed from observation.... His humanity is plain, practical, and manly. It is quite untainted with sentimentality. There is no mawkish wailing for ideal distresses—no morbid exaggeration of the evils incident to our lot—no disposition to excite unavailing discontent, or to turn our attention from remediable grievances to those which do not admit a remedy. Though he appeals much to our feelings, we can detect no instance in which he has employed the verbiage of spurious philanthropy.

He is equally exempt from the meretricious cant of spurious philosophy. He never endeavours to mislead our sympathies—to pervert plain notions of right and wrong—to make vice interesting in our eyes—and shake our confidence in those whose conduct is irreproachable, by dwelling on the hollowness of seeming virtue. His vicious characters are just what experience shows the average to be; and what the natural operation of those circumstances to which they have been exposed would lead us to expect. We are made to feel both what they are, and *why* they are what we find them. We find no monsters of unmitigated and unredeemable villany.... (pp. 75–8)

Good feeling and sound sense are shown in his application of ridicule. It is never levelled at poverty or misfortune; or at circumstances which can be rendered ludicrous only by their deviation from artificial forms; or by regarding them through the medium of a conventional standard. Residence in the regions of Bloomsbury, ill-dressed dinners, and ill-made liveries, are crimes which he suffers to go unlashed; but follies or abuses, such as would be admitted alike in every sphere of society to be fit objects for his satire, are hit with remarkable vigour and precision. Nor does he confine himself to such as are obvious; but elicits and illustrates absurdities, which, though at once acknowledged when displayed, are plausible, and comparatively unobserved. (p. 78)

The whole story of the action against Pickwick for breach of promise of marriage, from its ludicrous origin, to Pickwick's eventual release from prison, where he had been immured for refusal to pay the damages, is one of the most acute and pointed satires upon the state and administration of English law that ever appeared in the light and lively dress of fiction. The account of the trial is particularly good.... (p. 80)

The imprisonment of Pickwick affords an opportunity of depicting the interior of a debtor's prison, and the manifold evils of that system, towards the abolition of which much, we trust, will have been effected by a statute of the past session. The picture is excellent, both in intention and execution, and as it bears strongly an air of truth, it is necessarily a painful one. (p. 82)

Mr Dickens is very successful as a delineator of those manners, habits, and peculiarities which are illustrative of particular classes and callings. He exhibits amusingly the peculiar turn of thought which belongs to each; and, as if he had been admitted behind the scenes, brings to light those artifices which members of a fraternity are careful to conceal from the world at large. (p. 84)

Mr Dickens's characters are sketched with a spirit and distinctness which rarely fail to convey immediately a clear impression of the person intended. They are, however, not complete and finished delineations, but rather outlines, very clearly and sharply traced, which the reader may fill up for himself; and they are calculated not so much to represent the actual truth as to suggest it. Analyses of disposition, and explanations of motives will not be found, and, we may add, will be little required. His plan is, not to describe his personages, but to make them speak and act,—and it is not easy to misunderstand them. These remarks are not applicable to *all* his characters. Some are too shadowy and undefined,—some not sufficiently true to nature; in some the representations consist of trails too trivial or too few; and some are spoiled by exaggeration and caricature. Pickwick's companions, Winkle, Snodgrass, and

Tupman, are very uninteresting personages,—having peculiarities rather than characters—useless incumbrances, which the author seems to have admitted hastily among his *dramatis personae* without well knowing what to do with them. The swindler Jingle and his companion want reality; and the former talks a disjointed jargon, to which some likeness may be found in farces, but certainly none in actual life. The young ladies in the *Pickwick Papers* are nonentities. The blustering Dowler, and the Master of the Ceremonies at Bath, are mere caricatures. The medical students are coarsely and disagreeably drawn. Wardle, though a tolerably good country squire, is hardly a modern one; and it may be doubted if Mr Weller, senior, can be accepted as the representative of any thing more recent than the last generation of stage-coachmen.

On the other hand, there are many characters truly excellent. First stand Pickwick and his man Weller,—the modern Quixote and Sancho of Cockaigne. Pickwick is a most amiable and eccentric combination of irritability, benevolence, simplicity, shrewdness, folly, and good sense—frequently ridiculous, but never contemptible, and always inspiring a certain degree of respect even when placed in the most ludicrous situations, playing the part of butt and dupe. Weller is a character which we do not remember to have seen attempted before. He is a favourite, yet, in many respects, faithful representative of the Londoner of humble life,—rich in native humour, full of the confidence, and address, and knowledge of the world, which is given by circumstances to a dweller in cities, combined with many of the most attractive qualities of the English character,—such as writers love to show in the brave, frank, honest, light-hearted sailor. His legal characters, Sergeant Snubbin, Perker, Dodson, Fogg, and Pell, are touched, though slightly, yet all with spirit, and a strong appearance of truth. Greater skill in drawing characters is shown in *Oliver Twist* and *Nicholas Nickleby*, than in *Pickwick*. His Ralph Nickleby, and Mrs Nickleby, deserve to be noticed as peculiarly successful.

But Mr Dickens's forte perhaps lies less in drawing characters than in describing incidents. He seizes with great skill those circumstances which are capable of being graphically set before us; and makes his passing scenes distinctly present to the reader's mind. Ludicrous circumstances are those which he touches most happily; of which the *Pickwick Papers* afford many examples; such as the equestrian distresses of Pickwick and his companions, the pursuit of Jingle, and Pickwick's night adventures in the boarding-school garden,—incidents richly comic and worthy of Smollett; and which are narrated with Smollett's spirit, without his coarseness. His descriptions of scenery are also good, though in a minor degree; and among these the aspect of the town is perhaps better delineated than that of the country, and scenes which are of an unattractive kind with more force and effect than those which are susceptible of poetical embellishment. (pp. 84–6)

The *Pickwick Papers* are, as the author admits in his preface, defective in plan, and want throughout that powerful aid which fiction derives from an interesting and well constructed plot. *Nicholas Nickleby* appears to be commenced with more attention to this important requisite in novel-writing; and if the author will relieve the painful sombreness of his scenes with a sufficient portion of sunshine, it will deserve to exceed the popularity of Pickwick. But *Oliver Twist*, a tale not yet completed, is calculated to give a more favourable impression of Mr Dickens's powers as a writer of fiction than any thing else which he has yet produced. There is more interest in the story, a plot better arranged, characters more skilfully and carefully drawn, without any diminution of spirit, and without that tone of humorous exaggeration which, however amusing, sometimes detracts too much from the truthfulness of many portions of the *Pickwick Papers*. The scene is laid in the humblest life: its hero is a friendless, nameless, parish orphan, born in a workhouse; at a time when workhouses were not subjected, as now, to the control of a central superintending board, and when attention was comparatively little directed to the condition of the poor. (p. 86)

Unfinished as this tale still is, it is the best example which Mr Dickens has yet afforded of his power to produce a good novel; but it cannot be considered a conclusive one. The difficulties to which he is exposed in his present periodical mode of writing are, in some respects, greater than if he allowed himself a wider field, and gave his whole work to the public at once. But he would be subjected to a severer criticism if his fiction could be read continuedly—if his power of maintaining a sustained interest could be tested—if his work could be viewed as a connected whole, and its object, plan, consistency, and arrangement brought to the notice of the reader at once. This ordeal cannot be passed triumphantly without the aid of other qualities than necessarily belong to the most brilliant sketcher of detached scenes. We do not, however, mean to express a doubt that Mr Dickens can write with judgment as well as with spirit. His powers of observation and description are qualities rarer, and less capable of being acquired, than those which would enable him to combine the scattered portions of a tale into one consistent and harmonious whole. If he will endeavour to supply whatever may be effected by care and study—avoid imitation of other writers—keep nature steadily before his eyes—and check all disposition to exaggerate—we know no writer who seems likely to attain higher success in that rich and useful department of fiction which is founded on faithful representations of human character, as exemplified in the aspects of English life. (pp. 96–7)

Source: T. H. Lister, "Dickens' 'Tales,'" in *Edinburgh Review*, Vol. 68, No. 137, October 1838, pp. 75–97.

SOURCES

Alcott, Louisa May, *Little Women*, Chapter 10, Project Gutenberg, http://www.gutenberg.org/files/514/514-h/514-h.htm (accessed January 6, 2012).

Auden, W. H., "Dingley Dell & the Fleet," in *Dickens: A Collection of Critical Essays*, edited by Martin Price, Prentice-Hall, 1967, p. 69; originally published in *The Dyer's Hand*, Random House, 1962.

Chesterton, G. K., "The Pickwick Papers," in *The Dickens Critics*, edited by George H. Ford and Lauriat Lane, Jr., Cornell University Press, 1961, pp. 109, 118; originally published in *Charles Dickens: A Critical Study*, Dodd, Mead, 1906.

Chittick, Kathryn, *Dickens and the 1830s*, Cambridge University Press, 1990, p. 64.

Cody, David, "Dickens: A Brief Biography," in *Victorian Web*, http://www.victorianweb.org/authors/dickens/dickensbio1.html (accessed October 25, 2011).

Davis, Paul, "The Pickwick Papers," in *Critical Companion to Charles Dickens*, Facts On File, 2007, pp. 324–25.

"Dickens, Charles," in *Merriam-Webster's Encyclopedia of Literature*, Merriam-Webster, 1995, pp. 324–25.

Dickens, Charles, *The Pickwick Papers*, Oxford University Press, 1948.

"Five Ways to Compute the Relative Value of a U.K. Pound Amount, 1830 to Present," MeasuringWorth.com, http://www.measuringworth.com/ukcompare/result.php (accessed October 20, 2011).

"Industry Plans: England and Wales," Network Rail website, September 2011, p. 18, http://www.networkrail.co.uk (accessed October 20, 2011).

"The Law Relating to Breach of Promise of Marriage," Law Reform Commission of Ireland website, http://www.lawreform.ie/_fileupload/consultation%20papers/wpBreachofPromise.htm (accessed October 20, 2011).

Marcus, Steven, "Language into Structure: Pickwick Revisited," in *Modern Critical Views: Charles Dickens*, Chelsea House Publishers, 1987, p. 136; originally published in *Daedalus: Journal of the American Academy of Arts and Sciences*, Vol. 101, No. 1, Winter 1972, 183-202.

"Parliamentary Constituencies," UK Parliament website, http://www.parliament.uk/about/how/elections-and-voting/constituencies/ (accessed October 20, 2011).

"The Struggle for Democracy: Getting the Vote," in National Archives website, http://www.nationalarchives.gov.uk/pathways/citizenship/struggle_democracy/getting_vote.htm (accessed October 20, 2011).

"Surrey Iron Railway," in *Croydon Online*, http://www.croydononline.org/history/places/surreyiron.asp (accessed October 20, 2011).

Wilson, Angus, "The Heroes and Heroines of Dickens," in *Dickens: A Collection of Critical Essays*, edited by Martin Price, Prentice-Hall, 1967, p. 19; originally published in *Dickens and the Twentieth Century*, edited by John Gross and Gabriel Pearson, Routledge and Kegan Paul, 1962.

FURTHER READING

Clendening, Logan, *A Handbook to "Pickwick Papers,"* Knopf, 1936.

> This volume, while written decades ago, is still available—and still worth reading because Clendening retraces the wanderings of the Pickwickians through England, sharing with the reader his keen observations and asides with wit and good humor.

Kaplan, Fred, *Dickens: A Biography*, Johns Hopkins University Press, 1998.

> First published in 1988, Kaplan's biography of the author was named as a notable book of the year by the *New York Times*. Kaplan explores some of the contradictions and conflicts in Dickens's personality as he describes the novelist's successful career, his expansive circle of friends, and his unraveling marriage.

Pool, Daniel, *What Jane Austen Ate and Charles Dickens Knew: From Fox Hunting to Whist—the Facts of Daily Life in Nineteenth-Century England*, Touchstone, 1993.

> Modern readers can sometimes be puzzled by the details of Victorian life: diet, clothing, manners, transportation, personal hygiene. This volume looks at the details of everyday life among the Victorians and provides readers of *The Pickwick Papers* with a picture of the material circumstances in which the novel's characters lived.

Sutherland, John, *The Longman Companion to Victorian Fiction*, 2nd ed., Longman, 2009.

> First published in 1988, this volume is a massive compendium of information about Victorian fiction. It includes plot summaries of hundreds of novels as well as biographical information on the principal authors. Readers can use this volume to trace the impact Dickens had on other authors.

SUGGESTED SEARCH TERMS

Charles Dickens

Charles Dickens AND *Pickwick Papers*

debtors' prisons AND England

Industrial Revolution

parliamentary elections AND England AND 19th century

picaresque novel

reform bills AND England

serial publication

Victorian era

Victorian fiction

The Ramayana

R. K. NARAYAN

1972

The Ramayana is one of the great masterpieces of Sanskrit and of world literature, an epic poem that ranks alongside the *Iliad*, the *Odyssey*, and *Beowulf* from Western culture. At the same time, the Ramayana is a sacred text of Hinduism, narrating the incarnation of the god Vishnu on earth in the same way the Christian Gospels narrate the incarnation of Jesus. R. K. Narayan's prose version of the epic, *The Ramayana*, first published in 1972, retells the story in a brief novel in a highly modern style. Set in a mythical version of Indian history, the plot of *The Ramayana* unfolds like a fairy tale, belying its serious philosophical and theological purpose. The prince Rama is cheated out of his rightful inheritance of his father's kingdom and forced to flee into the wilderness, where his wife, Sita, is captured by the demon Ravana and can only be rescued by a band of flying monkeys. Rama is the incarnation of the god Vishnu as a mortal man who alone can save the world from Ravana. Composed by the early Indo-European invaders of ancient India, the Ramayana is a work that, though not well known in the West, contains many elements that will remind readers of Western legends and tales. L. Frank Baum, author of *The Wonderful Wizard of Oz* (1900), was a member of the Ramayana Brotherhood of the Theosophical Society and borrowed the flying monkeys for his own novel. The leader of the Ramayana's monkeys, the god Hanuman, is the basis for Sun Wukong—known in the West as the Monkey King—the hero of the medieval Chinese novel *Journey to the West*.

R. K. Narayan (© *Dinodia Photos / Alamy*)

AUTHOR BIOGRAPHY

Narayan's novel version *The Ramayana* comes at the end of a progression of literary development over two millennia long. Narayan's authorship cannot be disentangled from this tradition since he describes his own work as a "version" (i.e., an adaptation) of the traditional epic. The original composition of the Ramayana is attributed to the poet Valmiki, but this is, at best, an oversimplification. Bards in the Indo-European culture that conquered northern India about 1500 BCE produced the epic of the Ramayana as the foundation story of their civilization. This process was carried out over a thousand years through oral performances by generations of illiterate bards, until a full version of the story was written down from performances in the first century. The singer in question was not Valmiki, and the authorship remains unknown and may not have been a single individual. In fact, Valmiki is understood to be a fictional creation (he appears as a character in the

original version of the Ramayana), like the Greek Homer, invented to supply a poet to be, in the modern sense, responsible for the text, once the bardic nature of its composition history had been forgotten.

The next step in the chain of tradition followed by Narayan was the translation of the Sanskrit Ramayana into Tamil (a language of the pre-Indo-European population of India). This was completed by the twelfth century, but the result was not a simple translation. Rather, a number of different Tamil-speaking scholars employed by royal or noble patrons wrote their own versions of parts of the story in Tamil, producing an original text (edited together from the work of the various authors) that tells the same story as the Ramayana, but in about half the number of lines as the Sanskrit prototype. Very little is known about this process of adaptation, which is itself the subject of a pseudo-biographical literature filled with miracle stories. Kamban (sometimes Kambar) is the name given to one of these Tamil scholars. In any case, the Tamil Ramayana—properly called the Ramavataran—is generally attributed, as a kind of shorthand for the complicated tradition, to Kamban.

Finally Narayan, a native Tamil speaker, again distilled the Ramayana tradition into the succinct form of a modern English novel in 1972. Born in 1906 in Madras, Narayan became a protégé of the English novelist Graham Greene and was the breakthrough author who introduced Indian English-language literature (frequently called Indo-Anglian literature) to the West. Narayan's early career was devoted to a series of novels mostly set in his mythical city of Malgudi, in which he interrogates the injustices that tradition imposed on Indian society. In the 1960s, Narayan turned to Hindu religious texts as inspiration and, besides writing *The Ramayana* in 1972, produced *Gods, Demons, and Others* in 1964, a volume of short stories based on a variety of traditional sources, and a novelization of the other great Indian epic, *The Mahabharata*, in 1978. After a career that included many years teaching and lecturing abroad, an honorary PhD from the University of Leeds in 1967, and much speculation that he would win the Nobel Prize in Literature, Narayan died in Chennai (formerly Madras) on May 13, 2001.

PLOT SUMMARY

Prologue

The Ramayana begins with Dasaratha, the emperor of Kosala, which is a prosperous realm in northern India. His life is perfectly contented, except that none of his three wives, Kausayla, Kaikeyi, or Sumithra, has borne him a child. His sages advise him to perform a horse sacrifice, an ancient Indo-European custom. It is revealed in one of the sage's visions that this has all been arranged by the god Vishnu, who has been petitioned by the other gods to destroy the *rakshasa* (ogre) Ravana. This monster has magical protections against all harm, except against human beings, whom he considered too weak to threaten him. Therefore Vishnu and his entourage will be incarnated in human form, born as sons to Dasaratha's wives.

Chapter 1: Rama's Initiation

When Rama (son of Dasaratha and incarnation of Vishnu) is a young man, the sage Viswamithra comes to Dasaratha's court and asks the assistance of Rama in performing a sacrifice in a foreign land. The emperor is reluctant to dispatch Rama, since it will require crossing a desert inhabited by monstrous serpents, but is persuaded by the sage's holiness. Accompanied by his faithful brother Lakshmana, Rama is able to kill all the monsters with his bow, exhibiting clearly superhuman fighting skill. Viswamithra tells Rama a number of myths that relate to their quest as well as to later events in the story. The most important of these is a version of the episode of Sita's abduction by Ravana. It tells the same story, though in briefer form and concerning other characters, illustrating the original oral composition of the narrative as a whole and its tendency to tell a few basic stories repeatedly.

Chapter 2: The Wedding

Returning home, Rama passes through the kingdom of Mithila, ruled by King Janaka. Rama and Janaka's daughter Sita fall in love at first sight, since they are the incarnations of Vishnu and his consort Lakshmi. Sita, in fact, had been harvested by Janaka when she grew out of a plowed field. Janaka has the bow of the god Shiva, which no human being can string because of its difficulty. He has decreed that any man who would marry Sita must string the bow. He has fought a veritable war against his daughter's suitors, enraged by their failing the test. Not only can Rama string the bow, but it snaps like a toy from the strength of his hands. So the royal couple are married.

Chapter 3: Two Promises Revived

Having grown old and infirm, Dasaratha wishes to devolve his empire through his son Rama. But Kooni, a deformed woman kept as a sort of jester by Dasaratha's wife Kaikeyi, reminds her mistress that Kaikeyi had once saved her husband's life and in return was promised to have two of her wishes granted. Kooni urges Kaikeyi now to wish that Rama be exiled to the forest for fourteen years and that her own son Bharatha be made heir. Although Dasaratha seems to suffer a stroke upon hearing this request, he honors his promise and agrees to her wishes. Rama's brother Lakshmana wishes to stage a coup d'état in Rama's favor, but Rama is perfectly content to go and seek wisdom as a hermit in the forest, taking Lakshmana and Sita with him. Dasaratha dies that same night. When Bharatha, who had been visiting his grandfather, returns, he wants none of this and chases Rama down in the forest to ask him to return and rule. But since Rama is destined to fight and kill Ravana, a voice from the sky orders Bharatha to take up the throne during the fourteen years of Rama's exile.

Chapter 4: Encounters in Exile

Rama considers his exile a spiritual pilgrimage, and as he and his companions move south through the forest, they, for the most part, encounter hermits and sages who have found a secluded life of holiness in the forest. Rama takes it as his special purpose to fight and destroy the evil spirits (*asuras*) that also live in the forest. The *rakshasa* Soorpanaka becomes infatuated with Rama because of his beauty, but when she is rebuffed, she unleashes an army of ogres to kill him. Rama succeeds in destroying them all single-handedly.

Chapter 5: The Grand Tormentor

Soorpanaka reports her defeat to her brother Ravana, the king of all *rakshasas*, in his island fortress Lanka. He becomes desirous of Sita based on his sister's description. Ravana is so tormented by the fire his vision of Sita has lit inside him that he causes rains to fall and the winter to come out of season. He stops the whole process of time, but nothing can assuage him. Fearful of Rama, he decides to kidnap Sita through deception. He lures Rama and Lakshmana away from Sita with

MEDIA ADAPTATIONS

- Indian manuscripts of the Ramayana were frequently lavishly illustrated with full-color paintings that themselves make up some of the greatest masterpieces of Indian art. This tradition was the focus of the exhibition *The Ramayana: Love and Valour in India's Great Epic*, held in 2008 at the British Library and accompanied by the publication of a catalog of the same title.

- The Ramayana has traditionally been illustrated in relief sculpture in Hindu temples. This practice was surveyed in 2000 in *Narrative Sculpture and Literary Traditions in South and Southeast Asia*, edited by Jan Fontein and Marijke J. Klokke. Narayan's *The Ramayana* is illustrated by R. K. Laxman with drawings based on traditional reliefs of stories from the epic.

- Kutiyattam is a form of Indian ballet whose origins go back to the first century. One of its most famous pieces is the *Balivadham*, which tells the story of the rivalry between Vali and Sugreeva from the Ramayana. A production of this for Indian television is available on DVD, released by Invis Multimedia through India Video, and is posted in many places on the Internet under the title *Kutiyattam: Balivadham*.

- The Ramayana has provided the source material for innumerable shows on Indian television, but perhaps the most important was an adaptation of the entire epic that played from 1986 to 1988 under the direction of Ramanand Sagar. It is widely available in a 16-DVD set under the title *Ramayan*.

- Bollywood has frequently adapted the Ramayana in animation, mostly recently in *Ramayana: The Epic*, directed by Chetan Desai, in 2010.

- The American director Nina Paley made an animated reinterpretation of the Ramayana titled *Sita Sings the Blues* in 2009. Its soundtrack consists of songs by the 1920s blues singer Annette Hanshaw.

- One of the most recent of the numerous comic-book adaptations of the Ramayana is the *Ravanayan*, written by Vijayendra Mohanty and drawn by Vivek Goel in 2011, which retells the story from the point of view of the *rakshasa* king Ravana.

---

magical illusions. Ravana approaches Sita disguised as a sage and sings his own praises to her in the third person. He then reveals himself and proposes marriage to her, since he is under a curse whereby he will be destroyed if he ever touches a woman against her will. When he finds Sita disgusted, he carries her off in his flying chariot back to Lanka.

Chapter 6: Vali

Heading south in search of Sita, Rama and Lakshmana come to Kiskinda, a land inhabited by monkeys. They meet Sugreeva, brother of the monkey king Vali, and his general Hanuman. Sugreeva too has been exiled because of a disagreement with his brother, and he swears that, if Rama will help him kill his brother and put Sugreeva on the throne, he will then use his monkey army to find Sita and fight the *rakshasa* army. Rama agrees, and while the two monkey brothers are fighting a duel, he shoots Vali in the back with an arrow. When the dying Vali cries treachery, Rama tells him that he was only taking vengeance for his old unjust treatment of Sugreeva.

Chapter 7: When the Rains Cease

No search can be undertaken during the monsoon rains that fall in India each year, and further delays are caused by Sugreeva's drunkenness and devotion to pleasure. But soon the monkey army is assembled and sent to search for Sita. The band led by Hanuman comes to the coast opposite Lanka and is told by an eagle that Sita is on the island. Using his divine powers, Hanuman steps across to the island that lies over the horizon.

Chapter 8: Memento from Rama
Hanuman, shrunk to the size of an insect, searches Lanka and eventually finds Sita when she is on the verge of hanging herself in despair of ever seeing Rama again. He reassures her that Rama is coming. He leaves to report back to Rama, but not without inflicting considerable damage on the city as a warning to Ravana.

Chapter 9: Ravana in Council
After repairing the damage to Lanka, Ravana takes advice from his councilors on how to deal with Rama and the monkey army. Most of what he hears is flattery, and he mocks the few of his generals who advise him to return Sita and try to make peace. This is particularly true of Ravana's brother, Vibhishana, who is so certain of Ravana's defeat that he defects to Rama's side.

Chapter 10: Across the Ocean
Vibhishana, concluding that his brother is unjust, seeks asylum with Rama in his camp on the mainland opposite Lanka. Rama accepts him and makes him the head of a government-in-exile of Lanka. The monkey army builds a mole (a bridge made of rubble) to Lanka.

Chapter 11: The Siege of Lanka
This chapter, relating the siege, was originally published as a short story in *Gods, Demons, and Others*. Narayan does not describe the actual fighting in much detail but emphasizes that one after another of Ravana's generals and heroic warriors go forth to challenge Rama, or the most important monkey fighters, only to be killed. Rama and Lakshmana are briefly immobilized by poisoned darts but are revived by magic. Similarly, many of Ravana's most successful ploys are magical tricks, creating the impression that Rama or Sita is dead, or the illusion that all of his own dead warriors have come back to life.

Chapter 12: Rama and Ravana in Battle
Ravana finally has no choice except to enter the battle himself, and he and Rama fight against each other in flying chariots. The failure of his magical weapons forces Ravana to conclude that he is fighting a god rather than a man, although he cannot say which one:

> This is, perhaps, the highest God. Who could he be? Not Shiva, for Shiva is my supporter; he could not be Brahma, who is four faced; could not be Vishnu, because of my immunity from the weapons of the whole trinity. Perhaps this man is the primordial being, the cause behind the whole universe." Rama eventually kills Ravana after a titanic struggle.

Chapter 13: Interlude
This chapter was also originally published as a short story in *Gods, Demons, and Others*. When Sita is brought into Rama's presence after the victory, he exiles her, on the grounds that any woman who has lived in another man's house must be considered to have committed adultery. Instead, Sita commits *sati* (or *suttee*), throwing herself on a bonfire as was customary for the widows of Hindu aristocrats. But the god of the fire rejects her, and so Rama is satisfied that she is innocent.

Chapter 14: The Coronation
Narayan's voice breaks into the narrative to criticize Rama for testing Sita in this way, since he clearly holds her to a different standard than he did other female characters in the story. The fourteen years of exile are over, so Rama and his entourage fly back to Ayodhya for his coronation, sending Hanuman ahead as his herald.

Epilogue
In the epilogue, Narayan goes so far as to narrate the last book of Valmiki's *Ramayana*. He comments upon it from his post-modern perspective, assuming that his readers know the story.

CHARACTERS

Bharatha
Bharatha is the son of Dasaratha and Kaikeyi and the half brother of Rama. He rejects the unjust claim for his rule of Ayodhya made by his mother, but he is convinced by Rama and a voice from heaven to accept rule as a sort of viceroy for Rama. He swears to kill himself, however, rather than rule beyond Rama's period of exile, and is on the point of doing so when Rama returns years later.

Dasaratha

Dasaratha is the emperor of Kosala. He has three wives simultaneously. With Kausalya, he is the father of Rama. With Kaikeyi, he is the father of Bharatha. With Sumithra, he is the father of the twins Lakshmana and Sathrunga. He sets the story in motion when he decides to retire before his death and yield the rule of Kosala to Rama. Although he is a just ruler, he is forced against his will to exile Rama and make Bharatha his heir by an injudicious promise he once made to the latter's mother, Kaikeyi, pledging to grant any request she might make as a reward for saving his life. Once he is informed that he is obligated to disinherit and exile Rama, he suffers a stroke from his grief, and he dies shortly after Rama's departure.

Hanuman

Hanuman is the companion of Sugreeva and the general of the monkey army. In Rama's war against Lanka, he proves himself the most able helper of Rama. The son of the wind god, he is possessed of divine powers, including the power of flight. He was dedicated as a child to become the servant of Vishnu and his attribute *dharma*, or justice, and so becomes Rama's faithful ally. His chief exploit is the initial reconnaissance of Lanka, during which he uses his godlike powers to nearly overturn Ravana's kingdom on his own.

Janaka

Janaka, the king of Mathila, is the father of Sita. He received her grown from the earth, and he established a test for her suitors of drawing the bow of Shiva, even though the failure of any mortal to do so involved him in war with disgruntled suitors.

Kaikeyi

Kaikeyi is the wife of Dasaratha and mother of Bharatha. While, by nature, she seems simply pleasure-loving, her servant Kooni is able to stir up envy and fear in her at the time the kingdom is given to Rama rather than Bharatha.

Kausalya

Kausalya is the wife of Dasaratha and mother of Rama.

Kooni

Kooni is the maid to Kaikeyi and the source of Bharatha's unjust claim to privilege that sends Rama into exile and motivates the plot of *The Ramayana*.

Lakshmana

Lakshmana is a son of Dasaratha and Sumithra and the half brother of Rama. He is exceptionally devoted to Rama as his friend and follower throughout his adventures, voluntarily sharing his exile and acting as his right-hand man at every turn. He is, however, more rash than Rama, who must frequently restrain him from violence.

Rama

Rama is portrayed as a prince and, eventually, king of Kosala, a state in northeastern India in the early first millennium BCE. He is the main character of *The Ramayana*. The remarkable personality possessed by Rama is the driving force of the tale. Narayan places the main description of Rama in the mouth of his enemy the *rakshasa* Soorpanaka:

> Even if I had a thousand tongues, I could never fully explain his beauty and the grandeur of his personality. Even if one had a thousand eyes one could not take in the splendour of this being. His strength is unmatched. Single-handed he wiped out all our army.... His mission in life is to wipe out our whole family, clan, class from the face of the earth.

But even while he is kingly and warlike, Rama is self-restrained and humble beyond human possibility. Rama embodies all of the virtues of traditional Indian culture, particularly *dharma*, or (in this sense) duty. He does not question the commands of his father even when he is disinherited. His duty to obey his father in accepting his disinheritance towers above any idea of his own rights or needs. Later, Rama rejects his beloved wife at the mere rumor of scandal because he owes to his civilization the duty of having a pure wife. Rama is able to attack and kill the monkey king Vali in a way that might seem treacherous precisely because he owes no duty to him. But at the same time, whenever he meets any of the inhabitants of Ayodhya, he greets them by asking, "How are you? Are your children happy? Do you want any help from me?" though of course he has already done everything to provide for his subjects' happiness. Rama's inability to compromise his devotion to duty makes him seem inhuman, and in fact, he is an incarnation of the god Vishnu.

Ravana

Ravana is the villain of *The Ramayana*, whose desire for Sita and kidnapping of her creates the story's plot, resulting in the destruction of his kingdom of Lanka and his fatal duel with Rama. In Valmiki's Ramayana, Ravana is an ogre with ten heads and twenty arms, the king of the *rakshasas*, who can be compared to the monstrous earth spirits that live beyond the bounds of human habitation in the Western tradition (see, e.g., *Beowulf*, line 112; Geoffrey of Monmouth, *History of the Kings of Britain*, 1.11.76). He was a terrible monster, feared and hated by the gods as well as by his human neighbors, but his sphere of operation was limited to southern India and especially his own kingdom on the island of Lanka. But Narayan elevates him to the status of a cosmic ruler and menace: "Ravana, the supreme lord of this and other worlds, sat in his durbar hall. . . . The kings of this earth whom he had reduced to vassaldom stood about [him]. . . . He had also enslaved the reigning gods." His title is modeled after the description of Satan in the Christian New Testament, at 2 Corinthians 4:4, as the "god of this world." But Narayan's conception is more nearly Gnostic in presenting a cosmos that is ruled at every level by an evil power. When Ravana disguises himself to deceive Sita he inverts the cosmic order, saying of himself and his *rakshasas*, "They are good people, not harmful or cruel like the so-called gods. The rakshasa clan have been misrepresented and misunderstood." He wishes to replace a true characterization of the world with a false one supported by his authority and power. Recasting Ravana in this way allows Narayan to make his story more familiar to Western Christian readers. At the same time, turning Ravana into a cosmic oppressor invokes the sense of human alienation from the world that permeates modern Western literature but which is foreign to traditional systems of thought like Hinduism.

Sathrunga

Sathrunga is a son of Dasaratha and Sumithra, the twin of Lakshmana, and the half brother of Rama.

Sita

Sita is a human incarnation of the earth goddess Lakshmi, who grew out of a furrow in a plowed field. She was adopted by King Janaka and is frequently referred to by the patronymic "Janaki." Only Rama is able to pass the test set by her father of stringing the bow of Shiva and thus marry her. But she is abducted by the *rakshasa* Ravana, who desires her for himself. However, she is able to preserve her virtue until rescued by Rama and his army of monkeys owing to a curse long ago placed on Ravana that dooms him if he should ever rape a woman. She is an example of ideal womanhood as viewed by the early Indo-European culture of India: she is incapable of shaming her family by feeling adulterous desire, and at the same time she obeys the dictates of her husband even when she know them to be unjust. When she first sees Rama before their marriage, she feels desire for him and interprets this as a loss of her own shame, believing that she has no right to her own feelings in view of the role imposed on her by her culture and by her father.

Soorpanaka

Soorpanaka is the sister of Ravana. Just as Ravana desires Sita because of her perfect beauty, Soorpanaka is overcome by desire for Rama. Rama's first encounter with the *rakshasas* comes when he spurns Soorpanaka's advances and annihilates her bodyguard.

Sugreeva

Sugreeva is the brother of Vali, the king of the monkeys, who was reluctantly forced to take the throne when Vali was thought dead. When he finally returned, Vali considered this treason and exiled his brother. Sugreeva makes a pact with Rama that, once Rama has helped him kill his brother Vali and once more become king of the monkeys, he will use the monkey army to help rescue Sita. But he is distracted from his vows by his animalistic desire for pleasure.

Sumithra

Sumithra is the wife of Dasaratha and mother of the twins Lakshmana and Sathrunga.

Vali

Vali is the king of the monkeys of Kiskinda. After fighting a demon in his underground lair for two years, he assumes that his brother and regent Sugreeva had tried to bury him and punishes him with exile. During a later duel with Sugreeva, Vali is killed when Rama intervenes against him. Vali had dishonored Sugreeva by taking his wife, so Rama considers the murder a just retribution.

Vibhishana

Vibhishana is Ravana's brother who tries to convince him to make peace with Rama. Convinced that Ravana will be defeated, he seeks asylum with Rama and is eventually made king of the *rakshasas* by him.

Viswamithra

Viswamithra is the sage who instructs and helps Rama in his early adventures.

THEMES

Epic

The epic (*ithiasa* in Sanskrit) tradition is sometimes said to consist of poetry that deals with history, but that is not quite correct. Epic poems deal with a period in the remote past that the bard who sings the epic and his audience believe to be a formative time in their own national history, while the stories of the epic are generally accorded the highest possible truth value. In fact, the epic tradition may well have begun shortly after the privileged moment of the past, and it may contain many accurate reflections of that time; however, in general the tradition is so transformed by the constantly changing and amorphous form of the oral transmission of the epic between generations of bards that, by the time it is recorded in writing, the main features of the epic will have little to do with the past, incorporating older mythological traditions. For example, the bardic tradition in Bosnia studied in the 1930s by Milman Parry (reported in his *The Making of Homeric Verse*) concerned the Battle of Kosovo in 1389, a crushing victory for the Ottoman Turks that made them masters of most of the Balkan Peninsula; but in the epic version, the battle became a Serbian victory over the Turks. Similarly, the *Iliad* is rooted in the end of the Bronze Age in the Aegean region, about 1200 BCE, when invaders from the north destroyed nearly every major city in Greece and on the eastern shore of the Aegean Sea, but the epic represents this upheaval in a war waged by the whole of Greece against the single city of Troy as, one might say, an emblem of the wider destruction.

The golden age that *The Ramayana* looks back to is represented by the civilization established in and around Kosala in northeastern India, between the Ganges River and the Himalaya Mountains, in the first half of the first millennium BCE. The capital of the most

TOPICS FOR FURTHER STUDY

- Various kinds of dramas based on the Ramayana are frequently performed by amateur groups associated with Hindu temples in the United States. If possible, attend one of these or watch a video of one on the Internet, and write a review incorporating the knowledge you gained by reading Narayan's version.

- Read the Japanese traditional epic *The Tale of the Heiki* (several English translations have been made). Adapt a scene from it as a short story in the ironic modern style that Narayan adopted for his novel *The Ramayana*.

- Write and perform with your classmates a brief dramatic adaptation of a scene from *The Ramayana*. Film it and post it on the Internet.

- The other great Indian epic, the Mahabharata, contains (in book 3, stanzas 257-76) the Ramopakhyana, a version of the main story of the Ramayana that is about fifteen hundred verses long. It may be a bard's singing of the story in the scope of a single day's performance. It is similar to Narayan's novel version in telling a compressed, rather than expanded, version of the story. Write a paper comparing the choices that the singer of the Mahabharata and Narayan made in composing their versions. What was left out of the larger story? What new story did they tell through their shaping and refining of the larger narrative? How are the two texts alike and different?

- Read one of the many adaptations of the Ramayana as a graphic novel (for example *Ramayana: Divine Loophole*, by Sanjay Patel, from 2010). Once you have familiarized yourself with the style, make your own graphic adaptation of a scene from a different epic—for example, the scene of Odysseus's contest with the suitors from the *Odyssey*.

powerful kingdom in the area was the fortress of Ayodhya, and many ruling families in historic times (such as that of Siddhartha Gautama, the Buddha) claimed descent from the Ikshvaku, the royal house of Kosala (called the Solar dynasty by Narayan). While Kosala and Ayodhya existed, they serve as no more than a jumping-off point for the utterly fantastic story of *The Ramayana*. Nevertheless, this historical anchor differentiates *The Ramayana* as epic from myth, which takes place entirely in the divine world, and from fairy tale, which relies entirely on folk tradition, although the epic incorporates elements of both.

Reincarnation

The early Indo-Europeans believed that the truest part of a human being was an immaterial essence or spirit that was attached to the body but existed before birth and could go on existing after death. One associated belief was that the same spirit could become attached to a series of bodies, human or animal. Each such incarnation was a punishment or reward for behavior in past lives. This idea took form in Greece in the philosophy of Pythagoras and Plato but also became one of the most important religious ideas in India. Another Indo-European idea was that gods could manifest themselves on earth in the form of human beings or animals. In Greece, this was considered merely a disguise assumed by the god, but Indian theologians developed the idea as a kind of incarnation, in which the divine spirit attached itself to a human body in the same way as an ordinary human spirit.

In *The Ramayana*, the god Vishnu undergoes such an incarnation as Rama, becoming what is known in Sanskrit as an *avatar* (incarnation or theophany). This may be the prototype of the general idea of divine avatars in Hinduism. Once Vishnu determines that only a human being can destroy Ravana, he announces to the other gods that he and his retinue will become human beings:

> I shall incarnate as Dasaratha's son, and my conch and my wheel, which I hold in each hand for certain purposes, and my couch, namely Adisesha, the Serpent, on whose coils I rest, shall be born as my brothers.

Vishnu's consort, the earth goddess Lakshmi, is also incarnated, as Sita. Through visions given to the sages employed as religious experts by Dasaratha, Vishnu arranges for him to make a horse sacrifice for the sake of gaining offspring. At the

The Ramayana has been a part of Hindu and other Asian mythologies for centuries, as evidenced by this ancient medallion. (© Dwight Smith / Shutterstock.com)

end of this ritual, a miracle occurs: "an immense supernatural being emerged from the sacrificial fire bearing in his arms a silver plate with a bolus of sacramental rice on it." One of the sages performing the sacrifice interprets this miracle for Dasaratha: "Take the rice and divide it among your wives and they will have children." The divine essence enters the mortal women through their eating the rice cake. This supposed divine impregnation depends on the common analogy between the process of planting grains and human reproduction. It has often been suggested that Vishnu's incarnation offers a parallel to the Christian idea of Jesus's incarnation, and further, to the presence of Jesus in the bread eaten during the Christian Eucharist, but the universality of such ideas suggests that any relationship between them is neither genetic (that is, tracing back to a single source) nor one of influence (for example, through the reception of Hindu ideas by Christian authors).

STYLE

Oral Formulaic Poetry

One imagines a poet in the modern world sitting down in private to write a new and original work, generally meant to be read silently by individual readers, even if it will sometimes be read aloud to an audience. Whatever its debt to other poems and its conversation with other poetry, the poem is a new creation, and one that will not change from reading to reading. One may also imagine a modern singer giving a recital of, say, one of Franz Schubert's *lieder*, performing exactly the words and music written down in the music score. But these conditions of composition and performance have not always prevailed, and indeed, could not have prevailed in an illiterate society. There the singer and the poet are a single figure, generally known in English as a bard (*suta* in Sanskrit). The bard cannot simply recite or sing something written down, since he does not know what writing is. But at the same time, he cannot spontaneously create something entirely new every time he performs. Instead, the bard learns the traditional stories of the heroic age of the past that he takes for his epic subject, and for a given performance, he tells one or more of the stories in as long or as short a time as he has available, embellishing or stripping away detail as appropriate. He sings in what can be called a metalanguage of formulae (lines and half lines of verse) that he either learned from listening to the bards with whom he studied or composed himself. He holds his formulae in his memory and puts them together the same way words are strung together in ordinary speech. He combines them into new patterns and associations every time he performs, improvising and inventing new combinations of formulae in the same way that baroque and classical musicians did in the eighteenth century, or the way jazz musicians still do. For example, a bard will know a speech in which a subject appeals to a king for justice, or a scene in which a hero kills a monster. He will repeat the same basic elements every time his narrative requires it, but he will tailor them to the specific needs of the particular version of the story he is telling. Every time he sings a scene, it will be the same, but different, transformed with the appropriate names and details, and made shorter or longer according to its importance and the time available.

There is no written text in the bard's illiterate culture, but rather each performance of the same story is a unique work of art. The bardic style of performance is so different from anything in modern literate culture that, for a long time, scholars did not even suspect it existed. But in the 1930s, Milman Parry investigated the bards in

the semiliterate Serbian community in Bosnia, in a series of studies that have mostly been collected in his *The Making of Homeric Verse*. Parry died before he could complete his work, but his investigations were taken up by his student A. B. Lord in his *Singer of Tales*. They discovered that the Serbian bards, who sang about the battle at Kosovo that took place in the fourteenth century, sang in this highly improvisatory way, relying on their memories to constantly create new songs. They also found that oral formulaic poetry was highly repetitive, telling variations of the same story if it went on long enough, and repeating lines and half lines quite frequently. This discovery made clear that other poems that share the same characteristics must originally have been composed through the combination of oral formulae also.

While bardic verse is found in many cultures, it was a particular feature of the Indo-European culture that began in central Asia before 5000 BCE and spread to occupy Europe, Iran, and India. All of the great early Indo-European poems were oral formulaic compositions, including *Beowulf* in the Germanic world, the *Iliad* and the *Odyssey* in ancient Greece, and the Ramayana and Mahabharata in India. The Ramayana was originally a long poem of about 50,000 verses, transcribed from performances given probably in the first century. No single bard on a single occasion could possibly have narrated even the core five books of the Ramayana, so the written text probably began with an editor compiling transcripts of several performances, not necessarily all by the same bard. Narayan's version, *The Ramayana*, is a distillation of the traditionally received text of the poem into the more modern form of the novel.

Novelization

Although the modern novel has a clear antecedent in the ancient romances (e.g., Apuleius's *Metamorphoses* or Heliodorus's *Aethiopica*) as well as novel-like works in other cultures (including the Chinese *Journey to the West*, which is itself partially based on the Ramayana), it developed during the seventeenth and eighteenth centuries and became the dominant form of literature in the nineteenth century. The novel has many superficial similarities to the epic, including its length, its complexity of plot, and its possibilities for character development. But leaving aside the poetic structure of the epic, the historicizing, legendary subject matter of the epic is only a subset of the artistic possibilities opened up by the novel. As a result, while the epic was still a highly productive form in the seventeenth century (e.g., John Milton's *Paradise Lost*), after the rise of the novel the epic was dead as a literary form. The reaction embodied in the romantic epics of the eighteenth and nineteenth century (beginning with James Macpherson's *Ossian*) was to create purposefully artificial and fragmentary works that reflected the ruined state of the genre. Twentieth-century works like Ezra Pound's *Cantos* or Derek Walcott's *Omeros*, although they revive the epic form, are indistinguishable from the modern novel in content and sensibility. Such works, however, have led the way to the opposite tendency, to adopt epics into novels.

The novelization impetus has produced a vast spectrum of works, ranging from Robert Graves's *Homer's Daughter* to James Joyce's *Ulysses*, which share the property of reading their epic source through the modern interpretive lens of the author, whether it is Graves projecting feminism and (strangely) neo-paganism onto his text, or Joyce modernistic irony onto his. Narayan's *The Ramayana* is decidedly a work of this kind. Narayan not only tightens the narrative style and trims the extreme discursiveness and poetic language of the Sanskrit and Tamil Ramayana epics to produce a recognizably modern novel, but it is also clearly his purpose to include a postmodern commentary on the story he retells. This is perhaps most obvious in the ending of the epic, where the pregnant Sita, blameless as she is, is exiled by Rama merely because she has become the subject of gossip by a peasant woodcutter. This passage is deeply offensive to modern Indian feminists inasmuch as it typifies the misogyny of traditional culture, both in its inability to differentiate between rape and adultery and in the idea that the only value women have is as vessels of sexual purity guaranteeing the legitimacy of children. Narayan is well aware that his Indian audience knows the original ending, but he directly tells the reader that he is omitting Valmiki's ending because "this part of the story is not popular." The Ramayana is ordinarily read as an allegorical presentation of Rama as a symbol of uncompromised righteousness (*dharma*). The exile of Sita is the supreme reflection of this theme, as Rama does what he hates because he considers it right. By any modern standard, however, Rama's actions are unjust in the extreme, and this episode is often taken as a point of attack in modern feminist deconstructions of the Ramayana (such as in the cartoon *Sita Sings the Blues*). Narayan effects his own modernist criticism of the story by omitting Sita's exile on the grounds that it is not popular and is not in conformity with modern culture.

HISTORICAL CONTEXT

The Indo-European Invasion of India

The Proto-Indo-Europeans were a people living as animal-herding nomads on the great central Asian steppes between the Ukraine and the Gobi Desert at least as early as 5000 BCE. Their language was ancestral to the modern languages of India, Iran, and Europe, including English. By 1500 BCE, they had developed the chariot and used it to conquer the older established civilizations to their south. Between 1500 and 1200 BCE, they largely destroyed and absorbed the Mycenaean civilization in Greece, as well as the illiterate but sophisticated civilization in the Indus River valley in modern Pakistan, and raided extensively throughout the Near East, establishing the Hittite kingdom in central Anatolia. By about the year 1000 BCE in India, Indo-Europeans controlled the Ganges valley (and over the next millennium would conquer the rest of the subcontinent). The prominence of Kosala, the extensive use made of chariots in the epic, the Indo-European four-caste structure of farmers, priests, warriors, and kings, and numerous historical details, such as the thick forests of the Gangetic plain (which were quickly cut down and converted to farmland after 500 BCE), all mark the Ramayana as originating in this period. The earlier population of India, related to modern Tamils, who were conquered and to an extent replaced by the Indo-Europeans, probably also appear in the epic. These peoples are represented in the *Ramayana* as the *rakshasas* and anthropomorphic monkeys that Rama encounters. Indo-European culture was traditionally hostile to other ethnic groups and tended to represent them as human-animal hybrids or shape-shifting monsters. (These features merit comparison with the *lapiths* and centaurs of Greek myth and Greek stories about the Hyperboreans, barbarian tribes supposedly able to transform into crows, wolves, or other animals.)

COMPARE & CONTRAST

- **The Iron Age:** The idea of caste does not exist in the Indian society portrayed by the Ramayana, although the traditional Indo-European classes of kings, priests, warriors, and farmers, from which caste will grow, are present.

  Today: Where caste evolved from Indo-European classes, far differently from any social developments in the West, Indian society is organized into hundreds of hereditary castes based on trade or tribal affiliation that interact according to strict social rules, which often result in discrimination analogous to racial discrimination in the United States.

- **The Iron Age:** The Indo-European civilization dominated by Ayodhya does not extend much south of the plain of the Ganges.

  Today: India covers most of the subcontinent and organizes many cultural and language groups into a single nation.

- **The Iron Age:** Indian society is preliterate, and national memory is contained in the oral performances of bards.

  Today: Sanskrit and its modern descendant Hindi have a fully developed writing system. Despite India's emergence as a leading high-tech economy, overall literacy rates are very low (compared, for example, to Sri Lanka or China), although bilingualism with English as the second language is remarkably high.

Bardic Performance

Bardic performance was a traditional part of Indo-European society. Such performance had, in general, two social locations. In the first, a king was obliged to feed the warriors who fought for him, generally at a banquet that he laid out for them each evening. A bard would perform during and after dinner. This is reflected in Odysseus's performance at the court of the Phaeacians in the *Odyssey*, in the mead-hall setting of much of *Beowulf*, and in the mythic banquet that the god Odin provided for his army of the dead in Valhalla in the *Elder Edda*. The other occasion for performance was at a public sacrifice. Sacrifice was a religious festival that allowed kings and other nobles to give charity to the poor in the form of a free meal of meat distributed to peasants whose diet mostly consisted of gruel. In India, in particular, sacrifice was often accompanied by gifts of clothing and other goods from the rich to the poor. The festival atmosphere of a sacrifice would be heightened by singing and dancing, as well as by bardic performance. The Sanskrit Ramayana itself claims that the epic was first recited by Rama's

sons Kusa and Lava at a sacrifice performed after Rama became king of Kosala. Throughout later Indian history down to the present day, the written text of the Ramayana has been recited or read each year at the Rama Navami, a festival devoted to Rama centered on his mythic birthday of January 10.

CRITICAL OVERVIEW

The Ramayana is one of the most popular works of Indian literature and exists in thousands of manuscript copies dating back to the eleventh century. There is tremendous variety in the manuscripts, showing that Indian scribes had little hesitation in making their own additions to the text. Also at an early date, the work inspired paraphrases in other Indian languages and in the cultures of Southeast Asia. Owing to the work's great length, collections of excerpts and shortened versions are also well attested in early manuscripts. The Indian versions of the epic are covered by the essays in the 1991 collection *Many Ramayanas:*

The original epic of 24,000 verses was recorded on Sanskrit tablets. (© Anatoli Styf / Shutterstock.com)

The Diversity of a Narrative Tradition in South Asia, edited by Paula Richman, while the conference papers compiled by K. R. S. Iyengar in *Asian Variations in Ramayana* (1983) deal with versions that were written as far away as Thailand, Laos, and Java as early as the ninth century. New Ramayana-based literature continues to be produced in India, most recently the notable series of novels by Ashok Banker, beginning with *The Prince of Ayodhya* in 2003. In the postcolonial era, the Ramayana has become the subject of innumerable adaptations into forms such as the comic book and graphic novel, as well as adaptations for film and television.

The Ramayana first became known in western Europe in 1829 when August Wilhelm Schlegel (brother of the famous romantic philosopher Friedrich Schlegel) published an edition of the first three books together with a translation into Latin. The marked similarity of the Ramayana to the *Iliad* of Homer was immediately observed. In 1870, Albrecht Weber argued in his "On the Ramayana" that this was a case of direct influence, that Homer had become known in India because of the contact of the Hellenistic world with India, and that Valmiki had borrowed elements from the *Iliad* to make a larger epic incorporating also older Indian folktales. This idea was immediately refuted, first by the Indian scholar Kashinath Trimbak Telang in his *Was the Ramayana Copied from Homer?* (1873) and then by the English Indologist Arthur Anthony Macdonell in 1900 in his *A History of Sanskrit Literature*. The objections that both authors raise are largely chronological, that the absence of any mention of Buddhism in the Ramayana pushes at least the main part of its tradition back to a date before Greek influence could have been felt in the East. The oral character of the Ramayana, and hence the true character of its relationship to the *Iliad* and other European epics, began to be recognized in the 1960s based on work done on epics in ancient Greece and the modern Balkans by Milman Parry and his student A. B. Lord. John Brockington, in his 2000 overview "The Textualization of the Sanskrit Epics," summarizes works on the Ramayana especially by Russian scholars that "attempt systematically to apply the analytic techniques developed by Milman Parry for the Homeric epics."

Narayan's version *The Ramayana* has attracted little critical attention because it is difficult for Western readers, unfamiliar with the Indian epic tradition, to isolate Narayan's own contribution from the Ramayana per se. B. A. Van Nooten, in his review in the *Journal of the American Oriental Society*, limits his comments to noting places where Narayan follows Kamban rather than Valmiki and citing instances where he varies from both, censuring him almost as if his postmodern creativity were a student's errors in summarizing a set text. K. S. Narayana Rao, in his review in *World Literature Today*, judges that, in *The Ramayana*, "Narayan is not at his best" and finds that "instances of awkward English and expository comment interfering with a straight narrative are not wanting." He considers it a decline from Narayan's *Gods, Demons, and Others*.

CRITICISM

Bradley A. Skeen

Skeen is a classicist. In the following essay, he analyzes the Ramayana as an Indo-European work, examining parallels between it and epics and myths from other Indo-European traditions.

In the sixteenth and seventeenth centuries, Catholic missionaries in India recognized that Sanskrit, the ancient language of India in which the Ramayana is written, had important similarities to Greek and Latin. In the eighteenth century the British imperial bureaucrat William Jones noted that the similarities extended to the Slavic and Germanic languages (including English) and supposed that they all must therefore have had a common origin and properly constituted a group known as the Indo-European language family. Compare for example the similarity of the English *mother* with the Latin *mater* and the Sanskrit *matar*, or similarly *brother*, *frater*, and *bhratar*, or *swine*, *sus*, *sukara*. The descent of several languages from a common ancestor was familiar to Europeans because of the transformation of Latin into various local languages like French, Spanish, and Romanian once the populations of Latin speakers became isolated from each other with the collapse of the Roman Empire. As philologists and other scholars studied this phenomenon over the next two centuries, it became clear that all of the languages in Europe, Iran, and India (except for a few isolates from older populations, like Basque or Tamil) descended from a common language,

> BOTH THE *ILIAD* AND THE RAMAYANA MUST HAVE BEGUN WITH THE STORY OF THE DIVINE TWINS' RESCUE OF THEIR SISTERS FROM ACROSS THE OCEAN, AND THEY ELABORATE THE STORY FROM THE TREASURY OF INDO-EUROPEAN MYTH, PRODUCING TALES THAT ARE THE SAME BUT DIFFERENT."

known as Proto-Indo-European. This must have been the language of a single group of people living somewhere in central Asia several thousand years ago, one that was carried by waves of migration and conquest from the homeland to all of the territories in Europe and southwest Asia that those people's descendants now occupy. As groups moved out, the language changed over time because of isolation. Sometimes such change can be seen, as in the case of Latin and the Romance languages, or as in the case of Old English and the modern varieties of Scots and English, but for the most part, the change has to be inferred by reconstructing the older form of the language from its later descendants.

The Indo-Europeans also shared a common culture, of which their language was part and which evolved in the same way as its members spread into new areas, sometimes preserving common features and sometimes changing them. The use of chariots in warfare is an example of an element of Indo-European culture that spread with them through their conquests. But more to the point here, Indo-European forms of storytelling were closely linked to the language. In every Indo-European culture, one finds bards singing for the entertainment of warriors of the glorious deeds of their ancestors, in long songs that can go on for several days of performance. This form is the epic, exemplified in Greece by the *Iliad* and the *Odyssey*, in Scandinavia by *Beowulf* and the *Eddas*, and in India by the Ramayana and the Mahabharata. Many of the individual stories and even large narrative structures that make up an epic like the Ramayana go back to the original Indo-European culture. Just as Greek and Sanskrit as languages have similarities because of their common descent, so too do Greek and Sanskrit

WHAT DO I READ NEXT?

- In his 1964 volume *Gods, Demons, and Others*, Narayan adapted Hindu mythological sources into a series of short stories, some of which are based on the Ramayana and which were printed as chapters in his version of the epic.

- There is a long history in India of adapting scenes from the Ramayana in art, and since the 1960s, in the Western graphical form of the comic book. The most recent effort along these lines, which also reinterprets the story in the context of modern feminism, is *Sita's Ramayana*, a graphic novel aimed at young adults drawn by Moyna Chitrakar and written by Samhita Arni in 2011, which retells parts of the Ramayana from the point of view of Sita, the main female character.

- Besides appearing as a prominent character in the Ramayana, Hanuman is an important god in modern Hindu popular piety. The Indian American Cheeni Rao describes in his 2009 memoir, *In Hanuman's Hands*, how he believes his life, shattered by a loss of identity and drug addiction as he sought

the American dream as an undergraduate at the University of Chicago, was transformed by the saving power of Hanuman.

- David C. Conrad and Djanka Tassey Condé recorded songs from a family of *griots* (bards) in West Africa singing about the foundation of the medieval kingdom of Mali. They edited and translated their results into a single corpus, which they published as *Sunjata: A West African Epic of the Mande Peoples* in 2004.

- Margaret Atwood's 2005 volume *The Penelopiad* is a novelization of the *Odyssey* from Penelope's viewpoint, analyzing the original from a feminist perspective.

- The three-volume translation of The Ramayana by Manmatha Nath Dutt, published in 1891–1893, is the only complete version of the original poem in English. However, it is based on the traditional rather than a scholarly edition of the text and suffers from sometimes grotesque uses of schoolboyish idioms.

---

epics, and many small and large elements of the Ramayana find close parallels in European epic poetry. Parallels between Indo-European epics occur at every level, from individual words, to line-long formulae, to the largest ideas and story elements driving the plot. Narayan's version *The Ramayana*, passing through an adaptation into the non-Indo-European Tamil language, as well as the shift from poetry to prose, and above all the transformation from ancient epic to modern psychological novel, conserves only the largest parallel structures, such as similarities between the characters Rama, Lakshmana, and Sita and the Greek Dioscuri and Persephone, between Rama and Sita's wedding and the homecoming of Odysseus, and between the general plots of the Ramayana and the *Iliad*.

One of the most widespread and best conserved myths of Indo-European culture concerns the divine twins, most familiar as the Greek Dioscuri, Castor and Pollux. In origin, these brothers were in some sense part divine and part human (the details differ from story to story). Their sisters were the sun and the moon, and it was the duty of the brothers to rescue them from across the ocean. Swans were usually involved in the story: Jupiter took the form of a swan to conceive Castor and Pollux by their mortal mother Leda, while the Children of Lir in Celtic myth were transformed into swans. The divine twins are well known in older, more purely mythical Sanskrit literature such as the Rig Veda under the title *Divo napatah*, or "Sons of Dyaus" (an old sky god etymologically connected to Zeus/Jupiter), an exact translation of

Dioscuri. Rama, a divine incarnation, and his mortal brother Lakshmana have long been recognized as a reflex of the divine twins myth. They must rescue Sita (standing in for the sisters) after she has been abducted and carried over the ocean. Their years of wandering in exile are akin to the unjust exile imposed on the Children of Lir by their wicked stepmother.

Sita herself has a close kinswoman in Greece in Persephone, whose myth is given in the greatest detail in the Homeric Hymn to Demeter but whose antiquity is guaranteed by a briefer mention in Hesiod's *Theogony* (lines 912–14). Persephone is the daughter of Demeter, the goddess of agriculture, and represents the grain growing in the field. She is abducted by Hades and carried off to the underworld (which in early Greek myth lies across the ocean) but is eventually released on the orders of Zeus because, without the agricultural harvest each year, the world would starve. She is to spend six months each year with her mother and six with her husband Hades, ruling as queen of the underworld, reflecting the role of the seasons in the agricultural year. Sita is the daughter of Lakshmi, the earth goddess, as Narayan relates in *The Ramayana*: "Sita, as a baby girl, was a gift of Mother Earth to Janaka, being found in a furrow when a field was ploughed." She is then kidnapped by the demon Ravana and taken away to his fortress over the ocean, from where she is eventually rescued. But at the end of her life (in an episode Narayan suppresses as incompatible with modern taste), Sita is taken back down under the earth by her mother. So Sita is literally a crop (compare *sitos*, the Greek word for "grain") grown out of the earth and returned there (i.e., as a seed) after the fallow time of year represented by her captivity.

Sita's marriage to Rama is the subject of another striking parallel with a European epic. As Narayan relates, Sita's father, King Janaka, has a bow that had been used by the god Shiva and which is invoked as a test for Sita's suitors:

> King Janaka made it a condition that whoever could lift, bend, and string Shiva's bow would be considered fit to become Sita's husband. When her suitors took a look at the bow, they realized that it was a hopeless and unacceptable condition. They left in a rage, and later returned with their armies, prepared to win Sita by force.

But Janaka is able to defeat them. When Rama comes to Janaka's court as a guest, he is able to pass the test. Similarly, Odysseus owns a bow that was used by the hero Eurytus to compete in a contest with Herakles for the hand of Iole. During Odysseus's wanderings (compare Rama's exile), the local noblemen declare that he must be dead and so demand that his wife Penelope marry one of them. They invade his palace and feast on the wealth of his household for two years before his return, terrorizing Penelope and his son Telemachus. Finally, as recorded in book 21 of Richmond Lattimore's translation *The Odyssey of Homer*, Penelope is inspired by the goddess Athene to agree to marry the suitor who can bend Odysseus's bow:

> But now the goddess, gray-eyed Athene, put it in the mind
> of the daughter of Ikarios, circumspect Penelope,
> to set the bow before the suitors, and the gray iron,
> in the house of Odysseus: the contest, the beginning of the slaughter.

Penelope announces that she will marry the suitor who can string the bow and use it to shoot through the eyes of a dozen axe heads set up in a row as Odysseus used to do. Although he has to agree, Antinoös, the leader of the suitors, thinks the test is impossible:

> I do not think
> that this well-polished bow can ever be strung easily.
> There is no man among the lot of us who is such a one
> as Odysseus used to be.

One after one, the suitors fail, but Odysseus returns and disguises himself as a beggar. As a joke, the suitors let him have a turn and are amazed to see him succeed. Aided by Telemachus, Odysseus proceeds to use the bow to massacre the suitors. The outline of the stories in the Ramayana and the *Odyssey* is the same: a princess's suitors must pass the test of stringing a divine bow, and when the mass of suitors fail, they are defeated. The particulars of the stories are adapted to the larger plots of the two epics. The compound bow referred to in this story was originally invented by Turkic peoples in central Asia and was taken up by Indo-Europeans before their migrations to India and Europe. The story undoubtedly goes back to that early time.

The similarities in the plot of the *Iliad* (really with the larger myth of the Trojan War, some details of which are only contained in fragments of lost Greek epics) with that of the Ramayana were the first thing Western scholars noticed about the Indian epic. Since the realization that

The god Hanuman was an integral part of the location and battle for Sita. *(© criminalatt | Shutterstock.com)*

Indian and Greek civilization both descend from the Proto-Indo-European language and culture, this shared ancestry has presented an adequate explanation to account for these parallels in a meaningful way. Julian Baldick's *Homer and the Indo-Europeans: Comparing Mythologies* presents a synopsis of parallels between the Homeric poems and other epics, including the Ramayana.

Both the *Iliad* and the Ramayana must have begun with the story of the divine twins' rescue of their sisters from across the ocean, and they elaborate the story from the treasury of Indo-European myth, producing tales that are the same but different. Baldick observes, "As brothers who rescue a female figure, Agamemnon and Menelaus are, in one perspective, reflections of the Divine Twins." Helen is, in fact, the sister of the Dioscuri. As discussed above, the same is true of Rama and Lakshmana's quest for Sita. Paris is able to abduct Helen and take her to Troy, a city of wealth and luxury, because he is fair and persuasive. Ravana similarly is able to abduct Sita and take her to the luxurious Lanka because he uses his magic to dress himself in a fair form and deceive her. Baldick comments, "Thus there is an impressive

parallel with Paris and Troy." Agamemnon marshals the armies of all the princes of Greece to retrieve Helen from across the ocean, which he can do because all the princes had contended for Helen's hand and had sworn to guarantee the marriage of Helen with the victor in a footrace (who turned out to be Menelaus). Similarly, Rama assembles an army drawn from the animals that inhabit the forests of southern India (standing in for the non-Indo-European population), which he can do because he binds Sugreeva, the king of the monkeys, by an oath. One of the most prominent episodes of the *Iliad* is Odysseus's reconnaissance inside Troy, during which he speaks with Helen. Similarly, Hanuman pays a surreptitious visit to Sita inside the city of Lanka. Finally, Hanuman infiltrates and burns Lanka to achieve Rama's final victory, just as Odysseus captures Troy with the deception of the famous Trojan horse.

Source: Bradley A. Skeen, Critical Essay on *The Ramayana*, in *Novels for Students*, Gale, Cengage Learning, 2013.

Charles B. Dodson

In the following essay, Dodson explores similarities and differences between The Ramayana *and the* Iliad *and the* Odyssey.

"

ALL THIS SUGGESTS THAT IN THE WORLD

OF THE *RAMAYANA*, EVIL IS ONLY A TEMPORARY

ABERRATION FROM GOOD AND NOT A PERMANENT

ENTITY."

Using more familiar works as benchmarks can effectively expand students' understanding and enjoyment of unfamiliar nonwestern literary works. For example, by the time I get to Valmiki's Indian epic, the *Ramayana*, in a sophomore world literature survey, the class has already read, among other things, a large chunk of the *Iliad* and all of the *Odyssey*. I can then ask students to read the *Ramayana* with the Homeric epics in mind and to look for both general and specific likenesses and differences in cultural assumptions, content, and style. My hope is that in this way they will come to recognize and appreciate the delights of a work that is sometimes strikingly similar to, yet often exotically different from, the more familiar western ethos and manner of Homer.

I begin the course by assuming the students have little knowledge of the Homeric epics beyond a general awareness of the Trojan war, a few major characters, and probably some of the adventures of Odysseus. Our discussions stress, in addition to details of the action, such matters as the traits of the heroic figure, the position of women in Homeric times, the relationship of mortals to gods, Olympian politics, and the social and ethical values of the warrior society—for example, Achilles's complaint that Agamemnon has slighted him in the distribution of booty is not so much a matter of dollars and cents as of status. I use the Fagles translation of the *Iliad* and the Fitzgerald translation of the *Odyssey*. Many students find the stately pace and understated tone of the *Iliad* hard going, and the *Odyssey* not much easier. When we begin Valmiki's epic, they are relieved to see that the translation of the *Ramayana* I have chosen, R. K. Narayan's prose version, reads much like a modern novel. Because it is also relatively short, I can expect students to have completed reading it by the second day of discussion. As I had previously done for Homer, I hand out topics and questions for journal

writing and group discussion. . . . These lead students to read the *Ramayana* in the light of what we have already read and discussed about the Homeric epics. I begin with a few minutes of general background comments on the religious, cultural, and historical background of the *Ramayana*.

Students have no trouble identifying the more obvious parallels between the epics, in spite of the different religious, cultural, and geographic origins that underlie them. For example, like the legends from which the *Iliad* and *Odyssey* are drawn, the *Ramayana* tells of a great war caused by the abduction of a princess, a siege of the abductor's city, a confrontation between the abductor and the aggrieved husband, and the return of the princess to her home city. Both Homer and Valmiki frequently interrupt their narrative with digressions. Both set their stories in a heroic age peopled by legendary figures, and there are important religious and ethical overtones along with the action. Gods take an active role in both. Thus Indra's sending of his own chariot and charioteer for Rama's use in battling Ravana reminds some students of Athene's active intervention at crucial times in the *Odyssey*; of the shield and armor made specially for Achilles by Hephaestus; and of various gods' participation on both sides on the battlefield before Troy.

More perceptive students find parallels to particular episodes or passages from both the *Iliad* and the *Odyssey*. Vali's wife Tara warns him not to go out to accept Sugreeva's challenge in a way that recalls Andromache's fearful urging in Book 4 of the *Iliad* that Hector not return to the field of battle but instead rebuff the rampaging Achaians from defensive positions atop the battlements of Troy. In a passage that, except for the character's name, could almost have come from the *Iliad*, Ravana's gigantic lieutenant Mahodara, "intoxicated with war fever" (like an Achaian warrior in a frenzied *aristeia*), and eager for the glory that comes with victory over a famous opponent, resolutely attacks Rama. Like Achilles, Ravana pridefully stays out of the fight with Rama's forces until, infuriated by Rama's destruction of his brother and son (parallel to Hector's slaying of Patroclus), Ravana feels "a terrific rage rising within him," dons his "blessed armor," and rushes forth to challenge Rama, telling himself, "The time has come for me to act by myself again."

The *Ramayana* contains frequent parallels to the events of the *Odyssey* as well. Though the circumstances vary, both Rama and Odysseus endure long exiles—Rama for fourteen years, Odysseus the ten years of his return to Ithaka on top of the ten he spent at Troy. Rama's wife Sita staunchly resists Ravana's threats and blandishments while she is in captivity, just as Penelope puts off the suitors, who have made her a virtual prisoner in her own house. The similarities of the bow-stringing episodes in each story are obvious to even the least-attentive students. Those who read more closely also point out that Hanuman and Lakshmana, who endure exile with Rama and act as important lieutenants in the battle with Ravana, correspond to the loyal Telemachus, Eumaeus, and Philoetius, who all stand with Odysseus in the showdown with the usurping suitors. Soorpanaka's attempted seduction of Rama parallels Circe's and Calypso's more successful attempts to divert Odysseus from returning home. The final battle concluded, civic order is restored in both epics as Rama returns to Ayodhya in triumph to resume the coronation interrupted fourteen years before; and, in the *Odyssey*, when Odysseus has finally been reunited with Penelope and his father Laertes, Athene steps in to disperse the vengeance-bent relatives of the slain suitors.

But within this framework of similarity, the differences between the *Ramayana* and the Homeric poems are what the students find so uniquely interesting in Valmiki's epic. When I ask if they see anything modern in Rama, some point to an element of charisma in him that reminds them of the way we react to sports heroes or pop culture figures. As one pointed out, other characters fear and respect Achilles and Odysseus, but they love Rama. I ask the students to find examples of asceticism, contemplation, and restraint, which a Homeric character would probably consider odd, impractical, even weak. Thus Rama's training and rites of passage involve not only tests of courage and physical strength, but instruction in yoga, philosophy, and ethics. The question of whether he can destroy Thataka with propriety, because she is a woman, would probably not occur to Achilles—or to Odysseus, who orders the execution of the faithless maids without hesitation. Nor would Homer's characters pause to argue the propriety of Rama's becoming involved in the dispute between Vali and Sugreeva. The lengthy discussion of the ethical questions raised by Rama's shooting of Vali from ambush can provide the occasion for an in-class "debate" between two groups of students. Achilles's stubborn insistence

on his own worth is the wellspring of the *Iliad*, yet one of Rama's most admirable traits is his self-denial, as he accepts an unjust exile without rancor and humbly dons clothing made from tree bark. And the blood-thirsty Achaian warrior-chieftans of the *Iliad* would probably find strange indeed the words of King Dasaratha to his favorite son Rama: "Humility and soft speech—there could be really no limit to these virtues. There can be no place in a kings heart for lust, anger, or meanness."

Homer's warriors have no time for speculation; Rama has 14 years for it. For the Greek warrior, human suffering can be explained simply and easily: the gods are responsible. But to the Indian, such issues are the subject of debate and introspection. The transitory nature of human existence means only to the Greek warrior-hero that he does not have much time to make his mark; for him, death is always only one fated spear-thrust away, and life is all that matters. I direct students' attention to Achilles's bitter comment to Odysseus in the underworld episode of the *Odyssey*; "Better, I say, to break sod as a farm hand / for some poor country man, on iron rations, / than lord it over all the exhausted dead" (Book 11). As Robert Antoine has pointed out, "While the Greek hero feels that human existence is a gift which must be enjoyed, the Indian hero tends to see in it a bondage from which one should escape."

The students are quick to notice not only the sheer number and variety of divine and demonic beings in the *Ramayana* but the ambivalent powers of the gods as well. For example, the gods often lack precognition of the outcome of major events, such as the climactic battle with Ravana; whereas Homer provides us with the wonderful image of Zeus weighing the fates of Achilles and Hector on his golden scales (Book 22). As in Homer, the gods of the *Ramayana* take human form and go among humans, but would Zeus go to a human for help as did Indra, "the chief of all the gods," who sought aid at various times from Rama's father Dasaratha and from the sage Agasthya (9, 12)? Students are especially surprised when they discover that Valmiki's gods can even be defeated by a mortal—as we learn in one of the digressive tales, when King Mahabali conquers the whole of earth and heaven. The laws of nature are seldom violated in the Homeric epics. Exceptions in the *Odyssey* are Scylla and, probably, the floating rocks, though the latter may well be a metaphor for an essentially natural phenomenon, as is Charybdis, the whirlpool. The warriors of the *Iliad* fight only other warriors (plus the occasional god or goddess), and the cannibal Polyphemus, his size and single eye notwithstanding, is essentially human—monstrous in behavior, but not a monster. But in the *Ramayana* the laws of nature are altered or even dispensed with as the storyteller pleases: Thataka is alternately woman, desert, and dragon; Shiva's bow, which Rama wields with ease, is "so huge that no one could comprehend it at one glance;" Ravana and Soorpanaka, Rama's and Sita's chief opponents, are themselves demons with magical powers (and Ravana has 10 heads and 20 arms); Ravana, lovesick at the mere thought of Sita—whom he has never seen—changes the weather, banishes the seasons, and disrupts the very passage of time itself; even the sun and moon shine or not, as he commands; Hanuman can assume gigantic size at will; and in the closing battle, Rama's and Ravana's chariots not only fly but circle the globe.

In fact, the western tendency to exaggerate the virtues and prowess of the heroic figure is mild in comparison to the almost bizarrely superhuman deeds, characters, and events of the *Ramayana*. Thus Bhagiratha, "responsible for bringing the Ganges down to earth [. . .] prayed intensely for ten thousand years to Brahma, [. . .] prayed to Shiva for ten thousand years [. . .] and prayed to Ganga for five thousand years" before finally prevailing on Ganga to become the Ganges (19). Rama defeats Kara's 14 demon commanders, then Kara himself and his whole army of demons, single-handedly; and he similarly disposes of Ravana's whole army, "which stretched away to the horizon," before taking on Ravana himself in a battle that ranges over the whole earth.

Both Homer and Valmiki's epics share a digressive narrative mode, which students tend to find disconcerting, given the modern penchant (especially in popular movies and television series) for uncomplicated linear narrative. So I ask students to look for fairy-tale-like qualities in the interpolated stories in the *Ramayana*, in contrast to Homer's stolid histories of helmets and lineages. For example, in Mahabali's story, Vishnu restores the kingdoms of the gods by tricking Mahabali, first by taking dwarfish form and then by becoming so huge that he encompasses the earth and the heavens in two steps. Thataka's story explains how the desert came to be. Perhaps

Ahalya's story is the nearest to Greek myth in spirit, reminding students of Zeus's frequent infatuation with mortal women. The sage Gautama, having caught Indra ("the highest god among the gods") in the act of lying with Gautama's surpassingly beautiful wife Ahalya, decrees that Indra's body "be covered with a thousand female marks, so that in all the worlds," he tells Indra, "people may understand what really goes on in your mind all the time"; immediately, "every inch of Indra's body displayed the female organ." Gautama also punishes the blameless Ahalya—Indra had assumed Gautama's own form when he seduced her—by turning her to granite. She can only be freed from the enchantment when "Rama passes this way at some future date," which, of course, happens when some dust from Rama's feet falls on her as he is walking to Sita's city for his wedding.

This fairytale quality pervades much of Narayan's version of the epic, quite in contrast with the somber and often grimly bloody events of the Homeric poems. The *Iliad* is full of pain and suffering: its battle scenes are exciting and realistic, its killings depicted in graphic and bloody detail. In the *Odyssey* the slaughter of the suitors, the hanging of the treacherous maids, and the mutilation of the disloyal goatherd Melanthius are ghastly and have considerable emotional impact despite Homer's lofty style. But the *Ramayana*, for all its military action, violent death, and physical punishments, is somehow different. We feel the pain in Homer's battles, but not in the *Ramayana*'s. And indeed, one wonders if the final conflict between Rama and Ravana takes place in the external world of searing pain and bloody corpses at all, or rather in Rama's mind. I ask students to consider this description of the penultimate attack by Ravana, who is invoking a weapon called "Maya," designed to create illusions:

> With proper incantations and worship, he sent off the weapon and it created an illusion of reviving all the arm[y] and its leaders [. . .] and bringing them back to the battlefield. Presently Rama found all those who, he thought, were no more, coming on with battle cries and surrounding him. Every man in the enemy's army was again up in arms. [. . .] Rama asked, [. . .] "How are all these coming back? They were dead." Matali explained, "In your original identity you are the creator of illusions in this universe. Please know that Ravana has created phantoms to confuse you. If you make up your mind, you can dispel them immediately." [. . .] Rama at once invoked a weapon called

"Gnana"—which means "wisdom" or "perception." [. . .] And all the terrifying armies who seemed to have come on in such a great mass suddenly evaporated into thin air.

Shortly after, Rama delivers the lethal blow to Ravana in the form of Brahmasthra, a weapon devised by Brahma himself. Immediately Ravana is transformed, revealing a being "devout and capable of tremendous attainments," whose "face shone with serenity and peace":

> Rama's arrows had burnt off the layers of dross, the anger, conceit, cruelty, lust, and egotism which had encrusted his [Ravana's] real self, and now his personality came through in its pristine form.

All this suggests that in the world of the *Ramayana*, evil is only a temporary aberration from good and not a permanent entity. And in fact, we are told on the next page that Ravana's spirit will "go to heaven, where he has his place."

But there are no miraculous transformations of character when a Homeric personage dies. In the *Odyssey*, the shade of Achilles is as sullenly ferocious as ever (Book 11); the dead suitors are quickly conducted to their permanent dwelling in the underworld. And were it not for the direct intervention of Athene, the *Odyssey* would close on yet another cycle of retributive killing in response to the code of blood vengeance.

The students find other noteworthy differences between the Homeric and Indian epics. For example, there are occasional flashes of humor in the latter and an unselfconscious treatment of sex that today's generation of students finds amusing. There are no doubt other ways of conveying to American students the delights of the *Ramayana* and other unfamiliar works outside the European tradition, but I have found that asking them to observe closely both the similarities and differences between Homer and Valmiki succeeds admirably with most. In fact, in the informal poll that I often conduct at the end of the course, many students tell me the *Ramayana* was the work they enjoyed most.

Source: Charles B. Dodson, "Using Homer to Teach *The Ramayana*," in *Teaching English in the Two Year College*, Vol. 28, No. 1, September 2000, pp. 68–73.

SOURCES

Baldick, Julian, *Homer and the Indo-Europeans: Comparing Mythologies*, I. B. Tauris, 1994, pp. 14–96.

Banker, Ashok, *The Prince of Ayodhya*, Penguin, 2003.

Brockington, John, "The Textualization of the Sanskrit Epics," in *Textualization of Oral Epics*, edited by Lauri Honko, Mouton de Gruyter, 2000, pp. 193–226.

Homer, *The Odyssey of Homer*, translated by Richmond Lattimore, Harper & Row, 1975, pp. 309–34.

Iyengar, K. R. S., ed., *Asian Variations in Ramayana*, Sahitya Akademi, 2006.

Jamison, Stephanie W., "Penelope and the Pigs: Indic Perspectives on the *Odyssey*," in *Classical Antiquity*, Vol. 18, No. 2, 1999, pp. 227–72.

Jones, William, *The Works of Sir William Jones: With the Life of the Author*, Vol. 3, John Stockdale and John Walker, 1807, pp. 24–46.

Lord, A. B., *The Singer of Tales*, 40th Anniversary Edition, Harvard University Press, 2000, pp. 3–138.

Macdonell, Arthur Anthony, *A History of Sanskrit Literature*, W. Heinemann, 1900, pp. 307–308.

Mallory, J. P., *The Oxford Introduction to the Proto-Indo-European and the Proto-Indo-European World*, Oxford University Press, 2006, pp. 1–11, 408–41.

Mallory, J. P., and Douglas Q. Adams, eds., *Encyclopedia of Indo-European Culture*, Taylor & Francis, 1997, pp. 161–65.

Narayan, R. K., *The Ramayana: A Shortened Modern Prose Version of the Indian Epic*, Viking Press, 1972.

Van Nooten, B. A., "*The Ramayana* by R.K. Narayan," in *Journal of the American Oriental Society*, Vol. 95, No. 1, 1975, p. 153.

Parrinder, Geoffrey, *Avatar and Incarnation: The Divine in Human Form in the World's Religions*, Oneworld, 1997, pp. 223–50.

Parry, Milman, *The Making of Homeric Verse: The Collected Papers of Milman Parry*, edited by Adam Parry, Oxford University Press, 1987, pp. 266–364.

Rao, K. S. Narayana, "*The Ramayana* by R.K. Narayan," in *World Literature Today*, Vol. 52, No. 3, Summer 1978, pp. 521–22.

Richman, Paula, ed., *Many Ramayanas: The Diversity of a Narrative Tradition in South Asia*, University of California Press, 1991, pp. 3–172.

Telang, Kashinath Trimbak, *Was the Ramayana Copied from Homer? A Reply to Professor Weber*, Union Press, 1873, pp. 1–71.

Weber, Albrecht, "On the Ramayana," in *Indian Antiquary*, Vol. 1, 1872, pp. 120–27, 172–82, 239–53.

FURTHER READING

Alles, Gregory D., *The Iliad, the Ramayana, and the Work of Religion: Failed Persuasion and Religious Mystification*, Pennsylvania State University Press, 1994.

Alles focuses on how both epics treat the role of persuasive speech in the societies that produced them.

Goldman, Robert P., *The Ramayana of Valmiki: An Epic of Ancient India*, 6 vols., Princeton University Press, 1990–2009.

This heavily annotated scholarly translation of the Ramayana establishes a new standard in the rendering and explanation of the epic based on the modern critical edition of the original Sanskrit text. Only six of the proposed seven volumes have been completed.

Leslie, Julia, *Authority and Meaning in Indian Religions: Hinduism and the Case of Valmiki*, Ashgate, 2003.

Leslie investigates the figure of Valmiki, the putative author of the Ramayana, in Hindu popular piety, where, especially among the Hindu community in Great Britain today, Valmiki is worshiped as a savior god.

Narayan, R. K., *The Mahabharata*, Heinemann, 1978.

The Ramayana and the Mahabharata are the two great sacred Indian epics and come from closely related traditions. Narayan novelized the Mahabharata in the same style he had its companion.

Watkins, Calvert, ed., *The American Heritage Dictionary of Indo-European Roots*, Houghton Mifflin Harcourt, 2011.

This frequently revised reference work gives a list of roots from Proto-Indo-European, similar to ordinary dictionary entries, but focused on showing how they came to be the basis of English words. Although published separately, this brief text (with about 13,000 entries) is also bound in as an appendix to many editions of the *American Heritage Dictionary*.

SUGGESTED SEARCH TERMS

R. K. Narayan AND *The Ramayana*

Ramayana

Valmiki

Kamban

epic

Tamil

Sanskrit

Indo-European OR Indoeuropean

Indo-Anglian literature

The Song of the Lark

WILLA CATHER

1915

Much of Willa Cather's most highly regarded fiction is set in the American West and in the Great Plains. Her third novel, *The Song of the Lark*, opens in Moonstone, Colorado, a setting integral to the early development of the novel's protagonist, Thea Kronborg. Thea's deeply emotional connections to places and to landscapes—first to Moonstone and later to the canyons of Arizona—shape her character. In *The Song of the Lark*, Cather traces the evolution of Thea as an artist.

Thea's journey begins in a small town in Colorado, where her talent as a pianist and her awareness of her sense of self are first revealed. In pursuit of a career in music, Thea travels first to Chicago and later to New York and Germany. Several relationships are revealed to be fundamental to Thea's artistic development and later professional success, but throughout the work, Cather emphasizes Thea's firm belief in her own unique sense of identity and artistic potential as she blossoms from a child into a young woman and accomplished opera singer. Scholars have noted that Cather's own childhood informs some of the early portions of the novel and that the author was inspired by the career of opera singer Olive Fremstad in writing the latter half of the work.

The Song of the Lark was originally published in 1915 and is available in a 2004 edition published by Dover.

Willa Cather (© *AP Images*)

AUTHOR BIOGRAPHY

Born on December 7, 1873, in Back Creek Valley, Virginia, Cather was named Wilella Cather, after an aunt. The year after Cather's birth, her parents, Charles and Mary Cather, moved their young family to Cather's grandfather's sheep farm in Willow Shade, Virginia. Two brothers and a sister were born in subsequent years. In 1882, Cather began calling herself "Willa Love Cather," in honor of two men—an uncle who had died in the Civil War and the doctor who presided at her birth. In 1883, Cather and her family, including grandparents and cousins, moved to a farm in Nebraska. They remained on the family farm for a year, and then Cather's father moved his family to the prairie town of Red Cloud, Nebraska. Here, he opened a real estate office. Another brother was born in 1888.

In 1890, Cather graduated from Red Cloud High School and later that year moved to Lincoln to enroll in a University of Nebraska preparatory school, the Latin School. Another sister was born that same year. Cather entered the University of Nebraska in 1891 and, during her time there, regularly contributed essays and theater criticism to the *Nebraska State Journal*. After graduation in 1895, Cather secured a position as an associate editor for the Lincoln paper, the *Courier*. In 1896, Cather returned to Red Cloud for a short time before moving on to Pittsburgh, where she worked as the editor of *Home Monthly*. She began regularly publishing short fiction, poetry, and criticism in journals during this time. After resigning from *Home Monthly* in 1897, Cather began working as a staff writer for a Pittsburgh paper, the *Leader*.

Following a brief stint in Washington, D.C., as a translator, Cather began teaching in Pittsburgh's Central High School, in 1901. She traveled to Europe with her friend Isabelle McClung in 1902. Cather published her first poetry collection, *April Twilights*, in 1903, and her first short story collection, *The Troll Garden*, in 1905. Cather moved to New York in 1906 to work at *McClure's Magazine*. In 1911, after a period of work and travel, Cather returned to New York and resigned from *McClure's*. She published her first novel, *Alexander's Masquerade*, in installments in *McClure's*, beginning in 1912. The novel would later appear in book form under the title *Alexander's Bridge*. In 1913, Cather published the novel *O Pioneers!*, her first work to receive widespread critical acclaim. Also in 1913, Cather met the opera singer, Olive Fremstad, a figure who inspired a portion of the novel *The Song of the Lark*, which was published in 1915.

Cather continued to write and travel from then on, spending large amounts of time in the American West, as well as in France. Over the years, Cather was awarded a number of honorary doctorate degrees, along with the French literary prize, the *Prix Fémina Américain*. She published *My Ántonia* in 1918, *Death Comes for the Archbishop* in 1927, *Shadows on the Rock* in 1930, and *Lucy Gayheart* in 1935, among other works. In 1942, Cather underwent gallbladder surgery. Cather died in New York on April 24, 1947, of a cerebral hemorrhage.

PLOT SUMMARY

Part 1: Friends of Childhood, Chapters 1–5

As *The Song of the Lark* opens, Dr. Howard Archie is approached by Peter Kronborg, who summons the doctor to his home to help with the

MEDIA ADAPTATIONS

- An unabridged audio recording of *The Song of the Lark* was published by Tantor Media in 2010. The work, narrated by Pam Ward, is available as an MP3 download and as an audio CD.

- *The Song of the Lark* was adapted for television by PBS in 2001. Joseph Maurer wrote the teleplay based on Cather's novel, and the production was directed by Karen Arthur. The television movie was released on DVD in 2006.

- An unabridged audio recording of *The Song of the Lark*, available as an MP3 download or audio CD and read by Christine Williams, was published in 2012 by Blackstone Audio.

delivery of the seventh Kronborg child. After attending the birth of the infant, Thor, Dr. Archie checks in on one of the other Kronborg children, a young girl named Thea, whom Dr. Archie discovers to be ill with pneumonia. In his treatment of the girl, Dr. Archie reveals the high regard he has for the child above all the other Kronborgs. Likewise, Thea adores the doctor and responds eagerly to his preferential attention.

In the course of Thea's recovery, the reader is introduced to the other members of the large Kronborg family, which is descended from Scandinavian immigrants. The action begins to center exclusively on Thea, the novel's protagonist. A music student, Thea regularly makes her way to the home of Mr. and Mrs. Kohler, where her teacher, the German Professor Wunsch, also resides. Professor Wunsch instructs Thea in piano and admires her will and determination. As the fifth chapter closes, the social structures of the Colorado town of Moonstone are portrayed, and Dr. Archie's wife is introduced as a woman who dislikes company in her home and of whom Thea remains wary.

Part 1: Friends of Childhood, Chapters 6–10

Dr. Archie invites Thea to go with him into the Mexican portion of Moonstone, where he is looking in on Spanish Johnny, a musician who is habitually intoxicated and who leaves home for long periods of time. Thea considers herself Johnny's friend and is enamored with the music associated with Moonstone's Mexican population. Soon after this trip with Dr. Archie, Thea is invited to go on another trip, this time with the thirty-year-old railway worker Ray Kennedy, who plans to marry Thea when she is older (Thea is currently twelve). The trip to the sand hills just outside of town is also made by two of Thea's older brothers, Johnny, and Johnny's wife, Mrs. Tellamantez.

These chapters of the novel underscore Thea's unique nature by highlighting the unusual friendships she develops as a child. Her maturity is also emphasized when she begins taking on her own music students and using the money she earns to transform an attic room into her own bedroom. Thea's sense of herself begins to unfold; in the quiet of her own space, she is able to hear the "voice within herself" that is otherwise "drowned" by the chaos associated with her family. Thea's parents begin to acknowledge the remarkable nature of Thea's talent and personality, as does Professor Wunsch.

Part 1: Friends of Childhood, Chapters 11–15

With Professor Wunsch, Thea discusses her future and her dreams for herself, and she acknowledges out loud, for the first time, her understanding that there is something special about her. The result of this conversation is Thea's belief that she must study music in Germany if she is to make something of herself, and she confides these dreams to Dr. Archie. By the next summer, Thea has taken on four students.

Professor Wunsch is increasingly unavailable to give Thea her lessons because of his heavy drinking. He is discovered unconscious in a gulch and is later cared for by Dr. Archie in the Kohler home. Wunsch awakens in a mad frenzy and begins destroying Mr. and Mrs. Kohler's property. After Johnny goes for help, Wunsch is restrained and confined to his bed for ten days. He loses the remainder of his students after this incident and subsequently leaves Moonstone.

Mr. and Mrs. Kronborg decide that Thea should stop attending school and begin taking on more music students. By her fifteenth birthday the following summer, Thea has eight pupils. Ray advises Thea to save her money and go to Chicago to study, but Thea believes she will never have enough income to do so.

Part 1: Friends of Childhood, Chapters 16–20

Thea and her mother take a trip to Denver, riding in the caboose of Ray's train. Ray, who has traveled extensively in the West and Southwest, tells Thea about the Native American cliff-dwelling ruins he has visited. Later in the summer, Thea's family encourages her to participate more in church (her father is a minister). She is asked to sing at prayer meetings, a task she undertakes reluctantly.

Thea's devout sister Anna frowns upon Thea's lack of enthusiasm for religion and does not approve of the fact that Thea's friends are all older men (Spanish Johnny, Ray Kennedy, and Dr. Archie). Thea is further prompted to consider such religious issues as morality and divine judgment when a tramp wanders through town, is shunned by everyone, and later contaminates the city's water supply, resulting in an outbreak of typhoid fever.

Not long after, Ray Kennedy is injured and soon dies from injuries sustained in a railway accident. Dr. Archie reveals that Ray has left Thea six hundred dollars with instructions that she is to use the money to travel to Chicago and study music there. Dr. Archie volunteers to accompany her. Thea's parents reluctantly agree to let her go.

Part 2: The Song of the Lark, Chapters 1–5

After arriving in Chicago, Thea and Dr. Archie begin seeking lodging for Thea. She secures a position singing in a church choir and finds a room to rent with a widow, Mrs. Lorch, and her widowed daughter, Mrs. Irene Anderson. Dr. Archie arranges for Thea to begin studying piano with Andor Harsanyi. Harsanyi is impressed with Thea's talent. When Thea visits Harsanyi and his family for dinner one evening and sings for them, Harsanyi discovers that Thea is a truly gifted singer. Thea continues her piano instruction but also begins instruction in singing as well. At Mrs. Anderson's suggestion, Thea begins exploring the cultural offerings of Chicago.

Part 2: The Song of the Lark, Chapters 6–11

Harsanyi insists that Thea should begin taking instruction from the renowned instructor Madison Bowers. Before returning home to Moonstone for the summer, Thea takes twenty lessons from Bowers and is delighted with his voice instruction. At home, she begins to perceive that her family now treats her differently, and she ponders her own sense of her self and her potential as an artist. After spending time with Spanish Johnny and Moonstone's Mexican community, Thea is further distanced from her family, particularly by Anna and her brothers, who disapprove of her behavior. Before returning to Chicago, Thea visits the ever-supportive Dr. Archie.

Part 3: Stupid Faces, Chapters 1–7

The third portion of the novel opens with Thea having studied under Mr. Bowers for two months. Thea moves frequently, always seeking better accommodations with her limited income. In addition to taking lessons from Mr. Bowers, Thea works for him as a pianist in the afternoons, accompanying other singers. At Mr. Bowers's studio, Thea meets Philip Frederick Ottenburg, or Fred, the wealthy and successful son of a German brewer.

Fred takes an interest in Thea and attends her lessons. Impressed with Thea's voice, Fred begins to arrange singing engagements for Thea. In the spring, as Thea is recovering from a lingering cold, Thea expresses to Fred her sense of discouragement with the path her career is taking thus far, as well as boredom with the work she is doing. Fred offers her a chance to spend the summer at a ranch in Arizona. The sprawling desert estate is owned by a friend of Fred's family, Henry Biltmore. Thea agrees to take advantage of this opportunity.

Part 4: The Ancient People, Chapters 1–8

In Arizona at the Biltmore ranch, Thea enjoys living simply. She spends long stretches of her time exploring the native cliff dwellings of the type Ray Kennedy used to reminisce about. In the canyon, Thea has a revelation in which she perceives a connection between herself and the native women who used to inhabit the cliff dwellings so long ago. She likens her own throat and voice to the beautifully crafted water jugs that held the water so vital to the native people of the canyon. As she regains a sense of self, peace, and strength, Thea decides she will find a way to go to Germany to study.

Not long after, Fred arrives to visit Thea, and what was once a romantic interest blossoms into a romantic relationship. As the two ride and hike through the canyon, Thea discusses her notions of identity and independence. Caught in a storm at dusk during an excursion into the canyon, Thea and Fred reveal their feelings for one another. They leave Arizona on the same train, and their discussions of the future lead Fred to propose that they run away together. Impulsively he suggests they marry in Mexico, although he doubts Thea will agree. To his surprise, she does. Privately, he despairs, as he is already married.

The narration turns at this point to Fred's past, as his relationship with Edith Beers is recounted. He married her on a whim when she was escaping her impending marriage to another man. After a few years, Fred began to see Edith's true manipulative and shallow nature. Because Edith would not agree to a divorce, Fred turned to alcohol, until his mother intervened and brokered an agreement with Edith that landed the unwanted wife an estate in California, where Edith is largely left to her own devices.

Part 5: Doctor Archie's Venture, Chapters 1–5

The narrative shifts once again back to Dr. Archie, who is becoming increasingly invested in the mining industry. While in Denver, Dr. Archie receives a letter from Thea, asking him for money. Dr. Archie prepares to join her in New York immediately. In New York, Fred and Thea discuss Dr. Archie's impending arrival. It is gradually revealed that in Mexico, Fred confessed to Thea that he was already married and cannot, in fact, marry her. Once they arrived in New York, Thea resolved to borrow money from Dr. Archie in order to go to Germany, while Fred decided to once again try and divorce his wife. Once Dr. Archie arrives in New York, he, Fred, and Thea discuss Thea's plans. Dr. Archie agrees to loan Thea the money she needs while Fred arranges the details of her journey to Germany.

Part 6: Kronborg, Ten Years Later, Chapters 1–5

This section of the book opens ten years after Thea's departure for Germany. Dr. Archie now resides in Denver and has done so since the death of his wife. He is now fully invested in the mining industry and has become quite wealthy and successful in this endeavor. Fred arrives to visit Dr. Archie, and the men discuss Dr. Archie's

upcoming trip to New York. Thea has been studying in Germany for some time and has recently returned to New York. Once Dr. Archie arrives in New York, he attends a performance of Thea's and barely recognizes the girl he once knew. Fred, also in New York at the time of Dr. Archie's arrival, visits with Dr. Archie after the doctor watches Thea perform. The men discuss how drastically Thea has changed; Dr. Archie found that after the performance she seemed "pretty well used up," whereas Fred is exhilarated by Thea's progression as an artist.

Part 6: Kronborg, Ten Years Later, Chapters 6–11

Thea awakens the morning after her performance and mentally assesses herself. She initially dreads seeing Dr. Archie again but warms to the idea as the day progress. Dr. Archie arrives to visit her and is shortly followed by Fred. As they dine together, Thea receives word that a singer in another show has fallen ill, and Thea has been asked to replace her in the second act of the performance. Dr. Archie and Fred assist Thea in making it to the theater on time. Not long after, the three dine together once again and discuss an upcoming role in which Thea will star.

Later, Fred and Thea spend time alone together in Central Park. After reviewing their romantic history, they agree to part as friends. Thea spends the next week preparing for a challenging role. At the performance, several key figures from Thea's past are in the audience, including Harsanyi and Spanish Johnny. The narrative ends as Thea begins her career as a famous opera singer; the role has proven to be her breakthrough performance.

Epilogue

The novel's epilogue is set in Moonstone in 1909. Thea's Aunt Tillie is the only remaining Kronborg in Moonstone. Having kept abreast of her niece's career through the papers, Tillie now reads of Thea's marriage to Fred.

CHARACTERS

Mrs. Irene Anderson

Mrs. Anderson is one of the two widows with whom Thea resides when she first reaches Chicago. It is on Mrs. Anderson's suggestion that

Thea begins to take advantage of Chicago's cultural offerings.

Dr. Howard Archie

Dr. Archie is Moonstone's doctor. He is introduced as the novel opens, when he delivers Mrs. Kronborg's seventh baby, Thor. Throughout the course of the novel, his personal attachment to Thea is highlighted; she is not simply another patient or fellow Moonstone resident. Like other men who play a significant role in Thea's life, including Spanish Johnny, Professor Wunsch, and Ray Kennedy, Dr. Archie recognizes that Thea possesses a unique nature. He sees that, in addition to her musical abilities, Thea is independent and mature and that she possesses a sense of self-assuredness that transcends her years. He struggles at times to treat her as the child she is, and as she grows, his devotion to her remains intact. He escorts her to Chicago, where, with the money left to her by Ray Kennedy, Thea spends a winter studying the piano and singing for Harsanyi. Eager to help when Thea calls on him, Dr. Archie later travels to New York to give Thea the money she needs to go to Europe to study and returns to New York a decade later to watch Thea perform in a role that assures her place in New York's operatic scene.

Mrs. Archie

Mrs. Archie is Dr. Howard Archie's wife. She is particular about her home and does not enjoy guests. Thea dislikes her.

Henry Biltmore

Henry Biltmore is a friend of the Ottenburg family and the owner of a large ranch in the canyons of Arizona. At Fred's invitation, Thea spend a recuperative summer at the ranch.

Madison Bowers

Madison Bowers is an influential singing instructor in Chicago. At Mr. Harsanyi's urging, Mr. Bowers takes on Thea as a student.

Andor Harsanyi

Andor Harsanyi is a notable music teacher in Chicago from whom Thea takes lessons. After hearing Thea's singing voice, Mr. Harsanyi becomes instrumental in furthering Thea's career as a singer, first by coaching her himself and later by arranging lessons with the prominent Madison Bowers. Mr. Harsanyi later hears Thea sing in New York during her breakout performance.

Mrs. Harsanyi

Mrs. Harsanyi is the wife of Andor Harsanyi. She is kind and motherly toward Thea and perpetually encourages Thea in her artistic endeavors.

Mrs. Johnson

Mrs. Johnson is the president of the Moonstone Orchestra. She frowns on Thea's adult male friends and disapproves of the fact that Thea is "bold" with them.

Ray Kennedy

Ray Kennedy is a railroad worker in Moonstone. He has long-standing plans to marry Thea when she is old enough (Ray is eighteen years older than Thea). Ray treats Thea respectfully and plans for the day when she might be ready to marry him. He plans to ask her to marry him when Thea is seventeen, but asserts that he "would be willing to wait two, or even three years, until she was twenty, if she thought best." By then, he hopes he will have made enough money to support her properly. Ray, however, does not have the opportunity to follow through on his plans. He is injured in a railway accident and dies soon after. Before he dies, Ray instructs Dr. Archie regarding the money Ray has set aside for Thea. He insists that the several hundred dollars he has saved be used by Thea to travel to Chicago to study music. In this way, Thea embarks on her music career.

Fritz Kohler

Fritz Kohler is Moonstone's tailor and one of the town's first settlers. Professor Wunsch lives with Mr. and Mrs. Kohler, and it is through her association with Professor Wunsch that Thea comes to know the Kohlers. Mr. and Mrs. Kohler care for Professor Wunsch after his alcoholic episode and are saddened when their tenant and friend leaves Moonstone.

Paulina Kohler

Paulina Kohler is the wife of the town tailor. She shows Thea an abundance of maternal kindness when Thea visits her home for piano lessons with Professor Wunsch. Mrs. Kohler has additionally spent many years cultivating a lush garden, in which Thea enjoys spending time. Later in

Thea's life, she cherishes her memories of relaxing in Mrs. Kohler's garden.

Anna Kronborg

Anna is the eldest of the Kronborg children. She becomes pious as she gets older and is vocal in her disapproval of Thea.

Mrs. Anna Kronborg

Mrs. Kronborg is Thea's mother. Despite being the wife of the town's minister, Mrs. Kronborg is not a particularly religious woman. She is praised by her husband for her upbringing of the children and her privileged knowledge of her children's natures and talents. Decidedly supportive of Thea's artistic and professional endeavors, Mrs. Kronborg is regarded by Thea as her only ally in the family, particularly when Thea returns home after her summer in Chicago and is subjected to the harsh judgment of her siblings. Mrs. Kronborg becomes gravely ill when Thea is studying in Germany, and despite being contacted by Dr. Archie regarding the state of her mother's health, Thea decides not to return home. Mrs. Kronborg dies without seeing Thea one last time.

Axel Kronborg

Axel is one of Thea's brothers. Axel and another brother, Gunner, frequently accompany Thea on her excursions with Ray Kennedy.

Charley Kronborg

Charley is one of Thea's brothers.

Gunner Kronborg

Gunner is one of Thea's brothers. Along with Axel, Gunner frequently accompanies Thea on her excursions with Ray Kennedy.

Gus Kronborg

Gus is one of Thea's brothers.

Peter Kronborg

Peter Kronborg is Thea's father. Mr. Kronborg is the town's preacher. He is depicted as a man who takes pride in his schooling and is prone to using bookish language. He recognizes that Thea has special talents and strives to create opportunities for her to flourish.

Thea Kronborg

Thea is the novel's protagonist, and her journey to fame is chronicled throughout the course of the narrative. Even as a child, Thea has an awareness of her own unique talent as an artist, and she possesses a sense of self that is remarkably well defined for such a young child. It is to this quality that many adults in Thea's life are drawn. Her instructors, first Professor Wunsch and later Mr. Harsanyi, realize that accompanying this natural ability and sense of self is a desire to work hard and to accomplish challenging tasks. Thea pushes herself repeatedly toward greater achievements. She first tackles the complex musical score with which Professor Wunsch has challenged her and later travels to Chicago to study first as a pianist and then as a singer. Determined to study in Germany, Thea relies on the help of Dr. Archie for the funds necessary to achieve this goal. Dr. Archie's investment pays off, and when Thea returns to New York, she is an accomplished opera singer awaiting the role with which she can prove her talent. Near the novel's end, Thea is given this opportunity, and the narrative closes at the onset of her burgeoning career.

Thor Kronborg

Thor is Thea's youngest sibling, born just as the book opens. As Thor grows, he is often left in Thea's adoring care. As a young man, he works as a driver for Dr. Archie.

Tillie Kronborg

Tillie Kronborg is Thea's aunt and Peter Kronborg's sister. She lives with Thea's family and considers herself an actress and an artist, as she performs with a local theater company. She is considered somewhat eccentric by Thea's family, but like others, recognizes that Thea possesses special talent. Tillie adores her niece and follows Thea's career after Thea leaves Moonstone.

Mr. Landry

Mr. Landry, often referred to simply as Landry, works as Thea's accompanist and is also a singer himself. He studied with Thea in Germany and possesses some insight into Thea's time spent there.

Mrs. Lorch

Mrs. Lorch is one of the widows with whom Thea temporarily stays when she arrives in Chicago to study piano. She is the mother of Mrs. Anderson, who is also widowed.

Edith Beers Ottenburg

Edith Beers Ottenburg does not appear directly in the novel but does complicate Fred's relationship with Thea. Edith is his wife from whom he has been estranged for many years. He seeks divorce from Edith for a number of years, and by the novel's epilogue he has apparently succeeded, as he and Thea are finally wed.

Philip Frederick "Fred" Ottenburg

Fred Ottenburg first hears Thea sing when she is studying with Madison Bowers. Both romantically interested in Thea and possessed, like other men, with a desire to help Thea advance in her career because of her obvious natural talent, Fred befriends Thea and offers emotional support during her difficult second winter in Chicago. When Fred sees Thea's spirits falter, he offers her the opportunity to spend the summer at his friend's estate in Arizona. He later meets her there, and their romantic relationship progresses. Although Fred proposes to Thea that they run off together, he eventually confesses that he cannot marry Thea because he is already married to another woman (Edith Beers Ottenburg). After the two travel to New York, Fred arranges for Thea's transport to Germany. When Thea returns to New York to perform ten years later, Fred's continued interest in her is obvious. The novel's epilogue indicates that the two have finally married.

Juan "Spanish Johnny" Tellamantez

Juan Tellamantez, nicknamed "Spanish Johnny," is one of Moonstone's most well-known members of the Mexican community. A musician and a friend to Thea, Johnny invites Thea into his world. She values Johnny's friendship as it allows her access to musical traditions that differ greatly from those she has been taught by Professor Wunsch. Spanish Johnny appears at the novel's end when Thea delivers her pivotal operatic performance.

Mrs. Tellamantez

Mrs. Tellamantez is Spanish Johnny's wife. She is depicted as both patient and long-suffering in the way she endures Johnny's bizarre, alcohol-inspired episodes of crazed disappearances and behavior.

The Tramp

This unnamed character, referred to as a tramp and a vagabond, wanders through town during Thea's youth. The man is reviled by the townspeople because of his filth and stench. He attempts to put on a show as a means of begging a few dollars but is soon jailed. Upon his release, he bathes in the town's drinking water before he leaves Moonstone and is therefore blamed for the outbreak of typhoid fever that follows soon after his departure. The town's treatment of the man forces Thea to question her understanding of moral behavior.

Professor Wunsch

Professor Wunsch is Thea's piano instructor in Moonstone. The German instructor was once a pianist in his own right, and his transition in professional stature from artist to instructor is commonly regarded by the townspeople as a result of his abuse of alcohol. He recognizes Thea's prodigious artistic ability and attempts to aid her in her pursuit of her artistic endeavors to the best of his ability. After Professor Wunsch suffers an alcoholic binge, he loses most of his piano students and leaves Moonstone not long after.

THEMES

Self Identity

In *The Song of the Lark*, Cather explores Thea's sense of identity as an artist. From a young age, Thea had an understanding of her inner voice as a guiding element in her life. Even while she is still in school, Thea begins taking on her own music pupils, young girls whose mothers disapprove of Professor Wunsch's methods. Using the money earned from these Saturday lessons, Thea furnishes and decorates an attic room. Here, she escapes the chaos of life within a large family, noting that "the clamor about her drowned the voice within herself" and that the room provided refuge. When given the time and space to listen to this inner voice, Thea realizes that "pleasant plans and ideas occurred to her which had never come before. She had certain thoughts which were like companions, ideas which were like older and wiser friends."

On Thea's thirteenth birthday, she and Professor Wunsch discuss her future, and the professor prompts her to acknowledge her own gifts, hinting she might have a future as a singer. Privately, Thea contemplates her understanding of herself:

> She knew, of course, that there was something about her that was different. But it was more

TOPICS FOR FURTHER STUDY

- In *The Song of the Lark*, Cather bases some of Thea's experiences as a budding opera singer on the life of Swedish American opera singer Olive Fremstad. Research Fremstad's life and work, and compose a biographical essay in which you discuss the artist's youth, schooling and training, and subsequent operatic career. A number of biographical sources for both Cather and Fremstad include information on the association between the two women; be sure to include a summary of Fremstad's role in inspiring Cather's character and plot in *The Song of the Lark*. Remember to cite all of the sources you used to compile your essay.

- In the young-adult fictionalized autobiography, *Breaking Through* (2001), Francisco Jimenez traces his family's escape from Mexico and subsequent immigration to the United States and narrates his own coming-of-age story. With a small group, read Jimenez's novel. Like Thea in *The Song of the Lark*, Francisco comes from a large family, and both Thea and Francisco witness the discrimination faced by Mexicans in America, although Francisco experiences this bigotry firsthand. In what other ways are the worlds and characters depicted in the two works similar? How is Cather's American West of the 1890s and early twentieth century different from the American West of the 1950s and 1960s depicted in Jimenez's work? Create an online blog in which you and your reading group discuss such issues. Consider both authors' treatment of race and identity, along with the works' other structural and thematic concerns.

- Cather devotes considerable space in *The Song of the Lark* to discussing the industrial development of the American West, focusing on the mining and railway industries. Using online and print resources, research the way the mining and railway industries contributed to the settling and developing of the American Western frontier in the United States in the 1890s and in the early twentieth century. Compile a research paper in which you detail this history. Consider the effects of the industrial development on the environment, on Native Americans, and on Mexican Americans. Be sure to cite all of your sources.

- Although Cather's work was published in 1915, a year after World War I had begun, the novel is largely centered on Thea's development as an artist and does not touch on national or international events or politics. Cather would later focus on World War I in another novel, *One of Ours*. Research the events leading up to World War I in Europe and study the events that precipitated the entry of the United States into the war. Explore the decisive battles of the war and the involvement of the United States in these battles. Create a time line in which you discuss key dates and events from the beginning of the twentieth century to the close of the war. Your timeline may take the form of a poster or similar display, a web page, or a PowerPoint presentation. Include maps or photographs to enhance your audience's understanding of your presentation.

like a friendly spirit than anything that was part of herself. She brought everything to it, and it answered her.

Thea continues to listen to this inner voice as the novel progresses and seems secure in her

knowledge that she is destined for a future bigger than what most Moonstone residents imagine for themselves. After two years of study in Chicago, however, Thea becomes disheartened, though she confesses to Mr. Harsanyi her belief that she always understood that she had a unique gift. Recognizing Thea's potential, as well as the damaging effect on Thea of having her talents underutilized as she continues her lessons with Mr. Bowers, Fred Ottenburg offers Thea the chance to find herself once again during a trip to the West.

In the canyons of Arizona, Thea's sense of self is renewed. She finds, in the artifacts of the Native Americans, a connection to the land and in particular to the women who once lived there. Thea grows stronger, and her sense of purpose is renewed. She vows to travel to and study in Germany, certain that this is the proper path toward her future professional success. In Arizona, Thea realizes that "she had an appointment to meet the rest of herself sometime, somewhere. It was moving to meet her and she was moving to meet it."

When Thea performs in New York, in the role that she deems pivotal to her success, it becomes apparent that she has come into her own, that her divided sense of self is finally made whole; her potential as a singer is unified with a version of herself that has taken full advantage of study and opportunity. The importance of this sense of completion and unification is underscored by the fact that the men who played pivotal roles in Thea's artistic development, including Spanish Johnny, Mr. Harsanyi, and Dr. Archie, are present for this key, breakout performance.

Coming of Age

In many ways, *The Song of the Lark* focuses on Thea's coming of age. This expression refers to the physical, emotional, and artistic maturation of Thea. While her development as an artist is the main focus of the novel, her journey from girlhood to womanhood also plays a significant role. As a young girl, Thea possesses a quality to which adult men seem to be drawn. Other adults notice this, but Thea seems to shrug off the notion that there is anything unusual in her choice of friends. The president of the Moonstone Orchestra, when casting parts for the Christmas program, disapproves of the freedom Thea's parents allow her and notices that Thea's "chosen associates were Mexicans and sinners" and that Thea was "bold with men."

Thea's sister Anna also observes Thea's relationships with the men of the village. She considers Dr. Archie to be "fast" and maintains that "it was because he was 'fast' that Thea liked him. Thea always liked that kind of people." Anna furthermore maintains that Dr. Archie is "too free" with Thea and dislikes that he "was always putting his hand on Thea's head, or holding her hand while he laughed and looked down at her." Although Thea is aware that others disapprove of her older, male friends, her own understanding of what they view as inappropriate about these relationships is limited. Rather, she is drawn to their recognition of her own unique qualities. To Thea, the fact that Dr. Archie, Spanish Johnny, and Ray Kennedy respond to something in her reaffirms her own sense of herself as a person with special gifts.

By the time Thea is in the midst of her second winter in Chicago, however, she begins to become aware of the physical and emotional changes that are happening to her. "She had got used to living in the body of a young woman, and she no longer tried to ignore it and behave as if she were a little girl." As a young woman, Thea begins to fall in love with Fred Ottenburg; they confess their mutual romantic feelings in Arizona, and their relationship quickly progresses. When the complication of Fred's marriage is brought to the fore, however, Thea spends little time grieving. She focuses once again on her plans for her future career and makes arrangements to study in Germany. Later, once she has returned to New York, Thea and Fred discuss another relationship she pursued in Europe, but this proved to be something of little consequence to Thea. She seems oblivious to Dr. Archie's continued attachment and is happy to remain friends with Fred, who is also still in love with her. Although she has become a woman, her interest in adult romantic relationships is minimal.

The novel concludes with an off-hand reference to her marriage to Fred. That this marriage is conveyed to the reader via a newspaper article read by Aunt Tillie de-emphasizes its significance. The marriage itself and the events leading up to it do not play a role in the narrative in any way; the notion that Thea's life as an adult is governed by her own self interest, rather than by romantic relationships, is thereby underscored. Thea's coming of age is, in this way, depicted as a deeply personal, internal, and solitary journey.

Thea, the female protagonist, dreams of becoming an opera star. (© *Victorian Traditions /*
Shutterstock.com)

STYLE

Omniscient Third-Person Narration

Cather employs an omniscient third-person narrator in *The Song of the Lark*. An omniscient narrator is all-knowing, that is, privy to the thoughts of all the characters in the novel. This omniscient narrator exists outside of the action of the story and does not function within the narrative itself. In telling the story, the narrator uses the third-person voice, referring to the characters in the story as "she" and "he." (This stands in contrast to a first-person narrator, who would refer to him or herself as "I.")

Cather's narrator tells the story largely, but not exclusively, from Thea's perspective. The novel opens, for example, with the narrator focusing on Dr. Archie and his interactions with the Kronborg family. The reader later is offered the perspectives of other key characters,

including Thea's parents, Ray Kennedy, and Fred Ottenburg. By using this style of narration, Cather is able to provide key insights from a number of characters and at the same time allow the reader the access to Thea's full range of thoughts and emotions necessary to engage the reader in Thea's journey.

This style of narration additionally allows the narrator to weigh in on what is happening to the protagonist and predict future events. For example, when Thea enjoys a trip with her mother to Denver, riding in Ray Kennedy's caboose, the narrator observes that the "warm, sleepy feeling of the friendliness of the world" is one that "nobody keeps very long and which [Thea] was to lose early and irrevocably."

Bildungsroman and Künstlerroman

In *The Song of the Lark*, Cather explores Thea's journey from a child to an adult and from a young girl with musical potential to an accomplished opera singer. As such, the novel can be regarded as a novel of development or formation, the German word for which is *bildungsroman*. The term was first applied by German critics to a late eighteenth-century work by Wolfgang von Goethe and was subsequently ascribed to nineteenth-century and twentieth-century novels by such authors as Charles Dickens, Charlotte Brontë, and Thomas Mann.

The type of bildungsroman that traces the development of an artist is known as a künstlerroman. James Joyce's 1914–15 *A Portrait of the Artist as a Young Man* and William Somerset Maugham's 1915 *Of Human Bondage* epitomize this genre. In *The Song of the Lark*, Cather emphasizes Thea's early understanding of both her artistic talent and her sense of self identity. Thea's determination to succeed and her almost spiritual understanding of her talent are the driving forces of the plot and are evident from Thea's youth in Moonstone. As the novel progresses, Thea's pursuit of her artistic aims encompasses attempts at improving her technical abilities (in Chicago), as well as her effort to reconnect with her sense of musical intuition and instinct (in Arizona). Thea's artistic journey culminates in her operatic success at the close of the novel.

While Thea's personal relationships and her experiences in Chicago and Arizona all play a role in who she is and what she will become, Cather takes pains to emphasize throughout the novel that Thea's progression from the

Moonstone girl taking piano lessons with Professor Wunsch to the star of the New York opera scene is one driven largely by Thea's own ambition and instinct. Her development as an artist is explored as a unique, inner calling, one that the narrator stresses is difficult to transcribe. At the conclusion of the novel, the narrator notes, "The growth of an artist is an intellectual and spiritual development which can scarcely be followed in a personal narrative."

HISTORICAL CONTEXT

Mexican American Discrimination at the Turn of the Century

The Song of the Lark spans a period of many years, from approximately the early 1890s through 1909; it was published in 1915. The work is not an overtly political one, but Cather does make repeated reference to the Mexican American community in Moonstone and draws attention to the often negative perceptions the white residents of Moonstone possess regarding their Mexican neighbors. In the mid-nineteenth century, the expansionist efforts of the United States resulted in the colonizing of land that had previously been held by Mexico, specifically, "all or parts of what are the states of Arizona, California, Colorado, New Mexico, Nevada, Texas, Utah, and Wyoming," according to Laura E. Gomez, in *Manifest Destinies: The Makings of the Mexican American Race*. The Mexican residents living in these areas faced an increasing amount of discrimination and were often the targets of racial violence.

William D. Carrigan, in an article for the *Journal of Social History*, explores the history of such violence suffered by Mexicans at the hands of whites. Carrigan states that, in the United States, "Between 1848 and 1928, mobs lynched at least 597 Mexicans." Carrigan goes on to explain that lynching refers to "a retributive act of murder for which those responsible claim to be serving the interests of justice, tradition, or community good." Such murders were used as a tool by whites to ensure racial dominance in the newly colonized American West. Carrigan maintains, "Well into the twentieth century the majority white culture continued to utilize extra-legal violence against Mexicans as a means of asserting its sovereignty over the region."

The New Woman and the Development of the Female Bildungsroman Genre

During the late nineteenth and early twentieth centuries, American women were increasingly establishing their right to an education, careers outside the home, and the freedom to express their own identity. The type of woman to pursue this course of action came to be figured as a "New Woman," and the notion of the New Woman soon grew into its own movement. The literary corollary to this development was the increasing exploration among American authors of the bildungsroman novel featuring a female protagonist. (*Bildungsroman* refers to a genre developed in Germany during the late eighteenth and early nineteenth centuries and subsequently employed throughout the nineteenth and twentieth centuries. The bildungsroman novel is one that explores the coming of age or the emotional, sexual, or artistic blossoming of the protagonist.)

The higher educational experiences of the New Woman often featured prominently in the fiction of this time period by New Woman writers, notes Catharine R. Stimpson, Marilee Lindemann, and Martha Nell Smith in an article for *The Reader's Companion to U.S. Women's History*. The authors state,

> The college experience became a central element in the female *bildungsroman* and in the exploration of the character of the New Woman as women writers grappled with expanded opportunities made possible by education as well as lingering patterns of discrimination and dependence.

Esther Kleinbord Labovitz further explores the female bildungsroman in *The Myth of the Heroine: The Female Bildungsroman in the Twentieth Century: Dorothy Richardson, Simone de Beauvoir, Doris Lessing, Christa Wolf*. Labovitz argues that nineteenth-century heroines were often prevented from fully achieving the personal growth that is typical in a bildungsroman novel. Labovitz further asserts, "When cultural and social structures appeared to support women's struggle for independence, to go out into the world, engage in careers, in self-discovery and fulfillment, the heroine in fiction began to reflect these changes." When women were able to fully explore their potential in reality, Labovitz maintains, women writers began to create works that could truly be called female bildungsroman.

COMPARE & CONTRAST

- **1890s:** Mexicans living in territory recently ceded to the United States by the 1848 Treaty of Guadalupe-Hidalgo increasingly find themselves the targets of discrimination, despite the fact that the treaty has granted them U.S. citizenship.

  1915: The United States sees a flood of Mexican immigrants during the Mexican Revolution, which ravaged Mexico from 1910 to 1920. In an effort to protect their rights, Mexican immigrants and Mexican Americans become active members of civil-rights organizations designed to protect their safety and their rights as workers.

  Today: Mexican immigration and the rights of illegal Mexican immigrants remain topics of considerable political debate. Specifically, the education of the children of illegal immigrants and the voting rights of Mexican Americans, are areas of particular concern. Organizations such as the Mexican American Legal Defense Fund seek to protect the human rights and civil liberties of Mexican Americans and Mexicans living in America.

- **1890s:** The concept of the "New Woman" begins to take hold in American culture. Increasingly, women seek higher education, financial independence, and political equality, among other aims.

  1915: The New Woman movement continues to evolve and diversify. Suffragists organize into various groups in order to more effectively pressure Congress for voting rights for women. By 1915, two organizations, the Congressional Union, later known as the National Woman's Party, and the National American Woman Suffrage Association, lead the charge in attempting to secure a woman's right to vote.

  Today: Although women achieved the right to vote with the passage of the Nineteenth Amendment in 1920, women have fought since then for the passage of an amendment to the constitution that would guarantee women equality of rights. The Equal Rights Amendment, passed in 1972, has not become law because it has not yet been ratified by 38 states (the number of state ratifications necessary for the bill to become law).

- **1890s:** The bildungsroman novel, or novel of formation, becomes a prominent literary genre. Popularized in the mid-nineteenth century by writers such as Charles Dickens with *David Copperfield* (1850) and *Great Expectations* (1861), Charlotte Brontë with *Jane Eyre* (1847), and Gustave Flaubert with *Madame Bovary* (1857), the genre continues to be explored in the 1890s by writers such as Thomas Hardy with *Jude the Obscure* (1895) and Henry James with *What Maisie Knew* (1897).

  1915: The bildungsroman remains a popular genre among writers, who also focus on the development of the artist. This type of novel is a subset of the bildungsroman and is known as the künstlerroman. Authors penning künstlerroman works at this time include such writers as James Joyce with *A Portrait of the Artist as a Young Man* (1914–15), William Somerset Maugham with *Of Human Bondage* (1915), and Cather with *The Song of the Lark* (1915).

  Today: While the term *bildungsroman* is less commonly used in the twenty-first century than in decades passed, the term "coming-of-age novel" is commonly used to describe works with a format similar to that of the bildungsroman. Examples include Caroyln Coman's *Many Stones* (2000), Jandy Nelson's *The Sky is Everywhere* (2010), and Simon Rich's *Elliot Allagash* (2010).

*Thea dreams of escaping Moonstone, Colorado,
to the big city. (© Mark Hayes / Shutterstock.com)*

CRITICAL OVERVIEW

When *The Song of the Lark* was published in
1915, the novel received largely favorable
reviews. As James Woodress comments in
Willa Cather: A Literary Life, critics were
impressed in particular with the "authenticity
of the characterizations" and praised Cather's
work in depicting "not just the reality of the
protagonist, but also of the minor characters."
Woodress goes on, stating that, although the
novel

> is an enormously interesting and attractive
> novel, it is not without flaws. Some of the
> reviewers complained that the novel was over-
> written, though they agreed that the excessive
> detail was far overshadowed by the quality of
> the characterization.

John J. Murphy, in an essay for the *Dic-
tionary of Literary Biography*, similarly com-
ments on the novel's length and also identifies
the work's focus on Thea's artistic development

as being a key feature of the work. Murphy
observes,

> While this work is at times ponderous and
> preachy, its heroine's discovery of her artistic
> power while bathing in a stream in an Arizona
> canyon is highly original and important for
> understanding Cather's own development as
> an artist.

Bernice Slote likewise focuses on Cather's
dramatization of the life of the artist but also
praises Cather's technical skill as a writer. Slote
observes,

> If *The Song of the Lark* is primarily directed to
> power—the primitive, physical, and emotional
> involvements of art—it is craft which placed
> these elements in the marvelously related
> sequences of scenes, metaphors, and incremen-
> tal repetition.

Other critics have centered their studies on
issues of genre. Janet Sharistanian, in an intro-
duction to *The Song of the Lark*, notes that
"Cather's novel falls into the category of the
Künstlerroman or 'artist novel,' a subset of the
Bildungsroman or novel of formation." Sharista-
nian goes on to explore the way Cather's depiction
of a female heroine (Thea) of a künstlerroman is
unique, in that Cather "allows her to make a
decisive choice for art and rewards her with
success."

However, in *The Imaginative Claims of the
Artist in Willa Cather's Fiction*, Demaree C. Peck
challenges critics who regard *The Song of the
Lark* as bildungsroman or künstlerroman, main-
taining that "*The Song of the Lark* resembles the
realistic novel of the artist's education only in the
superficial trappings of its plot. Despite its appa-
rent scope, the novel subordinates all time,
space, and characters to Thea." Peck goes on to
state that the novel should rather be considered
as "a fairy tale, or wish fulfillment, in which
Thea's desire, like Willa Cather's in writing the
novel, has the magical power to reorganize the
world around the self."

CRITICISM

Catherine Dominic

*Dominic is a novelist and freelance writer and
editor. In the following essay, she explores Cath-
er's treatment of the role of emotion and intuition
in the artist's journey in* The Song of the Lark.

WHAT DO I READ NEXT?

- Cather's novel *My Antonia* was published in 1918 and is counted among Cather's greatest works. The novel is set in the prairies of Nebraska, a setting frequently used by Cather in her fiction.

- *One of Ours* was published by Cather in 1922. The novel is set during World War I and won Cather a Pulitzer Prize.

- William Somerset Maugham's *Of Human Bondage* was published, like *The Song of the Lark*, in 1915. A classic bildungsroman, *Of Human Bondage* was inspired by events in Maugham's own life and chronicles the experiences of Philip Carey, from the time when he was orphaned at the age of nine through his young adult struggles to find success as an artist in Europe.

- The 2010 coming-of-age novel *Girl in Translation*, by Hong Kong-born Jean Kwok, explores the childhood, adolescence, and young adulthood of Kimberly Chang, who, having emigrated from Hong Kong with her family at the age of five, eventually climbs her way out of poverty in Brooklyn by winning a scholarship to a prestigious college preparatory academy.

- Siobhan Dowd's 2009 young-adult novel *Solace of the Road* is the coming-of-age story of Holly Hogan, who journeys from innocence to experience in England and Ireland.

- The 2003 novel *The Kite Runner* by Khaled Hosseini, the first Afghan novel written in English, has been described as a modern bildungsroman in its focus on its Afghani protagonist Amir and his painful journey from childhood to emotional maturation and manhood.

In *The Song of the Lark*, Cather examines Thea's development as an artist as well as her growth from adolescence to womanhood. As such, the work is often described as a

> WHAT IS STRIKING ABOUT CATHER'S DEPIC-
> TION OF THIS PROCESS IS THE WAY CATHER, THROUGH
> THEA, UNDERSCORES THE WEIGHT OF INTUITION,
> INSTINCT, AND INSIGHT OVER TECHNICAL ABILITY
> AND THE RELATIONSHIP OF SUCH INSIGHT TO THEA'S
> PROFESSIONAL SUCCESS AND FULFILLMENT."

künstlerroman, a novel concerned with the coming of age of an artist. Cather's emphasis on the artist's journey is the subject of much of the criticism of the novel. What is striking about Cather's depiction of this process is the way Cather, through Thea, underscores the weight of intuition, instinct, and insight over technical ability and the relationship of such insight to Thea's professional success and fulfillment.

From early on in the novel, Thea's aversion to being told the "proper" way do something is contrasted with her instinct as an artist. When Cather first depicts Thea's piano lesson with Professor Wunsch, Thea grumbles to herself "about the way he had marked the fingering of a passage." Wunsch responds in a way that suggests his pupil's defiance is familiar and habitual, stating, "It makes no matter what you think. . . . There is only one right way." She then works diligently for the next hour.

Not long after this incident, Thea uses her own money (earned by teaching her own piano students) to make habitable an attic bedroom. The significance of Thea having a place to escape the noise and distraction her family creates is clear when Thea recognizes that "the acquisition of this room was the beginning of a new era in Thea's life." Here, she can listen to the "voice within herself" that is otherwise muted by the "clamor" of daily life. She considers the thoughts and plans that come to her in this space as "companions" with whom she is reunited at the end of a day. In this passage, Cather underscores the fact that Thea's sense of herself is a dual one: her private self is that which contemplates her future path, and this private, inner voice will later be equated with Thea's artistic intuition.

In another lesson with Professor Wunsch, Thea struggles over a challenging piece of music, regarding the piece as an "enemy." Only after Thea discusses the history of the piece with Wunsch, as well as his recollection of how it had been sung in the past, is Thea able to apply herself more successfully to the challenge the music presents. She must proceed to the emotional heart of a work to fully understand it. Wunsch asserts that, as an artist, Thea must have a certain kind of knowledge, and he further suspects that Thea possesses the indescribable quality he feels is so important to singing. She is unable to articulate what it is she intuits about the meaning of the music but understands to some degree what Wunsch describes. She observes that this quality was to her "like a friendly spirit. . . . She brought everything to it, and it answered her; happiness consisted of that backward and forward movement of herself."

Once Thea begins her formal musical education in Chicago under Mr. Harsanyi, she begins to feel frustrated and fears that she is beginning to lose that certain "friendly spirit" that had always been with her. "She had come to Chicago to be with it, and it had deserted her, leaving in its place a painful longing, an unresigned despair." When Harsanyi discovers that Thea, in addition to being an accomplished pianist, has an unusually beautiful singing voice, he vows to begin teaching her in this capacity as well, although he acknowledges that he knows little about "voice production." Harsanyi observes that Thea's relationship with the music she sings is an intuitive and emotional one. He recognizes that she must have a full comprehension of the piece before she could move forward: "After she once had her 'revelation,' after she got the idea that to her—not always to him—explained everything, then she went forward rapidly." Thea's work with Harsanyi exemplifies her approach to art as one based on an intuitive and emotional connection to the story the music tells. Her desire to work at a piece is based on this connection, and her desire for technical mastery, as it was under Wunsch, is secondary.

As Thea continues to study in Chicago, she gradually begins to explore the city. At the Chicago Art Institute, Thea becomes taken with a painting titled "The Song of the Lark." She establishes an emotional narrative to accompany the image and considers it "her picture. She imagined that nobody cared for it but herself, and that it waited for her." In considering what appeals to her about the painting, Thea thinks, "The flat country, the early morning light, the wet fields, the look in the girl's heavy face—well, they were all hers." Somehow, to Thea, the "picture was 'right.'" Although in the novel, Cather does not elaborate further on what is actually a painting by the French realist painter Jules Breton, she does comment on the Breton work elsewhere. James Woodress, in *Willa Cather: A Literary Life*, states that, in Cather's preface to the 1932 edition of *The Song of the Lark*, Cather "realized that the title [of the novel] had been a mistake, because readers thought the lark song referred to 'the vocal accomplishments of the heroine,' who was any thing but a sky lark." Woodress goes on to explain that in the preface Cather "also had to admit that the painting was second rate." Significantly, the painting that Cather recognizes as technically inferior is one that Thea is intuitively drawn to.

At Harsanyi's urging, Thea begins taking voice lessons from Madison Bowers. Of his methods, Thea reflects that Bowers "worked with a voice as if he were in a laboratory, conducting a series of experiments." Initially, this approach suits Thea, despite the fact that Harsanyi "declared that he [Bowers] had the soul of a shrimp, and could no more make an artist than a throat specialist could." After Thea has returned from a summer in Moonstone and resumes her instruction with Bowers, frustrations begin to develop. Resentful of seeing people less talented than herself succeed in their profession, often with Bowers's help, Thea confides her despair to Mrs. Harsanyi. She tells Mrs. Harsanyi that Mr. Harsanyi "was the teacher for me." Thea becomes increasingly dispirited throughout this time and begins to sense herself stagnating. She tells Fred Ottenburg, "Being bored eats the heart out of me." The technical instruction she receives from Bowers, while initially engaging for Thea, leads to an increasing sense of dissatisfaction. She feels no emotional connection to her art any longer.

Recognizing Thea's despair, Fred offers Thea an opportunity that will change the course of her career. Interestingly, it has nothing to do with music, art, or singing. Rather, Fred invites Thea to spend a summer at his friend's estate in the canyons of Arizona. The weeks she spends in Arizona provide Thea the chance to retreat back into herself. She becomes grounded once again and emotionally in tune with her sense of self. Having contemplated her failures, first under Harsanyi and later under Bowers, from whom she had learned things only of "secondary importance," Thea immerses herself in a landscape that fascinates her.

It is here, in the canyons and in the cliff dwellings of the Native Americans who once lived there that Thea rediscovers her sense of herself as an artist. In contemplating a shard of ancient pottery, Thea equates her voice to the water, the "shining, elusive element which is life itself," and her throat to the ancient vessel that once served as a means of carrying water for the Native women. "In singing," Thea thinks, "one made a vessel of one's throat and nostrils and held it on one's breath, caught the stream in a scale of natural intervals." Thea's sense that she is connected to something larger than herself, to an ancient past, renews her confidence in herself as an artist. She begins to feel "united and strong." Thea resolves to go to Germany to study as she had once dreamed of doing, and an increasingly intense romance with Fred does not deter Thea. The fact that their relationship is compromised by Fred's complicated past, that is, by the fact that he is already married, makes Thea's path toward Germany even clearer.

Cather chooses to not depict Thea's period of study in Germany. She returns to New York an accomplished opera singer. Mr. Landry, a singer and piano player who often works as Thea's accompanist, studied with Thea in Germany and discusses his understanding of Thea's talent with Fred. Landry asserts that what Thea brings to her roles is "a big personality—and all that goes with it. Brains, of course. Imagination, of course. But the important thing is that she was born full of color, with a rich personality." Landry goes on to discuss a particular role Thea played while in Germany, a part she was studying during her mother's fatal illness. Landry recalls, "I could see her anxiety and grief getting more and more into the part."

While Landry is quite a minor character in the novel, his understanding of Thea as she became known to him during her period of study in Germany is critical to Cather's thematic exploration of the artist. As Cather has emphasized throughout the novel, as an artist, Thea is extremely intuitive and must connect emotionally with her subject matter in order to progress.

Andor Harsanyi, Thea's piano teacher, is liberated by his interactions with her. (© byheaven / Shutterstock.com)

Thea does not eschew the technical aspects of her craft, but they are, as she states in reflection while in Arizona, of "secondary importance." Landry emphasizes the way in which Thea, after her study in Germany, incorporates her whole self, her personality and her past and her pain, into her work. Throughout the work, Cather has carefully depicted this aspect of Thea's artistry as a constant. Through Landry, the reader sees that, even after ten years of formal study abroad, the unique element Thea brings to her work is her personality—her full emotional involvement in a role, a connection she makes by drawing on her own insights and experiences—and it is this, in combination with her studies, with her "brains" and "imagination" that has resulted in Thea's success as a singer.

Cather closes the story here, having utilized the künstlerroman format and brought Thea from childhood to the blossoming of her career as an artist. As an artist herself, Cather stresses,

"Any account of the loyalty of young hearts to some exalted ideal, and the passion with which they strive, will always, in some of us, rekindle generous emotions." While the epilogue of the novel assures the reader that Thea and Fred are finally able to marry, Cather has throughout underscored Thea's emotional, passionate pursuit of an "exalted ideal," a pursuit that has placed both the intellectual component of such study as well as the artist's personal relationships as secondary to the artist's passion.

Source: Catherine Dominic, Critical Essay on *The Song of the Lark*, in *Novels for Students*, Gale, Cengage Learning, 2013.

Pamela Christine Wade

In the following chapter, Wade examines whether Cather went too far in allowing Thea to achieve too many of her goals in The Song of the Lark.

In *The Song of the Lark*, Cather presents her reader with the tale of the exceptionally driven Thea Kronborg. After escaping from her provincial upbringing, Thea discovers her true talent abroad and becomes a well-known opera singer. Every possibility that was imagined for Thea is gradually realized, and, for this reason, the novel has been criticized for taking fiction too far into fairytale. In fact, Judith Fetterley believes that it is the "least appreciated" of Cather's work because of "its uncompromising portrayal of a woman who grows up to get what she wants" (Fetterley 222). Laura Dubek called Cather's portrayal of her heroine "only a wish that comes true in fiction," and, while Dubek's assessment is fair, given Cather's admission that the novel was "her fairytale," we should resist the urge to regard Cather's comment as merely dismissive. Cather's words from the 1932 preface are almost always invoked to prove her dissatisfaction with continuing Thea's story into "the full tide of achievement." By drawing attention to the magic of her fairytale, it is possible that Cather was anticipating and hoping to ease the concerns of her readers. However, her agreement with the novel's primary criticism also adds to its ambiguity. Are we to read *The Song of the Lark* for the fairytale or does the fairytale become a curtain that prevents us from seeing something else? Even so, these possibilities rarely receive attention; rather, it is easier to overlook Cather's ambivalence about her own work and dismiss the novel as an unrealistic portrayal of "wish-fulfillment."

In the context of Cather's oeuvre, *The Song of the Lark* has been granted its exceptional status with far too much ease. As I mentioned before, O'Brien divides Cather's fiction into distinctive thematic categories of "life" and "death" and expansiveness and limitation that prevent us from discovering how these concepts flow together and depend on each other. O'Brien implies that the discovery of desire and the pursuit of opportunity exist only in the first half of life, during development. Ironically, critics never fail to notice how Cather sought to "transcend" dualisms, but they are eager to divide her fiction in a dualistic fashion. If Cather had to hide behind or escape within a masculine identity to transcend the categories of gender and reconnect with and reestablish an identity as a new kind of female, perhaps she also had to construct a fairytale as a kind of cover story in order to imagine the integration of this new gender identity with reality.

When Cather identified *The Song of the Lark* as a fairytale, it is possible that she conceived of a fairytale less as a story of fantasy than as a story that is very much aware of reality and intended to offer its reader the courage and means by which to cope in this life. It takes just a quick scan of popular children's fairytales to realize how these tales often consist of threatening characters, grim and gloomy forests, and an ominous foreboding of death. Although these stories often end with the familiar phrase: "And they lived happily ever after." Bruno Bettelheim reminds his reader that this ending is not intended to "fool the (reader) into believing that eternal life is possible" (Bettelheim 10). In *The Uses of Enchantment: The Meaning and Importance of Fairy Tales*, Bettelheim examines many well-known fairytales and explores the conscious and unconscious ways in which these stories speak to children. Bettelheim's purpose is to emphasize the significance of these texts in an individual's development; according to Bettelheim, the message of a fairytale is

> that a struggle against severe human difficulties in life is unavoidable, is an intrinsic part of human existence—but that if one does not shy away, but steadfastly meets unexpected and often unjust hardships, one masters all obstacles and at the end emerges victorious. (8)

Obviously, this is not always a person's experience, and obstacles are not always overcome. Bettelheim argues that a fairytale challenges its reader to "transcend the narrow confines of a self-centered existence. . . in order not to be at the mercy of the vagaries of life" (4). Yet the ability to "transcend" is found in the expression of privately felt fears and desires, and this aspect of the fairytale is just as important as its ability to inspire triumph. The fairytale's representation of life's evils as well as the existence of humanity's dark side is essential: it imagines and expresses a person's "severe inner pressures" in a way that can be understood and managed. Furthermore, when a person is denied the opportunity to confront these anxieties, Bettelheim suggests that he or she feels overwhelmed with fear, and that fear can also lead to a sense of hopelessness that will "succeed in wringing meaning out of. . . existence" (8). The fairytale not only offers the possibility that one can "master all obstacles," but, when faced with the knowledge that life is made up of constant struggles, it is also a source of relief because it provides its readers the space in which to acknowledge and release anxiety.

In her essay, "Willa Cather and the Fiction of Female Development," Judith Fetterley writes about the release of anxiety she experienced when reading *The Song of the Lark*. For Fetterley, reading *The Song of the Lark* was a genuinely meaningful and emotional experience. The novel spoke to the anxieties Fetterley was holding on to as a feminist and a lesbian, and she writes of nervously turning each page, expecting Thea to give in to Fred's marriage proposals and submit to the "conventional woman's story." *The Song of the Lark* seems to have been the fairytale Fetterley needed in order to live "happily ever after"; as Fetterley concludes her own essay, she writes, "for us *The Song of the Lark* can always lie ahead, helping us, like Thea, to realize the power of our desire" (233–4).

Fetterley suggests that *The Song of the Lark* is unique because it is a text that can continually "lie ahead" for readers, helping them to desire freely and with the expectation that these desires will one day materialize. She removes it from its status as one of Cather's earlier works, and thus makes it an ever-present reminder of "the power of our desire." For Fetterley, anxiety is the effect of repressed desires: the novel, first, helped her manage her anxiety, but it seems that it did so in such a way that it also gave her the courage to experience desire. In Fetterley's reading, desire becomes a source of power. Fetterley implies that power, born of desire, not only moves us

forward, but can potentially open up the future in a way that gives life continuity, and this implied connection between power and desire leads us to consider other ways in which desire might effect continuity. A fairytale allows its reader to confront her unconscious anxieties in a fictional context, and in the confrontation and release of these anxieties, she is free to "transcend. . .the vagaries of life" and experience the "power of desire." Of course, as I've already mentioned, an important aspect of this process is in the struggle to transcend, because that struggle is critical to the creation of the space in which one realizes the possibilities of change. Furthermore, it seems that the release of anxiety should also ease one's anxiety about reality, with its "unexpected and often unjust hardships." . . . Therefore, in a way, it is desire that structures a person's response to life, but, more importantly, it forges an implicit connection between fantasy and reality.

Source: Pamela Christine Wade, "*The Song of the Lark*: Fiction or Fairytale?" in *"As if it Mattered!": Discovering the Effect of the Fairytale in Willa Cather's "The Song of the Lark,"* PhD diss., Southern Methodist University, 2008, ProQuest (0549549382, 978054954983), pp. 8–12.

Katherine Boutry
In the following excerpt, Boutry describes the romantic imagery as well as the identity Thea finds through her voice in The Song of the Lark.

ISN'T IT ROMANTIC?
. . . The Romantic ideal of masculine intellect coupled with feminine inspiration to engender true art is consistent with the sexual crossing that I argue occurs in Cather's musical scenes. Cather borrows imagery from Wordsworth in the Die Walkure episode, as noted earlier, and from Coleridge in the Lucia di Lammermoor scene. Coleridge's "By woman wailing for her demon lover! . . . A mighty fountain momently was forced" is echoed in Cather's "at the acute moment, the soprano voice, like a fountain jet, shot up into the light" and in "[f]ervently she rose . . . until in a splendid burst . . . she christened him" ("Kubla Khan"; *Song of the Lark*). The internalization of Romantic literary theory would have reinforced Cather's suspicion that female artists needed a strong "masculine" element in order to balance their "too feminine" natures. Indeed, her artistically successful heroines always incorporate gender-typed

> THEA RECOGNIZES THAT HER VOICE HAS THE POWER TO UNEARTH THE SOCIETAL RESTRICTIONS KEEPING HIDDEN SELVES AND SEXUALITIES REPRESSED."

characteristics from both sexes. And in an effort to take the Romantic ideal of both gendered elements in "genius" to its metaphorically logical conclusion, Cather explicitly blends active and passive sexualities in her musical descriptions. Thea's embodiment of both "masculine" and "feminine" roles in her music (and body) is what makes her autonomous and powerful.

Music is the medium through which the two roles meet. Powerless, Spanish Johnny "pants" with excitement after he hears Thea sing, just as Coleridge's speaker longs to recapture his own fleeting memory of both a song and a beautiful woman pathetically phallacized in the earth's "fast thick pants":

Could I revive within me
Her symphony and song,
To such a deep delight t'would win me,
That with music loud and long,
I would build that dome in air,
That sunny dome! those caves of ice!
And all who heard should see them there,
And all should cry, Beware! Beware! . . .

Coleridge's speaker will take a passive experience of music and use that to create a world of paradox, of opposites powerfully reconciled. The artifice that music will empower is Cather's *Kingdom of Art*, a kingdom in which Bohemia wins out over Philistia and Art is the sacred mover. To come back to Suzanne Cusick's provocative statement with which I started, Cather's *Kingdom* is one in which "Artist" suffices as sexual identity, no questions asked.

It takes a particular setting to come out. The end lines of Cather's introductory poem to *O Pioneers!* ("'singing and singing' / Out of the lips of silence, / Out of the earthy dusk") foreshadow the "dusky voices" of the Mexicans in *The Song of the Lark* whose desire and musical sensibility will be equated with the earthiness and the canyon that provides Thea with

inspiration. Coleridge's feminine "savage place," his "holy and enchanted" "chasm" recalls Cather's feminized landscaping of Panther Canyon in *The Song of the Lark*, with its "V-shaped inner gorge," "deep groove" and "hollow (like a great fold in the rock)" (*Song of the Lark*), and creates a symbol for Romantic "feminine/Other" creativity as a source of artistic vision. Cather considers Harsanyi's, Kohler's, and Spanish Johnny's ethnicity and Thea's "difference" the key to their sensitivity and appreciation of music. Like Coleridge's speaker with the Abyssinian maid, part of Thea's enjoyment of the evening is her "passing" a cultural divide and finding a musical appreciation equal to her own. She is misunderstood by her sister and brothers, however, and when Thea protests that the Mexicans "know something about what I'm doing," her sister rebukes her for "throwing that at her family." "'Well,' she replied in a cold, even tone, 'I'll have to throw it at them sooner or later. It's just a question of when, and it might as well be now as anytime'" (*Song of the Lark*). This scene of her musical "coming out" to her family is brought about by her identification with an Other culture. She realizes that she will have to leave home (once identified as a "musician," she had already been given a room apart from the rest of the family) and that "Yes, she and It must fight it out together. The thing that looked at her out of her own eyes was the only friend she could count on" (*Song of the Lark*). Thea feels her difference and knows that her lover—"It"/ music—is within her. But she allows her true voice to be recognized only in unguarded moments with Spanish Johnny and Harsanyi, accepting her identity as a singer reluctantly.

For just as a threat rests behind the musical selections she chooses and the "Beware! Beware!" in Coleridge's poem, Cather could not shake the inevitability of suffering for art and love. Thea's trip to the opera house and Panther Canyon allow her temporary transgressions, but eventually she has to return. As Coleridge warns his readers, having drunk the milk of paradise does not endear artists to other mortals, and makes daily living difficult. Because of the categorizations Cather shared with society, music remained one of the few g[r]ay areas she permitted herself. But even music is confining. When Thea leaves Chicago to rest and commune with nature, "The old, fretted lines which marked one off, which defined her—made her

Thea Kronborg, Bowers's accompanist, a soprano with a faulty middle voice—were all erased" (*Song of the Lark*). Between the fretted lines of this passage is Olive Fremstad.

OLIVE FREMSTAD AND THE "FAULTY MIDDLE VOICE"

A discussion of the transgressive nature of music in Cather's fiction would not be complete without a consideration of the diva who informed Thea Kronborg's character. Elizabeth Wood has argued quite persuasively that Olive Fremstad's lesbianism as well as her ability to pass from a contralto to a soprano voice dependent upon the operatic role she was to play made her an attractive subject for Cather's kunstlerroman. For Fremstad's conscious cultivation of an "in between" or "long" voice was for her a source of vocal and gender defiance (Wood 33). Interestingly, neither Fremstad nor Cather's Thea has achieved a perfect passing voice. Thea must escape from her critics who claim she has "a faulty middle voice" (*Song of the Lark*). Since the author acknowledged that Thea was a composite of both Fremstad and herself, if Wood's suggestion that the novel provides a dialogue between the two lesbian artists is correct, Cather may be suggesting that her own "crossing" was not as smooth as she may have wished. Wayne Koestenbaum asks the important question,

> Are registers a fact of nature, or a figment of voice culture? They are, at least, a metaphorical way of describing and enhancing anatomical perimeters—of finding categories for a voice's uneven production as it moves from low to high. . . . However many registers a male or female voice possesses (and it is not clear whether a 'register' represents a zone of opportunity or of prohibition), register-theory expresses two central dualities: true versus false, and male versus female. ("The Queen's Throat" 219)

Surely Koestenbaum means the metaphoric value of the register as a zone of opportunity and prohibition, for like all liminal gender activities, value and threat come from being both simultaneously, from being between registers. For Wood, the lesbian space provided by what she terms the "Sapphonic voic[e]" "is a transvestic enigma, belonging to neither male nor female as constructed—a synthesis, not a split. . . . For listeners, the Sapphonic voice is a destabilizing agent of fantasy and desire" (32). Akin to Barthes' "grain of the voice," which is "the erotic relationship between voice and listener,"

something in the hearer responds to gender transgressions in the voice. Like Fremstad's, Thea's "faulty middle voice" becomes the source of her vocal power and her fame. No longer a source of embarrassment, her range makes her voice in the conclusion "as flexible as her body; equal to any demand, capable of every nuance," (*Song of the Lark*). The movie of the Italian castrato Farinelli illustrates what Marjorie Garber has said of Liberace's and Elvis's "androgynous" physical appeal. The music coupled with the hint of sexual transgression drives fans wild. Women swoon with desire and curiosity to know whether Farinelli/Liberace/Elvis can "perform" for them offstage despite the evidence to the contrary. While these same fans might be threatened by androgyny in the outside world, music allows this connection to occur. Certainly, Thea's power stems from this crossing place as well.

Contemplating the musical ability that constitutes a hidden, secret aspect of her identity, Thea wonders, "What if one's second self could somehow speak to all these second selves? . . . How deep they lay, these second persons, and how little one knew about them, except to guard them fiercely. It was to music, more than to anything else that these hidden things in people responded" (*Song of the Lark*). Thea recognizes that her voice has the power to unearth the societal restrictions keeping hidden selves and sexualities repressed. This underground communication between musician and hearer may be "bisexual," for Koestenbaum argues first that the vocal chords, like the female reproductive system, are hidden from view and hence have elicited curious speculation (dread?) as well as a feminine coding for the voice. Later in his essay, however, he makes an equally plausible case for the larynx as phallic. Suffice it to say, as he does, that the "voice may be, in fact, a symbol of a separate pleasure zone that offers Edenic, imaginary alternatives to dominant cultural models of what sex means" ("The Queen's Throat" 211–14). But alternatives like registers are freedom and confinement, pleasure and prohibition. Her vocal talent is described as a treasured but vulnerable sexuality: "Hitherto she had felt but one obligation toward it—secrecy; to protect it even from herself" (*Song of the Lark*).

By the end of the novel, however, "her inhibitions chanced to be fewer. . . . [S]he entered into the inheritance that she herself had laid up, into the fullness of the faith she had kept before she knew its name or its meaning" (*Song of the Lark*). Once she is a recognized artist, Thea's "secret" is passion. . . . It is an open secret, and perfectly safe" (*Song of the Lark*). As an older, more musically and sexually mature Thea/Cather recognizes and admits her talent, the vocal chords/genitals/musical talent/voice become actualized through use and exposure, through performance and sexual acts, and emerge despite or because of Cather's self-protective composition.

Source: Katherine Boutry, "Between Registers: Coming In and Out Through Musical Performance in Willa Cather's *The Song of the Lark*," in *Legacy: A Journal of American Women Writers*, Vol. 17, No. 2, June 2000, p. 187.

SOURCES

Carrigan, William D., "The Lynching of Persons of Mexican Origin or Descent in the United States, 1848 to 1928," in *Journal of Social History*, Vol. 37, No. 2, 2003, pp. 411–38.

Cather, Willa, *The Song of the Lark*, 1915, reprint, Dover, 2004.

Dumenil, Lynn, "The New Woman," in *The Modern Temper: American Culture and Society in the 1920s*, Hill and Wang, 1995, pp. 98–144.

Francis, Roberta W., "The History Behind the Equal Rights Amendment," http://www.equalrightsamendment.org/era.htm (accessed December 30, 2011).

Gomez, Laura E., Introduction to *Manifest Destinies: The Making of the Mexican American Race*, New York University Press, 2007, pp. 1–15.

Labovitz, Esther Kleinbord, Introduction to *The Myth of the Heroine: The Female Bildungsroman in the Twentieth Century: Dorothy Richardson, Simone de Beauvoir, Doris Lessing, Christa Wolf*, Peter Lang, 1988, pp. 1–11.

"Mission Statement," in *Mexican American Legal Defense and Educational Fund*, http://www.maldef.org/about/mission/ (accessed December 30, 2011).

Murphy, John J., "Willa Cather," in *Dictionary of Literary Biography*, Vol. 256, *Twentieth-Century American Western Writers, Third Series*, edited by Richard H. Cracroft, The Gale Group, 2002, pp. 31–45.

Overfelt, Robert C., "The Mexican Revolution," in *Handbook of Texas Online*, http://www.tshaonline.org/handbook/online/articles/pqmhe (accessed December 30, 2011).

Peck, Demaree C., "Thea Kronborg's 'Song of Myself': The Artist's Imaginative Inheritance in *The Song of the Lark*," in *The Imaginative Claims of the Artist in Willa Cather's Fiction*, Associated University Press, 1996, pp. 106–27.

Sharistanian, Janet, Introduction to *The Song of the Lark*, Oxford University Press, 2000, pp. vii–xxv.

Slote, Bernice, "The Kingdom of Art," in *The Kingdom of Art: Willa Cather's First Principles and Critical Statements*, University of Nebraska Press, 1966, pp. 31–112.

Smith-Rosenberg, Carroll, "The New Woman," in *The Reader's Companion to U.S. Women's History*, edited by Wilma Mankiller, Gwendolyn Mink, Marysa Navarro, Barbara Smith, and Gloria Steinem, Houghton Mifflin, 1998, p. 430.

Stacey, Lee, "Civil Rights in the United States," in *Mexico and the United States*, Marshall Cavendish, 2003, pp. 191–94.

Stimpson, Catharine R., Marilee Lindemann, and Martha Nell Smith, "Literature," in *The Reader's Companion to U.S. Women's History*, edited by Wilma Mankiller, Gwendolyn Mink, Marysa Navarro, Barbara Smith, and Gloria Steinem, Houghton Mifflin, 1998, pp. 345–50.

Woodress, James, "*The Song of the Lark*," in *Willa Cather: A Literary Life*, University of Nebraska Press, 1987, pp. 252–75.

FURTHER READING

Billington, Ray Allen and Martin Ridge, *Westward Expansion: A History of the American Frontier*, 6th ed., University of New Mexico Press, 2001.

> Billington and Ridge offer a detailed analysis of the way the American West was conquered, settled, and developed. The authors further explore the environmental and human costs associated with westward expansionism.

Dizikes, John, *Opera in America: A Cultural History*, Yale University Press, 1993.

> In this acclaimed work, Dizikes traces the history of opera in America, beginning with the introduction of opera in the early eighteenth century and focusing heavily on the growth of the art form in the nineteenth century.

Goldberg, Jonathan, *Willa Cather and Others*, Duke University Press, 2001.

> Goldberg offers an analysis of Cather's work, exploring in particular her investigations concerning gender and sexuality. Through the course of this study, Goldberg also touches on the careers of Cather's contemporary artists, including opera singer Olive Fremstad and photographer Laura Gipin.

Lewis, Edith, *Willa Cather Living: A Personal Record*, Knopf, 1953.

> Lewis was Cather's close friend and traveled with her extensively. Lee's biography of Cather details her personal life and her professional achievements.

SUGGESTED SEARCH TERMS

Cather AND *The Song of the Lark*

Cather AND American West

Cather AND Great Plains

Cather AND bildungsroman

Cather AND kunstlerroman OR künstlerroman

Cather AND Olive Fremstad

Cather AND opera

Cather AND Jules Breton

Cather AND New Woman

Cather AND Pulitzer Prize

The Tortilla Curtain

T. C. BOYLE
1995

The Tortilla Curtain was published in 1995 and became author T. C. Boyle's most widely read novel. With immigration a major theme of the book, its publication caused a stir as America struggled with illegal immigration and its effects on society. In a 59- to 41-percent vote, California had just passed a bill restricting illegal immigrants' rights to use certain public resources, such as non-emergency health care and public schools. Immigration concerns were on the minds of citizens and politicians alike.

Along with immigration, Boyle's novel explores themes of the American dream, racism, and the value of walls through the depiction of two distinct couples. Delaney and Kyra Mossbacher lead comfortable, middle-class lives in Topanga Canyon, an estate neighborhood in California. Just around the bend but in what might as well be a totally different planet live Cándido and América Rincón, illegal Mexican immigrants without money, a home, or jobs. The crossing of the two men's paths opens the novel and sets the rest of the story in motion.

Boyle's choice to switch narrators in alternating chapters gives readers a chance to understand and analyze themes and events from a variety of perspectives, particularly those of middle-class Americans and poverty-stricken Mexicans. In this way, the author communicates how cultural values and norms shape one's prejudices and beliefs, even as he neither takes any stance

T. C. Boyle *(© AP Images / Jim Cooper)*

nor presents any bias in his treatment of the main theme of immigration. Boyle does not shy away from tackling the seedier side of immigration and homelessness. Through instances of obscene language and a graphic rape scene, which results in life-altering consequences, the author provides a realistic portrayal of a side of life many would prefer to overlook.

AUTHOR BIOGRAPHY

Thomas John Boyle was born on December 2, 1948, in Peekskill, New York, to a janitor (father) and secretary (mother). Boyle changed his middle name to Coraghessan when he was seventeen years old. Initially intending to study music, he graduated with a bachelor's degree in English and history from the State University of New York at Potsdam in 1968. With no job lined up upon graduation, Boyle drifted for a while. He found himself pursuing a musical career after all as he played in a rock band, but the lifestyle proved too much to handle, and he developed a heroin addiction. The death of a close friend helped him

escape his own demons, and he memorialized that self-destructive period of his life in the short story "The OD and Hepatitis Railroad or Bust," published in the *North American Review* in the fall of 1972. The story gained him admission into the prestigious Iowa Writers' Workshop, from which he earned his master of fine arts degree in 1974 under the instruction of famous American writers such as John Irving and John Cheever. He followed that three years later with a PhD in nineteenth-century British literature from the University of Iowa. While studying for his PhD, Boyle served as fiction editor for the highly respected literary journal *Iowa Review*.

In 1978, Boyle accepted a position as assistant professor of creative writing at the University of Southern California; more than thirty years later, he was still teaching at the university, only now he was a distinguished professor of English with twenty-one works of fiction to his credit. The award-winning novel *The Tortilla Curtain* (1995) was his sixth. Known for what Barnes & Noble reviewer Arthur McCune calls his "acrobatic verbal skill," Boyle has been compared to numerous respected, prolific writers, among them Franz Kafka, Flannery O'Connor, Hunter S. Thompson, and James Joyce.

The list of literary awards Boyle has won is long and distinguished. He won the prestigious PEN/Faulkner Award in 1988 for his third novel, *World's End*, and several of his short stories won the O. Henry Award. *The Tortilla Curtain* won France's Prix Médicis étranger in 1997 for best foreign novel of the year, and Boyle's own audiobook narration of the novel won the Audie Prize for best narration by an author in 2007. In all, his writing has earned him nearly a dozen national or international prizes. Boyle, once deemed "America's most imaginative contemporary novelist" by *Newsweek* magazine (as cited on the Silicon Valley Reads website), lives with his wife and children in California and continues to teach English at the University of Southern California.

PLOT SUMMARY

Part One: Arroyo Blanco

CHAPTER 1

Delaney Mossbacher opens *The Tortilla Curtain* thinking about the car accident where he has just run into an older Mexican man with

MEDIA ADAPTATIONS

- *The Tortilla Curtain* was released as an audio-book by Blackstone Audiobooks in 2006, narrated by Boyle himself.

his expensive car. Unable to forget the image of the injured man, Delaney regrets that his first concerns were for his car and his insurance rates.

When he finally steps out of the car to check on the man, Delaney realizes that he hit him so hard that the impact knocked him off the canyon and into the creek below. Unable to find the man, Delaney is about to give up when he hears the man's moans. He is covered in food and broken glass, as well as his own blood, as he was hit while walking back to his camp from the grocery store. Delaney asks if he is okay, but the man does not speak or understand English.

Eventually, Delaney settles with the man with a twenty-dollar bill. Relieved that there were no witnesses and the man obviously is not going to press charges, Delaney returns to his car. Realizing that his victim is an illegal immigrant not even willing or able to seek necessary medical attention, he is filled with "a gulf of sadness that took Delaney out of himself for a long moment." His pity quickly morphs into outrage as he pieces together the clues—the food, shopping cart, location of the accident—and understands that this man, and probably many more like him, are camping in Topanga Canyon, polluting its waters and dumping their garbage.

Delaney drives directly to the dealership, where he is met by salesman Kenny Grissom. He lies and tells Kenny that he hit a dog, then realizes he is lying to cover up his shame. The guys in the shop repairs Delaney's car while he calls his wife, Kyra, to tell her about the accident. She is not convinced that the situation is so easily taken care of with twenty dollars, but Delaney reiterates that his victim is Mexican.

CHAPTER 2

Cándido Rincón is collapsed in the dirt, agonizing over his injuries as he tries to recall the events that occurred. His pregnant teenage wife, América, finds him when she returns from a day of (unsuccessfully) looking for work in Venice, California. She takes the twenty dollars and buys first-aid supplies. Her husband falls asleep but wakes up with a case of amnesia and blood in his urine. He sustained a concussion, and the pain of his other injuries is too excruciating for him to work. Beaten, Cándido shamefully watches América as she heads off for another day of job searching.

CHAPTER 3

Arroyo Blanco Estates is home to Delaney and Kyra Mossbacher and their son, Jordan. The community boasts a country club and community center and is close to Topanga State Park. The Delaneys have a Siamese cat named Dame Edith and two dogs, Osbert and Sacheverell. The family enjoys a healthy lifestyle that includes whole foods and regular exercise outdoors, although six-year-old Jordan makes his displeasure over his restricted diet known as often as possible.

Kyra Delaney is the breadwinner of the family and works long hours as a Realtor. Delaney stays home to care for his stepson and write his nature column, "Pilgrim at Topanga Creek." On the morning that opens chapter 3, a coyote clears the fence lining the perimeter of the yard and runs away with Sacheverell in his mouth. After Kyra goes to work and Jordan to school, Delaney tries to find the dog but manages to recover only a piece of his leg.

Furious that the neighbors must be leaving food out for these wild creatures, Delaney attends the emergency meeting of the property owners' association about the building of a gate at the entrance to Arroyo Blanco. Those who are against it feel strongly that it will increase dues and limit the open nature of the neighborhood. Other residents, like Jim Shirley and Jack Cherrystone, share crime stories in an effort to increase support for the gate. Nobody pays attention to Delaney. He leaves the meeting under duress and is stopped outside by Jack Jardine, Jr., who wants to know where the car accident happened. Delaney absentmindedly answers the teen and heads home.

CHAPTER 4

Unable to find work, América visits the labor exchange. She eventually finds work at the exchange, where she meets Mary, an alcoholic also in search of work. América is shocked to realize that even whites are out of work in their own country. She is disgusted by Mary's appearance and by her situation.

At the camp, Cándido hears voices approaching and drags himself to a secluded position. He watches as Jack Jardine, Jr., and his accomplice ransack their site. In paint, they write the words "Beaners Die" on the rocks.

CHAPTER 5

As Delaney walks home from the meeting, his anger subsides. But he is soon followed by an old, rumbling car. Once home, he thinks, "If there was a gate that car wouldn't have been there, and who knew what he'd just escaped—a beating, robbery, murder?"

Kyra heads out to work the next day, knowing she cannot sell houses when in such a funk over losing her dog. She finishes a showing and then makes the rounds to the five houses she locks up at the end of each day. Her favorite house is the Da Ros mansion, overlooking the canyon. It is a house Kyra would like to own.

The chapter closes with Delaney's nature column. In it, he shares a firsthand account of hiking and camping outdoors, and he ends the piece with an homage to the wildness of the coyote, whose cunning allows him to thrive under the most difficult circumstances.

CHAPTER 6

América and Cándido are running out of food and América chastises Cándido. He slaps her and calls her a whore. América leaves for the labor exchange.

There, she meets José Navidad, a light-skinned Mexican, and she accepts a cup of coffee. América grows ashamed that her emptiness, her hunger, caused her to accept the coffee, for now José seems to think he owns a piece of her. She tells him she is married, and soon after, she is chosen along with Mary to work for Jim Shirley, an American who looks down on Mexican immigrants.

Meanwhile, Cándido regrets the scene that morning. Deciding it best to move to a new campsite, he heads upstream. Exhausted from the trek, he selects a site behind a wrecked car on the beach, builds a shelter, and falls asleep. When he wakens, he worries that América will not know where to find him. While searching for his wife, he notices a man walking down the path toward him. It is José Navidad.

José wants to know all about Cándido and asks what happened to his face. Cándido deflects the stranger's questions and lies to him, telling him he does not live down in the canyon. José leaves, and Cándido continues to search but fails to find América.

After putting in more than nine hours of work, América is driven home by Jim Shirley.

CHAPTER 7

Delaney sees Jack Jardine at the grocery store, Jack comments on Delaney's emotional outburst at the meeting, and the two men argue about the gate until Jack, Jr., joins them. Outside, they hear a voice hurling racist insults, and to Delaney's surprise, the recipient is the man he hit with his car. The white man shoves Cándido. As he passes the three men, he apologizes and does not seem to recognize Delaney.

While writing his column the next morning, Delaney can only think about Cándido, whom he considers "*his* Mexican." Delaney now pegs Cándido for a bum and decides he himself had been swindled out of twenty dollars. Deciding to go for a hike, he notices sleeping bags dotting the landscape and garbage strewn everywhere. He runs into José Navidad and his companion, who claim to have been out hiking themselves. Delaney blames them for the mess in the canyon. He returns to his car—but his car has been stolen. In his mind, he sees Cándido driving away in the Acura.

CHAPTER 8

Cándido greets América in the parking lot where he had been shoved and is elated at her income. They purchase a feast and return to the new campsite, happier than in a long time. Both of them attempt to find work at the labor exchange the next day, but only América is successful, as Jim Shirley hires her once more.

América waits for Cándido in the parking lot of the supermarket again, but he does not return. She assumes he has found work and heads back to the campsite. José Navidad and his friend rape her. América is devastated.

Part Two: El Tenksgeevee

CHAPTER 1

At the dealership, Kenny is regaling Delaney with stories of immigrants stealing cars. Delaney is stressed out and decides to go for another hike. Again, he leaves his car parked, but this time he hides in the bushes to watch. No one steals his new car.

Kyra closes her deal and heads home where she is pleased by a new, taller fence she had built. She deciphers that the hired hand who limps and has other visible injuries must be her husband's victim.

Finding a shopping cart just inside the gate of the Da Ros property as she makes her nightly rounds to lock up homes, she investigates. She encounters José Navidad and his friend and yells at them to leave. Although her attitude is authoritative, she feels fearful.

CHAPTER 2

Cándido lands the construction job. He finishes his workday, and upon arriving at camp, he finds América, naked and mending her torn dress. Determined not to torment him with the truth, she tells him she was robbed by José and his companion. He forbids her to return to the labor exchange.

Cándido loses his construction job and turns to drinking, feeling guilty for the life he has thrust his wife into.

CHAPTER 3

After dinner, Kyra tells Delaney that she cleared immigrants from loitering around from around a gas station she noticed. Noticing her husband's discomfort, she explains that she is not proud.

Jack Jardine invites Delaney to the house of his friend Dominick Flood, a wealthy business investor whose questionable ethics landed him with house arrest. Also at the meeting are Jim Shirley and Jack Cherrystone, secretary of the association. As the three men overwhelm Delaney with horror stories of immigrant crimes, Delaney gradually realizes that they want his support in building a wall all around Arroyo Blanco Estates. Dom informs Delaney that he used his considerable political influence to put an end to the labor exchange.

Delaney cogitates as he returns home. Once there, he and Kyra talk. Suddenly outside, another coyote jumps the new fence and steals Osbert from the backyard.

CHAPTER 4

Cándido's hopes are bolstered by steady construction work and saving money. Despite his success, however, Cándido suddenly finds himself out of work and is dismayed that the labor exchange has been shut down.

América believes they can now move somewhere more permanent, but Cándido says they need to save more. Displeased, she sews their savings into the cuff of her husband's pants, and they set off for Canoga Park in search of work. There, a man says he knows an inexpensive place they can rent.

CHAPTER 5

Delaney's column is about the dangers of feeding coyotes. He recounts Osbert's demise and warns readers that coyotes should be regarded with caution.

CHAPTER 6

Kyra contemplates the Da Ros property as she locks it up for the night. Then she spends her evening canvassing Arroyo Blanco in favor of a stone wall around the community. Jack Jardine talked her into supporting the effort by playing on her raw sadness. She informs Delaney that she intends to support the campaign, starting a fight. Delaney tells her that Jardine wants the wall to keep Mexicans out, not coyotes. The fight goes on for days.

When she returns to the Da Ros place, she finds it vandalized. Kyra suspects José Navidad.

As he walks home, Delaney is approached by neighbor Todd Sweet, who tries to get Delaney to work with him on opposing the wall. He asks Delaney to help him write a counterargument, but Delaney resists and promises to call Todd without ever taking his phone number.

Delaney comes across José Navidad with a suspicious large white sack on his back. He tells José he is trespassing on private land and demands to know what is in the bag. José tells him, but Delaney refuses to believe him. When he looks, he realizes José has been hired to distribute the fliers for a meeting to vote on the wall.

CHAPTER 7

After waiting for Cándido for over an hour, América is shocked to see him appear bleeding in ripped clothes. The man and his friends mugged him and stole the couple's entire savings. They clean Cándido's wounds in a gas station bathroom, and then he dives into a dumpster to scrounge for food. América is disgusted and belittled.

CHAPTER 8
The community voted to build the wall, and Delaney did not protest. Now the wall construction crew is at his home, and he abandons writing to watch them work.

Cándido is worried about his wife, who refuses to bathe, eat, or speak. But Cándido finds work again, this time through Señor Willis, and he soon saves five hundred dollars. At the supermarket one evening, two young men in front of him are given a turkey for spending over fifty dollars. They also give a bird to a bewildered but grateful Cándido, who does not know what the holiday Señor Willis calls "Tanksgeevee" is. His good fortune cheers up his wife, and she begins to cook the turkey over a fire he made. Then Cándido realizes that the wind has picked up sparks and blown them into the canyon, which is set ablaze.

Part Three: Socorro
CHAPTER 1
Thanksgiving Day at Dominick Flood's includes a string quartet and sushi. The Mossbacher parents, along with Kyra's mother, Kit, join the party, which includes the Jardines. Kit flirts shamelessly with Dom. Suddenly, someone announces fire in the canyon, and Delaney, Kyra, and a reluctant Kit head home. The television reporter warns that the fire is heading toward Arroyo Blanco, so the Mossbachers consider evacuation.

CHAPTER 2
Cándido and América furiously scramble up a rock wall to safety. Once on the road, América refuses to go any farther. Cándido, terrified that they will be found and killed, asks her if she wants to die, and she says yes.

América's water breaks, and she goes into labor. Cándido sequesters her in an aluminum tool shed. Dame Edith, the Mossbachers' cat, joins the couple in the shed, and América decides that the cat is her saint, sent to guide her through childbirth.

CHAPTER 3
The Mossbachers and other residents stand together atop the canyon, evacuated from their homes. Delaney recognizes two men walking up the path—José Navidad and his companion. He settles on these two men as scapegoats. Before he can lay into them, police appear, and the Mexicans are handcuffed and taken away.

Shifting winds blow the fire in another direction before it reaches Arroyo Blanco, and everyone returns home. Kyra finds her own home intact, but a phone call tells her Da Ros has been destroyed. She is devastated, and at that moment, her mother appears and holds up Dom's ankle bracelet, which she found in her purse. He had been using Kit as part of his escape plan.

CHAPTER 4
América gives birth to a girl, whom she names Socorro ("help" in Spanish). Cándido finds enough supplies and tools to build a tiny shack behind the shrubs outside the wall. Dame Edith becomes a meal for the Rincóns.

CHAPTER 5
Kyra finds Da Ros burned to the ground. Certain that José Navidad and his friend destroyed the gate, she is furious that they were released from police custody. Delaney and Kyra begin looking for Dame Edith. As they search outdoors, they run into Jack Jardine, who asks them to go for a ride in his car.

Jack presents the graffiti marring the new wall. Taking action like a man possessed, Delaney sets up cameras by the wall. On the one night he declines to stand vigil, the camera is tripped, and the face in the developed film is Cándido's.

CHAPTER 6
Cándido returns to the canyon to find their savings burned. América believes he is cursed. She begs him to help get Socorro baptized, but all she truly wants is to return to Mexico. As she looks into her baby's eyes, she notices that Socorro does not look back. Is she blind?

Unable to find work but desperate to stay in California, Cándido takes comfort in having escaped the canyon, now ravaged by floodwaters. Downtrodden, Cándido stands alongside the road. Suddenly a car swerves, and out jumps Delaney, screaming at him not to move.

CHAPTER 7
Delaney plans to turn Cándido in to the police for the graffiti, but when Cándido steps into the road while Delaney calls for help, a truck swerves to miss him and hits Delaney's new car. Cándido runs off, and Delaney is ticketed for

obstructing traffic. He follows the immigrant's tracks and finds they lead to his gated community.

Back in his neighborhood, Delaney notices the wall again vandalized and is eager to see the pictures. He grabs his gun. Developing the film, he is shocked to discover not Cándido's face but those of Jack, Jr., and an accomplice. He destroys the evidence and resumes his hunt for Cándido. He finds the Rincóns' hideout.

CHAPTER 8

Cándido returns to the shack and tells América about Delaney. América reiterates to her husband the urgency of getting Socorro to a doctor because she thinks the baby is blind. When Cándido brushes off this fear as irrational, América finally acknowledges the rape and is afraid she caught a sexually transmitted disease that caused their daughter's blindness. Delaney then appears armed in their doorway.

Suddenly, floodwaters tear away the hut, the ground, and all four people. Socorro is washed away, but the forceful waters deposit Cándido against the U.S. Post Office. He climbs onto the roof and rescues his wife only to realize that their baby girl is gone forever. Cándido has every reason to plunge himself into the fatal waters; yet when Delaney's white hand reaches up for assistance, Cándido takes hold without hesitation, and the reader is left not knowing what happens next.

CHARACTERS

Jack Cherrystone

Jack Cherrystone is secretary of the Arroyo Blanco Estates Property Owners' Association. Though small in stature, he has a commanding presence bolstered by a booming voice. In addition to his secretarial duties, Cherrystone is a voice actor who makes his money recording Hollywood movie trailers. A self-professed liberal, he nevertheless quickly points out the perceived dangers presented by the Mexicans who live in the canyon. Cherrystone is the epitome of middle-class America.

Dominick Flood

Dom is a wealthy businessman whose unethical behavior led to three years of house arrest. A client of Jack Jardine's, Dom's personal charm and magnetism are showcased at the numerous social events he hosts at his mansion. These events allow Dom to retain a considerable degree of social influence and power within the community, and it is because of him that the labor exchange is abruptly shut down, leaving Cándido and his peers without work or hope. In a sleazy move, Dom uses Kyra's mother's obvious attraction to him as a way to escape the law when he cuts off his ankle bracelet and deposits it into her purse. Under the cover of the chaos caused by the fire, he escapes the country.

Kenny Grissom

Kenny Grissom is an obnoxious salesman at the Acura car dealership where Delaney bought the car he hits Cándido with. Though he tries to be affable, Grissom's loud, boisterous comments reveal his racism.

Jack Jardine

A friend of the Mossbachers, Jack Jardine is president of the Arroyo Blanco Estates Property Owners' Association and a legal consultant by trade. Jardine is the poster child for successful, white businessmen, and his vocal promotion of building the wall around Arroyo Blanco—it was, in fact, his idea—blurs the line between concern for the personal safety of the neighborhood's residents and blatant racism.

Jack Jardine, Jr.

Jack Jardine, Jr., is the teenage son of Jack Jardine and a menace to all of the novel's Mexican immigrants. He is symbolic of anti-immigration sentiment in general, reacting to immigration with mindless violence and hatred. Boyle leads the reader to believe it was Jack, Jr., who vandalized the wall at Arroyo Blanco (which he knew would be blamed on Mexicans), and the angry teen bullies and threatens immigrants throughout the unfolding of the story. Cándido Ricon mistakenly assumes Jack, Jr., is Delaney's son, intentionally sent to harass him and América.

Mary

Mary is a poor, overweight alcoholic who visits the labor exchange the same day as América. When she unsuccessfully tries to steal a job from América, the two women find themselves working together. But while América puts forth great effort to perform the job she has been hired to do, Mary's lazy work ethic is highlighted by her spending the day drinking from a flask and complaining. Still, América is horrified to realize that even white Americans are forced to find work through the labor exchange, and Mary's presence leaves América feeling hopeless for her own and her baby's future.

Delaney Mossbacher

Delaney Mossbacher is one of the main characters in the novel and represents white, middle-class America in the 1990s. He lives with his workaholic wife and stifled young stepson in Arroyo Blanco Estates, a community near Topanga Canyon in which all houses are white with orange rooftops, and all yards are dutifully maintained, primarily by illegal immigrants.

Delaney is a full-time stay-at-home dad whose love of and respect for nature lead him to write a monthly column called "Pilgrim at Topanga Creek" for the nature magazine *Wide Open Spaces*. His desire to connect with nature prohibits Delaney from supporting the idea of building a wall around his neighborhood, but in time, his suppressed attitudes of prejudice surface, belying his liberal facade and revealing his true beliefs. By the novel's end, Delaney betrays his liberal values and acts in concert with his conservative, immigrant-hating neighbors, even when hard evidence proves his anger should be focused elsewhere.

Jordan Mossbacher

Jordan Mossbacher is the son of Kyra Mossbacher, stepson of Delaney Mossbacher. The six-year-old spends most of his time playing video games and watching television, a direct rejection of his parents' values for nature and physical fitness. Although a minor character in the book, the few lines Jordan does have reflect the concept that humans are as much a product of society as a whole as they are of their upbringing.

Kyra Mossbacher

Kyra Mossbacher is a workaholic mother and wife who spends more time thinking about how to move houses than she does anything else. Like her husband Delaney, Kyra is dedicated to health and fitness. She runs and works out daily and belongs to nature-oriented clubs such as the Sierra Club and National Wildlife. On the surface, at least, Kyra values a feeling of kinship with nature. She loves and values her dogs, and when one of them is mauled to death by a coyote, his dramatic death leave her listless and forlorn. Ultimately, Kyra is in favor of building the wall around Arroyo Blanco, which would, in essence, separate her from the very nature she claims to respect and appreciate. This is because her love of nature is not as intense as her dislike and distrust of the illegal immigrants living in camps around Los Angeles and her neighborhood.

Kyra's goodness is largely superficial; she is, at heart, selfish and egotistical. She values appearances more than substance, a characteristic reflected in her obsession with her looks and her dream of owning an ostentatious mansion, complete with perfect gardens. Her family, on the surface, is worthy of admiration, yet son Jordan clearly does not share his parents' values, and the few lines in the book he is given betray his unhappiness at the lifestyle he is forced to live. Kyra's relationship with Delaney is not democratic, either, but one in which she is in control. For example, she determines when the couple has sex. And for her, the physical act of sex is not reflective of the love or passion she feels for her husband but is instead therapeutic, something she does to relieve stress.

José Navidad

José Navidad is a lost soul who is accepted by neither whites nor Mexicans. With skin light enough to pass for white, José presents himself in such a way that everyone—white or otherwise—distrusts and wants to avoid him. José is always wearing a poncho or *serape*, which is a traditional Mexican article of clothing, so the reader is encouraged to understand that he identifies with his Mexican roots and is not interested in fitting in with white society.

José is accused of several crimes throughout the novel because he is an easy scapegoat. Yet the one crime—the rape—he is certain of committing was against a member of his own race. In this fact, Boyle holds up José as an example of a hateful immigrant who, nevertheless, is not deserving of all the racial profiling to which he falls victim. Yes, he is a criminal, but he does not deserve to be blamed for those crimes he did not commit.

Candelario Pérez

Candelario Pérez is the liaison between American employers and those looking for work via the labor exchange. He is a rough man, accustomed to dealing with difficult people.

América Rincón

América Rincón is the seventeen-year-old sister of Cándido's first wife. She grew up in poverty in Mexico and ran away with Cándido after he found his first wife cheating on him. América naively believed Cándido's promises of a happy, easier life in the United States, so the reality of life with him in California goes beyond humiliating to defeating. Pregnant with a daughter who will be born blind as a result of a rape, América loses hope little by little as the story progresses until, in the end, she is literally fighting for her life, a life she is not even sure is worth living.

Cándido Rincón

Cándido Rincón immigrates illegally to California from Mexico with his young wife, América. Married once before to her sister, Cándido has dedicated his entire existence to building a better life, but the American Dream seems just out of reach.

After finding his first wife in bed with another man, Cándido turned to alcohol to ease his pain, but it was with renewed hope that he finally left Mexico for the United States. Life there, however, was nothing but one hardship after another. After being hit by the car Delaney Mossbacher was driving, Cándido could not seek much-needed medical attention because his illegal status would have been discovered and he would have been deported. So he tries to heal as best he can living outdoors in a campsite. Work is scarce, and even when he finally is able to save some money, it is stolen by Jack Jardine, Jr. It seems that, for every stroke of good luck Cándido has, something bad happens, and he is never able to get ahead.

By the novel's end, Cándido's makeshift shack is washed away in floodwaters, and he is fighting for his own life. It seems as though the American Dream will always be just out of reach for this immigrant.

Jim Shirley

Jim Shirley hires América and Mary to shine Buddhas for him in his shop. His attitude toward immigrants is obvious in that he finds them useful enough to perform manual labor for him in unfit conditions and for measly compensation, but he simultaneously promotes the building of the wall in his neighborhood, Arroyo Blanco Estates. Jim is often the source of the exaggerated crime stories involving immigrants that circulate among his neighbors. Sweaty and obese, Jim Shirley is representative of American hypocrisy.

Todd Sweet

Todd Sweet lives in Arroyo Blanco, but he is against the building of the gate and eventually the wall. A fit, attractive man, Todd is what Delaney believes himself to be.

Señor Willis

Señor Willis hires Cándido for construction projects after the labor exchange closes. An intelligent man, Señor Willis frequently goes on drinking binges, but he treats Cándido well and pays him wages that are more than fair. After the fire in the canyon, Cándido never hears from him again.

THEMES

Immigrant life

Immigrant life is arguably the most obvious theme in *The Tortilla Curtain*. Without ever stating as much outright, Boyle shows the reader how challenging and brutal life for illegal immigrants can be. He presents the reader a chance to view such lives from the inside, with Cándido and América struggling even as the lost and permanently damaged José Navidad continues to live his life in one hopeless, hateful act after another. And the author also allows the reader to view the immigrant experience from the outside, through the eyes of middle-class, white Americans who only see the surface and who misinterpret loneliness and desperation as corruption. For example, Delaney immediately assumes that Cándido had purposely run out in front of his car, probably so that he could collect money: "The man must have been crouching in the bushes like some feral thing, like a stray dog or bird-mauling cat, and at the last possible moment he'd flung himself across the road in a mad suicidal scramble." But the reader realizes that this was not how the accident happened at all, that this is nothing more than misguided assumption.

American Dream

The struggle to attain the American Dream is the theme that lies at the heart of Boyle's novel. It is a powerful thing, this dream, so much so that it motivates Cándido and América Rincón to gamble everything they have in hopes of achieving it. Cándido arguably has less to lose than the young América, who is close to her mother and family and young enough that the idea of journeying to a new and unfamiliar land is intimidating. But

TOPICS FOR FURTHER STUDY

- Research the lives of Mexican immigrants who come to America. Now research the lives of Chinese immigrants who landed on America's shores through Angel Island in California back in the 1800s. How were their experiences similar? How were they different? Using the computer software of your choice, develop a presentation that compares and contrasts the two cultural groups' immigrant experiences. Be sure to go beyond the surface to explore their fears, the challenges they faced in leaving behind all they held dear and coming to a new land, and the methods and strategies they used to organize and manage as the minority population.

- Choose one chapter from *The Tortilla Curtain* and rework it as a graphic novel. Let the illustrations tell the story. Do this assignment by hand using any medium you wish, or use illustration software like Adobe or Xara.

- Choose one Mexican character from Boyle's novel and write a poem that accurately portrays your emotions and thoughts of your experiences as an immigrant in America. If you are musically inclined, write a song instead of a poem, and put the lyrics to music. Be prepared to read your poem or sing your song to the class.

- Read the Newbery Award–winning young adult novel *Kira-Kira*, written by Cynthia Kadohata. Compare the tragedies that befall this Japanese immigrant family with those suffered by the Rincóns and other immigrants in Boyle's novel. What themes do the books share, and how are those themes portrayed in the texts? Write a paper citing these themes; be sure to support your claims with evidence from each text.

- The ending of *The Tortilla Curtain* does not provide closure to the story but serves rather to leave the fates of Delaney, Cándido, and América wide open to speculation. Rewrite the ending of the story, providing a new final chapter. Be prepared to explain why you chose the ending you did. Remember that the ending can involve just those main characters, or it can involve any and all characters in the story. Their fates now lie in your hands.

- Imagine Socorro had lived. Write a short story from her point of view as a fifteen-year-old girl. What happened after the flood? What was life in America like? Did she, in fact, stay in America? Did her parents stay together? Was she blind after all? Make her character come to life on the page with detail.

---

that dream—the idea that one can attain a comfortable middle-class existence—is the reason the Mexican couple stays the course. It is the reason they live like animals, the reason they accept manual labor for unfair wages. Even as that dream drifts further away as the events of the story unfold, Cándido and América hold out hope. For América, the breaking point is when Cándido must dumpster-dive in order to feed himself and his pregnant wife. She loses her last shred of hope at that point, only to regain it upon the birth of the couple's daughter, Socorro. But even then, the dream is shattered as América comes to discover her baby is blind. Cándido, despite his many misfortunes, keeps chasing the American Dream. It is not until the flood that he understands he will never succeed.

The Mossbachers chase their own version of the American Dream. They live in a gated community in a beautiful region of the country, in a comfortable house. Both have fulfilling careers and enough leisure time to pursue their personal interests of fitness and outdoor activities. Because of their station in life, the Mossbachers have the luxury of making time for things they enjoy doing and which are important to them. Their money allows them to spend more on things like cars, clothing, and even the foods they eat. They do not need to expend all their energy and time on just getting by. They truly have attained the American Dream; but now the efforts of illegal immigrants to attain the same is threatening the Mossbachers' sense of security.

Perhaps Boyle is making the statement that the American Dream is not so much a dream as it is a nightmare, because its many versions are not capable of coexisting in one society. And even when the dream is realized, satisfaction is not guaranteed, as evidenced by the Mossbachers and their eternal quest for material wealth. At the end of the day, then, the American Dream is merely illusion.

Racism

Racist attitudes and behavior run rampant through Boyle's novel. Delaney likes to think he is not racist, but even as early as the first chapter, his racism is evident when he assures his wife that there will be no legal or financial repercussions from the car accident. Kyra is in disbelief when her husband tells her he took care of the situation by paying the victim twenty dollars. When she questions his certainty, Delaney replies, "I told you—he was *Mex*ican." Even before those words escape his mouth, Delaney is struggling with the obvious conflict between his conscience and his actions: "He'd just left the poor son of a bitch there alongside the road, abandoned him, . . . relieved to buy him off with his twenty dollars' blood money. And how did that square with his liberal-humanist ideals?"

Jack Jardine is one of the more racist characters in the novel. A friend of Delaney's and the family's lawyer, Jack is Delaney's confidante after the accident. Jack is a staunch believer in the necessity of the community gate and wall, and he feeds Delaney's underlying racism and fear so that Delaney will change his mind and join the rest of the community promoting the wall. Jack, Jr., is clearly a product of his father's attitudes, and his racism takes a more physical form as he vandalizes property with racial slurs and destroys the Rincóns' campsite and all their worldly possessions. It is through the two Jack characters that Boyle illustrates how racism is bred into successive generations and why it is so difficult to eradicate.

Isolation

The theme of isolation is exemplified by the literal and figurative walls that appear throughout the book. The illegal immigrants entered the country by jumping the border, the dividing line, between Mexico and the United States. One of the main conflicts at the center of the story is whether or not to build first a gate and then a wall around the Arroyo Blanco Estates community. Using their cunning and instinct, the coyotes that kill the Mossbachers' dogs had to jump over the yard's fence (a different kind of division or wall) to get to the dogs, much like the immigrants jumped the fence into America. Even the canyon wall plays a role: It is the one thing that keeps Cándido and América outside the security and prosperity of white society.

Figuratively speaking, there is a wall between the immigrants and Americans, and it is one that seems to be built higher and higher as the story progresses. There is even a wall that begins to form between América and Cándido, as their time in Los Angeles serves up one tragedy after another, leaving the young pregnant wife resentful and hopeless. After she is raped, América builds a sort of wall between her and her husband in order to protect him. And Cándido builds his own walls, one after another and with each misfortune, to shield himself from the white world he has chosen to live in.

Walls serve two purposes: they keep things out or they keep things in. Either way, the result is isolation. The residents of Arroyo Blanco want to build a wall to keep out the illegal immigrants who have set up camp in the canyon, though ostensibly, they want it to keep out the coyotes and other dangers of semi-wilderness living. But an eight-foot wall is possible to scale, as Boyle demonstrates toward the end of the book when Cándido jumps the wall to procure items he needs to build his makeshift shack.

Those walls that keep things out also keep things isolated inside, a fact Delaney realizes when he hears Jack, Jr.'s racist talk. At that point, he understands that the wall he initially fought but eventually wants will force him into isolation with the likes of Jack, Jr., and all the hatred and racism that goes with him. Delaney is the one character who seems to fully acknowledge his moral demise as he lets go of the values he held in favor of a false sense of safety. No longer could he claim "that he stood apart from

Cándido and América must live in a temporary shelter in the Topanga Canyon after Cándido cannot get work. *(© William Allum | Shutterstock.com)*

his fellow men and women, that he saw more deeply and felt more passionately."

In this novel, the walls built to keep things out fail. The wall around Arroyo Blanco is jumped by Cándido, and so it is safe to assume it will be jumped by anyone else who is determined to get into the community. Eight feet may be high enough to keep out animals, but not humans. And the wall around Kyra's beloved Da Ros property? It is not enough to keep out the wayward José Navidad and his minion. All the walls serve to do in *The Tortilla Curtain* is isolate those on either side.

STYLE

Alternating Point of View

Boyle chose to tell his story from two primary points of view, those of Delaney Mossbacher and Cándido Rincón. He structured the novel so that the chapters alternate between these two protagonists and, in doing so, made it easier for readers to compare everything about the men:

family, lifestyle, beliefs, values, and so on. The reader is able to see how each couple responds to their circumstances as they happen.

For example, the novel opens with Delaney running into Cándido with his car. The reader is immediately given clues to Delaney's propensity for selfishness. Although he is concerned about having hit and hurt a pedestrian, he wonders why it had to "happen to him." This is a rather absurd thought, since it did not happen to him, it happened to Cándido. For Delaney, the event "ruined his afternoon," and the more he thought about why Cándido was even in the vicinity and how that must mean the man was actually living in the canyon, "Delaney felt his guilt turn to anger, to outrage." Here is a middle-class man, one who lives a comfortable life without struggle, who just ran into a poor, homeless immigrant with little else to his name besides the shirt on his back. And somehow, Delaney manages to be the one to feel righteous outrage. Cándido, conversely, has no thoughts of ill will toward Delaney; the chapter told from his point of view speaks only of the physical aspects of being run over—the pain, the mangled arm and face, the inability to move. Cándido experiences not anger or disbelief at his bad fortune but shame, because his young, pregnant wife must walk alone, for a long distance, to try to find work that will pay a meager wage at best while he lies immobile on the ground. Boyle's shifting of points of view consistently throughout the novel helps the reader understand the dueling perspectives on the various events as they unfold, which gives the story a sort of "real time" feel.

Cultural Contrasts

Through the switches in point of view, the reader of this novel is able to compare and contrast the central Mexican and American couples in terms of personality, lifestyle, and values. But Boyle is suggesting the reader make comparisons not only between Mexican and American cultures and attitudes but also within white society as well. He presents two sides of white America. The first—and more desirable, at least on some level—is that of the white American who is aware of the world around him and his place in it. He strives to reach his potential by working hard (perhaps too hard) and treating his body with respect. The reader sees this side through characters like the Mossbachers and their neighbors.

Another side of white America is depicted through Mary. She is fat and lazy, with an addictive personality that indicates lack of self-control and self-respect. Jim Shirley, owner of the shop who hires Mary and América to shine Buddhas, is also representative of this segment of American society. Using this compare-and-contrast technique, Boyle is encouraging his readers to turn the magnifying glass inward. Are whites really superior to the Mexican immigrants? Is it possible that is just a stereotype?

Symbolism

The Tortilla Curtain is rife with symbolism. Many of the characters themselves are symbolic of something more abstract, something greater than themselves. Jack Jardine, Jr., for example, is a rather minor character in Boyle's story; he is a belligerent, malicious teenage boy. But figuratively, his character is symbolic of America's highly pervasive anti-immigrant attitude. Jack, Jr., is the epitome of society's hateful intolerance of outsiders, of anyone who is in any way different from native-born Americans. Though he has no personal gripe against any of the immigrants living in the canyon, Jack, Jr., makes it his mission to harass and bully them, to vandalize and destroy their belongings. To what end?

Delaney and Kyra Mossbacher together are symbolic of the self-proclaimed liberal, left-leaning faction of society that espouses to believe in equality and the right of immigrants to strive for the American Dream, but which in time of crisis reveals a darker side. Delaney wants to believe he is a champion of the downtrodden, but as the novel progresses and events unfold, he steps further and further away from his purported ideals. By the end of the story, he even disbelieves hard evidence that someone—a white someone—other than Cándido is vandalizing Arroyo Blanco and hunts down the immigrant couple with a gun. The man is a whole-foods fitness nut, a nature lover who feels it is his duty to defend wildlife and preserve natural beauty, a live-and-let-live kind of guy. Yet he is stripped down to his most primitive, vengeful state as crisis and conflict mount. His idea of who he is turns out to be nothing more than delusion. Kyra is merely a more shallow version of her husband, and she struggles to a lesser degree with letting go of her delusion as her dogs are mauled and killed and the dream house she has coveted is destroyed.

The coyote in the story is an obvious symbol for the Mexican immigrants. Despite the fact that the family dog was killed by a coyote, Delaney writes one of his nature columns regarding the coyote with a kind of awe. He at once fears and respects the animal's wild instinct to survive as he refers to him as "the Trickster, the four-legged wonder who can find water where there is none and eat hearty among the rocks and the waste places." He again refers to the coyote in a later column, when he describes how the one who "makes his living on the fringes of my community...has learned to simply chew his way through the plastic irrigation pipes whenever he wants a drink." Later in the novel, Cándido himself sneaks into the walled community to steal those things he needs to survive. But it is not only Delaney who holds a loathing fascination for the coyote; his neighbors put out food for them, knowing this will attract them, and then complain and go into crisis mode when the coyotes actually make their way into the neighborhood. This is a direct parallel to the way they treat the Mexican immigrants: they hire them from the labor exchange to work in the community, but then they immediately blame and revile

COMPARE
&
CONTRAST

- **1990s:** Immigrants make up 7.9 percent of America's entire population.

  Today: Immigrants make up 12.9 percent of the country's population.

- **1990s:** By decade's end, 26.2 percent of California's population is foreign-born.

  Today: The foreign-born population of California has increased just 1 percent, to 27.2 percent.

- **1990s:** The treadmill is the most popular piece of fitness equipment in health clubs. The most popular form of exercise is lifting free weights.

  Today: The treadmill remains the most popular exercise of choice in gyms across the nation. Walking is the most popular form of exercise, with running being a close second.

them for anything that goes wrong. To the white Americans in the story, the Mexican immigrants are wild, untamed, primitive, just like the coyote. They live off the land, doing what they must to survive, and rather than be welcomed in the city, they are hunted.

HISTORICAL CONTEXT

Immigration
Published in 1995, *The Tortilla Curtain* revolves around what was arguably the most controversial topic of the time, immigration. Although the topic had been under debate since the earliest immigrants descended upon America's shores, the argument escalated in the 1990s, particularly in California, where, according to *Time* magazine, 40 percent of the nation's estimated 3.4 million illegal immigrants lived by year's end in 1994. Just one year before, California passed a bill called Proposition 187, which denied illegal immigrants public schooling, welfare, and other social programs. The bill passed 59 percent to 41 percent, and tension within the state was high.

According to an article published on December 5, 1995, in the *San Francisco Chronicle*, approximately 800,000 immigrants were entering the United States legally each year, while another 200,000 to 300,000 were crossing the nation's borders illegally. Three months later, the same newspaper reported that half of those

who immigrate legally end up illegal because they overstay their visas. It was a problem without an obvious solution or even compromise because, according to James Edwards, Jr., of the Center for Immigration, legal and illegal immigration had been moving in tandem since 1965: as legal immigration rose, so did the number of illegal immigrants. And by the end of the 1990s, more than half of all Mexicans living in the United States were of illegal status.

One of the major concerns regarding illegal immigrant populations was the effect on the unemployment rate of native-born Americans. A report published by the Cato Institute and the National Immigration Forum declared, "Immigrants have practically no negative effect in the labor market on any person except other immigrants. The effect on wages is modest by any appraisal, and the effect on unemployment apparently is zero." Despite these findings, Americans continued in their xenophobia (fear of foreign-born people) and demanded legal consequences and restrictions.

Fitness
The 1990s was a decade of increased and expanded awareness of the importance of physical fitness. With a degree of dedication harkening back to the 1970s, Americans turned their attention to exercise. California in particular was concerned with health and fitness, primarily for two reasons. One was that it was home to Hollywood, the land of beautiful actors and aspiring wannabes. In an

The Mossbachers live in a gated community in the Topanga Canyon area of Los Angeles. *(© Lynne Furrer / Shutterstock.com)*

industry that relies heavily on physical appearance, staying fit was key. But the 1990s found Californians consuming less milk (traditionally considered a nutrition benchmark) each year, as bottled and purified waters increased in popularity along with diet soda, health drinks, and the like.

To break the trend, the state's food and drug administration formed the California Milk Processor Board, the purpose of which was to market milk to the public. The board in turn hired an advertising agency that came up with the "Got Milk?" campaign in 1993. One year after the award-winning campaign was launched, California saw a 7-percent increase in the consumption of milk.

Boyle incorporated fitness and health themes into his story by making the Mossbachers nature lovers who take time each day to improve their fitness, either by working out or hiking or just staying active. By imbuing only the white, middle-class characters with these qualities, he insinuates that only the more fortunate have time and

energy to pay attention to physical fitness. The rest of the world is consumed with trying to make enough money just to survive, living day to day. For those less fortunate, good health is a luxury.

CRITICAL OVERVIEW

The Tortilla Curtain was controversial from the time of its publication in 1995 for its treatment of the issue of immigration. Some critics lamented that Boyle took no stance on the topic, that he offered no literary answers to this multilayered, politically charged conflict. In an interview with Boyle published on the Penguin Group publisher's website, Boyle responded to the accusation:

> People want a polemic. They want to raise their fist in the air and say, 'Yes, you're on our side.' Well, I'm not on your side. I am presenting a fable, a fiction, so that you can judge for yourself.

Scott Spencer, *New York Times* book critic, slams the novel for its author's failure to fully develop all the protagonists. While praising Boyle's depiction of the Rincón couple as first-rate, Spencer criticizes his portrayal of the Mossbachers:

> Why are we being asked to follow the fates of characters for whom he clearly feels such contempt?...Contempt is a dangerous emotion, luring us into believing that we understand more than we do....T. Coraghessan Boyle may be the most contemptuous of our well-known novelists.

For this critic, Boyle does appear to take sides, and his bias encourages readers not to care about some of the characters.

Still other critics simply found the storytelling dull. *SF Gate* reviewer David Eggers refers to Boyle's story as a contemporary fable that addresses the most explosive controversial topics of the era in a way that is at once urgent and full of good intentions. Yet he judges the writing style to be lacking: "Boyle has scrapped his energetic, lyrical style in favor of a stripped-down, dead-sober tone." Considering the characters shallowly depicted, Eggers claims Boyle has done them a disservice: "How can we hear the story of the 'illegals' when their voices sound so thin, their words so spiritless and hollow?"

Boyle was even brought to task for writing about Mexicans, presumably because he is white. In an interview with Chryss Yost, Boyle had this to say:

> That's the most racist thing of all. It's the same old line, that only Mexicans can write about Mexicans, only women can write about women, only dogs can write about dogs...where does it stop? I'm a writer. I write about people, all sorts.

Arguably, the book hit a nerve for its raw, realistic portrayal of a slice of the American Pie nobody really likes to think about. Even in the twenty-first century, Boyle's novel is causing conflict because some parents do not want it to be read in the classroom. They take offense at the profanity, the graphic rape scene, and the stereotype of Latino girls. As late as 2010, parents in California attempted to get the book banned from high-school classrooms, albeit unsuccessfully. Boyle was unfazed. About art, the writer told John Beck of *Press Democrat*,

> It's not supposed to make you feel good about your own prejudices and your own values; it's supposed to open you up in some way and get you outraged or make you happy or make you sad or whatever it's going to do.

CRITICISM

Rebecca Valentine

Valentine is an award-winning author whose writing has been published by Dell, St. Martin's Press, and Reader's Digest, among others. In the following essay, she suggests that the very aspect of Boyle's writing in The Tortilla Curtain *that draws the ire of critics is what makes this fable successful.*

Boyle has long been revered for his verve, his energy, his remarkable command of the English language. In a 1985 *New York Times* piece, Larry McCaffery wrote, "Mr. Boyle's literary sensibility...thrives on excess, profusion, pushing past the limits of good taste." His characters are often over the top in terms of behavior or personality, and as the number of his published novels progressed from one to three to five and then to *The Tortilla Curtain*, his sixth, readers and critics came to expect a certain style of writing from Boyle. His unpredictability had become predictable; one-dimensional characters did not fit his readers' understanding of who he was as an author.

So when he wrote a fable with political undertones and peopled it with stock, stereotypical characters, he threw everyone for a loop. Those who appreciate Boyle's literary eccentricities may have been surprised that he chose to develop "typical" characters, but those new to his masterful storytelling may instead have shaken their heads and wondered what all the fuss over this Boyle fellow was about.

But let's get something straight: Boyle did not write a political novel here. At least, not a traditional political novel, the very nature of which is inherently bent on presenting a particular viewpoint or side. He wrote *The Tortilla Curtain* to be read as a fable, that is, a narration intended to convey a useful truth. He explained in an interview with David Appell of *Auteurs.net*, "I wanted to do something different here. I wanted to produce a sort-of-fable, and to do that I had to curb some of the hyperbolic tendencies that I have." Traditional fables often include talking animals, or at least animals as main characters. Boyle does not go that far, but he certainly includes animals in his plot, using the coyotes as symbols and metaphors for humans and human behavior. In order to make room for readers to recognize the fable's useful truth, the author needed to develop characters that were representative of broader society. In doing so, he made them easy to recognize but also kept the

WHAT DO I READ NEXT?

- Pam Muñoz Ryan's award-winning young-adult novel *Esperanza Rising* (2000) tells the tale of thirteen-year-old Esperanza's experience as a Mexican immigrant moving to California during the Great Depression. Esperanza has to assimilate not only into a new culture but into a lower social class as well when she leaves behind her privileged life in Mexico to live on a farm as a migrant worker.

- Thanhha Lai's 2011 coming-of-age novel *Inside Out and Back Again*, written for adolescents, tells the story of Ha, whose ten years of life have been spent in Saigon. After realizing that the father who has been missing in action for nine years during the Vietnam War is probably not coming back, Ha, her mother, and her siblings flee to America and settle in Alabama, where she is safe from war but not from racism and cruelty. Hers is a tale of letting go, holding on, and growing up.

- *My Name Is Not Easy* (2011) is the story of Luke, a teenager forced to leave his arctic home to live at a Catholic boarding school two hundred miles away. Here Eskimos and Indians clash as their prejudice and racism are challenged daily. Set in the early 1960s, Debby Dahl Edwardson's novel portrays the coming-of-age stories of five boys who eventually overcome their differences in an effort to survive in an unfamiliar world.

- In 2004, Mae M. Ngai published *Impossible Subjects: Illegal Aliens and the Making of Modern America*. She traces history back to the origin of "illegal aliens" and deftly explains and illustrates how illegal immigration became the central topic of America's immigration policy. Her research includes Filipinos, Mexicans, and Asians and suggests that these ethnic groups may always remain "other" in America.

- Anne Fadiman published the award-winning book *The Spirit Catches You and You Fall Down: A Hmong Child, Her American Doctors, and the Collision of Two Cultures* in 1997, which looked into the personal lives of the close-knit Hmong community of Merced, California. Lia Lee was born into this displaced family, the thirteenth child. As her parents struggle to make ends meet and survive in this foreign Western universe, well-meaning doctors try to force them into treating their infant's seizure disorder with medicine. They prefer animal sacrifice, and as a result of their "neglect," little Lia is forcibly removed from their custody. This is a story of cultural miscommunication and misunderstanding.

- T. C. Boyle's eleventh novel, *Talk Talk*, is about a thirty-year-old deaf woman, Dana, whose identity is stolen by a villain who also happens to be a gourmet cook with a shopaholic girlfriend. Dana's do-good boyfriend leaves everything behind to join her on a cross-country hunt for the man who turned her into someone else. The 2006 title was hailed as an adventure-filled page turner.

focus on the moral of the story, not the players bringing the message.

Reviewer David Eggers wrote, "The characters fall somewhere between archetypes and stereotypes—either way, they lack depth." He points out the Rich People, the Poor People, the Good White People, and the Bad White People. There are the Good Mexicans and, for added measure, the Bad Mexicans, and Eggers is not happy with any of them.

But society is still significantly blanketed with intolerance and prejudice, its people willing to accept stereotypes as accurate. And most astute, mature readers understand what those stereotypes

> HIS UNPREDICTABILITY HAD BECOME
> PREDICTABLE; ONE-DIMENSIONAL CHARACTERS
> DID NOT FIT HIS READERS' UNDERSTANDING OF
> WHO HE WAS AS AN AUTHOR."

are. This understanding is, in fact, what makes the stereotypes offensive in the first place. When seen in print, it is hard to truly observe a person who shares one's beliefs and prejudices and not feel like the Ugly American. Still, stereotypes are universal and do not require concentrated effort to understand or identify with.

Had Boyle populated his novel with characters who surprise readers with their choices, he would have had a more difficult time communicating the moral or lesson of his fable. Take José Navidad, for example. A damaged, dangerous man who is light enough to "pass" for white but clearly of Mexican heritage, he is accepted and tolerated by no one. He is, literally and figuratively, a man without a country. It is a centuries-old story, and a believable one, given human nature. That kind of marginalization "just because" can make a man hard-hearted and hateful. And so we expect José to do the things he does: harass, sneer, intimidate, sneak, lie, and eventually, rape. He acts within the confines of our expectations, and in his doing so, we are able to see how truly frightening he is.

Kyra Mossbacher is another example of a character who is stereotyped and for good reason. With a comfortable lifestyle that affords her many luxuries, Kyra is a rather spoiled, shallow woman whose priorities include work, fitness, and family, in that order. She is all about keeping up appearances, so we are not surprised that she is a perfectionist who abhors clutter and is meticulous about the real-estate properties she works with. As the novel progresses, she is more easily able to let go of her espoused ideals than is her husband. She does not experience that same struggle with her conscience as she begins to think of the illegal immigrants as inferior, as she agrees to support the construction of the wall around Arroyo Blanco. Kyra was, by her very nature, already on her way to becoming a racist.

By the story's end, there is no doubt where she stands.

What readers and many critics seem to miss in their interpretation of *The Tortilla Curtain* is that it is a satire. By definition, satire uses irony and ridicule to expose and criticize people's vices and stupidity. In his novel, Boyle uses satire to illuminate the absurdity of stereotypes, and perhaps he is, simultaneously, using satire to reveal each reader's own prejudices. Historically, the author has not spared anyone his caustic wit; everyone is fair game in Boyle's world. He is not contemptible of his characters, as one critic accuses, but trying to figure out how he feels about the primary topic at hand, which is racism. As he told Appell, "This is the third book I've written on the subject of racism. . . . I just wanted to sort out my own feelings on the issue." And for him, the best way to come to do that is to force all those stereotypes together in one place and let them respond as they naturally would. If he can poke fun of them at the same time, point out their inconsistencies, then more power to him.

In 2010, parents of California high school parents tried to get the book banned from the classroom, in part because of the stereotypical portrayal of Latino girls. América most definitely fits the label of stereotype: She is young, homeless, and pregnant with an older man's baby. She is gullible, having believed Cándido's promises of a better, easier life in the United States. To unknowing outsiders, América appears to be nothing more than a naive Mexican girl. But Boyle subtly shows the absurdity of that assumption throughout the novel.

América misses her family; her ties to her mother and siblings are strong, capable of surviving long distances and grueling hardship. Her work ethic is admirable. Even pregnant, she walks long distances for the mere *hope* of finding work, often without success. Her persistence born of a desire to stay healthy for the sake of her baby is palpable, and she is not afraid of hard physical work that causes her pain, as when she shines the Buddha statues with acid-based cleaners that eat through her skin. When her husband is weak and turns to drink to drown his frustrations and sorrows, it is the young América who remains strong and steadfast.

And so Boyle, through his satire, portrays América as a stereotype but is quite clear that she is only so simplified by those unwilling to look

The "tortilla curtain" is an euphemism for the illegal Mexican border crossings. (© James Steidl / Shutterstock.com)

deeper into the true essence of her character. He is reflecting society's ideas of who she is.

The mimetic theory of literary criticism asks the reader to consider how a piece of literature imitates or reflects real life. *The Tortilla Curtain* is Boyle's exploration of racism via illegal immigration, an issue that was roiling American society when he wrote the novel in 1995 and continues to be controversial in the twenty-first century. From a mimetic perspective, the author's stereotypical characters are a direct and true representation of society. They are inexplicably absurd, but that is the essence of human nature. Boyle uses them so that his readers can recognize themselves within the pages of the book, and perhaps the most absurd aspect of this reading experience is that they do not even realize what they are processing until the cover is closed. It is not the characters we remember from *The Tortilla Curtain*; it is what they represent. And true to his nature, Boyle does not wrap up his story with a

neat, precise ending. That would be too easy. He gives us the tools to determine the outcome of the novel. It is up to us to figure it out.

Source: Rebecca Valentine, Critical Essay on *The Tortilla Curtain*, in *Novels for Students*, Gale, Cengage Learning, 2013.

James Knudsen

In the following review, Knudsen remarks that a "harder-edged look" in this social novel might have resulted in better results.

T. Coraghessan Boyle's most recent novel, *The Tortilla Curtain*, takes its epigraph from *The Grapes of Wrath*: "They ain't human. A human being wouldn't live like they do. A human being couldn't stand it to be so dirty and miserable." In so doing, Boyle makes clear his intention to write a novel of social consequence. Although the work contains many vividly rendered scenes of contemporary life in California as its citizens struggle with the issue of immigration and also boasts Boyle's usual finely crafted prose, there is a predictability to the characters, their situation, and the ultimate, ironic outcome of the plot that prevents the novel from being a total success.

The Tortilla Curtain tells the parallel stories of Delaney Mossbacher, an upper-middle-class nature writer, and Candido, an illegal immigrant from Mexico. As the novel opens, Delaney is leading a pleasant existence hiking in the hills surrounding his comfortable home in Arroyo Blanco Estates and writing about his adventures for a nature magazine. His wife Kyra is a very successful real-estate agent helping monied city dwellers escape to the developments that are gradually replacing the wilderness her husband celebrates. Candido and his pregnant wife America, as might be expected due to their lack of education and green cards, are living a generally miserable existence in a gutty not far from Arroyo Estates. They are victims of the weather, the Anglos who employ them, racist teen punks, and their own innocent dreams. These sections, written without a trace of irony, are quite affecting, even if we can guess their eventual outcome.

The sections about the Mossbachers, particularly Kyra, occasionally feel arch and seem similar in tone to Tom Wolfe's *Bonfire of the Vanities*. Though Boyle often scores comedically, it is difficult to care about these characters. In making Delaney a sensitive, thoughtful nature writer, Boyle sets up interesting possibilities for exploring the complex moral dilemma of what to do about illegal immigration. But we never understand why Delaney would have married the avaricious Kyra, who cannot look at a natural setting without immediately wondering what the subdivided lots would sell for, and he seems to get caught up too easily in the anti-immigrant hysteria of his wife and neighbors. The novel ends up on an ironic note that is more sentimental than resonant or believable.

Though Boyle's heart is on his sleeve here, at least his heart is in bountiful evidenced—a distinct improvement over his previous novel, *The Road to Wellville* (see *WLT* 68:1, p. 126). Boyle is unquestionably a gifted writer who creates memorable characters and manages their intersecting plotlines with great facility. He is clearly out to write a major social novel in the manner of Dickens (perhaps in response to Tom Wolfe's call some years ago for more social novels), and one can only applaud the effort. Perhaps if he had taken a harder-edged look, in the manner of Steinbeck,

instead of the sometimes facetious one we find here, the results would have been more deeply affecting.

Source: James Knudsen, Review of *The Tortilla Curtain*, in *World Literature Today*, Vol. 70, No. 3, Summer 1996, p. 690.

Scott Spencer

In the following review, Spencer declares that the dual structure of The Tortilla Curtain *hurts its value in either story.*

In *The Tortilla Curtains*, Mr. Boyle deftly portrays Los Angeles's Topanga Canyon, catching both its privileged society and its underlying geological and ecological instability. But while the book has heft, its story is slight, and not unfamiliar: an undocumented Mexican couple struggle for survival in the interstices of society and in the canyon itself, even as an affluent Anglo couple live their fearful, selfish existence behind the dubious protection of a walled development called Arroyo Blanco Estates.

We first meet Candido Rincon when he is hit by a car driven by the male half of the novel's Anglo couple, a self-styled Annie Dillard disciple named Delaney Mossbacher. Candido is in California with his young pregnant wife, America, having recently braved another crossing of the border. Candido and America are part of California's unacknowledged work force, cogs in the vast human machine that does the state's brute labor and without whom (Proposition 187 to the contrary) the state could probably not survive.

Mr. Boyle is first-rate in capturing the terror of looking for work in an alien society; as in this passage describing Candido's experience at a parking-lot labor exchange: "The contractors began to arrive, the white men with their big bleached faces and soulless eyes, enthroned in their trucks. They wanted two men or three, they wanted four or five, no questions asked, no wage stipulated, no conditions or terms of employment. A man could be pouring concrete one day, spraying pesticide the next—or swabbing out urinals, spreading manure, painting, weeding, hauling, laying brick or setting tile. You didn't ask questions. You got in the back of the truck and you went where they took you."

Mr. Boyle is convincing, and even stirring, in his telling of Candido and America's story, bringing to it an agitprop artist's perspective on both society's injustices and the cold implacability of the privileged classes, as well as a Brechtian vision of how those cast to the bottom of society blindly victimize one another. Indeed, the journey of the Rincons—from their desolate Mexican village to the terrors of exploitation on the undocumented edge of American society and finally into the whirling, pyrotechnically presented catastrophe toward which the story builds—more than confirms Mr. Boyle's reputation as a novelist of exuberance and invention, gained with such pop extravaganzas as *World's End* and *The Road to Wellville*. It also adds to his fictional range an open-hearted compassion for those whom society fears and reviles.

But Mr. Boyle was clearly not interested in merely writing a novel about illegal aliens scrabbling for a living. For he has divided his considerable narrative and stylistic gifts between the Rincons' story and that of Delaney and Kyra Mossbacher, the rather contemptible yuppie couple whose deeply unremarkable experiences are set in opposition to the Rincons'. It is here, alas, that Mr. Boyle undoes himself.

The great risk of a novel with a dual structure is that the reader will fasten one one of the stories at the expense of the other. In *The Tortilla Curtain*, the drama, feeling and stylistic bravado, the emotional reach that Mr. Boyle brings to the story of the Rincons so profoundly exceed what he brings to the Mossbachers that the book itself ends up feeling as disunited as the society Mr. Boyle is attempting to portray. And that's a pity, because there is life here and moments of very fine writing.

Source: Scott Spencer, Review of *The Tortilla Curtain*, in *Migration World Magazine*, Vol. 24, Nos. 1–2, January/ February 1996, p. 52.

Julie Wheelwright

In the following review, Wheelwright discusses the symbolism of the characters in The Tortilla Curtain.

Like *Bonfire of the Vanities*, Tom Wolfe's novel of hubris on Wall Street, the plot of *The Tortilla Curtain* hinges on a car accident that leads to a downward spiral of events. The parallel lives of naturalist-writer Delaney Mossbacher and Candido Rincon, an illegal Mexican immigrant, literally collide along a Pacific highway on the outskirts of Los Angeles. But just as Delaney's polished Japanese car with its personalised numberplates takes a knock when it bumps

Candido from the road, so a liberal's ideals are shattered.

Boyle has his finger firmly on the pulse of an American middle class whose fear of the iron curtain has been replaced by an obsession with one made of tortillas. The novel is replete with such ironies. Delaney writes a magazine column extolling the great outdoors but is married to Kyra, an estate agent with designs for rapacious development. They live in Arroyo Blanco, an exclusive housing estate surrounded by a high wall, with its own 24-hour security guard. While the residents' committee demands a strict adherence to a Spanish architecture and relies on Latinos for cheap, casual work, they banish the local labour exchange that supplies it.

The fear that moves the residents to build walls and post guards is palpable. Delaney and Kyra are horrified when a coyote leaps easily over their chain-link fence and makes off with their pet dog clenched in its jaws. There are rumours even in this supposedly tranquil LA suburb of break-ins and assaults, while strange graffiti appears on the guardhouse wall and Delaney stumbles across a makeshift camp in the canyon. All are read as portents of forthcoming disaster.

But as the gringos wait for the apocalypse, Candido and America, his 17-year-old, pregnant wife, are living it. And life is rough in every sense, as they work on the black, dodge immigration, are robbed by rich and poor alike and suffer in silence when ill. Boyle archly connects his characters across the gulfs that divide them, to contrast their experience. Two Mexican drifters rape America in the canyon, but they retreat under Kyra's glare when she encounters them on a deserted property. With her, they have too much to lose.

There is no going back for this other America, however. "She wanted. Of course she wanted. Everybody who'd stayed behind to dry up and die in Tepozltan wanted too—hell, all of Morelos, all of Mexico and the Indian countries to the south, they all wanted, and what else was new? A house, a yard, maybe a TV and a car too—nothing fancy, no palaces like the gringos built—just four walls and a roof. Was that so much to ask?" For Kyra and Delaney, the answer is a resounding yes, since it means an intrusion upon their comfortable existence.

Boyle explores powerful issues through his parallel characters, but they operate just shy of caricature. They are more symbolic figures than real inhabitants of a state wallowing in economic downturn. The Mexicans are naive, but essentially good, while their Anglo counterparts grow increasingly ugly with rage. The hand that Candido reaches out to Delaney in the novel's final passage, however, suggests that hope for reconciliation and renewal remains, even at this explosive end of California dreaming.

Source: Julie Wheelwright, Review of *The Tortilla Curtain*, in *New Statesman & Society*, Vol. 8, No. 378, November 10, 1995, p. 39.

SOURCES

"About the Author," T. C. Boyle website, http://tcboyle.com/page2.html?4 (accessed January 17, 2012).

Appell, David, "Earthquakes, Critics and the .600 Nitro: An Interview with T. Coraghessan Boyle," T. C. Boyle website, http://www.tcboyle.net/appell.html (accessed January 19, 2012); originally published in *Hayden's Ferry Review*, No. 18, Spring/Summer 1996.

Beck, John, "T. C. Boyle Talks about 'Tortilla Curtain' and Censorship," in *Press Democrat*, February 17, 2010, http://www.pressdemocrat.com/article/20100217/ENTERTAINMENT/100219567?p = 1&tc = pg (accessed January 17, 2012).

Boyle, T. C., *The Tortilla Curtain*, Penguin, 1995.

Camorta, Steven A., "A Record-Setting Decade of Immigration: 2000–2010," Center for Immigration Studies website, October 2011, http://cis.org/2000-2010-record-setting-decade-of-immigration (accessed January 18, 2012).

Cavazos, Miguel, "Most Popular Pieces of Exercise Equipment," February 3, 2011, http://www.livestrong.com/article/373299-most-popular-pieces-of-exercise-equipment/ (accessed January 18, 2012).

Condor, Bob, "Pumping Iron Was 1990s Top Exercise," in *Chicago Tribune*, January 7, 2000, http://articles.chicagotribune.com/2000-01-07/news/0101070423_1_personal-trainers-fitness-cardiovascular-exercise-equipment (accessed January 18, 2012).

Edwards, James R., Jr., "Two Sides of the Same Coin: The Connection Between Legal and Illegal Immigration," Center for Immigration Studies website, February 2006, http://www.cis.org/articles/2006/back106.html (accessed January 16, 2012).

Eggers, David, Review of *The Tortilla Curtain*, in *SF Gate*, September 10, 1995, http://articles.sfgate.com/1995-09-10/books/17814947_1_tortilla-curtain-delaney-mossbacher-coraghessan (accessed January 17, 2012).

"Foreign-Born Population and Foreign Born as Percentage of the Total US Population, 1850 to 2010," Migration Policy Institute website, http://www.migrationinformation.org/datahub/charts/final.fb.shtml (accessed January 18, 2012).

"Got Milk? Campaign," in *Marketing Campaign Case Studies*, April 21, 2008, http://marketing-case-studies.blogspot.com/2008/04/got-milk-campaign.html (accessed January 17, 2012).

"Immigration: The Demographic and Economic Facts; 4. Effects of Immigration on Native Unemployment," in *Cato Institute and the National Immigration Forum*, http://www.cato.org/pubs/policy_report/pr-imnative.html (accessed January 16, 2012).

McCaffery, Larry, "Lusty Dreamers in the Suburban Jungle," in *New York Times*, June 9, 1985, p. 15.

McCune, Arthur, "Meet the Writers: T. C. Boyle," Barnes and Noble website, http://www.barnesandnoble.com/writers/writerdetails.asp?cid = 881674 (accessed January 16, 2012).

McDonnell, Anne B., "Fitness—Top 20 Product Trends from the Past 20 Years," July 2005, http://athleticbusiness.com/articles/article.aspx?articleid = 2954&zoneid = 42 (accessed January 18, 2012); originally published in *Fitness Management*.

"New Americans in California," in *Immigration Policy Center*, American Immigration Council, http://www.immigrationpolicy.org/just-facts/new-americans-california (accessed January 18, 2012).

Norkiewicz, Nancy, "Walking Still Is Most Popular Form of Exercise," in *RunCoach*, http://www.sportscoach.netmx.co.uk/index.php?name = News&file = article&sid = 164 (accessed January 18, 2012).

"Reading Guides: *The Tortilla Curtain*," Penguin Group website, http://us.penguingroup.com/static/rguides/us/tortilla_curtain.html (accessed January 16, 2012).

Spencer, Scott, Review of *The Tortilla Curtain*, in *New York Times*, September 3, 1995, http://www.nytimes.com/books/98/02/08/home/boyle-tortilla.html?_r = 1 (accessed January 16, 2012).

"T. C. Boyle," University of Southern California website, http://dornsife.usc.edu/cf/faculty-and-staff/faculty.cfm?pid = 1003124 (accessed January 17, 2012).

"*The Tortilla Curtain*," in *Reading Group Guides*, http://www.readinggroupguides.com/guides_T/tortilla_curtain1.asp (accessed January 16, 2012).

"*The Tortilla Curtain*," in *Silicon Valley Reads*, http://www.siliconvalleyreads.org/2012-13/tortilla.asp (accessed January 16, 2012).

Yost, Chryss, "The Face on *The Tortilla Curtain*: T. C. Boyle Raises a Ruckus," http://www.sbbookfestival.org/boyle.html (accessed January 17, 2012); originally published in *Santa Barbara Independent*, Vol. 16, No. 820, August 3–15, 2002.

FURTHER READING

Bacon, David, *Illegal People: How Globalization Creates Migration and Criminalizes Immigrants*, Beacon Press, 2008.

Bacon's investigation into the cause-and-effect relationship between globalization and immigration earned this book a starred review from *Publishers Weekly*. An award-winning photojournalist and labor organizer, Bacon makes clear his contempt for political policy regarding immigration while simultaneously supporting his stance with logic, research, and thought-provoking analysis.

Chomsky, Aviva, *"They Take Our Jobs!": And 20 Other Myths about Immigration*, Beacon Press, 2007.

Historian Chomsky draws on economic analysis as well as immigration history to debunk common assumptions that fuel the current immigration debate. The text is well researched and presented in easy-to-understand terms.

Gleason, Paul William, *Understanding T. C. Boyle*, University of South Carolina Press, 2009.

This reference is divided into sections according to genre and years: one chapter is concerned with Boyle's short stories, while other chapters analyze his novels, decade by decade. Although not all-inclusive, this compendium of literary criticism does give coverage of *The Tortilla Curtain*.

Rodriguez, Gregory, *Mongrels, Bastards, Orphans, and Vagabonds: Mexican Immigration and the Future of Race in America*, Vintage Books, 2008.

Rodriguez, a columnist for the *Los Angeles Times*, has compiled a thorough and accessible history of Mexico, beginning with the adventures of Hernán Cortés in the 1500s. Although his column focuses on current immigration issues and consequences, this book emphasizes the history of the past five hundred years and provides a foundation for understanding how Mexican immigration got to where it is today.

Segersten, Alissa, and Tom Malterre, *The Whole Life Nutrition Cookbook: Whole Foods Recipes for Personal and Planetary Health*, 2nd ed., Whole Life Press, 2007.

Along with mouth-watering healthy recipes, this cookbook provides readers with evidence-based information on whole foods as well as strategies for eating well despite food allergies. The authors have extensive backgrounds in nutrition and health, and their approach to eating encourages smart food choices and wise food preparation for optimal health.

Urrea, Luis Alberto, *Across the Wire: Life and Hard Times on the Mexican Border*, Anchor Books, 1993.

This book is an account of the author's life along the Mexican American border from 1979 to 1991. A Mexican-born American himself, Urrea offers a stark, unemotional portrayal of refugee life just across the border, only twenty miles or so from San Diego. His is a gripping depiction of people trying to do nothing more than survive.

SUGGESTED SEARCH TERMS

T. C. Boyle

T. C. Boyle AND *The Tortilla Curtain*

The Tortilla Curtain AND review

illegal immigration AND T. C. Boyle

American dream AND *Tortilla Curtain*

Tortilla Curtain AND summary

Tortilla Curtain AND themes

illegal immigration AND 1990s

California AND illegal immigration history

When the Emperor Was Divine

JULIE OTSUKA

2002

When the Emperor Was Divine is a novel by American author Julie Otsuka that was published in 2002. Otsuka's first novel, it tells the story of the internment of Japanese Americans during World War II from 1942 to 1945. They were interned because the U.S. government thought they would be sympathetic to the Japanese cause and likely to participate in espionage or sabotage.

The story focuses on one family in particular, a mother and her two young children who are compelled to leave their home in California in the spring of 1942. They are sent to an internment camp in the remote desert at Topaz, in Utah. The father of the family was arrested in December 1941, immediately after the Japanese attack on Pearl Harbor, and his story forms part of the novel, too.

In a matter-of-fact, unemotional tone, Otsuka shows how Japanese Americans coped with the shock of being uprooted from their homes and forced to live in a makeshift camp with few amenities. The novel is valuable not only for the human story it tells but as a contribution to understanding an episode in U.S. history that is now universally regarded as a mistake and an injustice.

AUTHOR BIOGRAPHY

Otsuka was born on May 15, 1962, in Palo Alto, California, to Japanese American parents. Her father was an aerospace engineer and her mother

Julie Otsuka (© *Ulf Andersen | Getty Images*)

a lab technician. The family moved to Palos Verdes, California, when Otsuka was nine. She excelled in high school and attended Yale University, graduating in 1984 with a BA in art. She was particularly interested in painting and sculpture, and for several years tried to make a living at it while also working as a waitress. She entered an MFA program at Indiana University in 1987 but left the program after only three months. She moved to New York but, within a couple of years, abandoned her goal of becoming a painter. Instead, she began reading American literature widely and writing some sketches of her own. As her interest in writing developed, she enrolled in an MFA program at Columbia University in 1994. She graduated in 1999, having completed much of the work that would within a few years become her first novel, *When the Emperor Was Divine*, which was published by Knopf in 2002. The subject matter, the internment of Japanese Americans during World War, was a historical event that had affected her own family: her grandparents, her mother—

then eleven years old—and her uncle had been sent away from their homes to an internment camp in Topaz, Utah, during World War II. They spent three years at the camp.

When the Emperor Was Divine received many glowing reviews and was named a *New York Times* Notable Book, a *San Francisco Chronicle* Best Book of the Year, and a Barnes & Noble Discover Great New Writers finalist.

Otsuka's second novel, *The Buddha in the Attic*, was published in 2011. It is about the Japanese "picture brides" who came to the United States in the early 1900s in order to marry men whom they knew only through photographs.

As of 2012, Otsuka lives in New York City. She writes on her website that she spends the afternoons writing in her neighborhood café.

PLOT SUMMARY

Evacuation Order No. 19

When the Emperor Was Divine begins in Berkeley, California, in the spring of 1942. The United States has entered World War II the previous December. A middle-aged Japanese American woman sees a notice in a post office window stating that all Japanese Americans must leave their homes by a certain date. She begins packing immediately, and nine days later, she is still packing. She goes to a hardware store to buy a few supplies and then tries to find a duffel bag for sale, but all the stores are sold out. She goes home and decides she must finish packing, and she takes some things from the rooms of her ten-year-old daughter and seven-year-old son, wraps them up and puts them in boxes. The family has to leave the next day and they do not know where they are going. The woman's husband was arrested the previous December following the Japanese attack on Pearl Harbor and is now imprisoned in Texas.

The woman gives their cat away, kills the chicken, and then kills and buries the pet dog. When the children come home, she tells them that tomorrow they will only be allowed to take with them what they can carry. After the children have gone to bed, the woman releases their bird, a macaw, from its cage. That night the woman lies awake worrying about the leaky roof of the house.

Train

It is September 1942; this chapter is told from the point of view of the woman's daughter. The family is on a train, moving through Nevada, with other Japanese Americans. For the last two and a half months the family had been staying at an assembly center at Tanforan, a race-track near San Francisco. Now they are on their way to the Utah desert where they will be living in a camp. It is a Sunday and as they pass through a small town, the girl looks out the window until a soldier tells her to put the shades down, which they must do whenever they pass through a town. She talks briefly with another passenger, a man named Ted Ishimoto. She tells him that her father is in Lordsburg, New Mexico, and that he never writes to her, although the latter statement is not true; he sends her post-cards every week and she saves them all. The girl then observes some other passengers, talks to her mother, and looks out the window again. Now that they are out of the town, the shades have been raised again. She tries to play cards with her brother, but he is not interested. Her mother gives her brother an orange to eat, while the girl slips all the cards, one by one, out the window. When her brother sleeps, she looks at the postcards her father has sent. Part of what he wrote has been blacked out by government censors.

She tries to sleep but is awakened in the evening by the sound of breaking glass. Someone has thrown a brick through the window. She tells her mother she dreamt of her father.

They reach Utah at night. At a town called Delta, all the passengers get off the train and are put on buses that take them to the camp at Topaz, in the desert. The girl sees barbed-wire fences and soldiers.

When the Emperor Was Divine

It is late summer 1942 in the internment camp. It is hot and dry, and the wind blows up dust. The family adapts to the daily rhythms of their new home, in which the three of them live in one sparsely furnished room in a barrack. The boy misses his father. His mother tells him not to touch the barbed-wire fence or mention the Japanese emperor's name, but sometimes he whispers the name. The family passes the time as best they can, waiting for the mail and waiting for meals. They have no idea how long the war will last. The boy has nightmares and wonders whether he has done something bad that resulted in his being in the camp.

They receive censored letters from their father from Lordsburg. The boy sends replies and remembers his past interactions with his father. The boy hates the dust that is everywhere in the camp. Sometimes, in the evening, he and his sister go walking at the edge of the barracks to watch the sun set over the mountains.

In the fall, some of the people in the camp are recruited to work on farms in Idaho or Wyoming. When they return, they tell of the prejudice and abuse they encountered there. In the camp, the internees hear all kinds of wild rumors about what may happen to them, including being sterilized, shot, or deported to Japan.

A school opens in the camp in mid-October in an unheated barrack. The boy misses his father and remembers the night his father was taken away by the authorities. He remembers how, after that, curfews were imposed on Japanese American residents, as well as restrictions on how far they could travel.

There are dust storms in the fall, and snow falls as winter approaches. There is not much to do. There are rumors of spies in the camp, people who are thought to be government informers. In late November, some willow saplings are planted in the camp, and the boy takes a green leaf from one of them and sends it to his father.

The weather gets extremely cold. A man disappears and is found three days later frozen to death. At Christmas, turkey is served, as well as gifts for the children from the Quakers and the American Friends Service Committee. It is a long cold winter, and there is not enough bedding provided to stay warm at night. Illness is common. The boy's mother gets depressed and loses her appetite.

In February, army recruiters arrive looking for volunteers who will be willing to take a test of loyalty to the United States. In spring, the boy starts to take long walks on his own. In April, a man is shot dead near the border fence. The guard says the man was trying to escape, but many do not believe this. His funeral is attended by nearly 2,000 people.

The long hot summer arrives. The boy thinks of the day when his father will return.

In a Stranger's Backyard

In fall 1945, after the war has ended, the family returns to their home in Berkeley. The house has been neglected. The paint is peeling and most of their furniture is gone. They do not know who lived in the house while they were away. Outside, the town seems much the same but when they meet people they know in the street, those people turn away and pretend not to have seen them. Someone throws a whiskey bottle through a window of their home.

Gradually, the men from the neighborhood who fought in the war come home. Some of them who were prisoners of war in Japan have harsh things to say about the Japanese. The children's old friends from school no longer invite them home for supper. The boy and the girl respond to hostility or indifference at school by just keeping to themselves, careful not to cause any trouble. All this is quite different from the friendly reception they thought they would receive.

By November, the family is poor and the mother is turned down for almost every job she applies for. She ends up cleaning houses for a living and taking in people's washing and ironing to make extra money.

Their father finally returns in December. He looks much older, and the children can hardly believe he really is their father. He never says a word about what happened to him during his imprisonment. He is suspicious of people, and when he is outside, he does not speak unless spoken to. Small things make him lose his temper, but he is always pleased to see his children. When spring comes, he spends more and more time alone in his room. The children's lives gradually return to normal, and they face less hostility at school.

Confession

This short chapter is narrated in the first person by the father, who gives an account of what happened to him after he was taken away at night. In detention, he was told he had to talk to his interrogators. He gives a mock account of what happened, saying he admitted to being an enemy saboteur. He creates an absurd scenario in which he says he is guilty of everything from poisoning food to blowing up railroads, spying on airfields and neighbors, and many other things that are even more fantastic. He says he is like all the other Japanese in California who his interrogators know, and against whom they are prejudiced, thus implying that all the Japanese are guilty, a claim that he knows is absurd and will sound absurd. His bitterness is plain

from his tone. Finally, having admitted to everything, he asks if he can go home.

CHARACTERS

Daughter

The daughter is ten years old in 1942 when the family is first sent to the internment camp. Unlike her parents, she was born in America and has always lived in California. She has straight black hair and is as American as any other girl her age. She likes "Boys and black licorice and Dorothy Lamour" (Lamour was a movie star at the time) as well as her pet macaw. She pays attention at school, studies for tests, and also takes piano lessons. She is good at drawing and has won a school prize for her work. Her world changes completely when the she and her mother and brother are sent away. Like her brother, she misses her father, and once confesses to her brother that what worries her most is that sometimes she cannot remember his face. She matures physically during the three years she spends at the camp, and when she undresses at night, she asks her brother to look the other way. She also gets to hear about some of the less savory things that go on at the camp during the nighttime hours. Sometimes she gets up in the middle of the night and jumps rope. She goes dancing in the evenings and wins second prize in a jitter-bug contest in the mess hall, where she also takes part in games of bingo.

When she, her mother, and her brother return to their home in California after the war, they find they are shunned. At school, the other students will not sit with the girl or boy at lunchtime, and their old friends longer invite them to their homes for supper. The girl and her brother try to keep quiet and not bring attention to themselves. She goes out of her way to make sure she does not offend anyone.

Father

Before he is arrested by the authorities shortly after the Japanese attack on Pearl Harbor, the father, who like the other main characters is never identified by name, worked for a company. What he did for that company is never stated, but it obviously provided sufficient financial reward for him to establish a middle-class lifestyle for his wife and two children. The father was born in Japan, it would appear, and immigrated to the United States, where he must have lived for over twenty years. He is described as a "small handsome man with delicate hands and a raised white scar on his index finger." He dressed well, was always polite and punctual, and loved to play with the children. He also loved his adopted country; he once told his son that what he "loved most about America . . . was the glazed jelly donut."

The charges made against the father are never revealed. He is detained in a prison at Lordsburg for four years, during which time he writes affectionate letters to his children. He is finally released and returns home in December 1945, but he is far from the handsome, strong man his children knew. He has aged considerably in the four years he has been away. He is thin and bald, and he has lost all his teeth.

He is completely shattered by his experience of being imprisoned. He refuses to talk about it and never mentions politics. His personality has also deteriorated, and he has become suspicious and uncommunicative. Sometimes he will fly into a rage at the slightest provocation. His affection for his children remains, but he is a broken figure, retreating often to his room just to be alone. Sometimes he goes to bed as early as seven o'clock, immediately after supper.

Ted Ishimoto

Ted Ishimoto is a Japanese American man who is on the same train as the family as they travel to the internment camp. He has a friendly chat with the daughter.

Mrs. Kato

Mrs. Kato is an old Japanese American woman who lives in the internment camp. She lives with her son and his wife in the room next to the family. She talks to herself all the time and is confused about the situation she is in.

Mother

The mother of the two children was born in Japan into a large family. She had six older sisters and a younger brother. She has lived in the United States for nearly nineteen years in 1942. In the spring of 1942 she is forty-one years old, eleven years younger than her husband. By the standards of the day she had married late and had her children late, when she was in her thirties.

She is a practical woman who absorbs the shock of having her husband taken from her by the FBI and takes the necessary steps to ensure the family's smooth departure after she sees the relocation notice. She gives the cat away, kills and buries the family dog, and spends many days packing. She is also resourceful, burying the family silver in the garden so she can be sure it will be there on their return.

She feels no allegiance to Japan and has no difficulty passing the loyalty test that she is given in the internment camp. It is not that she has great patriotic feelings for the United States; she simply does not want to be sent back to Japan, and she wants to ensure that the family remains together. Since she lives in the United States, she wants to continue her life there.

In the internment camp she does her best to look after her children, but during the long cold winter she also gets worn down and depressed by the situation they are in. She does not bother to apply for any of the jobs that are available, and sometimes she just sits in her room doing nothing with an unopened book in her lap. She is haunted by the experience of having her husband suddenly taken from her with no explanation.

After she returns from the internment camp with the children, she must shoulder the responsibility of providing for her family. It will be several months before her husband returns, and he never works again. Facing prejudice because of her ethnicity, the mother is forced to take menial work cleaning houses. The work is hard and it ages her, but she does what she has to do for the sake of the family.

Elizabeth Morgan Roosevelt

Elizabeth Morgan Roosevelt is a young American girl with long yellow hair. She was a neighbor of the family that is sent to the internment camp. Elizabeth is a friend of the boy, and just before he goes away, she gives him a lucky stone from the sea. She writes to him at the camp, telling him all the news from Berkeley.

Son

The son is seven years old when the family is first sent to the internment camp. Like his sister, he is a typical young American; he likes baseball. However, in the months after Pearl Harbor before they are sent to the camp, he finds out what it is like to face discrimination because of his ethnicity. He learns to say that he is Chinese rather than Japanese so as to deflect this hostility. But on one occasion, having told a man he is

Chinese, he runs to the corner of the street and shouts out that he is "Jap! Jap!"

The son is an impressionable young boy who absorbs a lot of information from his older sister, whom he asks a lot of questions. At the assembly center before they go to the camp, they stay in former horse stalls behind the racetrack, and after that the boy talks about horses a lot. He dreams he is riding a horse.

At the camp he misses his father badly and, at first, thinks he sees him everywhere among the other Japanese American men. His father had always been very affectionate toward him, calling him names like Little Guy and Gum Drop. The boy writes postcards to his father from the camp.

The boy seems to find it hard to adjust to life in the camp. Sometimes he lies awake at night listening to the radio bulletins about the war. Sometimes he wakes up from a bad dream wondering where he is. He wonders why he is in the camp and sometimes thinks it must be because he did something bad, but he never knows what that might have been. He keeps himself amused by playing marbles and Chinese checkers, and roaming around the barracks with the other boys, playing games. He keeps a pet tortoise in a wooden box filled with sand.

THEMES

Prejudice

The Japanese Americans in the novel all face discrimination and prejudice based on their race. This becomes immediately apparent after the bombing of Pearl Harbor. The father is arrested and taken from his home at midnight even though he has done nothing wrong. He is not the only one. The boy hears of many other Japanese American fathers from the neighborhood who are arrested in similar fashion. Likewise, the families who are sent to the internment camps are innocent of wrongdoing. Many of them are U.S. citizens. Their only crime is to be of Japanese heritage. When some of the internees volunteer in the fall to work on farms in other states harvesting crops, they tell sad stories of prejudice when they return. Anti-Japanese sentiment is rampant, and they say they were shot at, spat upon, and refused entry to restaurants and movie theaters.

When the family returns to Berkeley after the war, they find the situation is much worse than before they left. No one welcomes them home, and people avoid them on the street. The children are picked on at school; their mother is unable to find anything other than menial work. The fear and dislike of Japanese Americans is typified by the employer who offers her a job only in a back room where no one will see her.

In spite of the prejudice they experience, the Japanese Americans are not shown reacting aggressively to it, even in their thoughts. They seem resigned to the situation. After their return, the children, for example, try to remain as inconspicuous as possible as long as the hostility continues. The only exception to this comes right at the end, when the father vents all his feelings of anger and frustration regarding the treatment he received.

Identity

The question of cultural identity is at the heart of the novel. The U.S. authorities assume that Japanese Americans are likely to side with their country of origin in the war, despite the lack of any evidence to support this notion. However, the mother, having lived in the United States for nearly twenty years, has no allegiance to the country of her birth. She has no difficulty in answering the loyalty questionnaire at the camp in a way that will keep her family together in the United States. She has no particular feelings of patriotism toward the United States, either; she just wants to keep the family together. Her lack of allegiance to Japan, however, does not mean that, as a first-generation immigrant, she does not retain some cultural ties to Japan. Before the order to evacuate comes, her home in Berkeley shows many signs of Japanese culture, including three silk kimonos she had brought with her from Japan, recordings of Japanese opera, a Japanese flag, and Imari dishes (Japanese porcelain). She feels compelled to destroy all these, however, to protect her family's safety. Not only does she feel the need to obliterate these signs of the family's Japanese origin, she even tells her children to deny their own heritage, just so they can stay safe. She instructs the children to say they are Chinese rather than Japanese.

There is a gap, though, between the first-generation immigrants such as the mother and father, who were born in Japan and retain something of their cultural origins, even if only in memory, and the second-generation Japanese Americans like the son and daughter who were born in the United States and know little of Japan. This is shown many times in the descriptions of the girl and

TOPICS FOR FURTHER STUDY

- What parallels are there between the situation faced by Japanese Americans in the 1940s and Muslims in the United States following the terrorist attacks in New York City and Washington, D.C., on September 11, 2001? In times of war or international terrorism, how should the U.S. government preserve the balance between homeland security and civil rights? What can we learn from the experience of Japanese American internment about how to treat U.S. citizens who belong to the same race or ethnic group as those who are attacking the United States? For example, how have Muslims and Arab Americans been treated since September 11, 2001? Give a class presentation in which you discuss this important issue.

- Read *The Children of Topaz: The Story of a Japanese-American Internment Camp; Based on a Classroom Diary* (1996), by Michael O. Tunnell and George W. Chilcoat, which contains a real classroom diary kept by a third-grade class at the Topaz internment camp. Imagine that you have been interned somewhere in the United States because of some hostile situation in the country that has affected your race or ethnic group. Write some diary entries that describe your interests and concerns. What do you remember most

from your life before internment? What do you miss most? What do you dream about? How do you spend your time? Upload your diary to your web log and share it with your classmates.

- Using Internet research, write an essay in which you discuss the typical differences between first- and second-generation immigrants to the United States. What sort of family issues are often raised when the parents were not born in the United States but their children were? What kind of issues are raised regarding a person's sense of identity?

- It is often said that the United States is a nation of immigrants, but immigrants of many different races and ethnic groups have often faced hostility and discrimination when they first arrived here, and prejudice sometimes continued for several generations. Give a class presentation in which you briefly discuss the difficulties faced historically by German, Irish, Polish, Italian, and Jewish immigrants, as well as the more recent waves of immigrants from Asia and Central America. What are the economic, cultural, and racial factors that have contributed to the prejudice faced by immigrants?

boy. They are typical American children. The boy likes baseball and reads American comic books. The girl likes to leaf through the Sears, Roebuck catalog. The boy imagines himself fighting in the war on the American side and being awarded a Purple Heart by General MacArthur. He has seen American movies, and when he thinks of his father, knowing he has been branded as the enemy, he imagines him as an outlaw from a cowboy movie, wearing cowboy boots and a Stetson hat and riding a big horse. The other Japanese American boys also identify with the American side. Their war games in the camp include the chant "*Kill the Nazis! Kill the Japs!*"

STYLE

Point of View

The story is told from a variety of points of view. The first three chapters are told by a third-person narrator. Chapter 1 focuses on the point of view of the mother as she prepares the family for departure; chapter 2 is told from the point of view of the girl as the family travels on the train to Utah, and chapter 3, set in the internment camp, focuses mostly on the point of view of the boy—his thoughts, dreams, and impressions. The type of narration changes in chapter 4, which is narrated in the first-person plural ("we") by the

The family was interned in a camp like Manzanar War Relocation Camp. *(© Sally Scott | Shutterstock.com)*

two children after they return home from the camp. The last chapter is also a first-person narration, this time by the father. The changes in focus enable the author to present a well-rounded picture of how each member of the family copes with the experience of internment.

Setting

The setting reflects the lives of the main characters. The camp in Utah is a barren place high in the desert. There are no trees. It rarely rains in summer, and the wind is hot and dry. There is dust everywhere from the dust storms that go on for hours and sometimes days. Temperatures are extreme. In winter, the temperature sometimes drops to twenty degrees below zero. One late November, the men in the camp plant tree saplings that have been delivered, but the mother says the soil is too alkaline for them to last the winter, and she is proved correct. The barren terrain acts as a metaphor for the bleak lives lived by the internees.

The setting changes on the return of the family to California. Images of nature in full flower—a magnolia tree in bloom and hyacinths and narcissus in their garden—appear when they begin to be fully accepted again by the community in the spring

of 1946. In May, the roses burst into bloom, and the children go searching for their mother's rosebush, which at some point was removed from where she had planted it in the front yard. The final image in that chapter is of the rosebush somewhere "blossoming madly, wildly, pressing one perfect flower after another out into the late afternoon light." Just as the desert landscape had suggested the empty nature of the lives the family was forced to endure, the rose image suggests that now the life force has reasserted itself and they can once more live full, happy lives.

HISTORICAL CONTEXT

Internment of Japanese Americans

After the surprise Japanese attack on the U.S. naval base at Pearl Harbor on December 7, 1941, the United States declared war on Japan and entered World War II. Japanese Americans immediately came under suspicion. It was thought that they might be loyal to Japan rather than to their adopted country and would act as spies or commit acts of sabotage. There had long

COMPARE
&
CONTRAST

- **1940s:** Japanese Americans face discrimination in the United States both during and after World War II.

  Today: As part of a larger group of Asian Americans, Japanese Americans have overcome past discrimination and are part of mainstream American society. They have made their mark in many fields of activity, including science and technology, literature and the arts, music, sports, and entertainment.

- **1940s:** According to the 1940 U.S. census, there are 126,947 Japanese Americans living in the United States. Of these, the vast majority live in the West, in California, Washington, and Oregon. Nearly two-thirds are U.S. citizens by birth.

  Today: According to the 2000 U.S. Census, there are 1,148,932 Japanese Americans in the United States, counting those who are Japanese American alone or in combination with one or more other races. Over 40 percent live in Hawaii or California.

- **1940s:** During World War II, Japan is an enemy of the United States. After the war, Japan is forced to accept U.S. occupation. The United States gives Japan a constitution, and the work of reconstructing the devastated nation begins.

  Today: Japan is a firm U.S. ally and the third-largest economy in the world, behind the United States and China.

been prejudice in the United States against Japanese immigrants. In 1924, for example, a law was passed that banned marriage between Japanese men and white women.

Acting on these fears, President Franklin D. Roosevelt issued Executive Order 9066 on February 19, 1942. The Executive Order revoked the civil rights of Japanese Americans despite the fact that two-thirds of them were U.S. citizens. Nearly 120,000 Japanese Americans from all over the Pacific coast were rounded up and sent to ten internment camps built by the War Relocation Authority in seven states. Most of the camps were built in remote places on Native American reservations. The camps were surrounded by barbed wire, and armed guards prevented anyone from leaving.

Internment proved a catastrophic experience for Japanese Americans, who were forced to abandon their homes and businesses. They lost everything that they had worked for since coming to the United States, where many of them had lived for thirty or forty years. They were given no time to ensure the safe storage of their possessions, and when they departed for the camps, they were allowed to take only what they could physically carry.

The camps themselves had been hastily and poorly constructed along the lines of military barracks. They were unpleasant places to live and offered inadequate protection against extreme heat in summer and bitter cold in winter. Internees worked at low-paying jobs. Faced with such conditions, the internees made extensive efforts to build their own sense of community that would combat their isolation and the undignified manner in which they were compelled to live. They formed civic associations and created opportunities for entertainment such as dances, theatrical performances, and athletic events. There were also schools, which functioned with a minimum of equipment and books.

In January 1943, the U.S. government decided to recruit second-generation Japanese immigrants into an all–Japanese-American combat unit. All males in the internment camps were required to answer a series of questions, which included whether they were willing to serve in the U.S. armed forces and whether they would swear allegiance to the United States, defend the country

From middle-class existences, the family was sent to live in substandard housing in the camps.
(© Sally Scott / Shutterstock.com)

against attack, and renounce obedience to the Japanese emperor. Most of the internees answered yes to these questions, but the several hundred who did not were sent to prison for disloyalty.

In 1944, the Supreme Court upheld Executive Order 9066, but the U.S. government finally rescinded it on January 2, 1945. All Japanese American prisoners were released from the internment camps, although it was some months before all of them were able to return to their homes. Some never made it back, since the U.S. government sent 4,724 Japanese Americans directly from the camps to Japan. Of these, 1,949 were U.S. citizens and almost all were under twenty years old. Some of them had expressed a desire for repatriation; others had renounced their U.S. citizenship.

CRITICAL OVERVIEW

The novel received a number of favorable reviews. For Reba Leiding, in *Library Journal*, it is a "spare yet poignant first novel." Donna Seaman in

Booklist commends the author, who "demonstrates a breathtaking restraint and delicacy throughout this supple and devastating first novel," in which she "universalizes [the characters'] experience of prejudice and disenfranchisement." The reviewer for *Publishers Weekly* comments, "The novel's honesty and matter-of-fact tone in the face of inconceivable injustice are the source of its power." *Kirkus Reviews* is less enthusiastic, acknowledging that the novel was "carefully researched" but arguing that it does not engage the reader emotionally: "The narrative remains stubbornly at the surface," detailing the injustices the detainees suffered, "but never finding a way to go deeper, to a place where the attention will be held rigid and the heart seized." Writing in the *New York Times Book Review*, Michael Upchurch has no such reservations. He calls it a "canny, muted first novel," and suggests that "Otsuka's portrait of the mother may be the book's greatest triumph. Almost everything in it is below the surface." Upchurch describes the "extraordinary" final chapter, in which the father speaks directly for the first time, as "a bitter tirade that is a burlesque version of what his supposed disloyalty would entail." What the reader is likely to notice most about the novel, in Upchurch's view, is

> how much Otsuka is able to convey—in a line, in a paragraph—about her characters' surroundings, about their states of mind and about the mood of our country at a time of crisis that did not, on this particular front, bring out the best in its character.

CRITICISM

Bryan Aubrey

Aubrey holds a PhD in English. In the following essay, he examines the historical background of When the Emperor Was Divine.

When the Emperor Was Divine is a novel, but the only thing fictional about it is the nameless mother, father, son, and daughter that author Julie Otsuka creates to allow the story to unfold. These four characters are anonymous because they are clearly meant to be representative of the Japanese American experience as a whole during the three to four years of internment during World War II. Otsuka takes an unusual step for a novelist in "A Note on Sources" at the end of the book, in which she names five books about the internment of the Japanese Americans that she used as source material during the writing of her novel.

Otsuka put her research to good use. Apart from the individual thoughts and actions she ascribes to her characters, which are her own invention, the facts of internment she recreates are entirely accurate. This bleak tale of people whose lives have been cruelly wrenched from their moorings was exactly, by all accounts, what internment was like for this American minority group that just happened to have been living on the West Coast at a traumatic and crucial time in U.S. history. Otsuka appears to have added nothing for dramatic effect, allowing the facts and the entirely plausible thoughts and feelings of the characters to speak for themselves about their experience. Even the tragic incident in the novel when a male internee is shot dead by a guard near the border fence because the guard claimed he was trying to escape is an account of a real incident that happened at Topaz in April 1943. A sixty-three-year-old man named James Wakasa was killed by a guard as he stood near the fence. According to J. Burton, M. Farrell, F. Lord, and R. Lord in "Topaz Relocation Center," Wakasa

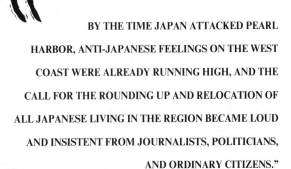

BY THE TIME JAPAN ATTACKED PEARL HARBOR, ANTI-JAPANESE FEELINGS ON THE WEST COAST WERE ALREADY RUNNING HIGH, AND THE CALL FOR THE ROUNDING UP AND RELOCATION OF ALL JAPANESE LIVING IN THE REGION BECAME LOUD AND INSISTENT FROM JOURNALISTS, POLITICIANS, AND ORDINARY CITIZENS."

was either deaf or distracted and so did not hear the guard's multiple warnings, which is exactly as Otsuka presents the incident in the novel. Other key details in the novel, such as the arrest of the father immediately after Pearl Harbor are presented with historical accuracy. By December 9, 1941, just forty-eight hours after the attack on Pearl Harbor, 1,212 Japanese Americans had been detained by the Federal Bureau of Investigation on suspicion of being dangerous and disloyal to the United States. Of that number, eighty-six were from the San Francisco Bay Area, the area from which the father in the novel is taken. Like the father, many were later imprisoned at the internment camp operated by the U.S. Army at Lordsburg, New Mexico, which housed about two thousand Japanese Americans.

After the war, it did not take long for a consensus to emerge that the internment of Japanese Americans was a chapter in American history of which no one could be proud. A grave mistake had been made in which misguided notions of military necessity had been allowed to violate the constitutional rights of American citizens—two-thirds of the detainees held citizenship status. As the website for the Topaz Museum bluntly describes it, "The internment of Americans of Japanese ancestry during WWII was one of the worst violations of civil rights in the history of the United States." Not many would quarrel with this judgment. The uprooting from their homes and forcible internment of thousands of people who had committed no crime was not a trivial act. Their incarceration was hard, long, cruel, and also pointless, since it is highly unlikely that any of the Japanese Americans who were interned presented any threat to the United States. No evidence has

WHAT DO I READ NEXT?

- *The Buddha in the Attic* (2011) is Otsuka's widely praised second novel. It tells the story of the Japanese women who came to San Francisco in the early twentieth century to marry American men. They were known as "picture brides" because the exchange of photographs was the only contact they had had with the men they agreed to marry. The novel tells their story from their arrival in an alien culture to their gradual adaptation to American life, including raising children who identify more with America than with their Japanese heritage.

- *Snow Falling on Cedars* (1995) by David Guterson is set in the 1950s and centers around a murder trial on an isolated island north of Puget Sound, Washington. The defendant is a Japanese American fisherman, and the novel takes place in the shadow of the World War II internment of Japanese Americans and the prejudice they faced then, which continued into the 1950s. This celebrated novel won the PEN/Faulkner Award. The book has some sexual content and obscenities, which might make it unsuitable for middle-school readers.

- *Farewell to Manzanar* (1973) is a memoir by Jeanne Wakatsuki Houston. A seven-year-old American-born child in World War II, she was sent with her family to an internment camp for Japanese Americans at Manzanar, California. Dealing with issues such as prejudice, isolation, and cultural identity, the memoir captures the impact internment had on Houston's family and on other Japanese Americans.

- The fifteen stories in *Seventeen Syllables and Other Stories* (2001), by Hisaye Yamamoto, a second-generation Japanese American, cover a wide range of the Japanese American experience, from the internment camps during World War II to the tensions between first-generation and second-generation immigrants. Yamamoto's stories also emphasize the lives of women.

- First published in French in 1956, *Night*, by Elie Wiesel, is a memoir of Wiesel's experiences during the Holocaust. The story is told by Eliezar, a fourteen-year-old Jewish boy, beginning in Transylvania (now Romania) in 1941. In 1944, Eliezar and his family are sent to concentration camps, where the boy is witness to innumerable horrors. He is the only member of his family to survive. This memoir has long been regarded as one of the most compelling ever written by a Holocaust survivor. It appeared in a new translation by Marion Wiesel, Wiesel's wife, in 2006.

- Ellen Levine's *A Fence away from Freedom: Japanese Americans and World War II* (1995) is a nonfiction book for young-adult readers about the internment of Japanese Americans. It consists of the testimonies of thirty-five people who were interned when they were children or adolescents. Their stories reveal what life in the camps was like and how people coped with it.

ever been uncovered that they did. Scorned outsiders, they were banished to remote parts of the country, finding out, as had Native Americans, African Americans, and other ethnic groups before them, what it was like when bad went to worse, when they were designated as the "other," a minority to be feared and despised by the dominant culture.

Nearly fifty years later, in 1988, the U.S. government formally recognized its error and did its best to make amends. Congress passed the Civil Liberties Act, also known as the Japanese American Redress Bill, which acknowledged the injustice inflicted on the internees and authorized Congress to pay each survivor $20,000 in reparations. President Reagan issued an apology to those who had been interned. Five years later, in October 1993, President Bill Clinton wrote a letter to the former detainees in which he said, "Today, on behalf of your fellow Americans, I offer a sincere apology to you for the actions that unfairly denied Japanese Americans and their families fundamental liberties during World War II." Thus was this distressing chapter in American history brought to a formal close.

But how was it ever allowed to occur? President Clinton referred in his letter to "racial prejudice" and "wartime hysteria" as being two of the principal causes. The Japanese, as well as Chinese immigrants to the West Coast, had long faced discrimination because they supposedly did not assimilate to white American culture and had a higher birth rate (so it was argued), which allegedly presented a threat to a future in California in which whites would eventually be in the minority. This was the reasoning behind legislation passed in the 1920s that was designed to curb Japanese immigration. By the time Japan attacked Pearl Harbor, anti-Japanese feelings on the West Coast were already running high, and the call for the rounding up and relocation of all Japanese living in the region became loud and insistent from journalists, politicians, and ordinary citizens. As Allan R. Bosworth explained in his book, *America's Concentration Camps*, there were three main justifications put forward for the evacuation of Japanese Americans by the Tolan Committee, a Congressional committee that met in February 1942. Suspicion fell first on the Japanese Language Schools, of which there were more than two hundred in California. Were they breeding grounds for Japanese nationalism? There was concern also about dual citizenship. Under Japanese law, if a child's father was a Japanese citizen, so was the child, wherever he or she lived. This meant that even those Japanese Americans who were born in the United States and were therefore U.S. citizens were also, according to Japanese law, Japanese citizens. According to views expressed to the Tolan Committee, these people were likely to be sympathetic to the Japanese cause. Last was the issue of the people known as *kibei*, who were American-born of Japanese parents but were sent to Japan for their education before returning to America. Where the loyalty of the *kibei* might lie was a concern of the committee. Bosworth explained how each of these factors was blown up out of all proportion, and the momentum toward the forced relocation of all Japanese Americans became a

steamroller that no one was willing or able to stop. As a result, 120,000 people were sent off to remote desert locations to endure their fate. Bosworth points out the injustice of it especially for the second-generation Japanese Americans:

> They had attended American schools and knew nothing but America; they liked hot dogs and football games and jazz, and were whizzes at playing baseball. Not one in ten could really speak Japanese. Their language was pure American, filled with colloquialisms and West Coast accents.

It made no difference if the Japanese Americans publicly proclaimed their loyalty to the United States. Bosworth's book includes a picture of the front of a grocery store in California that displays a huge message in the window, "I AM AN AMERICAN." But above the name of the store is another sign that says "Sold," and that tells the sad story. The owner was evacuated and had to sell his business. This happened to many of the internees, and their businesses were sold at a fraction of what they were actually worth. This is hinted at in the comment made by Ted Ishimoto in *When the Emperor Was Divine*, when the girl asks him if he is rich. "Not anymore," he replies. It is in small incidents like this that Otsuka creates the world of the internees, the ways they endured and the ways they suffered. She presents some disturbing insights, too, particularly concerning the seven-year-old boy. When he first arrives at the camp in Utah, he thinks he sees his father everywhere. As his thoughts pour out, it transpires that he has absorbed the racial stereotype with which the majority culture viewed the Japanese: "For it was true, they all looked alike. Black hair. Slanted eyes. High cheekbones. Thick glasses. Thin lips. Bad teeth. Unknowable. Inscrutable." Another significant moment comes when the boy acquires a pet tortoise. He does not give the tortoise a name but adopts the same practice that the authorities followed, in which families were referred to not by their names but by an identification number. Unthinkingly accepting this dehumanizing practice, the boy scratches his family's number on the shell of the tortoise.

One thing is noticeable in the accounts of the internment of the Japanese Americans in World War II, and that is the stoic and resourceful way in which they endured their treatment and made the best of a bad situation. This does not mean that there were no incidents of violence, and some such incidents involved internees turning

Those of Japanese descent in the United States were interned in camps after the bombing of Pearl Harbor on December 7, 1941. (© NeonLight | Shutterstock.com)

on one another. In *When the Emperor Was Divine*, Ishimoto, for example, is attacked by three men wielding lead pipes because he is suspected of being an FBI informant. But in general, it seems that the internees quietly accepted their situation because they could do nothing to alter it. This is why the final chapter of Otsuka's novel, in which the first-person narration of the father gives expression to the suppressed rage of an entire people, is so devastating, like a punch in the face from an unexpected source. Readers of this novel will likely understand the pent-up anger and reflect on a huge injustice that should never have happened.

Source: Bryan Aubrey, Critical Essay on *When the Emperor Was Divine*, in *Novels for Students*, Gale, Cengage Learning, 2013.

Courtney Lewis

In the following review, Lewis analyzes the role of the novel as a work of both psychological and historical fiction.

Otsuka has created an intriguing story about Japanese internment during WW II. This powerful book is characterized by sparse, contained prose detailing the lives of a Japanese American family in California. The reader never learns the names of the characters, just their roles in their family— mother, son, daughter, and later, father. As the mother walks around her neighborhood on her errands, she stops to read a notice and her demeanor changes. She begins packing, locking up some items and burying others. She gives away the cat and kills the dog prior to her children coming home from school. They take a train out to the desert and are interned in a concentration camp, all the while awaiting news from the father who was taken away one night in his bathrobe and slippers. Through the minute details of their lives and their memories of what life was like before the war, we get to know each character and their personalities. The father, reduced in most of the story to the author of an occasional postcard, finally rejoins his family as a shell of his former self, reduced to a fearful life of mere existence. The other members of the family, once returned home after the war, cannot look at their neighbors or even their home the same way. Each has invisible but lasting scars from their experience.

When the Emperor Was Divine could easily be categorized as psychological fiction as well as historical fiction with its in-depth look at the minds of its characters and how each of them copes with their situation. There is no reader's guide to the book, which would have increased its appeal, as the paperback version will undoubtedly inspire book clubs to adopt it as a selection. Senior high and public libraries will definitely want to add this work if they don't already own the hardcover edition.

Source: Courtney Lewis, Review of *When the Emperor Was Divine*, in *Kliatt*, Vol. 38, No. 1, January 2004, p. 19.

Barbara Riley

In the following review, Riley expresses that Otsuka "captures the unrelenting rawness of ostracization" in the internment process.

Evacuation Order No. 19 was an act of homeland security in 1942 that bears remembering in 2003, an act of political vivisection, if you will.

Julie Otsuka's distillation of one family's experience at Topaz, the internment camp for American citizens in the Utah desert, is fiction drawn from inescapable fact—a generation of men, women and children legally disenfranchised for the security implications of an epicanthic fold.

When the Emperor was Divine is a short novel. The pace is measured. Otsuka's characters live in Kafka-esque ordinariness. No pets. No destination. Husband disappeared wearing slippers and bathrobe. Hisaye Yamamoto, author of *17 Syllables*, offered this same world in her short stories from Manzanar, another internment camp. The fiction of Joy Kogawa chronicles horrific Canadian experiences of families of Japanese descent during the Second World War in her novel, *Obasan*.

Otsuka's story differs in looking with the same measured glance at the family's return home. This is the first day in school, when an 8-year-old who had been interned for three years writes an essay about being in a camp—and the teacher tells her in front of all the class that nothing like that ever happened. And the men, deemed especially subversive, return to lives where they will never work again as they were trained, where family fields were stolen with all the household furnishings. The return is not a return to the goodness of their former lives. Otsuka captures the unrelenting rawness of ostracization, a darkened train from which they cannot step down, on which generations will ride.

The security of a nation depended on this systematic dismantling of the rights of American citizens. Reading *When the Emperor was Divine*, stepping into the logic of unquestioned civil obedience, is a telling counterpoint to the implications of the Patriot Act of 2002.

Source: Barbara Riley, "Echoes from a Past Measure to Protect Homeland Security," in *Santa Fe New Mexican*, January 12, 2003, p. F2.

Donna Seaman

In the following review, Seaman notes that Otsuka brings home the Japanese American internment experience in the novel.

A woman sees the sign on a bright day in Berkeley, California, in 1942. Otsuka, who demonstrates a breathtaking restraint and delicacy throughout this supple and devastating first novel, does not explain what the sign says, or immediately reveal the woman's Japanese heritage. The woman has a smart and nervy daughter, and a bright and imaginative son. The man of the house, a successful businessman, has already been taken away. And so Otsuka launches her exquisite psychological tale, inspired by her own family's travails, of the internment of tens of thousands of innocent Japanese Americans during World War II. By illuminating the minds of each of her magnetic, wryly humorous characters, and by focusing on such details as the torment of having to abandon pets, the emblematic loss of an earring, the magical sight of wild mustangs out a train window at night, and the harsh Utah desert in which these gentle souls are forced to live in grim exile for more than three years, Otsuka universalizes their experience of prejudice and disenfranchisement, creating a veritable poetics of stoicism. (For another evocative approach to the subject, see Marnie Mueller's *Climate of the Country* [1999]).

Source: Donna Seaman, Review of *When the Emperor Was Divine*, in *Booklist*, Vol. 99, No. 1, September 1, 2002, p. 59.

Reba Leiding

In the following review, Leiding reveals the accessibility of the novel to readers of all ages.

Otsuka researched historical sources and her own grandparents' experiences as background for this spare yet poignant first novel about the ordeal of a Japanese family sent to an internment camp during World War II. Its perspective shifts among different family members as the story unfolds. We see the mother numbly pack up the family's middle-class belongings to leave behind in their Berkeley home. The dehumanizing train trip to the camp, and the bleak internment in the alkaline Nevada desert, as related by the young son and daughter, become mythic events. Their father, picked up for questioning immediately after Pearl Harbor and imprisoned throughout the war, returns a broken and bitter man. The family's humiliation continues beyond the war's end: after returning to their vandalized home, they are shunned for months by former friends and neighbors. The novel's themes of freedom and banishment are especially important as we see civil liberties threatened during the current war on terrorism. Otsuka's clear, elegant prose makes these themes accessible to a range of reading levels from young adult on. Highly recommended for all libraries.

Source: Reba Leiding, Review of *When the Emperor Was Divine*, in *Library Journal*, Vol. 127, No. 14, September 1, 2002, p. 215.

Publishers Weekly

In the following review, a contributor to Publishers Weekly *comments on the "matter-of-fact tone" of the novel.*

This heartbreaking, bracingly unsentimental debut describes in poetic detail the travails of a Japanese family living in an internment camp during World War II, raising the specter of wartime injustice in bone-chilling fashion. After a woman whose husband was arrested on suspicion of conspiracy sees notices posted around her neighborhood in Berkeley instructing Japanese residents to evacuate, she moves with her son and daughter to an internment camp, abruptly severing her ties with her community. The next three years are spent in filthy, cramped and impersonal lodgings as the family is shuttled from one camp to another. They return to Berkeley after the war to a home that has been ravaged by vandals; it takes time for them to adjust to life outside the camps and to come to terms with the hostility they face. When the children's father re-enters the book, he is more of a symbol than a character, reduced to a husk by interrogation and abuse. The novel never strays into melodrama—Otsuka describes the family's everyday life in Berkeley and the pitiful objects that define their world in the camp with admirable restraint and modesty. Events are viewed from numerous characters'

points of view, and the different perspectives are defined by distinctive, lyrically simple observations. The novel's honesty and matter-of-fact tone in the face of inconceivable injustice are the source of its power. Anger only comes to the fore during the last segment, when the father is allowed to tell his story—but even here, Otsuka keeps rage neatly bound up, luminous beneath the dazzling surface of her novel.

Source: Review of *When the Emperor Was Divine*, in *Publishers Weekly*, Vol. 249, No. 34, August 26, 2002, p. 44.

SOURCES

"About Julie Otsuka," Julie Otsuka website, http://www. julieotsuka.com/about/ (accessed December 4, 2011).

Bosworth, Allan R., *America's Concentration Camps*, W. W. Norton, 1967, p. 18.

Burton, J. M. Farrell, F. Lord, and R. Lord, "Topaz Relocation Center," in *Confinement and Ethnicity, an Overview of World War II Japanese American Relocation Sites*, http://www.cr.nps.gov/history/online_books/anthropology 74/ce12a.htm (accessed December 9, 2011).

"FDR and Japanese American Internment," Franklin D. Roosevelt Presidential Library and Museum website, http:// www.fdrlibrary.marist.edu/archives/pdfs/internment.pdf (accessed December 9, 2011).

Gibson, Campbell, and Kay Jung, "Historical Census Statistics on Population Totals by Race, 1790 to 1990, and by Hispanic Origin, 1979 to 1990, for the United States, Regions, Divisions, and States," U.S. Department of Commerce website, Bureau of the Census, September 2002, http://www.census.gov/population/www/documentation/ twps0056/twps0056.html (accessed December 5, 2011).

"Japan," in CIA: *World Fact Book*, 2011, https://www. cia.gov/library/publications/the-world-factbook/geos/ja. html (accessed December 5, 2011).

"Japanese American Demographics," Japanese American Citizens League website, http://www.jacl.org/about/ Japanese_American_Demographics.pdf (accessed December 5, 2011).

Kawano, Kelley, "A Conversation with Julie Otsuka," Random House website, http://www.randomhouse.com/bold type/0902/otsuka/interview.html (accessed December 4, 2011).

Leiding, Reba, Review of *When the Emperor Was Divine*, in *Library Journal*, Vol. 127, No. 14, September 1, 2002, p. 215.

"A More Perfect Union: Japanese Americans and the U.S. Constitution," Smithsonian Museum of American History website, http://americanhistory.si.edu/perfectunion/ non-flash/overview.html (accessed December 5, 2011).

Nakayama, William, "Simmering Perfection," in *GoldSea*, http://goldsea.com/Personalities/Otsukaj/otsukaj.html (accessed December 4, 2011).

Otsuka, Julie, *When the Emperor Was Divine: A Novel*, Knopf, 2002.

"Presidential Letter of Apology," PBS website, http://www.pbs.org/childofcamp/history/clinton.html (accessed December 10, 2011).

Review of *When the Emperor Was Divine*, in *Kirkus Reviews*, August 1, 2002, p. 1068.

Review of *When the Emperor Was Divine*, in *Publishers Weekly*, Vol. 249, No. 34, August 26, 2002, p. 44.

Seaman, Donna, Review of *When the Emperor Was Divine*, in *Booklist*, Vol. 99, No. 1, September 1, 2002, p. 59.

"Topaz Camp," Topaz Museum website, http://www.topazmuseum.org/ (accessed December 4, 2011).

Upchurch, Michael, "The Last Roundup: A Novel about a Japanese-American Family Sent to a Relocation Camp during World War II," in *New York Times Book Review*, September 22, 2002, p. 14.

prejudice against Asian Americans, the upholding by the Supreme Court of the evacuation, life in the internment camps, and the difficulties involved in resettling internees after the war.

Taylor, Sandra C., *Jewel of the Desert: Japanese Internment at Topaz*, University of California Press, 1993.
Otsuka named this book as one she had found helpful in writing her novel. It tells the story of Japanese Americans from the San Francisco area who were interned at the camp in Topaz, Utah. The book includes interviews with fifty people who lived at the camp.

Uchida, Yoshiko, *Desert Exile: The Uprooting of a Japanese-American Family*, University of Washington Press, 1984.
Noted by Otsuka as one of the books she read and valued as she was writing her novel, this is an autobiographical narrative about how Uchida, her parents, and her sister were sent to an internment camp in Utah.

FURTHER READING

Cooper, Michael L., *Fighting for Honor: Japanese Americans and World War II*, Clarion Books, 2000.
This is an account for young readers of the role played by Japanese Americans who joined the U.S. Army in World War II. More than 11,000 Japanese Americans fought in the 442nd Regimental Combat Team and many were decorated for their bravery. The book is based on diaries, autobiographies, and military records.

Daniels, Roger, *Prisoners without Trial: Japanese Americans in World War II*, Hill and Wang, 1993.
This is a concise account of the incarceration of Japanese Americans during World War II. Daniels discusses topics such as the historical

SUGGESTED SEARCH TERMS

Julie Otsuka

Executive Order 9066

Japanese American internment

Japanese American internment AND Tanforan Racetrack

Pearl Harbor

Topaz internment camp

Nisei AND World War II

Kibei

Japanese American Redress Bill

No-No boys

Japanese American loyalty questionnaire

Glossary of Literary Terms

A

Abstract: As an adjective applied to writing or literary works, abstract refers to words or phrases that name things not knowable through the five senses.

Aestheticism: A literary and artistic movement of the nineteenth century. Followers of the movement believed that art should not be mixed with social, political, or moral teaching. The statement "art for art's sake" is a good summary of aestheticism. The movement had its roots in France, but it gained widespread importance in England in the last half of the nineteenth century, where it helped change the Victorian practice of including moral lessons in literature.

Allegory: A narrative technique in which characters representing things or abstract ideas are used to convey a message or teach a lesson. Allegory is typically used to teach moral, ethical, or religious lessons but is sometimes used for satiric or political purposes.

Allusion: A reference to a familiar literary or historical person or event, used to make an idea more easily understood.

Analogy: A comparison of two things made to explain something unfamiliar through its similarities to something familiar, or to prove one point based on the acceptedness of another. Similes and metaphors are types of analogies.

Antagonist: The major character in a narrative or drama who works against the hero or protagonist.

Anthropomorphism: The presentation of animals or objects in human shape or with human characteristics. The term is derived from the Greek word for "human form."

Anti-hero: A central character in a work of literature who lacks traditional heroic qualities such as courage, physical prowess, and fortitude. Anti-heroes typically distrust conventional values and are unable to commit themselves to any ideals. They generally feel helpless in a world over which they have no control. Anti-heroes usually accept, and often celebrate, their positions as social outcasts.

Apprenticeship Novel: See *Bildungsroman*

Archetype: The word archetype is commonly used to describe an original pattern or model from which all other things of the same kind are made. This term was introduced to literary criticism from the psychology of Carl Jung. It expresses Jung's theory that behind every person's "unconscious," or repressed memories of the past, lies the "collective unconscious" of the human race: memories of the countless typical experiences of our ancestors. These memories are said to prompt illogical associations that trigger powerful emotions in the reader. Often, the emotional process is primitive, even primordial. Archetypes are the literary images that grow out of the "collective unconscious." They appear in literature as incidents and plots that repeat basic patterns of life. They may also appear as stereotyped characters.

Avant-garde: French term meaning "vanguard." It is used in literary criticism to describe new writing that rejects traditional approaches to literature in favor of innovations in style or content.

B

Beat Movement: A period featuring a group of American poets and novelists of the 1950s and 1960s—including Jack Kerouac, Allen Ginsberg, Gregory Corso, William S. Burroughs, and Lawrence Ferlinghetti—who rejected established social and literary values. Using such techniques as stream of consciousness writing and jazz-influenced free verse and focusing on unusual or abnormal states of mind—generated by religious ecstasy or the use of drugs—the Beat writers aimed to create works that were unconventional in both form and subject matter.

Bildungsroman: A German word meaning "novel of development." The *bildungsroman* is a study of the maturation of a youthful character, typically brought about through a series of social or sexual encounters that lead to self-awareness. *Bildungsroman* is used interchangeably with *erziehungsroman,* a novel of initiation and education. When a *bildungsroman* is concerned with the development of an artist (as in James Joyce's *A Portrait of the Artist as a Young Man*), it is often termed a *kunstlerroman.*

Black Aesthetic Movement: A period of artistic and literary development among African Americans in the 1960s and early 1970s. This was the first major African-American artistic movement since the Harlem Renaissance and was closely paralleled by the civil rights and black power movements. The black aesthetic writers attempted to produce works of art that would be meaningful to the black masses. Key figures in black aesthetics included one of its founders, poet and playwright Amiri Baraka, formerly known as LeRoi Jones; poet and essayist Haki R. Madhubuti, formerly Don L. Lee; poet and playwright Sonia Sanchez; and dramatist Ed Bullins.

Black Humor: Writing that places grotesque elements side by side with humorous ones in an attempt to shock the reader, forcing him or her to laugh at the horrifying reality of a disordered world.

Burlesque: Any literary work that uses exaggeration to make its subject appear ridiculous, either by treating a trivial subject with profound seriousness or by treating a dignified subject frivolously. The word "burlesque" may also be used as an adjective, as in "burlesque show," to mean "striptease act."

C

Character: Broadly speaking, a person in a literary work. The actions of characters are what constitute the plot of a story, novel, or poem. There are numerous types of characters, ranging from simple, stereotypical figures to intricate, multifaceted ones. In the techniques of anthropomorphism and personification, animals—and even places or things—can assume aspects of character. "Characterization" is the process by which an author creates vivid, believable characters in a work of art. This may be done in a variety of ways, including (1) direct description of the character by the narrator; (2) the direct presentation of the speech, thoughts, or actions of the character; and (3) the responses of other characters to the character. The term "character" also refers to a form originated by the ancient Greek writer Theophrastus that later became popular in the seventeenth and eighteenth centuries. It is a short essay or sketch of a person who prominently displays a specific attribute or quality, such as miserliness or ambition.

Climax: The turning point in a narrative, the moment when the conflict is at its most intense. Typically, the structure of stories, novels, and plays is one of rising action, in which tension builds to the climax, followed by falling action, in which tension lessens as the story moves to its conclusion.

Colloquialism: A word, phrase, or form of pronunciation that is acceptable in casual conversation but not in formal, written communication. It is considered more acceptable than slang.

Coming of Age Novel: See *Bildungsroman*

Concrete: Concrete is the opposite of abstract, and refers to a thing that actually exists or a description that allows the reader to experience an object or concept with the senses.

Connotation: The impression that a word gives beyond its defined meaning. Connotations may be universally understood or may be significant only to a certain group.

Convention: Any widely accepted literary device, style, or form.

D

Denotation: The definition of a word, apart from the impressions or feelings it creates (connotations) in the reader.

Denouement: A French word meaning "the unknotting." In literary criticism, it denotes the resolution of conflict in fiction or drama. The *denouement* follows the climax and provides an outcome to the primary plot situation as well as an explanation of secondary plot complications. The *denouement* often involves a character's recognition of his or her state of mind or moral condition.

Description: Descriptive writing is intended to allow a reader to picture the scene or setting in which the action of a story takes place. The form this description takes often evokes an intended emotional response—a dark, spooky graveyard will evoke fear, and a peaceful, sunny meadow will evoke calmness.

Dialogue: In its widest sense, dialogue is simply conversation between people in a literary work; in its most restricted sense, it refers specifically to the speech of characters in a drama. As a specific literary genre, a "dialogue" is a composition in which characters debate an issue or idea.

Diction: The selection and arrangement of words in a literary work. Either or both may vary depending on the desired effect. There are four general types of diction: "formal," used in scholarly or lofty writing; "informal," used in relaxed but educated conversation; "colloquial," used in everyday speech; and "slang," containing newly coined words and other terms not accepted in formal usage.

Didactic: A term used to describe works of literature that aim to teach some moral, religious, political, or practical lesson. Although didactic elements are often found in artistically pleasing works, the term "didactic" usually refers to literature in which the message is more important than the form. The term

may also be used to criticize a work that the critic finds "overly didactic," that is, heavy-handed in its delivery of a lesson.

Doppelganger: A literary technique by which a character is duplicated (usually in the form of an alter ego, though sometimes as a ghostly counterpart) or divided into two distinct, usually opposite personalities. The use of this character device is widespread in nineteenth- and twentieth-century literature, and indicates a growing awareness among authors that the "self" is really a composite of many "selves."

Double Entendre: A corruption of a French phrase meaning "double meaning." The term is used to indicate a word or phrase that is deliberately ambiguous, especially when one of the meanings is risqué or improper.

Dramatic Irony: Occurs when the audience of a play or the reader of a work of literature knows something that a character in the work itself does not know. The irony is in the contrast between the intended meaning of the statements or actions of a character and the additional information understood by the audience.

Dystopia: An imaginary place in a work of fiction where the characters lead dehumanized, fearful lives.

E

Edwardian: Describes cultural conventions identified with the period of the reign of Edward VII of England (1901-1910). Writers of the Edwardian Age typically displayed a strong reaction against the propriety and conservatism of the Victorian Age. Their work often exhibits distrust of authority in religion, politics, and art and expresses strong doubts about the soundness of conventional values.

Empathy: A sense of shared experience, including emotional and physical feelings, with someone or something other than oneself. Empathy is often used to describe the response of a reader to a literary character.

Enlightenment, The: An eighteenth-century philosophical movement. It began in France but had a wide impact throughout Europe and America. Thinkers of the Enlightenment valued reason and believed that both the individual and society could achieve a state of perfection. Corresponding to this essentially humanist vision was a resistance to religious authority.

Epigram: A saying that makes the speaker's point quickly and concisely. Often used to preface a novel.

Epilogue: A concluding statement or section of a literary work. In dramas, particularly those of the seventeenth and eighteenth centuries, the epilogue is a closing speech, often in verse, delivered by an actor at the end of a play and spoken directly to the audience.

Epiphany: A sudden revelation of truth inspired by a seemingly trivial incident.

Episode: An incident that forms part of a story and is significantly related to it. Episodes may be either self-contained narratives or events that depend on a larger context for their sense and importance.

Epistolary Novel: A novel in the form of letters. The form was particularly popular in the eighteenth century.

Epithet: A word or phrase, often disparaging or abusive, that expresses a character trait of someone or something.

Existentialism: A predominantly twentieth-century philosophy concerned with the nature and perception of human existence. There are two major strains of existentialist thought: atheistic and Christian. Followers of atheistic existentialism believe that the individual is alone in a godless universe and that the basic human condition is one of suffering and loneliness. Nevertheless, because there are no fixed values, individuals can create their own characters—indeed, they can shape themselves—through the exercise of free will. The atheistic strain culminates in and is popularly associated with the works of Jean-Paul Sartre. The Christian existentialists, on the other hand, believe that only in God may people find freedom from life's anguish. The two strains hold certain beliefs in common: that existence cannot be fully understood or described through empirical effort; that anguish is a universal element of life; that individuals must bear responsibility for their actions; and that there is no common standard of behavior or perception for religious and ethical matters.

Expatriates: See *Expatriatism*

Expatriatism: The practice of leaving one's country to live for an extended period in another country.

Exposition: Writing intended to explain the nature of an idea, thing, or theme. Expository writing is often combined with description, narration, or argument. In dramatic writing, the exposition is the introductory material which presents the characters, setting, and tone of the play.

Expressionism: An indistinct literary term, originally used to describe an early twentieth-century school of German painting. The term applies to almost any mode of unconventional, highly subjective writing that distorts reality in some way.

F

Fable: A prose or verse narrative intended to convey a moral. Animals or inanimate objects with human characteristics often serve as characters in fables.

Falling Action: See *Denouement*

Fantasy: A literary form related to mythology and folklore. Fantasy literature is typically set in non-existent realms and features supernatural beings.

Farce: A type of comedy characterized by broad humor, outlandish incidents, and often vulgar subject matter.

Femme fatale: A French phrase with the literal translation "fatal woman." A *femme fatale* is a sensuous, alluring woman who often leads men into danger or trouble.

Fiction: Any story that is the product of imagination rather than a documentation of fact. characters and events in such narratives may be based in real life but their ultimate form and configuration is a creation of the author.

Figurative Language: A technique in writing in which the author temporarily interrupts the order, construction, or meaning of the writing for a particular effect. This interruption takes the form of one or more figures of speech such as hyperbole, irony, or simile. Figurative language is the opposite of literal language, in which every word is truthful, accurate, and free of exaggeration or embellishment.

Figures of Speech: Writing that differs from customary conventions for construction, meaning, order, or significance for the purpose of a special meaning or effect. There are two major types of figures of speech: rhetorical figures, which do not make changes in the meaning of the words, and tropes, which do.

Fin de siecle: A French term meaning "end of the century." The term is used to denote the last decade of the nineteenth century, a transition period when writers and other artists abandoned old conventions and looked for new techniques and objectives.

First Person: See *Point of View*

Flashback: A device used in literature to present action that occurred before the beginning of the story. Flashbacks are often introduced as the dreams or recollections of one or more characters.

Foil: A character in a work of literature whose physical or psychological qualities contrast strongly with, and therefore highlight, the corresponding qualities of another character.

Folklore: Traditions and myths preserved in a culture or group of people. Typically, these are passed on by word of mouth in various forms—such as legends, songs, and proverbs—or preserved in customs and ceremonies. This term was first used by W. J. Thoms in 1846.

Folktale: A story originating in oral tradition. Folktales fall into a variety of categories, including legends, ghost stories, fairy tales, fables, and anecdotes based on historical figures and events.

Foreshadowing: A device used in literature to create expectation or to set up an explanation of later developments.

Form: The pattern or construction of a work which identifies its genre and distinguishes it from other genres.

G

Genre: A category of literary work. In critical theory, genre may refer to both the content of a given work—tragedy, comedy, pastoral—and to its form, such as poetry, novel, or drama.

Gilded Age: A period in American history during the 1870s characterized by political corruption and materialism. A number of important novels of social and political criticism were written during this time.

Gothicism: In literary criticism, works characterized by a taste for the medieval or morbidly attractive. A gothic novel prominently features elements of horror, the supernatural, gloom, and violence: clanking chains, terror, charnel houses, ghosts, medieval castles, and mysteriously slamming doors. The term "gothic novel" is also applied to novels that lack elements of the traditional Gothic setting but that create a similar atmosphere of terror or dread.

Grotesque: In literary criticism, the subject matter of a work or a style of expression characterized by exaggeration, deformity, freakishness, and disorder. The grotesque often includes an element of comic absurdity.

H

Harlem Renaissance: The Harlem Renaissance of the 1920s is generally considered the first significant movement of black writers and artists in the United States. During this period, new and established black writers published more fiction and poetry than ever before, the first influential black literary journals were established, and black authors and artists received their first widespread recognition and serious critical appraisal. Among the major writers associated with this period are Claude McKay, Jean Toomer, Countee Cullen, Langston Hughes, Arna Bontemps, Nella Larsen, and Zora Neale Hurston.

Hero/Heroine: The principal sympathetic character (male or female) in a literary work. Heroes and heroines typically exhibit admirable traits: idealism, courage, and integrity, for example.

Holocaust Literature: Literature influenced by or written about the Holocaust of World War II. Such literature includes true stories of survival in concentration camps, escape, and life after the war, as well as fictional works and poetry.

Humanism: A philosophy that places faith in the dignity of humankind and rejects the medieval perception of the individual as a weak, fallen creature. "Humanists" typically believe in the perfectibility of human nature and view reason and education as the means to that end.

Hyperbole: In literary criticism, deliberate exaggeration used to achieve an effect.

I

Idiom: A word construction or verbal expression closely associated with a given language.

Image: A concrete representation of an object or sensory experience. Typically, such a representation helps evoke the feelings associated with the object or experience itself. Images are either "literal" or "figurative." Literal images are especially concrete and involve little or no extension of the obvious meaning of the words used to express them. Figurative images do not follow the literal meaning of the words exactly. Images in literature are usually visual, but the term "image" can also refer to the representation of any sensory experience.

Imagery: The array of images in a literary work. Also, figurative language.

In medias res: A Latin term meaning "in the middle of things." It refers to the technique of beginning a story at its midpoint and then using various flashback devices to reveal previous action.

Interior Monologue: A narrative technique in which characters' thoughts are revealed in a way that appears to be uncontrolled by the author. The interior monologue typically aims to reveal the inner self of a character. It portrays emotional experiences as they occur at both a conscious and unconscious level. images are often used to represent sensations or emotions.

Irony: In literary criticism, the effect of language in which the intended meaning is the opposite of what is stated.

J

Jargon: Language that is used or understood only by a select group of people. Jargon may refer to terminology used in a certain profession, such as computer jargon, or it may refer to any nonsensical language that is not understood by most people.

L

Leitmotiv: See *Motif*

Literal Language: An author uses literal language when he or she writes without exaggerating or embellishing the subject matter and without any tools of figurative language.

Lost Generation: A term first used by Gertrude Stein to describe the post-World War I generation of American writers: men and women haunted by a sense of betrayal and emptiness brought about by the destructiveness of the war.

M

Mannerism: Exaggerated, artificial adherence to a literary manner or style. Also, a popular style of the visual arts of late sixteenth-century Europe that was marked by elongation of the human form and by intentional spatial distortion. Literary works that are self-consciously high-toned and artistic are often said to be "mannered."

Metaphor: A figure of speech that expresses an idea through the image of another object. Metaphors suggest the essence of the first object by identifying it with certain qualities of the second object.

Modernism: Modern literary practices. Also, the principles of a literary school that lasted from roughly the beginning of the twentieth century until the end of World War II. Modernism is defined by its rejection of the literary conventions of the nineteenth century and by its opposition to conventional morality, taste, traditions, and economic values.

Mood: The prevailing emotions of a work or of the author in his or her creation of the work. The mood of a work is not always what might be expected based on its subject matter.

Motif: A theme, character type, image, metaphor, or other verbal element that recurs throughout a single work of literature or occurs in a number of different works over a period of time.

Myth: An anonymous tale emerging from the traditional beliefs of a culture or social unit. Myths use supernatural explanations for natural phenomena. They may also explain cosmic issues like creation and death. Collections of myths, known as mythologies, are common to all cultures and nations, but the best-known myths belong to the Norse, Roman, and Greek mythologies.

N

Narration: The telling of a series of events, real or invented. A narration may be either a simple narrative, in which the events are recounted chronologically, or a narrative with a plot, in which the account is given in a style reflecting the author's artistic concept of the story. Narration is sometimes used as a synonym for "storyline."

Narrative: A verse or prose accounting of an event or sequence of events, real or invented. The term is also used as an adjective in the sense "method of narration." For example, in literary criticism, the expression "narrative technique" usually refers to the way the author structures and presents his or her story.

Narrator: The teller of a story. The narrator may be the author or a character in the story through whom the author speaks.

Naturalism: A literary movement of the late nineteenth and early twentieth centuries. The movement's major theorist, French novelist Emile Zola, envisioned a type of fiction that would examine human life with the objectivity of scientific inquiry. The Naturalists typically viewed human beings as either the products of "biological determinism," ruled by hereditary instincts and engaged in an endless struggle for survival, or as the products of "socioeconomic determinism," ruled by social and economic forces beyond their control. In their works, the Naturalists generally ignored the highest levels of society and focused on degradation: poverty, alcoholism, prostitution, insanity, and disease.

Noble Savage: The idea that primitive man is noble and good but becomes evil and corrupted as he becomes civilized. The concept of the noble savage originated in the Renaissance period but is more closely identified with such later writers as Jean-Jacques Rousseau and Aphra Behn.

Novel: A long fictional narrative written in prose, which developed from the novella and other early forms of narrative. A novel is usually organized under a plot or theme with a focus on character development and action.

Novel of Ideas: A novel in which the examination of intellectual issues and concepts takes precedence over characterization or a traditional storyline.

Novel of Manners: A novel that examines the customs and mores of a cultural group.

Novella: An Italian term meaning "story." This term has been especially used to describe fourteenth-century Italian tales, but it also refers to modern short novels.

O

Objective Correlative: An outward set of objects, a situation, or a chain of events corresponding to an inward experience and evoking this experience in the reader. The term frequently appears in modern criticism in discussions of authors' intended effects on the emotional responses of readers.

Objectivity: A quality in writing characterized by the absence of the author's opinion or feeling about the subject matter. Objectivity is an important factor in criticism.

Oedipus Complex: A son's amorous obsession with his mother. The phrase is derived from the story of the ancient Theban hero Oedipus, who unknowingly killed his father and married his mother.

Omniscience: See *Point of View*

Onomatopoeia: The use of words whose sounds express or suggest their meaning. In its simplest sense, onomatopoeia may be represented by words that mimic the sounds they denote such as "hiss" or "meow." At a more subtle level, the pattern and rhythm of sounds and rhymes of a line or poem may be onomatopoeic.

Oxymoron: A phrase combining two contradictory terms. Oxymorons may be intentional or unintentional.

P

Parable: A story intended to teach a moral lesson or answer an ethical question.

Paradox: A statement that appears illogical or contradictory at first, but may actually point to an underlying truth.

Parallelism: A method of comparison of two ideas in which each is developed in the same grammatical structure.

Parody: In literary criticism, this term refers to an imitation of a serious literary work or the signature style of a particular author in a ridiculous manner. A typical parody adopts the style of the original and applies it to an inappropriate subject for humorous effect. Parody is a form of satire and could be considered the literary equivalent of a caricature or cartoon.

Pastoral: A term derived from the Latin word "pastor," meaning shepherd. A pastoral is a literary composition on a rural theme. The conventions of the pastoral were originated by the third-century Greek poet Theocritus, who wrote about the experiences, love affairs, and pastimes of Sicilian shepherds. In a pastoral, characters and language of a courtly nature are often placed in a simple setting. The term pastoral is also used to classify dramas, elegies, and lyrics that exhibit the use of country settings and shepherd characters.

Pen Name: See *Pseudonym*

Persona: A Latin term meaning "mask." *Personae* are the characters in a fictional work of literature. The *persona* generally functions as a mask through which the author tells a story in a voice other than his or her own. A *persona* is usually either a character in a story who acts as a narrator or an "implied author," a voice created by the author to act as the narrator for himself or herself.

Personification: A figure of speech that gives human qualities to abstract ideas, animals, and inanimate objects.

Picaresque Novel: Episodic fiction depicting the adventures of a roguish central character ("picaro" is Spanish for "rogue"). The picaresque hero is commonly a low-born but clever individual who wanders into and out of various affairs of love, danger, and farcical intrigue. These involvements may take place at all social levels and typically present a humorous and wide-ranging satire of a given society.

Plagiarism: Claiming another person's written material as one's own. Plagiarism can take the form of direct, word-for-word copying or the theft of the substance or idea of the work.

Plot: In literary criticism, this term refers to the pattern of events in a narrative or drama. In its simplest sense, the plot guides the author in composing the work and helps the reader follow the work. Typically, plots exhibit causality and unity and have a beginning, a middle, and an end. Sometimes, however, a plot may consist of a series of disconnected events, in which case it is known as an "episodic plot."

Poetic Justice: An outcome in a literary work, not necessarily a poem, in which the good are rewarded and the evil are punished, especially in ways that particularly fit their virtues or crimes.

Poetic License: Distortions of fact and literary convention made by a writer—not always a poet—for the sake of the effect gained. Poetic license is closely related to the concept of "artistic freedom."

Poetics: This term has two closely related meanings. It denotes (1) an aesthetic theory in literary criticism about the essence of poetry or (2) rules prescribing the proper methods, content, style, or diction of poetry. The term poetics may also refer to theories about literature in general, not just poetry.

Point of View: The narrative perspective from which a literary work is presented to the reader. There are four traditional points of view. The "third person omniscient" gives the reader a "godlike" perspective, unrestricted by time or place, from which to see actions and look into the minds of characters. This allows the author to comment openly on characters and events in the work. The "third person" point of view presents the events of the story from outside of any single character's perception, much like the omniscient point of view, but the reader must understand the action as it takes place and without any special insight into characters' minds or motivations. The "first person" or "personal" point of view relates events as they are perceived by a single character. The main character "tells" the story and may offer opinions about the action and characters which differ from those of the author. Much less common than omniscient, third person, and first person is the "second person" point of view, wherein the author tells the story as if it is happening to the reader.

Polemic: A work in which the author takes a stand on a controversial subject, such as abortion or religion. Such works are often extremely argumentative or provocative.

Pornography: Writing intended to provoke feelings of lust in the reader. Such works are often condemned by critics and teachers, but those which can be shown to have literary value are viewed less harshly.

Post-Aesthetic Movement: An artistic response made by African Americans to the black aesthetic movement of the 1960s and early '70s. Writers since that time have adopted a somewhat different tone in their work, with less emphasis placed on the disparity between black and white in the United States. In the words of post-aesthetic authors such as Toni Morrison, John Edgar Wideman, and Kristin Hunter, African Americans are portrayed as looking inward for answers to their own questions, rather than always looking to the outside world.

Postmodernism: Writing from the 1960s forward characterized by experimentation and continuing to apply some of the fundamentals of modernism, which included existentialism and alienation. Postmodernists have gone a step further in the rejection of tradition begun with the modernists by also rejecting traditional forms, preferring the anti-novel over the novel and the anti-hero over the hero.

Primitivism: The belief that primitive peoples were nobler and less flawed than civilized peoples because they had not been subjected to the tainting influence of society.

Prologue: An introductory section of a literary work. It often contains information establishing the situation of the characters or presents information about the setting, time period, or action. In drama, the prologue is spoken by a chorus or by one of the principal characters.

Prose: A literary medium that attempts to mirror the language of everyday speech. It is distinguished from poetry by its use of unmetered, unrhymed language consisting of logically related sentences. Prose is usually grouped into paragraphs that form a cohesive whole such as an essay or a novel.

Prosopopoeia: See *Personification*

Protagonist: The central character of a story who serves as a focus for its themes and incidents and as the principal rationale for its development. The protagonist is sometimes referred to in discussions of modern literature as the hero or anti-hero.

Protest Fiction: Protest fiction has as its primary purpose the protesting of some social injustice, such as racism or discrimination.

Proverb: A brief, sage saying that expresses a truth about life in a striking manner.

Pseudonym: A name assumed by a writer, most often intended to prevent his or her identification as the author of a work. Two or more authors may work together under one pseu-

donym, or an author may use a different name for each genre he or she publishes in. Some publishing companies maintain "house pseudonyms," under which any number of authors may write installations in a series. Some authors also choose a pseudonym over their real names the way an actor may use a stage name.

Pun: A play on words that have similar sounds but different meanings.

R

Realism: A nineteenth-century European literary movement that sought to portray familiar characters, situations, and settings in a realistic manner. This was done primarily by using an objective narrative point of view and through the buildup of accurate detail. The standard for success of any realistic work depends on how faithfully it transfers common experience into fictional forms. The realistic method may be altered or extended, as in stream of consciousness writing, to record highly subjective experience.

Repartee: Conversation featuring snappy retorts and witticisms.

Resolution: The portion of a story following the climax, in which the conflict is resolved.

Rhetoric: In literary criticism, this term denotes the art of ethical persuasion. In its strictest sense, rhetoric adheres to various principles developed since classical times for arranging facts and ideas in a clear, persuasive, appealing manner. The term is also used to refer to effective prose in general and theories of or methods for composing effective prose.

Rhetorical Question: A question intended to provoke thought, but not an expressed answer, in the reader. It is most commonly used in oratory and other persuasive genres.

Rising Action: The part of a drama where the plot becomes increasingly complicated. Rising action leads up to the climax, or turning point, of a drama.

Roman à clef: A French phrase meaning "novel with a key." It refers to a narrative in which real persons are portrayed under fictitious names.

Romance: A broad term, usually denoting a narrative with exotic, exaggerated, often idealized characters, scenes, and themes.

Romanticism: This term has two widely accepted meanings. In historical criticism, it refers to a European intellectual and artistic movement of the late eighteenth and early nineteenth centuries that sought greater freedom of personal expression than that allowed by the strict rules of literary form and logic of the eighteenth-century neoclassicists. The Romantics preferred emotional and imaginative expression to rational analysis. They considered the individual to be at the center of all experience and so placed him or her at the center of their art. The Romantics believed that the creative imagination reveals nobler truths—unique feelings and attitudes—than those that could be discovered by logic or by scientific examination. Both the natural world and the state of childhood were important sources for revelations of "eternal truths." "Romanticism" is also used as a general term to refer to a type of sensibility found in all periods of literary history and usually considered to be in opposition to the principles of classicism. In this sense, Romanticism signifies any work or philosophy in which the exotic or dreamlike figure strongly, or that is devoted to individualistic expression, self-analysis, or a pursuit of a higher realm of knowledge than can be discovered by human reason.

Romantics: See *Romanticism*

S

Satire: A work that uses ridicule, humor, and wit to criticize and provoke change in human nature and institutions. There are two major types of satire: "formal" or "direct" satire speaks directly to the reader or to a character in the work; "indirect" satire relies upon the ridiculous behavior of its characters to make its point. Formal satire is further divided into two manners: the "Horatian," which ridicules gently, and the "Juvenalian," which derides its subjects harshly and bitterly.

Science Fiction: A type of narrative about or based upon real or imagined scientific theories and technology. Science fiction is often peopled with alien creatures and set on other planets or in different dimensions.

Second Person: See *Point of View*

Setting: The time, place, and culture in which the action of a narrative takes place. The elements of setting may include geographic location, characters' physical and mental environments, prevailing cultural attitudes, or the historical time in which the action takes place.

Simile: A comparison, usually using "like" or "as," of two essentially dissimilar things, as in "coffee as cold as ice" or "He sounded like a broken record."

Slang: A type of informal verbal communication that is generally unacceptable for formal writing. Slang words and phrases are often colorful exaggerations used to emphasize the speaker's point; they may also be shortened versions of an often-used word or phrase.

Slave Narrative: Autobiographical accounts of American slave life as told by escaped slaves. These works first appeared during the abolition movement of the 1830s through the 1850s.

Socialist Realism: The Socialist Realism school of literary theory was proposed by Maxim Gorky and established as a dogma by the first Soviet Congress of Writers. It demanded adherence to a communist worldview in works of literature. Its doctrines required an objective viewpoint comprehensible to the working classes and themes of social struggle featuring strong proletarian heroes.

Stereotype: A stereotype was originally the name for a duplication made during the printing process; this led to its modern definition as a person or thing that is (or is assumed to be) the same as all others of its type.

Stream of Consciousness: A narrative technique for rendering the inward experience of a character. This technique is designed to give the impression of an ever-changing series of thoughts, emotions, images, and memories in the spontaneous and seemingly illogical order that they occur in life.

Structure: The form taken by a piece of literature. The structure may be made obvious for ease of understanding, as in nonfiction works, or may obscured for artistic purposes, as in some poetry or seemingly "unstructured" prose.

Sturm und Drang: A German term meaning "storm and stress." It refers to a German literary movement of the 1770s and 1780s that reacted against the order and rationalism of the enlightenment, focusing instead on the intense experience of extraordinary individuals.

Style: A writer's distinctive manner of arranging words to suit his or her ideas and purpose in writing. The unique imprint of the author's personality upon his or her writing, style is the product of an author's way of arranging ideas and his or her use of diction, different sentence structures, rhythm, figures of speech, rhetorical principles, and other elements of composition.

Subjectivity: Writing that expresses the author's personal feelings about his subject, and which may or may not include factual information about the subject.

Subplot: A secondary story in a narrative. A subplot may serve as a motivating or complicating force for the main plot of the work, or it may provide emphasis for, or relief from, the main plot.

Surrealism: A term introduced to criticism by Guillaume Apollinaire and later adopted by Andre Breton. It refers to a French literary and artistic movement founded in the 1920s. The Surrealists sought to express unconscious thoughts and feelings in their works. The best-known technique used for achieving this aim was automatic writing—transcriptions of spontaneous outpourings from the unconscious. The Surrealists proposed to unify the contrary levels of conscious and unconscious, dream and reality, objectivity and subjectivity into a new level of "super-realism."

Suspense: A literary device in which the author maintains the audience's attention through the buildup of events, the outcome of which will soon be revealed.

Symbol: Something that suggests or stands for something else without losing its original identity. In literature, symbols combine their literal meaning with the suggestion of an abstract concept. Literary symbols are of two types: those that carry complex associations of meaning no matter what their contexts, and those that derive their suggestive meaning from their functions in specific literary works.

Symbolism: This term has two widely accepted meanings. In historical criticism, it denotes an early modernist literary movement initiated in France during the nineteenth century that reacted against the prevailing standards of realism. Writers in this movement aimed to evoke, indirectly and symbolically, an order

of being beyond the material world of the five senses. Poetic expression of personal emotion figured strongly in the movement, typically by means of a private set of symbols uniquely identifiable with the individual poet. The principal aim of the Symbolists was to express in words the highly complex feelings that grew out of everyday contact with the world. In a broader sense, the term "symbolism" refers to the use of one object to represent another.

T

Tall Tale: A humorous tale told in a straightforward, credible tone but relating absolutely impossible events or feats of the characters. Such tales were commonly told of frontier adventures during the settlement of the west in the United States.

Theme: The main point of a work of literature. The term is used interchangeably with thesis.

Thesis: A thesis is both an essay and the point argued in the essay. Thesis novels and thesis plays share the quality of containing a thesis which is supported through the action of the story.

Third Person: See *Point of View*

Tone: The author's attitude toward his or her audience may be deduced from the tone of the work. A formal tone may create distance or convey politeness, while an informal tone may encourage a friendly, intimate, or intrusive feeling in the reader. The author's attitude toward his or her subject matter may also be deduced from the tone of the words he or she uses in discussing it.

Transcendentalism: An American philosophical and religious movement, based in New England from around 1835 until the Civil War. Transcendentalism was a form of American romanticism that had its roots abroad in the works of Thomas Carlyle, Samuel Coleridge, and Johann Wolfgang von Goethe. The Transcendentalists stressed the importance of intuition and subjective experience in communication with God. They rejected religious dogma and texts in favor of mysticism and scientific naturalism. They pursued truths that lie beyond the "colorless" realms perceived by reason and the senses and were active social reformers in public education, women's rights, and the abolition of slavery.

U

Urban Realism: A branch of realist writing that attempts to accurately reflect the often harsh facts of modern urban existence.

Utopia: A fictional perfect place, such as "paradise" or "heaven."

V

Verisimilitude: Literally, the appearance of truth. In literary criticism, the term refers to aspects of a work of literature that seem true to the reader.

Victorian: Refers broadly to the reign of Queen Victoria of England (1837-1901) and to anything with qualities typical of that era. For example, the qualities of smug narrow-mindedness, bourgeois materialism, faith in social progress, and priggish morality are often considered Victorian. This stereotype is contradicted by such dramatic intellectual developments as the theories of Charles Darwin, Karl Marx, and Sigmund Freud (which stirred strong debates in England) and the critical attitudes of serious Victorian writers like Charles Dickens and George Eliot. In literature, the Victorian Period was the great age of the English novel, and the latter part of the era saw the rise of movements such as decadence and symbolism.

W

Weltanschauung: A German term referring to a person's worldview or philosophy.

Weltschmerz: A German term meaning "world pain." It describes a sense of anguish about the nature of existence, usually associated with a melancholy, pessimistic attitude.

Z

Zeitgeist: A German term meaning "spirit of the time." It refers to the moral and intellectual trends of a given era.

Cumulative Author/Title Index

Rölvaag, O. E.
  Giants in the Earth: V5
A Room with a View (Forster): V11
Roots: The Story of an American Family (Haley): V9
Roth, Philip
  American Pastoral: V25
Roy, Arundhati
  The God of Small Things: V22
Rubyfruit Jungle (Brown): V9
Rumble Fish (Hinton): V15
Rushdie, Salman
  Haroun and the Sea of Stories: V41
  Midnight's Children: V23
  The Satanic Verses: V22
Russo, Richard
  Empire Falls: V25

S

Sachar, Louis
  Holes: V37
Saint-Exupéry, Antoine de
  The Little Prince: V30
Salinger, J. D.
  The Catcher in the Rye: V1
  Franny and Zooey: V30
Saramago, José
  Blindness: V27
Saroyan, William
  The Human Comedy: V39
Sartre, Jean-Paul
  Nausea: V21
The Satanic Verses (Rushdie): V22
The Scarlet Letter (Hawthorne): V1
The Scarlet Pimpernel (Orczy): V31
Schaefer, Jack Warner
  Shane: V36
Schindler's List (Keneally): V17
Schindler's List (Motion picture): V38
Scoop (Waugh): V17
Scott, Walter
  Ivanhoe: V31
The Sea-Wolf (London): V35
The Secret Life of Bees (Kidd): V27
Seize the Day (Bellow): V4
Sense and Sensibility (Austen): V18
Sense and Sensibility (Motion picture): V33
A Separate Peace (Knowles): V2
Sewell, Anna
  Black Beauty: V22
Shaara, Michael
  The Killer Angels: V26
Shabanu: Daughter of the Wind (Staples): V35
Shane (Schaefer): V36
Shange, Ntozake
  Betsey Brown: V11
Shelley, Mary
  Frankenstein: V1
  Frankenstein (Motion picture): V37

Shields, Carol
  The Stone Diaries: V23
Ship of Fools (Porter): V14
The Shipping News (Proulx): V38
Shizuko's Daughter (Mori): V15
Sister of My Heart (Divakaruni): V38
Shoeless Joe (Kinsella): V15
Shogun: A Novel of Japan (Clavell): V10
Shute, Nevil
  On the Beach: V9
  A Town Like Alice: V38
Siddhartha (Hesse): V6
Silas Marner (Eliot): V20
Sijie, Dai
  Balzac and the Little Chinese Seamstress: V39
Silko, Leslie Marmon
  Ceremony: V4
Sinclair, Upton
  The Jungle: V6
Sister Carrie (Dreiser): V8
Slaughterhouse-Five (Vonnegut): V3
The Slave Dancer (Fox): V12
Smiley, Jane
  A Thousand Acres: V32
Smilla's Sense of Snow (Høeg): V17
Smith, Betty
  A Tree Grows in Brooklyn: V31
Smith, Zadie
  White Teeth: V40
Snow Falling on Cedars (Guterson): V13
So Far from the Bamboo Grove (Watkins): V28
Solzhenitsyn, Aleksandr
  One Day in the Life of Ivan Denisovich: V6
Something Wicked This Way Comes (Bradbury): V29
Song of the Lark (Cather): V41
Song of Solomon (Morrison): V8
Sons and Lovers (Lawrence): V18
Sophie's Choice (Styron): V22
Soul Catcher (Herbert): V17
The Sound and the Fury (Faulkner): V4
Spark, Muriel
  The Prime of Miss Jean Brodie: V22
Speak (Anderson): V31
Spiegelman, Art
  Maus: A Survivor's Tale: V35
Staples, Suzanne Fisher
  Shabanu: Daughter of the Wind: V35
Staying Fat for Sarah Byrnes (Crutcher): V32
Stead, Christina
  The Man Who Loved Children: V27

Stein, Gertrude
  Ida: V27
Steinbeck, John
  Cannery Row: V28
  East of Eden: V19
  East of Eden (Motion picture): V34
  The Grapes of Wrath: V7
  The Grapes of Wrath (Motion picture): V39
  Of Mice and Men: V1
  The Moon is Down: V37
  The Pearl: V5
  The Red Pony: V17
Steppenwolf (Hesse): V24
Stevenson, Robert Louis
  Dr. Jekyll and Mr. Hyde: V11
  Kidnapped: V33
  Treasure Island: V20
Stockett, Kathryn
  The Help: V39
Stoker, Bram
  Dracula: V18
  Dracula (Motion picture): V41
The Stone Angel (Laurence): V11
The Stone Diaries (Shields): V23
Stones from the River (Hegi): V25
Stowe, Harriet Beecher
  Uncle Tom's Cabin: V6
The Strange Case of Dr. Jekyll and Mr. Hyde (Stevenson): see *Dr. Jekyll and Mr. Hyde*
The Stranger (Camus): V6
Stranger in a Strange Land (Heinlein): V40
The Street (Petry): V33
Strout, Elizabeth
  Olive Kitteridge: V39
Styron, William
  Sophie's Choice: V22
Sula (Morrison): V14
Summer (Wharton): V20
Summer of My German Soldier (Greene): V10
The Sun Also Rises (Hemingway): V5
Surfacing (Atwood): V13
Swarthout, Glendon
  Bless the Beasts and Children: V29
The Sweet Hereafter (Banks): V13
Sweetgrass (Hudson): V28
Swift, Graham
  Waterland: V18
Swift, Jonathan
  Gulliver's Travels: V6

T

A Tale of Two Cities (Dickens): V5
The Talented Mr. Ripley (Highsmith): V27
Tambourines to Glory (Hughes): V21

Cumulative Nationality/Ethnicity Index

Cumulative Nationality/Ethnicity Index

Cumulative Nationality/Ethnicity Index

Subject/Theme Index

Subject/Theme Index

Revolts. *See* Rebellion
Right and wrong
 Donald Duk: 95
Rites of passage
 The Ramayana: 264
Rituals
 The Ramayana: 257
Roman Catholicism
 Benito Cereno: 40–41
Romantic love
 Doctor Zhivago: 47, 53–55, 57, 58,
  63–64, 67
 Feed: 124, 128, 130
 Haroun and the Sea of Stories: 149
 The Man in the Iron Mask: 195,
  198, 205, 206–207
 The Song of the Lark: 272
Romanticism
 Benito Cereno: 31–32
 The Man in the Iron Mask:
  208–209
Russian culture
 Doctor Zhivago: 54, 68–69
Russian history
 Doctor Zhivago: 55, 58–59,
  65–66, 69

S

Sacrifice
 The Ramayana: 257
Sadness
 Haroun and the Sea of Stories: 164
Sadomasochism
 Dracula: 117
Sarcasm
 Donald Duk: 78
Satire
 Haroun and the Sea of Stories: 160
 The Pickwick Papers: 228, 230,
  231–232, 241, 243
 The Tortilla Curtain: 308–309
Science
 Dracula: 107, 119
 The Pickwick Papers: 239–241
Seafaring
 Benito Cereno: 32
Seduction
 Doctor Zhivago: 53, 54
 Dracula: 100, 107–108, 120
Self-assuredness. *See* Confidence
Self deception
 Benito Cereno: 41
Self discipline
 Donald Duk: 91
Self hatred
 Donald Duk: 85, 89, 90
Self identity
 The Joys of Motherhood: 179
 The Song of the Lark: 268, 270,
  271, 274, 275–277, 282, 284,
  287, 288

Self image
 Donald Duk: 88
Self knowledge
 Donald Duk: 94
Self realization
 The Joys of Motherhood: 186
 The Song of the Lark: 279
Self Tradition
 Donald Duk: 85
Selfishness
 The Tortilla Curtain: 298, 302,
  308
Sensuality
 Dracula: 100, 111
Sentimentality
 Dracula: 121–122
 The Pickwick Papers: 229
Separation
 Haroun and the Sea of Stories:
  162–163
Setting (Literature)
 Doctor Zhivago: 58
 The Song of the Lark: 268
 When the Emperor Was Divine:
  321
Sex roles
 Donald Duk: 88–94
 Dracula: 111
 The Joys of Motherhood: 176–177,
  185, 187–193
 The Pickwick Papers: 235–237
 The Ramayana: 256
 The Song of the Lark: 286–289
Sexuality
 Dracula: 111, 118
 The Joys of Motherhood: 182
 The Song of the Lark: 287,
  288–289
Shame
 Donald Duk: 89
 The Tortilla Curtain: 303
Slavery
 Benito Cereno: 23, 28, 29, 32, 34,
  38–40
 The Joys of Motherhood: 189
Social class
 Benito Cereno: 29–30, 38
 Doctor Zhivago: 60
 Dracula: 121
 Feed: 130, 131–133, 137, 138
 The Pickwick Papers: 238, 243
 The Tortilla Curtain: 311
Social commentary
 Donald Duk: 85
 The Tortilla Curtain: 310
Social criticism
 Doctor Zhivago: 69
Spanish culture
 Benito Cereno: 32
Spirits (Supernatural beings)
 The Joys of Motherhood: 189

Spirituality
 The Ramayana: 248
Stereotypes (Psychology)
 Donald Duk: 86, 94
 Feed: 136
 The Tortilla Curtain: 306–309
Stoicism
 When the Emperor Was Divine:
  328
Storytelling
 Dracula: 115, 116
 Haroun and the Sea of Stories: 143,
  145, 150, 151–152, 157,
  160–162, 164, 165
 The Ramayana: 259
 The Tortilla Curtain: 306
Strength
 The Song of the Lark: 271
 The Tortilla Curtain: 308
Struggle
 The Man in the Iron Mask:
  195
Success
 The Song of the Lark: 281, 284,
  285
 The Tortilla Curtain: 297
Suffering
 The Man in the Iron Mask:
  206–207
 The Song of the Lark: 287
Suicide
 The Joys of Motherhood: 169,
  177
Superiority
 Benito Cereno: 39
 The Man in the Iron Mask: 213
Supernatural
 Dracula: 109
 Haroun and the Sea of Stories:
  153
 The Joys of Motherhood:
  187–190
Surrealism
 Donald Duk: 82
Survival
 A Bell for Adano: 20
 The Tortilla Curtain: 303
Suspicion
 The Man in the Iron Mask:
  204
Symbolism
 A Bell for Adano: 10
 Benito Cereno: 25, 45
 Doctor Zhivago: 53, 60
 Haroun and the Sea of Stories:
  163
 The Ramayana: 256
 The Song of the Lark: 288
 The Tortilla Curtain: 303,
  311–312
Sympathy
 Dracula: 121